DISABILITY IN THE CHRISTIAN TRADITION

Disability in the Christian Tradition

A READER

Edited by

Brian Brock *&* John Swinton

WILLIAM B. EERDMANS PUBLISHING COMPANY
GRAND RAPIDS, MICHIGAN

Wm. B. Eerdmans Publishing Co.
2140 Oak Industrial Drive NE, Grand Rapids, Michigan 49505
www.eerdmans.com

23 22 21 20 19 18 17   3 4 5 6 7 8 9

Library of Congress Cataloging-in-Publication Data

Disability in the Christian tradition: a reader / edited by Brian Brock & John Swinton.
    p.   cm.
    Includes bibliographical references and index.
    ISBN 978-0-8028-6602-8 (pbk.: alk. paper)
    1. People with disabilities — Religious aspects — Christianity.
    2. Theological anthropology — Christianity
    I. Brock, Brian, 1970-   II. Swinton, John, 1957-

BT732.7.D57   2012
261.8′324 — dc23

                         2012018109

With gratitude to Adam,
and our many other teachers

Contents

CONTENTS

Contributors

JANA BENNETT is Assistant Professor of Religious Studies at the University of Dayton in Dayton, Ohio. She is the author of "Being 'Stuck' between Stanley and the Feminists (the Proverbial Rock and a Hard Place)," in *Unsettling Arguments: A Festschrift on the Occasion of Stanley Hauerwas's 70th Birthday* (Eugene, Ore.: Cascade Press, 2010); and *Water Is Thicker than Blood: An Augustinian Theology of Marriage and Singleness* (New York: Oxford University Press, 2008).

CHRISTOPHER CRAIG BRITTAIN is Lecturer in Practical Theology at the University of Aberdeen and the author of *Adorno and Theology* (London: T&T Clark, 2010); and *Religion at Ground Zero: Theological Responses to Times of Crisis* (London and New York: Continuum, 2011).

BRIAN BROCK is Lecturer in Moral and Practical Theology at the University of Aberdeen. He is the author of "Autism, Care, and Christian Hope" in *The Journal of Religion, Disability and Health* 13, no. 1 (2009): 7-28; as well as the author and editor (with John Swinton) of *Theology, Disability, and the New Genetics: Why Science Needs the Church* (London: T&T Clark, 2007).

ALMUT CASPARY works in science management at a traditional medical research campus in the northeast of Berlin. She is the author of *In Good Health: Philosophical-Theological Analysis of the Concept of Health in Contemporary Medical Ethics* (Stuttgart: Franz Steiner, 2010); and co-author of a strategy proposal on religion and anti-discrimination practices in the NHS.

DEBORAH BETH CREAMER is Associate Dean for Academic Affairs, Associate Professor of Theological Bibliography, and Director of Library and Information Services at Iliff School of Theology. She is the author of *Disability and Christian Theology: Embodied Limits and Constructive Possibilities* (Oxford: Oxford University Press, 2009).

AMY LAURA HALL is Associate Professor of Christian Ethics at Duke University Divinity School. She is the author of *Kierkegaard and the Treachery of Love* (Cambridge: Cambridge University Press, 2002); and *Conceiving Parenthood: American Protestantism and the Spirit of Reproduction* (Grand Rapids: Wm. B. Eerdmans, 2007).

STEFAN HEUSER is Lecturer at the Chair of Ethics in the Institute for Systematic Theology at the University of Erlangen (Germany), and Vicar in the Evangelical Church of Hessen and Nassau. He is the author of "Dialogue between Science and Ethics: Phenomenological Considerations on Interdisciplinary Research into Scientific Discourses," in *Medicine at the Interface between Science and Ethics,* edited by Walter Doerfler (Halle: Saale, 2010), pp. 177-90; and editor, with Ralf K. Wüstenberg and Esther Hornung, of *Bonhoeffer and the Biosciences: An Initial Exploration* (Frankfurt/Main: Peter Lang, 2010).

MARJOLEIN DE MOOIJ is a Ph.D. student in the Faculty of Theology at the VU, Amsterdam, and Minister of Pastoral Care in a mental health institution.

HANS S. REINDERS is Professor of Ethics at the VU University, Amsterdam. He is the author of *The Future of the Disabled in Liberal Society* (South Bend: University of Notre Dame Press, 2000) and *Receiving the Gift of Friendship* (Grand Rapids: Wm B. Eerdmans, 2008); and the editor of *The Paradox of Disability: Responses to Jean Vanier and L'Arche Communities from Theology and the Sciences* (Grand Rapids: Wm. B. Eerdmans 2010).

MIGUEL J. ROMERO is a Th.D. candidate in moral theology at Duke Divinity School. His research concerns Aquinas on *misericordia,* and the moral witness of Christian communities willing to recognize and pursue the beauty of friendship with profoundly vulnerable and dependent persons. He is the author of "Liberation, Development, and Human Advancement: Catholic Social Doctrine in *Caritas in Veritate*" in *Nova et Vetera,* English edition, vol. 8, no. 4 (2010): 923-57.

JOHN SWINTON is Professor of Practical Theology and Pastoral Care at the University of Aberdeen, where he is the director of the University's Centre for Spirituality, Health, and Disability. Significant publications include *Raging with Compassion: Pastoral Responses to the Problem of Evil* (Grand Rapids: Wm. B. Eerdmans, 2007); *Living Gently in a Violent World: The Prophetic Witness of Weakness*, with Stanley Hauerwas and Jean Vanier (Downers Grove, Ill.: InterVarsity Press, 2008); and *Resurrecting the Person: Friendship and the Care of People with Mental Health Problems* (Nashville: Abingdon Press, 2000).

BERND WANNENWETSCH is Professor of Christian Ethics at the University of Aberdeen, and the author of "Angels with Clipped Wings: The Disabled as the Key to the Recognition of Personhood," in *Theology, Disability, and the New Genetics: Why Science Needs the Church*, edited by John Swinton and Brian Brock (London: T&T Clark, 2007), pp. 182-200; and *Political Worship: Ethics for Christian Citizens* (Oxford: Oxford University Press, 2004).

MARTIN WENDTE was Assistant Professor at the Department of Theology at the Eberhard Karls University, Tübingen, and is now curate in Württemberg, Germany. He is the author of *Gottmenschliche Einheit bei Hegel: Eine logische und theologische Untersuchung* (Berlin/New York: de Gruyter, 2007); and co-editor of *Hauptwerke der Systematischen Theologie: Ein Studienbuch* (Tübingen: UTB, 2009).

DONALD WOOD is Lecturer in Systematic Theology at the University of Aberdeen. He is the author of *Barth's Theology of Interpretation* (Aldershot: Ashgate, 2007).

INTRODUCTION:

Disability and the Quest for the Human

BRIAN BROCK

What does it mean to be human? Any approach to the topic of disability leads inexorably toward the "problem of the human." Westerners face this problem, however, in an intellectual universe that has kept its distance from sustained attention to what we now call disabling conditions. In discussions about what it means to be human, disability has most often appeared in the modern period under the heading of "special cases," outlying exceptions useful mainly for demarcating the outer boundaries of anthropological definitions. The images of the human constructed in this manner are aptly called "best-case anthropologies." But understanding all humanity through the lens of a best-case anthropology has the awkward effect of rendering disability largely invisible. Like gender, race, and culture, disability is a topic that one takes to be either a reality that impacts us all in some way, or an issue that is really only a pressing issue for a specific subgroup of our peers. The latter view is widespread today and almost always accompanied by the self-assured geniality with which people assume that upon meeting someone in one of these subgroups, his or her needs would of course be accommodated. What is true of Western society in general is also largely true of the church. "The times that I have asked ministers and pastors about members of their congregations who are disabled," writes the Dutch theologian Hans Reinders, "the most frequent response is 'We don't have them'" (Reinders 2008, 335).

Coming to terms with the simultaneous visibility and invisibility of disability is central for any modern anthropology because it raises the question of what it is that we are expecting to see. Often the language of gender, race,

1

and nationalism cloaks deeper assumptions that the health and well-being of societies depends on being able to spot the threat presented to them by broken or malfunctioning bodies and minds. Quests to root out perceived moral and cultural deficiencies can therefore all too easily intertwine with suspicions that there are deeper physical and mental deficiencies at their root (Hall 2008). It is therefore not far-fetched to claim that the polarity between able and disabled humanity underlies the whole range of prejudicial attitudes that have been resisted by activists over the last hundred years, misogyny, racism, and nationalism being the most prominent, views which rest on deeply held beliefs that the bodies of women, other races, or other cultures are somehow deficient, intrinsically misshapen, or lacking some basic capacities (Carter 2008, ch. 2). We already see a glimmer of the fertility of the Christian theological tradition when noticing that theologians have often resisted these connections in the face of best-case anthropologies run wild (cf. readings **1.9**, **2.13**, **8.1**, **11.10**, and **13.3**). Bernd Wannenwetsch encapsulates the dynamics of this Christian resistance in Chapter 10 of this volume by detailing the way that firsthand experience of persons living with various disabilities and worshiping together wholly reshaped Dietrich Bonhoeffer's presumptions about what it means to be human. This experience enabled him to perceive at once the inevitability of the slide from the desire to expel disabled people as enemies of society to the desire to expel or liquidate other minorities and reaching its logical terminus in war-breathing aggression against supposed external threats (**10.1**).

The persistence of the belief that some people are "broken" or "functionally deficient" is thus one of the core paradoxes of modernity. Because we are concerned with constructing just societies, we find it important to recognize that some humans face physical and intellectual challenges for which thoughtful societies will want to make provision. At the same time, we sense the immense dangers that modern history has taught us attend any culture's blanket designation of a class of persons as "partially functioning humans" (Bérubé 2003). These are the problematics of a society in which notions of freedom, self-determination, and equality are core to our collective identity and in which ideas about the cultivation of good citizens must rely on presuppositions about what constitutes "normal" and "abnormal" bodies and minds among those citizens (Nussbaum 2006, chs. 2-3).

In the modern era, the rise to dominance of the medical and psychological sciences has established their definitions as default accounts of the category of "disability" (Oliver 1996; Shakespeare 1998). Biological and psychological frameworks can designate individuals among us who should be considered to have well-functioning minds or bodies and those who do not and so, by definition, lie on the margins of human "normalcy." The activists who have taken these definitions and gone into battle for better care for those in need in society, and the professionals who have backed the rise of these definitions of disability over the last century or so, have always had practical and political aims — cure, rehabilitation, normalization, and political justice. But postmodern theorists have asked more probing questions of the theories that ground these medical discourses, questioning the justice of any such ascriptions of normalcy and deviance (Betcher 2007). Declaring that the paternalistic age of "speaking for minorities" is at its end (Badiou 2003, 13), they have tended in turn to glorify the self-expressions of those considered marginalized or different (Althaus-Reid 2003). Rather than too quickly choosing sides in this battle between modern traditionalists and reactionaries, it is probably better to hold this question open a bit longer by asking whether different accounts of disability in fact dismantle or further entrench the center-and-periphery conceptualizations of disability.

Within this intellectual landscape, the question remains for Christians: Ought they to join one or another of these camps or eschew the available options? Are these viable or even compatible ways for Christians to begin their thinking about the issues raised by the phenomena to which the label "disability" is most often attached? Are there any alternative conceptualities? On what grounds might the relative worth of various definitions of disability be assessed? The assumption that grounds this project is that there are indeed alternatives, readily discovered by investigating the writings that constitute the Christian tradition. The variations in human mental and physical capacities that characterize the human race have been named and explained in a wide variety of ways through the centuries, and have had no single meaning or significance (Yong 2007, Parts I and II). To note that within the long history of Christian thought conditions that are today considered disabling have been understood within a range of quite different frameworks is to be offered better access to one of the central questions facing Christians today: How should we think of and treat those human beings whom we experience as "other" than "us"?

The time has come to ask this question as self-consciously Christian theologians in dialogue with the communion of saints. Our suggestion is that Christian theology is able to place modern accounts of disability within a much broader canvas, so moving beyond polarized discourses that have grown sterile, whether of personal experience and autobiography or activism and application. In the last decades several notable efforts have been made to think about disability in theological terms, most notably in works by Jean Vanier, Frances Young, David Pailin, Brett Webb-Mitchell, Burton Cooper, Nancy Eisland, and Stanley Hauerwas. More recently, scholars such as Hans Reinders, Deborah Creamer, Kathy Black, John Gillibrand, Tom Reynolds, and Amos Yong have undertaken robustly theological explorations of disability. But to date there has been no serious or systematic effort to ask what Christians of other ages might bring to this inquiry. This reader remedies that deficit.[1]

There are many reasons why this approach has never before been explored, not least the modern conceit that on this issue, authors from previous ages are by definition backward and primitive. There is no doubt that strands of the Christian tradition have worked to stigmatize and marginalize those it deems disabled, and there is ample evidence of the reasons for this in the excerpts collected in this volume. When Christians throughout the ages have failed to transcend the prejudices of their ages, as they have often done, they demand the censure of contemporary Christians. But if past Christians were guilty of reproducing the prejudices of the age, this problem is not properly solved by a contemporary church that swallows wholesale the prejudices of modern secularity, which deems the Christian tradition as a whole to be largely anti-progressive, especially on the topic of social marginalization.

Such dismissals are neither historically nor intellectually tenable. They evade the investigative task of asking how Christians of earlier ages actually lived and thought in the short-sighted assumption that the history of the West can simply be left behind. An important aim of this reader is to indicate the *intellectual* beliefs that have allowed or justified Christian condescension toward or outright rejection of people with disabilities. This self-critical task is crucial for a modern church that all too often is indistinguishable from or even lags behind its secular counterparts in the welcome it offers to disabled people. At the same time, strands within the Christian tradition have also served to uphold, value, and include people that today might be labeled disabled. Moderns should be prepared to discover that this accepting stance of earlier Christians may have been undertaken with a grace that seems to suggest that contemporary accounts of the "problem" of disability as one, for instance, of "social justice" are rather lacking in ambition, scope, and clarity. By providing access to the primary sources, this reader thus counters contempo-

---

1. The research in this volume was supported by a grant from the College of Arts and Social Sciences at the University of Aberdeen and the excellent editorial work of Judith Heyhoe.

rary habits of thought in which nothing good ever came to the disabled from people of faith in the bad old days before modernity, as well as enabling readers to undertake the more constructive task of exposing and commenting on theological insights and ideas that might enrich contemporary thinking about the issue of disability.

Once we start looking, it is surprisingly easy to find reflections in the Christian tradition on the definition and meaning of variations in the human population. Such reflections may not have been a central preoccupation of Christian authors, but they recur throughout the ages, and when they do, they are often theologically astute and intellectually provocative. The attentive reader can detect traces everywhere of a will to embrace and include those we might call disabled. Following up these traces promises to increase our contemporary capacity to make fine-grained and theological distinctions about the definition of disability, and to give more appropriate accounts of how contemporary Christians and others concerned with disability issues ought to respond to it. It would be anachronistic to suggest that our authors comment directly on a concept that has emerged only in the last few decades. What they do offer, however, are insights and conceptualities that can sharpen our thinking today as we come to terms with disability in the twenty-first century. The power of studying any historical account is its invitation to explore different frameworks for perception. It is our hope that listening closely to the thoughts of Christians through the ages might yield a Christian community with new sensitivities for perceiving and responding to the physically and mentally marginalized in our societies, and, perhaps more importantly, for thinking about the inabilities of those who consider themselves "normal" to take the marginalized and their experiences seriously.

Tradition

Within the remit of such a project, the terms "disability" and "tradition" are both highly contentious terms. We have assumed that, in its most basic form, the *Christian tradition* is made up of the writings of a faith community on its scriptures. For that reason, we have not included a separate chapter on "disability in the Bible" (see Avalos et al. 2007; Monteith 2005, 2010), and we consider "the tradition" that range of interpretations which have emerged as the church tries to interpret its scriptures. This tradition is not an inert deposit that is simply "recovered." Rather, serious thought about any *contemporary* idea is impoverished if we confine our field in historically narrow terms. "Without the dialogue between the ages," Oliver O'Donovan comments, "we can frame no serious critical questions about the prejudgments with which our society approaches practical reasoning. These [prejudgments] *themselves* belong to the process of tradition. Tradition is judged through tradition" (Torrance and Banner 2006, 37). This raises the problem of the "Western canon," that familiar, venerable line-up of (presumably) white males who "made history" and so have become mandatory reading in university survey courses. We consider the selection of authors chosen for this volume to be not a definitive line-up, but only a beginning, a first sampling of what has traditionally been considered the main stream of Western Christendom.

For several centuries now, under the influence of thinkers like Immanuel Kant, theologians who consider themselves modern have tended to consider the notion of a "theological tradition" a problem to be overcome. As a result, those modern theologians most strongly devoted to care for the poor and the outsider have been especially prone to understanding past Christian thought to be an obstacle rather than a resource for fostering a more inclusive church. Walter Rauschenbusch, the founder of the Social Gospel movement and a classic post-Kantian, stated this prejudice in the bluntest possible terms. The task of theology is stripping away the husk of Christian interpretation to get to the kernel of the teachings of the historical Jesus and Paul. "When we have been in contact with the ethical legalism and the sacramental superstitions of the Fathers, we feel the glorious freedom and the pure spirituality of Paul like a mighty rushing wind in a forest of pines. When we have walked among the dogmatic abstractions of the Nicene age, the Synoptic Gospels welcome us back to Galilee with a new charm, and we feel that their daylight simplicity is far more majestic and divine than the calcium light of the creeds" (Rauschenbusch 1907, 115). Clearly, Rauschenbusch appreciates the ways that modern historical method has invited Christian self-criticism, but he embraces it so exuberantly that the very notion of an intellectual heritage is fatally corroded, and along with it any role for the shaping of perception that has long been the gift of religious traditions. If one central characteristic of modernity is a widespread suspicion of the value of previous ages, this reader challenges that premise by proceeding with the rival suspicion that there is more to learn from Christians of past ages than contemporary Christians have noticed. The lens of our interest in disability reveals quite a bit of neglected material in the Christian tradition, immediately provoking critical reflection on the reasons for this elision, not by way of cutting away tradition but by attending more closely to what it actually says.

The most difficult methodological problem in conceiving a volume of this type was achieving a balance between a survey of what "people in the past" thought, which would only be of antiquarian interest, and a project which just "mines" thinkers of the past for fresh concepts for use in the present, without letting the thought structures of these conversation partners emerge to challenge us. Because "disability" is a blatantly modern term, the strict historian's interest in objectivity and pure description untainted by our current concerns makes a project like this look like an imposition of our problems and questions on people who neither knew nor cared about them. Either we read the texts as they stand and try to understand them in their context, which is of course different in many ways to ours, or we try to force them to say something they never dreamed of saying, the historian concludes.

The idea of the communion of saints provides a way through this historiographical impasse. The historian must often terminate her investigation with the admission that the thinking of those in the past was so different from ours that we can't make any reasonable sense of it. We must simply admit that we are alienated from them and find it very difficult to learn from them. But it is precisely here that Christian theology is forced to take another route. Its study of those in the past takes place as a study of people under a shared Lord. Because Christians throughout the ages have read a single set of scriptures within a shared confession of the role of the person and work of Jesus Christ, they are provided with a theologically inflected understanding of the very concepts of tradition and history (Barth 2002, introduction). Christians are formed into a trans-temporal and trans-spatial community that Augustine called the "City of God," a "communion of saints." The vast cultural differences that make up this communion of saints remind modern Christians that in order to be part of this community, we must develop skills of listening and learning from others who strike us as almost incomprehensibly different from ourselves. This negotiation is part of the divine identity imprinted on the church as a social body (Bonhoeffer 2009).

These are the conceptual grounds for the strong moral imperative laid upon Christians both to study the breadth of the Christian tradition and to take seriously the problem of learning how to negotiate perceived difference. The special efforts required to come to terms with thinkers of previous ages thus parallel and foster the central contemporary skills of gracefully and appreciatively negotiating cultural, socioeconomic, gender, intellectual, and other kinds of otherness. A television age has made us familiar with the extension of our sympathy across space and cultures. Its instantaneous images can engage us in the distress of those who are far away and invite us to learn from them, often despite the fact that some facets of their cultures might appear repulsive to us. This reader is an invitation to extend this same hermeneutic of generosity back in time, to our own intellectual heritage and ecclesial progenitors. It requires a movement out of our familiar culture into another culture conceptually and practically configured in bewilderingly different ways. To accomplish such an immersive learning requires suspending our assumptions about how to take on board the perceptions of those we perceive as "others." Once we have done so, however, our ability to designate them as "other" quickly diminishes because we have been changed; "they" have become part of "us." This discipline of entering empathetically into the thought of other ages can only occur, however, if we are prepared to be surprised if and when Christians of past ages have clear insights into issues important to disability theology, and when they are more concerned with the marginalized than is usually assumed by moderns. It is within this framework that Christians must ask, What "disables" human beings? Who should be cared for in society? What constitutes care? Who are "we," as church?

It is important that this approach to the tradition not be made too quickly or easily, however, for many of the saints frame their discussions in quite unfamiliar terms. When premodern theologians, for instance, want to talk about what humans in this world are supposed to look like when they are flourishing, they talk about the Garden of Eden, or the resurrection body, or the body of Jesus. While such language may today appear sheer fantasy or rosy-tinted projection, to hear what is being said in these discourses requires becoming comfortable with the fact that it was in this way that our predecessors in the faith investigated what it means to be a creature, and what it means to be redeemed and healed. Such discussions are not "pie in the sky" imaginings, but a biblically and theologically informed mode of teasing out what is right about the world in which we live and to be upheld with our action, and what is evil and denuding. It is for these reasons that any efforts expended in coming to terms with their framing of the issues promise rich gains in insight as we learn to see what they saw. Most importantly, such new perceptions often reveal how our own ways of seeing have become somehow stale and fruitless.

Disability

A more complex problem is to find a working definition of disability that does not too quickly foreclose a proper investigation of what it might mean.

As it is used today, the term is a placeholder for a whole range of ideas and interests. The first issue this raises is terminological. How are we to refer to those with perceived impairments without denigrating them, so reinforcing the very problem we have set out to remedy? An important step is to avoid reducing people to their condition with single-word labels like "the disabled," "the blind," and so on. Right now the English-speaking world seems to be divided on the issue of appropriate terminology. The more mainstream usage is "people with disability," a designation emphasizing that people are whole as they are, that people come first, before any discussion can begin of any presumably standard human capacities they may or may not share. A more recent and radical trend has been to co-opt or even commandeer the language of disability, owning repressive language with pride in order to dramatize the way that society marginalizes certain people. The aim is to revel in the ontological difference that society seems to have bestowed on them, in order to make it clear that what is at stake in the ascription of disability is not an ontological but a social status. This volume will use neither of these terms exclusively, but it has a strong interest in uncovering what is at stake in this debate by taking it seriously and coming to terms with the whole scope of issues being raised around the question of the relation between the social and ontological levels of the discourse.

A full appreciation of this project will depend on staving off one of the foreshortenings induced by the very concept of "disability." Polarizations such as health-disability, normal-aberrant, or functioning-impaired assume that some people are at the center of normal humanity and others are on its margins. These polarities thus name in various ways the *human*. The heartland of this project is to look constructively and imaginatively at the human, understanding disability within the scope of a full and positive account of what it means to be a human, rather than resting content with disability and people with disabilities being understood as special problem cases lying at the edges of more basic or central discourses. This is one gain that the tradition offers a contemporary discussion which is rhetorically focused on "those" who have disabilities, rather than on what it means to be human. This is to suggest that disability is not a topic that is properly located as an elective in the university or seminary curriculum, but ought properly to be a core inquiry. To talk about disability, therefore, is not to take up a "marginal" issue at all, but to press a range of fresh questions on secular thinkers as well as modern Christian theology as a whole. The discourse of disability cannot be only a discourse about politics or disability studies, because it raises wide-ranging questions for constructive practical and dogmatic theology. At the same time, it also relies on the patient working habits of the church historian who brings up from the bowels of the library resources to liberate disability as a real feature of people's lives from the narrow confines and politics of university disability studies.

This criticism can be pushed one step further. Modern (especially academic) intellectual life is shaped by the secularization of knowledge. If in Christian theology the main topic is God and humans' relation to God, modern secular thought confines itself to what can be said about the natural processes of the universe. Anthropology is rendered the basic discipline of philosophy, an emphasis that has in most cases been absorbed in turn by modern theology. But a wholly philosophical anthropology makes it difficult to escape the polarizing categories that emphasize people's lack. In contrast, an ecclesial view escapes this problem by focusing on what each person *brings* and who we are *together* (Wannenwetsch 2004, Parts II and III). A theological account, therefore, can begin its investigation of the human with appreciation of every person in every form rather than with pity or by pointing out what individuals might lack (Kelsey 2009, 201-7). To return to the study of God and humans together thus promises a vantage point from which the Western tendency to work from best-case anthropologies can be overturned.

In sum, the second important methodological challenge facing a study of this type is to overcome the problem that "disability" is not in the Christian tradition because it is a modern idea. Christians through the ages will obviously have taken a range of conditions to hinder human flourishing in various ways, but these may well not be the ways we moderns might expect. John Swinton and I have thus asked contributors not simply to skim through writings from different ages to see what they had to say about the conditions that *seem to us today to qualify as* handicaps. We have asked rather for a more searching investigation of the sources to discover the conditions *they* considered disabling. The aim of this volume is for each contributor to expose how his or her author might fill out the term or even render it meaningless. What *content* is properly associated with this term? In some cases, various authors' positions may simply reflect the prejudices of the age; in other cases, not. But it is more instructive for our thinking to see *how* their positions are constructed than to simply fit them into our own preconceptions about the constitution of disability. The aim of the reader is not to promulgate a single definition of disability, but to allow unfamiliar theological constructions to open up fresh ways of thinking about it.

The task, then, is neither a purely descriptive exercise ("What those in the past once said") nor a purely constructive one ("Here is what this author said, on the basis of which we can say something more interesting today"). Each contributor's introduction to their chosen figure from the Christian tradition is structured by three questions. First, what did each thinker say directly about disabling conditions? Christians through the ages have often used terminology rendered problematic today, referring to monsters, idiots, madmen, and so on. Contributors will thus provide us with a view of the whole range of the thinker's own descriptions at their most discomforting and even conceptually confused as well as at its most insightful. The second question is, What is problematic about such an account? This question allows us to test ideas from other ages against modern ideas, demanding that we moderns become more self-aware about our own assumptions about disability. The third question is, What can we learn from such an account of disability? Here each contributor indicates the conceptual moves present in the work of the thinker they are introducing which they see as having the most direct or important contemporary relevance for a theology of disability. Naturally, the different contributors have weighted these tasks differently, some focusing more on historical description and others on revealing constructive resources. The main task of the reader is simply to give unmediated access to primary sources that bear on questions related to disability, and to suggest ways in which they might enrich contemporary thinking about the topic. Tracing the development of the tradition provides an opportunity to see precisely *which* ideas were added *when* in order to build up what we now know to be modern ways of thinking about disability. In the process, it will become clear *why* terms like "charity" became pivotal for Christians as they thought about people we would call disabled as we learn about the practices such charity was intended to displace. In so doing we gain a better sense of both how the modern tradition developed and how more incisively to direct our current intellectual efforts to understand and respond to disability.

Chapter Summaries

In broad overview, there are three intertwining questions to which Christians through the ages have continually returned when facing persons with what we would consider disabling conditions and the larger human phenomenon of mental and physical impairment.

- The first question is a practical and ethical one: "For whom are we to care, and what sort of care ought Christians to provide?" This question has fueled many different Christian experiments in the provision of social care over the centuries, and I will therefore refer to it as the *activist discourse*.
- The second question operates in a conceptual register and tries to come to terms with the definition or essence of disability: "What is sickness or disability in relation to what we know of human wholeness and health?" This second question has guided Christians as they have thought through how to name and recognize the features or capacities that humans ought properly to possess. It is a *discourse of definition*.
- The third question concerns human self-awareness and the demands placed on it by people who do not conform to our expectations: "What sort of people do we have to become in order to rightly perceive and love all people, including those whom we might wish to shun?" With this question, the focus shifts from what can we do for others, and also away from how others are defined and categorized, toward a more personal interest in having our perception of others transformed. I will call this third strand the *existential discourse*.

What this reader makes clear is that these three strands twist and intertwine, persisting right through the Christian tradition and into the modern discourse. This is in itself an important initial finding in a modern intellectual climate that does not often combine these views. Broadly speaking, the medical model of disability largely asks definitional questions, and the social constructivist approach to disability stresses the necessity for adjustments in our (existential) assumptions about what we consider disabling. Modern disability activism usually relies on one of these accounts of disability in the course of protest and reform, aiming to advance justice understood as increased social inclusion. Within the context of our collection it will be rare to find all three strands in a single thinker, but at several points explicit arguments are offered to explain why one of these strands is superior or another counterproductive. It is methodologically important to note that none of these three sorts of questions is finally silenced in the running conversation that is the communion of the saints.

Almut Caspary begins the reader by surveying the writings of the Church Fathers. Disfiguring conditions in classical Greece and Rome, especially congenital malformations, were largely ascribed to supernatural powers that needed to be exorcised and purified for the benefit of society as a whole. A person's value was largely defined in social terms, calibrated by reference to his or her potential to contribute both materially and through acquired virtues to the good of the family and society. Christianity thus marked a turning point in late antiquity in holding that every human life has intrinsic value. Early Christian theologians give testimony to a decidedly different attitude toward human life from beginning to end, enacting broad strategies of resistance to dominant attitudes toward the body and life more generally as valuable only in terms of its presumed future capacity to contribute to the public good. Without radically overhauling ancient conceptions of disability or disease, the Church Fathers, represented here by the writings of Basil the Great, Gregory of Nyssa, and Gregory of Nazianzus, nevertheless recognized the importance of a theoretically rich account of what was going on in the phenomena while strongly resisting the practice of discarding or shunning those considered social outcasts, be they children, the lame, the blind, the poor, or prostitutes. So while the Church Fathers of the late fourth century showed little interest in developing new theories of the origin or moral nature of physical differences, they found in the New Testament a witness that pressed for Christian action, to which they responded by strongly commending and modeling pastoral care and philanthropy toward the socially excluded.

My own contribution investigates the early fifth-century reflections of Augustine on issues related to disability and sickness, reflections that penetrate much more deeply into the conceptual questions raised by the high estimation of practical care for outsiders in the patristic period. A rich and diverse thinker, Augustine deeply shaped how the problem of disability was to be conceived in the Christian West for centuries to come. He gave theoretical explication to some relatively underdescribed earlier Christian practices, and as he did so, displayed a dual impulse that has been visible in Western Christian thought ever since. On the one hand, he entered the definitional discourse by seeking to define the "normal" human in the light of the one perfect human, Jesus Christ. The line he took here was to be highly influential for ages to come, as he tried to set out the features and functions of all "normal" humans. On the other hand, Augustine also had a strong sense that the Christian God has a remarkable tendency to overturn our ideas of who among us stands near the center of this human ideal and who is at its periphery, a concern of the existential discourse. Here he asked how disability questions our perceptual categories and requires our renewal as subjects in order to appreciate how God is at work in and through it.

Two medieval thinkers display the solidification of the discourse of definition and the rise of a more fully developed existential counter-discourse. Thomas Aquinas's highly intricate theological anthropology continues and develops the definitional strand with great subtlety and attention to detail. Miguel Romero traces Aquinas's elaboration and reshaping of Augustine's account of the soul as the form of the body. By exploring Aquinas's discussion of the *amentes* ("imbecile" or "mindless"), Romero shows how Aquinas was able to uphold the full validity of all human lives as well as their importance for the life of the church. Like Augustine, Aquinas has no interest in setting out criterion for whether or not a given person is a human being. He assumes that everyone born of a human bears the image of God and is complete and whole in his or her created soul. But because the complete operations of the soul may be thwarted by infirmities of the body or brain, Aquinas's emphasis is on developing a theology of bodily weakness. This account helps clarify how God gives grace to people who seem incapable of virtue or good works; it also sets the terms for the liturgical and pastoral care that the church owes to every human being.

Julian of Norwich is the first author in our collection whose theology as a whole we might think of as an extended reflection on disability. Julian is also the first representative in this collection of what I have called the existential strand of Christian thought about disability. Her central concern is to understand and evoke a renewal in the way disabling conditions are perceived. Amy Laura Hall traces Julian's understanding of the connection between her own suffering and the suffering of Christ. Writing as a woman in a time of male dominance in the world of letters and as a representative of the sex assumed to bear duty for the bodily care of others in a time of dreadful contagion, Julian explores the transgressive character of Christ's work and its power to break down our fear of contact with others, of entanglement in the messiness of their lives. In being "disabled" by Christ, Julian discovers Christ's heart for the outcast in herself and all the world. Hall suggests that this theology has direct implications for contemporary theological consideration of the way the work of Christ may be said to be the dissolution of the sinful human tendency to set up and maintain boundaries that promise to protect us but in fact cut us off from life in communion with others.

The two magisterial reformers of the early sixteenth century present us with decisive shifts in theological approach that will open up the road to modernity. The thought of Martin Luther remains very much within the orbit of a medieval world in which disability was experienced as an effect of demonic powers, but Stefan Heuser explains that precisely because sickness, suffering, and disability were so prevalent at this time, Luther's consideration of these themes displays particularly theological insight. For Luther, God may allow disability, but does not desire humans to be victimized by it. Because all people are spiritually disabled, the divine grace upon which every person must rely demands that we rethink what it means to be physically or mentally disabled. God uses both ability and disability for God's own purposes, meaning that the key theological question is not whether someone is disabled, but how it is that we can learn to attend to what God is bringing into the world through him or her. Here, activist and definitional discourses are firmly located within the existential discourse. In considering every human being a medium of God's own speaking, Luther offers a theology unencumbered by the modern entrapment in the normality-abnormality polarity.

In the work of Calvin we come closer to the conceptions of disability with which modern Christians are familiar. Calvin's approach is oriented by a definitional discourse in which disability emerges as an aspect of a positive theological definition of the human. Deborah Creamer begins her introduction by tracking Calvin's abiding activist interest in formalizing institutions to ensure care for disabled people in Geneva and their inclusion in the worship of the church. The doctrine of divine sovereignty suggests to Calvin that God makes distinctions among people for reasons that are futile to try to understand, but in doing so, God always stands on the side of the outcast and the outsider. Calvin therefore suggests that the church is to be a welcoming presence in society. Creamer finds that Calvin's theology frames important theological insights into conceptions of inclusion, equality, interdependence, and the importance of embodiment, but also raises questions about the model of charity he assumes and the rationalist anthropology that underpins it.

We now jump with a large leap from the Reformation to survey the work of three thinkers from the late eighteenth and early nineteenth century, often called the later Enlightenment period. Martin Wendte explains why G. W. F. Hegel affirms Christianity as the highest religion because it is the one best-suited to foster human freedom and autonomy. In Christianity, both reason and religion can thus be said to reach their pinnacle. Hegel understands human beings as primarily relational in nature, having been created by a God who is one as three persons. In light of this definitional investigation, Hegel concludes that what are genuinely disabling are mental conditions that place barriers in the way of human communication and communion. While Hegel's explicit account of mental illness and disability is rather narrow, Wendte suggests that his thought nevertheless offers us fresh ways of thinking about disability in its relation to the firmly held modern ideals of community and autonomy. We might also consider Hegel the first thinker in the Christian tradition to attempt to explicitly take into account the methodological problem of uniting definitional and existential strands of anthropological discourse by locating the existential as a constitutive part of the definitional.

It was on Christian grounds that Søren Kierkegaard believed it important to resist Hegel's account of Christianity, on the grounds that his solution does not take seriously enough the remaking of the subject's perception that disability demands. Christopher Craig Brittain traces Kierkegaard's linking of disabling conditions with the problem of estrangement from God, which he calls the "sickness unto death." A better understanding of this vertical relationship, Kierkegaard suggests, brings new insight to individuals that enables them to own the inevitable limitations that attend any human life while at the same time refusing the social values that may be ascribed to those limitations. This existential investigation of the transformation of the individual sufferer's perspective opens the way for humans to go beyond their tendencies to love only those images which they project onto other persons rather than the persons themselves, with all their unique and perhaps angular qualities.

In contrast to Kierkegaard's largely conceptual consideration of disability in Denmark, Willem van den Bergh was in the same time period deeply engaged in social activism in the Netherlands. Marjolein de Mooij explains how van den Bergh's founding of Holland's first institution for mentally disabled people grew out of Calvinist impulses. These impulses were, however, deeply inflected with the sensibilities of a romantic age fascinated by the mentally disabled, as well as a largely wholesale acceptance of contemporary medical and moral certainties about the origins of mental illness in immoral human behaviors. We are therefore provided with an example of the activist impulse implicitly shaping the definitional discourse. Van den Bergh's vision also rested on a distinctive political theology, a conservative political vision tied to a high valuation of local institutions set up by the church rather than the state or private philanthropy. What results is an account of Christian care for people with disabilities that deeply revises traditional Calvinist anthropology while understanding itself as a true expression of Calvin's core interest in the church's responsibility to provide diaconal care to everyone in society.

Bringing us into the twentieth century are the next pair of theologians, Dietrich Bonhoeffer and Karl Barth. One of the surprises of this volume is Bernd Wannenwetsch's suggestion that not only was the question of disability core to the theological anthropology and ecclesiology of Bonhoeffer, but that his firsthand experience of people with disabilities is the key to understanding his implacable and far-sighted resistance to the Nazi regime. On a 1933 visit to the Bethel Institute for the Physically and Mentally Handicapped, Bonhoeffer was overwhelmed by the reality of their gathering, "in which a proto-celestial mélange of epileptics and other disabled people, elderly tramps, deaconesses and theology students, doctors, and pastors and their families worshiped together" (see Wannenwetsch essay, p. 354). This was a moment that was to echo through Bonhoeffer's subsequent thought, propelling him in a quest to detoxify Christianity of its attraction to anthropologies that valorize strength or prowess as the main Christian attribute. In time these critical questions were extended to the point of raising serious questions of the long tradition of Christian benevolence. In the battle for "the least of these" that Wannenwetsch calls "Bethel vs. Buchenwald," the head of the Bethel asylum was to become a high-profile casualty, as was Bonhoeffer himself. In Bonhoeffer we see the definitional discourse turned back from disability toward the church: How do we understand the church and so humanity when we receive people with disabilities not as special cases, but as the rule of the church's truest gathering?

Because Karl Barth was the most widely influential Protestant theologian of the twentieth century, his work is particularly important to analyze in a survey of Christian understandings of disability. Donald Wood explains in his introduction how Barth's account of disability begins with the assumption that what is at stake in using any such ascription is coming to terms with the *relationships* between humans, trying to draw out the precise ways in which we are the same as, and different from, one another as revealed by the one relation with the God-man Jesus Christ. This opening move rests on a theocentric account of humanity that sharply resituates the contemporary concept of disability. It de-emphasizes the importance of contemporary cultural values and understandings of the human in the face of God's love for each person. The human sciences can describe aspects of the phenomena of the human, but in its engagement with the one real human, Jesus Christ, theology draws from revelation a deeper and more unifying definition of the human and so of the relationships between humans within which disability language does its work. This account generates a fundamental ethical insight that all human life claims respect, which Barth articulates not only in (activist) political and institutional aspects, but in personal (existential) terms as well — as the glad receipt of the life that each of us has been leant by God.

The three final chapters survey contemporary theologies of disability.

Jana Bennett traces the convergence of modern feminist concerns about the gendered moral prescriptions of the modern world and the Western intellectual tradition with those of Christians thinking about disability: for many centuries, to be a woman was itself considered a disability. In the works of Rosemary Radford Ruether, Nancy Eisland, and Sarah Coakley, Bennett finds special sensitivities to the intertwining of social exclusion and ecclesial rigidities as expressions of Christian doctrines of God and Christology. In the work of these three thinkers, the three strands of the Christian inquiry into disability intertwine in complex ways. Where the three thinkers meet is in their agreement that the work of the Trinitarian God can be understood to enable the struggle for justice in the public and legal sphere for those with disabilities, and also to offer a way out of those beliefs which estrange us from our own bodies. From the perspective of the half of humanity who have been so often considered disabled in Western best-case anthropologies, suggests Bennett, we can learn what is promising about giving up the all-too-seductive desire to claim "I am not disabled."

Jean Vanier is a special thinker in the collection in that his Christian vocation has been to spend his life intentionally with mentally disabled people. Hans Reinders explains how this life with the severely intellectually disabled has shaped his theology, not least by teaching him to write in plain, simple language. Vanier describes his own journey as the remaking of a complex and sophisticated man of action into one who seeks to know himself in order to be a gentle and perceptive conduit of divine love. His story presents the reader with an especially fertile example of the effects of bounding definitional and activist discourses within the orbit of the existential. Vanier's recurrent interest is in how we as subjects can learn about reality not by defining what constitutes the normal human, nor by offering "service" to those who are deficient on these terms, but by facing down the fears and resistances that make it impossible for us to love others. In learning to attend to the weakness in others, we may learn of our own weakness, and in learning about the weakness that characterizes both sides of such relationships, our illusions are stripped away, and we begin to understand the reality of God's grace.

Stanley Hauerwas reflects in more theoretical and definitional terms on the theological meaning of lives like that of Jean Vanier. John Swinton explains that Hauerwas's main interest is in uncovering the many ways in which profoundly intellectually disabled people challenge modern presumptions about what it means to be human, for societies to be just, and for the church to be the church. He asks after the conceptual and practical affirmations which sustain the modern sensibility that disability is a "problem" to be solved. The indirection of this approach to the topic allows Hauerwas to probe modern assumptions about the presumed suffering of the disabled and the inhumanities that can flow from it; his interest is in developing a better account of what it means for *all* of us to be human. In this he directly responds to the bias of Western anthropologies toward best-case scenarios, though in his conclusion Swinton wonders whether this fruitful inquiry into modern accounts of disability may depend more than necessary on unhelpful reifications of the concept of "the disabled."

Conclusion

What emerges, in overview, is that throughout the history of the West, Christian thinkers have been concerned to articulate in their own characteristic ways how humans are related to each other by Jesus Christ. This core interpretative assumption constitutes the continuity of a tradition that has construed both the probl⬛⬛⬛⬛⬛⬛g of disability in often quite different and sometimes⬛⬛⬛⬛⬛⬛ways. The centrality of this core theological theme in ⬛⬛⬛⬛ion together is thus especially important, a realizatio⬛⬛⬛⬛egained some prominence in disability theology (cf. Eisland ⬛⬛⬛ton 2000, Creamer 2009, Yong 2007, Reynolds 2008, and Reinders 2008). This contemporary renaissance of explicitly theological and doctrinal approaches to the question of disability offers a way beyond modern secular disability discourses which most often operate within a primary concept of equality, a concept always haunted by the spectre of homogeneity in having reasons both to use and to reject the very notion of nonfunctional or inadequate humanity. These contemporary thinkers have each reconsidered what it might mean to take a step back from definitional, existential, and activist discourses in order to think again about the deficiencies of any account of disability that divides humanity (including able-disabled) in ways that assume some humans are conceived as "outside." They return to the work of Christ in order to discern afresh the vast diversity that comprises our shared humanity.

Thinkers in the Christian tradition track most closely with the modern anthropological and medical definitions of disability when they ask the definitional question: What are the traits of the "normal" human? But one important lesson learned from the many Christians who have pursued this question in the past is that it is dangerous to define the human merely empirically. People with disabilities will always be a marginal phenomenon if "normal" humanity is a matter of statistical occurrence. But in Jesus Christ, thinkers like Augustine, Thomas, Calvin, and Barth insist, we know the real human in a way that often flies in the face of cultural assumptions about normalcy.

The muted but significant exploration by Augustine of the importance of the transformation of the subject rather than the definition of the objects of disability is further developed in the thought of Julian, Luther, and Vanier, and is clearly articulated by Kierkegaard: "It is a sad but altogether too common inversion to go on talking continually about how the object of love must be so it can be loveworthy, instead of talking about how love must be so it can be love" (Kierkegaard 1995, 159; cf. **8.10**). The thinkers who pursue this existential investigation of disability emphasize that in Christ Christians learn that to love is to receive with welcome and in a new way what is divinely given and therefore waiting to be embraced. It warns that without love for those with whom we are concerned, defining disability as a lack of certain common human capacities or engaging in activism on the behalf of disabled people will inevitably be a projection of our own wishes, a totalizing activity that cannot avoid becoming patronizing or even violent. In this they take up but extend the insights of the social critique of disability, which emphasizes how our own attitudes and expectations cause more suffering for others than their physical pain or the mechanical challenges presented by their own physiognomy. For these Christian thinkers, to learn to attend to people in the way Christ does is to know them and to respond to them (as well as ourselves) aright.

The activist strand of the Christian tradition insists that engagement with and care for those whom either society or physical conditions disable is not optional for Christians. To notice and make smooth the path of those among us with special conditions is constitutive of the Christian community's identity in Christ. From the very first, Christians recognized that a God who became incarnate calls for embodied, practical forms of love corresponding to his own care for the "least of these." While Christian activists from the patristic period (Gregory of Nyssa) to the modern (van den Bergh, Vanier) have explained their activism in very different ways, and even named the recipients of their special attention within contradictory definitional frameworks, it is impossible to find a thinker within the broad stream of the tradition who does not value and commend concrete acts of love toward those we would today call disabled.

In John the Evangelist's portrayal of the Last Supper, Jesus iconically displays his humble mission to serve humanity by washing his disciples' feet. Enacting once again the form which God's love takes, he points directly to its culmination in his laying down his life on the cross. His disciples had found this love difficult to grasp in their three years of living with him, and even at this Last Supper, Peter recoils at the man he had come to confess to be God taking the place of a servant rather than that of the sage or king which Peter believed better suited him. "For Peter this is impossible," comments Jean Vanier. It is impossible only because Peter still has not grasped the full scope of Jesus' form of love, which claims "to transform the model of society from a pyramid to a body, where each and every person has a place, whatever their abilities or disabilities, where each one is dependent upon the other" (Vanier, 2004, 227). Betrayed by their aspirations for the recognition they thought was due as a result of their "leadership" in the top tier of the kingdom they thought Jesus was establishing, the disciples revealed to all of us that they had not yet grasped its essence. It is certainly an essence easily lost to view. This reader is an attempt, once again, to hear this invitation afresh.

References Cited

Althaus-Reid, Marcella. 2003. *The Queer God.* New York: Routledge.

Avalos, Hector, Sara J. Melcher, and Jeremy Schipper, editors. 2007. *This Abled Body: Rethinking Disabilities in Biblical Studies.* Atlanta: Society of Biblical Studies.

Badiou, Alain. 2003. *Saint Paul: The Foundation of Universalism.* Translated by Ray Brassier. Stanford: Stanford University Press.

Barth, Karl. 2002. *Protestant Theology in the Nineteenth Century.* New edition. Grand Rapids: Wm. B. Eerdmans.

Bérubé, Michael. 2003. "Citizenship and Disability." *Dissent* (Spring): 52-57.

Betcher, Sharon. 2007. *Spirit and the Politics of Disablement.* Minneapolis: Fortress Press.

Black, Kathleen. 1996. *A Healing Homiletic: Preaching and Disability.* Nashville: Abingdon Press.

Bonhoeffer, Dietrich. 2009. *Sanctorum Communio: A Theological Study of the Sociology of the Church.* Dietrich Bonhoeffer Works, vol. 1, edited by Clifford Green. Minneapolis: Fortress Press.

Carter, J. Kameron. 2008. *Race: A Theological Inquiry.* Oxford: Oxford University Press.

Cooper, Burton. 1992. "The Disabled God." *Theology Today* 49, no. 2: 173-82.

Creamer, Deborah. 2009. *Disability and Christian Theology: Embodied Limits and Constructive Possibilities.* New York: Oxford University Press.

Eisland, Nancy. 1994. *The Disabled God: Toward a Liberatory Theology of Disability*. Nashville: Abingdon Press.

Gillibrand, John. 2010. *Disabled Church, Disabled Society: The Implications of Autism for Philosophy, Theology, and Politics*. London: Jessica Kingsley Publishers.

Hall, Amy Laura. 2008. *Conceiving Parenthood: American Protestantism and the Spirit of Reproduction*. Grand Rapids: Wm. B. Eerdmans.

Hauerwas, Stanley. 1986. *Suffering Presence: Theological Reflections on Medicine, the Mentally Handicapped, and the Church*. Notre Dame: University of Notre Dame Press.

Kelsey, David. 2009. *Eccentric Existence: A Theological Anthropology*. Louisville: Westminster John Knox Press.

Kierkegaard, Søren. 1995. *Works of Love*. Translated and edited by Howard V. Hong and Edna H. Hong. Princeton: Princeton University Press.

Monteith, Graham. 2005. *Deconstructing Miracles: From Thoughtless Indifference to Honouring Disabled People*. Glasgow and Edinburgh: Covenanters Press.

———. 2010. *Epistles of Inclusion: St Paul's Inspired Attitudes*. London: Grosvenor House Publishing.

Nussbaum, Martha. 2006. *Frontiers of Justice: Disability, Nationality, Species Membership*. Cambridge: Belknap Press.

O'Donovan, Oliver, and Joan Lockwood O'Donovan, editors. 1999. *From Irenaeus to Grotius: A Sourcebook in Christian Political Thought*. Grand Rapids: Wm. B. Eerdmans.

Oliver, Michael. 1996. *Understanding Disability: From Theory to Practice*. New York: St. Martin's Press.

Pailin, David. 1992. *A Gentle Touch: From a Theology of Handicap to a Theology of Human Being*. London: SPCK.

Rauschenbusch, Walter. 1907. "The Influence of Historical Studies on Theology." *The American Journal of Theology*, vol. 2 (January): 111-27.

Reinders, Hans. 2008. *Receiving the Gift of Friendship: Profound Disability, Theological Anthropology, and Ethics*. Grand Rapids: Wm. B. Eerdmans.

Reynolds, Thomas. 2008. *Vulnerable Communion: A Theology of Disability and Hospitality*. Grand Rapids: Brazos Press.

Shakespeare, Tom. 1998. *The Disability Reader: Social Scientific Perspectives*. London: Continuum.

Swinton, John. 2000. *From Bedlam to Shalom: Towards a Practical Theology of Human Nature, Interpersonal Relationships, and Mental Health Care*. New York: Peter Lang.

———. 2000. *Resurrecting the Person: Friendship and the Care of People with Severe Mental Health Problems*. Nashville: Abingdon Press.

Torrance, Alan, and Michael Banner, editors. 2006. *The Doctrine of God in Theological Ethics.* London: T&T Clark.

Vanier, Jean. 1989. *Community and Growth.* Revised edition. London: Darton, Longman & Todd.

————. 2004. *Drawn into the Mystery of Jesus through the Gospel of John.* London: Darton, Longman & Todd.

Wannenwetsch, Bernd. 2004. *Political Worship: Ethics for Christian Citizens.* Oxford: Oxford University Press.

Webb-Mitchell, Brett. 1994. *God Plays Piano, Too: The Spiritual Lives of Disabled Children.* New York: Crossroad.

Yong, Amos. 2007. *Theology and Down Syndrome: Reimagining Disability in Later Modernity.* Waco: Baylor University Press.

Young, Frances. 2007. *Brokenness and Blessing: Towards a Biblical Spirituality.* London: Darton, Longman & Todd.

————. 1986. *Face to Face: A Narrative Essay in the Theology of Suffering.* London: Epworth.

1 The Patristic Era: Early Christian Attitudes toward the Disfigured Outcast

ALMUT CASPARY

To explore the situation of disability in late antiquity and in the writings of the early church, one might start by recalling how different today's Western social practices are from ancient Greek or Roman societies in relation to the vulnerable at the fringes of their cities — the newborn, the elderly, the diseased, the injured, and the disfigured, as well as the poor. Greek philosophy valued order, balance, and harmony in nature and society; disorder, as represented by morbidity and poverty, indicated a menace or curse to nature and society. Disorder originates on another plane: that of the gods. In a world where diseases, injuries, malformation, and material misfortunes were often seen as signs of the ill will of the gods, scant public resources were allocated to disfigured citizens, and then first of all given to impaired and impoverished war veterans. Institutionalized medical care was largely absent in ancient societies, again with the possible exception of care for injured soldiers and veterans, which took place in Roman *valetudinaria* (cf. Stiker 1999; Miller 1985).

In a time of raging epidemics, famines, and wars taking enormous death tolls, the most vulnerable, disabled, impaired, and chronically ill within the societies of late antiquity did not constitute a group substantial enough to be reckoned with politically and institutionally. Medico-historical sources and skeletal finds document the frequent occurrence of life-threatening epidemics: types of fever such as viral influenza, typhoid fever, and malaria were widespread. Outbreaks of typhus and cholera were common not only in times of war. Meningitis together with diseases such as mumps and measles were frequent causes of death (cf. Hippocratic Writings, *Epidemics;* Lloyd 2003). Newborns as well as children and the elderly were among the most vulnerable, being less physically robust, along with those weakened by poverty.

Leaving aside causes of death largely beyond people's control, there is nonetheless a marked difference between the social practices of late antiquity and, if not today, certainly the Middle Ages as regards the attitude shown to babies born with disabilities. While in late antiquity (as in most pre-industrial and pre-clinical societies) both adult and infant mortality were generally high, the social practices of the time ensured a virtual death sentence for those born with a disabling condition. The exposure of *both* healthy and defective newborns was widely practiced in classical Greece and Rome. While the former were exposed for economic reasons and as a means of population control, the latter were left to die for social and eugenic reasons. The disfiguring conditions of monsters, as they were called (*prodigia* in Latin, *terata* in Greek), were largely ascribed to supernatural powers that needed to be exorcised and purified for the benefit of society as a whole. Often such monsters were seen as manifestations of supernatural powers foreboding danger for the community; divine signs, portents, or bad omens for their families and the polis at large (cf. Stiker 1999, ch. 3).

It is crucial to understand in this context that a person's value in antiquity was largely defined as social value: A human being was considered to be of value in view of his or her potential to contribute both materially and through acquired virtue to the good of the family and of society. Children were generally considered of value only to the extent that they had potential to make a virtuous contribution to the public good as adults. According to John Rist, "It was almost universally held in antiquity that a child has no intrinsic right to life in virtue of being born. What mattered was being adopted into a family or some other institution of the society" (Rist 1996, 141). The value of embryonic, newborn, or indeed infant human life was solely potential. "With the exception of a few late Stoics, there is little appreciation in the writings of the philosophers that childhood has any value of its own, that it might be judged on its own terms" (Rist, 142).

The advent of Christianity marked a turning point in late antiquity in its appreciation of human life as having intrinsic value. Following Christ's message and example, early Christian theologians gave testimony to a decidedly different attitude toward human life from beginning to end. Christians' countercultural social practices paved the way for public institutions of charity for the socially excluded. They reacted to, and often against, the dominant attitudes toward the body and toward life more generally as valuable only in terms of its contributions to the public good. They attacked the practice of exposure of infants, including defective newborns. They showed little interest in particular disabilities or diseases; the interest they did show (as in the case of leprosy) was in connection with a more general concern with social exclusion. Disabled or "crippled" people were of interest only because all social outcasts were of interest — be they children, the lame, the blind, the poor, or prostitutes. And while the Church Fathers of the late third and fourth centuries showed little if any theoretical interest in the physiological origin or moral nature of physical differences, they adamantly recommended pastoral care and philanthropy as exemplary responses to social exclusion as enjoined in the New Testament.

This introduction is divided into two sections and explores the writings of third-century and fourth-century Fathers from both West and East. The first section looks at the condemnation of the exposure of newborns through excerpts from writings of the North African Fathers Clement of Alexandria (d. ca. A.D. 215), Tertullian (ca. A.D. 155-230), and Lactantius (ca. A.D. 210-320). The second section examines the public care practiced by the three Cappadocian Fathers: Basil the Great (A.D. 329-379), his friend Gregory of Nazianzus (A.D. 329-389), and his brother, Gregory of Nyssa (A.D. 335-394). While both strands of these traditions take their orientation from the New Testament's message of God's love for humanity and of the intrinsic goodness of human life, the first strand refers more explicitly to the value of human life, whereas the second is more explicitly practical and pastoral in orientation, centering on the works of philanthropy that allow Christians to identify with Christ both as individuals and as participants in their communal liturgical practices. Given their greater length and conceptual development, excerpts from this second stream will make up the primary texts for this chapter.

Early Christian Attitudes toward Disfigured Newborns

It is beyond the scope of this introduction to undertake a detailed examination of ancient Greek and Roman attitudes to defective newborns, but a few comments will provide the background to the scattered comments made by Clement of Alexandria, Tertullian, and Lactantius in relation to early human life and the practices of abortion and exposure.

Plato's *Republic*, Aristotle's *Politics,* and Soranus's treatise *Gynecology* allow us to assume "that the *care* of defective newborns simply was not a medical concern in classical antiquity" and that "the morality of the killing of the sickly or deformed newborns appears not to have been questioned, at least not in extant sources, either by non-medical or by medical authors" (Amundsen 1996, 55). According to Darrell Amundsen, "It can be categorically asserted that there were no laws in classical antiquity, Greek or Roman, that prohibited the killing, by exposure or otherwise, of the defective newborn" (Amundsen, 55). The reason for such rejection of deformed newborn life seems to have been the negligibility of its contribution to the future public good.

Despite the growing humanitarianism of late antiquity, a by-product of broader philanthropic sentiments within Stoicism, the practice of exposure of both healthy and defective newborns was still common in the early Christian centuries. This practice now met with a theologically founded disapproval. Written testimonies to such disapproval are frequent, though made in passing and fragmentary in nature. The Christian writer Minucius Felix writes in a condemnatory tone in *Octavius* that "newly begotten sons [are] at times exposed to wild beasts and birds, or dispatched by the violent death of strangulation," and that women, "by the use of medicinal potions, destroy the nascent life in their wombs, and murder the child before they bring it forth" (*Octavius,* 30; cf. also Clement, *Paidagogos,* 173-74).

Arguments against these practices by Christian authors are not very detailed. Comments are situated primarily in the context of the prohibition of the taking of human life (or the shedding of human blood), even of animal life (or animal blood) more generally: "We however are not allowed either to witness or to hear of human slaughter, and the awe we have of human blood is so great that we do not even taste that of animals for food" (Minucius Felix, *Octavius,* 30). Similarly, Lactantius makes this argument in *The Divine Institutes:* "Therefore (when God forbids killing) no exception whatsoever must be made. It is always wrong to kill a man whom God has intended to be a sacrosanct creature. Let no one, then, think that it is to be conceded even that newly born children may be done away with, an especially great impiety! God breathes souls into them for life, not for death." In the context of killing, Lactantius also addresses the exposure of infants for economic reasons and recommends chastity as the only morally acceptable means of birth control. "Parricides," he says, "complain of the narrowness of their opportunities and pretend that they are not able to provide for bringing up several children, as if in truth, the opportunities are in the power of those possessing them, or as if God does not daily make the rich poor and the poor rich. So, if someone is not able to bring up children on account of poverty, it is more satisfactory that he refrain from intercourse with his wife rather than that he corrupt the works of God with defiled hands" (*Divine Institutes,* 20).

A general appreciation of the goodness of the body regardless of its state and of our responsibility toward it, as well as its spiritual inferiority to the soul, provides another context for early Christian arguments against abortion and exposure. When Tertullian attacks both practices for children healthy or defective, he underlines that there is no difference between an embryo, a baby, a child, or an adult as regards their humanness, based on the union of body and soul. "The fruit is present in the seed" (Tertullian 1950, *Apology*, 9), and the conceptus is a "human being from the moment when its formation is completed" (Tertullian, *On the Soul*, 37/2), by which Tertullian means "the joining of the seeds" (37/5), which for him is also the beginning of the union of body and soul. A degree of potentiality remains in that "the power of the soul which contains all its native potentialities gradually develops along with the body." Yet there is "no change in the initial substance which it received by being breathed into the man in the beginning" (37/5). Such a view clearly differs from the Roman view of human value as acquired gradually through training and education.

The hierarchical view of body and soul often also yields a downplaying of concern with bodily appearance. Clement of Alexandria says in *The Paidagogos*, "It is not the appearance of the outer man that should be made beautiful but his soul with the ornament of true virtue" (202). He condemns both female "decoration of body" and male attempts at "improving the ageing body" (212), and he finds it "absurd to those who have been made to the image and likeness of God to adopt some unnatural means of ornamentation, disfiguring the pattern by which they have been created, and preferring the cleverness of man to that of their divine Creator" (250). In a similar vein, Tertullian exhorts both men and women not to be overly concerned with their appearance. "By a defect of nature, there is inborn in men because of women (just as in women because of men) the desire to please; the male sex also has its own peculiar trickeries for enhancing their appearance: for instance, cutting the beard a bit too sharply, trimming it too neatly, shaving around the mouth, arranging and dyeing our hair, darkening the first signs of gray hair, disguising the down on the whole body with some female ointments, smoothing off the rest of the body by means of some gritty powder, then always taking occasion to look in a mirror, gazing anxiously in it. Are not all of these things quite idle and hostile to modesty once we have known God, have put aside the desire to please others and foresworn all lasciviousness?" (Tertullian 1959, *The Apparel of Woman*, 8). Might it follow from scorn for concern with bodily appearance that disfigurement was rendered also of no great concern? No direct references are made.

How then should humans meet bodily impairment and the suffering it might cause? One response can be found in Tertullian, who commends patience both in flesh and in spirit as the attitude humans should display in the face of what he understood to be an attack by the devil. With reference to Job, he explains, "Thus did that hero who brought about a victory for his God beat back all the darts of temptation and with the breastplate and shield of patience soon after recover from God complete health of body and the possession of twice as much as he had lost" (Tertullian 1959, *Patience*, 14). In general, Tertullian took the body to be the stage on which nature and the supernatural meet and interact. This view, in combination with his hierarchical understanding of the body's union with the soul, allowed him to recognize medicine as a means of health and at the same time to limit it by pointing out the greater importance of spiritual health, defined as relationship with God, the Creator.

Philanthropy to Disfigured Adults

"The hand is mutilated but it is not insensitive to assistance. The foot is gangrenous but always able to run to God; the eye is missing, but it discerns invisible goodness nonetheless, to the enlightenment of the soul" (Gregory of Nyssa, 1.10).

The second strand in early church attitudes toward disability is a concern with the attitude that humans show to the social outcast more generally, an issue approached from the perspective of communal responsibility. These theologians are less interested in how individuals are to face their own suffering (for instance, through patient endurance, as Tertullian recommended) and more concerned with how Christians should meet the suffering of others. Their orientation is pastoral. Following New Testament examples, they commend an attitude of love of humanity (philanthropy) as a response to disability (or disease or poverty). Philanthropy was not a new concept in the Hellenistic context, especially within the Stoic tradition (Daley 1999, 434), but with the advent of Christianity it was invested with new force through the connection "between an active, socially radical concern for humanity and all serious religious observance" (Daley, 436).

I will now focus on three Cappadocian Fathers: Basil the Great, bishop of Caesarea; Gregory of Nazianzus, his friend; and Gregory of Nyssa, his

29

brother. Each continued the work of the Alexandrian Father Athanasius (A.D. 295-373) by seeking the overthrow of Arian doctrines in Asia Minor in defense of Nicean faith and the unity of the church. Although the three are united by their common theological and ecclesiastical interests as well as "by the bonds of a close and life-long friendship . . . Basil is known as the man of action, Gregory of Nazianzus as the master of oratory, and Gregory of Nyssa as the thinker" (Quasten 1994, vol. III, 203).

The great project that seems to have underlain most of their preaching and letter-writing was the promotion of a way of life "characterized on the civic, public level in dramatically concrete ways by Christian *philanthropia,* specifically by the care of the poor" (Daley 1999, 439). Such an idea of life and Christian action was best realized in or near cities, Basil said, rather than in the silence of the desert (Daley, 439). They shared a belief in the reclamation of social outcasts. The social integration of the weak, the ill, the lame, the old, and the poor was seen as integral to the way of Christ and therefore of human redemption. In the words of Gregory of Nazianzus, philanthropy is "the single way towards the salvation both of our bodies and of our souls" (**1.16**).

Such an attitude is, of course, bound up with particular definitions of the body and soul and, crucially, of humans as created in the image of God. Indeed, Gregory says, the kindness that we show to physically disfigured people reminds us that we are clothed in the same "lowly body." He continues, "They have been made in the image of God in the same way you and I have, and perhaps preserve that image better than we, even if their bodies are corrupted. . . . Christ died for them as he did for us, taking away the sin of the whole world" (**1.21**). According to Gregory of Nyssa, disfigurement belongs to our material nature ("common nature," "life under the common biological law," and "common reality" are other terms Gregory uses), which is destined to die: "There is for all only one entrance into life: one way to live, to drink, to eat, only one physical make-up, a common biological law, only one physical death, only one return to dust. All are similarly bound to decomposition" (**1.10**).

This section, then, centers on the philanthropic activities reported by and about Basil the Great, and the sermons exploring the importance of philanthropy for a Christian life written by Gregory of Nyssa and Gregory of Nazianzus and preached around the time of Basil's project of building a new city for the social outcast. Brian Daley suggests that both Nyssa's homilies and Nazianzus's sermon can best be understood "if we suppose they were originally delivered in Caesarea during the years that Basil was developing and carrying out his philanthropic program" (Daley 1999, 448).

Basil's letters, his rule for monks ("The Long Rules," readings **1.1** to **1.7**), and Gregory of Nyssa's two homilies on the poor and disfigured lepers give us closer views of these men's account of philanthropy. Gregory of Nazianzus's *Oration 14* will focus our discussion, an oration written during 369-371 and most likely as an appeal for support for Basil's efforts in providing public care for the sick and the poor (though there is no direct evidence in the sermon of Basil's project). It is written as a homiletic appeal for moral action, enjoining individual participation in assisting those suffering from bodily disfigurement. It is not only the longest and most perfectly constructed sermon on the topic, but the most biblical and exhortative of all Cappadocian writings on social outcasts and philanthropy. Parallels, and even direct verbal parallels, are common with Basil's *Rules,* and while literary dependence is unquestionable, it is not entirely clear who was using whom as source, and hence, which sermon preceded which (cf. Daley 1999; Holman 2001).

Of the three Cappadocians' writings, it is Gregory of Nyssa's homily *On the Love of the Poor,* 2: "On the Saying, 'Whoever Has Done It to One of These Has Done It to Me'" that describes the sight of those suffering from disfiguring diseases such as leprosy and the effects it has on their lives. It is a "frightful malady" which robs humans of "their human form," turns them into "monsters," "beasts." Yet for humans such disfigurement is even worse, for "at least beasts preserve, in general, the appearance they had at birth until they die" (**1.8**). And what is more, disfigured humans are socially excluded and forced to live outside the city because of fear of contagion: "Alone, the sick are driven out from all countries, like designated enemies of the human race. They are not considered worthy of a roof, a common table, or any furniture" (**1.9**). The change in bodily appearance caused by leprosy makes it difficult to recognize the disfigured person's human face, his or her humanness. This has consequences for the respect shown to them. "You see a man and in him you have no respect for a brother?" (**1.8**) Against this, Gregory reminds his hearers that the disfigured are our brothers and sisters, that they are humans just like us, for they are made in God's image like us. He warns that we all might be victims of disfigurement and disease at some future point. "Don't count too heavily on the future. In condemning the sickness that preys upon the body of this man, you fail to consider whether you might be in the process condemning yourself and all nature. For you yourself belong to the common nature of all. Treat all therefore as one common reality" (**1.8**).

Against the background of this common reality, of humanity created in the image of God and created as material bodies, Gregory commends works of charity as the only appropriate response to the suffering of human kin. "Is it not necessary rather to let our compassion and love for one another shine forth radiantly in action? There is a difference between words and action as great as the difference between a painting and reality. The Lord affirms that we will be saved, not by our words but by our actions" (1.10). Such action consists not in isolating the afflicted from our communities, but in reaffirming their place as being "amongst us," in the midst of human communities.

In line with Gregory of Nyssa's arguments, Basil's focus on social outcasts, the disabled, the diseased, and the poor, appears to emphasize the role of social structures, the public response at an institutional level. This had not always been his emphasis. In search of the good life, the youthful Basil was drawn to solitude and monastic communities. However, when he saw the monks of Egypt, Palestine, and Syria, he was not only amazed by their ascetic heroics but "struck too by their failure to carry out the corporeal works of mercy" (Miller 1985, 119) and by their failure of *koinonia*, of community, in which service for the world is practiced. It was here that Basil was confronted with the question of the appropriate relationship of *praxis* and *theoria*.

For Basil, *theoria* — that is, teaching and preaching, praying and worshiping — always takes place within an ecclesial community. As *theoria* within a community, it would not only sustain human knowledge of God's presence but also provide humans with a community able to sustain proximity to those in pain. Drawing on his reading of the scriptures, Basil understood that Christ expected his followers *to be present* — that is, to feed the hungry, clothe the naked, and care for the sick, to carry out practical works of charity and *philanthropeia*. "Prayer and psalmody" are no excuses "for neglecting their work; it is necessary to bear in mind that for certain other tasks a particular time is allotted" (Basil, "The Long Rules," 37). In *Letter 150*, Basil explains that "instruction of how a Christian should live is not so much in need of speech as of daily example." Basil the Great thus turned his back on forms of ascetic life that ignored praxis, concluding that living the good life demands the integration of both *theoria* and *praxis*, both prayer and works of mercy, and within a community.

"The Long Rules," Basil's instruction for monks, starts with an exposition of the commandment of love of God and one's neighbor, elucidating its predominance for both *theoria* and *praxis* in the Christian life (1.1). Charity belongs to the very nature of human beings and is incipient in everyone, planted in anticipation of the Lord's requiring fruits of charity. Charitable acts are a means of recognizing Christ's disciples and are ultimately transferred to Jesus Christ Himself (1.3). In Rule Seven he explains how the phrase "If you live alone, whose feet will you wash?" pointedly highlights the distinctions between solitude and collective service as well as between the active life of *praxis* (deeds of charity in and for the community) and the life of *theoria* (worship, prayer within or outside a community): one who is alone will always fail to act out one of the many dimensions of charity (1.7).

Basil assumes that a monastic community sustaining a whole range of charitable institutions best serves the requirements of the good life, a life which takes seriously the example of Christ. Most likely in response to a famine in Asia Minor, in his early years as a bishop Basil founded a cluster of hospital and care buildings, a philanthropic institution or *ptochotropeion* (that is, in the literal sense, a house to shelter and nourish the poor and destitute) outside the gates of Caesarea during A.D. 368-372. Basil describes it in *Letter 94* as "inns for guests, both those visiting us on their journey and those needing some treatment in their illness." He stresses that the "necessary comforts" be provided, including "nurses, doctors, beasts of burden, and escorts." A hospital, in which both cure and care took place, was part of the cluster of different institutions. It definitely included physicians as part of its staff (Basil, *Letter 94*). The *Basileias* is considered the first hospital in Western civilization if by "hospital" is understood a formal institution devoted to the cure and care of the sick or wounded regardless of their profession, economic and social class, sex, age, and race (Miller 1985, 30-39).

In the funeral oration for his friend delivered in January 382, Gregory of Nazianzus refers to this institution as "the new city." He says, "Go forth a little from this city and behold the new city, the storehouse of piety, the common treasury of the wealthy where superfluous riches, sometimes even necessities, thanks to the exhortations of Basil, are laid up, unexposed to the moths and no source of joy for the thief, escaping the assault of envy and the corruption of time" (Gregory of Nazianzus, *On Basil*, 63).

Gregory's evocation of Basil's "new city" was not simply fourth-century rhetoric but represented a new Christian self-understanding combining the Hellenistic call to social and political leadership based on social class status with the call to be disciples of Christ through practical action as leaders in the church community. The "new city" was explicitly set up to put Christian charity into practice. It was the epitome of true Christian life insofar as it enabled humans to follow the highest commandment and live in discipleship to Christ. This new city was founded as a city *in* and *for* the world, not as a supposedly *heavenly* sphere detached from or distant to it. As Basil says in *Letter 94*, it was "a source of pride to the governor since words of praise redound upon him." Basil's foundation was for Gregory of Nazianzus "the most wonderful achievement of all, the short road to salvation and the easiest ascent to heaven" (Gregory of Nazianzus, *On Basil*, 63).

In this new city, the care of the sick played a crucial role. Gregory of Nazianzus in his funeral sermon does not refer explicitly to the care of poor people or strangers but says, "There, sickness is endured with equanimity, calamity is a blessing, and sympathy is put to the test" (Gregory of Nazianzus, *On Basil,* 63). Service to the sick is reckoned a deep expression of sympathy, charity, and love of humanity, an embodiment of the Christian calling to become God-like. For Eastern theologians, "God was above all *philanthropos,* 'one who loves humanity'" (Harakas 1999, 75). Reportedly, Basil took the care for the sick upon himself. "Others had their cooks and rich tables and enchanting refinements of cuisine, and elegant carriages, and soft flowing garments," Gregory says; "Basil had his sick, and the dressing of their wounds, and the imitation of Christ, cleansing leprosy not by word but in deed" (Gregory of Nazianzus, *On Basil,* 63).

There is a hierarchy of values implicated in Basil's answer to Question 55: Relationship with God is followed by spiritual goodness, which is at all times bound up with the good of the body. The primacy of God's relationship with humans, and of spiritual goodness over against bodily goodness, is understood to guide decision-making, providing humans with an understanding of the *telos* of their actions (namely, the "practice of piety" and the spiritual fulfillment of life) and a judgment on the means employed to achieve such *telos*. Most importantly, for Basil such decision-making is understood as a process which happens within the ecclesial community.

Basil reiterated the importance for human fulfillment and happiness of knowing the command of charity, which takes God to be the highest value and involves compassionate cure and care for the other, thus emphasizing "the sense of human corporateness and ecclesial unity" (Harakas 1999, 89).

The significance of care in the institutionalized public sense of the *Basileias* as well as in a more individual way is brought out most forcefully by Gregory of Nazianzus in *Oration 14,* entitled *Love of the Poor* (reading 1.12-23). While also looking at social exclusion and poverty more generally, the sermon largely deals with the misery of lepers — that is, those who are excluded from the encounter with others and society at large due to the visible effects that leprosy has on their skin and the perceived risk of contagion. The image of the poor body as Christ's body is present throughout the sermon.

Nazianzus sets out to examine the redemptive nature of "love of humanity." He begins by discussing which virtue might be supreme, and finds that love of the poor, compassion, and sympathy are the most excellent form of Christian charity. While he relies in part on a spiritualizing account of disability, in which physical affliction (here, leprosy) is used as metaphor for the illness of the soul, he is above all interested in real physical disfigurement that afflicts people against their will and the social exclusion that accompanies it. He explains that the kindness and compassion shown toward our brothers and sisters in misery "is the single way towards the salvation both of our bodies and of our souls" (1.16). He invites his audience to come into physical contact with lepers, for such touch — medically contagious though it was believed to be — is theologically salvific, effecting spiritual healing for those who are physically well.

Two points are interesting in this context. First, Gregory sees lepers (and the poor) in the light of their relationship to humanity: They are our *kin*, our brothers and sisters, both literally and metaphorically. Second, he views them in light of their relationship to the divine, so that the love we show to them as our kin is love shown to Christ.

While both Gregories and Basil focus on similar ideas (common humanity, the superiority of actions over words, and charity as the highest command), of the three writings we are considering in more detail it is the sermon on the poor by Gregory of Nazianzus that most explicitly recommends the philanthropic care for the disfigured as an action of love, the greatest of all virtues. He emphasizes a view of the poor and disfigured as images of Christ, concluding that our attitude toward them reflects our attitude to Christ. Here I will quote the pivotal passage in full:

> I revere greatly Christ's ointment box, which invites us to care for the poor, and the agreement of Peter and Paul, who divided up the preaching of the Gospel but made the poor their common concern, and the way of perfection of the young man, which was defined by the law of the giving what one has to the poor. . . . Let us take care of Christ while there is still time; let us minister to Christ's needs, let us give Christ nourishment, let us clothe Christ, let us gather Christ in, let us show Christ honor. . . . Let us give this gift to him through the needy, who today are cast down on the ground, so that when we all are released from this place, they may receive us into the eternal tabernacle, in Christ himself, who is our Lord. (*Oration 14*, 39-40)

This identification with Christ neither elevates the sick above other humans nor relegates them below the human per *imago Dei*: Gregory describes them as "brothers and sisters before God . . . who share the same nature with us . . . who have been put together from the same clay from which we first came, who are strung together with nerves and bones in the same way we are, who have put on flesh and skin like all of us. . . . They have been made in the image of God in the same way you and I have, and perhaps preserve that image better than we, even if their bodies are corrupted; they have put on the same Christ in the inner person, and have been entrusted with the same pledge of the Spirit" (**1.21**). Here, the last sentence deserves particular attention: it emphasizes a crucial anthropological aspect found throughout the writings of the Cappadocian Fathers, namely, of the hierarchical union of body and soul, or outer and inner man, with the soul or inner man being the superior part because relating immediately to the divine.

Does this turn those suffering from leprosy into passive objects? Or are they in any sense active gatekeepers of heaven? These are questions not dealt with in the sermon, which does not "imply a new social empowerment of the poor" and disfigured (Holman 2001, 152). "The donors were, as these texts ever remind us, patrons who gave to clients who remained clients; bishops who gave food, clothing, and medicine to wandering mendicants but did not (usually) ordain them" (Holman, 152).

Conclusion

Two strands are prominent in early church attitudes toward the disfigured, the diseased, and the social outcast more generally. On the one hand, there is a concern with the body from an ontological perspective (that is, "Who are we? What is distinctive about the human creature?"). The individual body is here approached in its relationship of subordination to "the soul" or "the spiritual." On the other hand, early church writers are concerned with the disfigured from an ethical perspective (that is, "How do we live well? How do we live well with our fellow humans?"). Here, the body is linked with the command of love and the liturgical community in which such *philanthropeia* or care of others (also bodily) is best practiced. Here the social dimension of sin is prominent, as Susan Holman points out: "This distribution of relief to the needy in a patronage-based culture, as also today in the 'rights-based' culture of the West, often acts as a gauge by which one may perceive the relative value of the individual body in that society. The value of the body is also a social value, in that it denotes the meaning of the body for a religious 'society'" (Holman 2001, 152).

Of course, questions will remain about the understanding of disability on view in these texts. For instance, is our only way of understanding our relationship to disability or those with disabling conditions through the conceptuality of philanthropy? Also, some of the more Stoic-influenced formulas seem to gain acceptance of disability by devaluing the body in relation to the soul. Yet these conceptual difficulties make the obvious and counter-cultural interest in practical care of those considered outcasts all the more striking in a world which thought of disability as something to be shunned or erased. Here we see the origins of a trajectory of care for the "afflicted" or "deformed" that not only grounds the projects of modern medicine but sets the stage for a discourse of concern with the outsider which we know today in its secular form as that of disability rights. Whatever the inadequacies of the theoretical framing of philanthropic activity here, for the first time in Western history an attentive and solicitous eye is turned on those who have been shunned from human communities or society, so challenging societies without any vision of social inclusion as itself a social *good*.

References

Primary Sources

Basil the Great. 1951. *Letters 1-185.* Translated by Sr. A. C. Way. Fathers of the Church, Vol. 13. Washington, D.C.: Catholic University of America Press.

———. "The Long Rules." 1950. In *Ascetical Works,* translated by Sr. M. M. Wagner. Fathers of the Church, Vol. 9. Washington, D.C.: Fathers of the Church, Inc.

Clement of Alexandria. 1954. *Christ the Educator [Paidagogos].* Translated by S. P. Wood. Fathers of the Church, Vol. 23. Washington, D.C.: Catholic University of America Press.

Gregory of Nazianzus. 1953. *On His Brother, St. Caesarius.* Translated by Leo P. McCauley. Fathers of the Church, Vol. 22. Washington, D.C.: Catholic University of America Press.

———. 1953. *On St. Basil the Great, Bishop of Caesarea.* Translated by Leo P. McCauley. Fathers of the Church, Vol. 22. Washington, D.C.: Catholic University of America Press.

———. 2006. *Oration 14.* Translated by Brian E. Daley, S.J. In Daley, *Gregory of Nazianzus.* The Early Church Fathers. London/New York: Routledge.

Gregory of Nyssa. 2001. *On the Love of the Poor,* 1: "On Good Works" [De beneficentia]. Translated by Susan R. Holman. In Holman, *The Hungry Are Dying.* Oxford: Oxford University Press, 193-99.

———. 2001. *On the Love of the Poor,* 2: "On the Saying, 'Whoever Has Done It to One of These Has Done It to Me'" [In illud: Quatenus uni ex his fecistis mihi fecistis]. Translated by S. R. Holman. In Holman, *The Hungry Are Dying.* Oxford: Oxford University Press, 2001, 199-206.

Hippocratic Writings. 1950. *Epidemics*. Translated by J. Chadwick and W. N. Mann. In *Hippocratic Writings,* edited by G. E. R. Lloyd. Oxford: Blackwell.

Lactantius. 1964. *The Divine Institutes, Books I-VII.* Translated by M. F. McDonald. Fathers of the Church, Vol. 49. Washington, D.C.: Catholic University of America Press.

Minucius Felix. 1950. *Octavius.* Translated by R. Arbesmann, Sr. E. J. Daily, and E. A. Quain. Fathers of the Church, Vol. 10. Washington, D.C.: Catholic University of America Press.

Tertullian. 1950. *Apologetical Works.* Translated by R. Arbesmann, Sr. E. J. Daily, and E. A. Quain. Fathers of the Church, Vol. 10. Washington, D.C.: Catholic University of America Press.

Tertullian. 1959. *Disciplinary, Moral, and Ascetical Works.* Translated by R. Arbesmann, Sr. E. J. Daily, and E. A. Quain. Fathers of the Church, Vol. 40. Washington, D.C.: Catholic University of America Press.

Secondary Sources

Amundsen, Darrell. 1996. "Medicine and the Birth of Defective Children: Approaches of the Ancient World." In *Medicine, Society, and Faith in the Ancient and Medieval Worlds,* edited by D. W. Amundsen. London/Baltimore: Johns Hopkins University Press, 50-69.

Daley, Brian E. 1999. "Building the New City: The Cappadocian Fathers and the Rhetoric of Philanthropy." *Journal of Early Christian Studies* 7, no. 3: 431-61.

Gorman, Michael J. 1982. *Abortion and the Early Church: Christian, Jewish, and Pagan Attitudes in the Greco-Roman World.* Downers Grove, Ill.: InterVarsity Press.

Harakas, Stanley. 1999. *Wholeness of Faith and Life: Orthodox Christian Ethics, Part One: Patristic Ethics.* Brookline, Mass.: Holy Cross Orthodox Press.

Holman, Susan R. 2001. *The Hungry Are Dying.* Oxford: Oxford University Press.

Lloyd, G. E. R. 2003. *In the Grip of Disease.* Studies in Greek Imagination. Oxford: Oxford University Press.

Miller, Timothy S. 1985. *The Birth of the Hospital in the Byzantine Empire.* London/Baltimore: Johns Hopkins University Press.

———. 1984. "Byzantine Hospitals." In *Dumbarton Oaks Papers,* Vol. 38, Symposium on Byzantine Medicine, 53-63.

Quasten, Johannes. 1994. *Patrology,* Vols. I-IV. Westminster, Md.: Christian Classics.

Rist, John. 1982. *Human Value: A Study in Ancient Philosophical Ethics.* Leiden: Brill.

———. 1996. *Man, Soul, and Body: Essays in Ancient Thought from Plato to Dionysius.* Aldershot: Variorum.

Stiker, Henri-Jacques. 1999. *A History of Disability.* Ann Arbor: University of Michigan Press.

Suggestions for Further Reading

Amundsen, Darrel W. 1996. *Medicine, Society, and Faith in the Ancient and Medieval Worlds.* London/Baltimore: Johns Hopkins University Press.

Boswell, John. 1988. *The Kindness of Strangers: The Abandonment of Children in Western Europe from Late Antiquity to the Renaissance.* Chicago: University of Chicago Press.

D'Irsay, Stephen. 1930. "Christian Medicine and Science in the Third Century." *Journal of Religion* 10, no. 4: 515-44.

Frings, H.-J. 1959. *Medizin und Arzt bei den griechischen Kirchenvätern bis Chrysostomos.* Ph.D. thesis, Bonn.

Harakas, Stanley. 2000. *Health and Medicine in the Eastern Orthodox Tradition.* New York: Crossroad.

Harnack, Adolf. 1892. "Medicinisches aus ältester Kirchengeschichte." In *Texte und Untersuchungen zur Geschichte der altchristlichen Literatur,* Vol. 8, pp. 37-152.

Numbers, Ronald L., and Darrel W. Amundsen, editors. 1998. *Caring and Curing: Health and Medicine in the Western Religious Traditions.* London/Baltimore: Johns Hopkins University Press.

Excerpts

1.1

Basil the Great. "The Long Rules." In *Ascetical Works.* Translated by Sr. M. M. Wagner. Fathers of the Church, Vol. 9. Washington, D.C.: Fathers of the Church, Inc., 1950, 232.

Q. 1. On order and sequence in the Lord's commandments.

. . . we require, first of all, to be informed as to whether the commandments of God have a certain order or sequence . . . so that one comes first, another, second, and so on; or whether all are interdependent and equal . . . so that one may begin at will wherever he likes, as with a circle.

R. Your question is an old one, proposed long ago in the Gospel when the lawyer came to the Lord and said: "Master, which is the first commandment in the law?" And the Lord answered: "Thou shalt love the Lord thy God with thy whole heart and with thy whole soul and with thy whole strength and with thy whole mind. This is the greatest and the first commandment. And the second is like to this: Thou shalt love thy neighbor as thyself" [Matt. 22:39 par.]. The Lord Himself, then, has established order in His commandments by designating the commandment of the love of God as the first and greatest commandment, and, as second in order and like to the first, but more as a fulfillment of it and as dependent upon it, the love of neighbor. With the aid of these and similar utterances which are handed down to us in the Holy Scripture, we can discover order and sequence in the whole series of the commandments.

1.2

"The Long Rules" (232-39)

Q. 2. Concerning the love of God, and showing that the inclination and the ability to keep the Lord's commandments belong to man by nature.

Speak to us first, therefore, of the love of God; for we have heard that we must love Him, but we would learn how this may be rightly accomplished.

R. The love of God is not something that is taught, for we do not learn from another to rejoice in the light or to desire life, nor has anyone taught us to love our parents or nurses. In the same way and even to a far greater degree is it true that instruction in divine law is not from without, but, simultaneously with the formation of the creature — man, I mean — a kind of rational force was implanted in us like a seed, which, by an inherent tendency, impels us toward love. This germ is then received into account in the school of God's commandments, where it is wont to be carefully cultivated and skillfully nurtured and thus, by the grace of God, brought to its full perfection. . . . We shall establish the fact that we have already received from God the power to fulfill all the commandments given us by Him, so that we may not take our obligation in bad part, as though something quite strange and unexpected were being asked of us, and that we may not become filled with conceit, as if we were paying back something more than had been given us. By means of this power, rightly and properly used, we pass our entire lives holily and virtuously, but through a perverted use of it we gradually fall prey to vice. Now, this is the definition of vice: the wrong use, in violation of the

Lord's command, of what has been given us by God for a good purpose. Similarly, the definition of the virtue which God requires of us is: the use with a good conscience of these same gifts in accordance with the Lord's command. This being the case, we shall apply the same principle also to charity. Having received, therefore, a command to love God, we have possessed the innate power of loving from the first moment of our creation. Of this, no external proof is required, since anyone can discover it of himself and within himself. We are by nature desirous of the beautiful, even though individual conceptions of the beautiful differ widely. Furthermore, we possess — without being taught — a love for those who are near and dear to us, and we spontaneously render to our benefactors a full measure of good will. Now, what is more admirable than Divine Beauty? What reflection is sweeter than the thought of the magnificence of God? What desire of the soul is so poignant and so intolerably keen as that desire implanted by God in a soul purified from all vice and affirming with sincerity, "I languish with love." Totally ineffable and indescribable are the lightning flashes of Divine Beauty. Words do not adequately convey nor is the ear capable of receiving [knowledge of them]. The rays of the morning star, or the brightness of the moon, or the light of the sun — all are more unworthy to be mentioned in comparison with that splendor, and these heavenly bodies are more inferior to the true light than is the deep darkness of night, gloomy and moonless, to brightest noonday. This Beauty, invisible to the eyes of the flesh, is apprehended by the mind and soul alone. Whenever it cast its light upon any of the saints, it left them with an intolerable pain of longing, and they would say, weary of life on earth: "Woe is me that my sojourning is prolonged" [Ps. 120:5]; "when shall I come and appear before the face of God?" [Ps. 42:2]; and again: "to be dissolved and to be with Christ, a thing by far the better" [Phil. 1:23]; also: "My soul hath thirsted after the strong living God" [Ps. 42:2] and "Now thou dost dismiss thy servant, O Lord" [Luke 2:29]. Since they felt the burden of this present life as an imprisonment, they were scarcely able to contain themselves under the impulses which the touch of Divine Love had made to stir within their souls. Indeed, by reason of their insatiable eagerness to enjoy the vision of Divine Beauty, they prayed that contemplation of the joy of the Lord would last as long as the whole of eternal life. Men are by nature, then, desirous of the beautiful. But, that which is truly beautiful and desirable is the good. Now, the good is God, and, since all creatures desire good, therefore, all creatures desire God.

So then, whatever is rightly done of free choice is also in us naturally, at least, in the case of those who have not perverted their rational faculty by iniquity. The love of God, therefore, demanded of us a strict obligation, and for a soul to fail in this is the most unendurable of all evils. Separation and estrangement from God are more unbearable than the punishment reserved for hell and more oppressive to the sufferer than the being deprived of light is to the eye, even if there be no pain in addition, or than the loss of its life is to an animal. If, moreover, the love of children for their parents is a natural endowment and if this love is noticeable in the behavior even of brute beasts, as well as in the affection of human beings in early infancy for their mothers, let us not appear to be less rational than infants or more savage than wild beasts by alienating ourselves from Him who made us and by being unloving toward Him. Even if we did not know what He is from His goodness, yet, from the very fact that we are made by Him, we ought to feel an extraordinary affection for Him and cling to a constant remembrance of Him, as infants do to their mothers. Furthermore, he who is our benefactor is foremost among those whom we naturally love. This gratitude is characteristic not of men only, but it is also felt by almost all animals, so that they attach themselves to those who have conferred some good upon them. "The ox knoweth his owner," says the Prophet, "and the ass his master's crib." God forbid that what follows these words should be said of us: "but Israel hath not known me and my people hath not understood" [Isa. 1:3]. As for the dog and many other animals, I need not speak of the great affection they show toward those who rear them. Now, if we bear a natural love and good will toward our benefactors and undergo any kind of hardship to make a return for what was first rendered to us, what words can fitly treat of the gifts of God? So many are they in number as even to defy enumeration. . . .

Let us, then, say nothing about the rising of the sun, the phases of the moon, climates, the alternation of the seasons, the water dropping from the clouds, other moisture rising from the earth, the sea itself, the whole earth and its produce, the creatures that live in the waters, those which inhabit the air, the countless varieties of animals — all beings destined to minister to our well-being. But what we may not pass over, even if we wished, that which it is quite impossible for one of sound mind and reason to be silent about — yet to speak of it adequately is more impossible — is the fact that God made man according to His image and likeness, that He deemed him worthy of the knowledge of Himself, that in preference to all the animals He adorned him with rationality, bestowed upon him the opportunity of taking his delight in the unbelievable beauties of paradise, and made him the chief of all the creatures on earth. Then, even after he was seduced by the serpent and fell into sin, and by sin into death and its attendant evils, God did not forsake him.

First, He gave to him the Law as an aid, appointed angels to watch over and care for him, sent prophets to refute evil and teach virtue, checked his impulses toward vice by threats, aroused his eagerness for the good by promises, revealed again and again the fate of each of the two classes [the good and the wicked], by making a prejudgment in the case of divers persons so as to warn the rest. In addition to all these and other favors equally great, He did not turn away from man when he persisted in disobedience. We have not been deserted by the Lord's goodness, nor have we impeded His love for us by our stupidity in treating our Benefactor contumeliously through not comprehending the greatness of the favors bestowed — nay, we have even been recalled from death and restored to life again by our Lord Jesus Christ Himself. Even the manner in which this favor was granted calls for the greatest wonder: "Who, being in the form of God, thought it not robbery to be equal with God; but emptied Himself, taking the form of a servant" [Phil. 2:6-7].

He has, moreover, taken upon Himself our infirmities and carried our sorrows. He was crucified for us that we might be healed by His bruises. He also redeemed us from the curse, "being made a curse for us" [Gal. 3:13], and endured the most ignominious death that He might restore us to the life of glory. Nor was He content with merely bringing back to life those who were dead, but He conferred upon them the dignity of divinity and prepared everlasting rest transcending every human concept in the magnitude of its joy. What, therefore, shall we render to the Lord for all the blessings He has bestowed upon us? He is so good, indeed, that He does not exact a recompense, but is content merely to be loved in return for His gifts. Whenever I call all these things to mind (if I may speak of my own feelings), I am struck by a kind of shuddering fear and a cold terror, lest, through distraction of mind or preoccupation with vanities, I fall away from God's love and become a reproach to Christ. For, he who now deceives us and endeavors by every artifice to induce us to forget our Benefactor through the attraction of worldly allurements, leaping at us and trampling us down unto our soul's destruction, will then, in the presence of the Lord, reproach us with our insolence and will gloat over our disobedience and apostasy. . . .

1.3

"The Long Rules" (239-41)

Q. 3. Of charity toward one's neighbor.

R. We have already said above that the law [of God] develops and maintains the powers existing in germ within us. And since we are directed to love our neighbor as ourselves, let us consider whether we have received from the Lord the power to fulfill this commandment also. Who does not know that man is a civilized and gregarious animal, neither savage nor a lover of solitude! Nothing, indeed, is so compatible with our nature as living in society and dependence upon one another and as loving our own kind. Now, the Lord Himself gave to us the seeds of these qualities in anticipation of His requiring in due time their fruits, for He says: "A new commandment I give unto you: that you love one another" [John 13:34]. Moreover, wishing to animate our soul to the observance of this commandment, He did not require signs or wonders as the means of recognizing His disciples (although He gave the power of working these also in the Holy Spirit), but He says: "By this shall all men know that you are my disciples, if you have love one for another" [John 13:35]. Further, He establishes so close a connection between the two great commandments that benefit conferred upon the neighbor is transferred to Himself: "For I was hungry," He says, "and you gave me to eat," and so on, adding: "as long as you did it to one of these my least brethren, you did it to me" [Matt. 25:35, 40].

It is, accordingly, possible to keep the second commandment by observing the first, and by means of the second we are led back to the first. He who loves the Lord loves his neighbor in consequence. "If anyone love me," said the Lord, "he will keep my commandments" [John 14:15]; and again, He says: "This is my commandment, that you love one another as I have loved you" [John 15:12]. On the other hand, he who loves his neighbor fulfills the love he owes to God, for He accepts this favor as shown to Himself. Wherefore, Moses, that faithful servant of God, manifested such great love for his brethren as to wish his name to be struck off the book of God in which it was inscribed, if the sin of his people were not pardoned. Paul, also, desiring to be, like Christ, an exchange for the salvation of all, dared to pray that he might be an anathema from Christ for the sake of his brethren who were his kinsmen according to the flesh. Yet, at the same time, he knew that it was impossible for him to be estranged from God through his having rejected His favor for love of Him and for the sake of that great commandment; moreover, he knew that he would receive in return much more than he gave. For the rest, what has been said thus far offers sufficient proof that the saints did attain to this measure of love for their neighbor.

1.4

"The Long Rules" (241)

Q. 4. *Of the fear of God.*
R. For those newly entered upon the way of piety, the basic discipline acquired through fear is more profitable, according to the counsel of Solomon, wisest of men: "The fear of the Lord is the beginning of wisdom" [Ps. 111:10; Prov. 1:7]. But, for you who have, as it were, passed through your infancy in Christ and no longer require milk but are able to be perfected according to the inner man by the solid nourishment of doctrine, loftier precepts are needed whereby the whole truth of the love which is in Christ is brought to fulfillment. . . .

1.5

"The Long Rules" (241-44)

Q. 5. *On avoiding distraction.*
R. This, at all events, must be recognized — that we can observe neither the commandment of the love of God itself nor that referring to our neighbor, nor any other commandment, if our minds keep wandering hither and yon. It is not possible to master an art or science if one is always starting on fresh subjects, nor even to excel in any single one without recognizing what pertains to the end in view; for one's action must be consistent with the aim, inasmuch as rational ends are not reached by irrelevant means. It is against the nature of things for one to become a master in metal-working by practicing the potter's art, and athletic crowns are not won by enthusiasm for playing the flute. As each kind of mastery demands its own specific and appropriate training, so the discipline for pleasing God in accordance with the Gospel of Christ is practiced by detaching oneself from the cares of the world and by complete withdrawal from its distractions. Therefore does the Apostle, although allowing marriage and deeming it worthy of blessing, oppose to it his

own preoccupation with the concerns of God, as if these two interests could not be compatible, saying, "He that is without a wife is solicitous for the things that belong to the Lord, how he may please God. But he that is with a wife is solicitous for the things of the world, how he may please his wife" [1 Cor. 7:32-33]. In the same manner, the Lord also bore witness to the guileless and single-hearted attitude of His disciples, when He said, "You are not of this world" [John 15:19]. On the other hand, He declared that it is impossible for the world to have knowledge of God or even to receive the Holy Spirit, saying, "Just Father, the world hath not known thee" [John 17:25] and "the spirit of truth, whom the world cannot receive" [John 14:17].

Whoever, therefore, would be truly a follower of God must sever the bonds of attachment to this life, and this is done through complete separation from and forgetfulness of old habits. Unless we wrest ourselves from both fleshly ties and worldly society, being transported, as it were, to another world in our manner of living, as the Apostle said: "But our conversation is in heaven" [Phil. 3:20], it is impossible for us to achieve our goal of pleasing God, inasmuch as the Lord said specifically: "So likewise every one of you that doth not renounce all that he possesseth cannot be my disciple" [Luke 14:33]. And having done this, we should watch over our heart with all vigilance not only to avoid ever losing the thought of God or sullying the memory of His wonders by vain imaginations, but also in order to carry about the holy thought of God stamped upon our souls as an ineffaceable seal by continuous and pure recollection. In this way, we shall excel in the love of God which at the same time animates us to the observance of the Lord's commands, and by this, in turn, love itself will be lastingly and indestructibly preserved. . . .

By these words He teaches us always to place before ourselves as our goal, in undertaking a task, the will of Him who has enjoined the work, and to direct our effort toward Him, as He says in another place: "I came down from heaven, not to do my own will but the will of him that sent me, the Father" [John 6:38]. As the secular arts are directed toward certain specific aims and adapt their particular activities to these aims, so also, inasmuch as our actions have as their rule and guide the keeping of the commandments in a manner pleasing to God, it is impossible to do this with exactitude unless it be done as He wills who gave [the commandments]. And by our painstaking zeal to do the will of God in our work, we shall be united to God through our memory. As the smith, when he is forging an axe, for example, thinks of the person who commissioned the task, and with him in mind calculates its shape and size, suiting his work to the wish of him who ordered it done (for if he is unmindful of this, he will fashion something quite different from what he was ordered to make), so the Christian directs every action, small and great, according to the will of God, performing the action at the same time with care and exactitude, and keeping his thoughts fixed upon the One who gave him the work to do. In this way, he fulfills the saying, "I set the Lord always in my sight; for he is at my right hand, that I be not moved" [Ps. 16:8], and he also observes the precept, "Whether you eat or drink or whatsoever else you do, do all to the glory of God" [1 Cor. 10:31]. But he who departs from the strict observance of the commandment in performing his actions clearly shows that he has given small thought to God. Mindful, therefore, of the voice of Him who said: "Do not I fill heaven and earth, saith the Lord?" [Jer. 23:24] and again: "Am I a God at hand and not a God afar off?" [Jer. 23:23]; also: "Where there are two or three gathered together in my name, there am I in the midst of them" [Matt. 18:20], we should perform every action as if under the eyes of the Lord and think every thought as if observed by Him. . . .

1.6

"The Long Rules" (245-46)

Q. 6. Concerning the necessity of living in retirement.

R. A secluded and remote habitation also contributes to the removal of distraction from the soul. Living among those who are unscrupulous and disdainful in their attitude toward an exact observance of the commandments is dangerous, as is shown by the following words of Solomon: "Be not a friend to an angry man and do not walk with a furious man; lest perhaps thou learn his ways and take snares to thy soul" [Prov. 22:24-25]. The words of the Apostle, "Go out from among them and be ye separate, saith the Lord" [2 Cor 6:17], bear also upon this point. Consequently, that we may not receive incitements to sin through our eyes and ears and become imperceptibly habituated to it, and that the impress and form, so to speak, of what is seen and heard may not remain in the soul unto its ruin, and that we may be able to be constant in prayer, we should before all things else seek to dwell in a retired place. In so doing, we should be able to overcome our former habits whereby we lived as strangers to the precepts of Christ (and it is no mean struggle to gain the mastery over one's wonted manner of acting, for custom maintained throughout a long period takes on the force of nature), and we could wipe away the stains of sin by assiduous prayer and persevering meditation on the will of God. It is impossible to gain proficiency in this meditation and prayer, however, while a multitude of distractions is dragging the soul about and introducing into it anxieties about the affairs of this life. Could anyone, immersed in these cares, ever fulfill that command: "If any man will come after me, let him deny himself" [Matt. 16:24 par.]? For, we must deny ourselves and take up the Cross of Christ and thus follow Him. Now, self-denial involves the entire forgetfulness of the past and surrender of one's will — surrender which it is very difficult, not to say quite impossible, to achieve while living in the promiscuity customary in the world. . . .

1.7

"The Long Rules" (247-52)

Q. 7. On the necessity of living in the company of those who are striving for the same objective — that of pleasing God — and the difficulty and hazards of living as a solitary.

R. I consider that life passed in company with a number of persons in the same habitation is more advantageous in many respects. My reasons are, first, that no one of us is self-sufficient as regards corporeal necessities, but we require one another's aid in supplying our needs. The foot, to cite an analogy, possesses one kind of power and lacks another, and without the cooperation of the other members of the body it finds itself incapable of carrying on its activity independently for any length of time, nor does it have wherewithal to supply what is lacking. Similarly, in the solitary life, what is at hand becomes useless to us and what is wanting cannot be provided, since God, the Creator, decreed that we should require the help of one another, as it is written, so that we might associate with one another. Again, apart from this consideration, the doctrine of the charity of Christ does not permit the individual to be concerned solely with his own private interest. "Charity," says the Apostle, "seeketh not her own" [1 Cor. 13:5]. But a life passed in solitude is concerned only with the private service of individual needs. This is openly opposed to the law of love which the Apostle fulfilled, who sought not what was profitable to himself but to many that they might be saved. Furthermore, a person living in solitary retirement will not readily discern his own defects, since he has no one to admonish and correct him with mildness and compassion. In fact, admonition even from an enemy often produces in a prudent man the desire for amendment. But the cure of sin is wrought with understanding by him who loves sincerely; for Holy Scripture says: "for he that loveth correcteth betimes" [Prov. 13:24]. Such a one it is very difficult to find in a solitude, if in one's prior state of life one had not been associated with such a person. The solitary, consequently, experiences the truth of the saying, "Woe to him that is alone, for when he falleth he hath none to lift him up" [Eccles. 4:10]. Moreover, the majority of the commandments are easily observed by several persons living together, but not so in the case of one living alone; for, while he is obeying one commandment, the practice of another is being interfered with. For example, when he is visiting the sick, he cannot show hospitality to the stranger and, in the imparting and sharing of necessities (especially when the ministrations are prolonged), he is prevented from giving zealous attention to [other] tasks. As a result, the greatest commandment and the one especially conducive to salvation is not observed, since the hungry are not fed nor the naked clothed. . . .

Besides, if all we who are united in the one hope of our calling are one body with Christ as our Head, we are also members, one of another [Rom. 12:5]. If we are not joined together by union in the Holy Spirit in the harmony of one body, but each of us should choose to live in solitude, we would not serve the common good in the ministry according to God's good pleasure, but would be satisfying our own passion for self-gratification. How could we, divided and separated, preserve the status and the mutual service of members or our subordinate relationship to our Head which is Christ? It is impossible, indeed, to rejoice with him who receives an honor or to sympathize with him who suffers when, by reason of their being separated from one another, each person cannot, in all likelihood, be kept informed about the affairs of his neighbor. In addition, since no one has the capacity to receive all spiritual gifts, but the grace of the Spirit is given proportionately to the faith of each, when one is living in association with others, the grace privately bestowed on each individual becomes the common possession of his fellows. "To one, indeed, is given the word of wisdom; and to another, the word of knowledge; to another, faith, to another, prophecy, to another, the grace of healing" [1 Cor. 12:8-9], and so on. He who receives any of these gifts does not possess it for his own sake but rather for the sake of others, so that, in the life passed in community, the operation of the Holy Spirit in the individual is at the same time necessarily transmitted to all. He who lives alone, consequently, and has, perhaps, one gift renders it ineffectual by leaving it in disuse, since it lies buried within him. . . .

Besides these disadvantages, the solitary life is fraught with other perils.

The first and greatest is that of self-satisfaction. Since the solitary has no one to appraise his conduct, he will think he has achieved the perfection of the precept. Secondly, because he never tests his state of soul by exercise, he will not recognize his own deficiencies nor will he discover the advance he may have made in his manner of acting, since he will have removed all practical occasion for the observance of the commandments.

Wherein will he show his humility, if there is no one with whom he may compare and so confirm his own greater humility? Wherein will he give evidence of his compassion, if he has cut himself off from association with other persons? And how will he exercise himself in long-suffering, if no one contradicts his wishes? If anyone says that the teaching of the Holy Scripture is sufficient for the amendment of his ways, he resembles a man who learns carpentry without ever actually doing a carpenter's work or a man who is instructed in metal-working but will not reduce theory to practice. To such a one the Apostle would say: "Not the hearers of the law are just before God, but the doers of the law shall be justified" [Rom. 2:13]. Consider, further, that the Lord by reason of His excessive love for man was not content with merely teaching the word, but, so as to transmit to us clearly and exactly the example of humility in the perfection of charity, girded Himself and washed the feet of the disciples [John 13:5-20]. Whom, therefore, will you wash? To whom will you minister? In comparison with whom will you be the lowest, if you live alone? How, moreover, in a solitude, will that good and pleasant thing be accomplished, the dwelling of brethren together in one habitation which the Holy Spirit likens to ointment emitting its fragrance from the head of the high priest [Ps. 133:2]? So it is an arena for the combat, a good path of progress, continual discipline, and a practicing of the Lord's commandments, when brethren dwell together in community. This kind of life has as its aim the glory of God according to the command of our Lord Jesus Christ, who said: "So let your light shine before men that they may see your good works and glorify your Father who is in heaven" [Matt. 5:16]. It maintains also the practice characteristic of the saints, of whom it is recorded in the Acts: "And all they that believed were together and had all things common" [Acts 2:44], and again: "And the multitude of believers had but one heart and one soul; neither did anyone say that aught of the things which he possessed was his own, but all things were common unto them" [Acts 4:32].

1.8

Gregory of Nyssa, *On the Love of the Poor*, 2: "On the saying, 'Whoever Has Done It to One of These Has Done It to Me.'" Translated by Susan R. Holman. In Holman, *The Hungry Are Dying*. Oxford: Oxford University Press, 2001, 199-206.

. . . You see these people, whose frightful malady has changed them into beasts. In place of fingernails, the disease has caused them to bear pieces of wood on hands and feet. Strange impressions are left on our paths! Who recognizes there a human foot? These people who yesterday stood upright and looked at the sky are here, today, bending to the earth, walking on four feet, practically changed into animals; listen to the rasping wheeze that comes from their chest. Thus it is that they breathe.

But we assert that this condition is worse than that of animals. At least beasts preserve, in general, the appearance they had at birth until they die. None of them experiences the effects of such an avatar, so profound a reversal. With men all happens as if they change in nature, losing the traits of their species to be transformed into monsters. Their hands serve them as feet. Their knees become heels; their ankles and toes, if they are not completely eaten away, they drag miserably like the launch boat that drags the ships. You see a man and in him you have no respect for a brother? No, you do not pity a being of your own race; his affliction only instills horror in you, his begging repels you, and you flee his approach like the assault of a wild beast. Think a little: . . . The Lord of the angels, the king of celestial bliss, became man for you and put on this stinking and unclean flesh, with the soul thus enclosed, in order to effect a total cure of your ills by his touch. But to you, you who share the nature of this brokenness, you flee your own race. No, my brothers, let not this odious judgment flatter you! Remember who you are and on whom you contemplate: a human person like yourself, whose basic nature is not different from your own. Don't count too heavily on the future. In condemning the sickness that preys upon the body of this man, you fail to consider whether you might be in the process condemning yourself and all nature. For you yourself belong to the common nature of all. Treat all therefore as one common reality.

1.9

On the Love of the Poor, 2

Why aren't you moved by any of the diseases you perceive happening to other people? You see the wandering men who are scattered along our roads like cattle foraging for a little nourishment, clothed in wretched rags, a wooden staff in their hands to arm and support them. Yet these are not their own fingers that they clasp, but a species of straps lying along their wrists. A torn scrip, a morsel of stale bread, that is their entire hearth, home, light, bed, barn, table, all the supplies of life. And do you know who it is who lives in this condition? Man born in the image of God, entrusted with the governance of the earth and the rule over all creatures, here so alienated by sickness that one hesitates to recognize him. He has none of the appearance of a man, nor those of a beast. Do you think about the man? But the human body disowns the hideous form. Do you try to see here an animal? But there is no species that takes the form of this monster. Alone, they dare to look at themselves among themselves, and they live in bands, united by their common sufferings. To outsiders they only awaken disgust. Among themselves necessity overrides the horror that they give themselves. Driven away from everywhere, they form a society apart and living, mixing together, closely [in a narrow space]. Can you distinguish their gloomy dances? Do you listen to their plaintive songs? How do they arrive to make a parade of their infirmities and give the crowds the spectacle of their crippled bodies? Macabre jugglers, exhibiting their diverse mutilations! Making sad melodies and gloomy chants, poets of a unique type of tragedy where, without any need of new subjects, they fill the stage with their own misfortunes. What expressions! What detailed descriptions! What events do we hear? They tell how they have been driven away by their own parents, without the least grief over their affliction, how they have been banished from the assemblies, festivals, the markets, treated like murderers and parricides, condemned like those to perpetual exile, but much worse yet. For criminals are always able to establish themselves abroad and live among the members of a collective group. Alone, the sick are driven out from all countries, like designated enemies of the human race. They are not considered worthy of a roof, a common table, or any furniture.

As if this is not bad enough, they are forbidden from the public fountains as well as the streams: they are likely to poison them, it is said. If a dog comes there to moisten his bloody tongue, it is not decreed that the water has been polluted. But if only a sick man approaches there, at once the stream is condemned because of him. Such are their stories and such their complaints. This is why, pressed by hunger, they come to throw themselves at the feet of the public and implore the first to appear.

This atrocious spectacle has often filled me with alarm; often I have felt deeply upset by it, and now it utterly confounds my thoughts. I see again this pitiable suffering, these scenes that force one to tears, these human beings dragging themselves along the road, half-dead, yet supremely human. Rather than men, theirs is a lamentable wreckage. Their malady has robbed them of the traits that would permit them to be identified. One is not able to recognize humans in them: they have lost the form. Alone among the living, they detest themselves and abhor the day they were born, since they have reason to curse these hours that have inaugurated such a horrendous existence. Human beings, I say, who are ashamed to answer to this common name, and who fear dishonoring the common nature by carrying the title. They pass their life ever groaning and never lack a good excuse for tears. All that they ever need to do to awaken their own plaintive cries is to look at themselves. For they do not know whether it is worse to lose their members or still to have them: should they be sad that nature sometimes spares them rather than mutilating them? Which is worse: to be able to see the evidence of their loss or to no longer have it in sight, the malady having rendered them blind? To have such misfortunes to be related, or to be dumb victims for whom the leprosy has eaten away their tongue? To feed miserably on a mouthful of bread or to have lost the form of the mouth altogether and no longer be able to eat like everyone else? To have the experience of the body rotting like carrion, or to be completely without nerve sensations? Where is their sight? Their smell? Their touch? . . .

1.10

On the Love of the Poor, 2

What then? Is one not sinning against the natural law by reducing this person's suffering to theatrical phrases, treating the disease with a speech and remembering it with a ballad? Is it not necessary rather to let our compassion and love for one another shine forth radiantly in action? There is a difference between words and action as great as the difference between a painting and the reality. The Lord affirms that we will be saved, not by our words but by our actions. Also, we ought not to short-change the commandment that enjoins us to help them [the poor]. But let no one say that some place far away from our life is perfectly sufficient and send them off to some frontier, supplying them with food. For a plan of this sort displays neither mercy nor sympathy but is designed, in the guise of goodwill, to banish these people utterly from our life. Are we not willing to shelter pigs and dogs under our roof? The hunters are often not separated, even at night, from their dogs. Look at the love the peasant has for his calf. Even better, the traveler washes his donkey's hoofs with his own hands, brushes his back, carries out his dung and cleans his stable. And will we disparage our own kin and race as baser than the animals? Let these things not be — no, my brothers! Resolve that this inhumanity will not triumph. Remember who they are on whom we meditate: on human beings, in no way distinct from common nature. "There is for all only one entrance into life": one way to live, to drink, to eat, only one physical make-up, a common biological law, only one physical death, only one return to dust. All are similarly bound to decomposition; the body lives bound to the soul; like a transitory bubble, the spirit clothes itself in the body. The bubble bursts without leaving a trace of our exit. Our memory remains on steles, tombstones, and epitaphs, but these also disappear eventually. Do not be exalted, as the apostle said, "but fear" [Rom. 11:20], lest the harsh lawgiver make you the first victim of the cruelty you practice. Do you flee, tell me, from the one who is sick? What repels you? That he has a weakness characterized by oozing of the rotten humors and blood infected by pus, followed by a flow of bile? For this is the medical explanation. Is it the sick person's fault if the frail fabric of his sickly nature exposes itself in these unfortunate ways? . . .

So why send these unfortunate away from us? This is why: no one fears the pronouncement, "Go, far from me, into the eternal fire. Of those whom you had given no aid, it is me you have failed to help" [Matt. 25:41, 45]. If we believe this, we would change our attitude toward the unfortunates; we would go back to them, without any trace of repugnance over caring for their illness. But if we have faith in the promise of God, it is our duty to obey these commandments: only our willingness can assure us of God's promised good will. Stranger, naked, hungry, sick, prisoner; this person carries all the misfortunes the gospel describes. He lives naked, without roof, and the addition of illness reduces him to the most tragic penury. He possesses nothing and has no power to get out of his suffering and provide for his life. He is a prisoner, chained by the illness. You have here the means by which to fulfill the whole law, rendering to the Lord all the things he demands if you show philanthropy to this person. Why then seek your own destruction? For God makes a home for those faithful to his law but deserts the hard-hearted. "Carry my yoke" (Matt. 11:29) — it is called yoke, obedience to the law.

Let us respond now to this summons: become Christ's beast of burden, strap on charity, and do not shake off this soft and gentle yoke that does not chafe the neck but rather caresses it. "Let us sow blessings in order to also reap blessings" (2 Cor. 9:6). This seed will yield a plentiful harvest. The crop of the Lord's law is abundant. The fruits of blessing are high indeed. Do you know how far they pile up? To the apex of heaven. All the good deeds that you have done will reap celestial fruit. Don't despair as a result of this saying, nor say that it is despicable to have a friendship with these people. The hand is mutilated but it is not insensitive to assistance. The foot is gangrenous but always able to run to God; the eye is missing, but it discerns invisible goodness nonetheless, to the enlightenment of the soul. Don't despise their misshapen body; yet a little while and you will contemplate a vision more astonishing than a complete miracle. Our frail nature is not prone to long-term endurance. As soon as there is no more weaving to be done on the corruptible and terrestrial body, the soul, delivered, will manifest its interior beauty. To that rich man of luxury, the life-giving hand of the poor man was not loathsome, but he expressed a desire that the formerly purulent fingers of the poor man might procure for him a drop of water, wanting to lick the wet thumb of the poor man with his tongue [Luke 16:19-31]. He would not have had to wish this if he had known enough to perceive the soul beyond the ugliness of the body. . . .

1.11

On the Love of the Poor, 2

But perhaps you will disagree with me that the commandments can be well trusted, and [you say that] these days it is important to avoid the risk of contagion. You imagine that therefore you escape involuntary ills by fleeing sicknesses. These words are made-up excuses by which you conceal your scorn for divine wishes. And they are not true. There is nothing to fear when one is following the commandment. Don't treat evil with evil. How often we see people who have devoted their lives to the sick from their youth to their old age, without their health being in the least affected. Nothing happens to them. . . .

But, you say, it is hard to master the loathing that most people naturally feel in the face of the sick. Truly, I am of your opinion: it is hard. But am I saying that if it is a worthy project, will there be no effort? God's law commanded much sweat and toil for the hope of heaven, and He teaches humankind — by the harder tasks and harshness of constraining circumstances on all sides — that the way to life is difficult. For it is said, "Narrow and restricted is the way that leads to life" [Matt. 7:14]. What then? Will we give up hope of blessing because it is incompatible with comfort? Let us ask the young people whether wisdom by effort does not seem to them more difficult than shameless abandonment to pleasures. Are we, with so much at stake, going to choose the pleasant, smooth path and beat a retreat in the face of the steep path of virtue? This decision offends the legislator who has forbidden us during our life to take the smooth road, easy and spacious. "Enter," he says, "by the restricted, narrow door" [Matt. 7:13]. Let us put our efforts into the exercise of the precepts that our lives so ignore: curing the natural aversion of the healthy by the persevering exercise of care for the sick. For hard exercise has a surprising effect even on the most difficult people, in that it creates a long-term sense of enjoyment. Let no one say this is laborious duty, for it is useful to those who perform it. In time we will change and laborious effort will become sweet. If I must make it more clear, sympathy toward the unfortunate is, in this life, profitable for the health. For it is beautiful for the soul to provide mercy to others who have fallen on misfortune. For all humanity is governed by a single nature, and no one possesses any guarantee of continual happiness. We ought never to forget the gospel precept that we treat others as we wish others to treat us [Matt. 7:12]. Insofar as you sail on tranquil waters, hold the hand of the unfortunate who have suffered shipwreck. You all sail on the same sea, prone to waves and tempests: and reefs, underwater breakwaters, and other dangers of the ocean evoke the same apprehension in all sailors. Insofar as you are floating, healthy and safe, on the calm sea of life, do not arrogantly pass by those who have shipwrecked their vessel on the reefs. What assurance do you have of always following your way on tranquil waters? You have not yet arrived at the safe port; you have not yet been dragged from the waves, you have not yet reached the shore; throughout your life you remain on the water. Your attitudes toward the unlucky person will determine the conduct of your fellow sailors toward you, yourself. Let us all go forward to attain the port of our rest and desire that the Holy Spirit grant us a serene haven at the end of our journey! Execute God's orders; let us conduct ourselves by the precept of love; guided in this way, let us go up and navigate [the way] to the promised land where the great city stands, whose architect and builder is our God, to whom be glory and power from age to age. Amen.

1.12

Gregory of Nazianzus. *Oration 14*. Translated by Brian E. Daley, S.J. In Daley, *Gregory of Nazianzus*. The Early Church Fathers. London/New York: Routledge, 2006, 76.

1. Brothers and sisters, poor with me — for all of us are beggars and needy of divine grace, even if one of us may seem to have more than others when measured on a small scale — accept my words on love of the poor, not in a mean spirit but generously, that you may be rich in God's Kingdom; and pray that we may bestow these words on you richly, and nourish your souls with our discourse, breaking spiritual bread for the poor. . . .

1.13

Oration 14 (78)

5. Each of these virtues is one path to salvation, and leads, surely, towards one of the blessed, eternal dwellings; just as there are different chosen forms of life, so there are many dwelling places with God, distributed and allotted to each person according to his merit. So let one person cultivate this virtue, the other that. . . . Let each one simply walk on the way, and reach out for what is ahead, and let him follow the footsteps of the one who leads the way so clearly. . . . And if, following the command of Paul and of Christ himself, we must suppose that love is the first and greatest of the commandments [Matt. 22:38], the crowning point of the law and the prophets, I must conclude that love of the poor, and compassion and sympathy for our own flesh and blood, is its most excellent form. For God is not served by any of the virtues as he is by mercy, since nothing else is more proper than this to God, "before whom mercy and truth march as escorts" [Ps. 85:13], and to whom mercy is to be offered as a sacrifice in preference to justice [Hos. 6:6; Prov. 21:3]; nor will human kindness be repaid with anything else than the same kindness, by him who makes just recompense and weighs our mercy with his balance and scales.

1.14

Oration 14 (78-79)

6. We must open our hearts, then, to all the poor, to those suffering evil for any reason at all, according to the Scripture that commands us to "rejoice with those who rejoice and weep with those who weep" [Rom. 12:15]. Because we are human beings, we must offer the favor of our kindness first of all to other human beings, whether they need it because they are widows or orphans, or because they are exiles from their own country, or because of the cruelty of their masters or the harshness of their rulers or the inhumanity of their tax-collectors, or because of the bloody violence of robbers or the insatiable greed of thieves, or because of the legal confiscation of their property, or shipwreck — all are wretched alike, and so all look towards our hands, as we look towards God, for the things we need. But of all these groups, those who suffer evil in a way that contradicts their dignity are even more wretched than those who are used to misfortune. Most especially, then, we must open our heart to those infected by the "sacred disease" [i.e., leprosy], who are being consumed even in their flesh and bones and marrow, just as some have been threatened by Scripture. They are being betrayed by this deceiving, wretched, faithless body! How I am connected to this body, I do not know, nor do I understand how I can be an image of God, and still be mingled with this filthy clay; when it is in good condition, it wars against me, and when it is itself under attack, it causes me grief! I love it as my fellow servant, but struggle against it as an enemy; I flee it as something enslaved, just as I am, but I show it reverence as called, with me, to the same inheritance. I long that it be dissolved, and yet I have no other helper to use in striving for what is best, since I know what I was made for, and know that I must ascend toward God through my actions.

1.15

Oration 14 (79)

7. So I treat it gently, as my fellow worker; and then I have no way of escaping its rebellion, no way to avoid falling, weighed down by those fetters that drag me or keep me held down to the earth. It is a cordial enemy, and a treacherous friend. What an alliance and an alienation! What I fear, I treat with

honor; what I love, I fear. Before we come to war, I am reconciled to it, and before we have made peace, I am at odds with it again. What wisdom lies behind my constitution? What is this great mystery? Is it God's will that since we are part of him, drawn in an upward stream, we should always look towards him from the midst of a fight and struggle with the body, so that we might not be lifted up by our own dignity and think ourselves so high that we begin to look down on our creator? Is this weakness with which we are joined a kind of training for that dignity, making us aware that we are both the greatest and the most lowly of creatures, earthly and heavenly, temporal and immortal, heirs of both light and fire, or even of darkness, depending on which way we may lean? Such is the blend of our nature, and for this reason, it seems to me, whenever we are exalted in spirit because of the image [of God], we are humbled because of earth. . . .

1.16

Oration 14 (79-80)

8. Now, however, as I feel pain at the weaknesses of my own flesh and sense my own weakness in the sufferings of others, what reason urges me to say this: brothers and sisters, we must care for what is part of our nature and shares in our slavery. For even if I lay charges against it, because of its possibility, still I stand by it as a friend, because of the one who bound me in it. And we must, each of us, care no less for our neighbors' bodies than our own, the bodies both of those who are healthy and of those who are consumed by this disease. "For we are all one in the Lord, whether rich or poor, whether slave or free" [Gal. 3:28], whether in good health of body or in bad; and there is one head of all, from whom all things proceed: Christ. And what the limbs are to each other, each of us is to everyone else, and all to all. So we must by no means overlook or neglect to care for those who experience our common weakness before we do, nor should we delight more in the fact that our bodies are in good condition than we grieve that our brothers and sisters are in misery. Rather, we must consider this to be the single way towards the salvation both of our bodies and of our souls: human kindness shown towards them. Let us examine this point together.

1.17

Oration 14 (80)

9. For most people, only one thing causes misery: something is lacking. Perhaps time, or hard work, or a friend, or a relative, or the passing of time has taken it away. But for the people I am speaking of, misery is present even more abundantly, in that the resources to work and to help themselves in need have been taken away along with their flesh, and the fear of growing weaker is always greater to them than the hope of recovery. Indeed, they find little support in hope, which is the only drug that really helps the unfortunate. In addition to their poverty, illness is a second evil: the most abominable and depressing evil of all. . . . And a third evil for them is the fact that no one will approach them, that most will not look at them, that all run away from them, find them disgusting, try to keep them at a distance. So that for them something still more burdensome than the disease is to perceive that they are hated because of their misfortune. I cannot bring myself to think about the suffering of these people without tears, and I am brought to confusion when I recall them; you should feel the same way yourselves, that you might put tears to flight with tears. I know, in fact, that those among you who love Christ and love the poor do feel this way; for you have received the gift of sharing God's mercy from God himself, and you give witness to your feelings yourselves.

1.18

Oration 14 (80-81)

10. There stands before our eyes a terrible, pitiable sight, unbelievable to anyone who did not know it was true: human beings both dead and alive, mutilated in most parts of their body, scarcely recognizable either for who they are or where they come from; they are, rather, wretched remnants of once human-beings. As marks of identification, they call out the names of their fathers and mothers, brothers and sisters and homes: "I am the son of so-and-so, so-and-so is my mother, this is my name, you were once my dear companion!" They do this because they cannot be recognized by their former shape; they are truncated human beings, deprived of possessions, family, friends, and their very bodies, distinctive in being able both to pity themselves and to hate themselves at once. They are uncertain whether to lament for the parts of

their bodies that no longer exist, or for those that remain — those which the disease has consumed, or those left for the disease to work on. The former have been consumed most wretchedly, the latter are still more wretchedly preserved; the former have disappeared before their bodies are buried, the latter have no one who will give them a burial. For even the kindest and most humane of neighbors is insensitive to them; in this instance alone, we forget that we are flesh, clothed in this lowly body, and we are so far from caring for our fellow creatures that we think the safety of our own bodies lies in fleeing from them. One approaches a body that has been dead for some time, even if it has begun to reek; one carries about the stinking carcasses of brute animals, and puts up with being full of filth; yet we avoid these lepers with all our might (what inhumanity!), almost taking offense at breathing the same air as they breathe.

1.19

Oration 14 (81)

11. Who could be more upright than a father? Who more sympathetic than a mother? But nature's operation is shut off even for them. The father looks at his own child, whom he begot and raised, whom alone he considered the light of his life, for whom he prayed often and long to God, and now both grieves over that child and drives him away — the first willingly, the second under compulsion. The mother recalls the pangs of childbirth and her heart is torn apart: she calls his name wretchedly, and when he stands before her she laments for her living child as if he were dead: "Unfortunate child of a miserable mother, bitter disease has come to share you with me! Wretched child, unrecognizable child, child whom I have raised only for the cliffs and mountaintops and desert places! You will dwell with wild beasts, and rock will be your roof; only the holiest of people will ever look on you!" Then she will utter those pitiable words of Job, "Why were you formed in the womb of your mother? Why did you not come forth from her belly and immediately perish, so that death and birth might have been simultaneous? Why did you not depart prematurely, before tasting the evils of life? Why did these knees receive you? Why were you allowed to suck at these breasts, since you were going to live so wretchedly, a life more difficult than death?" [Job 3:10-13, paraphrase]. So she speaks, and lets loose floods of tears; the unfortunate woman wishes to embrace her child, but fears his flesh, as if it were the enemy. From all the neigh-

bors come loud shouts and gestures, driving him away — cries not directed against criminals, but against the wretched. There have been instances when people have allowed a murderer to live with them, have shared not only their roof but their table with an adulterer, have chosen a person guilty of sacrilege as their life's companion, have made solemn covenants with those who have wished them harm; but in this person's case suffering, rather than any injury, is handed down as a criminal charge. So crime has become more profitable than sickness, and we accept inhumanity as fit behavior for a free society, while we look down on compassion as something to be ashamed of.

1.20

Oration 14 (81-82)

12. They are driven away from the cities, driven away from their homes, from the market-place, from public assemblies, from the streets, from festivals and private celebrations, even — worst of all sufferings! — from our water; not even the springs flow for them, though they are common property for everyone else, nor are the rivers allowed to wash off any of their impurities. Most paradoxical of all, we drive them away as bearers of pollution, yet we draw them back towards us again, as if they caused us no distress at all, by giving them neither housing, nor the necessary food, nor treatment for their lesions — by not cloaking their disease, as far as we can, with some form of covering. For this reason they wander around night and day, destitute and naked and homeless, showing their disease publicly, talking of the old times, crying out to their Creator, crafting songs that constrain us to pity, asking for a bit of bread or some tiny scrap of food, or for some tattered rag to protect their modesty and offer some relief to their sores. The kindest person, for them, is not someone who supplies their needs, but someone who does not send them off with a sharp stick. Most of them, too, are not ashamed to appear at festivals — just the opposite: they thrust their way into them because of their want. I am speaking both of public festivals and of the sacred ones that we have instituted for the care of our souls, when we come together either because of some mystery of faith or to celebrate the martyrs who witnessed to the truth, so that by paying honor to their struggles we might also imitate their piety. These people feel shame at their condition, surely, before their fellow human beings, since they are human themselves; they would wish to be hidden by mountains or cliffs or forests, or finally by night and

darkness. Yet they throw themselves into the midst of the crowd, nonetheless, a wretched rabble worthy of our tears. Perhaps this all has a reason: that they might remind us of our own weakness, and persuade us not to lean on any of the present things we see around us, as if it were stable. They throw themselves into our midst, some from a longing to hear the human voice, others to see a face, others in order to gather up some scanty provisions from those who are feasting — all of them making their laments public, in hope of tasting some form of gentleness in return.

1.21

Oration 14 (83)

14. This is how they are suffering, and much more miserably than I have said: our brothers and sisters before God (even if you prefer not to think so) who share the same nature with us, who have been put together from the same clay from which we first came, who are strung together with nerves and bones in the same way we are, who have put on flesh and skin like all of us, as holy Job says when reflecting on his sufferings and expressing contempt for our outward form. Or rather, if I must speak of greater things, they have been made in the image of God in the same way you and I have, and perhaps preserve that image better than we, even if their bodies are corrupted; they have put on the same Christ in the inner person, and have been entrusted with the same pledge of the Spirit; they share in the same laws as we do, the same Scriptural teachings, the same covenants and liturgical gatherings, the same sacraments, the same hopes. Christ died for them as he did for us, taking away the sin of the whole world; they are heirs with us of the life to come, even if they have missed out on a great deal of life here on earth; they have been buried together with Christ, and have risen with him; if they suffer with him, it is so they may share in his glory.

1.22

Oration 14 (85)

18. What do you make of all this, my friends, my brothers and sisters? Why do we suffer ourselves from this spiritual sickness — a sickness much more

serious than that of the body? I am convinced, after all, that as much as the one is involuntary, the other comes from our choice; as much as the one ends with this life, the other goes with us when we are brought to the next; as much as the one is pitiable, the other is hateful, for anyone of sound mind. Why do we not help our own natural kin, while we have time? . . .

1.23

Oration 14 (90-91)

27. For a human being has no more godlike ability than that of doing good; and even if God is benefactor on a grander scale, and humans on a less, still each does so, I think, to the full extent of his powers. He created us, and restored us again by setting us free; you must not overlook the one who has fallen. He has shown mercy to us in the greatest ways, above all by giving us the law and the prophets, and even before them the unwritten law of nature, the standard of judging all our deeds; he examines us, admonishes us, trains us, and finally he has given himself as a ransom for the life of the world. He has lavished on us apostles, evangelists, teachers, shepherds, healers, wonderful signs, a way that leads to life, the destruction of death, a trophy of victory over the one who had conquered us, a covenant in shadow and a covenant in truth, gifts that let us share in the Holy Spirit, the Mystery of new salvation. As for you, if you are also capable of greater things, do not fail to do good for the needy with the gifts which your soul is blessed, for God has made you rich in this way, too, if you only wish to be so. Give a share in these things, first and foremost, to the one who asks your help, even before he asks you; all day long, "have mercy and lend" [Ps. 37:26] him God's word, and earnestly demand your loan back, with the growth of the one you have helped as your "interest" — for he always adds something to the word you have given by letting the seeds of piety grow a little more within himself.

But if you cannot do this, give the secondary, smaller gifts, as far as it is in your power: come to his help, offer him nourishment, offer her a scrap of clothing, provide medicine, bind up his wounds, ask something about her condition, offer sage advice about endurance, give encouragement, be a support. . . .

2 Augustine's Hierarchies of Human Wholeness and Their Healing

BRIAN BROCK

Although in his own lifetime Augustine was an acclaimed figure, he was by no means a dominant political or ecclesial actor. But as subsequent chapters amply illustrate, his framing of any given question was to set the basic parameters within which centuries of Western Christians were to think. Later theologians have been prone to systematize his thought, finding their own unities amid the many arguments of his vast corpus, encouraged by his various speculative ruminations, his tendency to high-flown rhetoric (especially in preaching), and his willingness to reconsider and nuance previously held opinions. Although it would be highly anachronistic to suggest that he had any theology of disability, his assumptions about human nature, sickness, and health have deeply shaped what in later centuries would come to be called disability.

This introduction will present an Augustine who develops two quite different theological responses to conditions we would understand today as debilitating. A minor but highly suggestive strand of his thought emphasizes the ways in which our perception of other human beings must be illuminated or sanctified if we are to know them rightly and resist the temptation to approach people as little more than their apparent deficits of mind or body. This line of thought parallels the modern critique of disability as a social construction in pressing Christians to see beyond their habits of judging humans according to socially conditioned beliefs about what counts as a good human life. This reasoning, while suggestive, is not the dominant strand in Augustine's anthropology. I will begin by tracing a quite different trajectory in which Augustine explicitly develops a theological account of the perfection of the human body and mind. Standing much closer to modern medical accounts of disability, this latter strand expresses a concern to objectively define which human functions must be lost to render one disabled. I will suggest, in conclusion, that these trajectories are not entirely compatible, the former emphasizing a breaking open of Christian perception of other human beings in a manner that seeks to know people beyond their supposed disabilities, while the latter stands in a long tradition of conceiving those with physical and mental challenges as residing within a hierarchy of wholeness, at a greater or lesser distance from what we take to be human perfection.

Like most ancients, Augustine often faced physical challenges that strike us today as debilitating or borderline debilitating. His medical history is probably not atypical of most people living before the advent of modern medicine: as a boy he suffered a near-death experience as a result of a severe fever and chest infection which he contracted (Confessions, I.xi.17) and a similarly life-threatening fever shortly after his arrival as a promising young orator in Rome (Confessions, V.ix.16). This latter brush with death cut short a promising career as a rhetorician, dashed his hopes of joining the imperial court, and forced him to resign from his teaching post. His "lungs had begun to weaken. Breathing became difficult. Pains on the chest were symptoms of the lesion, and deprived me of the power to speak clearly for any length of time" (Confessions, IX.ii.4). In his letters we read that for the rest of his life his lungs were susceptible to the cold (Letter 124), a condition that worsened with age (Letters 151.13, 269), and was compounded by other common conditions such as hemorrhoids (Letter 38.1).

More important for our purposes are Augustine's keen observations on the social role of conditions we would consider debilitating. For instance, in a very early work, he illustrates a conceptual point about the relationship of signs to meaning with a reference to the communication of deaf people. In so doing he produced what is probably the earliest surviving account of communication between deaf people.

> Haven't you ever seen that men converse, as it were [quasi sermocinentur], with deaf people by gesturing? That deaf people themselves, no less by gesturing raise and answer questions, teach and indicate all the things they want, or at least most of them [indicent aut omnia, quae volunt, aut certe plurima]? When this happens, they show us without words not only visible things, but also sounds and flavors and other things of this sort. Even actors in the theatres unfold and set forth entire stories without words — for the most part, by pantomime. (The Teacher, 2.4)

In an even earlier work he describes witnessing firsthand communication between deaf and hearing people who, "by nods and gesture express the thoughts they have to communicate" — a reference to a young deaf man of Milan and to a deaf family of six or more people whom he knew. He also noted that a hearing child born to deaf parents communicates with signs learned from the parents (*The Magnitude of the Soul,* 18). In a later note Augustine was to make similar conceptual points by reference to mimes (*On Christian Doctrine,* 2.3.4).

Augustine is untroubled that his use of disabled people as illustrations in academic discussions is exploitative, but this ought not to be taken as a mark of insensitivity. We do glimpse in his regular comments on what he usually refers to as intellectual or physical "deformity" a keen awareness of the grief of loved ones at disabling conditions — especially of the intellect — suffered by their children or wards. Furthermore, he is acutely aware of the pain that is inflicted on these same parents or carers when the "morons" in their care are subjected to the crass and carnal amusement of the masses. His comments reveal much about the cultural context in which Augustine wrestled with these issues:

> We see, also, how those simpletons whom the common people call Moriones are used for the amusement of the sane; and that they fetch higher prices than the sane when appraised for the slave market. So great, then, is the influence of mere natural feeling, even over those who are by no means simpletons, in producing amusement at another's misfortune. Now, although a man may be amused by another man's silliness, he would still dislike to be a simpleton himself; and if the father, who gladly enough looks out for, and even provokes, such things from his own prattling boy, were to foreknow that he would, when grown up, turn out a fool, he would without doubt think him more to be grieved for than if he were dead. (*On the Merits and Forgiveness of Sins,* 66; cf. **2.2**)

It is clear from these opening observations that Augustine had suffered, seen and appreciated various disabling conditions, and felt the need to set them within a wider theological account of human existence. He did so with sympathy and awareness of the cruelty often heaped on the disabled, which he bluntly censored as carnal delight in others' misfortune. Thus far, however, we have seen Augustine assuming that physical or mental impairment is a lamentable state, an undertone that persists in most of his comments on these themes. Several counter-notes are also struck, but to hear them we must investigate Augustine's more conceptually dense attempts to explain the presence of such people in the world. In a striking inversion of the interpretations current at the time, he suggests that physical, sensory, and mental impairments, while still impairments (at least congenital impairments), are nevertheless not the work of evil spirits, because all humans are made by a Creator who creates only good things. In this strand of his thought we see him trying to overcome the human tendency to see the disabled as God's mistakes. The way in which his answers to this problem are framed, however, rests on a theological norm for human life which allows "deformity" to be identified.

Norming the Human

Augustine was always very clear that the human body and intellect are intended by God to be complete, and his definition of human completeness was based not on theory but empirical experience. "It is . . . clear what constitutes the natural norm in the majority of cases and what, in itself, is a marvelous rarity" (*City of God,* XVI.8; **2.13**). His elaborated theoretical account of the normal human was strongly influenced by ancient philosophical sensibilities: human perfection is marked by harmony, a unification of beauty and utility, of form, shape, and color (**2.21**). This account combined the commonsense observation that human beings generally have a set of familiar traits, such as two arms and two legs, which Augustine interpreted in Platonic terms as the expression of a "pattern" or "potential" woven into the fabric of the body, present from birth, and guiding its development (**2.13, 2.16**). In this sense humans do not differ from other living things: "For it is thanks to the activity of God continued even down to the present time that seeds display themselves and evolve from hidden and invisible folds, as it were, into the visible forms of beauty which we behold. It is He who brings about that wondrous combination and union of an incorporeal with a corporeal nature, with the former in command and the latter subjected to it, by which living being is made" (*City of God,* XXII.24; cf. **2.21**). The "soul" is the "pattern" for human development, but also the locus of a standard that allows Augustine to spot and quantify greater or lesser deviation from a human norm. It allows him to make assessments of the human like the following: "We know of men who were born with more than five fingers or five toes. This is a trivial thing and not any great divergence from the norm" (*City of God,* XVI.8; **2.13**).

Augustine was led into this line of reasoning by his belief that Christ, as the Wisdom or Logos of God, revealed the global norm for human flourishing. He firmly asserts that all speculation about the proper form of human life is necessarily Christological speculation. This was not a novel thought, but an expression of the common patristic belief that Christians must affirm the physical resurrection of every person, and that, for Christians at least, this resurrection happens only "in Christ" (2.17). This leaves Augustine with a complex equation: Because all humans will be resurrected in Christ, they will be resurrected in their true and eternal form. Affirming that the perfect human has appeared in Christ leads Augustine to deny the ascription of physical, intellectual, or volitional perfection to any human being. This is an important point, because it means that, for Augustine, every human falls short of the norm. No human can claim to be complete, wholly healthy. At best we see intimations of the perfect human spread through the best of humanity's diverse traits. This circuitous but powerful logic underlies all his anthropological speculations.

Because Christ is the sum of all human perfections, Augustine turns to the resurrection of Christ's body in order to explicate the perfection of resurrected human bodies (2.18). The perfect individual pattern hidden in humans from conception will be expressed in its fullness in the Resurrection, leading to the conclusion that in it all human infirmity will be healed. On this point Augustine is unambiguous. "Concerning monsters [monstra] which are born and live, however quickly they die, neither is resurrection to be denied them, nor is it to be believed that they will rise again as they are, but rather with an amended and perfected body. . . . And so all other births which, as having some excess or some defect or because of some conspicuous deformity [deformitate], are called monsters, will be brought again at the resurrection to the true form of human nature [humanae naturae figuram]" (*The Enchiridion,* 87). His account of the unfolding of the soul's pattern should be distinguished from modern genetic accounts: what guides development is not a biological structure but the immortal soul (*The Magnitude of the Soul,* 22). It also differs from the modern use of general social norms to describe human social and political activity: the Christological norm, in the form of the soul of each person, is not generic and uniform but particular, different for each person, underlying and sustaining the variation between individuals, and indeed, the sexes (2.17-20).

That Augustine's adaptation of a Neoplatonic doctrine of the forms is being rather firmly worked over in Christological and biblical terms is attested to by the remarkable fact that Augustine breaks with his age in refusing to call the female form a departure from an original perfect male form (**2.19**). In the Resurrection, individuals will both be given the body that fully expresses the perfect norm (that is, without impairments) and be granted full appreciation of the body each has received (*The City of God*, XXII.30). "Deformed" and "restored" to "normal shape" are conceived in this logic as straightforwardly physical terms. But that "normal shape" includes both women and men clarifies Augustine's comment that the Christological norm is not generic and uniform. It appears that Augustine's *principle of diversity* is based on his reading of the biblical promise that in the Resurrection "not a single hair will be lost"; that we will be made "like Christ" is his organizing principle of similarity and "normal shape." The whole discussion is focused on physical form rather than traits like rationality or sensation. Put in modern terms, in the resurrection the social constructions of disability will be erased as sinful barriers to communion, and physical impairments and deformities will be restored to the wholeness that is promised to each person in Christ, the perfect human.

This basic account of the "normal" human was no empty cipher for Augustine. In an early letter he wrote that God "has bestowed so many goods of his own creation on good and bad alike: their existence, their humanity, their flourishing senses, their health and strength, their overflowing wealth" (Letter 155). A later and more developed account of the normal human traits included having sensation, intellect, reproductive capacity, and capacity for developing virtue, ingenuity, and beauty (**2.21**). He typically uses a negative vocabulary for impairments to indicate that they are homologous with evil as a deprivation of the good. At the same time, Augustine insisted that, while the loss or lack of any of these traits was properly lamentable, life itself was a good not vitiated by the loss of any of these capacities (**2.14**; cf. Letter 155). Humans suffer impairment in the same way they suffer evil. Augustine is unhitching human happiness from human capacity or incapacity.

In summary, Augustine's theological norm for the human body rested upon judgments about ideal and real human capacities, but did not denigrate the lack of capacities he considered ideal. In most cases, however, he did assume that to lack some capacities was an inferior and mournful state. The function of Augustine's Christology was thus both to anchor and to validate his observations about the "average" way of being human, and to provide a conceptual mechanism allowing the affirmation of the eternal value of each human life, no matter how impaired. "Christ" does, then, function for Augustine as a promise of human wholeness, but not one that sets up a social norm against which individuals can be struck off the rolls of the human race. This is arguably true even of his ideas about intellectual impairment.

Rationality and the Image of God

A crucial aspect of Augustine's anthropological norm is his strong association of rationality with the essence of the human. Augustine not only thinks of the term "soul" as naming the enduring essence of the human, but insists that this essence is ineradicably rational. Augustine is not suggesting that those who do not express this essential human trait are sub-human. Structurally, the human soul is rational, even if this rational soul has not been expressed (**2.8**). Augustine stresses this point by disagreeing with the Origenist claim that souls pre-exist bodies and are only grudgingly forced into disabled bodies. Rather, each soul is specifically created for each body by God, and does not exist without it (**2.3**). Augustine does not clarify the mechanics of how a soul that will be resurrected with a whole body — and so is presumably the perfect pattern of the individual that will be restored — can nevertheless yield a "deformed" body or mind. The rationale that Augustine assumes for this occurrence is that it is an effect of the Fall, and he only tentatively speculates that its mechanics are related to the effects of a perfectly created soul being united to a body suffering the defects of the fallen world (**2.3**).

The high profile of rationality in this anthropology raises questions in a contemporary context. The first concerns the hierarchical logic of an anthropology and a moral psychology that not only names rationality as the human capacity separating humans from animals, but suggests that this trait is what makes them *superior* to animals (**2.6**; **2.11**; **2.21**). Such a reliance on rationality as a principle of superiority is bound to lead to the disparagement of the intellectually impaired: if "the divine principle is reason, the logic of Stoicism tends to include only the intelligent in the divine community," Reinhold Niebuhr once observed. "An aristocratic condescension, therefore, corrupts Stoic universalism" (Niebuhr 1956, 53). Augustine *wants* to say that all human life is valuable, but his basic account of God and humanity problematizes his achieving this aim. The second and more worrying implication of such an intellect-focused account of the human to post-Holocaust ears is that it appears to allow that those without intellect are sub-human, a claim seemingly bolstered by Augustine's definition of the commandment against murder solely by reference to rationality (**2.9**). Yet he ought not to be drafted too quickly as a defender of modern definitions of personhood that are solely indexed to possessed capacities. For Augustine, humans are beings with rational souls, in each and every case (**2.8**). His anthropological norm is never deployed to suggest that an individual's humanity is lost if his or her capacity to reason is lost, insisting rather on the opposite, that the loss of rationality is not the loss of humanity, or even of personhood, but is a loss of the *expression* of a central human trait. In addition, he warns that the reduction of human happiness to a matter of possessing a set of capacities has murderous implications (**2.14**; cf. Letter 155).

To be human is to be the bearer of a set of traits, including rationality, whether these are empirically expressed or not. The question of inclusion in the human family, then, is *not* a matter of expressed functional capacities, but descent by birth. All who descend from Adam and Eve by birth are human, regardless of their physical traits: "Anyone who is born anywhere as a man (that is, as a rational and moral animal), no matter how unusual he may be to our bodily senses in shape, color, motion, sound, or in any natural power or part or quality, derives from the original and first-created man; and no believer will doubt this" (*City of God,* XVI.8; **2.13**). Modern interpreters must at this point come to their own conclusions about the implications of Augustine's dual emphasis on humans as rational and his simultaneous insistence that none of the children of Adam and Eve may ever be decreed non-humans on the basis of an apparent lack of physical or mental capacities.

Impairment and the Remaking of Human Perception

Augustine's insistence that all humans are good as God's creations (**2.10**; **2.13**) generates another and quite different approach to the problem of human impairment. He is well aware of the human tendency to pity or shun those considered "monstrous" and believes that precisely because humans are rational souls, this sinful proclivity can be healed. Commenting on the creation of humans in the book of Genesis, Augustine concludes that "it was in the very factor in which he surpasses non-rational animate beings that man was made to God's image." Because humans are created rational, "the apostle too says: Be renewed in the spirit of your minds and put on the new man, who is being renewed for the recognition of God according to the image of him who created him (Rom. 12:2; Eph. 4:23-24; Col. 3:10) . . . he makes it plain enough just what part of man was created in God's image — that it was not in the features of the body but in a certain form of the illuminated mind" (*The Literal Meaning of Genesis,* III.20, 30). This juxtaposition of the work of creation and the work of redemption reveals that though the modern discourse about human rationality is concerned with basic human creaturely features, Augustine's interest is in the illumination of the mind as part of the sanctification necessary if sinful humans are to have a right relationship to all God's children. It is clear that

Augustine's reading here is not working from *created* human capacities, but develops the Genesis command to have dominion (Gen 1:28; cf. **2.9**) by focusing it through the Pauline insistence that a *redemptive* renewal of the mind is a necessary aspect of salvation (Rom. 12:2). For Augustine these texts again point to rationality as the locus of human transformation, and therefore as the fundamental and distinguishing feature of human nature — whether actually expressed or not (cf. **2.7**).

Augustine presses several speculations, none presented as definitive, about God's reasons for allowing human impairment. His basic belief is that all suffering and impairment are ultimately an effect of the Fall. Some individual cases he adjudges to be divine interventions in the lives of individuals for pedagogical purposes, and others he takes to be effects of the Fall on the functioning of the material world (**2.20**). His most interesting response to this question begins with his exhortation to note with wonder the unity and diversity even of the "non-impaired" population (**2.15**). Augustine suggests that those who have come to appreciate the diversity that attends all human life may discover humans who lie at the margins of his norm as divine acts of communication. His insistence that God's creations are always good leads him to a new construal of some cases of impairment as events that happened "so that the work of God might be displayed" (John 9:3). He calls these "strange vocations," and to illustrate his point cites an individual who is both intellectually impaired and Christian (**2.1**). In this discussion Augustine seems closest to transcending the sensibility of his age that intellectual disability is by definition a sad marring of the human visage. Affirming that God has created *all* human beings, and noting that God can reveal his glory through *any* created thing, he is drawn to the conclusion that some people's impairments are not, in cosmic terms, deficits:

> Such persons are predestinated and brought into being, as I suppose, in order that those who are able should understand that God's grace and the Spirit, "which bloweth where it listeth" (John 3:8), does not pass over any kind of capacity in the sons of mercy, nor in like manner does it pass over any kind of capacity in the children of Gehenna, so that "he that glorieth, let him glory in the Lord" (1 Cor. 1:31). (*Merits of Forgiveness of Sins*, 32; cf. **2.1**)

This admission that disability can be tied up with God's creation of "strange vocations" presages what is perhaps the most remarkable conceptual reversal of the patristic era. As Almut Caspary outlined in the previous chapter, in the ancient world the birth of disfigured infants was understood as the work of malevolent supernatural powers, bad omens for both family and nation. Early Christians expressed their rejection of the independent powers of the pantheon of gods and demons by repudiating the routine destruction of disfigured infants, and Augustine was able to give this clear but inchoate insight a rich theological explication. His thesis is as bold as it was novel in his context: because God has created each human, some impairments are to be understood positively as divine speech to the world. He systematically reconfigures "portent" and "monster" language to emphasize the revelatory function of non-standard bodies and minds. The result is the claim that the individual or group with non-standard physical or mental traits ought to be understood not as a forbidding omen but as a special "wonder," a divine communicative act challenging human expectations of worldly occurrence and so functioning as a sign of divine involvement in human affairs (**2.13; 2.15**).

Without stretching his train of thought here, I would suggest that this insight allows readers to draw a conclusion that moves in a different direction from his general assumption that all "deformity" is nothing more than a lack and evil, to be removed in the Resurrection. Here Augustine's thought suggests that some disabled people, like the martyrs, while being functionally healed, will retain the marks of their glorious roles as divine witnesses in the Resurrection (**2.20**). Augustine hints at a reconceptualization of impairment in a manner quite different from the other strand of his thought with its interest in defining all lack, brokenness, or estrangement as that from which we ought to hope for complete healing. His revolutionary thought is that an observer's shame or embarrassment in the presence of the handicapped is an artifact of disunion with his or her Creator, a mark of humanity's common guilt not easily overcome and certainly not by human powers. In showing themselves before and to us, people with disabilities both reveal our disunion with God and stand as a promise of his resurrecting and sanctifying power over it.

Responding to Impairment

Augustine is concerned not only with defining and reconceiving his readers' perceptions of human impairment, but also with the pastoral challenges it raises. His account of impairment as a divine work does not demand a stoic stance toward human feelings of loss and suffering associated with impairment. Human life is always good, even when capacities are lost (**2.14**), and even persons with impairments have something to give to others (*Expositions of the Psalms*, 125.12-13). Christians suffering lost capacity should therefore pray for resolution of their conditions or ask for patience and grace to deal with them. In this hopeful endurance, Christ's self-emptying in the Incarnation is exemplary:

> This is the reward of faithful souls, and in the hope of attaining [eternal blessedness] we pass through this temporal and mortal life, as something endurable rather than pleasurable, and we bear its evils courageously with a right understanding and with divine help when we rejoice in our confident hope of eternal goods, relying on the sure promise of God. The Apostle encourages us to do this when he says, "Rejoicing in hope, patient in tribulation" [Rom. 12:12] and by putting "rejoicing in hope" first he shows the reason for "patient in tribulation." This is the hope to which I exhort you through Jesus Christ our Lord. God Himself was our Master when He hid the majesty of His divinity, appearing in the weakness of flesh, and taught us not only by the prophetic utterance of His speech but also by the example of His Passion and Resurrection. By the one He showed us what we should bear, by the other what we ought to hope for. (*Letters,* vol. 20, p. 308)

Augustine appears to have modeled this patience himself, or at least to have commended it in his own physical sufferings. As he put it to a close friend near the end of his life, "In spirit, as far as it pleases the Lord, and as He deigns to give me strength, I am well, but in body, I am in bed, for I can neither walk nor stand nor sit because of the pain and swelling of hemorrhoids and chafing." In a comment that clarifies his understanding of spiritual perseverance in the face of physical suffering and impairment, he continues, "Even so, since it pleases the Lord, what else is to be said but that I am well?" (Letter 38.1).

A belief in intercessory prayer and healing was fundamental to Augustine's faith, and even his conversion. He interpreted his healing from his near-fatal sickness in Rome to the entreaties of his devout mother's prayers. Though still an unbeliever, Augustine was again confronted with the power of prayer when healed by God with "miraculous rapidity" (*Confessions,* V.ix.16). Here Augustine interprets a disabling sickness as divine chastisement. Later Augustine interpreted a toothache as another chastisement, "and when it became so bad that I lost the power to speak, it came into my heart to beg all my friends present to pray for me to you, God of health of both soul and body." As soon as his friends fell on their knees in prayer, the pain vanished: "What agony it was, and how instantly it disappeared!" (*Confessions,* IX.iv.12).

In recounting these experiences, Augustine is offering a narrative account of why believers ought to ask for the relief of physical pain and the gift of health. However, this account is tailored to pedagogical and temporary impairment rather than the congenital impairment he allows as a special case of divine communication. Petitionary prayers are concerned with the physical ailments that befall humans as sinners and mortals. Such prayers can be cries for divine mercy for oneself (*deprecatio*), as well as on behalf of others (*intercessio*), or invitations for God to enter one's being (*invocatio*). The first two forms of prayer mark the "tearful prayer for pardon from repentant sinners" (*Expositions of the Psalms*, 17.9), which arises out of the grievousness of the human condition. It is because of his high view of divine involvement in human affairs that Augustine can tie this view of intercessory prayer to a high estimation of medicine as a divine gift expressing human ingenuity, and interpreted as an ameliorative activity directed at individual suffering (2.21).

Conclusion

It is clear that Augustine's account displays divergent but not incompatible internal trajectories. Along the way it includes a range of suggestive insights about how Christians might perceive others who are marked by what he would think of as deviations from the human norm. However, all that he says is set within a firm insistence that God created each person and is not to be blamed that any given person does not fit the "normal" template. The way he constructs his case, furthermore, casts the burden of proof against any attempts to label others as non-persons or non-humans. He suggests that what may look to us like a deformity may actually be an artifact of a sinful inability to see God's working in all people to create a beautiful whole (2.13). Finally, and most promisingly, he proposes a form of eschatological perception which attends to the beauty and virtue of justice of people's character by looking beyond and within their physical traits even as it (problematically) draws attention to them (2.4). This transformation of subjective perception is a strong strand within an account that more regularly emphasizes a rather detailed, descriptive, and trait-oriented vision of human perfection. Such a doctrine becomes destructive only if Augustine's emphasis on the transformation of *our* perception is jettisoned and his anthropological norms are utilized to set up a standard of virtue that must be present if we are to consider people lovable. Augustine's insistence that it is appropriate to love the righteousness each person displays is an enabling doctrine when understood as he meant it, as a call to appreciate the virtues and patience visible in those who live gracefully with infirmity.

REFERENCES

Primary Sources

Augustine. 1995. *Against the Academicians* and *The Teacher*. Translated by Peter King. Indianapolis: Hackett.

————. 2001. *Augustine: Political Writings*. Edited by E. M. Atkins and R. J. Dodaro. Cambridge: Cambridge University Press.

————. 1991. *Confessions*. Translated by Henry Chadwick. Oxford: Oxford University Press.

————. 2000-2004. *Expositions of the Psalms*, 6 vols. In *The Works of Saint Augustine: A Translation for the 21st Century*, vols. 15-20. Edited by John Rotelle. Translated by Maria Boulding. New York: New City Press.

————. 1950. *Faith, Hope, and Charity* [*The Enchiridion*]. In *The Fathers of the Church: A New Translation, Saint Augustine*, vol. 2. New York: Fathers of the Church, Inc.

————. 2002. *On Genesis: A Refutation of the Manichees, Unfinished Literal Commentary on Genesis, The Literal Meaning of Genesis*. Edited by John Rotelle. Translated by Edmund Hill. New York: New City Press.

————. 1998. *The City of God against the Pagans*. Edited and translated by R. W. Dyson. Cambridge: Cambridge University Press.

————. 1991. *The Trinity*. Translated by Edmund Hill. New York: New City Press.

————. 1988. *Tractates on the Gospel of John, 1-10*. Translated by John Rettig. Washington, D.C.: Catholic University of America Press.

————. 1978. *A Treatise on the Merits and Forgiveness of Sins, and on the Baptism of Infants*. In *The Nicene and Post-Nicene Fathers*, vol. 5. Edited by Philip Schaff. Grand Rapids: Wm. B. Eerdmans.

————. 1978. Letter CLXVI to Jerome. In *The Nicene and Post-Nicene Fathers*, vol. 1. Edited by Philip Schaff. Grand Rapids: Wm. B. Eerdmans.

————. 1951-1956. *Letters*. In *The Fathers of the Church: A New Translation: Saint Augustine*, vols. 18-22. Translated by Wilfrid Parsons. New York: Fathers of the Church, Inc.

Secondary Sources

Amundsen, Darrel W. 1996. *Medicine, Society, and Faith in the Ancient and Medieval Worlds*. Baltimore: Johns Hopkins University Press.

Burnell, Peter. 2005. *The Augustinian Person.* Washington, D.C.: Catholic University of America Press.

Miles, Margaret R. 2005. "Sex and the City (of God): Is Sex Forfeited or Fulfilled in Augustine's Resurrection of Body?" *Journal of the American Academy of Religion* 73, no. 2 (June): 307-27.

Niebuhr, Reinhold. 1956. *An Interpretation of Christian Ethics.* New York: Meridian.

Stainton, Tim. 2008. "Reason, Grace, and Charity: Augustine and the Impact of Church Doctrine on the Construction of Intellectual Disability." *Disability and Society* 23, no. 5 (August): 485-96.

Sullivan, John. 1963. *The Image of God: The Doctrine of St. Augustine and Its Influence.* Dubuque: Priory Press.

Excerpts

2.1

A Treatise on the Merits and Forgiveness of Sins, and on the Baptism of Infants (written 412). In *The Nicene and Post-Nicene Fathers.* First Series, vol. 5. Edited by Philip Schaff. Grand Rapids: Wm. B. Eerdmans, 1978, 27-28.

Chapter 32

Now a good deal may be said of men's strange vocations — either such as we have read about, or have experienced ourselves — which go to overthrow the opinion of those persons who think that, previous to the possession of their bodies, men's souls passed through certain lives peculiar to themselves, in which they must come to this, and experience in the present life either good or evil, according to the difference of their individual deserts. . . . If we follow those persons who suppose that souls are oppressed with earthly bodies in a greater or a less degree of grossness, according to the deserts of the life which had been passed in celestial bodies previous to the assumption of the present one, who would not affirm that those had sinned previous to this life with an especial amount of enormity, who deserve so to lose all mental light, that they are born with faculties akin to brute animals — who are (I will not say most slow in intellect, for this is very commonly said of others also, but) so silly as to make a show of their fatuity for the amusement of clever people, even with idiotic gestures [*cerriti*], and whom the vulgar call, by a name, derived from the Greek, Moriones [that is, "fools," from the Greek μωρός]? And yet there was once a certain person of this class, who was so Christian, that although he was patient to the degree of strange folly with any amount of injury to himself, he was yet so impatient of any insult to the name of Christ, or, in his own person, to the religion with which he was imbued, that he could never refrain, whenever his gay and clever audience proceeded to blaspheme the sacred name, as they sometimes would in order to provoke his patience, from pelting them with stones; and on these occasions he would show no favor even to persons of rank. Well, now, such persons are predestinated and brought into being, as I suppose, in order that those who are able should understand that God's grace and the Spirit, "which bloweth where it listeth" (John 3:8), does not pass over any kind of capacity in the sons of mercy, nor in like manner does it pass over any kind of capacity in the children of Gehenna, so that "he that glorieth, let him glory in the Lord" (1 Cor. 1:31). They, however, who affirm that souls severally receive different earthly bodies, more or less gross according to the merits of their former life, and that their abilities as men vary according to the self-same merits, so that some minds are sharper and others more obtuse, and that the grace of God is also dispensed for the liberation of men from their sins according to the deserts of their former existence — what will they have to say about this man? How will they be able to attribute to him a previous life of so disgraceful a character that he deserved to be born an idiot, and at the same time of so highly meritorious a character as to entitle him to a preference in the award of the grace of Christ over many men of the acutest intellect?

2.2

A Treatise on the Merits and Forgiveness of Sins, and on the Baptism of Infants (41-42)

Chapter 66

I should, however, wish any one who was wise on the point to tell me what sin he has seen or thought of in a new-born infant, for redemption from which he allows baptism to be already necessary; what kind of evil it has in its own proper life committed by its own mind or body. If it should happen to cry and to be wearisome to its elders, I wonder whether my informant would ascribe this to iniquity, and not rather to unhappiness. What, too, would he say to the fact that it is hushed from its very weeping by no appeal to its own reason, and by no prohibition of any one else? This, however, comes from the ignorance in which it is so deeply steeped, by reason of which, too, when it grows stronger, as it very soon does, it strikes its mother in its little passion, and often her very breasts which it sucks when it is hungry. Well, now, these small freaks are not only borne in very young children, but are actually loved — and this with what affection except that of the flesh [*carnali*], by which we are delighted by a laugh or a joke, seasoned with fun and nonsense by clever persons, although, if it were understood literally, as it is spoken, they would not be laughed with as facetious, but at as simpletons? We see, also, how those simpletons whom the common people call Moriones are used for the amusement of the sane; and that they fetch higher prices than the sane when appraised for the slave market. So great, then, is the influence of mere natural feeling, even over those who are by no means simpletons, in producing amusement at another's misfortune. Now, although a man may be amused by another man's silliness, he would still dislike to be a simpleton himself; and if the father, who gladly enough looks out for, and even provokes, such things from his own prattling boy, were to foreknow that he would, when grown up, turn out a fool, he would without doubt think him more to be grieved for than if he were dead. While, however, hope remains of growth, and the light of intellect is expected to increase with the increase of years, then the insults of young children even to their parents seem not merely not wrong, but even agreeable and pleasant. No prudent man, doubtless, could possibly approve of not only not forbidding in children such conduct in word or deed as this, as soon as they are able to be forbidden, but even of exciting them to it, for the vain amusement of their elders. For as soon as children are of an age to know their father and mother, they dare not use wrong words to either, unless permitted or bidden by either, or both. But such things can only belong to such young children as are just striving to lisp out words, and whose minds are just able to give some sort of motion to their tongue. Let us, however, consider the depth of the ignorance rather of the new-born babes, out of which, as they advance in age, they come to this merely temporary stuttering folly — on their road, as it were, to knowledge and speech.

2.3

Letter CLXVI, "A Treatise on the Origin of the Human Soul," written to Jerome (415). In *The Nicene and Post-Nicene Fathers,* vol. 1. Edited by Philip Schaff. Grand Rapids: Wm. B. Eerdmans, 1978, 529.

17. What shall I say, moreover, as to the [difficulty which besets the theory of the creation of each soul separately at the birth of the individual in connection with the] diversity of talent in different souls, and especially the absolute privation of reason in some? This is, indeed, not apparent in the first stages of infancy, but being developed continuously from the beginning of life, it becomes manifest in children, of whom some are so slow and defective in memory that they cannot learn even the letters of the alphabet, and some (commonly called idiots [*moriones*]) so imbecile that they differ very little from the beasts of the field. Perhaps I am told, in answer to this, that the bodies are the cause of these imperfections. But surely the opinion which we wish to see vindicated from the objection does not require us to affirm that the soul chose for itself the body which so impairs it, and, being deceived in the choice, committed a blunder; or that the soul, when it was compelled, as a necessary consequence of being born, to enter into some body, was hindered from finding another by crowds of souls occupying the other bodies before it came, so that, like a man who takes whatever seat may remain vacant for him in a theatre, the soul was guided in taking possession of the imperfect body not by its choice, but by its circumstances. We, of course, cannot say and ought not to believe such things. Tell us, therefore, what we ought to believe and to say in order to vindicate from this difficulty the theory that for each individual body a new soul is specially created.

2.4

Tractates on the Gospel of John III.20-21 (written 411-416). In *Tractates on the Gospel of John, 1-10,* translated by John Rettig. Washington, D.C.: Catholic University of America Press, 1988, 91-92.

... My brothers, now we believe, we do not see; to see what we believe will be recompense for this faith.

The prophets knew this, but it was hidden before he [Christ] came. For in the psalm a certain lover says with a sigh, "One thing have I asked of the

Lord; this I shall seek after" (Ps. 27:4). . . . What is it that he seeks after? He says, "That I may dwell in the house of the Lord all the days of my life." And suppose that you dwell in the house of the Lord; whence will be your joy there? "That I may gaze," he says, "on the delight of the Lord."

My brothers, why do you shout, why do you exult, why do you love, except that a spark of this love is there? What do you desire, I ask you? Can it be seen with the eyes? Can it be touched? Is there some beauty which delights the eyes? Have not the martyrs been loved ardently? And when we commemorate them, do we not catch fire with love? What do we love in them, brothers? Their limbs mangled by wild beasts? What sight is fouler, if you should consult the eyes of the flesh? What is more beautiful if you should consult the eyes of the heart? How does a very handsome young man, but a thief, appear to you? How your eyes do stare in terror! Are the eyes of the flesh terrified? If you should consult them, there is nothing better structured than that body, nothing better arranged. The symmetry of the limbs and the loveliness of his complexion entice the eyes. And yet when you hear that he is a thief, you flee from the man because of your mind.

On the other side you see a bent-over old man, leaning on a cane, scarcely able to move, ploughed all over with wrinkles. What do you see that delights the eyes? You hear that he is just; you love him, you embrace him. Such rewards were promised to us, my brothers; love some such thing, sigh for such a kingdom, long for such a country, if you wish to attain that with which our Lord came, that is, grace and truth. But if you desire physical rewards from God, you are still under the Law and therefore you will not fulfill the Law itself. . . . If God gave grace to you, precisely because he gave it gratuitously, love gratuitously. . . . Fear not that you may fail of a surfeit; such will be the delight in beauty that it will always be present to you and you will never be sated — rather you will always be sated, and yet never be sated.

2.5

The Trinity, XI.1 (written 399-422/426). In *The Trinity*, translated by Edmund Hill. New York: New City Press, 1991, 305.

The sense of the eyes, however, is called a sense of the body precisely because the eyes too are parts of the body; and although an unconscious or lifeless body does not sense anything, yet it is through a bodily instrument that the conscious soul mixed with the body senses, and it is this instrument that is called a sense. When someone goes blind through some affliction of the body this sense is cut off and extinguished, but the consciousness remains the same; and though its intention, now that the eyes have been lost, has no sense of the body which it can join in the act of seeing to a body outside, and keep its gaze fixed on it once seen, nonetheless it shows by its very exertions that it neither perishes nor even diminishes with the loss of the bodily sense; the desire to see remains intact, whether this happens to be possible or not. So these three, the body, which is seen, and the actual sight, and the intention joining the two together, are clearly distinguished not only by what is proper to each but also by the difference of their natures.

2.6

The Trinity, XII.1.1-3 (322-23)

Let us see where we are to locate what you might call the border between the outer and the inner man. Anything in our consciousness that we have in common with animals is rightly said to be still part of the outer man. It is not just the body alone that is to be reckoned as the outer man, but the body with its own kind of life attached, which quickens the body's structure and all the sense it is equipped with in order to sense things outside. And when the images of things sensed that are fixed in the memory are looked over again in recollection, it is still something belonging to the outer man that is being done. In all these things the only way we differ from animals is that we are upright, not horizontal in posture. This is a reminder to us from him who made us that in our better part, that is, our consciousness, we should not be like the beast we differ from in our upright posture. Nor indeed that we should throw ourselves heart and soul into what is most sublime in our bodies; for to seek satisfaction for the will even in such noble bodies is to fell the consciousness into a prone position. But even just as our body is raised up by nature to what is highest in bodies, that is, to the heavens, so our consciousness being a spiritual substance should be raised up toward what is highest in spiritual things — not of course by the elevation of pride, but by the dutiful piety of justice.

So animals too can both sense bodies outside with the senses of the body, and remember them as fixed in the memory, and seek in them whatever is advantageous and shun whatever is harmful. But to take note of such things, and to retain not only what has been naturally caught in the memory but also what has been committed to it on purpose, and by recollection and thought to impress on it again things that were fast slipping into oblivion, so that just as thought is formed out of what the memory carries, what is in the memory is only fixed firmly there by thought; to compose fabricated sights by taking all sorts of things recorded from here and there and as it were sewing them together; to observe how in this kind of thing what is like truth is to be distinguished from what is actually true — in bodies I mean, not in spiritual things; all this kind of conscious activity, while it is carried on with sensible things and with what the consciousness has imbibed from them through the senses of the body, is nonetheless not without its share in reason, and so is not common to man and beast. But it pertains to the loftier reason to make judgments on these bodily things according to non-bodily and everlasting meanings; and unless these were above the human mind they would certainly not be unchanging, and unless something of ours were subjoined to them we would not be able to make judgments according to them about bodily things. But we do make judgments on bodily things in virtue of the meaning of dimensions and figures which the mind knows is permanent and unchanging.

. . . Just as among all the beasts there was not found for the man an assistant like himself, and only something taken from himself and formed into a consort could fit the bill, so too our mind, with which we consult the highest and innermost truth, has no assistant like it in the parts of the soul we have in common with the beasts, for making use of bodily things in a way to satisfy the nature of man.

2.7

The Trinity, XII.3.12 (328-29)

After all, the authority of the apostle as well as plain reason assures us that man was not made to the image of God as regards the shape of his body, but as regards his rational mind. It is an idle and base kind of thinking which supposes that God is confined within the limits of a body with features and limbs. And does not the blessed apostle say, be renewed in the spirit of your mind, and put on the new man, the one who was created according to God (Eph. 4:23); and even more clearly elsewhere, putting off the old man, he says, with his actions, put on the new who is being renewed for the recognition of God according to the image of him who created him (Col. 3:9)? If then we are being renewed in the spirit of our mind, and if it is this new man who is being renewed for the recognition of God according to the image of him who created him, there can be no doubt that man was not made to the image of him who created him as regards his body or any old part of his consciousness, but as regards the rational mind, which is capable of recognizing God.

2.8

The Trinity, XIV.2.6 (374)

Though the reason or understanding in it may appear at one moment to be in a coma, at another to be small, at another to be great, the human soul is never anything but rational and intellectual. And therefore if it is with reference to its capacity to use reason and understanding in order to understand and gaze upon God that it was made to the image of God, it follows that from the moment this great and wonderful nature begins to be, this image is always there, whether it is so worn away as to be almost nothing, or faint and distorted, or clear and beautiful. . . . Although it is a great nature, it could be spoiled because it is not the greatest; and although it could be spoiled because it is not the greatest, yet because it is capable of the greatest nature and can share in it, it is a great nature still.

2.9

City of God, I.20 (written 413-426). In *The City of God against the Pagans*, edited and translated by R. W. Dyson. Cambridge: Cambridge University Press, 1998, 33.

. . . When we read "Thou shalt not kill" [Exod. 20:13; Mark 10:19 par.], we are not to take this commandment as applying to plants, for these have no sensation. Nor does it apply to the non-rational animals which fly, swim, walk, or crawl, for these do not share the use of reason with us. It is not given to them to have it in common with us; and, for this reason, by the most just ordinance of their Creator, both their life and death are subject to our needs (cf. Gen. 1:28). What remains, then, is this: that, when it is said, "Thou shalt not kill," we must understand this as applying to man, and hence to mean "neither another nor thyself"; for he who kills himself kills what is no other than a man.

2.10

City of God, XI.10 (462-64)

There is, then, a Good which alone is simple, and therefore alone immutable, and this is God. By this Good all other goods have been created; but they are not simple, and therefore are not immutable. "Create" I say: that is, made, not begotten. . . . The incorruptible body which is promised to the saints at the resurrection does, indeed, have a quality of incorruption which cannot be lost; but the bodily substance and the quality of incorruption are still not the same thing. For the quality of incorruption exists entire in each single part of the body. . . . The body, then, which is not present in its entirety in each of its parts is one thing, whereas incorruptibility, which is completely present throughout the whole body, is something else; for every part of the incorruptible body, however unequal to the rest it may be in other respects, is equally incorruptible. . . . And so, although incorruptibility is inseparable from an incorruptible body, the substance by virtue of which it is called a body is nonetheless one thing, and the quality by virtue of which it is described as incorruptible is another; and so the body is not what it has. . . . Again, the soul itself, though it will be forever wise when redeemed in eternity, will be so by participation in an immutable Wisdom which is not itself. . . .

. . . In Holy Scripture, it is true, the Spirit of Wisdom is called "manifold" because it contains many things within itself (Wis. 7:22). What it contains, however, it also is, and, being one, it is all these things. For wisdom is not many things, but one thing, in which there are immense and infinite treasuries of intelligible things, and in which reside all the invisible and immutable forms of the visible and mutable things made by it. For God made nothing unknowingly; not even a human craftsman can rightly be said to do so. If He made everything with knowledge, however, then, surely, what He made He knew; and from this there occurs to the mind a wondrous, but nonetheless true, thought: that this world could not be known to us if it did not exist, but it could not exist if it were not known to God.

2.11

City of God, XI.16 (470)

For among those beings which have some measure of existence, and which are distinct from the God by Whom they were made, those which have life are placed above those which do not have life; and those that have the power of generation, or even of desiring it, are placed above those which lack this capacity. And among living things, the sentient are placed above those which do not have sensation: animals above trees, for instance. And, among the sentient, the intelligent are placed above those which do not have intelligence: men, for example, are above cattle. And, among the intelligent, the immortal, such as the angels, are placed above the mortal, such as men. These are the graduations which exist in the order of nature. But there are also various standards of value arising out of the use to which we put this thing or that; and, for this reason, we often prefer some things which lack sensation to some which have sensation.

2.12

City of God, XII.24 (534)

God, then, made man in His own image (Gen. 1:26). For He created for him a soul by virtue of which he might surpass in reason and intelligence all the creations of the earth, air, and sea, which do not have souls of this kind.

2.13

City of God, XVI.8 (707-10)

The histories of the nations tell of certain monstrous races of men (Gen. 1:24). If these tales are to be believed, it may be asked whether such monsters are descended from the sons of Noah, or rather from that one man from whom the sons of Noah themselves have come. Some of these are said to have only one eye, in the middle of their forehead. Others have feet which point backwards, behind their legs. Others combine in themselves the nature of both sexes, having the right breast of a man and the left of a woman, and, when they mate, they take it in turns to beget and conceive. Others have no mouths and live only by breathing through their nostrils. Others again are only a cubit high, and these are called Pygmies by the Greeks, after their word for a cubit, *pygme*. Elsewhere, we come across females who conceive at the age of five and who do not live to be more than eight years old. Again, there is a race whose feet are attached to a single leg which does not bend at the knee, yet they move with marvelous speed. These are called "Shadow-feet" because in hot weather they lie on their backs on the ground and take shelter in the shade of their feet. There are some men without necks, who have eyes in their shoulders; and other men, or man-like creatures, are depicted in mosaic on the marine parade at Carthage, taken from books as examples of the curious things to be found in natural history. And what am I to say of those dog-headed men whose dogs' heads and actual barking show that they are more beasts than men?

It is not, of course, necessary to believe in all the kinds of men which are said to exist. But anyone who is born anywhere as a man (that is, as a rational and moral animal), no matter how unusual he may be to our bodily senses in shape, color, motion, sound, or in any natural power or part or quality, derives from the original and first-created man; and no believer will doubt this. It is, however, clear what constitutes the natural norm in the majority of cases and what, in itself, is a marvelous rarity.

Moreover, the explanation which is given of monstrous human births among us can also be given in the case of some of these monstrous races. For God is the Creator of all things: He Himself knows where and when anything should be, or should have been, created; and He knows how to weave the beauty of the whole out of the similarity and diversity of its parts. The man who cannot view the whole is offended by what he takes to be the deformity of a part; but this is because he does not know how it is to be adapted or related to the whole. We know of men who were born with more than five fingers or five toes. This is a trivial thing and not any great divergence from the norm. God forbid, however, that someone who does not know why the Creator has done what He has done should be foolish enough to suppose that God has in such cases erred in allotting the number of human fingers. So, then, even if a greater divergence should occur, He whose work no one may justly condemn knows what He has done.

There is at Hippo Zaritus a man who has crescent-shaped feet with only two toes on each; and his hands are similar. If there were any race with these features, it would be added to our list of the curiosities and wonders of nature. But are we for this reason to deny that this man is descended from that one man who was created in the beginning?

Again, though they are rare, it is difficult to find times when there have been no androgyny, also called hermaphrodites: persons who embody the characteristics of both sexes so completely that it is uncertain whether they should be called male or female. However, the prevailing habit of speech has named them according to the superior sex, that is, the male; for no one has ever used the term "androgyness" or "hermaphroditess."

Some years ago, but certainly within memory, a man was born in the East with a double set of upper members but a single set of lower ones. He had two heads, two chests, and four arms, but only one belly and two feet, as if he were one man; and he lived long enough for his fame to draw many people to come and see him.

Again, who could call to mind all the human infants who have been born very unlike those who were most certainly their parents? It cannot be denied, however, that these derive their origin from that one man, Adam; and the same is therefore true of all those races which, by reason of their bodily differences, are said to have deviated from the usual pattern of nature exhibited by most — indeed by almost the whole — of mankind. If these races are included in the definition of "human," that is, if they are rational and mortal animals, then it must be admitted that they trace their lineage from that same one man, the first father of all mankind: if, that is, what we are told of the diversity of those races, and their great difference from one another and from us, is true. For if we did not know that monkeys and apes and baboons are not men but beasts, these historians who revel in curiosities might with unpunished vanity delude us into believing that they are kinds of men. If, however, the creatures of which these wondrous things are written are indeed men, why was it God's will to create some races in this way? Perhaps it was so that, when monsters are born of men among us, as they must be, we should not think them the work of an imperfect craftsman: perhaps it was so that we should not suppose that, despite the wisdom with which He fashions the nature of human beings, God has on this occasion erred. In which case, it ought not to seem absurd to us that, just as some monsters occur within the various races of mankind, so there should be certain monstrous races within the human race as a whole.

I shall, then, conclude my discussion of the question with a tentative and cautious answer. Either the written accounts which we have of some of these races are completely worthless; or, if such creatures exist, they are not men; or, if they are men, they are descended from Adam.

2.14

City of God, XIX.4 (918-24)

If, therefore, we are asked what . . . the City of God . . . believes concerning the Final Good and Evil, we shall reply as follows: that eternal life is the Supreme Good, and eternal death the Supreme Evil, and that to achieve the one and avoid the other, we must live rightly. For this reason it is written, "The just man lives by faith" (Hab. 2:4; Rom. 1:17; Gal. 3:11; Heb. 10:38). For we do not yet see our good, and hence we must seek it by believing. Moreover, we cannot live rightly unless, while we believe and pray, we are helped by Him who has given us the faith to believe that we must be helped by Him. The philosophers, however, have supposed that the Final Good and Evil are to be found in this life. . . .

. . . When, where, and how can what are called the primary objects of nature be possessed in this life with such certainty that they are not subject to the vicissitudes of chance? For is there any pain, the contrary of pleasure, any disquiet, the contrary of rest, that cannot befall a wise man's body? Certainly the amputation or decay of limbs undermines a man's soundness; deformity ruins his beauty, sickness destroys his health, weakness his strength, lassitude his vigor, torpor or lethargy his activity. And is there any of these which may not assail the flesh of the wise man? The postures and movements of the body, when they are comely and appropriate, are numbered among the primary gifts of nature. But what if some disorder causes the limbs to tremble? What if a man's spine is so curved as to bring his hands to the ground, so that he becomes a kind of quadruped? Will this not subvert all the body's beauty and grace, whether it be at rest or in motion? And what of the primary goods, as they are called, of the mind itself? The two placed first are sensation and intellect, because they enable us to grasp and perceive the truth. But what kind of sensation remains, and how much of it, if a man becomes blind and deaf, to say nothing of other disabilities [*ut alios taceam*]? And to what place will reason and intelligence withdraw, where will they slumber, if a man is driven insane by some sickness? The mad say and do many absurd things, most of which are foreign to their intentions and dispositions: certainly to their good intentions and normal dispositions. When we contemplate or see people in this condition, and when we consider their plight fully, we can hardly refrain from weeping: perhaps we cannot do so at all. And what shall I say of those who suffer attacks of demonic possession? Where does their own intelligence lie hidden and buried while the malignant spirit makes use of their soul and body according to his own will? And who is certain that such an evil cannot befall a wise man in this life? Again, how can we perceive the truth while we are in this flesh, and to what extent? For, as we read in the trusty book of Wisdom, "the corruptible body presseth down the soul, and the earthly tabernacle weigheth down the mind that museth upon many things" (Wis. 9:15). Moreover, as to that impetus or desire towards action — if this is the right way to express in Latin what the Greeks call *hormé* — which is also reckoned to be one of the primary goods of nature: is not this the very impulse which, when sensation is deranged and reason asleep, produces those unhappy gestures and actions of the insane at which we shudder? . . .

Again, that virtue whose name is fortitude, however great the wisdom with which she is accompanied, bears most evident witness to human ills; for it is precisely those ills which she is compelled to endure with patience. I wonder at the shamelessness of the Stoics. For they contend that such ills are not really ills at all, yet admit that if they should become so severe that a wise man cannot or should not bear them, he is compelled to put himself to death and depart from this life. Yet these men, in their stupid pride, believe that the Final Good is to be found in this life, and that they can achieve happiness by their own efforts. They believe that their wise man — that is, he whom, in their amazing vanity, they describe as such — even if he becomes blind, deaf, and dumb; even if he is enfeebled in limb and tormented with pain; even if he falls victim to every other ill that can be described or imagined; even if he is compelled to put himself to death: that such a man would not shrink from calling such a life, beset with such ills, a happy one! O happy life, that seeks the aid of death to put an end to it! If this is happiness, let him remain in it; but if these ills compel him to flee from it, how is it happy? . . .

There is great power in the evils which compel a man — and, according to those philosophers, even a wise man — to take away his own existence as a man. . . . Let them no longer suppose that the Final and Supreme Good is something in which they may rejoice while in this moral condition. For, in this condition, those very virtues than which nothing better or more advantageous is found in man clearly attest to his misery precisely by the great assistance that they give him in the midst of perils, hardships, and sorrows.

True virtues, however, can exist only in those in whom there is true godliness; and these virtues do not claim that they can protect those in whom they are present against suffering any miseries. . . . They do, however, claim that, though human life is compelled to be miserable by all the great evils of this world, it is happy in the hope of the world to come, and in the hope of salvation. . . . The apostle Paul, therefore — speaking not of men without prudence, without patience, without temperance, or without justice, but of those who live according to true piety, and whose virtues are therefore true virtues — says, "For we are saved by hope. Now hope which is seen is not hope; for what a man seeth, why doth he yet hope for? But if we hope for that we see not, then do we with patience wait for it" (Rom. 8:24). As, therefore, we are saved by hope, it is in hope that we have been made happy; and as we do not yet possess a present salvation, but await salvation in the future, so we do not enjoy a present happiness, but look forward to happiness in the future, and "with patience." We are in the midst of evils, and we must endure them with patience until we come to those good things where everything will bestow ineffable delight upon us, and where there will no longer be anything which we must endure. . . .

2.15

City of God, XXI.8 (1060-62)

. . . We read the following passage in the book of Marcus Varro entitled *De gente populi Romani*. I here cite it in his exact words: "There occurred a wondrous portent in the heavens," he says. "Castor writes that this great portent arose when the brilliant star Venus . . . changed its color, size, shape, and course. Such a thing had never occurred before, and has never happened since. The famous mathematicians Adrastus of Cyzicus and Dion of Naples both say that this took place during the reign of King Ogygus." So acute an author as Varro would not have called this a "portent" had it not seemed contrary to nature. Indeed, men say that all portents are contrary to nature. They are not so, however; for how is that contrary to nature which happens by the will of God, since the will of so great a Creator is certainly the nature of every created thing? A portent, therefore, is an occurrence contrary not to nature, but to nature as we know it.

Who can number the multitude of portents which are contained in the histories of the nations? . . . What is there so closely regulated by the Author of the nature of the heavens and the earth as the ordered course of the stars? What is there so securely established by laws so certain and unvarying? And yet, when He so wished — He Who rules what He has made with supreme authority and power — the star famed beyond all others for its magnitude and splendor altered its size and shape and, more wonderful still, the order and law of its course. . . .

As far as the knowledge of nature is concerned, therefore, let not unbelievers make things dark for themselves. Let them not think it impossible for something to occur in some object, through the exercise of divine power, which does not lie within their own human experience of that object. Even those things which are known to us most commonly in the natural order are no less wonderful, and would be a source of astonishment to all who consider them, if men were not accustomed to be amazed at nothing except what is rare. For example, who could fail to see, on rational consideration, how marvelous it is that, despite the innumerable multitude of men, and despite the great similarity of their nature, each individual man has his own particular appearance? If it were not for this similarity, man would not be a species distinct from other animals; but, without the differences, it would not be possible to distinguish one man from any others. Therefore, we acknowledge that men are alike, and, at the same time, we discover that they are different. But it is a consideration of the differences which ought to make us wonder; for similarity seems to be more consistent with our common nature. Yet because it is precisely when things are rare that they are wonderful to us, we are much more surprised when we find two people so much alike that we always or often make mistakes in trying to tell them apart.

2.16

City of God, XXII.14 (1142-43)

What, therefore, are we to say of infants, if not that they will not rise in that tiny body in which they died, but will receive, by the wondrous and most rapid operation of God, that body which they would have received in any case by the slower passage of time? For in that utterance of the Lord, where He says that "Not a hair of your head shall perish" (Luke 21:18), it is said that we shall not in future lack anything that we once had; but it is not said that we shall not then receive anything that we do not have now. The dead infant lacked the perfect stature of its body, for even the perfect infant lacks the perfection of bodily size because, unlike an adult, it has not yet achieved the greatest stature possible for it. There is, however, a sense in which this perfect stature is possessed by all when they are conceived and born: that is, they have it potentially, even though not yet in their actual size. In the same way, all the members of the body are latent in the seed, although some of them are lacking even after the child is born — teeth, for example, and things of that kind. Every material substance, then, seems to contain within itself what one might call a pattern of everything which does not yet exist — or, rather, which is as yet latent — but which in the course of time will come into existence, or, rather, into sight. In this sense, therefore, the child who is to be short or tall is short or tall already. According to this reasoning, then, we need fear no bodily loss in the resurrection of the body. Even if it is true that all are to be equal, so that all will attain the stature of giants, lest those who were largest in this life should lose anything of their stature and it should perish (for this would go against the assurance of Christ, who said that not a hair of their head should perish): even in this case, why should the Creator, the wondrous Artist Who made all things from nothing, not be able to make the additions that he knew to be necessary?

2.17

City of God, XXII.15 (1143)

When He rose from the dead, Christ's bodily stature was undoubtedly the same as it had been when He died. Nor is it permitted to say that, when the time comes for all men to rise, His body will, for the sake of equaling the tallest, assume a magnitude which it did not have when He appeared to His disciples in the form in which they knew Him. But if we say that the bodies of those who were larger than the Lord are to be reduced to the size of His body, then a great deal of their substance will perish from the bodies of many, even though He promised that not a hair of their head should perish. Therefore, it remains for us to conclude that everyone will receive back his own size: the size which he had in youth, if he died an old man, or that which he would have had, if he died before attaining it. As for what the apostle said of the "measure of the age of the fullness of Christ" (Eph. 4:13), we may understand this as referring to something else: namely, to the fact that the measure of the age of Christ will be completed when all the members among the Christian peoples are added to the Head. Alternatively, if the apostle was indeed speaking of the resurrection of the body, we may take him to mean that the bodies of all the dead will rise neither older nor younger than Christ, but at that age and vigor to which we know that Christ had attained. For the most learned men of this world have defined the prime of life as occurring at around the age of thirty years. When this period of time is over, a man begins to decline towards an increasingly infirm old age. Therefore the apostle was not referring to the measure of the body, or to the measure of stature, but to the "measure of the age of the fullness of Christ."

2.18

City of God, XXII.16 (1144)

Again, the apostle's words, "Predestinate to be conformed to the image of the Son of God" (Rom. 8:29), may be understood according to the inner man. . . . The apostle can also be taken to mean that, as Christ was conformed to us by mortality, so shall we be conformed to Him by immortality; and this, indeed, does have reference to the resurrection of the body. But if these words are also intended to instruct us as to the form of our risen bodies, then, as in the case of the "measure," this conformity to Christ is to be understood not in terms of size, but of age.

So then: all are to rise with a body of the same size as they had, or would have had, in the prime of life. But it would in any case be no hardship even if the form of the body were to be that of a child or an old man, provided that no infirmity of mind or body remained. Thus, even if someone contends that everyone will rise with the same kind of body as he had when he died, we need not devote too much effort to the task of arguing the point with him.

2.19

City of God, XXII.17 (1144-45)

. . . not a few people believe that women will not be resurrected as female in sex, but that all are to be men, because God made only man of earth, and the woman from the man. But it seems to me that the better opinion is that of those who do not doubt that both sexes are to rise. For then there will be no lust, which is now the cause of confusion. For before they sinned, the man and woman were naked, and were not ashamed (Gen. 2:25). Vice will be taken away from those bodies, therefore, and nature preserved. And the sex of a woman is not a vice, but nature. They will then be exempt from sexual intercourse and childbearing, but the female parts will nonetheless remain in being, accommodated not to the old uses, but to a new beauty, which, so far from inciting lust, which no longer exists, will move us to praise the wisdom and clemency of God, who both made what was not and redeemed from corruption what He made. . . . The woman, therefore, is the creation of God, just as the man is. But by the fact that she was made from the man's side, unity is commended to us; and, as we have said, the manner of her creation prefigured Christ and the Church. He, then, who instituted two sexes will restore them both. . . .

2.20

City of God, XXII.19 (1147-50)

What reply shall I now make concerning the hair and nails? Once it is understood that no part of the body will perish in such a way as to cause any bodily deformity, it will at the same time be understood that any bodily substance which would have given rise to deformity by its great quantity will be added to the body's total mass, but not to parts the form of which would thereby be spoiled. After all, suppose that, having made a clay pot, one were then to make it all over again, using the same clay, with the whole of the clay making the whole of a new pot, with nothing left over: it would not be necessary to remake the handle out of the same portion of clay which had formed the old handle, or the new bottom out of that which had formed the old bottom. Thus, if hair which has been cut and nails which have been trimmed would constitute a deformity if they were restored to the same places, they will not be restored. Nothing will perish at the resurrection, however, for every part of the body's substance will be restored to it, but altered in a way which is in keeping with the various parts of the body.

Moreover, what the Lord said, "Not a hair of your head shall perish" (Luke 21:18), might more aptly be understood as referring to the number of hairs, not to their length. Hence, He elsewhere says, "The hairs of your head are all numbered" (Luke 12:17). I do not say this because I think that anything which is naturally present in the body will perish. Rather, I believe that whatever deformity was present in it (and such deformity is present for no other reason than to show the penal condition under which mortal man exists) will be restored in such a way that, while the integrity of the body's substance is preserved, the deformity will perish. If an artist has for some reason made a flawed statue, he can recast it and make it beautiful, removing the defect without losing any of the substance. . . . And if a man can do this, what are we to think of the Almighty Artist? Will he not be able to remove and abolish all deformities of the human body, whether common ones or rare and monstrous, which, though in keeping with this wretched life, are not consistent with the future happiness of the saints? And will He not be able to do so in the same way that our natural but ugly excretions are removed, without any diminutions of the body's substance?

For this reason, let neither fat persons nor thin ones fear that their appearance at the resurrection will be other than they would have wished it to be here if they could. For all bodily beauty consists in the suitable arrangement of the parts, together with a certain pleasantness of color. Where there is not a suitable arrangement of the parts, this is displeasing either because something is lacking, or is too small or too large. But the deformity which arises when there is not a proper arrangement of parts will not exist in heaven. There all defects will be corrected. Whatever is less than fitting will be made good from resources which the Creator knows. Whatever is more than fitting will be removed, but without prejudice to the integrity of the body's substance. . . .

. . . the love we bear for the blessed martyrs makes us desire to see in the kingdom of heaven the marks of the wounds which they received for Christ's name; and it may be that we shall indeed see them. For this will not be a deformity, but a badge of honor, and the beauty of their virtue — a beauty which is in the body, but not of the body — will shine forth in it . . . the places where they have been struck or cut will retain the scars, but the limbs which were cut off will not be lost, but restored. While, therefore, no blemishes which the body has sustained will be present in the world to come, we are nonetheless not to deem these marks of virtue blemishes, or call them such.

2.21

City of God, XXII.24 (1159-64)

The human race's present condition of misery is a punishment for which we can only praise God's justice; yet in His goodness He has filled the whole of His creation with many good things of all kinds, which we must now consider.

The first blessing is that which He pronounced before Adam sinned, saying, "Increase, and multiply, and replenish the earth" (Gen. 1:28). He did not choose to diminish that blessing after Adam sinned. Rather, the fruitfulness which He had given remained even in the condemned stock. The blemish of sin, though it has brought down upon us the necessity of death, has not taken away from us that wondrous power of seed, or, rather, that even more wondrous power by which seed is produced: a power which is, in a manner of speaking, inscribed or woven into the human body. . . .

As we have said, then, these goods flow out from the goodness of God, as from a kind of fountain, even into a nature vitiated by sin and condemned to punishment. The first of them, propagation, God bestowed by His blessing during those first creative works from which He rested on the seventh day; while the second, conformation, He still gives in his continued activity up to the present time. Indeed, if God were to remove the efficacy of His power from things, they would not be able to go on and attain the kind of development assigned to them, or live out their allotted span; nor would they even remain in that condition in which they were created. . . .

But if conformation were not added to propagation, mankind would not continue to exhibit its own distinctive forms and modes of being. . . . "Neither is he that planteth anything, neither he that watereth, but God that giveth the increase" (1 Cor. 3:7). In the same way, we can say that neither is the sexual intercourse nor he that soweth anything, but God that giveth form; neither is the mother, who conceives, carries, bears, and feeds, anything, but God that giveth growth.

For it is thanks to the activity of God continued even down to the present time that seeds display themselves and evolve from hidden and invisible folds, as it were, into the visible forms of beauty which we behold. It is He who brings about that wondrous combination and union of an incorporeal with a corporeal nature, with the former in command and the latter subjected to it, by which living being is made. This is a work so great and marvelous as to astonish the mind that considers it well, and to call forth praise to the Creator. And this is true not only in the case of man, who is a rational being and therefore more excellent and outstanding than any other creature on earth, but even in the case of the minutest fly.

It is God who has given the human soul a mind. In the infant reason and intelligence are in a certain sense dormant, and it is as if they were not present at all. But they are soon to be awakened and exercised as the years pass; and in this way the individual becomes capable of knowledge and learning, able to perceive the truth and love the good. This capacity enables the mind to drink in wisdom and to achieve those virtues of prudence, fortitude, temperance, and justice by which a man is equipped to resist errors and the other vices implanted in him, and to conquer them by fixing his desires upon nothing but the Supreme and Immutable Good. A man may, indeed, not succeed in doing this; but who can adequately describe or imagine the glory of this work of the Almighty, and the marvelous benefit which He has divinely implanted in our rational nature in giving us even the capacity for such good?

But not only do we have this capacity to live well and to achieve immortal happiness by means of those arts which are called virtues, which are given only by the grace of God, which is in Christ, to the children of the promise and of the kingdom. In addition, there are the many great arts invented and exercised by human ingenuity, some for necessary purposes and others for pleasure. The mind and reason of man shows great excellence in contriving such things, even though they may be superfluous, or even perilous and hurtful; and is not this evidence of a great good which man has in his nature, whereby he is able to discover, learn, and exercise those arts? How wonderful, how astonishing, are the achievements of human industry in devising clothing and shelter! What progress man has made in agriculture and navigation! . . . And here we are speaking only of the natural capacities with which the human mind is adorned in this mortal life, not of the faith and the way of truth by which man achieves life immortal. . . .

Moreover, how clearly does the providence of our great Creator appear even in the body itself! This is so even though it has mortality in common with the beasts, and is in many respects weaker than they. For are not the sense organs and the other parts of the body so arranged, and the form and shape and stature of the whole body so disposed, as to indicate that it was made as the servant of the rational soul? We see that man has not been created like the animals which lack reason, whose faces are turned towards the ground. On the contrary, his bodily form is erect, facing towards heaven, to admonish him to dwell on things above. Then there is the wonderful mobility with which his tongue and hands are equipped, so that he is able to speak and write and accomplish so many other arts and crafts. And does not all this show us clearly enough the kind of soul of which a body of this kind was intended to be an adjunct? Moreover, even leaving aside the necessary functions of the parts, there is a harmonious congruence between them all, a beauty in their mutual arrangement and correspondence, such that one does not know whether the major factor in their creation was usefulness or beauty.

Certainly, we see that no part of the body has been created for the sake of usefulness which does not also have something to contribute to its beauty, and this would appear to us all the more clearly if we knew how all its parts are connected to one another and mutually related. Perhaps, indeed, human ingenuity could discover these relations, if it were given the task of doing so, by observing what appears on the body's surface only. For as to what is covered and removed from our scrutiny — the complex arrangement of veins and nerves and entrails and hidden vital organs — no one can come at it. . . . But as to those relations of which I speak, and which form the "togetherness" — what the Greeks call the *harmonia* — of the whole body, outside and in, as of some instrument: has anyone yet managed to find these? . . . If these could be known . . . then even the internal organs of the body, which make no show of beauty, would so delight the mind, which makes use of the eyes, with their rational beauty that we should prefer that beauty more than the merely visible beauty which pleases the eye alone.

Moreover, certain things are associated with the body in such a way as to have beauty but no use. Cases in point are the nipples on a man's chest and the beard on his face. The fact that the beard exists as a manly adornment and not for the purposes of protection is shown by the beardless faces of women, who are the weaker sex and for whom a beard would therefore be more suitable if it were a protective device. If it is true, therefore — and no one can doubt it — that, of all our members which are visible to us, there is not one in which beauty is sacrificed to usefulness, while there are others which have no use other than to contribute to the body's beauty, then we can, I think, readily understand from this that, when the body was created, dignity took precedence over necessity. After all, necessity is a transitory thing; whereas the time is coming when we shall enjoy each other's beauty without any lust: an enjoyment which will specially redound to the praise of the Creator, who, as it is said in the psalm, has "put on praise and comeliness" (Ps. 104:1 LXX). . . .

3 Aquinas on the corporis infirmitas: Broken Flesh and the Grammar of Grace

MIGUEL J. ROMERO

A human body is said to be weak when it is disabled or hindered in the execution of its proper action, through some disorder of the body's parts, so that the humors and members of the human body cease to be subject to its governing and motive power. Hence a member is said to be weak when it cannot do the work of a healthy member, the eye, for instance, when it cannot see clearly. . . .

Summa Theologica, 1-2.77.3, response

Just as bodily blindness is the privation of the principle of bodily sight, so blindness of mind is the privation of the principle of mental or intellectual sight. Now [mental or intellectual sight] has a threefold principle. One is the light of natural reason, which light, since it pertains to the species of the rational soul, is never forfeit from the soul, and yet, at times, it is prevented from exercising its proper act, through being hin-

The basic thesis of this essay materialized by way of formal and informal exchanges with Reinhard Hütter, Stanley Hauerwas, Fr. Fergus Kerr, and Amy Laura Hall. Sarah Sanderson-Doughty offered helpful comments on the first draft of this essay. An early draft was read and commented upon at the Duke Theology and Ethics Colloquium, and I am especially grateful to Paul Griffiths, Warren Kinghorn, Matthew Whelan, Sheryl Overmyer, and Sean Larson for their thoughtful comments and suggestions there. Later drafts benefited from commentary and suggestions offered by Colin McGuigan, Sean Larson, John Slotemaker, and Reinhard Hütter.

> *dered by the lower powers which the human intellect needs in order to understand, for instance, in the case of imbeciles and madmen.*
>
> *Summa Theologica,* 2-2.15.1, *response*

This chapter introduces St. Thomas Aquinas's understanding of corporeal infirmity in the context of his philosophy and theology. Aquinas did not compose a treatise on the bodily damage, dysfunction, and decay to which all human creatures are subject. Nevertheless, formal reflections on corporeal infirmity and related themes appear frequently in Aquinas's writings, and these treatments usually refine or develop the contours of some major thesis. For that reason, although Aquinas did not leave behind a "theory of disability," the systematic character of what he says about corporeal infirmity implicates the whole of his thought and, in this way, alludes to a consistent and versatile "theology of bodily weakness."

This essay is no more than a sketch of Aquinas's construal of corporeal infirmity. Its purpose will be achieved if it inspires readers to explore the relevance of his thought to contemporary theologizing around the theme of disability. Tangential to that primary aim is my desire to address criticisms of Aquinas related to the theme of disability.

In the first section, I outline Aquinas's account of the human creature, who is the image of God and who is graced with an inviolable nature. In the second section, I show how Aquinas uses the term "corporeal infirmity" and how that concept relates to his understanding of "evil suffered" in the human body. For the purpose of this introduction, I highlight Aquinas's reflections on the condition *amentia* (a profound cognitive impairment, literally "mindlessness"), which is an evil suffered in the body of a person whom Aquinas calls the *amens* (usually translated "imbecile"). In the third section, I sketch the implications of Aquinas's "grammar of grace" in relation to the condition of the *amens* — in particular, Aquinas's view that *amentia* cannot decisively foreclose on the attainment of the ultimate good of the *amens* as one created in the image of God. In the fourth section, I review Aquinas's various descriptions of how the *amens* participates in the life of the church. Correspondingly, I map Aquinas's claim that *amentia* does not impede the "infusion" of supernatural virtue, nor does the condition warrant the exclusion of the *amens* from the communal life of the Body of Christ.

I. The Human Creature: Image of God and Human Nature

Aquinas's account of "corporeal infirmity" (when a body has been rendered weak by damage, dysfunction, or decay) presumes the standard Christian view that the human creature is made in the image and the likeness of the Triune God. Aquinas explains that the image of God relates to God in two ways (*Summa Theologica,* 1.93.1). First, the human creature is related to God by origination, where God is the beginning of every particular human being (i.e., the "production" of the image, the first perfection). Second, the human creature is related to God by ordination, where God is the ultimate good of every particular human being (i.e., the "purpose" of the image, the final perfection) (see Merriell 2005, 123-42).

Aquinas maintains that the image of God is such that the human creature has an essential and incorruptible aptitude for knowledge and love of God (**3.9**; cf. *ST,* 1.45.7). Aquinas takes as his own Augustine's animated insistence that newborns, the comatose, and profoundly demented persons all reflect the dynamic life of the Trinity — always capable of knowing and loving God (*Commentary on De Trinitate of Boethius,* 2.3.1, *reply 4;* see Augustine, *De Trinitate,* XIV.13; cf. XIV.6-8, 18, 19). For Augustine and Aquinas, it is one thing to have a sense of self (an inner or hidden life) and a wholly other thing to reason discursively about one's self (cf. Reinders 2008, 21).

Following Augustine, Aquinas designates three states or degrees of relational intimacy between the image of God and God *(ST,* 1.93.4, *response).* These degrees presume the creature-Creator relationship between the *imago Dei* and the divine source of the image, ordination (cf. Kerr 2002, 125). The first state is the always-active natural aptitude for knowledge and love, which is the basic condition of the human creature's capacity for relationship with God. For Aquinas, at all stages, the dynamic inner life of the human creature is animated with desire for its creator. The second state is when the Triune God objectively draws the image of God into the dynamic life of the Father, Son, and Holy Spirit. For Aquinas, this happens at baptism, when God elevates the always-active capacity of the human creature above its natural condition and moves it toward participation (albeit imperfect) in the goodness and beauty of God *(ST,* 1-2.110.1, *response).* The third state is the perfect actualization of human potential, which Aquinas calls "beatitude" (the perfect happiness of our supernatural union with God). Aquinas associates this third state only with the bodily resurrection of believers (see *response* in **3.11**; cf. **3.44**). The dynamism and relational trajectory that Aquinas presumes at the root of the three states of intimacy between God and the image of God condition his anthropological account of the essential and unchanging structure of human nature (see Torrell 2003, 80-83).

Aquinas uses Aristotle to distinguish between what a human being is (i.e., its form, essential structure, or metaphysical composition) and what the human creature is for (i.e., its telos, final end, or purpose) (*Compendium Theologiae*, 154; cf. Merriell 2005, 125). Aquinas's description of "human nature" is a conceptual snapshot, so to speak, of what a human being is (*ST*, 1.75-89). In Aquinas's *Summa*, this descriptive picture outlines the terms or analytic premises for his theological articulation of the human creature's ordination for relationship with the Triune God (*ST*, 1.1.7, *response*; cf. Stump 2003, 238-41). Although Aquinas appropriates Aristotle's conceptual vocabulary to describe human nature (principally, *De Anima*), Aquinas radically repurposes Aristotle's categories by way of Augustine's understanding of the human creature as the image of God (principally, *De Trinitate*; see Pieper 1962, 43-54).

Like Augustine, Aquinas gives an account of human nature that is not a set of criteria for determining if a being is or is not a *human* being (cf. *City of God*, XVI, 8). Without ambiguity, Aquinas maintains that individuals are members of the human species because they come from human parents (*ST*, 1.98.1; 1.100.1). For Aquinas, the species membership of a particular person is objective, while the notional attributes of the human species as a biological kind is amendable according to descriptive convention (see Porter 2005, 103-25, esp. 107-8).

Aquinas accepts the standard Christian view that the human being is a composite creature: a unity of immaterial and material properties, an immortal soul and animal body (*ST*, 1.75.4; see *response* in **3.5**). In Aquinas's terms, the theologian describes human nature (i.e., what a human being is) principally by way of the soul, which is the configuration (i.e., the shape or the "form") of the human body (*ST*, 1.75, *prologue*; 1.76.5, *response*). Aquinas describes the human soul as a "subsistent form," which means that the soul has immaterial properties that operate (in a limited way) independent of the body (*ST*, 1.75.2-3; *CT*, 152). Such are the properties of "intellect" (the capacity to know) and "will" (the capacity to love what is known) (cf. *ST*, 1.45.7, *response*). Although immaterial, these properties are configured to cooperate with the body *(ST*, 1.75.7; 1.76.5, *response)*. Aquinas's account of the relation between the rational soul and the human body entails a fundamental affirmation of the body. In particular, God directly creates the human soul for embodiment *(De Malo*, 4.1, *response; ST*, 1.76.7, *sc)*.

Aquinas uses the terms "intellectual soul" and "rational soul" interchangeably in his discussion of the "human soul." It is important to be clear on the distinctive way Aquinas uses notions like the "rational soul" and concepts like "the operation of reason." Most important, the status or "whatness" associated with the term "rational" does not principally refer to the cognitive operations we call intelligence, understanding, or reason. Rather, for Aquinas, the term "rational" is shorthand for the full spectrum of characteristics that distinguish "humans" as a unique species. According to Aquinas, although accidental characteristics and qualities tend to follow from species membership, species membership is not a question of characteristics and qualities. Thus, to claim, as Aquinas does, that "the rational soul is the principle of human nature" is very different from the (false) claim which identifies the capacity for discursive reason or purposive action as constitutive of human nature and personhood (contra Reinders 2008, 22; cf. *ST,* 1.78.4, *response*).

For Aquinas, what is "rational" about the rational soul is the image of God in the human creature — insofar as the rational creature is always capable of knowledge and love, and cannot be rendered incapable of kowing and loving. Moreover, this capacity "rationality" does not originate from an instrumental faculty belonging to some bodily organ, that is, the brain (see *reply 1* in **3.5**; cf. **3.4**; cf. Pasnau 2002, 284-86; 342-44). Aquinas vehemently rejects all attempts to reduce human nature to a corporeal operation, while affirming the goodness and beauty of our existence as embodied creatures (**3.11**; cf. *ST,* 1.75.4; *ST,* 1.76.5; cf. Yong 2007, 264-66).

For Aquinas, the operation of reason in the human creature involves both the powers of the rational soul and the sensory powers of the human body *(ST,* 1.78.4, *response)*. This operation is variously termed "intellection," "cogitation," and "understanding."

As it is relevant to his reflections on profound cognitive impairment, it is important to briefly summarize Aquinas's nuanced account of human cognition. For Aquinas, under descriptively "normal" operation, there are four parts to the unified operation called cognition (see Brennan 1941, 45-63; Stump 2003, 268-70). First, the "external sense organs" of the human body (eyes, ears, nose, etc.) undergo material changes in response to environmental stimulation — let us say the stimulation generated when a dog is present. Second, an "internal sense organ" Aquinas associates with the brain organizes the various sense impressions of the thing (sight, sound, smell, etc.) into a dynamic and unified bodily experience, which Aquinas calls a "phantasm" (**3.7**; cf. *response* in **3.5**; *ST,* 76.5, *response; ST,* 79.8-9). Third, the power of the human soul called intellect acts upon the bodily phantasm by drawing forth "dog-ness" (the "form" of the dog) from the raw sense experience (*ST,*

1.85.1-2). Finally, the intellect ascribes a "mental concept" or "internal word" to the experienced form, analogous to saying or thinking the word "dog" (*ST,* 1.85.3, *reply 1*).

For Aquinas, the mental concept is what enables us to "re-cognize" one sense experience as corresponding to an earlier sense experience. Moreover, although these mental concepts are ordinarily associated with an occurrent awareness of notions like "dog" or "pet," for Aquinas the mental concept is not constituted by an occurrent awareness of such notions, nor is it conditioned by the capacity to think or utter the words normally associated with such notions.

The human creature understands what her senses perceive because the rational soul illuminates the substance and significance of what is perceived. Thus, according to Aquinas, the conventional operation of the human intellect manifests the essentially rational nature of the human creature; however, the manifestation of these capacities is not constitutive of any particular person's status as a rational creature (see Stump 2003, 244-76. Stump helpfully illustrates the nuances of Aquinas's view of human cognition by way of the neurological conditions called "blindsight" and "agnosia").

Constitutive Limitations and Operative Limitations

It is necessary to distinguish with Aquinas between the constitutive limitations of embodiment and a body with operative limitations (*DM,* 1.3). In his treatise *De Malo,* Aquinas discusses the appropriateness of death and corporeal corruption to the nature of human beings (**3.43**). Aquinas explains that because all matter is subject to change and variation, the human body is intrinsically subject to the contingencies of causality (*DM,* 4.1, *response*). For that reason, the human species exhibits a broad range of capacities for enactment and, in Aquinas's view, this spectrum is not a defect; rather, the diversity communicates the beauty of the created order (*ST,* 1.96.3, *response; CT,* 141; cf. *City of God,* XI.18, 22; XII, 5-4). For Aquinas, the dependency and vulnerability of human creatures are intrinsic to our mortal creatureliness — these are the constitutive limitations of embodiment and a good common to all human beings (**3.48**; *ST,* 1.99.1, *response;* cf. MacIntyre 1999, x-xi).

Before the Fall, according to Aquinas, the human creature lived in a state of graced intimacy with God. One gift associated with this state was that God's grace "overflowed" from the soul into the body (*DM,* 5.1; see *response* in **3.49**). For Aquinas, this overflow of grace entailed, among other things, a preternatural incapacity of the human creature to suffer corporeal infirmity (see *reply 1* in **3.49**). When humanity lost the divine help of supernatural grace, the human body was set in a state of disorder in relation to the soul — that is to say, the human body ceased to operate according to its grace-elevated nature (**3.19**). As a consequence, the finite organic systems of the human body were made susceptible to damage, dysfunction, and decay. These *operative limitations* unequally affect particular bodies and are identified as "weaknesses" insofar as the body is not subject to reason's governing power (**3.39**); moreover, these "afflictions" are experienced as evil by the human creature, and such bodily sufferings are proper objects of fear (*ST,* 1-2.35.1, *reply 3*).

Aquinas's account of corporeal infirmity concerns the bodies of particular people who are "afflicted" with operative limitations. Considering Aquinas's view of the operational limitations of the human body in light of his account of the human creature, one preliminary point immediately stands out: When particular operations of the body are hindered or impaired, the cooperation between the soul and those operations is likewise affected. For example, a defect or disorder of a body's internal sense organ would certainly affect the operation of reason — insofar as the immaterial powers of the soul are configured to cooperate with the internal sense organ in the illumination of the phantasm (**3.10**; *ST,* 1.75.3, *reply 2; De Veritate,* 18.8, *reply 2*). However, according to Aquinas, no defect or disorder of the body can ever impair the principal operation and flourishing of the rational soul in its communication with God, which is an immaterial act of the soul (**3.13**; *ST,* 1.75.6; cf. *ST,* 3.69.4-6; contra Reinders 2008, 106-7).

II. Privation of the Good, Evil Suffered, and Corporeal Infirmity

An account of the generically infirm or weakened human body is for Aquinas but one inflection of a broader thesis regarding how Christians use the word "evil." For Aquinas, the word "evil" *(malum)* signifies the undesirable absence or defection of a good that is due (an operative limitation), and the word is used to express all degrees of undesirable privation of a good (*ST,* 1.14.10, *response*). In the various places he treats evil, Aquinas distinguishes between *malum poenae* ("affliction" or "evil suffered") and *malum culpae* ("evil of fault"), which roughly correspond to the contemporary notions "natural evil" and "moral evil" (*ST,* 1.48.5, 6).

When it comes to corporeal infirmity, it is crucial for Aquinas that the term "evil" in properly Christian speech does not signify any being or form of creaturely existence (*ST*, 1.48.1, *response; CT*, 117). Rather, for Aquinas, the evil called "affliction" is always discussed as parasitic upon a more determinative good (*ST*, 1.49.3; *CT*, 118). It follows for Aquinas that insofar as a suffering human being exists, that person is good — and any evil suffered in the body by that person is a privation of that person's relative good as a human creature (*ST*, 1.48.6, *response*; 1.48.3, *response*; cf. 1.5.1).

For Aquinas, affliction is the relative privation of a corporeal good, and not the absolute negation of the goodness of corporeality. On that basis, Aquinas carefully distinguishes between the process of corruption and the simple state of corruption (*ST*, 1-2.73.2). For Aquinas, bodily corruption is a matter of more or less, not a matter of simple negation. On Aquinas's terms, a person cannot, in fact, "simply be profoundly disabled" (contra Reinders 2007, 173). Moreover, for Aquinas, not every defect of good is evil (i.e., a constitutive limitation), but only the privation of a good which is naturally due (*ST*, 1.48.5, *response; CT*, 114). Because corporeal incorruptibility is not a good inherent to human nature, the potential of any particular human being for the perfect actualization of some corporeal capacity is a proximate good, relative to that person's ultimate good (*ST*, 1.5.1; cf. Reinders 2007, 171-73).

Aquinas understands the bodily suffering of human beings to be the concomitant consequence of existing as composite creatures (a unity of material and immaterial properties) in a good world disordered by sin (see *reply 7* in **3.42**; *ST*, 1.48.2, *response*; 1.48.5, *reply 1*; 1.22.2, *reply 2*). In this way, Aquinas affirms that to suffer a corporeal infirmity is to experience evil, while ardently rejecting any suggestion that the person afflicted somehow becomes essentially or inherently "defective." For Aquinas, the evil suffered in corporeal infirmity does not reduce, destroy, or transform the suffering person's essential nature into something subhuman, marginally human, or non-human. To be clear, for Aquinas, corporeal infirmity, even in the form of a profound intellectual disability, does not result in an "anthropological minor-league" (*pace* Reinders 2007, 181n.26).

Aquinas approaches the damage, dysfunction, and decay of the human body as having to do with the unambiguously *human* experience of affliction. In Aquinas's way of thinking, affliction concerns the full spectrum of undesirable conditions to which human beings are subject, from pimples to plagues, and Aquinas gives special attention to injury, illness, and what we today might call congenital cognitive impairments or disorders.

Aquinas famously illustrates his understanding of evil suffered by way of the corporeal infirmity experienced by people who are blind (*ST*, 1.48.1-

6). When a person lacks the good of sight, that person suffers evil — that is to say, the privation of a good that naturally belongs to members of the human species. Aquinas explains that because evil is a privation of a good and not a thing in itself, the evil called "blindness" cannot entirely destroy the threefold good upon which it is parasitic: the good which is opposed to evil (as sight is to blindness), the good which is the subject of evil (the human creature who is blind), and the ultimate good which is the potential of the subject for actualization (the ordination of the person who is blind to friendship with God) (**3.2**; **3.38**; cf. MacIntyre 1999, 66-67). For although blindness deprives its subject of the good of sight, the person who is blind continues to exist as a human creature, and she cannot lose her essential capacity to respond to the movements of divine grace *(ST,* 1.5.5, *reply 3).*

Aquinas maintains a commonsense view of corporeal infirmity in that the evil suffered by way of blindness will certainly hinder or impair the actualization of one or several potentialities for proximate goods related to the "mode" and "species" of the person afflicted (*DM,* 1.1, *reply 1; CT,* 119). However, according to Aquinas, no corporeal affliction can decisively impact the actualization of the immaterial potential of the human creature pertaining to her highest good and ultimate end (cf. *ST,* 1.5.5, *response*).

For example, on Aquinas's terms, the affliction experienced by a woman with a profound mental disorder will certainly hinder the actualization of her potential for the proximate goods that follow from the conventional operation of human cognition. However, no measure of impairment can destroy or diminish the essence of that woman as *imago Dei,* nor can the affliction halt the actualization of her ultimate good in response to the movements of divine grace (**3.21**; **3.24**; cf. *ST,* 1-2.110.3-4; 1.93.9, *response;* contra Byrne 2000, 148). For Aquinas, this basic understanding of corporeal infirmity — and the threefold good of the human creature upon which corporeal affliction is parasitic — appertains to all manner and degree of evil suffered in the bodies of human beings (*DM,* 5.4, *response*).

Aquinas vigorously maintains that no measure of bodily affliction — including mental illness, profound cognitive impairment, and severe dementia — can decisively frustrate the highest good and ultimate end of the human creature. Some contemporary readers resist this interpretation of Aquinas. However, such hesitations are rooted in the baseless assumption that, according to Aquinas, those who suffer from these sorts of afflictions in this life are simply and absolutely corrupted — as if the good of the body is the final and ultimate good of the human creature (*ST,* 1-2.2.5, *response;* 2-2.55.1, *response;* cf. Stump 2003, 578n.59; contra Reinders 2008, 115-19; contra Byrne

2000, 147-48). Aquinas's view is that there are simply some things that the human creature cannot lose (**3.11**; **3.12**; see *reply 4* in **3.21**; cf. **3.5**).

When it comes to the broad spectrum of corporeal weaknesses that human beings might suffer, Aquinas's terminology is flexible; nevertheless, important distinctions emerge in his thought. Pertinent to the aim of this introduction, these distinctions are clearest at those points where Aquinas is keen to reject arguments suggesting that there are types of corporeal infirmity which affect or otherwise impair the realization of the ultimate good for particular human beings, which is the beatific vision (**3.11**; **3.47**; cf. **3.44**).

Aquinas considers corporeal infirmity — as one aspect of evil suffered — in three distinct ways, corresponding to the particular member (or systems) of the body that is rendered weak by disorder, damage, or decay (see *response* in **3.4**; see *response* in **3.30**). The first type concerns instrumental infirmities having to do with the proportionality and operational integrity of a particular body part or organic system. For example, both a person with legs described as "lame" *(claudus)* and someone who is described as "mute" *(muti)* have appendages or organs that do not operate as they should (**3.3**; *DM*, 3.2, *response*). Aquinas regards the propensity for seizure *(epileptica)* and the condition of paralysis *(paralytica)* as instances of instrumental infirmity.

The second type of corporeal infirmity that Aquinas discusses is *external sensorial infirmities* having to do with those sense organs disposed to receive external stimuli. For Aquinas, this type is most commonly discussed as the privation of sight, in the case of blindness *(caecitas)*, and as the privation of hearing, in the case of deafness *(surdi)* (*ST*, 1.5.5, reply 3; cf. **3.18**). With this second class of infirmity, by Aquinas's reasoning, in addition to the bare instrumental infirmity of the sense organ, someone who is deaf (or blind) is additionally hindered in their apprehension of the sense impression corresponding to the ordinary operation of the sense organ, which is sound (or sight).

The third type of corporeal infirmity is the most complex and differentiated for Aquinas, and pertains to internal sensorial infirmities (cf. Simonnet 1971). Internal sensorial infirmities have to do with the organ called the brain *(ST*, 1.78.4, *response)*. For Aquinas, the proper operation of the brain is toward the production of phantasms — which are necessary for common sense, the imagination, and the estimative and memorative faculties *(ST*, 1.91.3, reply 1). Aquinas recognizes that the instrumental and sensorial faculties of the brain, like those of all bodily organs, are subject to deterioration, damage, and decay (**3.7**; 1.84.8, reply 2).

Under this third type, Aquinas identifies a variety of conditions analogous to what we today might call diseases, disorders, and dysfunctions of a mental, intellectual, or neurological nature. In Aquinas's use, these conditions include, but are not limited to, mindlessness *(amentia)*, violently disposed madness *(furor)*, a generically unhealthy mind *(insanes)*, an unusual alienation from faculties crucial to human cognition *(alienates a mente, alienates a sensibus)*, an arrested or seized mind *(captus mentis)*, a condition underlying frenzied or wild behavior *(phreneticus)*, and a condition underlying lethargic or listless behavior *(lethargicus)*. Aquinas refers to persons who lack sufficient understanding to manage their own affairs (in various ways and to various degrees) as "half-wits" and "fools" *(moriones* and *stulti)*, and he carefully distinguishes between culpable foolishness (which is a moral evil) and natural foolishness (which is an evil suffered due to bodily impairment) (**3.1; 3.23; 3.26; 3.27; 3.28**). Moreover, Aquinas regularly refers to those who "lack the use of reason," which he generally associates with the condition *amentia* (cf. **3.36; 3.37**). Aquinas uses the term "insanity" *(insania)* to describe the unhealthy mental state wherein one lapses from a condition of "soundness" of mind to "unsoundness" of mind (**3.35**). Contrary to the common prejudice against medieval psychologies, we note that Aquinas's understanding of "demon possession" *(arreptitiis)* is unambiguously distinct from his account of internal sensorial infirmities — that is to say, Aquinas does not confuse the two conditions (see *reply* 2 in **3.37**; *ST,* 1-2.80.3, *response;* 1.115.5; cf. *Summa Contra Gentiles,* 3.154.14-15, 16, 23).

For the purposes of this introduction, I will focus on the condition Aquinas calls *amentia,* which is an affliction suffered by a person Aquinas calls the *amens.* Of the fifty or so instances where Aquinas directly discusses the *amens,* the term is most often translated as "imbecile" and on occasion (confusingly) as "madman," "idiot," and "insane." Aquinas defines *amentia* as a privation of "mental sight" due to a bodily impediment, and his technical use of the term corresponds to what we might call a profound cognitive impairment (**3.24; 3.26; 3.27; 3.28**).

The severity of *amentia* illuminates the most important aspects of Aquinas's "theology of bodily weakness" — insofar as *amentia* profoundly impairs the actualization of potentialities for proximate goods proper to the human creature, pertaining to mode and species. Viewed by way of the mechanisms of human cognition, as Aquinas understands them, the *amens* suffers a corporeal infirmity in which the lower powers of the human body necessary for the operation of reason (sensation and phantasm) do not cooperate with the immaterial intellect in the exercise of its proper act in relation to the phantasm, which is to understand (**3.24**). What is not hindered in the *amens* is her active imaging of God (which is an immaterial operation of the rational soul), nor is she prevented (as we shall see) from participating in the supernatural life — which is a foretaste of the beatific vision. Aquinas maintains that *amentia* cannot keep a human creature from responding to God's grace, nor is the condition able to impair the *amens* in the realization of her ultimate good.

In line with Aquinas's definition of the *amens* and the condition *amentia*, the picture I would like us to keep in mind is of a person who is congenitally unable to communicate, who manifests no capacity for discursive reasoning or intentional acts, and is entirely dependent upon others for her proximate well-being.

III. The Grammar of Grace and *Amentia*

Original Justice, Original Sin, and Unruly Flesh

Humanity was created for friendship with God, where "friendship" is understood as a relationship of likeness between the image of God and Triune God (*ST*, 2-2.23.1). For Aquinas, intrinsic to humanity's self-separation from God at the Fall was the loss of the "original justice" or right relationship with God (*DM*, 4.8). In the act of sin, humanity damaged the harmony of our friendship with God. As a consequence, God withdrew sanctifying grace, which is the elevation of the rational creature above the condition of its nature into a participation in the divine good. According to Aquinas, the common heritage of all human beings in relation to the withdrawal of sanctifying grace is called "original sin" (*DM*, 4.1, *response*). Moreover, as a consequence of that impaired relationship with God, Aquinas believes that without exception every rational creature needs the divine help of restorative and sanctifying grace in order to attain perfect happiness (**3.41**). In Christ, grace is restored through the sacrament of baptism, which entails the hope for bodily resurrection (*ST*, 3.69.3, *response;* **3.45**). For Aquinas, Christian reflection on the corruptible flesh begins with the rational creature as one ordained to live in a state of grace, yet as one who is likewise implicated in the effects of original sin and the drama of redemptive history (*DM*, 5.5, *sc*).

One further consequence of the Fall in Aquinas's understanding is the varying degrees to which and the modes by which the lower powers of the body were put in a state of disorder in relation to the higher powers of the rational soul (**3.42**; see *reply 1* in **3.20**). In the state of original grace,

the body was elevated with the soul to a supernaturally perfect cooperation in response to God's goodness and beauty (*ST,* 1-2.81.2, *response*).
However, wounded by sin, the broken relationship between creature and
Creator impaired the orderly operation of the soul in relation to the human body (*DM,* 5.1). In Aquinas's understanding, the breach of this immaterial relationship led to a material disorder, insofar as the soul lost the supernatural means to govern the body toward the actualization of both the
natural and the ultimate good of the human creature (**3.6**; **3.44**; cf. 1.97.1,
response; 1-2.81.5, *reply* 2).

The body and soul of fallen humanity retain their natural endowments
and powers, although these endowments and powers are retained and
passed on in a state of disorder *(DM,* 5.2, *response).* For Aquinas, this material disorder of the body in relation to the soul is passed from parent to child
in a manner that coincides with, but is not constituted by, the biological
transmission of life from parent to child (**3.19**; *DM,* 4.6, 8).

Most directly, the original sin that is passed from parent to child radically impairs the attainment of the good proportionate to human nature,
which includes the orderly operation of the bodily faculties related to the
proximate good of the human creature (**3.8**). Nevertheless, original sin did
not destroy the capacity of the human creature to be moved by grace toward
her ultimate good, which is beyond and above human nature: that is, our
participation in the life and love of Triune God (**3.9**).

The salvation wrought by Christ on the cross resolved and restored
what was lost at the Fall: original justice and the unmerited gift of grace. In
Christ, we are made friends with God. Among other things, the Christian
hope for bodily resurrection anticipates the divine restoration of the orderly
operation of the soul and its body (*ST,* 3.69.3; *CT,* 158; **3.45**).

Proximate Goods, Human Flourishing, and Beatitude

For Aquinas, the human body is configured by a rational soul and, as such,
the body is always in a state of potency in relation to the soul — a subjectivity that does not exist on the part of the soul in relation to the body *(ST,*
1.76.6, *response).* Among other things, this means that no organic or operational impairment of the body can ever impair the principal operation and
flourishing of the rational soul in its communication with God and imaging
of God (**3.41**; *ST,* 1.76.3, *reply* 1). Moreover, it means that the perfect happiness and ultimate flourishing of the human creature (a unity of material

and immaterial properties) does not consist principally in goods of the body (*ST*, 1-2.2.5). However, because the rational soul is created for embodiment and perfected in operation by way of the body, in a narrow sense the proximate flourishing of the human creature can be impaired by a corporeal infirmity (**3.42**).

Although the ultimate good and flourishing of the human creature requires the body, for Aquinas the perfection of human flourishing is not determined by goods or ills experienced in the body (**3.47**). In particular, baptism elevates the condition of the person whose bodily operations are insurmountably impeded or profoundly impaired to a supernatural status operative according to the economy of divine grace: the ultimate human flourishing called faith, hope, and love (cf. *ST*, 3.69.3-4). The restored participation of the baptized in the goodness and beauty of God is hindered, however, insofar as human creatures continue to suffer the corporeal wounds of original sin and anticipate the bodily resurrection of the dead.

Nevertheless, no degree of dysfunction or disorder of the normal internal sensory operations proper to the human creature can ultimately impair the self-communicating intercourse between God and the image of God, which is our capacity for participation in the life of God through Christ (**3.26**; *ST*, 1.45.7, *response*; 3.4.1, *reply 2*; 3.6.2, *response*). Communication between God and the image of God is not contingent upon an operational function or sensory faculty of the brain (*ST*, 3.69.4-6). This is an important argument of Aquinas's that is often overlooked, insofar as it illuminates what of "nature" must be intact in order to be perfected by divine grace.

For Aquinas, it is human nature, corresponding to the very structure of our constitution as composite creatures, that our capacity to perceive and understand the world requires the sensory apparatus of our animal bodies — this is how we realize our natural good. However, it is likewise constitutive of human nature that our capacity to supernaturally perceive, understand, and participate in the divine life by way of our incorporation into Christ cannot be destroyed or ultimately obliterated by original sin, the consequences of original sin, or the limitations of embodiment.

According to Aquinas, persons who have even the most profound sorts of cognitive impairment are capable of receiving and responding to the movements of divine grace, operative in the sacraments of the church. It is in this way that Aquinas grounds his theological understanding of the *amens* (and the doctrinal significance of *amentia*) in the life of the Body of Christ: where damaged bodies and wounded souls are drawn toward their ultimate perfection in Christ, the Crucified One.

IV. The Life of the Church: Sacraments, Mercy, Virtue, and Resurrection

Sacraments: Baptism, Eucharist, and Reconciliation

Aquinas is profoundly agnostic regarding what we can reasonably speculate concerning the hidden or inner life of the *amens* in relation to God (*ST,* 1.57.4, *response* and *reply 1*). Nevertheless, for Aquinas, the Christian faith entails a primary certainty that God can and does objectively communicate with the human creature, including the *amens,* in the sacramental life of the Church (*ST,* 2-2.45.5; 2-2.91.2, *reply 5;* 3.69.4-6; *DV,* 11.3).

On Aquinas's view, the participation of persons with *amentia* in the divine nature is understood primarily through their membership and participation in the Body of Christ (*ST,* 3.73.3, *response;* 3.80.3, 9, 11). For that reason, the logic of Christian baptism is essential to Aquinas's figuration of the *amens.* The effects of baptism are twofold in Aquinas's understanding. First, baptism entails the restoration of harmony ("original justice" or righteousness) to the human creature in relation to God (*ST,* 3.69.1-2). Second, in baptism we receive the gifts of supernatural grace and virtue, which are our membership and incorporation into the Body of Christ (*ST,* 3.69.4-5).

There is no doubt for Aquinas whether or not Christians should baptize "madmen and imbeciles." He writes that "imbeciles [*amentes*] who never had, and have not now, the use of reason, are baptized, according to the Church's intention, just as, according to the Church's ritual, they believe and repent" (see *reply 1* in **3.36**; *DV,* 28.3). Aquinas presumes the objective effect of baptism upon a person who lacks, or has yet to develop, the use of reason. Likewise, Aquinas presumes that grace makes possible a supernatural life by way of the infused virtues independent of a particular measure of occurrent awareness, as in the case of children and the *amens* (*ST,* 3.69.6, *response*). There is nothing about the condition of a person with a profound cognitive impairment like the *amens* that would somehow exclude him or her from being brought into the communion of the Body of Christ (*Scriptum super libros Sententiarum magistri Petri Lombardi,* IV, 4.3.1, qc 3; IV, 6.1.2, qc 3, ad 2).

In relation to baptism, it is worth noting that Aquinas addresses why the bodily disorder consequent of original sin is not taken away by baptism (**3.40**). That is to say, if the circumstance of disharmony in relation to God is overcome and healed in baptism, why do our bodies continue to suffer the effects of original sin *(ST,* 3.69.3, *reply 3)*? Aquinas's answer is that because the consequences of original sin experienced in the body correspond to the material donation of the parents in the process of human procreation, the overcoming of those consequences requires a divine gift of bodily restoration — which is the Resurrection (**3.20**). Specifically, according to Aquinas, Christians are baptized into Christ's passion, and the evil we continue to suffer in the body is perfected in and through Christ's suffering (3.69.3, *response*); yet, we are also baptized into Christ's resurrection, of which we will partake when our bodies are restored and raised to their supernatural glory (**3.46**).

As he did with his treatment of baptism, Aquinas devotes an entire article to the Eucharist and "those who lack the use of reason." Despite that fact, Aquinas's understanding of how the *amens* is involved in the eucharistic life of the Church is comparatively more difficult to parse out than his understanding of Baptism. Aquinas answers the objection that those who "lack the use of reason" should not be given Eucharist (**3.37**; cf. *SSS*, IV, 9.1.5, qc 3).

In his response, Aquinas distinguishes between, on the one hand, "those who are said" to absolutely never *(nunquam)* have had the use of reason — that is, the *amens* in principle. (The superlative *nunquam* means "never" in the same way that "cattle never had a nature capable of heavenly bliss" [*ST*, 2-2.165.2, *reply 4*]; and "never" to the same degree that Christ never sinned [*ST*, 3.34.1, *reply 2*].) On the other hand, Aquinas identifies "those who seem" to lack the use of reason in various ways and to different degrees — that is, the *amens* in fact (cf. **3.15**, where Aquinas discusses the process of corruption and the simple state of corruption). Aquinas grants that those baptized Christians "who are said" to absolutely never *(nunquam)* have had the use of reason from birth (i.e., never, in principle, developed past the stage of a newborn infant) should not be given the Eucharist. In such a case, Aquinas reasons, the "open cause" for "robbing" these Christians of their baptismal "right" to receive the Eucharist is the supposed impossibility of their having "devotion" toward the sacrament (cf. 3.80.6, *response*). This is crucial in Aquinas's view because a Christian who consumes the Eucharist without devotion or reverence to the real presence of Christ eats and drinks to his or her own condemnation (*ST*, 3.80.4, *response*; cf. 1 Cor. 11:29).

As Aquinas understands it, a person has devotion when she surrenders herself to the service of God (*ST*, 2-2.82.1, *response*). This devotional surrender is an interior act of directed attention toward God, which is exhibited in an "exterior humbling of the body" called adoration (*ST*, 2-2.84.2, *response*). Thus, by Aquinas's description, a priest has open cause to withhold the Eucharist from a baptized Christian if her body does not exhibit signs of interior humility before the sacramental body of Christ, according to the sense of

Psalm 120:1-2 (*ST,* 2-2.82.3, *response*). Aquinas also notes that "in simple souls . . . devotion abounds by repressing pride" (*ST,* 2-2.82.3, *reply 3;* cf. **3.32**).

At first blush, Aquinas's response seems to advocate a view that contradicts the normative position articulated by the Council of Orange in the *sed contra,* which reads, "All things that pertain to piety are to be given to the insane [*amentibus*]." However, when read in context, Aquinas's position can be read as twofold. First, Aquinas distinguishes between, on the one hand, the unique way a newborn lacks the use of reason and, on the other hand, the unequal and various ways that congenitally impaired adults do, in fact, lack the use of reason. Second, Aquinas sketches how the diverse ways in which adults can lack the use of reason correspond to an equally diverse field of pastoral concerns and responses. In particular, he addresses the privation of the use of reason experienced by people with lifelong *amentia,* irregular bouts of "mental insanity," and age-associated dementia.

This twofold distinction provides a fluid means for a priest to pastorally assess the eucharistic devotion of someone like the *amens,* about whom the procedural question of 3.80.9 is directly concerned. This is certainly a recognizable pastoral problem if we recall that, for Aquinas, the *amens* is congenitally unable to communicate, manifests no capacity for discursive reasoning or intentional acts, and is entirely dependent upon others for her proximate well-being. When it comes to newborn infants, the priest has a measure of certainty that the child has yet to develop the use of reason necessary for devotion. However, the priest has no way of knowing if someone with an *amentia*-like condition is capable of eucharistic devotion. The obscurity of the inner or hidden life of the *amens,* on Aquinas's terms, poses a pastoral problem — which is sufficiently complex to warrant both speculative and pastoral consideration. Understood in that way, and when read in light of Aquinas's wider theology of the Eucharist, the implications of 3.80.9 are more easily discernable.

To summarize Aquinas's view: *In principle,* someone who completely lacks the use of reason should not be given the Eucharist, because there is no direct way to know from the exterior movements of the body if there is or ever was an interior act of devotion on the part of the *amens.* As with the comatose and the demented elderly, such a "giving" would occur with the priest directly placing the Eucharist in the person's mouth. However, it likewise follows from that logic that there is no principled way to know, from either (1) bodily mannerisms (except for spitting or vomiting) or (2) the failure of the *amens* to develop mentally according to her age, if there is not and absolutely never *(nunquam)* was occurrent devotion to the sacrament.

Thus, Aquinas affirms the plain sense of the *sed contra,* and makes the following distinction. On the one hand, there is the concrete pastoral matter regarding children and "those who seem" to be completely devoid of the use of reason. On the other hand, there is the principled speculative concern about "those who are said" absolutely never *(nunquam)* to have had the use of reason from birth. For Aquinas, when it is a matter of principled speculation, the priest should not give the sacrament to someone who "lacks the use of reason"; however, in every other case — be it wildly erratic movements or psychological delirium — the priest should give the sacrament to a baptized Christian (unless there is a danger of spitting or vomiting). The question is whether or not the principal conditions for withholding the Eucharist can ever, in fact, obtain on Aquinas's terms. I am inclined to think that according to Aquinas we cannot know if those principled conditions are ever the case (cf. *ST,* 2-2.8.2, *response).*

In any case, it is clear from elsewhere in Aquinas's writings that he is not concerned with policing who does and does not have a right to consume the Eucharist, because all Christians have a duty and a right to approach the Lord's Table *(ST,* 3.80.6, *response).* If anything, Aquinas is worried that the Eucharist will be placed in the mouth of someone who does not desire the sacrament. Furthermore, under the logic of Aquinas's eucharistic theology, all baptized Christians receive the sacramental grace of the Eucharist during the Mass, insofar as they possess an interior devotion to the sacrament. This sacramental grace is received regardless of whether or not the Christian actually consumes the sacramental elements *(ST,* 3.73.3 *reply 2).*

Aquinas stopped working on his *Summa* midway through his treatise on the sacrament of Penance *(ST,* 3.84-90). Nonetheless, some important inferences can be made about Aquinas's understanding of sin in relation to persons who have an internal sensorial infirmity. Here also, Aquinas's distinction between the *amens* in principle and the *amens* in fact is pertinent. In essence, Aquinas understands moral culpability to correspond to what a person is able to understand and thereby enact by way of free will *(liberum arbitrium)* (**3.24;** *ST,* 1-2.88.6, *response;* 2-2.154.5, *response).* This means that in principle a Christian with *amentia* is incapable *(nunquam)* of sin, having been freed from the stain of original sin (by way of baptism) and having been elevated by grace to a supernatural participation in the beauty and goodness of God (**3.22; 3.17;** cf. **3.16**). However, as with the Eucharist, there is a real question on Aquinas's terms if those principled conditions can ever, in fact, be known to obtain (cf. *ST,* 1-2.77.7, *response).* Thus, for Aquinas, *those* *who seem* to lack the use of reason (which is a matter of degree) are obliged like all Christians to partake in the sacrament of Reconciliation to the extent that they are able to understand an action as sinful *(ST,* 1-2.89.6, *response;* cf. *ST,* 1-2.73.6, *reply 3).*

Related to this obligation, Aquinas held that if a contrite Christian desires to confess and atone for her mortal sin, yet is impeded from partaking in the sacrament of Penance (e.g., due to a profound impairment of the faculties required for communication), in response to her contrition, God's past mercies provided reason to believe that God would absolve her of the spiritual penalties of her self-separation from divine grace *(ST,* 3.90.2, *replies 1, 4;* cf. *ST,* Sup. 10.1-2). Presumably, in the case of profound *amentia*-like conditions, the penitent would desire sacramental absolution for "inward" or "hidden" sins (cf. *ST,* 2-2.54.3, *reply 3).*

The Christian Vocation in Relation to Corporeal Infirmity: Mercy, Protection, Limitation, and Care

According to Aquinas, "mercy" or "compassion" has two aspects: it is something we feel, and it is something we do (cf. MacIntyre 1999, 119-28). Aquinas's way of saying this is that mercy is both a "passion" and a "virtue" *(ST,* 2-2.30.3, *response).* As a passion, mercy is an involuntary displeasure that human beings experience when we recognize the suffering or affliction of another. As a virtue, mercy is the habit of choosing to respond to the suffering of another as if the affliction were being experienced in one's own person. In particular, virtuous mercy seeks to relieve another's suffering by removing the cause of the suffering or by providing what is missing. According to Aquinas, the disposition to mercy is an interior act of charity; and as an external act, mercy is the greatest of all the virtues pertaining to the love of neighbor *(ST,* 2-2.30.4, *response).*

Aquinas calls the acts of merciful or compassionate love of neighbor "almsgiving," and the particular need we are confronted with in the person of our neighbor determines the alms that are due to him or her *(ST,* 2-2.32.2, *response).* For Aquinas, merciful acts are a matter of moral precept, and neglecting to perform merciful acts when appropriate is a grave mortal sin *(ST,* 2-2.32.5, *sc).*

In Aquinas's view, when there is a difference between the actual need and the expressed need, Christian mercy always responds to the actual need — insofar as the actual need is knowable. For example, Christians are responding to an actual need and not an expressed need when, through the use of physical force, they subdue someone afflicted with a mental disorder who resists urgent medical treatment *(ST,* 2-2.33.6, *reply 1;* cf. 2-2.32.3, *response).* Similarly, a weapon is not to be returned to a person who is caught in a temporary state of "madness," even if that person is the rightful owner of the weapon *(ST,* 2-2.57.2, *reply 1;* 2-2.62.5, *obj/reply 1;* 2-2.120.1, *response).*

Aquinas articulates two kinds of need that oblige an act of mercy: some needs are corporeal, such as those needs which arise from sickness, injury, or disability; and other needs are spiritual, which affect the soul. Mercy responds to corporeal needs by supplying what is deficient: for example, leading the blind, supporting the lame, and visiting the sick (**3.25**). Mercy responds to spiritual needs by supplying what is deficient: praying for God's help, comforting those who grieve, and relieving deficiencies on the part of the intellect. Aquinas writes that if a "deficiency be in the speculative intellect, the remedy is applied by 'instructing,' and if in the practical intellect, the remedy is applied by 'counseling'" *(ST,* 2-2.32.2, *response).* Because *amentia*-like conditions impede the operations of practical rationality, Christians are obliged by the precepts of mercy to counsel those who lack "sufficient knowledge for the guidance of life" *(ST,* 1.23.7, *reply 3;* cf. MacIntyre on "proxy," 1999, 130, 138-39, 147-54).

Aquinas notes various limitations that Christians ought to observe and/or enforce in relation to particular corporeal infirmities. For example, people with severe *amentia*-like conditions are debarred from making solemn religious vows and contracting marriage, so long as the state of "madness" or "insanity" persists (**3.33**; *SSS,* IV, 34.1. *prologue;* IV, 23.2.2, qc 3, *response).* Similarly, such persons are debarred from acting as legal advocates (see *response* in **3.30**); have qualified credibility as legal witnesses *(ST,* 2-2.70.3, *response);* and are debarred from some of the works of mercy, such as counseling or teaching (see *reply 1* in **3.30**). Nevertheless, for Aquinas, most of these limitations are provisional and are outweighed by necessity *(ST,* 2-2.71.2, *response).*

By Aquinas's reckoning, it is a mortal sin (i.e., "worthy of hell fire") to call someone a name reserved for "natural fools" *(fatue) (ST,* 2-2.72.2, *sc).* A contemporary example of this might be using the word "retarded" as a pejorative epithet. Similarly, Aquinas considers it a mortal sin to mock or to make fun of a person who is a "natural fool" *(stultorum),* on account of their affliction (**3.31**). Aquinas maintains that "natural fools" (such as the *amens)* are due "greater respect." In the case of a "natural fool," derision is a mortal sin precisely because the person who is the object of the mocking is weak and vulnerable due to bodily affliction *(ST,* 2-2.75.2, *response).*

The Life of Virtue

The indelible and immaterial capacity of the rational soul to receive divine grace and to respond to divine grace has implications for how Aquinas understands the life of virtue of the *amens*. The question is what might we know, in Aquinas's terms, about the supernatural life of the *amens*, a baptized person with a lifelong and profound cognitive impairment. Clearly such a person would be capable of perfect happiness and participation in the divine nature — there is no question of that for Aquinas (*ST,* 1-2.2.5; cf. **3.13**). But how exactly does this happen in Aquinas's understanding; how are we to speak of such a person's virtue?

Aquinas distinguishes between different kinds of virtue. Most importantly, he distinguishes between, on the one hand, moral virtue (or "acquired" virtue), which is a proximate good with respect to our final end; and, on the other hand, supernatural virtue (or "infused" virtue), which is an ultimate good corresponding to our final end. Aquinas's understanding of acquired moral virtue relies heavily upon Aristotle's account of the virtues, the habituated dispositions of a good human life (flourishing as *eudaimonia*): prudence, courage, justice, and fortitude. Following Aristotle, Aquinas understands the moral virtues as acquired only by way of bodily faculties. The implications of this are that a person like the *amens* would not *in principle* be capable of developing moral virtue because she lacks the use of reason — and, therefore, is not capable of purposive (i.e., rational) acts.

In distinction from Aristotle, Aquinas follows Augustine in describing the ultimate good of the human life (flourishing as beatitude) as a supernatural participation in the life of God, characterized by the supernatural virtues called faith, hope, and love. For Aquinas, the infusion of faith, hope, and love at baptism is the foundation of his account of the acquired moral virtues in the Christian life. Because the supernatural virtues are not acquired by way of the body, but infused in a direct act of God, for Aquinas the *amens* is capable of attaining her highest good — even if the natural good that is the life of moral virtue is somehow stymied or hindered.

Although the *amens* is hindered in her acquisition of moral virtues like prudence, in baptism she receives supernatural habits of moral virtue (*ST,* 3.69.6, *response;* cf. 1-2.113.3, *response;* **3.22**; see *response* in **3.26**). In this way, Aquinas soberly acknowledges the profundity of the affliction experienced in the body of the *amens,* as it impairs the development of moral virtue, while concurrently developing an understanding of how the *amens* virtuously participates in the life of the Body of Christ. It is unclear what it means in practical terms for someone with *amentia* to have an infused disposition for moral virtue; nevertheless, Aquinas maintains that "half-wits and fools" receive supernatural wisdom and supernatural prudence when they are baptized (**3.26**; **3.29**; **3.14**). Additionally, according to Aquinas, those who courageously bear infirmities of the flesh exemplify the virtue of courage, and the perfection of that virtue is in the acknowledgment of one's own infirmity (i.e., weakness) in relation to God, which is the essence of humility (**3.34**).

The Life to Come

Death is the absolute privation of bodily life (**3.15**). For Aquinas this means that death is the most severe evil suffered in the body by the human creature (*ST*, 1-2.37.4, *reply 3; SCG*, 3.48.6). Because human beings are composite creatures, Aquinas maintains that the final cessation of the body's operations places the immortal soul in an unnatural state of separation from its body (*ST*, 1.89.1, *response;* see *reply 2* in **3.11**). Nevertheless, the human soul subsists, desirously awaiting the resurrection of its body (*ST*, 1.89.2, *reply 1;* see *reply 4* in **3.11**). There are two points related to the theme of corporeal infirmity that stand out in Aquinas's speculation on the bodily resurrection of the baptized. First, the glorification of the human creature at the Resurrection entails the perfection of the soul as it is united with its body (see *response* in **3.12**; *ST*, 2-2.18.2, *reply 2*). Aquinas maintains that there is an essential continuity between our mortal body and our resurrection body: it is the same body because the soul is its form. What is different is that the perfection of the glorified soul "overflows" to the body, perfecting and glorifying the body in its operations (*ST*, 3.7.4, *reply 2;* 3.15.10, *response; CT*, 167). Second, Aquinas identifies four perfections which belong only to the resurrected and glorified body: harmonious docility to the glorified soul; flawless expression of the soul's beauty; incapacity to suffer bodily affliction; and perfect responsiveness in movement to the intentions of the soul (**3.46**; *Commentary on 1 Corinthians*, lect. 6, §980-83).

Conclusion

Within the contours of Aquinas's thought resides a versatile "theology of bodily weakness." In addition to his illuminating treatment of the damage, dysfunction, and decay to which all human creatures are subject, Aquinas provides a way for us to understand the theological significance of a serious impairment of the ordinary cognitive operations associated with "the use of reason." According to Aquinas, an impairment of that sort has no direct implication upon a person's capacity for relationship with God. As in the case of the *amens,* such a person would be related to God by way of origination and ordination. For the *amens,* as with all human creatures, the realization of her ultimate potential for God begins at baptism, when she is made a member of the Body of Christ and is drawn into the goodness and beauty of the Triune God; her likeness of virtue in faith, hope, and love is a likeness unto Christ, the one, true, and perfect image of God; and her bodily perfection and ultimate happiness are anticipated, as with all believers, through our hope in the promise of bodily resurrection.

I hope this introduction to Aquinas on the theme of disability will inspire some to explore how contemporary theological engagements with the nature and significance of "disability" might be enlarged and enriched in light of St. Thomas Aquinas's theological vision.

REFERENCES

Primary Sources

Aquinas, Thomas. 1987. *Commentary on De Trinitate of Boethius (Expositio super librum Boethii De Trinitate).* English translation by Armand Maurer. Mediaeval Sources in Translation, 32. Toronto: Pontifical Institute of Medieval Studies.

———. n.d. *Commentary on the First Epistle to the Corinthians.* English translation by Fabian Larcher. Albany, N.Y.: Magi Books.

———. 1993. *The Compendium of Theology (Compendium Theologiae).* English translation by Cyril Vollert, S.J. St. Louis: B. Herder, 1947. Reprinted with editorial revisions as *Light of Faith: The Compendium of Theology.* Manchester: Sophia Institute.

———. 2003. *On Evil (De Malo).* English translation by Richard Regan; edited and with an introduction and notes by Brian Davies. New York: Oxford University Press.

———. 1994. *On Truth (De Veritate).* English translation by Robert W. Mulligan, James V. McGlynn, and Robert W. Schmidt. 3 vols. Library of Living Catholic Thought. Chicago: Regnery, 1952-54. Reprint, Indianapolis: Hackett.

———. 1929. *Scriptum super libros Sententiarum magistri Petri Lombardi.* Volumes I and II edited by R. P. Mandonnet. Paris: Lethielleux. Volumes III and IV edited by Maria F. Moos. Paris: Lethielleux, 1956.

————. 1975. *Summa Contra Gentiles*. English translation by Anton C. Pegis, James F. Anderson, Vernon J. Bourke, and Charles J. O'Neil. 5 vols. Notre Dame: University of Notre Dame Press.

————. 1981. *Summa Theologica*. English translation by the Fathers of the English Dominican Province. New York: Ave Maria Press.

Literature

Brennan, R. E. 1941. *Thomistic Psychology: A Philosophic Analysis of the Nature of Man*. New York: Macmillan.

Byrne, Peter. 2000. *Philosophical and Ethical Problems in Mental Handicap*. New York: St. Martin's Press.

Chesterton, G. K. 1974. *Saint Thomas Aquinas: The Dumb Ox*. New York: Doubleday.

Feser, Edward. 2009. *Aquinas: A Beginner's Guide*. Oxford: Oneworld Publications.

Journet, Charles. 2002. *The Meaning of Grace*. English translation by Geoffrey Chapman. London: Scepter Publishing, 1996.

Kerr, Fergus. 2002. *After Aquinas: Versions of Thomism*. Oxford: Blackwell.

Kopp, Paul. 1935. "Psychiatrisches bei Thomas von Aquin: Beiträge zur Psychiatrie der Scholastik II." In *Zeitschrift fur die gesamte Neurologie und Psychiatrie* 152: 178-96.

Krapf, E. Eduardo. 1943. *Tomas de Aquino y la psicopatologia: contribucion al conocimiento de la psiquiatria*. Buenos Aires: Editorial Index.

Lauand, Luiz Jean. 2001. "Fools in Aquinas's Analysis." In Quodlibet Journal 3, no. 1 (Winter). English translation by Alfredo H. Alves.

MacIntyre, Alasdair. 1999. *Dependant Rational Animals: Why Human Beings Need the Virtues*. Chicago: Open Court.

Merriell, D. Juvenal. 2005. "Trinitarian Anthropology." In *The Theology of Thomas Aquinas*. Edited by Rik Van Nieuwenhove and Joseph Wawrykow. Notre Dame: University of Notre Dame Press, pp. 123-42.

Pasnau, Robert. 2002. *Thomas Aquinas on Human Nature*. Cambridge: Cambridge University Press.

Pieper, Joseph. 1962. *Guide to Thomas Aquinas*. San Francisco: Ignatius Press.

Porter, Jean. 2005. *Nature as Reason: A Thomistic Theory of the Natural Law*. Grand Rapids: Wm. B. Eerdmans.

Reinders, Hans S. 2007. "Life's Goodness." In *Theology, Disability, and the New Eugenics: Why Science Needs the Church*. New York: T&T Clark, pp. 163-81.

————. 2008. *Receiving the Gift of Friendship: Profound Disability, Theological Anthropology, and Ethics*. Grand Rapids: Wm. B. Eerdmans.

Roth, Gottfried. 1960. "Thomas von Aquin in der neueren und neuesten Psychiatrie." In *Confinia Psychiatrica* 3: 180-86.

Simonnet, Jacques. 1971. *Du concept de maladie mentale chez saint Thomas d'Aquin.* Dissertation, Université de Paris.

———. 1983. "Folie et notations psychopathologiques dans l'oeuvre de Saint Thomas d'Aquin." In *Nouvelle histoire de la psychiatrie.* Edited by Jacques Postel and Claude Quétel. Toulouse: Privat.

Stump, Eleonore. 2003. *Aquinas.* Arguments of the Philosophers Series. New York: Routledge.

Torrell, Jean-Pierre, O.P. 2005. *Aquinas's "Summa": Background, Structure, and Reception.* Washington, D.C.: Catholic University Press.

———. 2003. "Image and Beatitude." In *Saint Thomas Aquinas: Spiritual Master,* vol. 2. Translated by Robert Royal. Washington, D.C.: CUA Press, pp. 80-100.

Yong, Amos. 2007. *Theology and Down Syndrome: Reimagining Disability in Late Modernity.* Waco: Baylor University Press, pp. 264-66.

Excerpts: Aquinas on the corporis infirmitas

Summa Theologica. English translation by the Fathers of the English Dominican Province. New York: Ave Maria Press, 1981.

3.1

ST, 1.23.7

Reply 3: . . . the majority of men have a sufficient knowledge for the guidance of life; and those who have not this knowledge are said to be half-witted or foolish [*moriones vel stulti*]. . . .

3.2

ST, 1.48.4

Response: Evil cannot wholly consume good. To prove this we must consider that good is threefold. One kind of good is wholly destroyed by evil, and this is the good opposed to evil, as light is wholly destroyed by darkness, and sight by blindness. Another kind of good is neither wholly destroyed nor diminished by evil, and that is the good which is the subject of evil; for by darkness the substance of the air is not injured. And there is also a kind of good which is diminished by evil, but is not wholly taken away; and this good is the aptitude of a subject to some actuality.

3.3

ST, 1.49.1

Response: . . . In the action evil is caused by reason of the defect of some principle of action, either of the principal or the instrumental agent; thus the defect in the movement of an animal may happen by reason of the weakness of the motive power, as in the case of children, or by reason only of the ineptitude of the instrument, as in the lame [claudis].

3.4

ST, 1.54.5

Response: In our soul there are certain powers whose operations are exercised by corporeal organs; such powers are acts of sundry parts of the body, as sight of the eye, and hearing of the ear. There are some other powers of the soul whose operations are not performed through bodily organs, as intellect and will: these are not acts of any parts of the body.

3.5

ST, 1.76.1

Response: We must assert that the intellect which is the principle of intellectual operation is the form of the human body. . . . Thus from the very operation of the intellect it is made clear that the intellectual principle is united to the body as its form.

The same can be clearly shown from the nature of the human species.

For the nature of each thing is shown by its operation. Now the proper operation of man as man is to understand; because he thereby surpasses all other animals. . . . The ultimate happiness of man must consist in this operation as properly belonging to him. Man must therefore derive his species from that which is the principle of this operation. But the species of anything is derived from its form. It follows therefore that the intellectual principle is the proper form of man.

But we must observe that the nobler a form is, the more it rises above corporeal matter, the less it is merged in matter, and the more it excels matter by its power and its operation; hence we find that the form of a mixed body has another operation not caused by its elemental qualities. . . . Now the human soul is the highest and noblest of forms. Wherefore it excels corporeal matter in its power by the fact that it has an operation and a power in which corporeal matter has no share whatever. This power is called the intellect.

Reply 1: . . . the intellectual power does not belong to a corporeal organ, as the power of seeing is the act of the eye; for understanding is an act which cannot be performed by a corporeal organ, like the act of seeing. But it exists in matter so far as the soul itself, to which this power belongs, is the form of the body, and the term of human generation.

3.6

ST, 1.76.5

Reply 1: . . . before sin the human body was immortal not by nature, but by a gift of Divine grace; otherwise its immortality would not be forfeited through sin. . . .

3.7

ST, 1.84.7

Response: In the present state of life in which the soul is united to a passable body, it is impossible for our intellect to understand anything actually, except by turning to the phantasms. First of all because the intellect, being a power that does not make use of a corporeal organ, would in no way be hindered in its act through the lesion of a corporeal organ, if for its act there were not required the act of some power that does make use of a corporeal organ.

Now sense, imagination, and the other powers belonging to the sensitive part, make use of a corporeal organ. Wherefore it is clear that for the intellect to understand actually, not only when it acquires fresh knowledge, but also when it applies knowledge already acquired, there is need for the act of the imagination and of the other powers. For when the act of the imagination is hindered by a lesion of the corporeal organ, for instance in a case of frenzy [*phreneticus*], or when the act of the memory is hindered, as in the case of lethargy [*lethargicus*], we see that a man is hindered from actually understanding things of which he had a previous knowledge.

3.8

ST, 1.91.3

Response: All natural things were produced by the Divine art, and so may be called God's works of art. Now every artist intends to give to his work the best disposition; not absolutely the best, but the best as regards the proposed end; and even if this entails some defect, the artist cares not: thus, for instance, when man makes himself a saw for the purpose of cutting, he makes it of iron, which is suitable for the object in view; and he does not prefer to make it of glass, though this be a more beautiful material, because this very beauty would be an obstacle to the end he has in view. Therefore God gave to each natural being the best disposition; not absolutely so, but in the view of its proper end. . . . Now the proximate end of the human body is the rational soul and its operations; since matter is for the sake of the form, and instruments are for the action of the agent. I say, therefore, that God fashioned the human body in that disposition which was best, as most suited to such a form and to such operations. If defect exists in the disposition of the human body, it is well to observe that such defect arises as a necessary result of the matter, from the conditions required in the body, in order to make it suitably proportioned to the soul and its operations.

3.9

ST, 1.93.8

Reply 3: The meritorious knowledge and love of God can be in us only by grace. Yet there is a certain natural knowledge and love as seen above [cf. *ST,* 1.12.12; 56.3; 60.5]. This, too, is natural that the mind, in order to understand God, can make use of reason, in which sense we have already said that the image of God abides ever in the soul; "whether this image of God be so obsolete," as it were clouded, "as almost to amount to nothing," as in those who have not the use of reason; "or obscured and disfigured," as in sinners; or "clear and beautiful," as in the just; as Augustine says [*De Trinitate,* XIV.6].

3.10

ST, 1.101.2

Response: As above stated [*ST,* 1.84.7], the use of reason depends in a certain manner on the use of the sensitive powers; wherefore, while the senses are tired and the interior sensitive powers hampered, man has not the perfect use of reason, as we see in those who are asleep or delirious [*dormientibus et phreneticis*]. Now the sensitive powers are situated in corporeal organs; and therefore, so long as the latter are hindered, the action of the former is of necessity hindered also; and likewise, consequently, the use of reason.

3.11

ST, 1-2.4.5

Response: Happiness [*beatitudo*] is twofold; the one is imperfect and is had in this life; the other is perfect, consisting in the vision of God. Now it is evident that the body is necessary for the happiness of this life. For the happiness of this life consists in an operation of the intellect, either speculative or practical. And the operation of the intellect in this life cannot be without a phantasm, which is only in a bodily organ, as was shown [*ST,* 1.84.6-7]. Consequently that happiness which can be had in this life depends, in a way, on the body. But as to perfect Happiness, which consists in the vision of God . . .

it is evident that the souls of the saints, separated from their bodies, "walk by sight," seeing the Essence of God, wherein is true Happiness.

Again this is made clear by reason. For the intellect needs not the body for its operation, save on account of the phantasms, wherein it looks on the intelligible truth, as stated [*ST*, 1.84.7]. Now it is evident that the Divine Essence cannot be seen by means of phantasms, as stated [*ST*, 1.12.3]. Wherefore, since man's perfect Happiness consists in the vision of the Divine Essence, it does not depend on the body. Consequently, without the body the soul can be happy.

We must, however, notice that something may belong to a thing's perfection in two ways. First, as constituting the essence thereof; thus the soul is necessary for man's perfection. Secondly, as necessary for its well-being: thus, beauty of body and keenness of perfection belong to man's perfection. Wherefore though the body does not belong in the first way to the perfection of human Happiness, yet it does in the second way. For since operation depends on a thing's nature, the more perfect is the soul in its nature, the more perfectly it has its proper operation, wherein its happiness consists. . . .

Reply 1: Happiness is the perfection of the soul on the part of the intellect, in respect of which the soul transcends the organs of the body; but not according as the soul is the natural form of the body. Wherefore the soul retains that natural perfection in respect of which happiness is due to it, though it does not retain that natural perfection in respect of which it is the form of the body.

Reply 2: . . . the human soul retains the being of the composite after the destruction of the body . . . after being separated from the body it has perfect being and consequently it can have a perfect operation; although it has not the perfect specific nature.

Reply 4: One thing is hindered by another in two ways. First, by way of opposition; thus cold hinders the action of heat: and such a hindrance to operation is repugnant to Happiness. Secondly, by way of some kind of defect, because, to wit, that which is hindered has not all that is necessary to make it perfect in every way: and such a hindrance to operation is not incompatible with Happiness, but prevents it from being perfect in every way. And thus it is that separation from the body is said to hold the soul back from tending with all its might to the vision of the Divine Essence. For the soul desires to enjoy God in such a way that the enjoyment also may overflow into the body, as far as possible. And therefore, as long as it enjoys God, without the fellowship of the body, its appetite is at rest in that which it has, in such a way, that it would still wish the body to attain to its share.

3.12

ST, 1-2.4.6

Response: . . . If we speak of that happiness which man can acquire in this life, it is evident that a well-disposed body is of necessity required for it. For this happiness consists, according to Aristotle [in the *Nicomachean Ethics*, §1102a 5-6], in "an operation according to perfect virtue"; and it is clear that man can be hindered, by indisposition of the body, from every operation of virtue. But speaking of perfect Happiness [in the beatific vision], some have maintained that no disposition of body is necessary for Happiness; indeed, that it is necessary for the soul to be entirely separated from the body. . . . But this is unreasonable. For since it is natural to the soul to be united to the body, it is not possible for the perfection of the soul to exclude its natural perfection.

Consequently, we must say that perfect disposition of the body is necessary, both antecedently and consequently, for that Happiness which is in all ways perfect. . . . [Thus,] from the Happiness of the soul [in the beatific vision] there will be an overflow on to the body, so that this too will obtain its perfection.

Reply 1: Happiness does not consist in bodily good as its object: but bodily good can add a certain charm and perfection to Happiness.

3.13

ST, 1-2.4.7

Response: For imperfect happiness, such as can be had in this life, external goods are necessary, not as belonging to the essence of happiness, but by serving as instruments to happiness, which consists in an operation of virtue. . . . For man needs in this life the necessaries of the body, both for the operation of contemplative virtue, and for the operation of active virtue, for which latter he needs also many other things by means of which to perform its operations.

On the other hand, such goods as these are nowise necessary for perfect Happiness, which consists in seeing God. The reason of this is that all such-like external goods are requisite either for the support of the animal body; or for certain operations which belong to human life, which we perform by means of the animal body: whereas that perfect Happiness which consists in seeing God will be either in the soul separated from the body, or in the soul united to the body then no longer animal but spiritual. Consequently these external goods are nowise necessary for that Happiness, since they are ordained to the animal life.

3.14

ST, 1-2.58.4

Reply 2: A man may be virtuous without having full use of reason as to everything, provided he have it with regard to those things which have to be done virtuously. In this way all virtuous men have full use of reason. Hence those who seem to be simple, through lack of worldly cunning, may possibly be prudent, according to Matthew 10:16: "Be ye therefore prudent as serpents, and simple as doves."

3.15

ST, 1-2.73.2

Response: . . . if we consider the matter carefully, we shall see that there are two kinds of privation. For there is a simple and pure privation, which consists, so to speak, in "being" corrupted; thus death is privation of life, and darkness is privation of light. Such like privations do not admit of more or less, because nothing remains of the opposite habit; hence a man is not less dead on the first day after his death, or on the third or fourth days, than after a year, when his corpse is already dissolved. . . . There is, however, another privation which is not simple, but retains something of the opposite habit; it consists in "becoming" corrupted rather than in "being" corrupted, like sickness, which is a privation of the due commensuration of the humors, yet so that something remains of that commensuration, else the animal would cease to live: and the same applies to deformity and the like. Such privations admit of more or less on the part of what remains of the contrary habit. For it matters much in sickness or deformity, whether one departs more or less from the due commensuration of humors or members.

3.16

ST, 1-2.74.5

Reply 1: . . . with regard to the case when it is a defect of knowledge about something which one is unable to know: . . . defect of reason is not a sin, and excuses from sin, as is evident with regard to the actions of madmen [*furiosi*]. If, however, the defect of reason be about something which a man is able and ought to know, he is not altogether excused from sin, and the defect is imputed to him as a sin.

3.17

ST, 1-2.76.3

Reply 3: If the ignorance be such as to exclude the use of reason entirely, it excuses from sin altogether [*totaliter usum rationis excluderet, omnino a peccato excusaret*], as is the case with madmen and imbeciles [*furiosus et amentibus*]: but such is not always the ignorance that causes the sin; and so it does not always excuse from sin altogether.

3.18

ST, 1-2.77.3

Response: . . . A human body is said to be weak when it is disabled or hindered [*debilitatur vel impeditur*] in the execution of its proper action, through some disorder of the body's parts, so that the humors and members of the human body cease to be subject to its governing and motive power. Hence a member is said to be weak when it cannot do the work of a healthy member, the eye, for instance, when it cannot see clearly. . . .

3.19

ST, 1-2.81.1

Response: . . . Since the body is proportionate to the soul, and since the soul's defects redound into the body, and vice versa, in like manner, say [some writers], a culpable defect of the soul is passed on to the child, through the transmission of the semen, albeit the semen itself is not the subject of the guilt. But all these explanations [as to how the original sin of our first parents could be transmitted biologically to their descendants] are insufficient. Because, granted that some bodily defects [defectus corporales] are transmitted by way of origin from parent to child, and granted that even some defects of the soul [defectus animae] are transmitted in consequence, on account of a defect in the bodily habit [corporis indispositionem], as in the case of idiots begetting idiots [fatuis fatui generantur]; nevertheless, the fact of having a defect by the way of origin seems to exclude the notion of guilt, which is essentially something voluntary. . . .

Therefore we must explain the matter otherwise by saying that all men born of Adam may be considered as one man, inasmuch as they have one common nature, which they receive from their first parents. . . . In this way, then, the disorder which is in this man born of Adam is voluntary, not by his will, but by the will of his first parent, who, by the movement of generation, moves all who originate from him, even as the soul's will moves all the members to their actions. Hence the sin which is thus transmitted by the first parent to his descendants is called "original," just as the sin which flows from the soul into the bodily members is called "actual."

3.20

ST, 1-2.81.3

Reply 1: Original sin is taken away by Baptism as to the guilt, in so far as the soul recovers grace as regards the mind. Nevertheless, original sin remains in its effect as regards the [means of transmission], which is the disorder of the lower parts of the soul and of the body itself, in respect of which, and not of the mind, man exercises his power of generation. . . .

Reply 3: Just as Adam's sin is transmitted to all who are born of Adam corporally, so is the grace of Christ transmitted to all that are begotten of

Him spiritually, by faith and Baptism: and this, not only unto the removal of sin of their first parent, but also unto the removal of actual sins, and the obtaining of glory.

3.21

ST, 1-2.110.4

Response: . . . grace, as it is prior to virtue, has a subject prior to the powers of the soul, so that it is in the essence of the soul. For as man in his intellective powers participates in the Divine knowledge through the virtue of faith, and in his power of will participates in the Divine love through the virtue of charity, so also in the nature of the soul does he participate in the Divine Nature, after the manner of a likeness, through a certain regeneration or re-creation.

Reply 4: Since the powers of the soul are natural properties following upon the species, the soul cannot be without them. Yet, granted that it was without them, the soul would still be called intellectual or rational in its species, not because of having these powers actually [*non quia actu haberet has potentias*], but on account of the essence of such a species, from which these powers naturally flow.

Translation amended in accord with Cambridge
University Press, 2006; v. 30, Cornelius Ernst.

3.22

ST, 1-2.113.3

Reply 1: Infants are not capable of the movement of their free-will [*non sunt capaces motus liberi arbitrii*]; hence it is by the mere infusion of their souls that God moves them to justice. Now this cannot be brought about without a sacrament; because as original sin, from which they are justified, does not come to them from their own will, but by carnal generation, so also is grace given them by Christ through spiritual regeneration. And the same reason holds good with madmen and idiots [*furiosis et amentibus*] that have never had the use of their free-will [*qui nunquam usum liberi arbitrii habuerunt*].

But in the case of one who has had the use of his free-will and afterwards has lost it either through sickness or sleep [*per infirmitatem vel per somnum*], he does not obtain justifying grace by the exterior rite of Baptism, or of any other sacrament, unless he intended to make use of this sacrament, and this can only be by the use of his free-will.

3.23

ST, 2-2.8.6

Reply 1: . . . it is *dullness of mind* [*hebetudo mentis*] that renders the mind unable to pierce into the heart of a thing. A man is said to be a fool [*stultus*] if he judges wrongly about the common end of life, wherefore folly [i.e., the condition of the *stultus*] is properly opposed to wisdom, which makes us judge aright about the universal cause. Ignorance [*ignorantia*] implies a defect in the mind, even about any particular things whatever, so that it is contrary to knowledge, which gives man a right judgment about particular causes. . . .

3.24

ST, 2-2.15.1

Response: Just as bodily blindness is the privation of the principle of bodily sight, so *blindness of mind* is the privation of the principle of mental or intellectual sight. Now this has a threefold principle. One is the light of natural reason, which light, since it pertains to the species of the rational soul, is never forfeit from the soul, and yet, at times, it is prevented from exercising its proper act, through being hindered by the lower powers which the human intellect needs in order to understand, for instance, in the case of imbeciles and madmen [*amentibus et furiosus*].

3.25

ST, 2-2.32.2

Reply 2: . . . needs are reduced to [the seven corporeal needs enumerated in Matthew 25:35-36], for blindness and lameness are kinds of sickness, so that to lead the blind, and to support the lame, come to the same as visiting the sick. On like manner to assist a man against any distress that is due to an extrinsic cause comes to the same as the ransom of captives.

3.26

ST, 2-2.45.5

Objection 3: Now many that have grace are naturally foolish [*naturaliter stulti*], for instance, madmen who are baptized [*amentibus baptizatis*] or those who without being guilty of mortal sin have become insane [*amentiam incidunt*]. Therefore wisdom is not in all that have grace. . . .

Response: The wisdom of which we are speaking . . . denotes a certain rectitude of judgment in the contemplation and consultation of Divine things, and, as to both of these, men obtain various degrees of wisdom through union with Divine things. For the measure of right judgment attained by some, whether in the contemplation of Divine things or in directing human affairs according to Divine rules, is no more than suffices for their salvation. This measure is wanting to none who is without mortal sin through having sanctifying grace, since if nature does not fail in necessaries, much less does grace fail: wherefore it is written (1 John 2:27): "(His) unction teacheth you of all things."

Reply 3: Baptized idiots [*amentes baptizati*], like little children, have the habit of wisdom, which is a gift of the Holy Ghost, but they have not the act, on account of the bodily impediment [*impedimentum corporale*] which hinders the use of reason in them.

3.27

ST, 2-2.46.1

Reply 4: To be unconcerned when one is injured is sometimes due to the fact that one has no taste for worldly things, but only for heavenly things. . . . Sometimes, however, it is the result of a man's being simply stupid about everything [*simpliciter circa omnia stupidus*], as may be seen in idiots [*amentibus*], who do not discern what is injurious to them, and this belongs to folly simply [*stultitiam simpliciter*].

3.28

ST, 2-2.46.2

Response: Folly, as stated above [2-2.46.1], denotes dullness of sense in judging, and chiefly as regards the highest cause, which is the last end and the sovereign good. Now a man may in this respect contract dullness in judgment [*stuporem in iudicando*] in two ways. First, from a natural indisposition, as in the case of idiots [*amentibus*], and such like folly [*stultitia*] is no sin. Secondly, by plunging his sense into earthly things, whereby his sense is rendered incapable of perceiving Divine things, according to 1 Corinthians 2:14 . . . and such like folly is a sin.

3.29

ST, 2-2.47.14

Reply 3: Acquired prudence is caused by the exercise of acts, wherefore "its acquisition demands experience and time," hence it cannot be in the young, neither in habit nor in act. On the other hand, gratuitous prudence is caused by divine infusion. Wherefore, in children who have been baptized but have not come to the use of reason, there is prudence as to habit but not as to act; this is also the case with imbeciles [*sicut et in amentibus*]; whereas in those who have come to the use of reason, it is also as to act, with regard to things necessary for salvation.

3.30

ST, 2-2.71.2

Response: In two ways a person is [licitly] debarred from performing a certain act: first because it is impossible to him, secondly because it is unsuitable to him: but, whereas the man to whom a certain act is impossible is absolutely debarred from performing it, he to whom an act is unsuitable is not debarred altogether, since necessity may do away with its unsuitability. Accordingly, some are debarred from the office of advocate because it is impossible to them through lack of sense — either interior, as in the case of madmen [*furiosi*] and minors — or exterior, as in the case of the deaf and dumb [*surdi et muti*].

For an advocate needs to have both interior skill so that he may be able to prove the justice of the cause he defends, and also speech and hearing, that he may speak and hear what is said to him. Consequently, those who are defective in these points are altogether debarred from being advocates either in their own or in another's cause. . . . A person may become unsuitable to exercise the office of advocate for two reasons. The first is that he has a higher obligation . . . the second reason is that he suffers from some personal defect, whether a physical one, like blindness, the possession of which would make it hard for a person to appear in court. . . .

Reply 1. Certain persons are sometimes debarred by unbecomingness, and others by inability from performing works of mercy: for not all the works of mercy are becoming to all persons: thus it ill becomes a fool to give counsel, or the ignorant to teach [*sicut stultos non decet consilium dare, neque ignorantes docere*].

> Translation amended in accord with Cambridge
> University Press, 2006; v. 38, Marcus Lefébure.

3.31

ST, 2-2.75.2

Response: . . . When somebody makes fun of or ridicules another's evil or defect because it is a small evil in itself, the corresponding sin is of its kind a venial and minor sin, whereas when the reason for treating such an evil or defect is the person involved, after the manner in which we are accustomed to treat the defects of a child or a fool lightly [*stultorum*], then ridiculing or making fun of somebody is to belittle him to the point of dismissing his misfortunes and treating them as a joke. This latter sort of derision is a mortal sin.

> Translation amended in accord with Cambridge
> University Press, 2006; v. 38, Marcus Lefébure.

3.32

ST, 2-2.83.13

Response: . . . there are three kinds of attention that can be brought to vocal prayer: one which attends to the words, lest we say them wrong, another which attends to the sense of the words, and a third, which attends to the end of prayer, namely, God, and to the thing we are praying for. That last kind of attention is most necessary, and even idiots [*idiotae*] are capable of it.

3.33

ST, 2-2.88.9

Response: . . . a simple vow takes its efficacy from the deliberation of the mind, whereby one intends to put oneself under an obligation. That such an obligation be of no force may happen in two ways. First, through defect of reason, as in madmen and imbeciles [*furiosus et amentibus*], who cannot bind themselves by vow so long as they remain in a state of madness or imbecility [*furia vel amentia*].

3.34

ST, 2-2.123.1

Reply 1: The virtue of the soul is perfected not in the infirmity of the soul, but in the infirmity of the body [*infirmitate carnis*], of which the Apostle was speaking [in 2 Corinthians 12:9: "Virtue is perfected in infirmity"]. Now it belongs to fortitude of the mind to bear bravely with infirmities of the flesh [*infirmitatem carnis fortiter ferat*], and this belongs to the virtue of patience or fortitude, as also to acknowledge one's own infirmity, and this belongs to the perfection that is called humility.

3.35

ST, 2-2.157.3

Reply 3: "Unsoundness" [*insania*] is corruption of "soundness." Now just as soundness of body is corrupted by the body lapsing from the condition due to the human species, so unsoundness of mind [*insania . . . animam*] is due to the mind lapsing from the disposition due to the human species.

3.36

ST, 3.68.12

Whether madmen and imbeciles should be baptized?

Objection 1: It seems that madmen and imbeciles [*furiosi et amentes*] should not be baptized. For in order to receive Baptism, the person baptized must have the intention, as stated above. But since madmen and imbeciles lack the use of reason, they can have but a disorderly intention. Therefore they should not be baptized.

Objection 2: Further, man excels irrational animals [*bruta animalia*] in that he has reason. But madmen and imbeciles lack the use of reason [*furiosi et amentes non habent usum rationis*], indeed in some cases we do not expect them ever to have it, as we do in the case of children. It seems, therefore, that just as irrational animals are not baptized, so neither should madmen and imbeciles in those cases be baptized.

Objection 3: Further, the use of reason is suspended in madmen and imbeciles more than it is in one who sleeps. But it is not customary to baptize people while they sleep. Therefore it should not be given to madmen and imbeciles.

On the contrary: Augustine says (*Confess.* iv) of his friend that "he was baptized when his recovery was despaired of": and yet Baptism was efficacious with him. Therefore Baptism should sometimes be given to those who lack the use of reason.

Response: In the matter of imbeciles and madmen [*amentes et furiosi*] a distinction is to be made. For some are so from birth, and have no lucid intervals, and show no signs of the use of reason. [*Quidam enim sunt a nativitate tales, nulla habentes lucida intervalla, in quibus etiam nullus usus rationis apparet.*] And with regard to these it seems that we should come to the same decision as with regard to children who are baptized in the Faith of the Church, as stated above [3.68.9, reply 2]. But there are others [*amentes*] who have fallen from a state of sanity [*sana mente*] into a state of insanity [*amentiam inciderunt*]. And with regard to these we must be guided by their wishes as expressed by them when sane: so that, if then they manifested a desire to receive Baptism, it should be given to them when in a state of madness or imbecility [*in furia vel amentia constitutis*], even though then they refuse.

If, on the other hand, while sane they showed no desire to receive Baptism, they must not be baptized. Again, there are some who, though mad or imbecile from birth [*nativitate fuerint furiosi et amentes*], have, nevertheless, lucid intervals, in which they can make right use of reason. Wherefore, if then they express a desire for Baptism, they can be baptized though they be actually in a state of madness [*amentia constituti*]. And in this case the sacrament should be bestowed on them if there be fear of danger; otherwise, it is better to wait until the time when they are sane, so that they may receive the sacrament more devoutly. But if during the interval of lucidity they manifest no desire to receive Baptism, they should not be baptized while in a state of insanity [*amentia constituti*]. Lastly there are others who, though not altogether sane [*non omnino sanae mentis existant*], yet can use their reason so far as to think about their salvation, and understand the power of the sacrament. And these are to be treated the same as those who are sane, and who are baptized if they be willing, but not against their will.

Reply 1: Imbeciles [*amentes*] who never had, and have not now, the use of reason [*nunquam habuerunt nec habent usum rationis*], are baptized, according to the Church's intention, just as according to the Church's ritual, they believe and repent; as we have stated above of children. But those who have had the use of reason at some time, or have now, are baptized according to their own intention, which they have now, or had when they were sane.

Reply 2: Madmen and imbeciles lack the use of reason accidentally, i.e., through some impediment in a bodily organ; but not like irrational animals through want of a rational soul. Consequently, the comparison does not hold. [*furiosi vel amentes carent usu rationis per accidens, scilicet propter aliquod impedimentum organi corporalis, non autem propter defectum animae rationalis, sicut bruta animalia. Unde non est de eis similis ratio.*]

Reply 3: A person should not be baptized while asleep, except he be threatened with the danger of death. In which case he should be baptized, if previously he has manifested a desire to receive Baptism, as we have stated in reference to imbeciles: thus Augustine relates of his friend that "he was baptized while unconscious," because he was in danger of death (*Confess.* iv).

3.37

ST, 3.80.9

Whether those who have not the use of reason ought to receive this sacrament [i.e., the Eucharist]?

Objection 1: It seems that those who have not the use of reason [*non habentes usum rationis*] ought not to receive this sacrament. For it is required that man should approach this sacrament with devotion and previous self-examination, according to 1 Cor. 11:28: "Let a man prove himself, and so let him eat of that bread, and drink of the chalice." But this is not possible for those who are devoid of [the use of] reason [*carent usu rationis*]. Therefore this sacrament should not be given to them.

Objection 2: Further, among those who have not the use of reason are the possessed, who are called energumens. But such persons are kept from even beholding this sacrament, according to Dionysius. Therefore this sacrament ought not to be given to those who have not the use of reason.

Objection 3: Further, among those that lack the use of reason [*carentes usu rationis*] are children, the most innocent of all. But this sacrament is not given to children. Therefore much less should it be given to others deprived of the use of reason [*carentibus usu rationis*].

On the contrary: We read in the First Council of Orange (Canon 13); and the same is to be found in the Decretals (xxvi, 6): "All things that pertain to piety are to be given to the insane" [*amentibus quaecumque sunt pietatis, sunt conferenda*]: and consequently, since this is the "sacrament of piety," it must be given to them.

Response: Men are said to have not the use of reason in two ways [*aliqui dicuntur non habere usum rationis dupliciter*]. First, when they are feeble-minded [i.e., have a hindered use of reason; *quia habent debilem usum rationis*], as a man who sees dimly is said not to see: and since such persons can conceive some devotion towards this sacrament, it is not to be denied them.

In another way men are said not to possess fully the use of reason [*dicuntur aliqui non habere totaliter usum rationis*]. Either, then, they never had the use of reason, and have remained so from birth [*nunquam habuerunt usum rationis, sed sic a nativitate permanserunt*]; and in that case this sacrament is not to be given to them, because in no way has there been any preceding devotion towards the sacrament: or else, they were not always devoid of reason [*non semper caruerunt usu rationis*], and then, if when they formerly had their wits [*quando erant suae mentis compotes*] they showed devotion towards this sacrament, it ought to be given to them in the hour of death; unless danger be feared of vomiting or spitting it out. Hence we read in the acts of the Fourth Council of Carthage (Canon 76); and the same is to be found in the Decretals (xxvi, 6): "If a sick man ask to receive the sacrament of Penance; and if, when the priest who has been sent for comes to him, he be so weak as to be unable to speak, or becomes delirious, let them, who heard him ask, bear witness, and let him receive the sacrament of Penance; then if it be thought that he is going to die shortly, let him be reconciled by imposition of hands, and let the Eucharist be placed in his mouth."

Reply 1: Those lacking the use of reason [*carentes usu rationis*] can have devotion towards the sacrament; actual devotion in some cases, and past in others.

Reply 2: Dionysius is speaking there of energumens [i.e., the demon-possessed] who are not yet baptized, in whom the devil's power is not yet extinct, since it thrives in them through the presence of original sin. But as to baptized persons who are vexed in body by unclean spirits [*corporaliter ab immundis spiritibus vexantur*], the same reason holds good of them as of others who are demented [*amentibus*]. Hence Cassian says (*Collat.* vii): "We do not remember the most Holy Communion to have ever been denied by our elders to them who are vexed by unclean spirits."

Reply 3: The same reason holds good of newly born children as of the insane who never have had the use of reason [*amentibus qui nunquam habuerunt usum rationis*]: consequently, the sacred mysteries are not to be given to them. Although certain Greeks do the contrary, because Dionysius says (Eccl. Hier. ii) that Holy Communion is to be given to them who are baptized; not understanding that Dionysius is speaking there of the Baptism of adults. Nor do they suffer any loss of life from the fact of our Lord saying (John 6:54), "Except you eat the flesh of the Son of Man, and drink His blood, you shall not have life in you"; because, as Augustine writes to Boniface (Pseudo-Beda, Comment. in 1 Cor. 10:17), "then every one of the faithful becomes a partaker," i.e., spiritually, "of the body and blood of the Lord, when he is made a member of Christ's body in Baptism." But when children once begin to have some use of reason so as to be able to conceive some devotion for the sacrament, then it can be given to them.

On Evil (De Malo). English translation by Richard Regan. Edited and with an introduction and notes by Brian Davies. New York: Oxford University Press, 2003.

3.38

On Evil, 1.2

Response: . . . we speak of the good in three ways. For we in one way call the very perfection of a thing good, as, for example, we call accurate vision the eyes' good, and virtue the good of human beings. In the second way, we call good the thing that has its proper perfection, as, for example, we call good human beings who are virtuous, and eyes that see accurately. In the third way, we call good the very subject as it has potentiality for perfection, as, for example, we call good the soul that has potentiality for virtue, and eyes that have potentiality for accurate vision. And as I have said before, evil is only the privation of a due perfection, and privation is only a potential being, since we say that things that nature designs to possess a perfection they do not have are deprived. . . . But evil deprives things of the good that is perfection. And so there cannot be evil in such a good. And evil lessens the good composed of a subject and its proper perfection insofar as the perfection is removed and the subject remains. For example, blindness takes away sight and lessens the eyes' power of sight and belongs to the substance of the eyes and even to the very animal as the deprived subject.

3.39

On Evil, 3.9

Response: . . . we need to understand the term weakness. And we should understand the term by analogy to bodily weakness [*infirmitatis corporis*]. And the body is weak when a fluid is not subject to the governing power of the whole body. . . . we should note that some bodily changes restrict the exercise of reason, so that reason either considers nothing at all or cannot freely reflect, as is evidently the case with those asleep and the insane [*dormientibus et phreneticis*].

3.40

On Evil, 4.6

Reply 4: Original sin is the contrary of original justice. And by that reason of original justice, the higher power of the soul both was joined to God and commanded lower powers and could even preserve the body from corruption. Therefore, baptism takes away original sin regarding the gift of grace, which unites the superior part of the soul to God, but baptism does not give the soul the power to be able to preserve the body from corruption, or the higher part of the soul the power to be able to preserve the lower powers from every kind of rebellion.

3.41

On Evil, 5.1

Response: . . . rational creatures surpass every other kind of creature in being capable of the highest good in beholding and enjoying God, although the sources from their own nature do not suffice to attain it, and they need the help of God's grace to attain it.

And we should note regarding this point that every rational creature without exception needs a particular divine help, namely, the help of sanctifying grace, in order to be able to attain perfect happiness. . . . But in addition to this necessary help, human beings needed another supernatural help because of their composite nature, for human beings are composed of soul and body, and of an intellectual and sensory nature. And if the body and the sense be left to their nature, as it were, they burden and hinder the intellect from being able freely to attain the highest reaches of contemplation. And this help was original justice, by which the mind of human beings would be so subject to God that their lower powers and their very bodies would be completely subject to them, nor would their reason impede them from being able to tend toward God. And as the body is for the sake of the soul, and the sense for the sake of the intellect, so this help whereby the body is under the control of the soul, and sense powers under the control of the intellect, is almost a disposition for the help whereby the human mind is ordained to see and enjoy God. And original sin takes away this help of original justice. . . .

3.42

On Evil, 5.4

Response: In accord with the Catholic faith, we undoubtedly need to hold that death and all such ills of our present life are punishment for original sin. But we should note that there are two kinds of punishment: one, indeed, as a penalty for sin; the second as something concomitant. . . . For God bestowed on human beings in their original condition the help of original justice, which preserved them from all such ills. And the whole human nature was indeed deprived of that help because of the sin of our first parents. . . . And different ills result from the privation of this help, and different persons have these deficiencies in different ways, although they equally share the moral fault of original sin. . . . For inasmuch as an offspring is part of its father regarding the body that it takes from its father but not regarding its soul, which God directly creates, it is not improper that an offspring for the sin of its father suffer corporeal punishment but not spiritual punishment, which belongs to the soul. . . . But the very fact that human beings are in such a condition that such ills or deficiencies help them either to avoid sin or to develop virtue is due to the weakness of human nature, which weakness results from the sin of our first parent. Just so, the fact that the body of a human being is so disposed as to need surgery in order to cure it belongs to its weakness. And so all these ills [and deficiencies] correspond to original sin as a concomitant punishment. . . .

Reply 7: Original justice, although it belonged to the soul, preserved the proper relationship of the body under control of the soul. And so bodily ills properly result from original sin, which took away original justice.

3.43

On Evil, 5.5

Response: . . . some things are natural to human beings regarding their form, for example, understanding, willing, and the like, and other things are natural to them regarding their matter, that is, their body. . . . Inasmuch as the human soul is potentially intellectual, it is united to the body so that it may through the senses acquire intelligible forms, by means of which it actually understands. For the union of the soul with the body is for the sake of the soul, not for the sake of the body, since matter exists for the sake of form, not form for the sake of matter . . . the disintegration of the elderly and all deficiencies are contrary to the particular nature of a particular thing as determined by its form, although in accord with the whole of nature, by whose power matter is brought into the actuality of every form for which matter has potentiality. . . . The dissolution resulting from a necessity of matter is in a special way unbefitting the form that is the rational soul. For other forms can pass away at least incidentally, but the rational soul can pass away neither intrinsically nor incidentally. . . . And likewise there can be no body composed of elements that is by the nature of matter indissoluble; an organic but dissoluble body is by nature suitable for the soul that cannot pass away. . . . Therefore, death and dissolution are natural to human beings by reason of a necessity of matter, but immortality would befit them by reason of the form's nature. And yet natural sources do not suffice to provide immortality. Rather, a natural disposition for it indeed befits human beings by reason of their soul, and supernatural power fulfills it.

The Compendium of Theology (Compendium Theologiae). English translation by Cyril Vollert, S.J. St. Louis: B. Herder, 1947; reprinted with editorial revisions as *Light of Faith: The Compendium of Theology*. Manchester: Sophia Institute, 1993.

3.44

CT, 109

All this brings to light the different relationship that God and creatures have to goodness. We may examine this difference from the standpoint of the two kinds of goodness discerned in creatures. Since the good has the nature of perfection and of end, the twofold perfection and end of the creature disclose its twofold goodness. A certain perfection is observed in the creature inasmuch as it persists in its nature. This perfection is the end of its generation or formation. The creature has a further perfection which it reaches by its motion or activity. This perfection is the end of its movement or operation. . . . Likewise, all creatures receive their perfect goodness from an end extrinsic to them. For the perfection of goodness consists in attainment of the ultimate end. But the ultimate end of any creature is outside the creature. This end is the divine goodness, which is not ordained to any ulterior end.

3.45

CT, 160

God, in restoring the risen body . . . will supply whatever is wanting to the proper amount of matter. . . . Although some may have lacked certain of their members during this life, or may not have attained to perfect size, the amount of quantity possessed at the moment of death makes no difference; at the resurrection they will receive, through God's power, the due complement of members and quantity.

3.46

CT, 168

[Regarding] the condition of the bodies of the blessed [at the resurrection: Because] the blessed soul, owing to its union with the first principle of all things, will be raised to the pinnacle of nobility and power, it will communicate substantial existence in the most perfect degree to the body that has been joined to it by divine action. And thus, holding the body completely under its sway, the soul will render the body subtle and spiritual. The soul will also bestow on the body a most noble quality, namely, the radiant beauty of clarity. Further, because of the influence emanating from the soul, the body's stability will not be subject to alteration by any cause; which means that the body will be impassible. Lastly, since the body will be wholly submissive to the soul, as a tool is to him who plies it, it will be endowed with agility. Hence the properties of the bodies belonging to the blessed will be these four: subtlety, clarity, impassibility, and agility. This is the sense of the Apostle's words in 1 Corinthians 15:42. . . .

3.47

CT, 173

. . . the goods and ills of this life are found to serve some purpose. External goods, and also bodily goods, are organically connected with virtue, which is the way leading directly to beatitude, for those who use such goods well. . . . Similarly the ills opposed to such goods (such as sickness, poverty, and the like) are an occasion of progress in virtue for some but aggravate the viciousness of others, according as men react differently to such conditions. But what is ordained to something else cannot be the final end, because it is not the ultimate in reward or punishment. Therefore neither ultimate happiness nor ultimate misery consists in the goods or ills of this life.

On Truth (De Veritate). English translation by Robert W. Mulligan, James V. McGlynn, and Robert W. Schmidt. 3 vols. Library of Living Catholic Thought. Chicago: Regnery, 1952-54; reprint, Indianapolis: Hackett, 1994.

3.48

On Truth, 18.8

Reply 1: The soul can be restricted by the body in two ways. One is by way of opposition. . . . The other is by way of incapacity and defect, namely, insofar as the body is unable to execute all that the soul would be capable of considered in itself. And there was nothing to keep the soul from being restricted by the body in this way in the state of innocence. For it is thus evident that by reason of the body the soul is hindered [as a consequence of original sin] from passing through things thrust in its path and from changing its location with as much ease as it does when separated from the body. In this way, also, it is kept from being able to have perfect use of its powers. . . .

3.49

On Truth, 26.10

Response: . . . because of the conjunction of the powers of the soul in one essence and of the soul and body in the one existence of the composite, the higher powers and the lower, and even the body and the soul, let flow from one to the other whatever superabounds in any one of them. . . . For this reason too there occurs an overflow from the very glory of the soul into the body, glorifying it . . . contrariwise the alteration of the body overflows into the soul. For a soul joined to a body imitates its make-up in point of insanity or docility and the like [*amentiam vel docilitatem*]. . . .

Reply 1: Just as God is the good and the life of the soul, so the soul is the good and life of the body, but not contrariwise so that the body should be the good of the soul. Now the ability to suffer is a sort of barrier or harmful factor as regards the union of the soul with the body. Thus the body cannot be blessed in its own way while still able to suffer, having a barrier to participation in its own good. For this reason impassibility is a part of the glory of the body. The soul's blessedness, however, consists entirely in the enjoyment of its own good, which is God. Hence the soul which enjoys the possession of God is perfectly happy, even if it happens to be passible from the point of view of its being united to the body, as was the case in Christ. . . .

4 A Ravishing and Restful Sight: Seeing with Julian of Norwich

AMY LAURA HALL

For the others,
         of whom I am one,
                  miracles (ultimate need, bread
of life) are miracles just because
         people so tuned
                  to the humdrum laws:
gravity, mortality —
         can't open
                  to symbol's power
unless convinced of its ground,
         its roots
                  in bone and blood.
We must feel
         the pulse in the wound
                  to believe . . .

Denise Levertov, "On Belief in the
Physical Resurrection of Jesus"

The author wishes to dedicate this essay to Anna Poulson.

Humdrum Laws

In her poem, Denise Levertov suggests that there may be those faithful for whom the resurrection of Jesus is symbolic, "an internal power, but not a matter of flesh." Like "epiphytes," a type of plant able to "flourish high in the canopy," there may be those Christians who can thus "subsist on the light, on the half of metaphor that's *not* grounded in dust, grit, heavy carnal clay." With Levertov, I am tuned to the humdrum laws of embodied life. My most faithful questions grow from the reality of *this particular* child's broken tooth, *this specific* teenage boy's new stutter, *this* precious toddler's inability to keep her cigarette-scarred hands from lashing out. I am a moral theologian who hungers for earthy miracles, who wishes daily to taste, as Levertov writes, "bread at Emmaus that warm hands broke and blessed" (Levertov 1993, 79-80).

Much of my teaching and research has involved noting a death-dealing split in dominant "decider" culture in the West: a split between those who can pass as functionally ethereal — above the fray — and those who are marked as simply incarnate, merely mortal. The crisscross net of cultural signals by which some human lives become *not worth hearing, not worth knowing, not worth living,* catches up individuals and whole neighborhoods, supposed "races" and entire peoples. This net, what Sharon L. Snyder and David T. Mitchell have termed "the Eugenic Atlantic," is so much a part of the Western academy that it seems, at times, Christian scholars are caught in something that we must also, at the same time, unravel (Snyder and Mitchell 2006, 100-131). The work of disability and theology is particularly fraught. By Snyder and Mitchell's reckoning, the distinction between those who are *able* and those who are *unable* acted as a "primary catalyst for collaboration" among peoples of *high* culture during much of the twentieth century, not only those in Germany during the Third Reich. This specific division between fit and unfit people is, by their estimation, even more "elusive" to analysis than other deadly markers of difference because of "its political and scientific ubiquity" (Snyder and Mitchell, 103). Who can argue with the scientific "facts" of a test, whether genetic or scholastic?

Writing academic prose about disability is potentially a self-defeating effort. Put plainly, for every supposedly excellent essay I publish, I shore up the legitimacy of an institution that excludes individuals bearing genetic marks for which the majority of women in my denomination choose to abort. How may I write well on a struggle that is so often excluded from what is considered to be proper, scholarly theological prose, without, by writing *well,* contributing further to an exclusion I believe is death-dealing?

One practice has been essential in answering this quandary. I return every year to read Julian of Norwich's *Revelations of Divine Love* — for her disturbing and blessed vision of the bodily Christ.

Within this little book on God's work in Jesus, Julian sorts through an extraordinary vision of lavish, abundant love flowing from Christ's very body into our own particular bodies, the rendered church body, the dismembered social body, and into the crevices of creation itself. Her text describes charity as not only *symbolic* friendship with God but a blood-and-flesh consanguinity that brings us to his very side. In this way, Julian may be read as intensifying and maternalizing the account of grace in the *Summa Theologica* of Thomas Aquinas, by describing Christ's blood as that which feeds, nourishes, joins, and transforms us. In this fourteenth-century vision, not only are our own bodies transformed, but the social body is also to be altered. Julian's vision of Christ's profuse, abundant, prodigal love is to stretch the reader's own vision of the boundaries regarding who *counts* for knowing, birthing, saving, hearing. The charity we are to envision with Julian is a love that blends our social and physical boundaries, a love that is to occasion the bleeding together of boundaries that we keep in our attempt to stay justified.

This has practical implications for real people living with disabilities and the real people who love people with disabilities, as well as for those who currently live in systemic or unacknowledged *fear of* disability. As Mary Jo Iozzio writes in her new work on "radical dependence," the most difficult problems facing people who live with disabilities are not bodily in a simple, physical sense, but related in a complicated way to their inclusion or exclusion within the social body. Physical pain is less often the presenting issue than is "marginalization, exclusion, and/or oppression." Iozzio explains, "People with disabilities manage this physical pain as well or as poorly as the non-disabled manage chronic and/or acute pain — with medication and with a kind of companioning or with substance abuse and a kind of violent anger." What singles out people living with disabilities is their "isolation," and the ways that they are perceived and treated as objects of "avoidance" or of dehumanizing upkeep (Iozzio, forthcoming, 29-30). Julian's vision undermines an understanding of danger that, in Western culture, has occasioned a carefully administered division between the fit and the unfit, the independent and the need-ridden. Her vision pulls together those who wish to function as relatively disembodied minds — disconnected from bone and blood themselves — and those of us whose bodies are marked in ways that register us as mortals in the world of grit and clay. To employ Iozzio's crucial term, Julian shows that all humans are marked by "radical dependence."

The woman known as Julian of Norwich received a series of visions in 1373, and she recounted them in the text known simply as *The Short Text (ST)*. For decades after, she spent her time praying, receiving, and writing what is known as *The Long Text (LT)*. I have included a slightly abridged version of *The Short Text* in the primary readings, but I will read it alongside the develoments in *LT*, where Julian digs more deeply into God's meaning with each chapter. In what follows, I will refer to sections of the text by whether they are in the *ST* or the *LT*, and by the standard numbering for the chapters in these two texts.

To Be Lovers of Christ

> Although our Lord showed me that I would sin, by me alone I understood everyone. At this I began to feel a quiet fear, and to this our Lord answered me as follows: "I am keeping you very safe." This promise was made to me with more love and assurance and spiritual sustenance than I can possibly say, for just as it was previously shown that I would sin, the help was also shown to me: safety and protection for all my fellow Christians. (**4.15**)

Julian's text is dedicated to "all those who wish to be lovers of Christ." For those readers who hope to receive the "revealing" of this love, our first task is to receive the "vivid perception of Christ." At what cost are readers to perceive reality with her? As the text opens, Julian asks for wounds, for sickness, and for participation in the pain of Christ's death. And at thirty, she receives this strange gift (**4.2**). The perception of her revelation as of *love* rather than self-delusion turns on the fulcrum of this gift. By seeking the marks of suffering and human sin, she may be read to reveal herself as a self-destructive poseur. Has she tried to substitute her own suffering for Christ's own? By seeking to know Christ's work *bodily,* rather than in a primarily scholastic way, has she proven herself guilty of the worst sort of masochistic works-righteousness? Has she sought suffering for her own salvation? There is no definitive answer to these questions. Julian's case cannot be disputed, proven, closed. But if one reads her open to the possibility of a strange gift, one may receive Christ through her words. One may receive, as her "fellow Christian," both safety and protection.

This text requires looking plainly at the "homely" blood of the incarnate Lord. As Elizabeth Spearing explains in her Translator's Note, the word was to convey familiarity, friendliness, even intimacy (Spearing 1998, xxxix).

Julian's access to the Lord comes not only through his infinite power, but through his kinship — his at-home-ness — with her. Her simple description of her reception is significant for her meaning. On her bed, Julian anticipates her own death, and a parson sets the cross in front of her. While propped up on pillows she tries to resist the parson's suggestion that she look straight at the cross, wishing instead to look past the cross, to keep her eyes upward, fixed high toward heaven. She explains that she finally, in exhaustion, supposes it just easier to look straight ahead at the crucifix, and, in the interest of this physical convenience, she accepts humbly the parson's cross and looks into the face of Christ. This simple shift in perception is blessed. Julian is granted "suddenly" the blood of Christ pouring from his brow, "all hot, freshly, plentifully, and vividly," the fruit of this "same who suffered for me" (4.3). Through this drenched vision, shown to her "without any intermediary," Julian receives bodily assurance that she, and "every creature living that would be saved, could have strength to resist all the fiends of hell and all spiritual enemies" (4.3).

It is significant that Julian's text is the first text in English known to have been written by a woman. Even if she was not a wife or a mother (and she may, for all we now know, have been both), she was raised by women in a society divided clearly along gender lines. This facet of her life is helpful to understand the form and content of her vision of Christ. Her gender and her life as a woman who cooked for kin, nursed infants, and cleaned wounds is intertwined with the revelation of Christ granted to her by God. Her imagery is often domestic, in a way that involves a home where people consume real food, where they embrace, weep tears, menstruate, defecate, give bloody birth, nurse drooling infants, and wipe the perspiring face of the dying. We do not know her name before she took the name of the church in which she became an anchoress in Norwich, England. We know her therefore by the name that notes her seemingly unproductive labor of contemplative prayer and spiritual counsel while she lived in a small room attached to the church. And we know her most importantly by the precious, bleeding Jesus whom she knows as *safety*. The cover of her text should feature a marked, risen Jesus.

Changed into Glory

By asking for the wounds of Christ, a woman comes to receive his blood directly, "without any intermediary" (4.3). Through the profligate, redeeming blood of Jesus, she receives bodily assurance of her safety and the safety of all that is. In one of her early visions, she is granted either senility or sanity by looking evil personified squarely in the face and scoffing at its power (4.20). Laughing at the devil himself, knowing him now to be, as she sees it, *nothing,* as "nought," she is granted a radical word about her neighbors. She finds "that the love of God unites us to such an extent that when we are truly aware of it, no man can separate himself from another" (*LT,* 65). Those attempts to protect one's own skin and soul from the pain and/or vice of another, or from a whole group of *others,* become in her vision silly; these attempts become foolish in an unholy sense. Through her vision, much of that which passes for civilized culture is seen as paltry hawking, as the miserable machinations of a force truly powerless to save us from pain and sin. (Here, in teaching Julian to future pastors, I often pull out — from my own purse — a bottle of anti-bacterial hand gel, naming it as a liturgical tool of supposed safety used by middle-class mothers across the United States after our children have had to cross social boundaries and use a *public* restroom.) To see with Julian is to know something about sin itself: that which separates us does not keep us safe. Her revelations are, I believe, significant even out of her own historical context. But in order to perceive the full significance of her visions, it is helpful to note a few features of the turn from the fourteenth to the fifteenth century.

Frederick Bauerschmidt explains that the Eucharist at this time in England was by no means a celebration of the profligate blood of Christ. The blood which Julian receives in her vision is hardly the same sort of affair as the sanctified liturgy occurring at the church down her way. As Bauerschmidt describes it, the mass was "a complex rite that depended on the participants properly performing their distinct functions," which included details such as a strictly hierarchical reception of the body and the restriction of the blood to the clergy (Bauerschmidt 1999, 18-19). During her time, laymen and laywomen simply *did not receive* the blood of Christ during the Eucharist. Julian receives profligate, abundant, floor-soaking blood directly from the brow and side of Christ. Also, at the time when Julian received her revelation, people maintained a kind of obsessive control of blood itself. This period of English history is marked by a fear of the mixing of bloodlines and, in a related sense, a fear of contamination through bodily humors. Those who irregularly (or even rather regularly) bled were marked as signs of *dis*ordered creation. Christendom stood against chaos by punishing the transgression of boundaries, both individual and corporate. There was a cultural consensus about incarnation: bodies and the social body itself were fragile and therefore in need of regulation. Bauerschmidt suggests that, by stark contrast, Julian's "images of the human body seem to exploit that fragility's capacity for openness and generativity" (Bauerschmidt, 64).

Julian underscores Christ's identity as a servant at a time of peasant revolts, including the significant Peasant Revolt of 1381. She receives her first visions of the bloody consanguinity of all Christians during a time when peasants, calling for an end to serfdom, burned buildings and even invaded the Tower of London. She envisions solidarity through Christ's blood at the same time that England is experiencing ruptures in the political body, including the ecclesial challenges of John Wycliffe and those perceived by the church to be his unrepentant followers, the Lollards, some of whom were excommunicated or burned at the stake near Norwich itself. And, not incidentally, Julian finds our safety in the flow of blood and tears at a time when a horrific plague had killed millions in England alone. "People died, horribly and suddenly and in great numbers," writes Grace Jantzen.

> It was so contagious that one contemporary witness describes how anyone who touched the sick or the dead immediately caught the disease and died himself, so that priests who ministered to the dying were flung into the same grave with their penitents. It was impossible for the clergy to keep up with all those who required last rites, and to die unshriven was seen as a catastrophe of eternal proportions. Nor could the people who died be buried with dignity. . . . The psychological impact on the survivors was incalculable, made worse in subsequent years by the further outbreaks which occurred at unpredictable intervals. (Jantzen 1988, 8)

During such a time, fear of one another and the desire precisely for one man to "separate himself from another" seem quite reasonable. Julian's perspective on atonement disallows separation, as God tells her explicitly when she struggles to understand her initial vision of universal kinship (*LT*, 65).

But should not a prudent believer separate herself from those who are in error, even separate herself from those whose suffering might tempt her toward the vice of despair? Julian envisions the world held safe in such a way that "sin is not shameful to man, but his glory" (4.15). In this passage, Julian touches upon one of the most radical implications of her text: the glory of those whose lives are obviously marked by the Fall and suffering of humanity. Naming David, Peter and Paul, Thomas and Magdalene, Julian concludes that "it is no shame to them that they have sinned . . . for there [in heaven] the badge of their sin is changed into glory" (4.15). Fear of the suffering brought on by the Fall and even fear of the Fall itself are transformed as Christ pulls all near. As we Christians come to Christ's side, we suffer *but are not to fear* his own proximity to sin. Drawing on this passage, Bauer-schmidt believes that, in Julian's vision, "the structure of the social body of Christ gives pride of place not to those who possess the most power, but to those who have been most in need and received the greatest mercy" (Bauer-schmidt 1999, 123).

Beside the Cross

> And thus our good Lord answered all the questions and doubts I could put forward, saying most comfortingly as follows: "I will make all things well, I shall make all things well, I may make all things well and I can make all things well; and you shall see for yourself that all things shall be well." (4.13)

In Julian's "bodily sight," she is intertwined with suffering, pain, and safety. While enduring grief and approaching death, she embodies the Fall. In this way she also comes into contact with the one whose fall is our safety. Her whole being is immersed in the "vivid" blood of Christ, and she receives the "bodily sight" of Christ "our clothing." "Hanging about us in tender love," he becomes so much a part of his beloved faithful that "he can never leave us" (4.4). The vision abruptly changes again, and Julian beholds a "little thing" in which all that is is held in God's palm. Draped with Christ as her garment, soaked in Christ's blood, held as a tiny thing on a little thing that is all that is made, Julian is brought to see that she is, in a blessed, gratuitous way, "really nothing," and that she is "in oneness of love" with all that God loves (4.6).

What about sin? How can Julian attest with such assurance that God is keeping all her fellow Christians safe? She envisions the world as a hazelnut. Yet how may we be rolled together in a little ball the size and smooth texture of a hazelnut, given the rampant ramifications of the fracture? She receives another vision at the point of this question; she watches as not the brow but the whole body of Christ begins to bleed, "so abundantly that it seemed to me that if at that moment it had been natural blood, the whole bed would have been blood-soaked and even the floor around" (4.7). She reflects here on the strange fittingness that God gives us "holy blood to wash away our sins," given that "it is so plentiful and it shares our nature" (4.7). Yet, again, what about sin? Does it remain? How does his blood conquer the sin passed down through our inheritance from Adam? She receives the words "By this is the Fiend overcome." This — the abundant, plentiful blood of Christ's body in distress and darkness — is the way that God "holds fast all the Devil's power," "scorn[s] his wickedness and set[s] him as nought" (4.7). As she gropes toward the significance of this vision, she receives the assurance that, through this blood, "all manner of things shall be well," and that through this blood those beloved by Christ are "filled with compassion" for others (4.11). For, as Christ's blood enters her, washes her, and clothes her, she is made compassionate — part of his passion and part of Christ's love for all others.

Julian returns repeatedly to the problem of sin. How can sin be naught until it is brought to naught at the end of time? Is sin not real in the suffering of God's children, obvious in home and barrio, in the grinding clash of war, for anyone with compassionate eyes to see? Is not sin real in willed ignorance and vice, obvious in person and society, for anyone with caring eyes to see? How can Julian be anything other than a royally duped woman, a woman who has shielded her vision to the horror around her? In answering, God grants a confusing temporal collapse, as all time prior and hence meets instantly at the cross: "for this atonement is incomparably more pleasing to God and more glorious in saving mankind than Adam's sin was ever harmful" (4.12). The Atonement forms the present. Past, current, and future sin, each and every indeed *real* pain of your suffering and my own, collide in time with the safety wrought by Christ's work. As she has written already in the text, Julian is told that there is now "nothing between the cross and heaven":

> At this point I wanted to look away from the cross, but I dared not, for I well knew that while I contemplated the cross I was safe and sound; therefore I was unwilling to imperil my soul, for beside the cross there was no safety, but the ugliness of fiends. Then a suggestion came from my reason, as though a friendly voice had spoken, "Look up to his Father in heaven." Then I saw clearly with the faith that I felt, that there was nothing between the cross and heaven which could have distressed me, and either I must look up or I must answer. I answered and said, "No, I cannot, for you are my heaven." (4.9)

We are told in the longer text that it takes Julian twenty years to understand how this equating of heaven and the cross can be so, given the palpable suffering all around her (and us) as well as her (and our) undeniable culpability: "For I knew through the universal teaching of Holy Church and through my own experience that the guilt of our sin weighs us down continually" (*LT,* 50). By one plausible reading, Julian receives a horrible curse of illness and confusion, even near-death and delusion, and she writes an elaborate justification to defend both God's goodness and Christian reason in the wake of her pain and psychosis. By another reading, she receives a blessed, strange gift of both bodily and cognitive solidarity with Christ, and thus with all of those for whom Christ suffered and died. Her gift of Christoform consanguinity brings the Fall, the Atonement, and the promise of heaven speeding toward one point in time, the moment that is true safety.

It is only in the parable of a fallen servant and a loving, gracious lord that she is able to make some sense of human guilt, our painful predicament, and the safety of the crucifixion. Given that this vision occurs between her writing of the *Short Text* and the *Long Text,* I will here give (excerpted) one significant portion of the vision from the *Long Text:*

> And then our kind Lord answered by showing in very mysterious images a wonderful parable of a lord who has a servant, and he gave me sight to aid my understanding of both. . . . The lord sits with dignity, in rest and peace: the servant stands, waiting reverently in front of his lord, ready to do his will. The lord looks at his servant lovingly and kindly, and he gently sends him to a certain place to do his will. The servant does not just walk, but leaps forward and runs in great haste, in loving anxiety to do his lord's will. And he falls immediately into a slough and is very badly hurt. And then he groans and moans and wails and writhes, but he cannot get up or help himself in any way. And in all this I saw that his greatest trouble was lack of help; for he could not turn his face to look at his loving lord, who was very close to him, and who is the source of all help. . . . (*LT,* 51)

Is the servant the same earth creature who followed the serpent's lead? How could it be that God would grant as clarity such a story to describe the Fall, given that the servant is described as waiting, *ready to do his will?* In an extensive meditation on this vision, Julian discovers that both Adam and Christ have been united in the person of the servant: the suffering of Adam's fall and Christ's dutiful suffering become so mixed as to be undistinguishable. "And thus our good Lord Jesus has taken upon himself all our guilt; and therefore our Father neither may nor will assign us any more guilt than he does to his own son, dearly loved Christ" (*LT,* 51). By Julian's vision, the *imago Dei,* the fall of Adam, and sin and suffering are seen through the prism of the collapsed, salvific moment that is Christ. The doctrines are bled together in the bleeding of the new Adam. In this way, she comes to realize how "wretched sin" is, truly, *nothing*.

Healed Wounds

At a time when bloodlines and kinship were enforced by law and by custom, Julian's vision bleeds the boundaries into kinship with Christ. At a time when fear of sin and suffering led to suspicion of blood and of unruly bodies, Julian receives the word that Christ's suffering and unruly blood are the means of safety. The task is thus not to ensure that one's own supposed blood-kin will be able to climb toward the high-culture canopy that subsists on merely symbolic faith, but to live in the risk-taking faith that God has poured out in Christ's blood. We are all kin, and, according to a potent reading of Julian, in such a manner that *those on the margins of goodness and coherence are God's favored ones.* To employ the work of Snyder and Mitchell for my own particular purposes, the body of Christ is that which crisscrosses the globe, replacing the death-dealing "political and scientific ubiquity" of what they term "the Eugenic Atlantic" with the power of homely grace (Snyder and Mitchell 2006, 103). The work of the faithful is not to climb our way up toward freedom, rung by rung, away from suffering and sin, but to free-fall. We are to embody kinship with even those most marked with disability, through the bodily knowledge that God has conquered the fiend. For, as Julian says, "although a man has the scars of healed wounds, when he appears before God they do not deface but ennoble him" (**4.15**). Bound up with Christ, we may be enabled to risk mercy, to the point of physical and even spiritual danger. The decision to be kin with only one out of ten women, women who discern a call to carry a chronically different fetus to term, may seem less a curse than a gift. Seeing with Julian, a decision to carry to term even an imminently terminal infant may be read as something other than a sign of sadomasochism. (For an interpretation of women who carry such pregnancies to term as religiously deluded, see especially Chapter Ten, "The Unexpected Baby," pp. 263-302, in Rapp, *Testing Women, Testing the Fetus,* 2000.) If Julian's perception is possible, the decision to be kin with disability may seem less a sign of mania and more a sign of hope.

Revelations of Divine Love may also be read to inspire our chosen field of inquiry: disability and theology. Julian receives a vision that likens seemingly disparate notions. She laughs at the devil. Sin is rendered as naught. The broken edges of fallen creation become smoothed like a hazelnut. Julian does not give a disputation, arguing her way forward with *sic et non,* leading pupils toward the definitive truth of the doctrinal matter at hand. (This was the standard theological/pedagogical method of her time.) Rather, Julian *likens* her way into a prayerful, vulnerable understanding of what she has seen. There is no sealed, clear way to adjudicate the truth of what she sees, or how she interprets what she has seen. She is either tragically deluded or beautifully inspired. But, even if she is inspired, the form of her inspiration is one of apparent weakness. In this way, the form of Julian's text sounds much like the words of some who write on disability. To write and speak from a position that is inescapably of *gravity, mortality* (to use again Levertov's poem), is, for some, to write and speak about the daily difficulty, even at times horror, of such a position while even simultaneously praising God for the perspective that this grants.

We are to envision that Christ's suffering is our safety, that we may even mock the evil that afflicts us from within and without, that we are bound up with one another in Christ. But this does not seal us up against pain. Here I would suggest that one of the most important words Julian grants at the intersection of disability and theology is patient, hopeful endurance with one another, even in the midst of what appears to be unendurable rupture from one another. What some people with disability most fear is that someday their disability will become *too much* for their loved ones to bear. What frightens some people called to live together with a person with disability is that they will indeed come to the end of their capacity to love, that they will reach a point past which there will be nothing holding them together. It is in this crux of need and fear and pain that physical struggle can result in the irresolvable suffering of alienation, one from another. And it is in this crux that Christians are called most resolutely to a life of what Mary Jo Iozzio calls "solidarity." Iozzio narrates this work of resilient kinship as indicative of a "God who stands in solidarity with humankind from the moment of kenosis and conception in Mary's womb until today" (Iozzio, forthcoming, 17). Pulling together here Iozzio's suggestion and Julian's text, we may see that the blood of the Crucified One does not grant secure impermeability so much as it reveals "radical dependence" (Iozzio's phrase). God's work in Christ enters through our permeability to create hope, merciful wisdom, and a courage sufficient for presence at the times of rupture. Julian received a vision that may be of use even for a family struggling toward solidarity in the midst of alienation and the often-resultant rage and/or depression. For, as Julian reminds us, "He did not say, 'You shall not be tormented, you shall not be troubled, you shall not be grieved,' but he said, 'You shall not be overcome'" (**4.19**).

References

Primary Sources

Julian of Norwich. 1998. *Revelations of Divine Love.* Translated by Elizabeth Spearing. London: Penguin. This edition is abridged.

——. 1961. *Revelations of Divine Love.* Translated by James Walsh. London: Burns & Oates. This edition contains the full text.

Secondary Sources

Bauerschmidt, Frederick Christian. 1999. *Julian of Norwich and the Mystical Body Politic of Christ.* Notre Dame: University of Notre Dame Press.

Iozzio, Mary Jo. Forthcoming. *Radical Dependence.* I worked with drafts of the Introduction and Chapter One.

Jantzen, Grace M. 1988. *Julian of Norwich: Mystic and Theologian.* New York and Mahwah, N.J.: Paulist Press.

Levertov, Denise. 1993. *The Stream and the Sapphire: Selected Poems on Religious Themes.* New York: New Directions.

Rapp, Rayna. 2000. *Testing Women, Testing the Fetus: The Social Impact of Amniocentesis in America.* New York: Routledge.

Snyder, Sharon L., and David T. Mitchell. 2006. *Cultural Locations of Disability.* Chicago: University of Chicago Press.

Excerpts

4.1

Julian of Norwich. *Revelations of Divine Love (The Short Text).* Abridged edition. Translated by Elizabeth Spearing. London: Penguin, 1998.

This is a vision shown, through God's goodness, to a devout woman, and her name is Julian, and she is a recluse at Norwich and is still alive in the year of our Lord 1413; in this vision there are many comforting and very moving words for all those who wish to be lovers of Christ.

RDL, 1

I asked for three graces of God's gift. The first was vivid perception of Christ's Passion, the second was bodily sickness, and the third was for God to give me three wounds. I thought of the first as I was meditating: it seemed to me that I could feel the Passion of Christ strongly, but yet I longed by God's grace to feel it more intensely. I thought how I wished I had been there at the crucifixion with Mary Magdalene and with others who were Christ's dear friends, that I might have seen in the flesh the Passion of our Lord which he suffered for me, so that I could have suffered with him as others did who loved him. . . .

As for the second gift, there came to me with contrition, freely, without any effort on my part, a strong wish to have of God's gift a bodily sickness. And I wanted this bodily sickness to be to the death, so that I might in that sickness receive all the rites of Holy Church, that I might myself believe I was dying and that everyone who saw me might believe the same, for I wanted no hopes of fleshly or earthly life. I longed to have in this sickness every kind of suffering both of body and soul that I would experience if I died, with all the terror and turmoil of the fiends, and all other kinds of torment, except for actually giving up the ghost, because I hoped that it might be to my benefit when I died, for I longed to be soon with my God.

I longed for these two things — the Passion and the sickness — with one reservation, for it seemed to me that they went beyond the common course of prayers; and therefore I said, "Lord, you know what I would have. If it is your will that I should have it, grant it to me. And if it is not your will, good Lord, do not be displeased, for I only want what you want." I asked for this sickness in my youth, to have it when I was thirty years old.

As for the third gift, I heard a man of Holy Church tell the story of Saint Cecilia; from his description I understood that she received three sword wounds in the neck from which she slowly and painfully died. Moved by this, I conceived a great longing, praying our Lord God that he would grant me three wounds in my lifetime: that is to say, the wound of contrition, the wound of compassion, and the wound of an earnest longing for God. Just as I asked for the other two with a reservation, so I asked for the third with no reservation. The first two of the longings just mentioned passed from my mind, and the third stayed with me continually.

4.2

RDL, 2

And when I was thirty and a half years old, God sent me a bodily sickness in which I lay for three days and three nights; and on the fourth night I received all the rites of Holy Church and did not believe that I would live until morning. And after this I lingered on for two days and two nights. And on the third night I often thought that I was dying, and so did those who were with me. But at this time I was very sorry and reluctant to die, not because there was anything on earth that I wanted to live for, nor because I feared anything, for I trusted in God, but because I wanted to live so as to love God better and for longer, so that through the grace of longer life I might know and love God better in the bliss of heaven. For it seemed to me that all the short time I could live here was as nothing compared with that heavenly bliss. So I thought, "My good Lord, may my ceasing to live be to your glory!" And I was answered in my reason, and by the pains I felt, that I was dying. And I fully accepted the will of God with all the will of my heart.

So I endured till day, and by then my body was dead to all sensation from the waist down. Then I felt I wanted to be in a sitting position, leaning with my head back against the bedding, so that my heart could be more freely at God's disposition, and so that I could think of God while I was still alive; and those who were with me sent for the parson, my parish priest, to be present at my death. He came, and a boy with him, and brought a cross, and by the time he came my eyes were fixed and I could not speak. The parson set the cross before my face and said, "Daughter, I have brought you the image of your Savior. Look upon it and be comforted, in reverence to him that died for you and me." It seemed to me that I was well as I was, for my eyes were looking fixedly upwards into heaven, where I trusted that I was going. But nevertheless I consented to fix my eyes on the face of the crucifix if I could, so as to be able to do so for longer until the moment of my death; because I thought that I might be able to bear looking straight ahead for longer than I could manage to look upwards. After this my sight began to fail and the room was dim all around me, as dark as if it had been night, except that in the image of the cross an ordinary, household light remained — I could not understand how. Everything except the cross was ugly to me, as if crowded with fiends. . . .

4.3

RDL, 3

And it suddenly occurred to me that I should entreat our Lord graciously to give me the second wound, so that he would fill my whole body with remembrance of the feeling of his blessed Passion, as I had prayed before; for I wanted his pains to be my pains, with compassion, and then longing for God. Yet in this I never asked for a bodily sight or any kind of showing of God, but for fellow-suffering, such as it seemed to me a naturally kind soul might feel for our Lord Jesus, who was willing to become a mortal man for love. I wanted to suffer with him, while living in my mortal body, as God would give me grace.

And I suddenly saw the red blood trickling down from under the crown of thorns, all hot, freshly, plentifully, and vividly, just as I imagined it was at the moment when the crown of thorns was thrust on to his blessed head — he who was both God and man, the same who suffered for me. I believed truly and strongly that it was he himself who showed me this, without any intermediary, and then I said, "Benedicite dominus!" Because I meant this with such deep veneration, I said it in a very loud voice; and I was astounded, feeling wonder and admiration that he was willing to be so familiar with a sinful being living in this wretched flesh. I supposed at that time that our Lord Jesus of his courteous love would show me comfort before the time of my temptation. For I thought it might well be, by God's permission and under his protection, that I would be tempted by fiends before I died. With this sight of the blessed Passion, along with the Godhead that I saw in my mind, I saw that I, yes, and every creature living that would be saved, could have strength to resist all the fiends of hell and all spiritual enemies.

4.4

RDL, 4

And at the same time that I saw this bodily sight, our Lord showed me a spiritual vision of his familiar love. I saw that for us he is everything that is good and comforting and helpful. He is our clothing, wrapping and enveloping us for love, embracing us and guiding us in all things, hanging about us in tender love, so that he can never leave us. And so in this vision, as I understand it, I saw truly that he is everything that is good for us.

And in this vision he showed me a little thing, the size of a hazel-nut, lying in the palm of my hand, and to my mind's eye it was as round as any ball. I looked at it and thought, "What can this be?" And the answer came to me, "It is all that is made." I wondered how it could last, for it was so small I thought it might suddenly disappear. And the answer in my mind was, "It lasts and will last for ever because God loves it; and in the same way everything exists through the love of God." In this little thing I saw three attributes: the first is that God made it, the second is that he loves it, the third is that God cares for it. But what does that mean to me? Truly, the maker, the lover, the carer; for until I become one substance with him, I can never have love, rest, or true bliss; that is to say, until I am so bound to him that there may be no created thing between my God and me. And who shall do this deed? Truly, himself, by his mercy and his grace, for he has made me and blessedly restored me to that end. . . .

4.5

RDL, 5

And during the time that our Lord was showing in spiritual sight what I have just described, the bodily sight of the plentiful bleeding from Christ's head remained, and as long as I could see this sight I kept saying, "Benedicite dominus!" In this first showing from our Lord I saw six things in my understanding: the first is the signs of Christ's blessed Passion and the plentiful shedding of his precious blood; the second is the Maiden who is his beloved mother; the third is the blessed Godhead that ever was, is, and ever shall be, almighty, all wisdom and all love. The fourth is all that he has made; it is vast and wide, fair and good, but it looked so small to me because I saw it in the presence of him that is Maker of all things; to a soul that sees the Maker of all, all that is made seems very small. The fifth thing I understood is that he made everything that is made for love; and the same love sustains everything, and shall do so for ever, as has been said before. The sixth is that God is everything that is good, and the goodness that is in everything is God. . . .

4.6

RDL, 6

... I am not good because of the showing, unless I love God better, and so may and should everyone that sees it and hears it with good will and true intention. . . . For it is universal and addressed to all because we are all one, and I am sure I saw it for the advantage of many others. Indeed it was not shown to me because God loved me better than the lowest soul that is in a state of grace, for I am sure that there are very many who never had a showing or vision, but only the normal teaching of Holy Church, and who love God better than I do. For if I look solely at myself, I am really nothing; but as one of mankind in general, I am in oneness of love with all my fellow Christians; for upon this oneness of love depends the life of all who shall be saved. . . .

And if any man or woman ceases to love any of his fellow Christians, then he loves none, for he does not love all; and so at that moment he is not saved, for he is not at peace; and he who loves all his fellow Christians loves all that is; for in those who shall be saved, all is included: that is all that is made and the Maker of all; for in man is God, and so in man is all. And he who loves all his fellow Christians in this way, he loves all; and he who loves in this way is saved. And thus I wish to love, and thus I love, and thus I am saved. (I am speaking in the person of my fellow Christians.) And the more I love with this kind of love while I am here, the more like I am to the bliss that I shall have in heaven without end, which is God, who in his endless love was willing to become our brother and suffer for us. And I am sure that whoever looks at it in this way will be truly taught and greatly comforted if he needs comfort. . . .

4.7

RDL, 8

And after this I saw with my bodily sight in the face of Christ on the crucifix which hung before me, which I was looking at continuously, a part of his Passion: contempt and spitting, which soiled his body, and blows on his blessed face, and many lingering pains, more than I can tell, and frequent changes of color, and all his blessed face covered at one time in dry blood. I saw this bodily in distress and darkness, and I wished for better bodily light to see it more clearly. And I was answered in my reason that if God wanted to show me more he would, but I needed no light but him.

And after this I saw God in an instant, that is, in my understanding, and in seeing this I saw that he is in everything. I looked attentively, knowing and recognizing in this vision that he does all that is done. I marveled at this sight with quiet awe, and I thought, "What is sin?" For I saw truly that God does everything, no matter how small. And nothing happens by accident or luck, but by the eternal providence of God's wisdom. Therefore I was obliged to accept that everything which is done is well done, and I was sure that God never sins. Therefore it seemed to me that sin is nothing, for in all this vision no sin appeared. So I marveled no longer about this but looked at our Lord to see what he would show me. . . .

And after this I saw, as I watched, the body of Christ bleeding abundantly, hot and freshly and vividly, just as I saw the head before. And I saw the blood coming from weals from the scourging, and in my vision it ran so abundantly that it seemed to me that if at that moment it had been natural blood, the whole bed would have been blood-soaked and even the floor around. God has provided us on earth with abundant water for our use and bodily refreshment, because of the tender love he has for us, yet it pleases him better that we should freely take his holy blood to wash away our sins; for there is no liquid created which he likes to give us so much, for it is so plentiful and it shares our nature.

And after this, before God revealed any words, he allowed me to contemplate longer all that I had seen, and all that was in it. And then, without any voice or opening of lips, there were formed in my soul these words: "By this is the Fiend overcome." Our Lord said these words meaning overcome by his Passion, as he had shown me earlier. At this point our Lord brought into my mind and showed me some part of the Fiend's wickedness and the whole of his weakness, and to do so he revealed how with his Passion he defeats the Devil. God showed me that he is still as wicked as he was before the Incarnation and works as hard, but he continually sees that all chosen souls escape him gloriously, and that grieves him; for everything that God allows him to do turns into joy for us and into pain and shame for him; and that is because he may never do as much evil as he would wish, for God holds fast all the Devil's power in his own hand. I also saw our Lord scorn his wickedness and set him at nought, and he wants us to do the same.

At this revelation I laughed heartily, and that made those who were around me laugh too, and their laughter pleased me. I wished that my fellow Christians had seen what I saw, and then they would all have laughed with me. But I did not see Christ laughing. Nevertheless, it pleases him that we should laugh to cheer ourselves, and rejoice in God because the Fiend has been conquered. And after this I became serious, and said, "I can see three things: delight, scorn, and seriousness. I see delight that the Fiend is defeated; I see scorn because God scorns him and he is to be scorned; and I see seriousness because he is defeated by the Passion of our Lord Jesus Christ and by his death, which took place in all seriousness and with weary hardship."

4.8

RDL, 10

After this Christ showed me the part of his Passion when he was near death. . . . I saw such pains that everything I could say would be quite inadequate, for they were indescribable. But every soul, as Saint Paul says, should feel in himself what was in Jesus Christ. This showing of Christ's pain filled me with pain, though I knew well he only suffered once, yet he wanted to show it to me and fill me with awareness of it as I had wished previously.

My mother, who was standing with others watching me, lifted her hand up to my face to close my eyes, for she thought I was already dead or else I had that moment died; and this greatly increased my sorrow, for in spite of all my suffering, I did not want to be stopped from seeing him, because of my love for him. And yet, in all this time of Christ's presence, the only pain I felt was the pain of Christ. Then I thought to myself, "I little knew what pain it was that I asked for"; for I thought that my pain was worse than bodily death. I thought, "Is any pain in hell like this pain?", and I was answered in my mind that despair is greater, for that is spiritual pain, but no bodily pain is greater than this. . . . Here I truly felt that I loved Christ so much more than myself that I thought bodily death would have been a great relief to me.

Here I saw part of the compassion of our Lady Saint Mary, for Christ and she were so united in love that the greatness of her love caused the intensity of her pain; for just as her love for him surpassed that of anyone else, so did her suffering for him; and so all his disciples, and all those who truly loved him, suffered greater pain than they would for their own bodily death;

for I am certain, from my own feelings, that the humblest of them loved him much better than themselves.

Here I saw a great union between Christ and us; for when he was in pain, we were in pain. And all creatures who were capable of suffering, suffered with him. And as for those who did not know him, their suffering was that all creation, sun and moon, withdrew their service, and so they were all left in sorrow during that time. And thus those that loved him suffered for love, and those that did not love him suffered from a failure of comfort from the whole of creation.

At this point I wanted to look away from the cross, but I dared not, for I well knew that while I contemplated the cross I was safe and sound; therefore I was unwilling to imperil my soul, for beside the cross there was no safety, but the ugliness of fiends. Then a suggestion came from my reason, as though a friendly voice had spoken, "Look up to his Father in heaven." Then I saw clearly with the faith that I felt, that there was nothing between the cross and heaven which could have distressed me, and either I must look up or I must answer. I answered and said, "No, I cannot, for you are my heaven." I said this because I did not wish to look up, for I would rather have suffered until Judgment Day than have come to heaven otherwise than by him; for I well knew that he who redeemed me so dearly would unbind me when he wished.

4.9

RDL, 11

Thus I chose Jesus as my heaven, though at that time I saw him only in pain. I was satisfied by no heaven but Jesus, who will be my bliss when I am there. . . . No tongue may tell, nor heart fully imagine, the pains that our Savior suffered for us, considering the majesty of the highest, most worshipful King and the shameful, insulting, and painful death; for he who was highest and most majestic was brought lowest and most truly despised. But the love that made him suffer all this is as much greater than his pain as heaven is above the earth; for the Passion was a deed performed at one particular time through the action of love, but the love has always existed, exists now, and will never end. . . .

4.10

RDL, 12

Then our Lord spoke, asking, "Are you well pleased that I suffered for you?" "Yes, my good Lord," I said. "Thank you, my good Lord, blessed may you be!" "If you are pleased," said our Lord, "I am pleased. It is a joy and a delight and an endless happiness to me that I ever endured suffering for you, for if I could suffer more, I would suffer." As I became conscious of these words my understanding was lifted up into heaven, and there I saw three heavens, a sight which caused me great amazement, and I thought, "I saw three heavens, and all of them of the blessed Manhood of Christ . . ."

For the first heaven Christ showed me his Father, in no bodily likeness, but in his nature and his action. This is how the Father acts: he rewards his son, Jesus Christ. This gift and this reward give Jesus such great joy that his Father could have given no reward that pleased him better. The first heaven, that is, the pleasing of the Father, appeared to me like a heaven, and it was full of great joy, for he is greatly pleased with all the deeds he has done to promote our salvation; because of these we do not just belong to Jesus by redemption, but also by his Father's generous gift. We are his joy, we are his reward, we are his glory, we are his crown. What I am describing causes Jesus such great pleasure that he thinks nothing of all his hardship and his bitter suffering and his cruel and shameful death. And in these words, "If I could suffer more, I would suffer more," I saw truly that if he might die once for each man who shall be saved as he died once for all, love would never let him rest until he had done it. And when he had done it, he would still think nothing of it out of love; for everything seems a trifle to him in comparison with his love. And he showed me this very seriously, saying these words, "If I could suffer more." He did not say, "If it were necessary to suffer more," but "If I could suffer more"; for if he could suffer more, he would, even if it were not necessary. This deed and this action for our salvation was ordered as well as he could order it; it was done as gloriously as Christ could do it. And here I saw complete joy in Christ, but this joy would not have been as complete if it could have been done any better than it was done.

And in these three sayings, "It is a joy, a delight, and an endless happiness to me," three heavens were shown to me, as follows: by the joy I understood the pleasure of the Father; by the delight, the glory of the Son; and by the endless happiness, the Holy Ghost. The Father is pleased, the Son is glorified, the Holy Ghost rejoices. Jesus wishes us to consider the delight which the Holy Trinity feels in our salvation, and wishes us to delight as much, through his grace, while we are on earth. And this was shown in these words, "Are you well pleased?" In the other words that Christ spoke, "If you are pleased, I am pleased," he revealed the meaning, as if he had said, "It is joy and delight enough to me, and I ask nothing more of you for my hardship but that I give you pleasure." This was shown to me abundantly and fully. Think hard too about the deep significance of the words "That I ever endured suffering for you," for in those words was a great sign of love and of the pleasure that he took in our salvation.

4.11

RDL, 13

Very happily and gladly our Lord looked into his side, and gazed, and said these words, "Look how much I loved you"; as if he had said, "My child, if you cannot look at my Godhead, see here how I let my side be opened, and my heart be riven in two, and all the blood and water that was within flow out. And this makes me happy, and I want it to make you happy." Our Lord revealed this to make us glad and joyful. . . .

Afterwards, our Lord reminded me of the longing I had had for him; and I saw that nothing kept me from him but sin, and I saw that this is so with all of us. And I thought that if sin had never existed, we should all have been pure and like himself, as God made us. . . .

He answered with this assurance: "Sin is befitting." With this word "sin" our Lord brought to my mind the whole extent of all that is not good: the shameful scorn and the utter humiliation that he bore for us in this life and in his dying, and all the pains and sufferings of all his creatures, both in body and in spirit — for we are all to some extent brought to nothing and should be brought to nothing as our master Jesus was, until we are fully purged: that is to say until our own mortal flesh is brought completely to nothing, and all those of our inward feelings which are not good. He gave me insight into these things, along with all pains that ever were and ever shall be; all this was shown in a flash, and quickly changed into comfort; for our good Lord did not want the soul to be afraid of this ugly sight.

. . . He supports us willingly and sweetly, by his words, and says, "But all shall be well, and all manner of things shall be well." These words were shown very tenderly, with no suggestion that I or anyone who will be saved was being blamed. It would therefore be very strange to blame or wonder at God because of my sins, since he does not blame me for sinning.

Thus I saw how Christ feels compassion for us because of sin. And just as I was earlier filled with suffering and compassion at the Passion of Christ, so was I now also partly filled with compassion for all my fellow Christians; and then I saw that whenever a man feels kind compassion with love for his fellow Christian, it is Christ within him.

4.12

RDL, 14

But you must apply yourself to this: contemplating these things in general, sad and grieving, in my mind I said to our Lord with great reverence, "Ah, my good Lord, how could all be well, given the great harm that has been done to humankind by sin?" And here I prayed, as much as I dared, for some clearer explanation to ease my mind over this. And our blessed Lord answered most compassionately and in a very friendly way, and showed me that Adam's sin was the greatest harm that ever was done, or ever shall be, until the end of the world; and he also showed me that this is publicly acknowledged through all Holy Church on earth. Furthermore, he taught me that I should consider the glorious atonement; for this atonement is incomparably more pleasing to God and more glorious in saving mankind than Adam's sin was ever harmful.

So what our blessed Lord's teaching means is that we should take heed of the following: "Since I have turned the greatest possible harm into good, it is my will that you should know from this that I shall turn all lesser evil into good."

He made me understand two aspects of this. One of them is our Savior and our salvation; this aspect is blessed and is clear and bright, light and beautiful and abundant, for all men who are or shall be of good will are included in it; we are bidden to it by God, and drawn to it, admonished and taught inwardly by the Holy Ghost and outwardly by Holy Church by the same grace; our Lord wishes our minds to be filled with this, rejoicing in him because he rejoices in us; and the more abundantly we are filled with this, reverently and humbly, the more we deserve his thanks and the more we benefit ourselves, and thus we may say, rejoicing, our Lord is our portion.

The second aspect is closed to us and hidden (that is to say, everything which is not necessary for our salvation); for it is our Lord's privy counsel, and it is proper to the royal lordship of God that his privy counsel should be undisturbed, and it is proper for his servants, out of obedience and reverence, not to know his counsel too well. . . .

And here I was taught that we must rejoice only in our blessed Savior Jesu and trust in him for everything.

4.13

RDL, 15

And thus our good Lord answered all the questions and doubts I could put forward, saying most comfortingly as follows: "I will make all things well, I shall make all things well, I may make all things well, and I can make all things well; and you shall see for yourself that all things shall be well." I take "I may" for the words of the Father, I take "I can" for the words of the Son, and I take "I will" for the words of the Holy Ghost; and where he says "I shall," I take it for the unity of the Holy Trinity, three persons in one truth; and where he says, "You shall see for yourself," I understand it as referring to the union with the Holy Trinity of all mankind who shall be saved. And with these five sayings God wishes to be surrounded by rest and peace; and thus Christ's spiritual thirst comes to an end; for this is the spiritual thirst, the love-longing that lasts and ever shall do until we see that revelation on Judgment Day.

For we that shall be saved, and shall be Christ's joy and his bliss, are still here on earth, and shall be until that last day. Therefore this is the thirst, the incompleteness of his bliss, that he does not have us in himself as wholly as he will have then. All this was shown me as a revelation of compassion, and his thirst will cease on Judgment Day. Thus he has pity and compassion for us, and he has longing to have us, but his wisdom and love do not permit the end to come until the best time.

And thus I understand the five sayings mentioned above — "I may make all things well," etc. — as a powerful and comforting pledge for all the works of our Lord which are to come; for just as the Holy Trinity made all things from nothing, so the Holy Trinity shall make all well that is not well. It is God's will that we should pay attention to all the deeds he has done, for he wants us to know from them all he will do. . . . It is God's wish that we should know in general terms that all shall be well; but it is not God's wish that we should understand it now, except as much as is suitable for us at the present time, and that is the teaching of Holy Church.

4.14

RDL, 16

God showed me the very great pleasure he takes in men and women who strongly and humbly and eagerly receive the preaching and teaching of Holy Church; for he is Holy Church; he is the foundation, he is the substance, he is the teaching, he is the teacher, he is the goal, he is the prize which every true soul works hard to win; and he is known and shall be known to every soul to whom the Holy Ghost reveals it. And I am sure that all those who are seeking this will succeed, for they are seeking God. . . .

4.15

RDL, 17

Although our Lord showed me that I would sin, by me alone I understood everyone. At this I began to feel a quiet fear, and to this our Lord answered me as follows: "I am keeping you very safe." This promise was made to me with more love and assurance and spiritual sustenance than I can possibly say, for just as it was previously shown that I would sin, the help was also shown to me: safety and protection for all my fellow Christians. What could make me love my fellow Christians more than to see in God that he loves all who shall be saved as though they were one soul? For just as there is an animal will in our lower nature which can have no good impulses, there is a godly will in our higher nature which, no less than the persons of the Holy Trinity, can will no evil, but only good. . . .

God also showed me that sin is not shameful to man, but his glory; for in this revelation my understanding was lifted up into heaven; and then there came truly into my mind David, Peter and Paul, Thomas of India and the Magdalene — how they are famous in the Church on earth with their sins as their glory. And it is no shame to them that they have sinned, any more than it is in the bliss of heaven, for there the badge of their sin is changed into glory. In this way our Lord God showed them to me as an example of all others who shall come there.

Sin is the sharpest scourge that any chosen soul can be struck with; it is a scourge which lashes men and women so hard, and batters them and destroys them so completely in their own eyes, that they think they only deserve to sink down into hell. But when the touch of the Holy Ghost brings contrition, it turns the bitterness into hope of God's mercy; and then their wounds begin to heal and the soul begins to revive into the life of Holy Church. The Holy Ghost leads a man on to confession, and he earnestly shows his sins, nakedly and truly, with great sorrow and great shame that he has so befouled the fair image of God. Then, in accordance with the basic teaching which the Church has received from the Holy Ghost, his confessor imposes a penance on him for each sin. By this medicine every sinful soul needs to be healed, especially of sins that are in themselves mortal. Although a man has the scars of healed wounds, when he appears before God they do not deface but ennoble him. And as on the one hand sin is punished here with sorrow and suffering, on the other it shall be rewarded in heaven by the generous love of our Lord God almighty, who does not want the toils and troubles of any who come there to be wasted. . . . And so all shame will be turned into glory and into greater joy. And I am sure, by what I feel myself, that the more every well-natured soul sees this in the kind and generous love of God, the more loath he is to sin.

4.16

RDL, 18

But if you are moved to say or think, "Since this is true, then it would be a good idea to sin in order to have the greater reward," beware of this impulse, for it comes from the Enemy, for any soul that chooses to follow this impulse can never be saved until he has been healed of this as if it were a mortal sin. . . . Sin is neither a deed nor a pleasure, but when a soul deliberately chooses to sin (which is punishment in God's eyes), in the end he has noth-ing at all. That punishment seems to me the hardest hell, for he does not have his God. A soul can have God in all sufferings except sin.

And God is as eager to save man as he is strong and wise; for Christ himself is the foundation of the whole law of Christian men, and he taught us to return good for evil. Here we can see that he himself is love, and he treats us as he wishes us to treat others, for he wants us to be like him in completeness of unending love for ourselves and our fellow Christians. Just as his love for us does not fail because of our sin, he does not want our love for ourselves and our fellow Christians to fail; we must feel naked hatred for sin and unending love for the soul, as God loves it. This assertion of God's is an endless help and comfort, which keeps us very safe.

4.17

RDL, 19

After this our Lord gave a revelation about prayer. I saw two qualities in those who pray, like those I have felt in myself. One is that they do not wish to pray for anything that may be, but only for things which are God's will and his glory. The second thing is that they set themselves strongly and continu-ally to pray for things which are his will and his glory. . . . And so we pray for all our fellow Christians, and for all manner of men, according to God's will, for we wish that all manner of men and women were in the same state of vir-tue and grace that we ought to desire for ourselves. But yet, for all this, often we do not trust God almighty fully for it seems to us that, because of our un-worthiness, and because we are feeling absolutely nothing, we cannot be cer-tain that he is hearing our prayers. For often we are as barren and as dry after our prayers as we were before, and so we feel our folly is the cause of our weakness; I have felt like this myself. . . .

Thus our Lord wants us both to pray and to trust, for the purpose of the preceding statements is to strengthen us against weakness in our prayers. . . . He wants us to pray with sure trust, for prayer pleases him. . . . Prayer unites the soul to God; for though the soul is always like God in nature and sub-stance, yet because of sin on man's part, it is often in a state which is unlike God. Prayer makes the soul like God; when the soul wills what God wills, it is then in a state like God, as it is like God in nature. . . . And thus prayer makes accord between God and man's soul, though while man's soul is near to God, there is no need for him to pray, but reverently to contemplate what he says. For during all the time of my showing, I was not moved to pray, but always to have this good in mind for my comfort, that when we see God, we have what we desire, and then we do not need to pray. But when we do not see God, then we need to pray because we lack something, and to make ourselves open to Jesus; for when a soul is tempted, troubled and isolated by distress, then it is time to pray and to make oneself pliable and submissive to God. . . .

4.18

RDL, 20

Before this time I often had a great longing, and desired that as a gift from God I should be delivered from this world and this life, so as to be with my God in bliss where, through his mercy, I hope to be surely for ever. For I often saw the grief which is here and the well-being and bliss which is existence there. And even if there had been no sorrow in this life except for the absence of our Lord, I sometimes thought it more than I could bear, and this made me grieve and earnestly yearn. Then God said to me, to bring me comfort and patience, "You shall suddenly be taken from all your suffering, from all your pain and from all your woe. And you shall come up above, and you shall have me as your reward, and you shall be filled with joy and with bliss. And you shall have no kind of suffering, no kind of sickness, no kind of displeasure, no unfulfilled desires, but always joy and bliss without end. Why should you fret about suffering for a while, since it is my will and my glory?" And at these words, "You shall suddenly be taken," I saw how God rewards man for the patience he shows in awaiting God's will in his lifetime, and I saw that man's patience extends throughout the time he has to live, because he does not know the time of his passing. This is a great advantage, for if a man knew his time, he would not have patience over that time. And God wishes that while the soul is in the body it should seem to itself always about to die, for all this life of distress which we have here is only a moment, and when we are suddenly taken from suffering into bliss, then it will be nothing. . . .

And therefore if a man is suffering so much pain, so much woe, and so much distress that it seems he can think of nothing but the state he is in and what he is feeling, he should pass over it lightly and set it at nought as soon as he can. And why? Because God wishes to be known. For if we knew him and loved him, we should have patience and be completely at rest, and everything that he does should be pleasing to us. . . .

4.19

RDL, 22

. . . then our Lord opened my spiritual eyes and showed me my soul in the middle of my heart. I saw my soul as large as if it were a kingdom; and from the properties that I saw in it, it seemed to me to be a glorious city. In the center of that city sits our Lord Jesu, true God and true man, glorious, highest Lord; and I saw him dressed imposingly in glory. He sits in the soul, in the very center, in peace and rest, and he rules and protects heaven and earth and all that is. The Manhood and the Godhead sit at rest, and the Godhead rules and protects without any subordinate or any trouble; and my soul was blissfully filled with the Godhead, which is supreme power, supreme wisdom, supreme goodness. In all eternity Jesus will never leave the position which he takes in our soul; for in us is his most familiar home and his favorite dwelling. . . . the sight of this sitting gave me certainty that he dwells there eternally. And I knew for certain that it was he who had shown me all that went before. And when I had considered this carefully, our Lord gently revealed words to me, without any voice or opening of his lips, as he had done before, and he said very seriously, "Know well that what you saw today was no delirium; accept and believe it, and hold to it, and you shall not be overcome."

And this teaching and true comfort applies without exception to all my fellow Christians. . . . He did not say, "You shall not be tormented, you shall not be troubled, you shall not be grieved," but he said, "You shall not be overcome." God wants us to pay attention to his words and wants our certainty always to be strong, in weal and woe; for he loves and is pleased with us, and so he wishes us to love and be pleased with him and put great trust in him; and all shall be well.

And soon after this it was all over and I saw no more.

4.20

RDL, 23

After this the Fiend came again with his heat and his stench and distressed me greatly. . . . I set my bodily eyes on the same cross in which I had seen comfort before, and my tongue to speaking of Christ's Passion and reciting the faith of Holy Church, and I fixed my heart on God with all my trust and with all my strength. . . . They kept me occupied all that night and in the morning until it was just after sunrise. And then at once they were all gone and passed away, leaving nothing but a stench; and that persisted for a while. And I thought of them with contempt. And thus I was delivered from them by the power of Christ's Passion, for that is how the Fiend is overcome, as Christ said to me before.

Ah, wretched sin! What are you? You are nothing. For I saw that God is all things: I saw nothing of you. And when I saw that God has made all things, I saw nothing of you; and when I saw that God is in all things, I saw nothing of you. . . . And when I saw our Lord Jesu sitting so gloriously in our souls, and loving and liking and ruling and guiding all that he has made, I saw nothing of you. And so I am certain that you are nothing; and all those who love you, and like you, and follow you, and choose you at the end, I am certain that they shall be brought to nothing with you, and endlessly overthrown. God protect us all from you. Amen, for the love of God. . . .

4.21

RDL, 24

God showed me that we suffer from two kinds of sickness, of which he wishes us to be cured: one of them is impatience, because we find our trouble and suffering a heavy burden to bear, and the other is despair, or doubtful fear. . . .

And our Lord very humbly revealed to me the patience with which he bore his terrible Passion and also the joy and delight which that Passion gave him because of his love. And he showed by his example that we should bear our sufferings gladly and lightly, because that pleases him greatly and benefits us for ever. And we are troubled by them because we do not recognize love. Though the persons of the Holy Trinity are all equal in nature, what was shown me most clearly was that love is nearest to us all. . . . So, of all the properties of the Holy Trinity, it is God's wish that we should place most reliance on liking and love; for love makes God's power and wisdom very gentle to us; just as through his generosity God forgives our sin when we repent, so he wants us to forget our sin and all our depression and all our doubtful fear.

5 The Human Condition as Seen from the Cross: Luther and Disability

STEFAN HEUSER

The theology of Martin Luther (1483-1546) provides suggestive ways of responding to the challenges of disability. However, in order to fully understand Luther's position, we need to explore two controversial images of his stance toward disability issues before assessing the role that disability actually played in Luther's world (A and B). We will soon notice that Luther's thought quickly leads us beyond a center-and-periphery conceptualization of disability, thereby opening up a new theological hermeneutics and an ethics of disability. I will develop two particular aspects of his thought. The first is a complex of theological ideas that sets up a critique of the contemporary tendency to think of disability as confinable by and to a discourse, and the second draws on Luther's theology of the Word to understand how others in their particularity function as a medium of God's action (C). Next, I will take up Luther's critique of self-chosen works to show how the reformer describes the calling to become the medium of God's good works for another person (D). I will conclude with a brief summary (E). I have selected primary texts that display Luther's opinions, both insightful and misguided, about disabling conditions (F). This introduction attempts to engage Luther through a systematic conversation rather than a strict historical reconstruction of comments on the topic (see Miles 2001 for a historical analysis).

A. Monster and Saint: Two Images of Luther

Luther's comments on issues of disability have resulted in two common but divergent images of the reformer. For some, Luther is the monster of *Table Talk*, No. 5207 (**5.17**) whose suggestion to suffocate a twelve-year-old boy from Dessau, presumably suffering from Prader-Willi Syndrome, was — together with many other of Luther's comments — seized upon by National Socialists to vindicate the legalization of the killing of disabled people and the creation of the euthanasia program of the Third Reich (Wolf 1964, 685-702). While the Nazi exegesis of Luther continues to draw the reformer into disputes, social scientists and historians often judge Luther's comments on "changelings" or offspring of the devil as evidence of a lamentable medieval superstition, but one that has long been overcome (see Gewalt 1974, 105).

However, a contrasting image of Luther also exists, and perhaps can be best understood by considering a key scene in the 2003 movie *Luther*. On 31 October 1517, while at Wittenberg, the young Luther is approached by a young peasant mother of a crippled girl called Grete. The mother, radiant with joy, shows Luther a letter of indulgence that she had bought from a preacher and which certifies the salvation of Grete from purgatory. The preacher has told the mother, Hanna, that it is within her reach to make crippled Grete walk to heaven through her purchase of the indulgence. Luther's eyes fill with compassion, then with anger. "It's just paper, Hanna," he says. "These words mean nothing. You must put your trust in God's love. Save your money to feed Grete." Luther repays the surprised Hanna the costs for the indulgence letter, then rushes to his desk to compose the 95 Theses later hammered to the gate of Wittenberg Castle church. And so the Reformation begins.

The vast bulk of research on the genesis of Luther's thoughts on the Reformation gives us, of course, a quite different story (see Lohse 1968, 1988). His was a complex and multifaceted struggle, not least one that took place at the writing desk of the Wittenberg Doctor of Biblical Exegesis. Luther gained his insights first of all from struggling with the biblical witness. His discovery of God's justifying grace, the significance of the divine promise, and the distinction between law and gospel, as well as his breaking of the scholastic synthesis of nature and grace, his dismissal of the doctrine of the free will, and his passion for the knowledge of God and humanity were all mediated by his listening to Scripture (Bayer 1969, 115-50). Figuratively speaking, Luther found his place at the foot of the cross very close to St. Paul's, a place from which he was able to respond to issues of disability in an extremely stimulating way, despite his various blunders. Notwithstanding its religious kitsch, the movie of Luther's life does convey the liberating dimension of Luther's ethics for human life, which is, to varying degrees, shot through with disabilities. Although the scene depicting the purchase of indulgences is fictional, it does illuminate Luther's ethical sensibility about disability. Nevertheless, the man who emphasized that the children, the poor, the sick, the suffering, the humiliated, and the sinners, rather than the pious, the noble, and the perfect, belong to Christ (WA[1] 5, 649 [*Operationes in Psalmos,* on Psalm 22]: Walch 1346 (No. 364, on verse 30) and 1341 (No. 348, on verse 27), was also the same man who could suggest the killing of a severely disabled boy, and maintain judgments about disabled people that appear to us as indefensible. Whether as monster or as saint, Luther remains for us a highly ambiguous figure when it comes to the issue of disability.

B. Disability in Luther's World

The apparent conflict in Luther's comments on topics related to disability might be explained with reference to his psychology, to his historic, cultural, and social context, or by simply stating that he made a mistake (see Gewalt 1974, 103-13). However, in light of recent analyses of the eugenic mentality (see Reinders 2000) and the ideology of reproductive technologies (see Hall 2007), Luther's suggestion that the disabled boy be killed appears symptomatic not only of medieval superstition but of beliefs that are very much alive in contemporary responses to disability.

In the most trustworthy of the three versions of *Table Talk* (the Latin version; Mülhaupt 1964, 81-88), Luther justifies his suggestion to suffocate a twelve-year-old boy who did nothing other than eat and excrete: "I simply think he's a mass of flesh without a soul. Couldn't the devil have done this, inasmuch as he gives such shape to the body and mind even of those who

---

1. The *Weimarer Ausgabe* (abbreviated throughout this chapter as WA) is the most complete edition of Luther's works, and its numbering has become a standard reference system. The standard English translation of Luther's works excerpts the WA: Jaroslav Pelikan and Helmut Lehmann, general editors, *Luther's Works: American Edition,* 55 volumes (Philadelphia: Fortress Press, and Saint Louis: Concordia Publishing House, 1955-1986); this translation will hereafter be abbreviated LW. If the translation of Luther's original Latin and German texts that appear in this chapter are contained in LW, only that reference will be provided; if not, the WA reference will be used. The translation of some quotations from Luther in this introduction are the author's own renderings of WA, though LW references are supplied.

have reason that in their obsession they hear, see, and feel nothing? The devil is himself their soul" (**5.17**). Luther's position therefore rests on his assumption that the boy is not of human origin but a child of the devil, and that killing the child is a means of fighting the devil.

A comparison with Luther's frequent comments on the issue of changelings (**5.8-9, 14, 20**),[2] to whom he denied human status on the basis of their presumed descent from the devil, gives us little reason to downplay *Table Talk* 5207. However casual the suggestion to kill the changeling might have been in this instance (see Wolf 1964, 685-702), I will suggest that such a conclusion is paradigmatic of any discourse that rests on the separation of "the disabled" from "the normal."

However, it is important to note that Luther's comments on changelings operate within a discourse seeking to distinguish between human beings and devil's children, not between "normal" and "disabled" human beings, or between human beings and something human, as in the modern disability discourse. His judgment was not yet informed by the modern project of normalization and standardization. We may today regard Luther's premodern attempts to account for his experiences by means of a worked-out theory of the demonic to be aberrant, but it is certainly open to question whether our own ways of distinguishing between "the normal" and "the disabled" are any less so. Contemporary secular thought draws heavily on an Enlightenment anthropology that assumes a homogenous, tamed, and subjected body and a rational mind (see Foucault 1967), and attempts to label and place every individual in the order of "normalcy." When otherness is thus recognized, defined, and categorized, emancipation from it or even eradication of it becomes not only conceivable, but attractive.

In Luther's times, however, it was taken for granted that human physical existence was a burden: grotesque, painful, dirty, oozing, stinking, sick, formless, and, due to its manifold desires, knit up with an equally messy world (see Bakhtin 1984). Luther therefore saw disabling conditions as inseparable from human life. Anomalous cases, such as that of the boy at Dessau, he assumed were not human life at all. He thus had no category of human life as "disabled," in the sense of the contemporary use of that term, because disability was an ineradicable part of *all* human life.

Today's disability discourse generates a dialectic that confirms or even

---

2. In addition, see, WA 1, 410, 7-12; WA 40 I, 314, 6; WA TR 2, 504, 3-6 (2528b); WA TR 2, 505, 22-25 (2529b); WA TR 3, 516, 3-12f (3676); WA TR 4, 357, 38-358, 14 (4513); WA TR 6, 218, 16-18 (6831); and WA TR 516, 3-12 and 517, 30-44 (3676).

widens the rift between "the normal" and "the disabled." Judgments about difference inevitably raise questions about moral superiority, and any discourse of disability runs the danger of becoming another means of dominating the disabled and an exercise of the will to power. Paradoxically, the more the dignity of the disabled is confirmed, the more likely it is that a group called "the disabled" will be isolated and instrumentalized.

For Luther, however, the problem of humanity is not disability, sickness, or otherness — barriers that drive a rift between human beings or divide the internal life of the individual; his interest is in fallen humanity who cannot achieve their salvation, but must expect it from God (5.12). The lack of a concept of disability in no way blurred Luther's attentiveness to the variety of disabling conditions in which human beings find themselves. The importance of these conditions for Luther does not rest on disabilities as such, but arises from his expectation that they are one of many means by which God rules people. For Luther, human ailments cannot be chosen or interpreted in anthropocentric terms of their value for bringing people into contact with God. God leads people against their choice and interpretations by intervening in their lives, allowing humans to suffer his works as works of *grace.* For Luther, the world is God's workshop and is marked by the revivifying power of God as he rewrites human plans. It is for this reason that we find such a rich vocabulary of German and Latin terms for the disabling conditions humans suffer that God's interventions reveal in overcoming them: Luther does not hesitate to speak of the deaf, crooked, paralytic, lame, misshapen, impotent, monstrous, paralyzed, deformed, spastic, and epileptic, or even the stupid, moronic, foolish, mad, and possessed.

From today's point of view, Luther's belief in the role of the devil or of evil spirits in the genesis of diseases and disabilities may appear outlandish (5.7-8, 10, 14, 20), but Luther had no doubt that the devil would be powerless without God's permission for his deeds (see especially 5.7). Luther circumvented the implication that he was teaching a dualism of powers by insisting that the devil is God's medium to punish people with diseases and disabilities. Of course, the danger of this thought is that it can be used as a vindication of disrespect for disadvantaged people. But Luther holds that God's judgment on a human being cannot be transformed into one human's judgment on another. Any thought that the sick or those suffering disability had fallen out of the hands of God is not to be countenanced. Disability, like other experiences not freely chosen but endured (cf. LW 14:152), is a means by which God leads people on the way of the cross, drawing them to himself. In Luther's view, it is consoling to believe that one's ailments ultimately come from God's hand. A world in which "disabilities" become free-standing, self-subsistent realities would no longer be God's world. Disabilities as punishment cannot, therefore, be God's final word. In downplaying the stand-alone category of disability by refusing to allow it to appear as a reality that determines the lives of people, Luther does not thereby render them theologically invisible, but instead places individual incapacities in the story of salvation.

In addition to his experience of a world full of diseases and disabilities (Midelfort 1999, Metzler 2005; see, however, Luther's comment in **5.15**), Luther could also draw on a rich experience of his own illnesses, such as constipation, hemorrhoids, and liver stones (**5.4, 16**), and he is believed to have suffered in his later years from Morbus Meniere, a disease of the inner ear causing dizziness, hearing loss, and ear pain (see Feldmann 1989, 26-44). Luther also had in his own household several people with disabling conditions, including Wolfgang Sieberger, Luther's personal assistant, who seemed to have been of low intelligence and weak-armed. Nevertheless, he was treated like a family member and was to be given a house of his own after Luther's death (**5.11**).

Although Luther often commented on the ailments caused by impairments, disabilities, and handicaps, these comments did not coalesce into a developed emphasis in his ethical thought. His central ethical focus on divine consolation meant that he spoke on disability only when it arose as an issue for those with whom he corresponded. Indeed, his comments on ethical issues are remarkable in that they were always directed to specific audiences and in the mode of pastoral care (Bayer 2004, 281-82).

C. Luther's Critique of the Rendering of Disability as Discourse: The Other as Medium of God's Word

Why read Luther on disability? First, because Luther provides a theological semantics which stands against the turning of disability into a discourse in which a group called "the disabled" is constituted, classified, and separated from "the normal." Luther's theology is suggestive precisely because it takes for granted that disability is entrusted to humankind just as much as ability.

Contemporary disability discourses, which frequently theorize polarizations of alienness and similarity, distance and proximity, and inclusion and discrimination, tend to render people with disabilities as objects of recognition. Thus, while recognition discourses deploy the distinction between "normal" and "different" in order to insure that the specific needs and conditions of the disabled are not neglected, they must keep this judgment in check by means of some concept of the universal kinship of all human beings. The disability discourse therefore faces the inevitable dialectic of either identifying disabled people by particular attributes that constitute the criterion for inclusion or exclusion, or operating with a reciprocal, universal recognition that evades the question of what becomes articulate through them in their particularity. The recognition discourse is liable to become a means to discriminate against and objectivize the disabled, unless "recognition" assumes a different semantics. This is where young Luther's theology of the cross becomes helpful for a critique of disability discourses.

According to Luther, human beings have a blurred perception of God's reality, and a spoiled ability to make value judgments when it comes to evaluating the reality of other humans. They adjudge suffering, disgrace, and disability as things that are intrinsically bad. As Luther put it in his famous Heidelberg Disputation, every human being is a born theologian of glory (using theology to aggrandize one's self) who "calls evil good and good evil," while the theologian of the cross (who learns in the cross that one's own reason and desire are corrupt) "calls the thing what it actually is" (LW 31:53, thesis 21). Luther says, "That person does not deserve to be called a theologian who looks upon the invisible things of God as though they were clearly perceptible in those things which have actually happened [Rom. 1:20]. He deserves to be called a theologian, however, who comprehends the visible and manifest things of God seen through suffering and the cross" (LW 31:52, theses 19 and 20). In opposition to scholasticism, Luther contends that there is no route from the perception of the visible creation to comprehension of the invisible world that does not involve a misinterpretation of God's works (LW 31:52-53, conclusion of thesis 20). For this reason God chose to make himself and man visible in the Incarnation, and at the cross (**5.1**). Human reason cannot understand this on its own. It will always search for the truth about God and man in the invisible world. But the Incarnation, Christ's suffering, and the cross call for understanding that God is hidden in his visible appearance.

This is not to suggest that Luther looks for God's manifestations in the noumenal, spiritual world. God's appearance is in the real, phenomenal world. God turns toward humans, makes himself known through humans, and promises to restore humans to the image of God: "Therefore man in this life is God's pure material for the future form of his life. Just as the whole creature, which is now subjected to nothingness [Rom. 8:20], is God's material for its future glorious form," Luther writes in *The Disputation Concerning Man*. "And as earth and heaven related to the form that was completed after six days, that is as their material, so man relates in this life to his future form, when the image of God will be restored and perfected" (LW 34:139-40, theses 35-38). While "man is God's creature . . . made from the beginning in the image of God" (LW 34:138, thesis 21), he cannot himself work toward his own renewal, because "after the fall of Adam he is subjected to the power of the Devil, sin and death, which are both evils that cannot be overcome by his own power, and that are eternal" (LW 34:138, thesis 22). Humans cannot construct their own ethics, but can only receive an ethical orientation from God. The human creature "can be freed and given eternal life only through the Son of God, Jesus Christ (if he believes in him)" (LW 34:138, thesis 23). Luther's definition of man is "man to be justified by faith" (LW 34:139, thesis 32). What human beings are is hence not defined by their attributes, their disposition, or their capabilities, but by the image that God has promised to bestow on them in Christ. Mankind is unified neither by constructing a morality nor by fleeing from differences into universalism, nor by expelling those who do not seem to fit in the image of man, but by the visitation of the One True Man on the cross to restore those whose image is lost.

From this vantage point we can see that Luther would adjudge it a perverted perception to place people with disabilities on a scale of normality because such a scale does not exist. Also, as with any phenomenon of human life, disability too may become an instrument of God to disrupt, turn around, and transform human beings. Luther asks us to take for granted that disability belongs to each of us, and to ask what of human beings appears in those lives we encounter that are likewise marked by disability. In doing so, he provokes a shift of attention from the question of whether "the disabled" belong to "us" to the question of the extent to which diseases and disability belong to humankind, and are entrusted to humans just as much as health and abilities (see Bach 2006). As he does this, Luther does not allegorize disability and never lets it disappear into the alleged equality of human beings. He holds that God makes the real human being in his or her physical particularity an instrument with which he addresses other human beings. Lutherans have tended to spiritualize Luther, while Luther himself holds that bodily appearance really matters to the extent that it becomes the material for God's addressing and claiming humanity for his way of being.

In a remarkable passage in his sermon on the man born blind (5.1), Luther argues that human beings, when left on their own, simply cannot find the right judgment of the other, because after the Fall, their eyes were *opened*. They were no longer blind. For Luther, ability (seeing), not disability (blindness), is the problem of the human condition. On these grounds Luther supported the admission of the deaf and dumb to the Lord's Supper and their full political recognition (**5.2, 3**; see also Gewalt 1970, 93-100). Adamic humanity cannot see the hidden dignity of the human being as an instrument of God's grace because they have lost the blindness of innocence and the grace to see with the eyes of God. According to Luther, human beings are not defined by their abilities or disabilities since, in the light of God's work in Christ, everyone falls short of what he or she should be:

> For we are all blind and our light and our illumination come solely from Christ, our good and faithful God. . . . For God has established a fixed rule: everything that is high and praised of men is disregarded and abominable in the sight of God. . . . If [one] hears something amusing, sweet, lovely, that's what he calls it. But God turns all this upside down. Everything we call beautiful, jolly, rich, etc., he calls poor, sick, weak, impotent. . . . That's what happened also in this Gospel. The blind man was a sign of the blindness that lay hidden in our hearts. . . . So our eyes have been opened, which really means that we have become totally blind, so that, as was said a moment ago, we consider the sham to be good and what is poor and misshapen to be evil. . . . But Christ came to teach these eyes to see and to take away the blindness, in order that we should not make this distinction between young and old, beautiful and ugly, and so on. Rather, all are equal, wise man or simpleton, sage or fool, man or woman; it is enough that he is a man with our flesh and blood, a body common to all (**5.1**; LW 51:36, 37, 39).

This could be read as a proto-Nietzschean "transvaluation of values," but what Luther is in fact pointing toward is not a new table of *values,* but the transformation of the *human being* who makes blurred value judgments.

Of course, the danger will remain that we will transform this divine work into a morality: a "morality of slaves" (Nietzsche 2009, First Essay, section 7). However, the weak and poor are the chosen ones not because weakness and poverty are good in themselves, but because God chose them. Hence, disability cannot be claimed as something generally valuable. The salient question is what message is heard from a disabled person. This cannot be the message of his or her disability, but a message through which he or she in his or her condition becomes a medium. Attending to a disabled person entails the expectation that this person makes something known that cannot be assigned to him or her in advance without stigmatizing that person.

According to Luther, human beings naturally see the good as evil and the evil as good. They misunderstand what they perceive. While anyone can become an instrument of God's message, Luther points out that there are theological reasons why people will expect this least of all from those with disabilities: they presume to hear the message from the strong, or from those they take to be strong. The theology of the cross entails a new attentiveness to the human being in his or her reality. What is at stake, for Luther, is not the identification and recognition of "the disabled," but the perception of how God works on human beings through the various gifts and burdens he has bestowed upon them. What is central is the question of how human beings are liberated from their natural perceptions about disability to discern the message that is conveyed to them *through* people with disabilities, and to become in turn the medium of God's works and word for persons with disabilities.

Luther sees two opposing states of consciousness that are in constant conflict with each other: the mediated perceptions of God's appearance and what Nietzsche would later call the "will to power" — the attempt to permanently enhance power by instrumentalizing other people. "The disabled" serve as the background against which people can assure themselves of their "normalcy," while simultaneously being blind to their own errors. Luther's hope is that people's perverted perception of reality and will to power will be overwhelmed by God's Word reaching through one human toward another. This hope calls all humans to attend to the other in the expectancy that he or she may become the medium of a message that frees, consoles, and reveals the proximity of God's rule.

Luther sees it as characteristic of the "old Adam" that when confronted with claims that contradict his own, he will express his unwillingness openly, or hide it, even in activity and care. It is impossible for the old Adam to *want* the other in his or her actual, given reality. For Luther, unless God's grace overwhelms them, humans do not want to live with the poor, the suffering, and the disabled, and least of all with God, and they will do so only if they believe they can garner some kind of benefit (cf. LW 31:9-17). Luther shows that service to those who are disadvantaged and a life shared with others depend not on the *will* but on *grace*, on the overcoming of man's will to power by the child in the cradle.

What Luther calls true recognition means not judging the other in the light of her differences or adequacies, but living with her in attentiveness to her becoming the medium of what God says about human beings and to human beings (**5.1**). To recognize the other is not to judge her, but to attend to her in the expectation of what will become articulate through her from God. Human beings need to be freed to become attentive to the way God makes himself and humankind known through the other, and for the other. Luther defines this freedom as a state of consciousness in which the works of Christ for us, not our works, determine who we are. "This Christian or evangelical freedom is a freedom of conscience, through which conscience is liberated from works not so that none are performed, but that one relies on none. Because conscience is not a power of acting, but a power to judge, which judges the works. . . . It grasps the works of Christ and repeatedly says as such: Through them I will be justified and saved and liberated of all sins and evil" (LW 44:298-99).

D. Luther's Critique of Self-Chosen Works: Becoming the Medium of God's Works for Others

For Luther, the specific problem of ethics is that the "old Adam" wants to live on his own works instead of Christ's work, the cross: ". . . for through the cross works are destroyed and the old Adam, who is especially edified by works, is crucified" (LW 31:53). Adam's consciousness is always directed toward his works, making them the criterion by which his own worth and that of others is judged (LW 44:297-316). In this attempt to understand themselves and others on the basis of their works, "human beings abuse the cognition of God through works" (LW 31:52). Man chooses only those works that he deems valuable for himself and for the sake of his own moral perfection (LW 31:363). Hence, without grasping and receiving Christ and his works, human beings perform works that are inevitably done not for others but for themselves (WA 10/1/2, 431, 1ff. [Sommerpostille 1526. Evangelium am 24. Sonntag nach Trinitatis Mt 9:18-20]). One's own righteousness thus becomes the paradigmatic good work, not Christ and what he has done "for me" (see Iwand 1954, 120-25). In distinguishing the works that human beings choose from the works to which they are called (by the abundance from which they live and by the need that they encounter in the other), Luther's ethics provides a fundamental critique of contemporary ways of describing the good life as one founded on the possibility of choice.

Writing within the contemporary disability debate, Hans Reinders has argued that a preoccupation with "choice" renders human beings unable to simply accept disability as being part of human life. Over against the capitalist culture as a "context of choice" (Reinders 2000, 198ff.), Reinders directs attention to the question of "what it means to say that life is good as it is, not because we chose it, or would have chosen it had there been a choice, but simply because it is what it is" (Reinders 2007, 164). Reinders develops this thought with reference to the doctrine of divine providence: life is good because God has chosen it. In Luther's line of thought, this would mean that human life is good insofar as it becomes the medium through which God's goodness reaches into the world.

Reinders refers to a passage in Christopher De Vinck's book *The Power of the Powerless* that tells the story of the author's severely disabled brother, Oliver, who was tied to bed all his life without any ability to talk or move. Oliver's mother comments:

> For many, many years, I was confined to the house, alone and without the support of relatives or friends. José [her husband] was at work all day and I was with Oliver and the other five children. This enforced seclusion was difficult for me; I had a restless, seeking spirit. Through Oliver, I was held still. I was forced to embrace a silence and a solitude where I could "prepare the way of the Lord." Sorrow opened my heart, and I "died." I underwent this "death" unaware that it was a trial by fire from which I would rise renewed — more powerfully, more consciously alive. (De Vinck 1990, 94)

This is what Luther calls "theologia crucis." In a passage that describes how a human being is led by the Word, Luther seems to quote Oliver's mother: "I am led back into the void and I know nothing. I wander in obscurity and darkness and I see nothing. In faith, hope, and love I only live and I fade away in weakness [that means I suffer] because when I am weak, then I am strong" (WA 5, 176, 26 [Operationes in Psalmos]). For Luther, the human being who lives on his or her works needs to be crucified and bereft of the works in order to be prepared to grasp the works of Christ and enter into the passive life of faith: "The passive life has to be added that kills and dismantles the whole active life, so that no merit remains, in which the arrogant could extol himself" (WA 5, 165, 35 [Operationes in Psalmos]). God frees people by overwhelming their values, works, and will to power, thereby giving way to his guidance.

In his exegesis of the seven penitential psalms, Luther depicts God addressing humans as follows:

> Behold, that is the way of the cross. You cannot find it, but I must lead you like a blind man. Therefore not you, not a man, not a creature, but I, through My Spirit and the Word, will teach you the way you must go. You must not follow the work which you choose, not the suffering which you

devise, but that which comes to you against your choice, thoughts, and desires. There I call; there you must be a pupil; there it is the time; there your Master has come. . . . (LW 14:152)

The direction of the will to God — believing, hoping, and loving — "is a way of being moved, being abducted, being led by the word of God and in a certain way a continuous purgation and renewal of the mind and of the senses from day to day to the cognition of God" (WA 5, 177, 12 [Operationes in Psalmos]).

This Word of God leads humans to do good works for their neighbors. For Luther, this is the origin of ethics. God's Word frees human beings from their moralistic, self-righteous, and self-centered selves. It is not the poor and disadvantaged themselves who initiate the works of charity, a trigger condition for the moral improvement of the rich, as in medieval ethics (Priddat 2002, 20ff.). Neither need nor disability have any intrinsic power in themselves to evoke charity, nor does human attentiveness to mere physical states of affairs; but God's calling to people through them and through everything good that he does for human beings does have this power. Christ's work is thus to free the soul to serve the neighbor: "Then the soul no longer tries to be justified before itself, but has Christ as its justice. Therefore it searches only the happiness of the others" (WA 2, 147, 30-32 [Sermo de duplici iustitia]). God's judgment of humans overwhelms their judgments of others, creating a new life in neighborly love (LW 31:364-65). Hence ethics does not originate in the human subject. Good works live from faith, while faith lives from God's promise to be with those who listen to his commandments: "God's Word is the first of all; faith follows it, and love follows faith. Love finally does every good work, for it does not cause harm, it is the fulfilling of the law. But the person can in no other way accord to or act with God than through faith" (LW 36:39). Only those works may be called "good" in which the human actor becomes the instrument of God's works.

Ulrich Bach, a German pastor with poliomyelitis who spent most of his life in a wheelchair, tells the story of a holiday with a friend who helped him by carrying him up and down stairs, putting him in a boat, and so on. When Bach attempted to thank him for this help, the friend replied that Bach should not thank him: "During these weeks let my legs be your legs — two legs are enough for us" (Bach 2006, 16). Good works do not aim to "fix" the world, but are expressions of service to each other. Their purpose is to uphold life that can be borne: a life open to experiencing, expecting, and articulating God's works, and to praising God for what he does for his creatures.

E. Summary

Luther's theology of the cross offers a potent criticism of discourses that label some as "disabled" and others as "normal," and of the ethics of choice. His theology paves the way for a new form of expectation about what becomes articulate through the other and what this calls us to do for others. For Luther, human beings enter into the exploration of a life that can be borne whenever they are freed to live with the other, a life in which they become attentive to the good works that they receive and hand on to the other. In the common life of all who are made equal by God's judgment, human beings are not judged on the basis of their abilities or disabilities. They are properly encountered in attentiveness to the message they might bring from God, and with the message from God that may become articulate for them. Over against a moralizing perception of the other, who is either judged by the value of his or her attributes or by the absolute value of his or her origin, Luther shifts the focus of the debate from the metaphysical or physical qualities of people to their permeability to God's working. The true human being is not to be found where human beings search for it, but where God searches it out: not with the saints, but with the sinners; not with the dignified, but with the humiliated. Human beings are clothed with dignity whenever they let go of their assumed divine shape and take up the shape of servants.

For a theology of the disabled, it may be sufficient to work with a "weak" anthropology that sharpens attentiveness to the phenomena of human becoming. The "human condition" cannot be the foundation for the recognition of the other, but is God's material to be transformed into his original image. It is thus a means through which humanity is dignified by God. This entails the contradiction of those powers that operate within the distinction between normal and disabled human beings. For Luther, because Christians see the true human being in the cradle and on the cross, it is their calling to become the medium of this contradiction, and of the necessary good works that favor all who are disadvantaged.

F. Luther Readings

To give the reader an impression of Luther's preaching on disability, the first reading is a complete Lenten sermon that Luther preached at Wittenberg in March 1518. This sermon is a genuine expression of his early theology and ethics of the cross. The other readings are taken from various texts and genres, and give an impression of some of the ambiguities of Luther's thought on disability issues.

References

Primary Sources

Luther, Martin. 1883-2009. *D. Martin Luthers Werke: kritische Gesamtausgabe*. 120 volumes. Weimar (though imprints vary; later volumes were published by H. Böhlaus Nachfolger).

Luther, Martin. 1955-1986. *Luther's Works: American Edition*. 55 volumes. Jaroslav Pelikan and Helmut Lehmann, general editors. Philadelphia: Fortress Press, and Saint Louis: Concordia Publishing House.

Works Cited

Bach, Ulrich. 2006. *Ohne die Schwächsten ist die Kirche nicht ganz. Bausteine einer Theologie nach Hadamar*. Neukirchen-Vluyn: Neukirchener Verlag.

Bakhtin, Mikhail M. 1984. *Rabelais and His World*. Bloomington: Indiana University Press.

Bayer, Oswald. 1969. "Die reformatorische Wende in Luthers Theologie." *Zeitschrift für Theologie und Kirche* 66: 115-50.

———. 2004. *Martin Luthers Theologie: Eine Vergegenwärtigung*. Tübingen: Mohr Siebeck.

De Vinck, Christopher. 1990. *The Power of the Powerless*. New York: Doubleday.

Feldmann, Harald. 1989. "Martin Luthers Anfallsleiden." *Sudhoffs Archiv. Zeitschrift für Wissenschaftsgeschichte* 73: 26-44.

Foucault, Michel. 1967. *Madness and Civilization: A History of Insanity in the Age of Reason*. London: Tavistock.

Gewalt, Dietfried. 1974. "Sonderpädagogische Anthropologie und Luther." In *Lutherjahrbuch* 41. Göttingen: Vandenhoeck & Ruprecht, 103-13.

———. 1970. "Taube und Stumme in der Sicht Martin Luthers." *Luther: Zeitschrift der Luthergesellschaft* 2: 93-100.

Hall, Amy Laura. 2007. *Conceiving Parenthood: The Protestant Spirit of Biotechnological Reproduction*. Grand Rapids: Wm. B. Eerdmans.

Iwand, Hans Joachim. 1954. "Wider den Mißbrauch des 'pro me' als methodisches Prinzip in der Theologie." *Evangelische Theologie* 14: 120-25.

Lohse, Bernhard, editor. 1968. *Der Durchbruch der reformatorischen Erkenntnis bei Luther*. Darmstadt: Wissenschaftliche Buchgesellschaft.

———, editor. 1988. *Der Durchbruch der reformatorischen Erkenntnis bei Luther — Neuere Untersuchungen*. Stuttgart: Steiner-Verlag.

Metzler, Irina. 2005. *Disability in Medieval Europe: Thinking about Physical Impairment in the High Middle Ages, c. 1100–c. 1400.* London: Routledge.

Midelfort, Erik H. C. 1999. *A History of Madness in Sixteenth-Century Germany.* Stanford: Stanford University Press.

Miles, M. 2001. "Martin Luther and Childhood Disability in 16th-Century Germany: What did he write? What did he say?" *Journal of Religion, Disability, and Health* 5, no. 4: 5-36. (A revised version of this paper can be found at http://www.independentliving.org/docs7/miles2005b.html.)

Mülhaupt, Erwin. 1964. "Spiegel, Stern, und Luther." *Luther: Zeitschrift der Luther-Gesellschaft* 35, no. 2: 81-88.

Nietzsche, Friedrich. 2009. *On the Genealogy of Morals.* New York: Oxford University Press.

Priddat, Birger P. 2002. *Theoriegeschichte der Wirtschaft.* Munich: Wilhelm Fink Verlag.

Reinders, Hans S. 2000. *The Future of the Disabled in Liberal Society: An Ethical Analysis.* Notre Dame: University of Notre Dame Press.

———. 2007. "Life's Goodness: On Disability, Genetics, and 'Choice.'" In John Swinton and Brian Brock, editors. *Theology, Disability, and the New Genetics: Why Science Needs the Church.* London and New York: T&T Clark, 163-81.

Wolf, Ernst. 1964. "Das Problem der Euthanasie im Spiegel evangelischer Ethik." In Erich Dinkler, editor. *Zeit und Geschichte, Dankesgabe an Rudolf Bultmann.* Tübingen: Mohr, 685-702. (This essay can also be found in *ZEE* 10 [1966]: 345-61.)

Excerpts

5.1

LW 51:35-43. "Sermon on the Man Born Blind, John 9:1-38." 17 March 1518. Translated by J. W. Doberstein. (WA 1:267-73)

You well know, dear friends of Christ, that I do not understand much about preaching and therefore I shall preach a foolish sermon; for I am a fool and I thank God for it. Therefore I must also have foolish pupils; anybody who doesn't want to be a fool can close his ears. This Gospel compels me to take this attitude; for you have heard in this Gospel that Christ is dealing only with the blind. And Christ also concludes that all who see are blind and all the wise and prudent are fools. These are his words. If I were to say it, I would be reviled as a new prophet. But Christ will not lie. Now listen to what St. Augustine says in his exposition of this Gospel: All that Christ did is both works and words; works, because they happened and were done by him; words, because they signify and teach something. Now this is an event, because the blind man received his sight. But it is also a word, for it signifies every man born of Adam. For we are all blind and our light and our illumination comes solely from Christ, our good and faithful God.

To distinguish these from one another, works and words, requires an enlightened mind; for how many there were who saw this work and yet did not see its significance. They looked upon it as a work, but the word, the significance, remained hidden from them. But if they had recognized it, they undoubtedly would have said, "Oh, I am far more blind than he is." And that's the right understanding of it; and so it is to this day, that the number of them is great even among those who shine before the world in their great power, culture, wisdom, piety, holiness, chastity, purity, and so on. But it is certain that always it has been so ordained that with a powerful man there is found an outcast, with the wise a fool, with the pious an impious, with the holy an unholy, with the healthy a sick man, with the handsome an ugly man, and so on. Just look at the human race and you will find rich and poor, beauty and ugliness, gaiety and dreariness, joy and sorrow, culture and stupidity, wisdom and foolishness, piety and wickedness, and whatever else you may name, crooked and straight, high and low, and so on.

And it is not without cause that God in his unspeakable wisdom should so desire to cast down the rule of the proud and the wise. Therefore let each one take heed, whether he be blessed with many or few of these gifts, that he by no means regard himself, but rather his neighbor, who does not possess the gift. Then he will say, "Ah, dear God, I am learned, or devout, and so on; but in the sight of God I am ignorant and full of sin, like this my brother"; then that person will find out what is his real condition. For God has established a fixed rule: everything that is high and praised of men is disregarded and abominable in the sight of God. Isaiah writes: God does not judge by the sight of his eyes or the hearing of his ears, but rather he will judge righteously [cf. Isa. 11:3-4]. It is as if he wanted to say: A man, because he is a man, judges no further than he sees or hears. So if he sees a rich man, a powerful man, a handsome man, a devout man, etc., that's what he calls him, just as he sees him. If he hears something amusing, sweet, lovely, that's what he calls it. But God turns all this upside down. Everything we call beautiful, jolly, rich, etc., he calls poor, sick, weak, impotent.

So let every man, if he has received a blessing or gift from God, learn to divest himself of it, shun it, give it up, in order that he may not look to himself, but rather note how his neighbor looks and how his neighbor is reflected in himself. Then he will surely say, "Ah, there God has hung a mirror before my eyes, and a book in which I am to learn to know myself. Ah, God, now I see clearly that what my brother is outwardly, I am inwardly." Thus he learns to know himself and not to exalt himself. So it is ordained, and nobody can evade it. For we see in all the words and works of Christ nothing but pure humility.

That's what happened also in this Gospel. The blind man was a sign of the blindness that lay hidden in our hearts. And it follows from this that what Augustine said is true, that the works of Christ are words and the words are works. Therefore at the end of this Gospel, when the aloof and spiritual Jews said, "Are we also blind?" our Lord concludes, "If you were blind, you would have no guilt; but now that you say, 'We see,' your guilt remains" [John 9:40-41]. Look, what an upside-down judgment that is for Christ to make! Therefore one must try to understand all the gifts that a man can have. Those whom we think are learned are ignorant in the sight of God. And anybody who does not know this will have a bad time of it in the judgment of God.

This is what Paul says to the Ephesians [Phil. 2:5-8]: Oh, dear brethren, your attitude should be like that of Christ, who did not exalt himself in the form of God, even though he could be equal with the Father, but emptied himself and utterly lowered himself, and took on the form of a servant, and was found in every degree and way a man and like a man, like him even in that he died for the sake of obedience to his Father. Note, dear friends of Christ, what a choice, profound saying that is. We should all be equal. For he speaks, not as a mere man, but as one in whom is the form of God, the very presence of power, honor, righteousness, wisdom, piety, and purity, who never did evil, who is full of every virtue even in his humanity, who desired to be equal with us, not with God, not like Lucifer, who desired to snatch the image of God, nor like the proud, who so look down on their neighbors that they can scarcely recognize them as grasshoppers. This Christ did not do: he put off the form of God and was found in the form of man, in sinful flesh, though he never sinned; nor could he ever sin. So he became a fool, the object of mockery, reproach, and derision by all the people; he bore our misfortune, and in him were found all the titles of our poverty. And this he did in order that we might freely follow him.

This, then, is the meaning: He who finds in himself the form of God, that is, has title to the gifts we spoke of above, let him not exalt himself but rather abase himself and sincerely believe that he is the lowest in all the world. And this must happen, if he is ever to get to heaven, whether it happens voluntarily or against his will. Thus his works are words. And therefore he [i.e., Augustine] is right when he says, "He who does not see the mystery of God is blind. Therefore this man is not merely blind, but is rather a figure of the blindness which is within the soul." This means that he who does not see and know God's hidden holiness is blind. And therefore this man in the Gospel is only a figure of that other blindness which is in the soul.

But then, the reason why all this is said and what causes it, says Augustine, is the transgression of Adam, to whom the devil said, "Your eyes will be opened, and you will be like God, knowing good and evil" [Gen. 3:5]. Oh, you villain, scoundrel, and betrayer! You see what he is doing; he is trying to lead them to the form of God, so he says, "Your eyes will be opened," that is, they will become blind. Before their eyes were closed, but after the Fall they were opened.

The consequence of this, as Origen, the wise and acute schoolmaster, teaches, is that man has two kinds of eyes, his own eyes and God's eyes. But the fact is that both kinds of eyes, our inward eyes and our outward eyes, are God's. Indeed, all our members and everything that is in us are instruments of God, and nothing is ours if they are ruled by God. But they are ours when God forsakes us. This means that, as Christ says, we must pluck out the eye that scandalizes and offends us and throw it away [Matt. 5:29]. That's why it is that we would rather see what is fine and pretty and well-formed rather than what is gold or silver, rather a young Jill or a young Jack than an old woman or an old Jack. And this is the mousetrap that dupes our minds, as is written of Adam in the book of Genesis. So our eyes have been opened, which really means that we have become totally blind, so that, as was said a moment ago, we consider the sham to be good and what is poor and misshapen to be evil. This the devil taught us, and it is his eyes that do it. But Christ came to teach these eyes to see and to take away the blindness, in order that we should not make this distinction between young and old, beautiful and ugly, and so on. Rather all are equal, wise man or simpleton, sage or fool, man or woman; it is enough that he is a man with our flesh and blood, a body common to all. For such perception one must have a fine, acute, and well-trained mind.

Christ pays no attention to distinctions we make, for he bestows children and honor upon an old, unattractive woman just as readily as upon a beautiful woman, which is clearly illustrated in Rachel and Leah [Gen.

29:21–30:24]. It makes no difference to him wherein he allows his work to appear. Therefore God says, "I will destroy the wisdom of the wise, and the cleverness of the clever I will thwart" [1 Cor. 1:19; Isa. 29:14]. Isaiah says, "I will choose what they mock at and despise." Also Paul says, "Thus is the call of God, that it receives the sick and the fools, in order that he may confound and shame the wise" [1 Cor. 1:27].

So because Christ does this and considers that evil which we consider good and vice versa, he takes away that which we delight in and gives everything that vexes us. This Christ practiced and proved; for God became man, as was said above. And in his last days we find what we consider the worst of all evils: we find him dying a shameful death. And when we view his whole life, we do not find that he undertook anything that the world considered good. Once he rode into Jerusalem with great honor, but his joy was embittered with sorrow. Now the most precious thing God has is death and dying; and Christ accepted it in love, joyfully and voluntarily, out of obedience to his Father. We flee it and consider life more precious than death. He embraced it as a thing of sweetness and gave his life unto death, and just because he is to ascend to the throne of glory and reign eternally with the Father, he must (and he does it willingly) die on the cross; he lets go of life and accepts death.

Now, if Christ did this, then fie on everyone who would try to get to heaven without following his example. And this is the true holy relic, of which the prophet says, *"In reliquiis tuis praeparabis vultum eorum."* "In thy relic," or in thy testament, which consists in cross and suffering, "wilt thou prepare their face." This is so holy and so sublime that it cannot be put into any monstrance, in any silver or gold. It is not the wood, stone, or vesture which he touched, but rather the suffering, the cross, which he sends to his devout children. All the goldsmiths together cannot make a vessel to enclose this relic. It requires a spiritual, living, eternal monstrance. For this sacred relic is a living thing like the soul of man. Therefore, it is the inward relic we must seek, not the outward. Nevertheless, we ought to encase the bones of saints in silver; this is good and proper. Many things, like images and the like, may be permitted for the sake of the sucklings which must be forbidden to others. Therefore those who are farther along should pay little regard to these things and lift their eyes higher; for Christ will bring to their very door something better than they can find anywhere in the world. For he will send them reverses, tribulation, anxiety, care, grief, poverty, ill will, and so on. He will send you sickness, and at the end of your life, in the throes of death, the devil will assault you unceasingly and terrify you so cruelly that you will well nigh despair. Indeed, he will press you to the point where he will snap his fingers at you and jeer: Yes, good pal, do what you will, you are mine any-how. You have to listen with Christ to this mockery: "If he is the son of God, let him come down from the cross" [Matt. 27:40]. He will read you a lecture all right, and with spite too. Then let each one of us pay heed to what is pleasing to God in order that we may joyfully say: Oh, my dear God, I firmly believe that thou art sending this to me. Welcome, beloved relic. I give thanks to thee, my faithful God, that thou dost consider me worthy of what was most precious in thy life. Ah, my beloved, faithful Christ, help me and I bravely accept it, and freely imitate thee in the surrender of my will. Then all the power of the devil will forthwith fall to the ground.

This is the most precious relic of all, *quod obviis ulnis et osculis debemus accipere,* which we ought to accept lovingly and gratefully. For this relic God himself hallowed and blessed with his most precious will, and with the approval of his Father. But now — God save the mark! — we see our bishops and leaders fleeing from this relic. If you take something away from them or speak too plainly to them, they would rather tear the whole place down than give in. So far has this childish veneration and holiness gone that they have started this game of excommunication, and the letters are flying about like bats, all because of a trifling thing. Their defense of this is: It is proper that we should guard and preserve the patrimony and legacy of Christ and St. Peter; we are doing it because it is right. O you poor Christ, O you wretched Peter! If you have no inheritance but wood and stone and silver and gold, you are of all the most needy.

Ah, but the good God wants what Isaiah speaks of in the last and also the first chapter [Isa. 66:1-2 and 1:10-17]. These things are all the works of his hands, which he has made. Therefore he does not need our goods, say David and Job [Ps. 34:16-21; 40:8-11; 50:8-15; 51:18-19; Job 22:23-27; 5:17-19; 2 Sam. 7:6-11, 18-29]. But when God sends it to us, we run away and flee from it. He wants to give it to us, but we don't want it. Nor are all of us worthy of it. In fact, it is the peculiar mark of faithful children of God. He bestows it often, but we do not know what to do with it. And so it comes about that we think we see clearly and yet are totally blind, so that we call evil what Christ calls good.

Therefore God the Father adorned his Son, as the bride in the Song of Solomon says, "Go forth, O daughters of Zion, and behold your King, Christ, with the crown and the ornament with which his mother adorned and crowned him on the day of his espousal and wedding and on the day of the gladness of his heart" [cf. Song of Sol. 3:11]. That is, because Christ was about to receive the kingdom and the power to reign, and be a king above all kings, he had the greatest honor and glory and joy in his heart when he died on the cross. This we do not see, and therefore we are rightly called blind and foolish by Christ.

But we persist in our evil way of seeing things and see no difference whatsoever. Augustine says, "Christ speaks of the blind man and of birth, whereby he clearly indicates that this is what we are from Adam's birth and that blindness adheres to us by nature," and this blindness can be taken away by none but Christ. Here is where all who undertake to do something of themselves are compelled to submit and be conquered. For the blind man did not imagine that he would be made whole; as the text says, "Never has it been heard that a blind man should receive his sight" [John 9:32]. We must despair of everything that we can do. But those who say, Ah, but I have done as much as I possibly can; I have done enough, and I hope that God will give me grace — they set up an iron wall between themselves and the grace of God. But if you feel within yourself the urge to call upon God and pray and plead and knock, then grace is already there; then call upon it and thank God. Grace can never forsake him who despairs of himself. For many passages declare: To the humble He gives grace, but He denies it to the proud [Prov. 3:34; James 4:6; 1 Pet. 5:5]. The fact is that nobody can do anything except freely surrender himself to God no matter what happens, and despair of himself. But those who say: All right then, I'll wait until grace comes, are turning it around. Ah, you fool, when you feel what has been effected within you, then grace is already there; just go on and follow. Thus you retire and you no longer stand and walk by yourself. God cannot endure our wanting to see; we needs must be blind. For God is wholly present in all creation, in every corner; he is behind you and before you. Do you think he is sleeping on a pillow in heaven? He is watching over you and protecting you. But as soon as Christ anointed the eyes of the blind man with spittle, his will concurred and desired what he had never dreamed of before, as the Evangelist shows. What the spittle is and the meaning of the washing in the pool of Siloam we shall save for another time.

5.2

LW 27:248-49. "Lectures on Galatians." 1519. Translated by R. Jungkuntz. (WA 2:508)

Here, however, St. Jerome is again concerned with the question how the deaf become Christians [*Ftn.* 15: Jerome, *Commentarius*, 374-75], especially since

Romans 10:14 says: "How are they to hear without a preacher? How are they to believe in Him of whom they have never heard?" And, as the apostle's step-by-step sequence puts it in that passage, first there is a sending, then preaching, then hearing, then believing, then an invoking, and thus the attaining of salvation. I shall add: How are infants saved, and how are they baptized, when they themselves do not hear? Jerome answers first that faith's coming from hearing can be taken as being partial or entire. But Paul overcomes this argument. "How," he says, "are they to believe in Him of whom they have never heard?" (Rom. 10:14). Secondly, Jerome says that the deaf can learn the Gospel from the attitude and the behavior of others. But where does this leave the infants? Therefore I follow the opinion he mentions last, namely, that to the Word of God nothing is deaf [*quod verbo dei nihil surdum*] and that it speaks to those ears of which it is said, "He who has ears to hear, let him hear" (Matt. 11:15). I like this argument very much, because the Word of God is not heard even among adults and those who hear unless the Spirit promotes growth inwardly. Accordingly, it is a Word of power and grace when it infuses the Spirit at the same time that it strikes the ears. But if it does not infuse the Spirit, then he who hears does not differ at all from one who is deaf.

5.3

LW 35:110-11. "A Treatise on the New Testament, that is, the Holy Mass." 1520. Translated by J. J. Schindel. Revised by E. T. Bachman. (WA 6:377-78)

Some have asked whether the sacrament is to be offered also to the deaf and dumb. Some think it a kindness to practice a pious fraud on them and think they should be given unblessed wafers. This mockery is not good; it will not please God, who has made them Christians as well as us. They deserve the same things that we do. Therefore if they are rational [*vornunfftig* = modern *vernünftig*] and can show by indubitable signs [*ausz gewissen zeichen mercken kan*] that they desire it in true Christian devotion, as I have often seen, we should leave to the Holy Spirit what is his work and not refuse him what he demands. It may be that inwardly they have a better understanding and faith than we [*Es mag sein, das sie inwendig hoeher vorstandt und glauben haben denn wir*], and this no one should maliciously oppose. Do we not read of St. Cyprian, the holy martyr, that in Carthage where he was bishop he even had both elements given to the children, although — for reasons of its own — that has now ceased? Christ had the children come to him and would not allow anyone to hinder them [Mark 10:14]. In like manner he withheld his blessings neither from the dumb nor the blind nor the lame. Why, then, should not his sacrament also be for those who heartily and in a Christian spirit desire it?

5.4

LW 48:217, 255, 257, 268, 307, 316. "Letters, I." 1521. Translated by G. G. Krodel. (WA Br. Nos. 77, 84, 85, 87, 96, 99)

LW 48:217: To Philip Melanchthon: "The Lord has afflicted me with painful constipation. The elimination is so hard that I am forced to press with all my strength, even to the point of perspiration, and the longer I delay the worse it gets. Yesterday on the fourth day I could go once, but I did not sleep all night and still have no peace. Please pray for me. This affliction will be intolerable if it continues as it has begun." (From Wartburg, *12 May 1521*)

LW 48:255: To George Spalatin: "The trouble from which I was suffering at Worms has not left me but rather has increased. I am more constipated than ever in my life, and despair of remedy. The Lord thus afflicts me, that I may not be without a relic of the cross. May he be blessed. Amen." *(10 June 1521)*

LW 48:257: To Melanchthon: "If this thing does not improve, I shall go directly to Erfurt. . . . There you will see me, or I you, for I shall consult doctors or surgeons. It is impossible that I endure this evil any longer; it is easier to endure ten big wounds than this small sign of a lesion." *(13 July 1521)*

LW 48:268: To Spalatin: "I tried the pills according to the prescription. Soon I had some relief and elimination without blood or force, but the wound of the previous rupture isn't healed yet, and I even had to suffer a good deal because some flesh extruded, either due to the power of the pills, or I don't know what." *(15 July 1521)*

LW 48:307: To Spalatin: "Today, on the sixth day, I had elimination with such difficulty that I almost passed out. Now I sit aching as if in labor confinement, wounded and sore, and shall have no — or little — rest this night. Thanks be to Christ, who has not left me without any relic of the holy cross." *(9 Sept. 1521)*

LW 48:316: To Spalatin: "At last my behind and my bowels have reconciled themselves to me. Therefore I need no further medication, and I am again completely healthy as before. Thanks be to God!" *(7 Oct. 1521)*

5.5

LW 15:65. "Notes on Ecclesiastes" 4:5. 1526. Translated by J. Pelikan. (WA 20:77-78)

The fool folds his hands and eats his own flesh. "Fool" in this passage does not mean, as we usually understand it, a man who is stupid or silly, but one who is wicked and good-for-nothing, one whom in German we call "a useless reprobate." Such are, for example, those envious people who, while they themselves are incapable of anything, nevertheless trouble and hinder others. Such good-for-nothings, without industry or ability, have no other purpose in life than to be a nuisance to others, as, for example, the foolish and ignorant preachers who teach or learn badly. Among the craftsmen there are those drones whom we call "bunglers," who only get into other people's way since they themselves do not do anything right. . . . *The fool folds his hands;* he is not an energetic worker. He is not watchful, but drowsy and lazy, a man who is not seriously concerned about his own work, but instead hinders, despises, and slanders others. . . . On the other hand, it is said of an industrious and energetic housewife (Prov. 31:19), "Her hands hold the spindle," that is, she grasps it. Therefore God arouses these stupid and good-for-nothing men for us to frustrate our counsels and efforts.

5.6

LW 15:74-76. "Ecclesiastes" 5:1-2. 1526. (WA 20:87-88)

To draw near to listen is better than to offer the sacrifice of fools. . . . And here you see what "fool" means to the Hebrews, namely, not the one whom we call a moron, but one who does not listen to the Word of God or does not believe it whole-heartedly, even though in other ways he may be very wise. . . . *For they do not know that they are doing evil.* With these words he himself interprets the word "fools." For certainly no one is so evil that he would do evil if he knew that it is so evil in the sight of God. That is why he calls them fools, ignorant and blind men, who do many things as though they were good, and do them with great seriousness, but do not know that these sacrifices, which they carry out with such zeal, are utterly wicked. Thus Christ called the Pharisees "blind" (Matt. 23:26) because they sacrificed much, tormented themselves with words, but neglected faith and love, in fact, did not even know about them, calling evil good and vice versa. Therefore it was right for him to call them fools.

5.7

LW 43:124-25; 127-29; 131-33. "Whether One May Flee from a Deadly Plague." 1527. Translated by C. J. Schindler. (WA 23:339-79)

According to Holy Scripture God sent his four scourges: pestilence, famine, sword, and wild beasts. If it is permissible to flee from one or the other in clear conscience, why not from all four? Our examples demonstrate how the holy fathers escaped from the sword; it is quite evident that Abraham, Isaac, and Jacob fled from the other scourge, namely, hunger and death, when they went to Egypt to escape famine. . . . I hear people say, "If war or the Turks come, one should not flee from his village or town but stay and await God's punishment by the sword." That is quite true; let him who has a strong faith wait for his death, but he should not condemn those who take flight. By such reasoning, when a house is on fire, no one should run outside or rush to help because such a fire is also a punishment from God. Anyone who falls into deep water dare not save himself by swimming but must surrender to the water as to a divine punishment. Very well, do so if you can, but do not tempt God and allow others to do as much as they are capable of doing. Likewise, if someone breaks a leg, is wounded or bitten, he should not seek medical aid, but say, "It is God's punishment. I shall bear it until it heals by itself." Freezing weather and winter are also God's punishment and can cause death. Why run to get inside or near a fire? Be strong and stay outside until it becomes warm again. We should then need no apothecaries or drugs or physicians because all illnesses are punishments from God. Hunger and thirst are also great punishments and torture. Why do you eat and drink instead of letting yourself be punished until hunger and thirst stop of themselves? . . .

I am of the opinion that all the epidemics, like any plague, are spread among the people by evil spirits who poison the air or exhale a pestilential breath which puts a deadly poison into the flesh. Nevertheless, this is God's decree and punishment to which we must patiently submit and serve our neighbor, risking our lives in this manner as St. John teaches: "If Christ laid down his life for us, we ought to lay down our lives for the brethren" [1 John 3:16]. When anyone is overcome by horror and repugnance in the presence of a sick person, he should take courage and strength in the firm assurance that it is the devil who stirs up such abhorrence, fear, and loathing in his heart. . . . And we should arm ourselves with this answer to the devil: "Get away, you devil, with your terrors! Just because you hate it, I'll spite you by going the more quickly to help my sick neighbor. . . ." Service to God is indeed service to our neighbor. It is proved by experience that those who nurse the sick with love, devotion, and sincerity are generally protected. Though they are poisoned, they are not harmed. . . . A person who attends a patient because of greed, or with the expectation of an inheritance or some personal advantage in such services, should not be surprised if eventually he is infected, disfigured, or even dies before he comes into possession of that estate or inheritance. . . .

Others sin on the right hand. They are much too rash and reckless, tempting God and disregarding everything which might counteract death and the plague. . . . This is not trusting God but tempting him. God has created medicines and provided us with intelligence to guard and take good care of the body so that we can live in good health. If one makes no use of intelligence or medicine when he could do so without detriment to his neighbor, such a person injures his body and must beware lest he become a suicide in God's eyes. . . . No, my dear friends, that is no good. Use medicine; take potions which can help you; fumigate house, yard, and street; shun persons and places wherever your neighbor does not need your presence or has recovered, and act like a man who wants to help put out the burning city. If in the Old Testament God himself ordered lepers to be banished from the community and compelled to live outside the city to prevent contamination [Leviticus 13–14], we must do the same with this dangerous pestilence so that anyone who becomes infected will stay away from other persons, or allow himself to be taken away and given speedy help with medicine. Under such circumstances it is our duty to assist such a person and not forsake him in his plight, as I have repeatedly pointed out before. Then the poison is stopped in time, which benefits not only the individual but also the whole community, which might be contaminated if one person is permitted to infect others.

5.8

LW 26:190. "Lectures on Galatians." 1531/1535. Translated by J. Pelikan. (WA 40:313)

Through his witches, therefore, he [the devil] is able to do harm to children, to give them heart trouble, to blind them, to steal them, or even to remove a child completely and put himself into the cradle in place of the stolen child. I have heard that in Saxony there was such a boy. He was suckled by five women and still could not be satisfied. There are many similar instances. Therefore witchcraft is nothing but an artifice and illusion of the devil, whether he cripples a part of the body or touches the body or takes it away altogether. He can do this uncommonly well, even in the case of old people. No wonder, then, that he bewitches children this way. Nevertheless, this is nothing but some sort of illusion; for they say that he is able to heal what he has crippled with his wiles.

5.9

LW 54:44-45. "Table Talk." 1532. Translated by T. G. Tappert. (WA TR 1:133, No. 323)

[*Recorder: Dietrich*] When we were discussing monstrous beings to which women sometimes give birth, there was mention of an offspring which was like a mouse when it was born and tried to run under a stool into a mousehole in the wall. He [Martin Luther] said, "That is a demonstration that the power of the mind is so great that it can even change the body." When I said that I could not believe this, he answered, "You do not know what the power of the mind is." When somebody asked whether monstrosities of this kind ought to be baptized, he replied, "No, because I hold that they are only animal life." Later somebody else asked whether they have souls, and he responded, "I don't know. I haven't asked God about it."

5.10

LW 54:53. "Table Talk." 1532. (WA TR 1:157, No. 360)

[*Recorder: Dietrich*] In all grave illnesses the devil is present as the author and cause. First, he is the author of death. Second, Peter says in Acts that those who were oppressed by the devil were healed by Christ. Moreover, Christ cured not only the oppressed but also the paralytics, the blind, etc. Generally speaking, therefore, I think that all dangerous diseases are blows of the devil. For this, however, he employs the instruments of nature. So a thief dies by the sword, Satan corrupts the qualities and humors of the body, etc. God also employs means for the preservation of health, such as sleep, food, and drink, for he does nothing except through instruments. So the devil also injures through appropriate means. When a fence leans over a little, he knocks it all the way down to the ground. Accordingly, a physician is our Lord God's mender of the body, as we theologians are his healers of the spirit; we are to restore what the devil has damaged.

5.11

Luther's Letters. 1535. Translated by M. Currie (1908), 309. (WA Br. 7:171, No. 2186)

[*To Augustin Himmel, about Wolfgang Sieberger*] I should like a little house to be bought for my good Wolf, into which he might retire after my death, as he has a weak arm, and needs a roof of his own, so that he may not have to seek refuge in an institution, poor and forsaken. (From Wittenberg, on 5 April 1535)

5.12

LW 1:61. "Lectures on Genesis Chapters 1–5": 1:26. 1535-1536. Translated by G. V. Schick. (WA 42:45-46)

[*Discussing humankind "made in the image of God"*] I am afraid that since the loss of this image through sin we cannot understand it to any extent. Memory, will, and mind we have indeed; but they are most depraved and seriously weakened, yes, to put it more clearly, they are utterly leprous and unclean. If these powers are the image of God, it will also follow that Satan was created according to the image of God, since he surely has these natural endowments, such as memory and a very superior intellect and a most determined will, to a far higher degree than we have them. Therefore the image of God is something far different, namely, a unique work of God. If some assert nevertheless that these powers are that image, let them admit that they are, as it were, leprous and unclean. Similarly, we still call a leprous human being a human being even though in his leprous flesh everything is almost dead and without sensation, except that he is rather violently excited to lust.

5.13

LW 1:118-19. "Genesis" 2:18-19. 1535-1536. (WA 42:89-90)

In Paradise that union [i.e., of man and woman] would have taken place without any bashfulness, as an activity created and blessed by God. It would have been accompanied by a noble delight, such as there was at that time in eating and drinking. Now, alas, it is so hideous and frightful a pleasure that physicians compare it with epilepsy or falling sickness. Thus an actual disease is linked with the very activity of procreation. We are in a state of sin and of death; therefore we also undergo this punishment, that we cannot make use of woman without the horrible passion of lust and, so to speak, without epilepsy.

5.14

LW 2:10-11. "Genesis Chapters 6–14": 6:1-2. 1535-1536. (WA 42:269-70)

It delights Satan if he can delude us by taking on the appearance either of a young man or of a woman. But that anything can be born from the union of a devil and a human being is simply untrue. Such an assertion is sometimes made about hideous infants that resemble demons very much. I have seen some of these. But I am convinced either that these were deformed, but not begotten, by the devil, or that they are actual devils with flesh that they have either counterfeited or stolen from somewhere. If with God's permission the devil can take possession of an entire human being and change his disposition, what would be so remarkable about his misshaping the body and bringing about the birth of either blind or crippled children?

5.15

LW 24:73-74. "Sermons on the Gospel of St. John": 14:11. 1537. Translated by M. H. Bertram. (WA 45:527)

But [God] rules in such a way that even physically we always see more of His grace and blessing than of His wrath and punishment. For we find a hundred thousand healthy people for every ailing, blind, deaf, paralytic, or leprous person. And even if one member of the body has a defect, the entire person, still endowed with body and soul, shows forth nothing but God's goodness.

5.16

LW 54:346. "Table Talk." April 1539. (WA TR 4:334-35, No. 4479)

[*Recorder: Lauterbach*] On this day he [Martin Luther] was also troubled by kidney stones and said: "This ailment attaches in a peculiar way to Germans, just as the gout is said to be the disease most frequently encountered in England. Various kinds of sickness have been directed at this wretched body of ours, and oh, the pain by which we have been quite broken! Cramps seem to be the least of the ailments, but I think epilepsy is a kind of spasm that occurs in the brain. When it occurs in the legs, a spasm makes motion and travel difficult." Then he also spoke about bewitching and how the bodies of men are also afflicted by this.

5.17

LW 54:396-97. "Table Talk." 1540. (WA TR 5:8-9, No. 5207)

[*Recorder: Mathesius*] In Dessau there was a twelve-year-old boy like this: he devoured as much as four farmers did, and he did nothing else than eat and excrete. Luther suggested that he be suffocated. Somebody asked, "For what reason?" He [Luther] replied, "Because I think he's simply a mass of flesh without a soul. Couldn't the devil have done this, inasmuch as he gives such shape to the body and mind even of those who have reason that in their obsession they hear, see, and feel nothing? The devil is himself their soul. The power of the devil is great when in this way he holds the minds of all men captive, but he doesn't dare give full vent to the power on account of the angels."

5.18

LW 54:460-61. "Table Talk." 1543. (WA TR 5:264, No. 5588)

[*Recorded by Heydenreich*] A question was put to the doctor [Martin Luther]. "There is a chaplain who can't baptize because his left hand is shaky or because he can't use it for other reasons." He [Luther] was asked whether the chaplain could have the verger hold the child and pour water with his other hand, which he could use. Luther replied, "If the chaplain preaches well and the congregation hears him gladly, this may be done, especially if the common people are not offended by it. If they approve of it, it's permissible." Then someone else suggested, "How would it be if he took hold of the child with both hands and dipped only his feet into the water?" The doctor replied, "Ah, no! Innovation isn't good. If the chaplain can't baptize, the pastor ought to do it himself."

5.19

LW 7:295. "Lectures on Genesis Chapters 38–44": 42:38. 1544. (WA 44:518)

Now because sleep is a customary thing, no one shrinks from it, as we are wont to shudder at the sight or mention of some unusual or horrible sickness, such as epilepsy. If men are seized by this sickness, they are deprived even of all feeling and movement so far as this life is concerned. Indeed, they seem to have descended into another life, to such a degree that they feel nothing at all, see nothing, and hear nothing, either when burned with fire or plunged beneath the waves. Consequently, epileptics are dead even though they are alive.

5.20

LW 8:316. "Lectures on Genesis Chapters 45–50": 49:33. 1545. (WA 44:812-13)

Above I adduced a rather crude analogy concerning the life of the fetus in the womb. For no one of those who are alive today knows where he was during the first two years, when he lived either in the womb, or when, after being brought into the light of day, he sucked his mother's milk. He knows nothing about the days, the nights, the times, and the rulers. Yet he lived at that time, and he was a body joined to a soul — a body adapted to all natural functions. Therefore this is most certain proof that God wants to preserve man in a wonderful manner altogether unknown to him. Look at the wretchedness and the paroxysms because of which epileptics and madmen are beside themselves to such an extent that they seem destitute of all their senses.

6 *John Calvin and Disability*

Deborah Beth Creamer

Introduction

When we think of John Calvin, it is far too easy to begin with overly simplistic images of his doctrines of the Fall, providence, and predestination. From such a perspective, we might not expect Calvin to have much of interest to offer to conversations about disability, either in his own time or in the present day. For example, we might imagine that he would simply tell us that God has predestined each of us to ability/disability or other embodied and social experiences, perhaps adding that we are wrong to try to understand why God has made such decisions or to try to change the path to which we have been called. While the idea that one's path has been chosen by God can help give meaning and purpose to one's life, such understandings can also be used in ways that are both personally distressing and politically dangerous for people with disabilities or others who may lack social power, if such claims are used to deny agency or the right to seek change, instead telling us just to accept things (including social injustices) just the way they are.

As with all caricatures, there is, not surprisingly, some degree of truth in this picture of Calvin, in that predestination and other related themes do figure strongly in his reflections. However, even a brief examination of the vast scope of his writings and teachings shows us that Calvin's use of these ideas is far more complex than this, and that he has much more to offer than this simplistic picture. As we shall see in the sections that follow, Calvin's own writings are complex, creative, and full of possibilities for contemporary reflection, even as they also force us to wrestle with sometimes problematic and challenging notions of the natures of God, humans, and the world.

Born in France in 1509, Calvin is one of the most influential pastors and theologians of the second generation of Protestant Reformers. (For his full biography, see Parker 1975, or McGrath 1990). He spent most of his professional life in the city of Geneva, where he served as a lecturer and preacher until his death in 1564. He survives for us today primarily through his prolific writings, which we will explore below, as well as in the later traditions of Calvinism and in the structures of presbyterian polity. As we engage his works, it is interesting to note that Calvin did not believe that he was establishing a new doctrine or even a new church; rather, he was attempting to restore the church to the structures and practices of early Christianity (see, for example, *Institutes* IV.18.9). Thus, even though we think of him today as one of the most significant systematic theologians from the Protestant Reformation, this cannot be separated from his interest in church order and in restoring the church to its scriptural roots.

It is clear that Scripture serves as the grounding for Calvin's central theological claims. For example, Calvin is often known today for his discussion of predestination. He builds this argument from the concept of election in Romans 9–11 (see, for example, *Institutes* III.11). From his reading of this text, Calvin argues for what is sometimes called double predestination, in that not only are some individuals chosen by God for eternal life, but also some are chosen for eternal damnation. As we will see in the excerpts below, Calvin believes that human nature became thoroughly corrupted as a result of the Fall, and so salvation must come only from God, not from our own faith or good works. In and of ourselves, we cannot become deserving of God. Yet human knowledge is still significant: as he writes in the opening lines of each edition of the *Institutes* (6.3), it is human knowledge of our own brokenness that makes us aware of the greatness of God, just as it is the awareness of God through both Scripture (the living words of God) and providence (the continued action of God in the world) that leads us to understand our own brokenness. For Calvin, our only sensible response to this recognition of God is piety, the attitude and practice that puts God at the center of one's life. Thus Calvin sees the role of the pastor as far more than just explaining an intellectual fact of human fallenness; indeed, it is one of encouraging us to live a life of piety in response to the assurance of God's presence and goodness. As he writes in *Institutes* I.14.4, "The theologian's task is not to divert the ears with chatter, but to strengthen consciences by teaching things true, sure, and profitable." Thus the role of the pastor (and Calvin's own goal) is to teach in such a way that reminds the community of the presence and power of God, and to encourage us to live out of such assurance.

While his theological writings are voluminous, we only have access to a few biographical details about Calvin's adult life. We do know that he experienced a series of hardships throughout his life, including his experience of perpetual exile from France. All of his children died in infancy, and his wife, whom he married when he was in Strasbourg in 1540, died in 1549 after a long illness. He experienced a variety of significant illnesses throughout his life, including migraines, hemorrhoids, consumption, gout, kidney stones, and tuberculosis (Cottret 2000; McGrath 1990). Biographers suggest that, given the scope of these conditions, it was perhaps not surprising that he often thought of the body as a prison (see McKee's introduction in Calvin 2001). However, apart from short and dispassionate descriptions of his own physical conditions that appear occasionally in his correspondence, we have little record of how Calvin interpreted or reflected upon his own embodied experiences. As we explore his theological writings, then, we must remember that these come from a particular man writing from a particular time and context, even though we lack a clear sense of whether or how he might have connected his own embodied experiences to his theological reflections.

Engaging Calvin and Disability

As we examine possible references to disability in Calvin's writings, at least four distinct categories emerge. As we have discussed above, Calvin often builds his own arguments through a close reading of biblical texts. In his theological treatises, biblical commentaries, sermons, and elsewhere, we see Calvin engaging issues of disability whenever such issues come up in Scripture. One way, then, of finding Calvin's references to disability is to look for biblical texts that relate to disability themes, and then review the ways he responds to such passages. As we will see in Selections **6.8** and **6.9**, Calvin sometimes interprets such themes in ways that match with specific physical conditions (e.g., "blind" meaning a person who cannot physically see), but at other times uses these terms metaphorically (e.g., that we are all "blind" to God's truth). Similarly, we could identify other scriptural passages that might relate to specific aspects of disability experiences (such as exclusion, alienation, suffering, and healing) and then examine Calvin's use of or responses to such themes. A second way to examine his understandings of disability is to look closely at his writings on church structure and organization.

In these writings Calvin shows a clear interest in those who are sick or who are otherwise on the margins of community, such as the prisoner or the widow. This appears most clearly in the "Draft Ecclesiastical Ordinances" (Selections **6.1** and **6.2**), but this interest in charity and inclusion is apparent elsewhere in his writings as well. In a third category, we discover that certain themes about the value of the human body are found throughout his writings, particularly so in the *Institutes* (Selections **6.3** through **6.6**). For example, one might look to the references he makes to the body as a prison (*Institutes* II.7.13; *Institutes* III.9.4) as well as those that affirm the beauty and value of creation (*Institutes* III.10.1-3). Finally, we can also see significance for disability in the ways in which he uses metaphors of ability in his descriptions of theology, as when he compares our inability to see God with the need for those with vision impairments to use spectacles (*Institutes* I.14.1), or when he asks whether it is better to think of God as a physician or as a judge *(Sermons on Jeremiah).*

Yet even as we look at individual passages within Calvin's writings, it is more challenging to uncover his underlying attitudes or beliefs about disability. A thorough reading of the *Institutes,* for example, shows an overall concern with community rather than the rights or experiences of discrete individuals. Calvin tends to discuss issues of impairment either in ways that relate to all people (e.g., that none of us can clearly see or understand God's grace) or in ways that exaggerate or exemplify a condition that any of us might experience (e.g., the profound suffering experienced by Job). He rarely talks about disability in and of itself, making it seem that he had little interest in disability either as a concept or as an experience. Yet, even though it is a challenge to determine what he does or does not think about disability, it is useful to seek out his underlying beliefs about the human experience which may complement or challenge contemporary theologies of disabilities, as well as to be attentive to underlying assumptions about human experience which may or may not make sense to us today in light of disability experiences. This is the project we will undertake as we explore the selections below.

Reading Calvin

Selections **6.1** and **6.2** come from Calvin's "Draft Ecclesiastical Ordinances," written in 1541 as a governing document for the church in Geneva. While the final version of this document has been lost to time, this draft gives us a clear picture of Calvin's ideals for church structure and ecclesiastical reform. Of particular interest is his description of the four orders of office for church leadership: pastors, doctors (teachers), elders, and deacons (**6.1**). All four, he notes in the opening to the Ordinances, are "instituted by our Lord for the government of his Church," coming to us from the ancient church, and thus having a profound sense of legitimacy. As described in this text, deacons have primary responsibility for issues of social welfare, including care of the poor and the sick. In Calvin's model, deacons are not considered a lower class of clergy, but rather serve communion right along with the pastors. While contemporary readers might be appropriately uncomfortable with Calvin's charity model or with the distinction between "healthy" clergy and "sick" subjects, it is also important to recognize some of the other implications of Calvin's model. The role of deacon is defined here as being central to church organization. Providing service to the "sick" or to anyone in need is seen as vital to the role of the church, no less important than any other church function. Calvin's commitment here is that the church is not just to be a place for inward reflection but must also be committed to the proclamation of the gospel through action and service to others. In addition, a strong connection between church and society emerges, with the church inextricably engaged in the public life of the city and the larger world.

In selection **6.2**, Calvin turns his attention to the sacraments. Here he makes the argument that all who are sick or who are in prison ought to be given access to Scripture, and that it is the responsibility of the clergy, as well as of the larger community, to make this available to them. He also reminds the community that this access must be given "before it is too late" — in other words, this is to be not merely a ceremonial visit by a member of the clergy, but rather a legitimate opportunity for the individual to hear and respond to the word of God. This demonstrates Calvin's interest in including all members of the community in the larger church, arguing that we must not deny access to Scripture (and, thus, access to the knowledge of God) based on physical condition or legal status. Similarly, in his discussion of children, we see his demand that *all* citizens and inhabitants are to bring their children to catechism, without any limit based on economic or educational status or any other criteria. In many ways, this mirrors Calvin's emphasis on inclusivity through the practice of infant baptism, which also does not demand any action or accomplishment on the part of the recipient. However, we also see in this passage the restriction that children are not to receive the sacraments until after they have been "well enough instructed" and are able to recite the whole of the catechism. This emphasis on the ability to recite the catechism would serve as a significant barrier to many individuals with cognitive differences, thus limiting access to the sacraments to those who are "smart enough" or who have particular capacities for memorization and recall. Thus, this excerpt reveals a tension between Calvin's affinity for inclusiveness in church community on the one hand, and his creation of barriers to full inclusion of people with certain disabilities or impairments on the other.

Selections **6.3** through **6.6** come from the *Institutes of the Christian Religion,* Calvin's most significant theological work. The first draft of the *Institutes,* written in six chapters in 1536, was designed as a basic catechism of the Christian faith. Calvin expanded this work to seventeen chapters in 1539 and to twenty-one chapters in 1543. In 1559, he published the version we see here today, in the form of four books totaling eighty chapters. Each book focuses on a central element of the Apostles' Creed: the knowledge of God the Creator, the knowledge of God the Redeemer in Christ, the way we receive the grace of Christ, and the Holy Catholic Church. The text is systematic and comprehensive, and has been described as the most thorough and complete exposition of Calvin's theology.

Selection **6.3** comes from the opening section of Book I of the *Institutes.* We see here Calvin's description of the knowledge of God as integrally related to the knowledge of self, and of the knowledge of self as integrally related to the knowledge of God. This section of text begins to give the flavor and style of writing that is found throughout Calvin's works, particularly in the way he uses Scripture to support and extend his own arguments. We also see here some of his attitudes toward the human condition, including an emphasis on depravity and corruption resulting from the Fall, as well as on the nature of God's majesty and goodness. Finally, we see embedded in this text a variety of assumptions about human intellectual capacity. Calvin acknowledges that none of us have perfect understanding, but he fails to reflect on the genuine diversity of human intellect, seeming instead to assume that we all share similar degrees of pride, vanity, and cognitive capacity. This is an example of a recurring and problematic theme throughout Calvin's work, where he simultaneously appears to value and equalize all people (we have all fallen and yet we all have sacred worth) and yet (intentionally or not) does not truly include all people in this vision, particularly excluding those who differ from his expectation of normal rationality or intellectual capacity.

Selections **6.4** and **6.5** come from Book II of the *Institutes.* In selection **6.4**, we begin to get a clearer picture of Calvin's perspective on the nature of the human condition, and particularly the role of rationality. As he writes here, we humans have rationality that distinguishes us from "brute beasts," but this rationality is choked with ignorance. This text, like the previous one, makes clear assumptions about intellectual status as being a defining characteristic of what it is to be human, in a way that is particularly troubling to those attentive to cognitive differences. This text might lead one to wonder, for example, whether Calvin would consider a person with Down syndrome or autism as belonging to the category of "mankind" or rather to one of "brute beasts." We also see in this passage Calvin's use of the idea of "madmen" as a contrast to that which is sensible or true, again raising the question of who does and does not belong in his category of human being.

In selection **6.5**, we see one of Calvin's clearest discussions of the question of theodicy: If God is all-powerful, how is it that evil (or suffering) exists in the world? Calvin gives us here an image which demonstrates how the same act can be attributed simultaneously to God, Satan, and the human, each having a completely different purpose in the midst of the same act. Thus, we see how God's providence can work through any situation, and so we ought not to blame God for acts that we might interpret as being wicked. This analogy functions well as an alternative to theodicies which either blame the subject for his or her own suffering or suggest that God is absent during times of suffering, both of which can be problematic from a disability perspective, as these beliefs function in ways that separate the person with a disability from God. This perspective argues instead that God is present even if we are unable to understand God's intentions or role in a situation. This can serve as a productive starting point for a theology of disability, showing that God is present in the midst of disability without necessarily attributing to God the cause of disability.

Selection **6.6** comes from Book III of the *Institutes,* and presents Calvin's understanding of anthropology (what the human is like) and eschatology (what the realm of God is like). Calvin states here that the human life is like smoke or shadow, and thus we ought not to be too attached to it. He also describes God as responsible for human miseries, as these help detach us from the vanities of this life. Calvin states that God permits us injuries, diseases, and perils that show how unstable and fleeting our lives are. He goes on, however, to argue that even as we recognize our own vanities, we ought to also consider human life as a blessing, a gift from God, in both its good and its difficult times. From a disability perspective, this passage raises some of the ambiguity that comes with human embodiment — that it includes both pain and joy, both what we might reject and what we ought to embrace — and is a helpful way of expressing the mixed experiences many of us have in our bodies. At the same time, however, we note that Calvin is again only speaking of humans in a rather generic sense, without addressing the real levels of complexity that come from genuine experiences of impairment or exclusion. This also opens him to challenges on his claim that God "permits" us to have such experiences, a position which people with disabilities might find to be trite or even offensive. Thus, this excerpt shows some of the valuable complexity within Calvin's understanding of the human experience of embodiment, while simultaneously revealing his lack of attention to concrete embodied experiences.

Selections **6.7** through **6.10** come from Calvin's *Biblical Commentaries*. As mentioned earlier, one could look in his commentaries for any passage that relates to disability, sickness, embodiment, suffering, exclusion, interdependence, diversity, or a host of other related themes in order to further unpack his teachings about disability. Here we have included four passages that might be productively examined from a disability perspective. In selection **6.7**, we see in his commentary on John a discussion of what it means that Christ (the Word) was made flesh. Here Calvin explains that this embodiment was not simply symbolic; rather, God actually took on human flesh. This could be especially interesting for those who might consider images of the Disabled God, such as proposed by Nancy Eiesland, insofar as it supports the view that God in Christ had real experiences with human limitation, pain, impairment, and even death, and thus that God has a real connection to people who experience disability. This perspective also affirms God's presence in embodiment more generally, not in an idealized way, but in the full messiness and complexity of what it is to be a body, which can also serve to sustain other theologies that take embodiment seriously.

Selection **6.8** looks at the story of the man born blind from John 9. Here Calvin gives his explicit reaction to the question asked in this passage: Who sinned, the man or his parents? Calvin reminds the reader that *all* have sinned; the question becomes absurd if we ask it as "Who did *not* sin, the man or his parents?" At the same time, Calvin argues that we cannot understand God's actions, which are far more complex than we could ever know, and thus it is pointless to try to assess why it is that one person is "afflicted" (to use Calvin's term) and another is not. This passage helps to critique those who would try to give a single answer to the question of the cause of suffering, and highlights again the notion that we cannot fully understand God's intentions in our lives.

In selection **6.9**, we see Calvin's reflection on Matthew's text which states that God's truth is hidden from the wise and revealed to the babes (to

which Calvin also adds "ignoramuses and uncultivated men"). As with earlier passages, this text not only highlights Calvin's overarching themes of
God's power and of human corruption, but also reveals some of his disparaging attitudes related to intelligence and socio-economic status. It states
that God has the ability to reach any person, which suggests that no person
is beyond the reach of God, regardless of intellectual or emotional status,
which may serve as an affirmation to people who experience the world quite
differently than others of us do. It also reinforces the idea that God makes
distinctions among people for God's own reasons, which we cannot even try
to understand.

Remembering that discussion of disability ought not to be limited to ex-
aminations of sickness or suffering, we have included selection **6.10,** which
looks at Calvin's claims about oppression and exclusion. As with Selection
6.2 from the "Draft Ecclesiastical Ordinances," we see here a commitment to
inclusion and justice. This passage includes an affirmation that God will vindicate those who are treated unjustly, and a declaration that God is on the
side of the outcast, a claim similar to the claims we find in liberation theology. We also see a reminder that "neighbor" includes, in Calvin's language,
"the whole of mankind," and thus that we must particularly love those who
are most in need of being loved. This speaks not only to inclusion but also to
advocacy, suggesting that God is on the side of people who experience disability and thus that the church ought to respond accordingly, becoming a
welcoming presence while simultaneously acting to challenge and remove
barriers and impediments wherever they may be found.

Selection **6.11,** from a sermon delivered in 1555, shows a variety of
themes and images which could be productively explored from a disability
perspective. For example, the declaration that we are all made in the image
of God can serve both to break down the dichotomy between "us" and
"them" when we talk about people with disabilities, and to highlight the
truth that people with disabilities, like all people, are of sacred worth. Additionally, the idea that we are all in the image of God raises some interesting
questions about God — for example, whether God's image includes disability or limits. (Calvin might not agree, but this sort of language at least raises
that question.) The claim that we are all members of Christ's body, "without
any distinction," similarly serves as a foundation for claims of equality in
access and in attitude, such as proposing that churches need to be accessible
to all, given that we are all part of the body of Christ. The proposal that we
ought not to despise our own flesh is particularly interesting from the perspective of disability, such that one might consider bodily experiences of

pain or impairment as something to be accepted and embraced rather than as cause for despair. This selection also demonstrates an interesting mingling of Calvin's commitments to justice, as he proposes that we must not abuse those who are under our hand while he simultaneously refuses to challenge the idea of slavery itself. At one level, this reminds us that any analysis of disability perspectives is insufficient without a corresponding analysis of sexism, racism, classism, and related issues, as these issues also affect people with disabilities. At another level, it suggests that Calvin might not be particularly willing to challenge social structures and distinctions between people even in the midst of his claim that we are all in the image of God.

Selection **6.12** comes from Calvin's correspondence. Throughout his time in Geneva, Calvin remained in constant contact with friends, other reformers, former students, members of the nobility, and many others. These letters give us a glimpse of the personal side of Calvin (through descriptions of his interests and emotions, for example) which is often lacking in his formal writings. This letter, from April 1541, describes Calvin's reaction to the death of a student (Louis) and his tutor (Claude Féray), and is addressed to the father of the deceased boy. Calvin's letter emphasizes that it is not only permissible but in fact good to feel grief and other natural human emotions. One might connect the descriptions found in this letter to experiences of disability that are encountered as loss — as, for example, in the case of a parent who did not expect to have a disabled child, or someone who experienced disability as the result of illness or accident. In these situations, we might imagine a Calvin who is open to the human experiences of grief, anger, confusion, and disappointment, and yet one who is simultaneously steadfast in his belief in the presence of God in and through such events.

Concluding Thoughts

We find in Calvin a complex constellation of perspectives relevant to disability studies. We have encountered intriguing and even positive themes such as inclusion (the "sick" and the prisoner are to be included in the larger church community), equality (all people are in the same state of sinfulness and depravity, regardless of ability or other conditions), interdependence (it is important to focus on community rather than individual piety), and the relevance of embodiment in the midst of God's created world (even though Calvin simultaneously argues that we should value God rather than earthly creation). At the same time, however, we have identified a number of dangerous themes (such as those related to predestination, depravity, and charity), an expectation of rationality and intellectual capability, and problematic language ("blind," "sick," "mad") that may underscore further biases against disability. Overall, from this examination we seem to have found a Calvin who is complicated and full of possibilities for contemporary reflection, even as we also cannot simplistically dismiss the problematic images, beliefs, assumptions, and doctrines found throughout his work. Perhaps the most significant insight to be gained from reflection on Calvin's work is that disability scholars ought not be afraid of his writings, or dismiss him out of turn for stereotypic assumptions about his teachings. Instead, a close reading of his texts shows us that his work is rife with possibilities for contemporary theological reflection on issues of disability even as it also gives us important insights into the complex relationships between Christian history and our interpretations of disability in the past and today.

References

Primary Sources

Calvin, John. 1958. *Calvin: Commentaries.* Translated and edited by Joseph Haroutunian in collaboration with Louise Pettibone Smith. Library of Christian Classics. Philadelphia: Westminster Press.

———. 1954. *Calvin: Theological Treatises.* Translated and with introductions and notes by J. K. S. Reid. Library of Christian Classics. Philadelphia: Westminster Press.

———. 1960. *Institutes of the Christian Religion.* Edited by John T. McNeill. Translated and indexed by Ford Lewis Battles. Library of Christian Classics. Philadelphia: Westminster Press.

———. 1980. *John Calvin's Sermons on the Ten Commandments.* Edited and translated by Benjamin W. Farley. Grand Rapids: Baker.

———. 1990. *Sermons on Jeremiah.* Translated by Blair Reynolds. Lewiston, N.Y.: Edwin Mellen Press.

———. 2001. *Writings on Pastoral Piety.* Edited and with translations by Elsie Anne McKee. The Classics of Western Spirituality. New York: Paulist Press.

Secondary Sources

Cottret, Bernard. 2000. *Calvin: A Biography.* Grand Rapids: Wm. B. Eerdmans.

McGrath, Alister E. 1990. *A Life of John Calvin: A Study in the Shaping of Western Culture.* Oxford: Basil Blackwell.

McKim, Donald K., editor. 2004. *The Cambridge Companion to John Calvin.* Cambridge: Cambridge University Press.

———, editor. 2006. *Calvin and the Bible.* Cambridge: Cambridge University Press.

Parker, T. H. L. 1995. *Calvin: An Introduction to His Thought.* Louisville: Westminster John Knox Press.

———. 1975. *John Calvin: A Biography.* Philadelphia: Westminster Press.

Partee, Charles. 2008. *The Theology of John Calvin.* Louisville: Westminster John Knox Press.

Excerpts

THE DRAFT ECCLESIASTICAL ORDINANCES

Selections 6.1 and 6.2: "Draft Ecclesiastical Ordinances." In *Calvin: Theological Treatises,* translated and with an introduction and notes by J. K. S. Reid. Philadelphia: Westminster Press, 1954. The following selections are taken from 58, 62, 63, 64-66, and 68-69.

6.1

Of the Four Orders

There are four orders of office instituted by our Lord for the government of his Church. First, pastors; then doctors; next elders; and fourth, deacons. Hence if we will have a Church well ordered and maintained, we ought to observe this form of government.

As to the pastors, whom Scripture also sometimes calls elders and ministers, their office is to proclaim the Word of God, to instruct, admonish, exhort, and censure, both in public and in private, to administer the sacraments, and to enjoin brotherly corrections along with the elders and colleagues. . . .

Concerning the second order, which we have called Doctors

The office proper to doctors is the instruction of the faithful in true doctrine, in order that the purity of the Gospel be not corrupted either by ignorance or by evil opinions. As things are disposed today, we always include under this title aids and instructions for maintaining the doctrine of God and defending the Church from injury by the fault of pastors and ministers. So to use a more intelligible word, we will call this the order of the schools. . . .

Concerning the third order, which is that of Elders

Their office is to have oversight of the life of everyone, to admonish amicably those whom they see to be erring or to be living a disordered life, and, where it is required, to enjoin fraternal corrections themselves and along with others. . . .

The fourth order of ecclesiastical government, that is, the Deacons

There were always two kinds in the ancient Church, the one deputed to receive, dispense, and hold goods for the poor, not only daily alms, but also possessions, rents, and pensions; the other to tend and care for the sick and administer allowances to the poor. This custom we follow again now, for we have procurators and hospitallers.

The number of procurators appointed for this hospital seems to us to be proper; but we wish that there be also a separate reception office, so that not only provisions be in time made better, but that those who wish to do some charity may be more certain that the gift will not be employed otherwise than they intend. And if the revenue assigned by their Lordships be insufficient, or should extraordinary necessity arise, the Seigneury will advise about adjustment, according to the need they see.

The election of both procurators and hospitallers is to take place like that of the elders; and in electing them the rule proposed by Paul for deacons is to be followed.

With regard to the office of procurator, we think the rules which have already been imposed on them by us are good, by means of which, in urgent affairs, and where there is danger in deferment, and chiefly when there is no grave difficulty or question of great expense, they are not obliged always to be meeting, but one or two can do what is reasonable in the absence of the others.

It will be their duty to watch diligently that the public hospital is well maintained, and that this be so both for the sick and for the old people unable to work, widowed women, orphaned children, and other poor creatures. The sick are always to be lodged in a set of rooms separate from the other people who are unable to work, old men, widowed women, orphaned children, and the other poor.

Moreover, care for the poor dispersed through the city should be revived, as the procurators may arrange it.

Moreover, besides the hospital for those passing through which must be maintained, there should be some attention given to any recognized as worthy of special charity. For this purpose, a special room should be set aside to receive those who ought to be assisted by the procurators, which is to be reserved for this business.

It should above all be demanded that the families of the hospitallers be honorably ruled in accordance with the will of God, since they have to govern houses dedicated to God.

The ministers must on their side enquire whether there be any lack or want of anything, in order to ask and desire the Seigneury to put it in order. To do this, some of their company with the procurators should visit the hospital every three months, to ascertain if all is in order.

It would be good, not only for the poor of the hospital, but also for those of the city who cannot help themselves, that they have a doctor and a surgeon of their own who should still practice in the city, but meanwhile be required to have care of the hospital and to visit the other poor.

As for the hospital for plague, it should be wholly separate and apart, and especially if it happen that the city be visited by this scourge of God.

For the rest, to discourage mendicancy, which is contrary to good order, it would be well, and we have so ordered it, that there be one of our officials at the entrance of the churches to remove from the place those who loiter; and if there be any who give offense or offer insolence to bring them to one of the Lords Syndic. Similarly for the rest of the time, let the Overseers of Tens take care that the total prohibition of begging be well observed. . . .

6.2

___

Of the Sacraments

Of the Visitation of the Sick

There are many people negligent in comforting themselves in God by his Word when they are afflicted with sickness, and so many die without the admonition or teaching which is more salutary for a man then than at any other time. It will be good therefore that their Lordships ordain and make public that no one is to be totally confined to bed for three days without informing the minister, and that each be advised to call the ministers when they desire it in good time, in order that they be not diverted from the office which they publicly discharge in the Church. Above all it is to be commanded that parents, friends, and attendants do not wait until the patient is about to die, for in this extremity consolation is in most cases hardly useful.

Of the Visitation of Prisoners

It will be good that their Lordships ordain a certain day each week on which admonition be given to prisoners, to reprove and exhort them; and if it seem good to them, let them depute someone of their company in order that no fraud be committed. If they have anyone in irons, whom it is not desirable to take out, if it seems good to them, they could give entry to some minister to console him in their presence as above. For if one waits until they are about to die, they are often so preoccupied with fear of death that they can neither receive nor listen. The day for doing this, it is decided, will be Saturday after dinner.

The Order to be observed in the case of little Children

All citizens and inhabitants are to bring or convey their children on Sundays at midday to Catechism, of which something has been said.

A definite formulary is to be composed by which they will be instructed, and on this, with the teaching given them, they are to be interrogated about what has been said, to see if they have listened and remembered well.

When a child has been well enough instructed to pass the Catechism, he is to recite solemnly the sum of what it contains, and also to make profession of his Christianity in the presence of the Church.

Before this is done, no child is to be admitted to receive the Supper; and parents are to be informed not to bring them before this time. For it is a very perilous thing, for children as for parents, to introduce them without good and adequate instruction; for which purpose this order is to be used. . . .

THE INSTITUTES OF THE CHRISTIAN RELIGION

6.3

Selection 6.3: "The Knowledge of God the Creator." In *Institutes of the Christian Religion*, Book I, Chapter 1. Edited by John T. McNeill. Translated and indexed by Ford Lewis Battles. Library of Christian Classics. Philadelphia: Westminster Press, 1960, 35-39.

Book I, Chapter 1

1. Without knowledge of self there is no knowledge of God

Nearly all the wisdom we possess, that is to say, true and sound wisdom, consists of two parts: the knowledge of God and of ourselves. But, while joined by many bonds, which one precedes and brings forth the other is not easy to discern. In the first place, no one can look upon himself without immediately turning his thoughts to the contemplation of God, in whom he "lives and moves" [Acts 17:28]. For, quite clearly, the mighty gifts with which we are endowed are hardly from ourselves; indeed, our very being is nothing but subsistence in the one God. Then, by these benefits shed like dew from heaven upon us, we are led as by rivulets to the spring itself. Indeed, our very poverty better discloses the infinitude of benefits reposing in God. The miserable ruin, into which the rebellion of the first man cast us, especially compels us to look upward. Thus, not only will we, in fasting and hungering, seek thence what we lack; but, in being aroused by fear, we shall learn humility. For, as a veritable world of miseries is to be found in mankind, and we are thereby despoiled of divine raiment, our shameful nakedness exposes a teeming horde of infamies. Each of us must, then, be so stung by the consciousness of his own unhappiness as to attain at least some knowledge of God. Thus, from the feeling of our own ignorance, vanity, poverty, infirmity, and — what is more — depravity and corruption, we recognize that the true light of wisdom, sound virtue, full abundance of every good, and purity of righteousness rest in the Lord alone. To this extent we are prompted by our own ills to contemplate the good things of God; and we cannot seriously aspire to him before we begin to become displeased with ourselves. For what man in all the world would not gladly remain as he is — what man does not remain as he is — so long as he does not know himself, that is, while content with his own gifts, and either ignorant or unmindful of his own misery? Accordingly, the knowledge of ourselves not only arouses us to seek God, but also, as it were, leads us by the hand to find him.

2. *Without knowledge of God there is no knowledge of self*

Again, it is certain that man never achieves a clear knowledge of himself unless he has first looked upon God's face, and then descends from contemplating him to scrutinize himself. For we always seem to ourselves righteous and upright and wise and holy — this pride is innate in all of us — unless by clear proofs we stand convinced of our own unrighteousness, foulness, folly, and impurity. Moreover, we are not thus convinced if we look merely to ourselves and not also to the Lord, who is the sole standard by which this judgment must be measured. For, because all of us are inclined by nature to hypocrisy, a kind of empty image of righteousness in place of righteousness itself abundantly satisfies us. And because nothing appears within or around us that has not been contaminated by great immorality, what is a little less vile pleases us as a thing most pure — so long as we confine our minds within the limits of human corruption. Just so, an eye to which nothing is shown but black objects judges something dirty white or even rather darkly mottled to be whiteness itself. Indeed, we can discern still more clearly from the bodily senses how much we are deluded in estimating the powers of the soul. For if in broad daylight we either look down upon the ground or survey whatever meets our view round about, we seem to ourselves endowed with the strongest and keenest sight; yet when we look up to the sun and gaze straight at it, that power of sight which was particularly strong on earth is at once blunted and confused by a great brilliance, and thus we are compelled to admit that our keenness in looking upon things earthly is sheer dullness when it comes to the sun. So it happens in estimating our spiritual goods. As long as we do not look beyond the earth, being quite content with our own righteousness, wisdom, and virtue, we flatter ourselves most sweetly, and fancy ourselves all but demigods. Suppose we but once begin to raise our thoughts to God, and to ponder his nature, and how completely perfect are his righteousness, wisdom, and power — the straightedge to which we must be shaped. Then, what masquerading earlier as righteousness was pleasing in us will soon grow filthy in its consummate wickedness. What wonderfully impressed us under the name of wisdom will stink in its very foolishness. What wore the face of power will prove itself the most miserable weakness. That is, what in us seems perfection itself corresponds ill to the purity of God.

3. Man before God's majesty

Hence that dread and wonder with which Scripture commonly represents the saints as stricken and overcome whenever they felt the presence of God. Thus it comes about that we see men who in his absence normally remained firm and constant, but who, when he manifests his glory, are so shaken and struck dumb as to be laid low by the dread of death — are in fact overwhelmed by it and almost annihilated. As a consequence, we must infer that man is never sufficiently touched and affected by the awareness of his lowly state until he has compared himself with God's majesty. Moreover, we have numerous examples of this consternation both in the Book of Judges and in the Prophets. So frequent was it that this expression was common among God's people: "We shall die, for the Lord has appeared to us" [Judg. 13:22; Isa. 6:5; Ezek. 2:1; 1:28; Judg. 6:22-23; and elsewhere]. The story of Job, in its description of God's wisdom, power, and purity, always expresses a powerful argument that overwhelms men with the realization of their own stupidity, impotence, and corruption [cf. Job 38:1ff.]. And not without cause: for we see how Abraham recognizes more clearly that he is earth and dust [Gen. 18:27] when once he had come nearer to beholding God's glory; and how Elijah, with uncovered face, cannot bear to await his approach, such is the awesomeness of his appearance [1 Kings 19:13]. And what can man do, who is rottenness itself [Job 13:28] and a worm [Job 7:5; Ps. 22:6], when even the very cherubim must veil their faces out of fear [Isa. 6:2]? It is this indeed of which the prophet Isaiah speaks: "The sun will blush and the moon be con-

233

founded when the Lord of Hosts shall reign" [Isa. 24:23]; that is, when he shall bring forth his splendor and cause it to draw nearer, the brightest thing will become darkness before it [Isa. 2:10, 19].

Selections 6.4 and 6.5: "The Knowledge of God the Redeemer." In *Institutes of the Christian Religion,* Book II, Chapters 2 and 4. Edited by John T. McNeill. Translated and indexed by Ford Lewis Battles. Library of Christian Classics. Philadelphia: Westminster Press, 1960, 270-71, 273-75, 276-77, and 309-11.

6.4

Book II, Chapter 2

12. *Supernatural gifts destroyed; natural gifts corrupted; but enough of reason remains to distinguish man from brute beasts*

And, indeed, that common opinion which they have taken from Augustine pleases me: that the natural gifts were corrupted in man through sin, but that his supernatural gifts were stripped from him. For by the latter clause they understand the light of faith as well as righteousness, which would be sufficient to attain heavenly life and eternal bliss. Therefore, withdrawing from the Kingdom of God, he is at the same time deprived of spiritual gifts, with which he had been furnished for the hope of eternal salvation. From this it follows that he is so banished from the Kingdom of God that all qualities belonging to the blessed life of the soul have been extinguished in him, until he recovers them through the grace of regeneration. Among these are faith, love of God, charity toward neighbor, zeal for holiness and for righteousness. All these, since Christ restores them in us, are considered adventitious, and beyond nature: and for this reason we infer that they were taken away. On the other hand, soundness of mind and uprightness of heart were withdrawn at the same time. This is the corruption of the natural gifts. For even though something of understanding and judgment remains as a residue along with the will, yet we shall not call a mind whole and sound that is both weak and plunged into deep darkness. And depravity of the will is all too well known.

Since reason, therefore, by which man distinguishes between good and evil, and by which he understands and judges, is a natural gift, it could not be completely wiped out; but it was partly weakened and partly corrupted, so that its misshapen ruins appear. John speaks in this sense: "The light still shines in the darkness, but the darkness comprehends it not" [John 1:5]. In these words both facts are clearly expressed. First, in man's perverted and degenerate nature some sparks still gleam. These show him to be a rational being, differing from brute beasts, because he is endowed with understanding. Yet, secondly, they show this light choked with dense ignorance, so that it cannot come forth effectively.

Similarly the will, because it is inseparable from man's nature, did not perish, but was so bound to wicked desires that it cannot strive after the right. This is, indeed, a complete definition, but one needing a fuller explanation. . . .

15. *Science as God's gift*

Whenever we come upon these matters in secular writers, let that admirable light of truth shining in them teach us that the mind of man, though fallen and perverted from its wholeness, is nevertheless clothed and ornamented with God's excellent gifts. If we regard the Spirit of God as the sole fountain of truth, we shall neither reject the truth itself, nor despise it wherever it shall appear, unless we wish to dishonor the Spirit of God. For by holding the gifts of the Spirit in slight esteem, we contemn and reproach the Spirit himself. What then? Shall we deny that the truth shone upon the ancient jurists who established civic order and discipline with such great equity? Shall we say that the philosophers were blind in their fine observation and artful description of nature? Shall we say that those men were devoid of understanding who conceived the art of disputation and taught us to speak reasonably? Shall we say that they are insane who developed medicine, devoting their labor to our benefit? What shall we say of all the mathematical sciences? Shall we consider them the ravings of madmen? No, we cannot read the writings of the ancients on these subjects without great admiration. We marvel at them because we are compelled to recognize how pre-eminent they are. But shall we count anything praiseworthy or noble without recognizing at the same time that it comes from God? Let us be ashamed of such ingratitude, into which not even the pagan poets fell, for they confessed that the gods had invented philosophy, laws, and all useful arts. Those men whom Scripture [1 Cor. 2:14] calls "natural men" were, indeed, sharp and penetrating in their investigation of inferior things. Let us, accordingly, learn by their example how many gifts the Lord left to human nature even after it was despoiled of its true good. . . .

17. Summary of 12-16

To sum up: We see among all mankind that reason is proper to our nature; it distinguishes us from brute beasts, just as they by possessing feeling differ from inanimate things. Now, because some are born fools or stupid, that defect does not obscure the general grace of God. Rather, we are warned by that spectacle that we ought to ascribe what is left in us to God's kindness. For if he had not spared us, our fall would have entailed the destruction of our whole nature. Some men excel in keenness; others are superior in judgment; still others have a readier wit to learn this or that art. In this variety God commends his grace to us, lest anyone should claim as his own what flowed from the sheer bounty of God. For why is one person more excellent than another? Is it not to display in common nature God's special grace, which, in passing many by, declares itself bound to none? Besides this, God inspires special activities, in accordance with each man's calling. Many examples of this occur in the Book of Judges, where it is said that "the Spirit of the Lord took possession" of those men whom he had called to rule the people [ch. 6:34]. In short, in every extraordinary event there is some particular impulsion. For this reason, Saul was followed by the brave men "whose hearts God had touched" [1 Sam. 10:26]. And when Saul's consecration as king was foretold, Samuel said: "Then the Spirit of the Lord will come mightily upon you, and you shall be another man" [1 Sam. 10:6]. And this was extended to the whole course of government, as is said afterward of David: "The Spirit of the Lord came upon him from that day forward" [1 Sam. 16:13]. The same thing is taught elsewhere with respect to particular actions. Even in Homer, men are said to excel in natural ability not only as Jupiter has bestowed it upon each, but "as he leads them day by day." And surely experience shows that, when those who were once especially ingenious and skilled are struck dumb, men's minds are in God's hand and under his will, so that he rules them at every moment. For this reason it is said: "He takes understanding away from the prudent [cf. Job 12:20] and makes them wander in trackless wastes" [Job 12:24; cf. Ps. 107:40]. Still, we see in this diversity some remaining traces of the image of God, which distinguish the entire human race from the other creatures.

6.5

Book II, Chapter 4

1. Man stands under the devil's power, and indeed willingly

Unless I am mistaken, we have sufficiently proved that man is so held captive by the yoke of sin that he can of his own nature neither aspire to good through resolve nor struggle after it through effort. Besides, we posited a distinction between compulsion and necessity from which it appears that man, while he sins of necessity, yet sins no less voluntarily. But, while he is bound in servitude to the devil, he seems to be actuated more by the devil's will than by his own. It consequently remains for us to determine the part of the devil and the part of man in the action. Then we must answer the question whether we ought to ascribe to God any part of the evil works in which Scripture signifies that some action of his intervenes.

Somewhere Augustine compares man's will to a horse awaiting its rider's command, and God and the devil to its riders. "If God sits astride it," he says, "then as a moderate and skilled rider, he guides it properly, spurs it if it is too slow, checks it if it is too swift, restrains it if it is too rough or too wild, subdues it if it balks, and leads it into the right path. But if the devil saddles it, he violently drives it far from the trail like a foolish and wanton rider, forces it into ditches, tumbles it over cliffs, and goads it into obstinacy and fierceness." Since a better comparison does not come to mind, we shall be satisfied with this one for the present. It is said that the will of the natural man is subject to the devil's power and is stirred up by it. This does not mean that, like unwilling slaves rightly compelled by their masters to obey, our will, although reluctant and resisting, is constrained to take orders from the devil. It means rather that the will, captivated by Satan's wiles, of necessity obediently submits to all his leading. For those whom the Lord does not make worthy to be guided by his Spirit he abandons, with just judgment, to Satan's action. For this reason the apostle says that "the god of this world has blinded the minds of the unbelievers," who are destined to destruction, that they may not see the light of the gospel [2 Cor. 4:4]; and in another place that he "is . . . at work in the disobedient sons" [Eph. 2:2]. The blinding of the impious and all iniquities following from it are called "the works of Satan." Yet their cause is not to be sought outside man's will, from which the root of evil springs up, and on which rests the foundation of Satan's kingdom, that is, sin.

2. *God, Satan, and man active in the same event*

Far different is the manner of God's action in such matters. To make this clearer to us, we may take as an example the calamity inflicted by the Chaldeans upon the holy man Job, when they killed his shepherds and in enmity ravaged his flock [Job 1:17]. Now their wicked act is perfectly obvious; nor does Satan do nothing in that work, for the history states that the whole thing stems from him [Job 1:12].

But Job himself recognizes the Lord's work in it, saying that He has taken away what had been seized through the Chaldeans [Job 1:21]. How may we attribute this same work to God, to Satan, and to man as author, without either excusing Satan as associated with God, or making God the author of evil? Easily, if we consider first the end, and then the manner, of acting. The Lord's purpose is to exercise the patience of His servant by calamity; Satan endeavors to drive him to desperation; the Chaldeans strive to acquire gain from another's property contrary to law and right. So great is the diversity of purpose that already strongly marks the deed. There is no less difference in the manner. The Lord permits Satan to afflict His servant; He hands the Chaldeans over to be impelled by Satan, having chosen them as His ministers for this task. Satan with his poison darts arouses the wicked minds of the Chaldeans to execute that evil deed. They dash madly into injustice, and they render all their members guilty and befoul them by the crime. Satan is properly said, therefore, to act in the reprobate over whom he exercises his reign, that is, the reign of wickedness. God is also said to act in His own manner, in that Satan himself, since he is the instrument of God's wrath, bends himself hither and thither at His beck and command to execute His just judgments. I pass over here the universal activity of God whereby all creatures, as they are sustained, thus derive the energy to do anything at all. I am speaking only of that special action which appears in every particular deed. Therefore we see no inconsistency in assigning the same deed to God, Satan, and man; but the distinction in purpose and manner causes God's righteousness to shine forth blameless there, while the wickedness of Satan and of man betrays itself by its own disgrace.

6.6

Selection 6.6: "The Way We Receive the Grace of Christ." In *Institutes of the Christian Religion,* Book III, Chapter 9. Edited by John T. McNeill. Translated and indexed by Ford Lewis Battles. Library of Christian Classics. Philadelphia: Westminster Press, 1960, 712-15.

Book III, Chapter 9

1. *The vanity of this life*

Whatever kind of tribulation presses upon us, we must ever look to this end: to accustom ourselves to contempt for the present life and to be aroused thereby to meditate upon the future life. For since God knows best how much we are inclined by nature to a brutish love of this world, he uses the fittest means to draw us back and to shake off our sluggishness, lest we cleave too tenaciously to that love. There is not one of us, indeed, who does not wish to seem throughout his life to aspire and strive after heavenly immortality. For it is a shame for us to be no better than brute beasts, whose condition would be no whit inferior to our own if there were not left to us hope of eternity after death. But if you examine the plans, the efforts, the deeds, of anyone, there you will find nothing else but earth. Now our blockishness arises from the fact that our minds, stunned by the empty dazzlement of riches, power, and honors, become so deadened that they can see no farther. The heart also, occupied with avarice, ambition, and lust, is so weighed down that it cannot rise up higher. In fine, the whole soul, enmeshed in the allurements of the flesh, seeks its happiness on earth. To counter this evil the Lord instructs his followers in the vanity of the present life by continual proof of its miseries. Therefore, that they may not promise themselves a deep, secure peace in it, he permits them often to be troubled and plagued either with wars or tumults, or robberies, or other injuries. That they may not pant with too great eagerness after fleeting and transient riches, or repose in those which they possess, he sometimes by exile, sometimes by barrenness of the earth, sometimes by fire, sometimes by other means, reduces them to poverty, or at least confines them to a moderate station. That they may not too complacently take delight in the goods of marriage, he either causes them to be troubled by the depravity of their wives or humbles them by evil offspring, or afflicts them with bereavement. But if, in all these matters, he is more indulgent toward them, yet, that they may not either be puffed up with vainglory or exult in self-assurance, he sets before their eyes, through diseases and perils, how unstable and fleeting are all the goods that are subject to mortality.

Then only do we rightly advance by the discipline of the cross, when we learn that this life, judged in itself, is troubled, turbulent, unhappy in countless ways, and in no respect clearly happy; that all those things which are judged to be its goods are uncertain, fleeting, vain, and vitiated by many intermingled evils. From this, at the same time, we conclude that in this life we are to seek and hope for nothing but struggle; when we think of our crown, we are to raise our eyes to heaven. For this we must believe: that the mind is never seriously aroused to desire and ponder the life to come unless it be previously imbued with contempt for the present life.

2. Our tendency to leave unnoticed the vanity of this life

Indeed, there is no middle ground between these two: either the world must become worthless to us or hold us bound by intemperate love of it. Accordingly, if we have any concern for eternity, we must strive diligently to strike off these evil fetters. Now, since the present life has very many allurements with which to entice us, and much show of pleasantness, grace, and sweetness wherewith to wheedle us, it is very much in our interest to be called away now and again so as not to be captivated by such panderings. What, then, I beg of you, would happen if we enjoyed here an enduring round of wealth and happiness, since we cannot, even with evil continually goading us, be sufficiently awakened to weigh the misery of this life?

That human life is like smoke [cf. Ps. 102:3] or shadow [cf. Ps. 102:11] is not only obvious to the learned, but even ordinary folk have no proverb more commonplace than this. And since they counted this something very profitable to know, they have couched it in many striking sayings. But there is almost nothing that we regard more negligently or remember less. For we undertake all things as if we were establishing immortality for ourselves on earth. If some corpse is being buried, or we walk among graves, because the likeness of death then meets our eyes, we, I confess, philosophize brilliantly concerning the vanity of this life. Yet even this we do not do consistently, for often all these things affect us not one bit. But when it happens, our philosophy is for the moment; it vanishes as soon as we turn our backs, and leaves not a trace of remembrance behind it. In the end, like applause in the theater for some pleasing spectacle, it evaporates. Forgetful not only of death but also of mortality itself, as if no inkling of it had ever reached us, we return to our thoughtless assurance of earthly immortality. If anyone in the meantime croaks the proverb "Man is the creature of a day," we indeed admit it: but with no attention, so that the thought of perpetuity nonetheless remains fixed in our minds. Who, then, can deny that it is very much worthwhile for all of us, I do not say to be admonished with words, but by all the experiences that can happen, to be convinced of the miserable condition of earthly life; inasmuch as, even when convinced, we scarcely cease to be stunned with a base and foolish admiration of it, as if it contained in itself the ultimate goal of good things. But if God has to instruct us, it is our duty, in turn, to listen to him calling us, shaking us out of our sluggishness, that, holding the world in contempt, we may strive with all our heart to meditate upon the life to come.

3. Gratitude for earthly life!

But let believers accustom themselves to a contempt of the present life that engenders no hatred of it or ingratitude against God. Indeed, this life, however crammed with infinite miseries it may be, is still rightly to be counted among those blessings of God which are not to be spurned. Therefore, if we recognize in it no divine benefit, we are already guilty of grave ingratitude toward God himself. For believers especially, this ought to be a testimony of divine benevolence, wholly destined, as it is, to promote their salvation. For before he shows us openly the inheritance of eternal glory, God wills by lesser proofs to show himself to be our Father. These are the benefits that are daily conferred on us by him. Since, therefore, this life serves us in understanding God's goodness, should we despise it as if it had no grain of good in itself? We must, then, become so disposed and minded that we count it among those gifts of divine generosity which are not at all to be rejected. For if testimonies of Scripture were lacking, and they are very many and very clear, nature itself also exhorts us to give thanks to the Lord because he has brought us into its light, granted us the use of it, and provided all the necessary means to preserve it.

And this is a much greater reason if in it we reflect that we are in preparation, so to speak, for the glory of the Heavenly Kingdom. For the Lord has ordained that those who are one day to be crowned in heaven should first undergo struggles on earth in order that they may not triumph until they have overcome the difficulties of war, and attained victory.

Then there is another reason: we begin in the present life, through various benefits, to taste the sweetness of the divine generosity in order to whet our hope and desire to seek after the full revelation of this. When we are certain that the earthly life we live is a gift of God's kindness, as we are beholden to him for it we ought to remember it and be thankful. Then we shall come in good time to consider its most unhappy condition in order that we may, indeed, be freed from too much desire of it, to which, as has been said, we are of ourselves inclined by nature.

Calvin's Biblical Commentaries

Selections 6.7 through 6.10: *Calvin: Commentaries.* Translated and edited by Joseph Haroutunian in collaboration with Louise Pettibone Smith. Philadelphia: Westminster Press, 1958. The following selections are taken from 163, 282, 295-97, and 330-31.

6.7

And the Word was made flesh. John 1:14.

The Evangelist has already spoken of Christ's coming. He now tells us that he came putting on our flesh and showing himself openly to the world. He touches briefly upon the ineffable mystery that the Son of God put on human nature. Even though brief, he is astonishingly clear. At this point, some mad people amuse themselves with frivolous subtleties and make fools of themselves. They say, The Word is said to have been made flesh in the sense that God conceived the Son in his own mind and then sent him into the world as a man; as though the Word were I do not know what sort of shadowy image. But we have shown that the statement refers to a real hypostasis in the essence of God.

By saying "flesh," the writer expresses himself more forcibly than if he had said *He was made man.* He means to state that the Son of God, for our sakes, left the height of his heavenly glory and humbled himself to a state at once low and abject. When Scripture speaks of man with contempt, it calls him *flesh.* In spite of the vast distance between the spiritual glory of the

Word of God and the stink of our filthy flesh, the Son of God stooped so low as to take upon himself this same flesh which is subject to so many miseries. *Flesh* here means not, as so often with Paul, our nature corrupted by sin, but mortal men in general. Still, it refers to our nature with disdain as frail and perishing; so we read in Scripture in Ps. 78:39, *Thou art mindful that they are flesh,* and in Isa. 40:6, *All flesh is grass.* (There are other passages of this kind.) At the same time, however, we must notice that this is a figure of speech: [flesh], which is one part of man, stands for him as a whole. Therefore Apollinaris was foolish to fancy that Christ put on a human body without the soul.

6.8

And his disciples asked him saying, Master, who did sin, this man, or his parents, that he was born blind? John 9:2.

First, since Scripture testifies that all the troubles of humanity arise from sin, whenever we see anyone in misery it naturally occurs to us at once that his distress is a punishment inflicted by the hand of God. Thus we err in three ways. First, few judge themselves as severely as they do others. If my brother meets adversity, right away I see the judgment of God in it. When God chastises me with an even heavier rod, I shut my eyes to my sins. But in passing judgment, a man ought to begin with himself; he ought not to spare himself more than others. If we would be just in this matter, we ought to be quicker to discern evil in ourselves than in others. Secondly, excessive rigor is wrong. No sooner do we find someone meeting disaster at God's hand than we jump to the conclusion that it is because God hates him. We turn his faults into crimes and almost despair of his salvation. On the contrary, we so belittle sins in our own case that we hardly see as little faults what we ought to confess as gross wickedness. In the third place, we sin by freely casting off as damned those whom God is trying with a cross.

It is true, as we said above, that all misery arises from sin. But it is also true that God afflicts his own for various reasons. Now, God does not avenge certain crimes in this world, but postpones punishment to the next, to deal with them all the more severely; conversely, he often deals severely with his faithful people, not because they have sinned greatly, but in order to mortify the sin of the flesh. At times he overlooks their sins; he tries their obedience

243

and trains them in patience. Take the case of Job, who suffered more calamity than other men; God was not concerned with his sins. His purpose was rather to make a better trial of Job's faith through his various afflictions. Therefore, the interpreters who attribute all suffering indiscriminately to sin are fools — as though all were punished equally, or as though in afflicting men, God had regard only to each man's desert!

6.9

At that time, Jesus answered and said, I thank thee, O Father, Lord of heaven and earth, because thou hast hid these things from the wise and prudent, and hast revealed them unto babes. Even so, O Father, so it seemed good in thy sight. Matt. 11:25-26.

It is certain that he gave thanks to the Father on their behalf and for their sakes, so that they might not be offended because the church appears so lowly and mean. We are always looking for splendor, and nothing seems more absurd than that the Heavenly Kingdom of the Son of God, the glory of which is celebrated with such magnificence by the prophets, should consist of the dregs and nobodies of low-class peoples. And surely it is an amazing counsel of God that when he had the whole earth in his hands he chose his people out of the contemptible folk, rather than out of the upper classes who might have brought the name of Christ greater credit through their own excellencies. But here Christ sets his disciples apart from the proud, from the high and mighty, so that they will not dare to despise the mean and obscure condition of the church with which he himself is well pleased and happy. Besides, in order to suppress more effectively the curiosity which is constantly creeping into people's minds, he goes beyond the realm of cause and effect, and contemplates the secret judgments of God, in order to lead others to wonder at them with him. Even though God's judgment shows him certainly to be of a mind quite different from our own, our pride is nonetheless insanely blind if we cry out against God's judgment while Christ who is our Head bows his head to it and adores it. But let us consider further the statement *I acknowledge to thee, O Father*. With these words, he testifies to his acquiescence in the decree of the Father, which accords so ill with the mind of man. There is here a hidden contrast between the praise which he renders to God and the malicious calumnies, and even the insolent barkings, of the world. It is clear that he glorifies the Father, because even though he is the Lord of the whole world, he has preferred babies and simple folk to those who are wise. Now, in this context, it is not without significance that he calls the Father *the Lord of heaven and earth*. In this way he declares that the distinction between the wise who act as blind men, and the uncouth and ignorant who embrace the mysteries of the gospel, depends on nothing else than the will of God. There are many other passages of this kind, where God shows that those who attain salvation are the ones whom he himself has chosen freely; for he is the Creator and Fashioner of the world, and all nations are his own.

This verse is impressive in two respects. The fact that not all receive the gospel is not due to the impotence of God, who could readily make all creatures submit to his empire. Secondly, that some arrive at faith, while others remain stupefied and obstinate, is due to his free election. He draws some to himself and passes others by; and in so doing, he himself distinguishes among men, whose situation by nature is the same. It is for his own glory that he elects little children rather than the wise. The flesh is much too zealous to set itself up. If clever and learned men were to have an advantage, then everybody would assume that faith is acquired by human skill, or industry, or knowledge. There is no other way in which the mercy of God can stand out more clearly than in God's way of choosing; for thus it becomes evident that men come to God empty-handed. Therefore, it is right that the wisdom of men should be overthrown; because in this way it will not obscure the glory of God's grace.

But someone will ask, Whom does Christ call the wise, and whom, little children? Experience teaches us clearly that not all those who are ignoramuses and uncultivated men receive the light and believe; and not all who are prudent or literate are left to their blindness. Therefore, they who are here called prudent and wise are those who, inflated with the devil's own arrogance, cannot bear to hear Christ speaking to them from his own height. And yet, as we are taught by the example of Paul, whose fierce zeal was overcome by Christ, it is not always the case that God reprobates those who have too high an opinion of themselves. And when we go down and look at the uncultivated crowd, we find that the majority of them are poisonously mean, and left for destruction together with those who are great men and noble. . . . Christ is the master of the humble, and the first principle of faith is, "Let none be wise in his own eyes." But what matters is not the willingness of men to become like children. Rather, Christ's discourse enlarges upon the grace of the Father, who does not disdain to go down to the weak, and to pull the paupers out of their filth. . . .

Even so, Father. These words remove every excuse for the kind of unlawful nosiness which always pleases us. Nothing is more difficult for God than to draw out of us an unquestioning acceptance of his will as rational and just. He teaches us often that his judgments are a deep abyss; and still we are impetuous enough to plunge headlong into its depths. And when anything does not suit us, we growl and murmur against him; and many break out in open blasphemy. Against all this, God has laid down the rule that we accept whatever pleases him as right. Sober wisdom is precisely this, that one good pleasure of God is more than a thousand reasons. Christ certainly could have brought out many reasons for the distinctions God makes among the people. But, satisfied with God's good pleasure, he did not search further into God's calling children rather than others to salvation; nor did he ask why God wills to fill his Kingdom with these sheep and nobodies. It is evident from this that people rage against Christ himself when they raise a hue and cry upon hearing that by the will of God some are freely chosen and others are rejected; they do it because they cannot bear to let God have his way.

6.10

The foreign born you shall not oppress nor plunder; for you were foreigners in the land of Egypt. You shall not afflict widows and orphans. Exod. 22:21-22; Lev. 19:33-34. (Calvin's wording.)

Before passing on to other iniquities, I thought it best to insert here the commandment which requires the people to deal justly with all without exception. If no mention had been made of the foreign born, the Israelites would have thought that when they harmed no one of their own race they had discharged their duty. But when God includes guests and resident aliens as well as members of their own families, they know that justice must be practiced always toward all.

And there is need for God to set himself and his guardianship against injury to foreigners. For they have no one willing to incur hatred in their defense, and are the more subject to the violence and oppression of the wicked because they lack the protections possessed by the native born.

Widows and orphans are in the same situation. The woman on account of her sex is exposed to various injuries unless she is sheltered in the shade of her husband. And many people take advantage of orphans as if they were legitimate prey because they have no adviser. But God hastens to bring his help when they are without human aid, and he declares that he will be their vindicator if they are unjustly treated.

In the first passage (Exod. 22:21-23), the law joins orphans and widows with the foreign born; in the second (Lev. 19:33-34), only the foreign born are mentioned. But the principle is the same. All those who are orphaned or otherwise deprived of earthly resources are under the guidance and guardianship of God and are protected by his hand. This ought to restrain the boldness of those who think that their crimes will remain unpunished if no one on earth takes action against them.

Truly no iniquity will remain unpunished by God. But there is a special reason why God declares that he takes the foreign born, the widows, and the orphans as his wards. Where evil is more flagrant, there is more need of potent remedy. . . .

In the second passage, it is said further that they are ordered to love outsiders and the foreign born as themselves. Hence it is clear that the term *neighbor* is not restricted to those of the same blood or to those who are the same sort of people, among whom the need of love is more obvious. *Neighbor* includes the whole of mankind, as Christ showed in the person of the Samaritan who took pity on an unknown man and showed him human kindness when he had been neglected by a Judean, and even by a Levite.

CALVIN'S SERMONS ON THE TEN COMMANDMENTS

6.11

Selection 6.11: "Sermon Six: Deuteronomy 5:13-15." From *John Calvin's Sermons on the Ten Commandments*. Edited and translated by Benjamin W. Farley. Grand Rapids: Baker, 1980. This selection is taken from 126-27.

Now nonetheless it is true that the rich can certainly help the poor. When a man has servants and chambermaids working for him, he does not set his servant above himself at table, nor does he permit him to sleep in his bed. But in spite of any [right of] superiority which might exist, it is essential that we always arrive at this point: that we are united together in one flesh as we are all made in the image of God. If we believe that those who are descended of Adam's race are our flesh and our bone, ought that not make us subject to humanity, though we behave like savage beasts toward each other? When the prophet Isaiah wants to persuade men of their inhumanity, he says: "You shall not despise your flesh." That is how I must behold myself in a mirror, in light of how many human beings there are in the world. That is one point.

But there is still more: that is that the image of God is engraved in all men. Therefore not only do I despise my [own] flesh whenever I oppress anyone, but to my fullest capacity I violate the image of God. Therefore let us carefully note that God willed in this passage to point out to those who are in authority and who receive esteem, who are richer than others and who enjoy some degree of honor, that they must not abuse those who are under their hand; they must not torment them beyond measure. They must always reflect on the fact that we are all descended from Adam's race, that we possess a common nature, and that even the image of God is engraved on us. That is what we have to note. Moreover, our Lord Jesus Christ has descended to earth for the purpose of being entirely destroyed in order to condemn all pride and to show that there is no other means of serving God except in humility. That being the case, he has made us all members of his body, including slaves and those who are masters and superiors, without any distinction.

CALVIN'S LETTER TO MONSIEUR DE RICHEBOURG

6.12

Selection 6.12: "Letter to Monsieur de Richebourg." From *John Calvin: Writings on Pastoral Piety.* Edited and with translations by Elsie Anne McKee. New York: Paulist Press, 2001. This selection is taken from 293-94, 298-99, 300-301.

When I first received the intelligence of the death of Master Claude [Féray] and of your son Louis, I was so utterly overpowered that for many days I was fit for nothing but to weep. And although I was somehow comforted and upheld before the Lord by those aids wherewith He sustains our souls in affliction, with regard to human society, however, I felt as if I were not at all myself. So far at least as regards my discharge of duty, I appeared to myself quite as unfit for it as if I had been half dead. . . .

With reference to my own feelings, if your children had never come hither at all, I should not now be feeling grief on account of the death of Master Claude and Louis. However, this most crushing sorrow, which I suffer on account of both, should never cause me to regret that day on which they were brought hither to us, by the hand of God rather than led by any settled purpose of their own; when that friendship commenced which has not only continued to the end, but which from day to day was rather increased and confirmed. Therefore, given the character they had, I rejoice that they lived under the same roof with me. And since it was appointed them to die, I rejoice also that they died under my roof, where they rendered back their souls into the hands of God more composedly, and in greater circumstances of quiet, than if they had happened to die in those places where they would have experienced greater annoyance from the importunity of those by whom they ought to have been assisted, than from death itself. On the contrary, it was in the midst of pious exhortations, and while firmly calling upon the name of the Lord, that these faithful spirits left this world below, gladly in Christ's company. Nor would I desire now to be free from all this sorrow at the cost of never having known them. I hope to hold their memory ever sacred to me, and even sweet and comforting, to the end of my days.

But what advantage, you will say, is it to me to have had a son of so much promise, since he has been torn away from me in the first flower of his youth? As if, forsooth, Christ had not merited by His death the supreme dominion over the living and the dead. And if we belong to Him (as we ought), why may He not exercise over us the power of life and of death? However brief, therefore, either in your opinion or in mine, the life of your son may have been, it ought to satisfy us that he has finished the course which the Lord had marked out for him. Moreover, we may not reckon him to have perished in the flower of his age, who had grown ripe in the sight of the Lord. For I consider all to have arrived at maturity who are summoned away by death; unless perhaps we would contend with Him, as if He can snatch away anyone before his time. This, indeed, holds true of everyone; but in regard to Louis, it is yet more certain on another and more peculiar ground. For he had arrived at that age when by true evidences he could prove himself a member of the body of Christ: having put forth this fruit, he was taken from us and transplanted. Yes, instead of this transient and vanishing shadow of life, he has gained the real immortality. Nor can you consider yourself to have lost him, whom you will recover in the blessed resurrection in the kingdom of God. For they had both so lived and so died, that I cannot doubt but they are now with the Lord; let us, therefore, press forward toward this goal which they have reached. There can be no doubt but that Christ will bind together both them and us in the same inseparable society, in that incomparable participation in His own glory. Beware, therefore, that you do not lament your son as lost, whom you acknowledge to be preserved by the Lord, that he may remain yours forever, who, at the pleasure of His own will, lent him to you only for a season. . . .

It is difficult, notwithstanding, you will say, so to shake off or suppress the love of a father, as not to experience grief on occasion of the loss of a son. Neither do I insist upon your laying aside all grief. Nor, in the school of Christ, do we learn any such philosophy as requires us to put off that common humanity with which God has endowed us, that, being human, we should be turned into stones. These considerations reach only so far as this, that you set bounds and, as it were, temper even your most reasonable sadness; that, having shed those tears which were due to nature and to fatherly piety, you by no means give way to senseless wailing. Nor do I by any means interfere because I am distrustful of your prudence, firmness, or high-mindedness; but only lest I might here be wanting and come short in my duty to you. Although, however, this letter shall be superfluous (which I can suppose), you will nevertheless take in good part, because of your distinguished and kindly courtesy, this my perhaps over-anxious importunity — pardonable, however, notwithstanding, because it proceeds from my unbounded affection toward you. Moreover, I have requested Melanchthon and Bucer [with him at the colloquy in Ratisbon] that they would also add their letters to mine, because I entertained the hope that it would not be unacceptable that they too should afford some evidence of their goodwill toward you.

Adieu, most distinguished sir, whom I much respect in the Lord. May Christ the Lord keep you and your family, and direct you all with His own Spirit, until you may arrive where Louis and Claude have gone before.

7 To Develop Relational Autonomy:
On Hegel's View of People with Disabilities

MARTIN WENDTE

"Hegel? Shouldn't he be shelved under 'fiction'?" a friend once asked me. He argued that the appropriate answer would be yes, for two reasons. First, many readers have thrown up their hands and declared Hegel a waste of time, too difficult to be reconstructed in a rational way. Second, what we can understand cannot be taken seriously today, not least Hegel's contention that an entity called "World Spirit" or "Absolute Spirit" rules the whole of history, a history culminating in the Prussian State of the nineteenth century that is in turn presented as the embodiment of God with humans. It is tempting at times to agree with my friend's first point: Hegel is quite often (but not always) a difficult read. Nevertheless, in this introduction I want to show why reading him is worth the effort, and how he remains one of the most interesting thinkers of all time in opening up new perspectives on many facets of reality, including the reality of those with disabilities. Hegel's project is on the cutting edge of modernity and shows how the whole tradition of modern thinking can be taken seriously in a Christian theology. He does present, however, a strongly biased view of disabled people. By emphasizing that a person is *spirit,* Hegel is able to render *physical* disability irrelevant. But at the same time, he classes *mentally* disabled people as inferior, even as mad, because they do not partake in higher stages of the spirit's development. In the conclusion of this essay I will suggest ways to read Hegel against Hegel, discovering potential in his thought that is much more hospitable to those with mental disability. I will argue that the development of the spirit (as Hegel's main insight into human nature) is something in which all humans partake, including people with mental disabilities. I will further argue that

Hegel's own understanding of the form and content of Christianity opens the way to the inclusion of mentally disabled people in one of the highest stages of the development of spirit, religion, because Christianity is the paradigm of religion because it takes forms open to everyone such as narratives and liturgies.

Understanding Hegel's remarks on disabled people will require a bit of stage-setting. Therefore, I will first locate Hegel in the development of modernity in order to indicate what a radical and relevant thinker he is (I). Second, I will briefly reconstruct his famous dialectical method, which shapes his approach to every material discussion, including his thoughts on disabled people (II). Third, I will sketch how his system as a whole develops out of his method, locating his texts on disabled people within the system (III). These wider perspectives will facilitate a thorough exegesis of Hegel's remarks on disabled people (IV), before allowing me to conclude with some suggestions about what Hegel could have said about disability had he applied some of his deeper insights in a more sympathetic way (V).

I. Reflexivity's Reflexivity: On Hegel's Place in Modernity

"Modernity" is a term for an extremely complex phenomenon that touches and molds every dimension of human life. The early Enlightenment was the philosophical strand of early modernity that tried to express its inner core, making explicit what, implicitly, shapes or should shape all other aspects of modernity, such as politics, economics, the public, and so on. The philosophical thought that shapes modernity as a whole is freedom, or autonomy. The latter term has Greek roots. It consists of the two words "autos" and "nomos," "your own" and "law." Thus, it emphasizes that in the realm of theoretical reason, reason is giving itself its own laws which it then has to follow. Reason could be thus compared to a game, with rules that determine how it works, and reason does not only play the game, but also provides its own rules for it. This has two implications. Nothing ought to be taken as true just because a certain authority (such as the tradition or the church) says so. Instead, all knowledge has to be critically examined by reason. And reason itself, as the entity which critically examines all knowledge, is grounded in nothing but itself. Thus, the standard for measuring reason is not a holy scripture or an order of the cosmos. Reason sets forth its own standards. In the realm of practical reason, humans should live according to their self-given rules. They should follow any authority (the tradition, the church, the state) only insofar as its rules are reasonable. This is to bring into view a theme around which the rest of this introduction will orbit: The anthropology connected to the Enlightenment often is cognitivistic, emphasizing the human faculty of reason and sometimes underplaying the fact that humans are first of all living, embodied beings.

With the work of Immanuel Kant (1724-1804), Enlightenment reason reached a new stage, becoming reflexive, that is, more self-conscious. Kant did not just criticize all traditional claims by autonomous reason, but examined more closely how reason functions. If all knowledge is judged by reason, and if reason is grounded in nothing outside of itself, how does reason itself work? Kant's main work, the *Critique of Pure Reason* (1781), is an extended answer to this question. Kant's "Copernican revolution" was the claim that reason is self-grounded and autonomous because reason itself brings the way we structure reality (i.e., the categories) to reality. For example, when we see an apple, our senses provide us with raw data only, and reason structures these data so that we see the apple *as* an apple, a red, round fruit (Kant 1993, 15 [B XVI]). This does not imply that we structure our sense impressions in a merely subjective way, but does in the end admit that there is a final gap between our thoughts and reality as it is apart from our thoughts about it, which Kant names the "thing-in-itself" *(Ding an sich)*. We cannot know about the thing-in-itself, but merely about how reality appears as a phenomenon, or object of our perception.

The work of Georg Wilhelm Friedrich Hegel (1770-1831) grows from two fundamental criticisms of the Kantian self-examination of reason (criticism which implies that reflexivity itself becomes reflexive). First, Hegel rejects Kant's idea of the thing-in-itself, reaffirming that our mental categories do in fact meet reality as it is in itself. Because our thoughts and reality are marked by the same categories, we do not just know about the phenomena of the world, but also about the thing-in-itself. Second, rational categories are not simply given, invariably innate in our mind. Rather, humankind develops them throughout history and in the communities in which it lives. With this move the Enlightenment reaches another turning point, because Hegel emphasizes the historical and relational side of reason. Reason enters history. Our autonomy takes place in a range of relationships; our autonomy is relational.

Three aspects of Hegel's relational autonomy deserve further attention. First: How is relational autonomy performed? According to Hegel, human beings are mainly spirit *(Geist)*. Although humans are spirit in connection to their bodies, Hegel does not escape the cognitivistic tendency of the earlier

Enlightenment. Spirit is characterized by what Hegel calls "negation." Humans as spirit leave themselves (they negate their unreflective initial starting point, which Hegel calls their immediacy) and move toward somebody or something else: they meet somebody or work on something. In this relationship they are truly themselves in gaining relational autonomy. Think of love: If we are in love, we are truly ourselves by being together with the beloved one. In this way, humans remain present to themselves in the other, integrating the other into their spirit. Relational autonomy is gained via this logic of negation, or via this dialectic movement. From a philosophical perspective, this process of remaining present to oneself in the other happens if the philosopher discovers reason in reality. But the moment in which humans discover that reality out there is formed by reason, the abstract otherness of reality is overcome, and reality is integrated into reason.

Second: Before we take a closer look at this dialectical movement, it is important to emphasize that Hegel understands it as continually operating, integrating ever-new aspects of otherness into spirit. History as a whole is this process of negating immediacy, the integration of otherness. Philosophy is the process of becoming aware of these processes. Thus, Hegel understands his philosophy as the culmination of the whole of history, of the history of philosophy, and therefore, of modernity, because his philosophy integrates all of reality, all otherness into his system. Reason enters history so that all of history may be encompassed into reason. Hegel is called an "idealist" for casting his whole project as encompassing all finite reality into spirit (cf. Hegel 1969, 154-55).

Third: In this relational, dynamic manner, Hegel develops a philosophical foundation in which reason gains true autonomy. Considering this philosophical foundationalism and its emphasis on autonomy, one might ask what is left for theology to do? In what sense is Hegel a theologian? Hegel approaches religion from a foundational philosophical point of view, trying to find reason in religion. In contrast to many contemporary theologians, and contrasting especially with those who follow the ideas of Karl Barth, Hegel does not first accept revelation as an absolute authority and then attempt to think it through. Taking a philosophical perspective, he is interested in ascertaining whether a religion is rational, whether there is any reason in religion. Where he finds reason in religion, he sees it as integrated into spirit. Hegel finds much that is rational in Christianity, which he understands as embodying his dialectical method in the realm of religion. The life of Jesus Christ begins with the Incarnation, which is itself negated on the cross, before resurrection shows that Christ remains present to himself in the other. Then Pentecost brings this dynamic, relational identity to all humanity. In other words, Christianity is the religion in which we discover that we are spirit, and as such, we are free, autonomous. Therefore, for Hegel, Christianity is the absolute religion. In it, reason and revelation or modernity and religion coincide.

Before we sketch Hegel's all-encompassing system in section III and his statements about disabled people within his system in section IV, I shall briefly develop his dialectic method which drives the system as a whole and therefore his remarks on disability.

II. Remaining Present to Himself in the Other: On Hegel's Dialectical Method

Hegel develops his dialectical method in the final chapter of his *Science of Logic,* entitled "Absolute Idea" (cf. Hegel 1969, 824ff.). Dialectics unfolds in three steps: thesis, antithesis, and synthesis. These three steps are to be understood as naming a process in which a simple, static entity (the thesis) negates itself. By negation, by becoming its other and thereby encompassing its other or its antithesis, the initial thesis gains its true identity as relational, dynamic, autonomous totality: it becomes the synthesis.

We can translate this structure into the main characteristics of Hegel's anthropology. Human beings, who are at first dominated by their immediate, natural surroundings (thesis), gain autonomy by negating their immediate state (antithesis). They develop relationships, become more and more conscious and self-conscious, and remain present to themselves in the other. In this they develop their true nature, spirit, as relational autonomy (synthesis). Thus Hegel presents an account of the human oriented around what humans develop into — their telos — in which its cognitive character is emphasized. The rule governing this process is that the stronger the moment of otherness or negation is, the better the spirit develops. It is of special importance for Hegel's view of disabled people to note that in our lived lives, this mediating process can fail. Humans can get stuck in the initial, static determination by nature. They can resist their integration into the totality of the dialectic process by which they gain their true identity. In this they contradict the process of gaining their true selves as spirit. According to Hegel, this phenomenon lies at the heart of madness and mental disability. One further comment is required if we are to properly understand Hegel's commentaries on disability.

III. The True Is the Whole: On the Architecture of Hegel's System

The aim of Hegel's dialectic method is to understand the whole of reality and integrate it into his conceptual system. As he famously put it, "The True is the whole" (Hegel 1977, 11), and his system is designed to do justice to the True as it unfolds in the three steps of his dialectic method. Its first part dwells on the thesis and is called *Science of Logic*. Here Hegel develops all the categories which form our thoughts and the world alike and therefore also the other two parts of the system. The second part addresses the antithesis and is called *The Philosophy of Nature*. Here logic becomes its other, nature. Finally, in the third part, logic and nature find their synthesis in humans, which Hegel reconstructs as *The Philosophy of Spirit* (often translated in English as *Phenomenology of Spirit*). Each of the three parts is once more divided into three subparts (and each of the subparts is divided into three sub-subparts, and so on). For our purpose, it suffices to note that *The Philosophy of Spirit* is divided into *The Subjective Spirit, The Objective Spirit,* and *The Absolute Spirit*. All three subparts deal with humans, but from different perspectives. The task of *The Subjective Spirit* is to gain self-knowledge. In it, via dialectic processes, human beings understand that they are not determined by nature, but that they are spirit, and as such are free, autonomous. Accordingly, it deals with their souls as they are embedded into nature (Hegel calls this part *Anthropology*), with consciousness as it is related to others *(Phenomenology of Spirit)*, and with reason as it is in itself *(Psychology)*. The task of *The Objective Spirit* is to see how humans use their freedom in their relationships to other people, thereby creating a communal world. Accordingly, it deals with the law *(Law)*, with questions of morality *(Morality)*, and with family, society, and the state *(Ethics)*. In *The Absolute Spirit*, spirit becomes reflexive — humans consciously deal with their true nature, spirit. This takes place in the form of art *(Art)*, in the form of religion, *(The Revealed Religion)*, and in the form of philosophy *(Philosophy)*.

This extended introduction to Hegel's thought in general is necessary because all of his concrete discussions are determined both by his dialectical method and by its place in his conceptual architecture.

IV. Hegel on Disabled People

IV.1. Text 7.1. and 7.2.: Mentally Disabled People as Madmen

Disabled people do not appear at the center of Hegel's thought, and the quantity and type of comments he makes about them bear this out. In fact, he makes only five scattered comments on disability. In none of the three editions of his main work, the *Encyclopedia in Outline* (published in 1817, 1827, and 1830), do we find any remarks on disabled people. Even in the parts of the system that Hegel developed at length and published as independent books, we find, in a peripheral discussion, just one very brief remark on disabled people. This is the remark ("Anmerkung") to §120 in his *Philosophy of Right,* which is an extended account of his teaching on *The Objective Spirit* (**7.6**). The other remarks we find in the lectures that Hegel gave on the different parts of his system. These lectures are extended commentaries on his *Encyclopedia,* illuminating the dark passages therein. These are not Hegel's revised manuscripts; they are student lecture notes collected after his death.

Nevertheless, these rather informal commentaries are especially interesting, because in them we find remarks on disabled people in relation to the three main parts of his system, *The Subjective Spirit, The Objective Spirit,* and *The Absolute Spirit.*

Texts **7.1-5** (located in the *Anthropology* as the first part of the *Subjective Spirit*) are Hegel's most important statement on mentally disabled people, whom, following the terminology of his time, he calls "idiots" or "cretins." Here Hegel describes how the soul — his term for the early stage of our spirit in the process of awakening to self-consciousness and gaining freedom from what was naturally and originally given — slowly frees itself from being determined by nature. Our text is located in the second part of the *Anthropology,* the *The Feeling Soul,* which describes how the feeling soul remains far from conscious knowledge, but the soul is immediately present in the form of feeling. *The Feeling Soul* once more develops in three steps. Our text is part of the description of the second stage, which Hegel calls "self-feeling." Here, the soul is still immersed in its contents, but connects these feelings with itself as center. We thus reach the stage in which two entities come into view: the particular feeling and the soul itself as the center or totality. As §407 states: "The sensitive totality is, in its capacity as individual, essentially the tendency to distinguish itself, and to wake up to the *judgment in itself,* in virtue of which it has *particular* feelings and stands as a *subject* in respect of these aspects of itself" (**7.1**, 122). The conceptual movement is outlined in text 7.1: a particular entity (in this case a feeling) is "idealized," that is, integrated into a totality in which it finds its true self. Or, as Hegel describes it: "The subject as such gives these feelings a place as *its own* in itself. In these private and personal sensations it is immersed, and at the same time, because of the 'ideality' of the particulars, it combines itself in them with itself as a subjective unit" (7.1, 122). This process can fail, and does so when the particular is not integrated into the totality, but pretends to be itself the totality, contradicting its true self as a being properly integrated into a greater whole. As such, it is an isolating sickness, a madness: "In this way the subject finds itself in contradiction between the totality systematized in its consciousness, and the single phase or fixed idea which is not reduced to its proper place and rank. This is Insanity or mental Derangement" (Hegel 1971, 123; 7.2).

As Hegel explains, madness appears in three forms (7.4): as *idiocy* (i.e., mental disability), as the *distracted mind,* and as the *rambling mind.* The rambling mind is the stage in which the soul is aware of the contradiction between the particular and totality. The distracted mind is a prior step, a state in which a soul is totally dominated by a certain, particular content. Idiocy, the most primal of these states, is, however, still characterized by immediacy: it is "the quite indeterminate state of self-absorption" (7.4, 131). Hegel distinguishes between different forms of idiocy. He characterizes natural idiocy as follows: "This is incurable. Particularly what is called *cretinism* comes under this head. This disease is partly sporadic in its occurrence and partly endemic in certain areas, especially in narrow valleys and marshy districts. Cretins are misshapen, deformed persons, often afflicted with goiter; their completely stupid facial expression singles them out, and their undeveloped soul can often find expression only in quite inarticulate sounds" (7.4, 132). Then there is idiocy which is caused by a misfortune such as an epileptic shock or other accident. These permanent forms of idiocy have to be distinguished from its temporal form, because the latter can be healed.

Text 7.6 also addresses mental disability and is best understood as making explicit an implication of texts 7.1-5. This comment is part of *The Objective Spirit,* and is part of Hegel's discussion of how humans use their freedom in their relationships to other people to create a communal world. After presenting (in the first part of *The Objective Spirit*) *The Law* as an entity which abstractly stands over against humans, Hegel deals with *Morality* as the stage in which humans' own free will comes into focus and, along with it, elements such as responsibility and guilt. Accordingly, the second part of *Morality* is called *Intention and Welfare.* Intention is an important aspect of an action that is willed freely by humans, because "the *right of intention* is that the *universal* quality of the action shall have being not only *in itself,* but shall be *known* by the agent and thus have been present all along in his subjective will" (Hegel 1991, 148). This implies that "the *responsibility* of children, imbeciles, lunatics, etc. for their action is either totally *absent* or diminished" (7.6, 148). Because Hegel has already laid great importance on the ability to be held responsible as a crucial aspect of an autonomous self, the irresponsibility of imbeciles is a rather grave problem, because it "allow[s] us to deny the agent the dignity of being a thinking individual and a will" (7.6, 149).

To be mentally disabled, then, means to be stuck at the very beginning of the long process of the spirit in which human reason frees itself and gains true, conscious autonomy. Measured by a cognitivist anthropology, mental disability is a form of madness because it is characterized by the same structure: the soul as the unconscious, not-yet-developed totality of spirit is unable to integrate its particular elements. But it differs from other forms of madness in its immediacy: mentally disabled people are totally self-absorbed. As such they are unable to partake in a responsible way in public life and lack the dignity of being thinking individuals with wills.

IV.2. Text 7.3 to 7.5: Physically Disabled People as Being Dominated by Spirit

A different picture emerges in Hegel's thoughts on bodily impairment. Text 7.7, located in the beginning of the Ethics as the third part of *The Objective Spirit,* can be read as a counterpart to the comments we have so far examined in emphasizing the equality of every human being, irrespective of qualities. Here Hegel defines the state as the way humans realize their freedom, bringing the famous definition that the state "consists in the march of God in the world" (7.7, 279). This state stands in the world and "hence in the sphere of arbitrariness, contingency, and error, and bad behavior may disfigure it in many respects" (7.7, 279). He presses this point by setting up an equivalence that is important for our purposes: "But the ugliest man, the criminal, the invalid, or the cripple, is still a living human being; the affirmative aspect — life — survives in spite of such deficiencies, and it is with this affirmative aspect that we are here concerned" (7.7, 279).

Text 7.8 (an excerpt from Hegel's *Lectures on the Philosophy of Religion* and part of *The Absolute Spirit*) outlines the processes of the spirit becoming reflexive and provides a new perspective on physically disabled people. As spirit, physically disabled humans can also have faith, and having faith renders a physical disability insignificant:

> For example, Christ healed a withered hand [Mark 3:1-5 par.], and at the wedding in Cana he changed water into wine [John 2:1-11]. Whether the guests at the marriage of Cana received more wine or not does not matter in the slightest; that is a wholly insignificant content, and it is no less a matter of contingency whether the man with the withered hand was healed. One ought not to begrudge a man an undamaged hand, but that occurrence carries no special weight, for millions of people go about with withered or crippled limbs, and no one healed *them*. . . . When God speaks, what he says is spiritual, for spirit reveals itself only to spirit. (**7.8**, 338-39)

Hegel thus allows that a miracle may provide a starting point for faith, but to build faith on miracles contradicts our nature as spirit. "Christ himself spoke out, however, against miracles, reproaching the Jews for demanding miracles from him, and telling his disciples 'The Spirit will lead you into truth'" (**7.8**, 338). In this, Hegel reiterates the Enlightenment consensus that miracles are an untenable basis for genuine faith, because the true nature of humans is spirit. For spirit, true communication with oneself, with other people, and with God takes place only via spirit, rendering crippled hands insignificant: "spirit witnesses only concerning spirit, not about external things" (**7.8**, 337). Hegel happily affirms that bodily disabilities are, in themselves, no barrier to true relational autonomy.

Text **7.9**, an excerpt from a later passage of Hegel's *Lectures on the Philosophy of Religion,* emphasizes this dominance of spirit even further and reiterates the irrelevance of miracles for true faith. Hegel now explains how miracles work: "Miracles [are], in general, effects produced by the power of spirit on the natural nexus" (**7.9**, 148). Such action is nothing extraordinary, though: "Speaking generally, spirit is this absolute intervention" (**7.9**, 148). We see it in all kinds of phenomena — for example, in people who die because they are afraid — and in all the phenomena we once called miracles: "In all ages, [there is] infinite faith, infinite trust, [the influence of] spirit unto spirit; cripples are healed, the blind see, the deaf hear, right up to the present day. Unbelief in such effects is based on a superstitious belief in the so-called powers of nature and their independence vis-à-vis spirit" (**7.9**, 148). From the perspective of *The Absolute Spirit,* people, whose true nature is spirit, are characterized by the domination of their nature by their spirit to the extent that physical disabilities are not merely rendered insignificant, but may even be healed by the spirit.

V. Process and Negation: What Did Hegel Say?
What Could He Have Said?

How, then, are we to assess Hegel's views today? Hegel judges disabled people by the standard of his modern, teleological, cognitivistic anthropology, formed by his dialectical method. By these standards, mentally disabled people are seen as inferior, mad, irresponsible beings who are unable to develop their true nature. In contrast, physically disabled people are seen as being able to reach true relational autonomy, for their disability is rendered irrelevant or is even overcome by their true nature, spirit. In these conclusions we can discern the main lines of modern accounts of disability with their teleological and cognitivistic anthropologies.

Happily, there are also resources in Hegel's thought that enable us to draw a different picture. My suggestion is that there are two such resources, both of which are formed by his dialectical method and draw on the embedding of process and negation in Hegel's anthropology. All humans are beings defined by the unending process of becoming spirit. This process is advanced by negation, or resistance, according to one rule: the more negation someone experiences, the more her spirit develops. This implies that *physically* disabled people develop their true nature, spirit, to a greater degree than non-disabled people, because they work their way through more resistance and negation. Accordingly, those without disability can learn from the physically disabled what true relational autonomy is.

Perhaps an alternative view of *mentally* disabled people is also available by drawing on other Hegelian resources, but only if two important corrections are applied. First, we know today that mentally disabled people are not just "self-absorbed" but know and learn much more than they were believed to two centuries ago. Like all people, they too participate in the process of becoming spirit. Second, we have become more aware in the last two centuries that humans as spirit are always closely connected to their bodily faculties. In these respects the disparagement of the mentally disabled in cognitivistic anthropologies needs to be rewritten. With such corrections in place, it would be possible to develop Hegel's emphasis on process and negation by linking it to his reading of Christianity in such a way as to discover in Hegel's thought the following view: In section I we saw that, for Hegel, Christianity is the absolute religion because Christianity perfectly incarnates the dialectical method in the realm of religion. The life of Jesus Christ starts with the Incarnation (as thesis), negates itself on the cross (as antithesis), and is then shown as remaining present to Jesus himself in the resurrected other (as synthesis). By suffering death, Jesus Christ undergoes the most radical otherness possible; in his resurrection, he includes all otherness into the totality of the spirit who, in Pentecost, has come to everyone. Accordingly, mentally disabled people are also freed from being viewed as inferior beings stuck in their particularity, unable to develop. Instead, their process can be appreciated as the open, unending process that characterizes all human life. What follows is, first, to recognize the mentally disabled as communal beings who partake in the realm of the objective spirit, as all humans do. Accordingly, it is the task of the public to enable them to partake in public life and to provide assisting institutions that support their overcoming of their isolation in their particularity. But mentally disabled people can also participate in the realm of the absolute spirit, especially in the form of religion. For religion is not merely the place where humans symbolically deal with their nature as spirit, but is also the place where this content is not presented in the form of a concept, as in philosophy, but in perceptible forms: in narratives, symbols, liturgies. This perceptible form of the Truth of reality is accessible to children, to ordinary people, and, we might add, to mentally disabled people. Accordingly, it is the task of all Christians to enable mentally disabled people to partake in religious life, a claim that assumes that mentally disabled people are to partake in their own way in relational autonomy also.

This sympathetic combination of Hegel's dialectical process of development with his reading of Christianity counteracts his explicit comments on mentally disabled people and suggests new perspectives on disability. Although this perspective will always be threatened by Hegel's cognitivism, if we bring together the modern consciousness of autonomy with Christianity, new and illuminating approaches for a contemporary theology of disability come into being. Mentally disabled people now appear as unities of body and spirit, their spirit being engaged in the unending process of development, in common with the spirit of all humans. The form of religion in general and the content of Christianity in particular would thus appear as an invitation and an obligation to enable mentally disabled people to take part in the sphere of the absolute spirit. Christianity facilitates the development of the relational autonomy which is adequate to them.

REFERENCES

Primary Sources

Hegel, Georg Wilhelm Friedrich. 1991. *Elements of the Philosophy of Right.* Edited by A. W. Wood. Translated by H. B. Nisbet. Cambridge: Cambridge University Press.

————. 1984. *Lectures on the Philosophy of Religion,* Vol. I: *Introduction and the Concept of Religion.* Edited by Peter C. Hodgson. Translated by R. F. Brown, P. C. Hodgson, and J. M. Stewart, with the assistance of J. P. Fitzer and H. S. Harris. Berkeley and Los Angeles: University of California Press.

————. 1985. *Lectures on the Philosophy of Religion,* Vol. III: *The Consummate Religion.* Edited by Peter C. Hodgson. Translated by R. F. Brown, P. C. Hodgson, and J. M. Stewart, with the assistance of H. S. Harris. Berkeley and Los Angeles: University of California Press.

————. 1977. *Phenomenology of Spirit.* Translated by A. V. Miller. Oxford: Oxford University Press.

————. 1971. *Philosophy of Mind: Being Part Three of the "Encyclopaedia of the Philosophical Sciences"* (1830). Translated by William Wallace. Oxford: Clarendon Press.

————. 1969. *Science of Logic.* Translated by A. V. Miller. Atlantic Highlands, N.J.: Humanities Press.

Secondary Sources

Kant, Immanuel. 1993. *Critique of Pure Reason. A Revised and Expanded Translation Based on Meiklejohn.* Edited by Vasilis Politis. Everyman's Library. London: J. M. Dent.

Suggestions for Further Reading

Drüe, Hermann, et al. 2000. *Hegel's "Enzyklopädie der philosophischen Wissenschaften" (1830). Ein Kommentar zum Systemgrundriß.* Frankfurt: Suhrkamp. For those who read German, this book contains lucid commentaries on each part of Hegel's system.

Gamm, Gerhard. 1997. *Der Deutsche Idealismus: Eine Einführung in die Philosophie von Fichte, Hegel, und Schelling.* Stuttgart: Reclam. My reading of modernity in section I is partly built on Gamm's book; see especially 7-35.

Hodgson, Peter C. 2005. *Hegel and Christian Theology: A Reading of the Lectures on the Philosophy of Religion.* Oxford: Oxford University Press. A very good reconstruction of Hegel's philosophy of religion.

Lewis, Thomas A. 2005. *Freedom and Tradition in Hegel: Reconsidering Anthropol-*

ogy, Ethics, and Religion. Notre Dame: University of Notre Dame Press. An excellent monograph on Hegel's anthropology in general and on *The Subjective Spirit* in particular.

Pinkard, Terry. 2000. *Hegel: A Biography.* Cambridge: Cambridge University Press. The authoritative biography that reconstructs both Hegel's life and thought.

Pippin, Robert. 1999. *Modernism as a Philosophical Problem: On the Dissatisfaction of European High Culture.* 2d ed. Oxford: Blackwell. My reading of modernity in section I is partly built on Pippin's book; see especially 1-77.

Taylor, Charles. 1975. *Hegel.* Cambridge: Cambridge University Press. Still the most important, classic, but very long philosophical reconstruction of Hegel's system as a whole in the English-speaking world.

Wendte, Martin. 2007. *Gottmenschliche Einheit bei Hegel: Eine logische und ontologische Untersuchung.* Berlin/New York: de Gruyter. This book reconstructs the dialectical movement as the logical background of the system, applies it to Hegel's philosophy of religion, and ends with an extended critique of Hegel.

Excerpts

7.1

Hegel's *Philosophy of Mind: Being Part Three of the "Encyclopaedia of the Philosophical Sciences"* (1830). Translated by William Wallace. Oxford: Clarendon Press, 1971, 122-39.

(β) *Self-feeling (sense of self)* [Selbstgefühl]

§ 407

(αα) The sensitive totality is, in its capacity as individual, essentially the tendency to distinguish itself in itself, and to wake up to the *judgment in itself,* in virtue of which it has *particular* feelings and stands as a *subject* in respect of these aspects of itself. The subject as such gives these feelings a place as *its own* in itself. In these private and personal sensations it is immersed, and at the same time, because of the "ideality" of the particulars, it combines itself in them with itself as a subjective unit. In this way it is *self-feeling*, and is so at the same time only in the *particular feeling*.

7.2

§ 408

(ββ) In consequence of the immediacy, which still marks the self-feeling, i.e., in consequence of the element of corporeality which is still undetached from the mental life, and as the feeling too is itself particular and bound up with a special corporeal form, it follows that although the subject has been brought to acquire intelligent consciousness, it is still susceptible of disease, so far as to remain fast in a *special* phase of its self-feeling, unable to refine it to "ideality" and get the better of it. The fully furnished self of intelligent consciousness is a conscious subject, which is consistent in itself according to an order and behavior which follows from its individual position and its connection with the external world, which is no less a world of law. But when it is engrossed with a single phase of feeling, it fails to assign that phase its proper place and due subordination in the individual system of the world which a conscious subject is. In this way the subject finds itself in contradiction between the totality systematized in its consciousness, and the single phase or fixed idea which is not reduced to its proper place and rank. This is Insanity or mental Derangement.

In considering insanity we must, as in other cases, anticipate the full-grown and intelligent conscious subject, which is at the same the *natural* self of *self-feeling*. In such a phase the self can be liable to the contradiction between its own free subjectivity and a particularity which, instead of being "idealized" in the former, remains as a fixed element in self-feeling. Mind as such is free, and therefore not susceptible of this malady. But in older metaphysics mind was treated as a soul, as a thing; and it is only as a thing, i.e., as something natural and existent, that it is liable to insanity — the settled fixture of some finite element in it. Insanity is therefore a psychical disease, i.e., a disease of body and mind alike: the commencement may appear to start from the one more than the other, and so also may the cure.

The self-possessed and healthy subject has an active and present consciousness of the ordered whole of his individual world, into the system of which he subsumes each special content of sensation, idea, desire, inclination, etc., as it arises, so as to insert them in their proper place. He is the *dominant genius* over these particularities. Between this and insanity the difference is like that between waking and dreaming: only that in insanity the dream falls within the waking limits, and so makes part of the actual self-feeling. . . . It is the evil genius of man which gains the upper hand in insanity, but in distinction from and contrast to the better and more intelligent part, which is there also. Hence this state is mental derangement and distress. The right psychical treatment therefore keeps in view the truth that insanity is not an abstract *loss* of reason (neither in the point of intelligence nor of will and its responsibility), but only derangement, only a contradiction in a still subsisting reason — just as physical disease is not an abstract, i.e., mere and total, loss of health (if it were that, it would be death), but a contradiction in it. This humane treatment, no less benevolent than reasonable (the services of Pinel towards which deserve the highest acknowledgment), presupposes the patient's rationality and in that assumption has the sound basis for dealing with him on this side — just as in the case of bodily disease the physician bases his treatment on the vitality which as such still contains health.

7.3

Zusatz. What follows may serve to elucidate the above Paragraph:

Already in the *Zusatz* to § 402, we interpreted insanity as the second of the three developmental stages passed through by the feeling soul in its struggle with the immediacy of its substantial content to raise itself to the self-related simple subjectivity present in the "I," whereby it becomes completely self-possessed and conscious of itself. This interpretation of insanity as a necessarily occurring form or stage in the development of the soul is naturally not to be understood as if we were asserting that *every* mind, *every* soul, must go through this stage of extreme derangement. Such an assertion would be as absurd as to assume that because in the Philosophy of Right crime is considered as a necessary manifestation of the human will, therefore to commit crime is an inevitable necessity for *every* individual. Crime and insanity are *extremes* which the human mind *in general* has to overcome in the course of its development, but which do not appear as extremes in every individual but only in the form of limitations, errors, follies, and offenses not of a criminal nature. This is sufficient to justify our consideration of insanity as an essential stage in the development of the soul.

But as regards the determination of the *Notion* of insanity, . . . in insanity the relationship of the psychical element to the objective consciousness is no longer one of mere difference, but of direct opposition, and therefore the two are no longer *mixed*. We will demonstrate here the truth of this statement by a more detailed treatment and thereby prove the rational necessity of the progress of our exposition from the magnetic states to insanity. The necessity of this progress lies in the fact that the soul is already *in itself* the contradiction of being an *individual*, a *singular*, and yet being at the same time immediately identical with the *universal* natural soul, with its substance. This opposition existing in the soul in the contradictory form of identity must be made *explicit* as opposition, as contradiction. This first happens in insanity; for it is first in this state that the subjectivity of the soul not merely separates itself from its substance . . . but comes into direct opposition to it, into complete contradiction with the objective consciousness, thereby becoming a purely formal, empty, abstract subjectivity, and in this its one-sidedness arrogates to itself the significance of a veritable unity of the subjective and the objective. Therefore, the unity and separation in insanity of the opposed sides just mentioned is still an imperfect one. This unity and this separation only exist in their perfection in the rational, actually objective consciousness. When I have raised myself to rational thinking I am not only *for myself, objective to myself*, and therefore a *subjective* identity of the subjective and objective, but I have also *separated* this identity from myself, set it over against me as an actually *objective* identity. In order to achieve this complete separation, the feeling soul must overcome its *immediacy*, its *naturalness* and *corporeality*, must convert this into an ideal moment, appropriate it to itself, thereby transforming itself into an *objective* unity of the subjective and objective and in doing this not only freeing itself from its Other but at the same time discharging this Other from its immediate identity with the feeling soul. But at the stage we are now considering, the soul has not yet reached this goal. Insofar as it is insane, it clings to a *merely subjective* identity of the subjective and objective, rather than to an *objective* unity of these two sides; and only insofar as, with all its folly and derangement, it is still rational and stands therefore on a level *other* than the one now to be considered, does the soul attain to an objective unity of the subjective and objective. In insanity proper, in fact, the two modes of finite mind — the immanently developed, rational consciousness with its objective world, and the world of inner feeling which clings to itself and has its objectivity *within* it — are each developed into a separately existing *totality*, into a separate *personality*. The *objective* consciousness of the insane shows itself in the most diverse ways; they know, for example, that they are in a lunatic asylum; they know their attendants; they also know that the other people there are insane; make fun among themselves of their madness; are employed on all kinds of duties, sometimes even being appointed overseers. But at the same time they are *dreaming while awake* and are *dominated* by a *fixed idea* which they cannot harmonize with their objective consciousness. . . . In insanity proper, on the other hand, the two different personalities are not two different states but are in one and the same state; so that these *negatively* related personalities — the psychical and the intellectual consciousness — have mutual contact and are aware of each other. The insane subject is therefore in communion with himself in the negative of himself; in other words, his consciousness immediately contains the negative of itself. This negative is not vanquished by the insane person; the duality into which it is split up is not brought back to unity. Consequently, though the insane person is *in himself* or *implicitly* one and the same subject, yet he does not know himself objectively as a self-accordant, inwardly undivided subject, but as a subject disrupted into two different personalities.

The *specific* meaning of this derangement, of this self-communion of mind in the *negative* of itself, requires still further elucidation. In insanity this negative requires a concreter significance than it has possessed hitherto in our exposition; just as the self-communion of mind must be taken here in a richer, concreter sense than the being-for-self hitherto attained by the soul.

In the first place, therefore, we must distinguish this negative of the soul characteristic of insanity from the other kind of negative. To illustrate: when we suffer, for example, aches and pains we are also communing with ourselves in a negative, but we need not therefore be mad. This we would be only if we endured the aches and pains without having a rational aim which could only be attained by means of them. For example, a journey to the Holy Sepulcher undertaken for the purpose of fortifying one's soul may be regarded as the act of a lunatic, because such a journey is quite useless for the end in view and is therefore not a necessary means for procuring it. For the same reason, the journeys across whole countries made by Indians crawling on their stomachs can be pronounced the acts of lunatics. The negative endured in insanity is, therefore, one in which only the *feeling,* not the *intellectual* and *rational,* consciousness finds itself again.

But in insanity the *negative* constitutes, as we have just said, a determination which belongs both to the psychical and to the intellectual consciousness in their mutual relation. This relation of these two opposed modes of the *self-communion* of mind likewise requires a more precise characterization to prevent its being confused with the relation in which *mere error* and *folly* stand to the *objective,* rational consciousness.

... Error and folly only become madness when the individual believes his merely subjective idea to be objectively present to him and clings to it in face of the actual objectivity which contradicts it. To the madman, his purely subjective world is quite as real as the objective world. In his merely subjective idea, for example in the fancied belief that he is someone who, in fact, he is not, he has the *certainty of himself,* and his *being* clings to this idea. When addressing a madman one must therefore always begin by reminding him of all the facts and circumstances of his situation, of his concrete actual world. Then, if in spite of being made aware of this objective interrelated whole he still sticks to his false idea, there can be no doubt that such a person is insane.

It follows from what has just been said that an idea can be called *insane* if the madman regards an empty abstraction and a mere possibility as something concrete and actual; for, as we have seen, in this idea abstraction is made from the concrete actual world of the madman. If, for example, I take myself to be a king, although I am very far from being one, this idea which is in contradiction with my total actual world and is therefore insane, has no other ground and content whatever than the indeterminate general possibility that since a man, in general, can be a king, I myself, this particular man, am a king. . . .

In the deranged consciousness, the contradiction between the abstract universality of the immediate, passive "I" and a particular, isolated idea severed from the total actual world, is unresolved. This consciousness is, therefore, not a true self-communion but a self-communion which remains fixed in the negative of the "I." An equally unresolved contradiction prevails here between this particular, isolated idea and the abstract universality of the "I" on the other hand, and the inwardly harmonious total actual world, on the other. This explains why the proposition "What I think is true," which is rightly disputed by a rational intelligence, receives in the mentally deranged a wrong, an irrational meaning and becomes just as false as the counter assertion made by the unintelligence of the abstractive intellect, that the subjective and objective are *absolutely separate.* There is more rationality in even the mere *feeling* of the *healthy* soul than in the said unintelligence or in insanity, since it contains the *actual* unity of the subjective and objective. As we have already said, this unity, however, only receives its perfect form in speculative Reason; for *only* what is thought by *this* is true in regard both to its form and to its content — a *perfect* unity of Thought and Being. In insanity, on the contrary, the unity and the difference of the subjective and the objective still have a merely *formal* significance from which the concrete content of the actual world is excluded.

We wish at this stage to repeat in a more condensed and, if possible, more exact form, something which has already been touched on several times in the above Paragraph and Remark, partly on account of the context and partly with the aim of more fully elucidating it. The point is that insanity must be grasped essentially as an illness *at once mental and physical,* and for this reason, that the unity of the subjective and the objective which prevails in insanity is still wholly *immediate* and is not as yet the outcome of infinite mediation; because the "I" afflicted with insanity, no matter how acute this point of self-feeling may be, is still a natural, immediate, passive "I," and consequently the moment of *difference* can become fixed as a passive, simply affirmative being; or, to put it still more specifically, because in insanity a particular feeling which conflicts with the objective consciousness of the insane person is *held fast,* is *not* transformed into an *ideality,* this feeling consequently having the form of a *simply affirmative,* hence *corporeal,* being, with the result that a *duality of being* is produced in him which is not overcome by his objective consciousness, a difference which remains purely *affirmative* and which becomes for the insane person a fixed limitation. . . .

From what was said at the beginning of this Anthropology about the necessity of starting the philosophical consideration of subjective mind with the natural mind, and from the *Notion of insanity* developed above in all its aspects, it will be sufficiently clear why insanity must be discussed before the healthy, intellectual consciousness, although it has that consciousness for its *presupposition* and is nothing else but the extreme limit of sickness to which the latter can succumb. We had to discuss insanity already in Anthropology because in this state the psychical element, the natural self — abstract, formal subjectivity — gains the mastery over the objective, rational, concrete consciousness, and consideration of the abstract, natural self must precede the exposition of concrete, free mind. . . .

This concludes the remarks we had to make at this point about the Notion of insanity as general.

As regards the various forms of insanity, these are usually classified not so much according to an *inner* characteristic as according to the *manifestations* of this illness; but this is inadequate for the philosophical treatment of the subject. We must recognize that even insanity is a state which is *differentiated within itself* in a *necessary* and therefore rational manner. But a necessary differentiation of this psychical state cannot be derived from the *particular* content of the formal unity of the subjective and the objective present in

insanity; for this content is something infinitely manifold and therefore contingent. On the contrary, therefore, it is on the quite general differences of
form appearing in insanity that we must fix our attention. To this end, we
must refer back to our characterization of insanity as a state in which the
mind is shut up within itself, has sunk into itself, whose peculiarity . . . consists in its being no longer in *immediate contact* with actuality but in having
positively *separated itself* from it.

Now this state in which mind has sunk into itself is, on the other hand, the
general feature in *all* forms of insanity; on the other hand, when it remains this
indeterminate, vacuous state, it forms a *particular* kind of insanity. It is with
this that we have to begin our consideration of the various forms of insanity.

But if this quite indeterminate being-within-self acquires a definite content, is linked to a merely subjective, particular idea and takes this to be
something objective, then we have the second form of insanity.

The third and last form of this illness appears when that which *confronts*
the soul's delusion is also *for* the soul, when the lunatic *compares* his merely
subjective idea with his objective consciousness, discovers the sharp difference existing between the two, and thus obtains the unhappy feeling of his
self-contradiction. Here we see the soul in the more or less despairing effort
to overcome the *discord* which, though already present in the second form of
insanity, is there felt only slightly or not at all, and to restore its *concrete self-
identity*, the inner *harmony* of the self-consciousness which remains unshak-
ably fixed in the *one* center of its actuality.

Let us now consider in more detail these three main forms of insanity.

7.4

1. *Idiocy, the distracted mind, and the rambling mind*

The first of these three main forms, the quite indeterminate state of self-
absorption, appears in the first place as

Idiocy

This takes different forms. There is *natural* idiocy and this is incurable. Particularly what is called *cretinism* comes under this head. This disease is

partly sporadic in its occurrence and partly endemic in certain areas, especially in narrow valleys and marshy districts. Cretins are misshapen, deformed persons, often afflicted with goiter; their completely stupid facial expression singles them out, and their undeveloped soul can often find expression only in quite inarticulate sounds.

But besides this natural idiocy there is also an idiocy which can be caused either by an underserved misfortune or by a person's own fault. With regard to the former class, Pinel cites the example of a congenital idiot whose dull-wittedness was believed to be the result of an extremely violent fright experienced by her mother during pregnancy. Idiocy is often a consequence of frenzy, in which case there is very little hope of cure; epilepsy, too, often terminates in idiocy. But this state is no less frequently brought on by excesses. We may also add that idiocy occasionally manifests as catalepsy, as a complete paralysis of both physical and mental activity. Idiocy occurs, too, not only as a permanent, but also as a transitory, state. For instance an Englishman fell into a state of indifference to everything, first to politics and then to his own affairs and to his family. He would sit quietly, looking straight in front of him and for years did not utter a word, and he appeared to be so dull-witted that it was doubtful whether he knew his wife and children or not. He was cured when someone else, dressed exactly like him, sat opposite him and imitated him in everything he did. This threw the patient into a violent frenzy which forced him to attend to things outside of him and drove him permanently out of his state of self-absorption.

The distracted mind

A further modification of the first main form of insanity under discussion is *distraction*. This consists in a non-awareness of the immediate present. This non-awareness is often the beginning of insanity; but there is also a lofty distractedness far removed from insanity. This can occur when the mind, by profound meditation, withdraws its attention from everything relatively unimportant. Archimedes, for instance, was once so absorbed in a geometrical problem that for several days he seemed to have forgotten everything else and had to be roused by force out of this concentration of his mind on a single point. But distractedness, properly speaking, is an absorption in a quite *abstract self-feeling*, a lapse of the self-possessed objective consciousness into inactivity, into a non-awareness of things of which it should be aware. A person in this state confuses his true situation in a particular case with a false one, apprehends external circumstances in a one-sided manner, not in the totality of their relationships. One of many amusing instances of this psychical state is that of a French count who, when his wig got caught on a chandelier, laughed heartily and looked around to see whose wig had been pulled off and who was showing a bald pate. Another instance of this kind is recorded of Newton. This savant is supposed on one occasion to have taken hold of a lady's finger in order to use it as a tobacco-stopper for his pipe. Such distractedness can be the result of excessive study; it is not uncommon to find it in scholars, especially those of past times. But distractedness is often the outcome, too, of the desire to be universally esteemed, which results in individuals being obsessed with their subjectivity, and in the process forgetting the objective world.

The rambling mind

In contrast to the distracted mind, the rambling mind interests itself in everything. This springs from an inability to *fix* one's attention on anything definite, and consists in the malady of stumbling from one object to another. This malady is mostly incurable. Fools of this kind are the most troublesome. Pinel tells of such a person who was a perfect type of chaos. He says: "This patient approaches me and swamps me with his chatter. Immediately afterwards he does the same thing to someone else. When this individual comes into a room he turns everything in it upside down, shakes chairs and tables and puts them in the wrong places without betraying any particular aim. You have hardly turned your eyes when he is already out in the neighboring street, behaving there just as aimlessly as in the room, chattering, throwing stones, pulling up plants, going on further, turning back, without knowing why." The rambling mind always stems from a weakening of the power of the rational consciousness to hold together the totality of its mental representations. But rambling minds often suffer from delirium — therefore, not merely from a non-awareness of what is immediately present to them but from unconsciously turning it topsy-turvy. So much for the first main form of insanity.

2. *The second main form of insanity — madness proper*

This occurs when the natural mind which is shut up within itself and whose various modifications we have just considered acquires a *definite* content and this content becomes a *fixed idea,* the mind which is not as yet fully self-possessed becoming just as much absorbed in it as in *idiocy* it is absorbed in its own self, in the abyss of its *indeterminateness.* It is hard to say exactly where madness proper begins. For example, in small towns one finds people, especially women, who are so absorbed in an extremely limited circle of particular interests and who feel so comfortable in this narrow life of theirs that we rightly call them crazy. But madness in the narrower meaning of the word implies that the mind is fixed in a single, merely subjective idea and accords it objective significance. This psychical state mostly comes about when someone who is dissatisfied with his actual world shuts himself up in his subjectivity. The passion of vanity and pride is the chief cause of this psychical self-imprisonment. Then the mind which is thus nestled in its interior life easily loses its understanding of the actual world and is at home only in its subjective ideas. This behavior can soon give rise to complete madness. For should there be any vitality in this solitary consciousness, the latter will readily be led to create some content or other from its own resources and to regard this purely subjective content as objective and to *fix* it as such. For whereas, as we have seen, in idiocy and in the rambling mind the soul does not possess the power to hold on to anything definite, this power *is* possessed in madness proper and by this very fact demonstrates that it is still consciousness, that in madness there is, therefore, still a *differentiation* of the soul from its content, from its *fixed* idea. Therefore, although on the one hand this content forms part of the madman's consciousness, yet, on the other hand, the latter's universal nature enables it to transcend the particular content of the insane idea. Therefore madmen, beside their craziness on one point, at the same time possess a proper, rational consciousness, a correct appreciation of things and the ability to act rationally. This, in addition to the suspicious reserve of madmen, makes it possible that sometimes a madman is not at once recognized as such and, in particular, that there can be doubts about his cure and consequent discharge.

The differences between madmen are mainly determined by the multifarious ideas which become fixed in them.

Disgust with life can be reckoned as one of the most indefinite forms of madness when it is not caused by the loss of loved and worthy persons or by a breakdown in the ethical sphere. An indefinite, unfounded disgust with life is not an *indifference* to it, for in the latter case life is endured; rather is it the inability to endure it, a fluctuation between desire for and aversion to everything pertaining to the actual world, an imprisonment in the fixed idea of the loathsomeness of life associated with an effort to overcome this idea. It is mostly the English who succumb to this quite irrational disgust with the actual world, as well as to other forms of madness; perhaps because with them the tenacious clinging to subjective particularity is so prevalent. In the English, this disgust with life is manifested mainly as *melancholy,* the state in which the mind constantly broods over its unhappy idea and is unable to rise to spontaneous thought and action. Not infrequently this psychical state develops into an uncontrollable impulse to commit suicide; sometimes this impulse has only been eradicated by the victim being violently taken out of himself. For instance, the story is told of an Englishman who was on the point of drowning himself in the Thames when he was attacked by robbers; he offered the fiercest resistance, and suddenly feeling that life was worthwhile, he lost all thoughts of suicide. Another Englishman who had hanged himself, on being cut down by his servant not only regained the desire to live but also the disease of avarice; for when discharging the servant, he deducted twopence from his wages because the man had acted without instructions in cutting the rope with which his master had hanged himself.

Over against the indeterminate form of mental derangement just delineated in which all spontaneity is extinguished, there is an endless variety of forms of insanity having a *single, isolated* content, in which the patient is vividly, passionately interested. In some cases this content depends on the particular passion which occasioned the insanity; but it can also be determined by some other chance circumstances. In the first group we should have to include those lunatics who, for example, take themselves to be God, or Christ, or a king. The second group, on the other hand, comprises lunatics who, for example, imagine themselves to be a grain of barley, or a dog, or to have a carriage in their stomach. But in both cases the *simple* lunatic has no *definite awareness* of the *contradiction* which exists between his fixed idea and the objective world. We alone are aware of this contradiction; the lunatic himself is not tormented by the feeling of his inner disruption.

3. *The third main form of insanity — mania or frenzy*

Only in this third form do we find that the maniac himself is aware of the disruption of his consciousness into two mutually contradictory modes, that the maniac himself has a vivid feeling of the contradiction between his merely subjective idea and the objective world, and yet cannot rid himself of this idea but is fully intent on making it an actuality or on destroying what is actual. It is implied in this notion of mania that it need not spring from an empty conceit, but can be brought about especially by a stroke of great misfortune, by a derangement of a person's individual world, or by the violent upheaval and putting out of joint of the general state of the world if the individual lives with his feelings exclusively in the *past* and is thus unable to find himself in the *present* by which he feels himself alike repelled and bound. In the French Revolution, for example, the almost complete collapse of civil society caused many people to become insane. Religious causes can often produce the same effect in the most frightful manner, when the individual is plunged into absolute uncertainty whether God's grace has been granted to him.

But in maniacs, the feeling of their inner disruption can equally well be a *tranquil* pain as it can also develop into a rage of reason against unreason and vice versa, and thus become a *frenzy*. For this unhappy feeling of the maniac very easily joins itself not only to a hypochondriacal mood which torments him with whims and fancies, but also to a suspicious, false, jealous, mischievous, and malicious disposition, to a furious resentment against the restraints imposed on him by his actual environment, against those from whom he suffers a limitation of his will; just as, conversely, in those *spoilt* individuals who are accustomed to getting their own way in everything, their rambling, headstrong nature easily turns to mania when the rational will which desires the universal opposes a dam to their caprice, a dam which their overweening subjectivity is unable to break through. Fits of ill-will occur in everyone; but the ethical, or at least prudent, person knows how to subdue them. But in mania, where one particular idea usurps the authority of the rational mind, the particularity of the subject manifests itself unchecked, and the natural impulses and those developed by reflection belonging to this particularity consequently throw off the yoke of the moral laws rooted in the truly universal will, with the result that the dark, infernal powers of the heart are set free. The madman in his rage often develops a positive mania for injuring others and, though he may have a horror of murder, may even be seized with a sudden irresistible desire to kill those whom otherwise he loves tenderly. But as we have just indicated, the malice of the maniac does not prevent him from having moral and ethical feelings; on the contrary, just because of his distress, just because he is mastered by the *unmediated opposition* present in him, these feelings can have an increased intensity. Pinel expressly states that nowhere has he seen more affectionate spouses and fathers than in lunatic asylums.

As regards the *physical* side of mania, its manifestation is often connected with general changes in Nature, especially with the course of the sun.

Very hot and very cold seasons exercise a particular influence in this connection. It has also been noticed that the approach of storms and abrupt changes in the weather produce temporary disturbances and outbursts among lunatics. With regard to age, it has been observed that mania does not usually occur before the age of fifteen. As regards other physical differences, it is known that in strong, muscular persons with black hair, fits of rage are usually more violent than in blond individuals. But to what extent insanity is connected with a morbid condition of the nervous system is a point which does not come within the purview of the physician who considers insanity from the outside, or of the anatomist.

7.5

The cure of insanity

The last point we have to discuss in connection with mania and insanity relates to the curative method to be applied to both diseases. This method is partly physical and partly psychological. In some cases the former alone is sufficient; but in most cases it is necessary to supplement this by psychological treatment which, in its turn, can sometimes effect a cure by itself. There is no known remedy universally applicable for the physical side of treatment. The medical remedies employed are, on the contrary, for the most part empirical and therefore uncertain in their action. But this much is certain, that the worst method of all is the one formerly practiced at Bedlam, which was limited to a thorough purging of the lunatics four times a year. Sometimes, though, the mentally deranged have been physically cured by the very thing that is liable to cause insanity in those not afflicted, namely, by falling heavily on their heads. The celebrated Montfaucon is said to have been cured of his imbecility in this way in his youth.

But the most effective treatment is always psychological. While this is unable to cure idiocy, it can often be successful in the treatment of insanity proper and mania because in these psychical states consciousness is still spontaneously active, and along with an insanity connected with a *particular* idea, there also exists a consciousness which in its other ideas is rational, and from this a skillful psychiatrist is able to develop sufficient power to overcome the particular fixed idea. (It is the merit of Pinel in particular to have grasped this residue of rationality in lunatics and maniacs as the foundation of treatment and to have conducted his treatment of such persons accordingly. His paper on this subject must be considered the best in this sphere of medicine.)

In the psychological treatment of the insane, it is more important than anything else to win their confidence. This can be won because the insane are still moral beings. But the surest way to win their confidence is to be quite frank with them yet at the same time not to let this frankness degenerate into a direct attack on their insane idea. Pinel relates an example of this method of treatment and of its successful outcome. A hitherto amiable man became insane, and to prevent him doing injury to others he had to be locked up. This put him in a rage and he had to be bound, which made him even more furious. He was therefore put in a lunatic asylum. Here the warden entered into a quiet conversation with him and gave in to his absurdities, which calmed him. He then ordered his bonds to be removed, led him into his new house, and by continuing this kind of treatment cured this lunatic in a very short time. After the confidence of the insane has been won, one must try to obtain a proper authority over them and to awaken in them the feeling that there are, in general, things of importance and worth. The insane feel their mental weakness, their dependence on the rational person. This makes it possible for the latter to win their respect. In learning to respect the one who is treating him, the lunatic acquires the ability forcibly to restrain his subjectivity, which is in conflict with the objective world. So long as he is unable to do this himself, others have forcibly to restrain him. Consequently if, for example, a lunatic refuses to eat, or even destroys things around him, then obviously this cannot be tolerated. It is particularly necessary — and this is often very difficult in the case of persons of rank, such as George III, for instance — to humble the conceitedness of the proud maniac by making him feel his dependence. Pinel gives a noteworthy example of this form of mania and of the method of treating it.

An individual who took himself to be Mahomet arrived at the lunatic asylum full of pride and arrogance, demanded homage, issued daily a host of decrees of banishment and death, and raved in royal fashion. Now although his delusion was not corrected, he was forbidden to give way to raving, as this was unbecoming, and when he did not obey he was locked up and reprimanded for his conduct. He promised to improve his behavior, was discharged, but began again to give way to fits of rage. This "Mahomet" was now roughly dealt with, again locked up, and informed that he must expect no more mercy. But the warden's wife, by an agreed arrangement, pretended to be touched by his earnest entreaties for liberty and asked him to promise faithfully not to abuse his freedom by giving way to outbursts of rage because this caused her unpleasantness. He gave his promise and was then released. From this moment onwards he behaved well. If he fell into a rage, a glance from the warden's wife was sufficient to send him to his room to hide his rage there. The respect he had for this woman and his determination to conquer his fits of rage restored him to sanity in six months.

As in the case just cited, it is most important always to remember that if at times it is necessary to deal severely with the insane, *in general* they deserve considerate treatment because their rational nature is not yet entirely destroyed. For this reason, the restraint which has to be applied to these unfortunates should always be of such a kind as to have the moral significance of a just punishment. Lunatics still have a feeling of what is right and good; they know, for example, that one should not harm others. Consequently they can be made aware of the wrong they have committed, can be made accountable for it and punished for it, and can be made to see the justice of the punishment meted out to them. Thereby their better self is encouraged, and when this happens they gain confidence in their own moral strength. Having reached this point, they become capable by associating with good people of recovering completely. On the other hand, the moral self-feeling of the insane can be so easily wounded by harsh, arrogant, contemptuous treatment that they fly into the most furious rage and frenzy. Also, one should not be so imprudent, especially in the case of religious maniacs, as to let anything come in their way which could serve to strengthen their mania. On the contrary, one should strive to get lunatics to think about other things and so make them forget their fancies. A specially effective way of dispelling the fixed idea is to compel the insane to occupy themselves mentally and especially physically; by working, they are forced out of their diseased subjectivity and impelled towards the real world. A case of this kind is that of a Scottish farmer who became noted for curing the insane, although his method was simply and solely to harness them, half a dozen at a time, to a plough and make them work until they were completely tired out. Of the remedies acting primarily on the body, the see-saw especially has proved efficacious, particularly with raving lunatics. The see-saw movement induces giddiness in the patient and loosens his fixed idea. But a great deal can also be achieved for the recovery of the insane by sudden and powerful action on their fixed idea. It is true that the insane are extremely distrustful when they notice that attempts are being made to wean them away from their fixed idea. Yet at the same time they are stupid and are easily taken by surprise. They can therefore not infrequently be cured by someone pretending to enter into their delusion and then suddenly doing something in which the patient catches a glimpse of liberation from his imagined complaint. There is a well-known case of an Englishman who believed he had a hay-cart with four horses in his stomach and who was freed from his delusion by a doctor who, having assured him that he could feel the cart and horses and so gained his confidence, persuaded him that he possessed a remedy for reducing the size of the things supposedly in his stomach. Finally, he gave the lunatic an emetic and made him vomit out of the window just as, with the doctor's connivance, a hay-cart was passing by outside which the lunatic believed he had vomited. Another way of effecting a cure of insanity consists in getting lunatics to perform actions which directly refute the *specific* delusion which plagues them. Thus, for example, someone who imagined he had glass feet was cured by a feigned attack by robbers, when he found his feet extremely useful for running away. Another who held himself to be dead, did not move and would not eat, came to his senses again when someone pretended to share his delusion. The lunatic was put in a coffin and laid in a vault in which was another coffin occupied by a man who at first pretended to be dead but who, soon after he was left alone with the lunatic, sat up, told the latter how pleased he was to have company in death, and finally got up, ate the food that was by him, and told the astonished lunatic that he had already been dead a long time and therefore knew how the dead go about things. The lunatic was pacified by the assurance, likewise ate and drank, and was cured. Sometimes lunacy can also be cured by a word or by a joke acting directly on the delusion. For instance, a lunatic who believed that he was the Holy Ghost recovered when another lunatic said to him: How can you be the Holy Ghost? *I* am it. An equally interesting instance is that of a watch-maker who imagined he had been guillotined although innocent. The remorseful judge ordered that his head be given back to him, but through an unfortunate mishap a different, much worse, thoroughly useless head had been put back on him. As this lunatic was once defending the legend according to which St. Dionysius had kissed his own severed head, another lunatic retorted: You arrant fool, with what did St. Dionysius kiss his head, with his heel perhaps? This question so shook the lunatic watch-maker that he completely recovered from his delusion. A joke of this kind will, however, completely dispel the delusion only if this malady has already diminished in intensity.

7.6

Elements of the Philosophy of Right. Edited by Allen W. Wood. Translated by H. B. Nisbet. Cambridge: Cambridge University Press, 1991, 148-49.

§ 120

The *right of intention* is that the *universal* quality of the action shall have being not only *in itself,* but shall be *known* by the agent and thus have been present all along in his subjective will; and conversely, what we may call the right of the *objectivity* of the action is the right of the action to assert itself as known and willed by the subject as a *thinking agent.*

> The right to such insight implies that the *responsibility* of children, imbeciles, lunatics, etc. for their actions is either totally *absent* or diminished. But just as actions, in their external existence [*Dasein*], include contingent consequences, so also does *subjective* existence contain an indeterminacy as far as the power and strength of self-consciousness and presence of mind are concerned. This indeterminacy, however, can be taken into account only in connection with imbecility, lunacy, etc., and with childhood, because only such pronounced conditions as these can annul [*aufheben*] the character of thought and free will and allow us to deny the agent the dignity [*Ehre*] of being a thinking individual and a will.

7.7

Elements of the Philosophy of Right, edited by Wood, 275, 279.

§ 258

The state is the actuality of the substantial *will,* an actuality which it possesses in the particular *self-consciousness* when this has been raised to its universality; as such, it is the *rational* in and for itself. This substantial unity is an absolute and unmoved end in itself, and in it, freedom enters into its highest right, just as this ultimate end possesses the highest right in relation to individuals [*die Einzelnen*], whose *highest duty* is to be members of the state.

Addition (G).

The state in and for itself is the ethical whole, the actualization of freedom, and it is the absolute end of reason that freedom should be actual. The state is the spirit which is present in the world and which *consciously* realizes itself therein, whereas in nature, it actualizes itself only as the other of itself, as dormant spirit. Only when it is present in consciousness, knowing itself as an existent object [*Gegenstand*], is it the state. Any discussion of freedom must begin not with individuality [*Einzelheit*] or the individual self-consciousness, but only with the essence of self-consciousness; for whether human beings know it or not, this essence realizes itself as a self-sufficient power of which single individuals [*die einzelnen Individuen*] are only moments. The state consists in the march of God in the world, and its basis is the power of reason actualizing itself as will. In considering the Idea of the state, we must not have any particular states or particular institutions in mind; instead, we should consider the Idea, this actual God, in its own right [*für sich*]. Any state, even if we pronounce it bad in the light of our own principles, and even if we discover this or that defect in it, invariably has the essential moments of its existence [*Existenz*] within itself (provided it is one of the more advanced states of our time). But since it is easier to discover deficiencies than to comprehend the affirmative, one may easily fall into the mistake of overlooking the inner organism of the state in favor of individual [*einzelne*] aspects. The state is not a work of art; it exists in the world, and hence in the sphere of arbitrariness, contingency, and error, and bad behavior may disfigure it in many aspects. But the ugliest man, the criminal, the invalid, or the cripple is still a living human being; the affirmative aspect — life — survives [*besteht*] in spite of such deficiencies, and it is with this affirmative aspect that we are here concerned.

7.8

Lectures on the Philosophy of Religion, Vol. I: *Introduction and the Concept of Religion.* Edited by Peter C. Hodgson. Translated by R. F. Brown, P. C. Hodgson, and J. M. Stewart, with the assistance of J. P. Fitzer and H. S. Harris. Berkeley and Los Angeles: University of California Press, 1984, 337-39.

Spirit witnesses only concerning spirit, not about external things. Finite things have their mediation only through external grounds. The authentic ground of faith is itself, the witness of spirit concerning spirit; and the witness of spirit is certainly something inwardly alive — this inward mediation. Cognition is the exposition [of this witness]; it is essential to hold fast to this. The verification [of faith] *can* appear in this external formal way, but this external formality must [eventually] fall away.

Thus it can be that faith in a specific religion starts from such testimonies, from miracles; the appearance of the divine occurs in a finite content. Christ himself spoke out, however, against miracles, reproaching the Jews for demanding miracles from him, and telling his disciples, "The Spirit will lead you into truth."[1]

With respect to the verification of faith, then, there are external modes and stories that provide a starting point for what turns into faith. Belief in these external modes is also called faith, but it is still formal. This belief may be what faith begins from, but authentic faith must then take its place — the faith which is the witness of spirit concerning spirit. If this distinction is not made, then people are expected to believe things which those who stand at a certain level of culture no longer *can* believe. For example, they are supposed to believe in miracles, and this is supposed to be a ground for the highest faith, faith in Christ. It may be a means for it, but this belief is also always required on its own account, as belief in a content of this kind. The belief in miracles, however, is faith demanded for a content that is "contingent,"[2] and hence it is not true faith, for true faith has no contingent content. This is especially noteworthy with respect to the Enlightenment, which took "faith" in this sense, and stuck to this sense, and proved its mastery over this mode of faith. If orthodoxy demands faith of this kind, it is powerless to maintain it once people view

1. The quotation is from John 16:13, but it is in the Synoptic Gospels (Mark 8:11-13 and parallels) that Christ "reproached the Jews for demanding miracles of him" — i.e., the controversy over seeking a sign. [*Ed.*]

2. *Thus also* W1; W2 *(Var) reads:* finite and contingent. [*Ed.*]

things in a certain way, for it is just a formal belief, a faith in a content that is not by nature divine, nor the spirit, nor any moment of the spirit. This is especially to be noted in regard to miracles. For example, Christ healed a withered hand[3] and at the wedding in Cana [he changed water into wine].[4] Whether the guests at the marriage of Cana received more wine or not does not matter in the slightest; that is a wholly insignificant content, and it is no less a manner of contingency whether the man with the withered hand was healed. One ought not to begrudge a man an undamaged hand, but that occurrence carries no special weight, for millions of people go about with withered or crippled limbs, and no one heals *them*. We are told other stories — for example, in the Old Testament, that in the exodus from Egypt the doors of the Jewish houses were marked with red, that the angel of the Lord might spare those within.[5] If, indeed, it *is* the angel of the Lord who smites the firstborn, ought he not to have recognized the Jews even without this sign? When [belief in] a content of this kind is demanded, that is no witness of the spirit; Voltaire's bitterest attacks are directed against the demand for this sort of belief. He says, among other things, that it would have been better if God had taught the Jews about immortality of the soul rather than teaching them to go to the privy *(aller à la selle)*.[6] This is to make latrines part of the content of faith. This is an unspiritual content, and, though there may perhaps be a place for it in these circumstances, [there is] an enormous contrast between God and it. When God speaks, what he says is spiritual, for spirit reveals itself only to spirit.

3. See Mark 3:1-5 and parallels. [*Ed.*]

4. See John 2:1-11. [*Ed.*]

5. See Exodus 12:12-13, 23. Contrary to Hegel's version, it is the Lord himself, not the angel of the Lord, who requires the sign, although according to v. 23 at least, it is the angel ("the destroyer") who does the slaying. [*Ed.*]

6. See Deuteronomy 23:12-14. Voltaire's attack is found in his *Examen important de Milord Bolingbroke (Oeuvres complètes* [1784], 33:18), and *La Bible enfin expliquée* (London, 1776), p. 209 (*Oeuvres complètes* 34:173). [*Ed.*]

7.9

Lectures on the Philosophy of Religion, Vol. III: *The Consummate Religion*. Edited by Peter C. Hodgson. Translated by R. F. Brown, P. C. Hodgson, and J. M. Stewart, with the assistance of H. S. Harris. Berkeley and Los Angeles: University of California Press, 1985, 147-48.

Faith, however, rests on the witness of the Spirit, not on miracles but on the absolute truth, on the eternal idea and its content, and from this standpoint the miracles have little interest. They can be cited as subjective reasons of an incidental and edifying character, or they can be left aside. [It is of] no interest [to faith] to investigate what the wedding guests at Cana really drank, and if it was wine, whose wine.[7] Miracles are supposed to attest, and [yet] they have to be attested themselves [first]. What is supposed to be attested by them is the idea; [but that] has no need of them, and therefore no need to attest *to* them.

There still remains this to be said: miracles [are], in general, effects produced by the power of spirit on the natural nexus, a higher intervention in the natural process, in the eternal laws of nature. Speaking generally, spirit is this absolute intervention. Life itself is already an intervention in these so-called eternal laws of nature. Life digests, i.e., it supersedes the eternal laws of physics [*Mechanismus*] and chemistry. Food, [as] material, behaves in accord with the eternal laws of physics, and as chemical, [with those] of chemistry; life puts an end to this. Still more marked is the effect on life of the power of spirit and its weakness. [There is such a thing as] death caused by fright; [people can become] sick from grief. In the same way joy and trust also [can bring life and health]. Animal magnetism [i.e., hypnosis] has disclosed these powers to us in a more familiar form. In all ages, [there is] infinite faith, infinite trust, [the influence of] spirit upon spirit; cripples are healed, the blind see, the deaf hear, right up to the present day.[8] Unbelief in such effects is based on a superstitious belief in the so-called powers of nature and their independence vis-à-vis spirit.

7. See John 2:1-11. [*Ed.*]
8. See Jesus' response to the disciples of John the Baptist in Matthew 11:5. [*Ed.*]

8 Between Necessity and Possibility: Kierkegaard and the Abilities and Disabilities of Subjectivity

CHRISTOPHER CRAIG BRITTAIN

The fact that Søren Kierkegaard was a financially independent bourgeois European of the nineteenth century, who had no concept of "disability" in the contemporary sense, does not, perhaps, make him an obvious conversation partner for a theology of disability. But Kierkegaard's thought does help us to reflect on *how* we might approach the question of disability, and what it might mean to reflect *theologically* on this issue from a perspective rooted in the Christian tradition.

Biographical Background

Søren Kierkegaard was born on 5 May 1813 in Copenhagen, Denmark. The son of a wealthy merchant, he was the youngest of seven children. His family was no stranger to tragedy and illness: five of his siblings died young, as did his father's first wife, and his surviving brother's first spouse. Kierkegaard himself was physically frail, although the exact status of his health is unclear. Describing his own condition, he wrote, "Slight, thin, and weak, denied in almost every respect the physical basis for being reckoned a whole person, comparable with others; melancholic, sick at heart, in many ways profoundly and internally devastated" (Garff 2005, 431). Various theories exist regarding the precise nature of his frailness, which he often referred to as the "thorn in my flesh." Some argue that he suffered from epilepsy; other scholars suggest that his physical weakness was due to a childhood fall from a tree. In *Kierkegaard the Cripple,* the German philosopher Theodor Haecker suggests that Kierkegaard was "physically handicapped from birth. *He was weakly, deformed, he had a hump, he was infirm*" (Haecker 1948, 1). Whatever the precise nature of Kierkegaard's physical well-being, Louis Dupré notes that Kierkegaard "felt that he was almost completely lacking in what physically characterizes a normal man" (Dupré 1964, 5). Assuming that he would die before the age of thirty-six, young Søren quickly spent most of the inheritance left by his father, only to be astonished (and left financially insecure) on his thirty-seventh birthday.

Kierkegaard never married. He was engaged for one year to Regina Olson, but broke off the relationship suddenly with no explanation. He continued to write about her in his journals for the rest of his life, and to this day scholars puzzle over how to interpret his relationship with her and the reasons for his decision not to marry.

Although the historical record about his physical condition remains unclear, later in life Kierkegaard was mocked in public for his odd appearance and mannerisms. The Danish satirical newspaper *The Corsair* published a series of attacks making fun of his clothes, manner of walk, voice, and habits, reserving particular ridicule for the fact that one of his trouser legs was shorter than the other. The portrait became the popular perception of him in Copenhagen, and he found himself being mocked and pointed at when in public.

The author of twenty-one books in twelve years, Kierkegaard is often credited with being the founder of existentialist philosophy and theology. Much of his thought and work wrestles with what it means to be a Christian, articulating a piety of an intense and personal nature. He aggressively criticized institutional religion (though also seriously considered becoming a pastor on a number of occasions). He accused the established church in Denmark (Lutheran) of becoming a complacent social club for polite society, conforming to the fashions of culture rather than the faithful living demanded in the Christian Gospel.

Kierkegaard's thought was developed in opposition to a number of intellectual fashions of his age, particularly speculative philosophical systems such as that of G. W. F. Hegel. Hegel's philosophy was understood by his contemporaries as demonstrating that human life involves a continuous progression toward a goal and an ideal, whereas Kierkegaard insisted that human beings live in a state of uncertainty and anxiety, which interrupts any possibility of consistent progress. Rather than celebrate a notion of a developing humanistic ideal, Kierkegaard argued that the individual must make a "leap of faith" and reach an eternal moment of truth. But this achievement is not the result of a single act or situation, but must be regained over and over through passionate living in whatever context one finds oneself. Much of his writing, therefore, centers on the importance of the self, and emphasizes the self's relation to the world as being grounded in self-reflection and introspection. For Kierkegaard, truth is not something that can be governed by universal standards and objective reason, but can be appropriated only by the subjective individual.

At the time of Kierkegaard's writing, Danish society was experiencing a massive and turbulent process of transformation, as the country rapidly moved from a largely feudal agrarian society to a modern capitalist state. Watching rapidly changing social hierarchies and the dramatic urban growth and expansion of the bourgeois middle class, Kierkegaard observed that this new culture was generating a rather stereotypical and conformist sort of identity. Social roles and values were becoming very fluid and unstable, and so the new bourgeois lived in pursuit of the latest fashions and fads. Kierkegaard criticized this unreflective form of existence — the mentality of "the crowd," as he called it. He challenged this form of imitative subjectivity, which praised the Hegelian idea of "cultivation" *(Bildung)*, and amounted to a mere herd mentality. In his view, to be cultivated is not to adopt the norms and values of one's culture: rather, it is to catch up with oneself; to take responsibility for one's own existential choices; and to commit to a way of life not merely dictated by the surrounding culture.

The Christian faith plays a central role in developing an authentic individual identity. For Kierkegaard the only objective truth is the identity of God, as demonstrated through the death and resurrection of Jesus Christ. It is the question of the subject's relation to this truth (whether through commitment or indifference) that is the issue at the core of his theology and philosophy. Theologians as diverse as Karl Barth, Rudolf Bultmann, Paul Tillich, and Hans Urs von Balthasar have considered Kierkegaard a significant influence on their work.

On 11 November 1855, after a month in the hospital, Kierkegaard died in Copenhagen at the age of forty-two. Some scholars suggest that his decline may have been the result of complications related to his frail physical condition (Garff 2005, 793).

Kierkegaard and Disability

A theological engagement between Kierkegaard and disability theory must admit at the outset that the particular challenges that face people with physical or mental disabilities are not issues that are central to Kierkegaard's thought. From the perspective of his philosophy of existence, physical and mental challenges and limitations are largely beside the point. They neither prevent the individual from living a complete and authentic life, nor assist her or him to do so. Such disabilities, in other words, do not inhibit what Kierkegaard thinks matters most about human existence.

In Kierkegaard's view, the sole disability that truly represents a problem and limitation for human flourishing is ultimately the problem of sin. Under the weight of sin, all human beings are effectively "disabled." Sin impedes human self-understanding; it disrupts relationships with others and prevents wholeness of living. For Kierkegaard, it is not limitation or sickness that ultimately threatens human well-being, but rather what he calls "sickness unto death," or, the desire not to be oneself. In his exegesis of John 11:4, Kierkegaard emphasizes that Jesus says of the sickness of Lazarus that it "does not lead to death; rather it is for God's glory" (Kierkegaard 1980, 7). But if illness and even death are seen as only minor events in the context of a belief in eternal life, pain and the fear of death do often lead individuals to despair. It is such a "sickness of the spirit" or "sickness unto death" that is, in Kierkegaard's view, the central threat to human well-being and flourishing. Such fear and depression prevent individuals from embracing responsibility for their own lives. They disrupt relationships with others, particularly with the God who embraces all things.

If Kierkegaard largely regards the general challenges of physical and mental disabilities as marginal issues with regard to the principal problem of human existence, what then does his thought have to offer to a theology of disability? Here the oddness of Kierkegaard's character and the dissonance that his thought had with his own time and culture prove fruitful. For what Kierkegaard was trying to accomplish, and, perhaps more importantly, what his theology is self-consciously trying *not* to do, resonate with a number of concerns within disability theory. Consideration of three prominent concerns within disability studies serve to illustrate that Kierkegaard's approach to individual identity and the nature of faith has some interesting overlap.

Critique of the Ideal of Human "Normalcy"

Clearly one of the principal issues in disability theory is to confront the modern tendency to assume that a person with a disability is a deviation from the norm of human existence. Part of the struggle of naming the category of human individuals who are "differently-abled" is to try to avoid imposing a label upon them which inherently suggests that they have an inferior status of "ableness" compared to other individuals in society. The concern is to avoid treating a person with a disability as an imperfect or incomplete human being, or as someone who is somehow uniquely flawed in comparison with others. This complex theoretical task finds encouragement in Kierkegaard's writing.

This might not be the first impression of a casual reader. Kierkegaard rather frequently employs what might be taken as pejorative terms: "sufferers," "the weak," "the imperfect," "those wronged from birth," "lowliness," and so on. He is not concerned with contemporary sensibilities about such labels, and often articulates himself with a determined bluntness. What is significant from the perspective of disability studies, however, is how such terms function in his writing. Kierkegaard's attitude toward this phraseology is noteworthy because what his theology is emphasizing as truly important (being oneself, inwardness, a leap of faith) considers all of these labels or states largely irrelevant. Kierkegaard places no emphasis on a person's physical health or ability to perform certain acts; in his view, these are largely irrelevant for living as an authentic individual. Secondly, even though he does refer to some physical conditions as making an individual "lowly," "weak," or classified as a "sufferer," he also frequently describes completely "healthy" individuals with exactly the same terms (**8.1**). This is to suggest that his references to illness and weakness are not primarily comments on individuals' physical abilities and health, but on their relationship to sin — that is, their relationship to God, fellow human beings, and especially their own inward relation to themselves.

The issue of what to call people with disabilities aside, in the concern to resist the imposition of a normative standard of human normalcy upon disabled persons, disability studies encounters a friend in Kierkegaard. He has no investment in a theological anthropology concerned to establish a standardized form of human existence. His emphasis is consistently on becoming the sort of human being God intends you to be, which has little in common with social and cultural standards and norms. He reserves harsh criticism for those who simply mime the behavior and values of those around them, or who place their confidence in the potential of human endeavor. A theology of disability which is seeking to articulate a theological anthropology that avoids being grounded on a universal standard of "humanness" (based on ability, skill, rationality, independence, etc.) will find Kierkegaard an intriguing resource.

Disability and Its Relationship to Illness and Suffering
(Medical Model)

Closely related to the concern to challenge a standardized norm for human "ableness" is disability theory's effort to challenge an approach to disability based on approaches referred to as the "individual," "medical," or "personal tragedy" models of disability (Barnes et al. 2002, 4). In such treatments, a person who has a disability not only is conceived as being incomplete or "defective," but is understood as living in a state of sickness and suffering. Such a view, which often naively assumes that it represents a compassionate concern for the well-being of persons who are disabled, presupposes that the individuals in question consider themselves unwell, and that, given the opportunity, would welcome being "healed" or "restored" to full human "ableness." Such an assumption is criticized for re-imposing a normative standard of human nature, but also for frequently underwriting a paternalistic attitude toward the concerns and interests of people with disabilities.

Kierkegaard's writing again represents an intriguing resource to theology for thinking about the needs of people with disabilities that might avoid making physical or mental suffering, or their cure, the central matter at issue. On this point, dialogue with Kierkegaard will need to proceed with some caution and attention to nuance, since, as mentioned above, he often employs sickness and illness as central tropes in his argument. Kierkegaard is highly alert to suffering, and is compelled to address it frequently. But the thrust of his writing is to treat suffering as a matter of fact. To him, suffering is a regrettable (sometimes torturous) reality, but his concern is not to discover ways to escape it; nor does he imagine that human existence can avoid it (**8.9**). Thus, one would encounter nothing in Kierkegaard's writing which would encourage a response to "disability" that emphasizes seeking a "cure" that would restore the individual to a more normative "able-ness."

Kierkegaard's journals are saturated with reports of his physical ailments and depressions (Kierkegaard 1978). One way to interpret this is to suggest that, for Kierkegaard, writing represented a way of dealing with his condition. But despite this weighty attention to the problem of suffering, his theology is not overburdened by the questions of theodicy. Determining some meaning for suffering is not his primary problem. Pain and death are for him simply tragic realities of life which all individuals must confront in one way or another. The real threat to human flourishing and Christian spirituality is the individual's relationship with herself. Spiritual illness, or "sickness unto death," is, for Kierkegaard, far more significant a concern than physical or mental illness (Kierkegaard 1980). In his view, the many physical sufferings and ailments that human beings may have operate in a different register from emotional and spiritual anxieties. Engaging with his perspective on this may help support a theology of disability that is concerned to de-center the issue of suffering in its approach to disability, and to encourage an approach that focuses on the individual's agency and responsibility for responding to the world from his or her specific situation and condition.

Social Disenfranchisement (Minority Model)

As a response to the so-called "medical model" of disability, many theorists now emphasize an alternative approach to disability, which focuses on how society constructs barriers to human beings with certain physical or mental limitations. This perspective challenges how these limitations are subsequently perceived as impairments only because society is unable (or unwilling) to accommodate the needs involved. "Rather than identifying disability as an individual limitation, the social model identifies society as the problem" (Barnes et al. 2002, 5).

Kierkegaard's thought has an ambiguous relationship with this model of disability theory. On the one hand, he is concerned to criticize how the social norms of his age resulted in prejudice, hypocrisy, and social marginalization. Below, in the excerpt from *The Present Age* (**8.3**), Kierkegaard criticizes the manner in which "the public" imposes its norms on all members of society, enforcing a "leveling" that reduces all things to a conformitive "sameness." His primary philosophical intent is to oppose this "destruction of the individual" and to encourage people to become themselves, rather than a mere copy of the latest fashion.

But this defense of the single individual against the crowd, while powerfully useful for challenging some universal standard for human normalcy, also presents a critical lens with which to examine the "minority model" of disability theory, which contains the risk that it might sometimes result in the construction of a self-enclosed identity politics. While Kierkegaard's writing challenges social stereotypes, it also warns that even minority identities can potentially become stereotypical and rigid in their own way. While Kierkegaard would support those who have managed to liberate themselves from a problematic conception of what it means to be a "complete" human being, he might also caution those who have accepted a minority model against the risk of imposing on it a rigid and enclosed self-understanding of what it means to be "disabled." This is to say that Kierke-gaard's thought shares the basic concern raised by disability theory against imposing socially constructed norms on a minority of individuals in soci-ety, but his thought also resists achieving this on the basis of an alternative standpoint grounded in a collective minority identity. As some activists have warned, a "minority" model can sometimes encourage an identity pol-itics founded on a sense of "victimization," or on some essential traits of a specific disability, which fails to assist people to escape the boundaries of societal norms. What society had constructed as negative is now reversed and turned into a positive identity, but this is but the other side of the same coin. The basic power dynamic of the "disabled" person's relationship to so-ciety remains in place.

Kierkegaard's emphasis on the singular individual intends to penetrate deeply into this complex dialectic. The opening paragraphs of *The Sickness Unto Death* extracted below (see **8.5**) describe the individual self not as a pure singular entity, but as a synthesis, the result of a relation to something beyond itself. Clearly the philosopher argues that the authentic individual does not define herself according to the "crowd." But adopting a self-understanding based on a "minority" identity is not, in Kierkegaard's view, any more authentically autonomous. He writes, "If the relation that relates itself to itself is established by another, then the relation is indeed the third."

Kierkegaard's resolution of this dilemma involves emphasizing the im-portance of what he calls "inwardness" and its relation to the religious. It is at this point that an engagement between disability theory and the philosophy of Kierkegaard points toward the theological. I will develop this point fur-ther below in some more direct comment on the excerpted selections from his writing.

Selections from Kierkegaard's Writing

The sample texts below are intended as brief illustrations of Kierkegaard's thought, and to encourage further engagement with his writing in a more sustained manner. The first two selections are letters written to disabled rel-atives. They serve as examples of how Kierkegaard might address such indi-viduals, as well as how he applies the key terms and emphases of his philoso-phy to their situation. It is possible that, on first reading, some of his comments might be taken as presenting a paternalistic call to quietism or resignation, or even as offering some form of sentimental consolation. The reader is encouraged, therefore, to read them carefully and to seek to understand Kierkegaard's intended meaning through the lens of his more general philosophy and theology, which the subsequent excerpts intend to illustrate.

The selection from *The Present Age* (**8.3**) offers an example of Kierkegaard's reasons for emphasizing the category of the individual, which, as discussed above, is principally related to his critique of the abstract "leveling" that society frequently imposes on people. This is followed by two selections (**8.4-5**) which begin to outline Kierkegaard's positive program for his concept of "inwardness." This aspect of his thought has been severely criticized by some philosophers, and thus there is reason for disability studies to approach it with caution. Theodor Adorno, for example, has said of Kierkegaard's view of inwardness, "The world of things is for him neither part of the subject nor independent of it. Rather, this world is omitted. It supplies the subject with the mere 'occasion' for the deed, with mere resistance to the act of faith" (Adorno 1989, 29).

Rather than ignoring social context, Kierkegaard is concerned to avoid the opposite problem: allowing the external world to dictate the meaning of human being. In his view, the only way to challenge a worldview and philosophical system that claim to be all-inclusive in their description and understanding of the world is to assume a position outside of them. This motivates his emphasis on the individual, and at this point, his approach to subjectivity and identity shares a common aim with disability theory. Kierkegaard's central interest is in behavior that amounts to either what he calls "aesthetic existence" (the use of artifice, irony, and imagination to recreate the world in one's own image) or "ethical existence" (the observance of prevailing social customs and values). These "stages on life's way" (as he calls them) are not without value, but they are also deeply flawed ways to engage one's life. Human anxieties and uncertainties disrupt us, and the social customs we inhabit are incomplete and sometimes destructive, but far too often people simply go along with them in order to avoid the nuisance that results from trying to swim against the current. Thus, Kierkegaard deploys the concept of "inwardness" as a metaphor for the centrality of the self. It is not externalities that ultimately determine the individual (social position, reputation, results of one's actions, natural endowments, etc.), but the self's individual "becoming" — its concerns (enthusiasms, passions, interests), and what flows from these (emotions, etc).

Kierkegaard argues that the individual can only truly become himself or herself through or in the person of Jesus Christ. It is at this point that the significance of his Christology comes into view. In *Works of Love,* for example,

Christ is presented as the One who alone offers "genuine love," so that human beings fall into error when they fail to recognize that we love only through Christ. For Kierkegaard, the authentic individual, and the genuine love relationship, can be achieved only in relation to God. To be a person, he says, is achieved only "before God" (Kierkegaard 1962, 124). Such a manner of being is modeled to human beings by the person of Christ.

The human self is, for Kierkegaard, a "synthesis." It is matter, and body, and social context; but not exclusively so. The self is also spirit and mind, commitment and faith. The approach to truth and subjectivity articulated in these excerpts illustrates his insistence that "empirical being" is not the sum total of the human, and thus his philosophy is a resource that offers disability theory an approach to human identity that avoids determinism, empiricism, and consequentialist reductionism. In this vision, there can be no standard for the "human," nor any scale of ability with which to measure the value of a person. Kierkegaard reserves such matters for the inward relationship that an individual has with herself.

These passages also demonstrate Kierkegaard's concern to present human subjectivity as the product of a dialectical tension between the self and an other. Far from seeking to articulate an individualistic or anti-social worldview, he aims to show that communication and cooperation are possible only when people are taken as genuinely finite individuals. Preserving this appreciation of the finite requires a respect for difference and limitation. Such respect for differences among people, as well as for their individual value and dignity, implies that no single human being can serve as the model for all others; nor can any individual understand himself or herself as complete.

Excerpts **8.6** to **8.9** illustrate the extent to which theology serves a central role in Kierkegaard's approach to subjectivity. The truth cannot simply exist alone in the subjective individual, any more than it rests with the abstract public. He refers to such an imagined direct relation to the truth as either "lunacy" or "paganism." God, for Kierkegaard, is the source of both human community and the individual self, for the actuality of God interrupts the banal social customs that shape inauthentic conformism, as well as self-absorbed conceit.

The potential that this perspective has for challenging socially problematic attitudes toward disability is, hopefully, clear. Excerpt **8.7** from *The Sickness Unto Death* may also suggest a more positive contribution. For beyond offering another critique of determinism and fatalism, the passage presents an intriguing description of the subject as mutually constituted by necessity and possibility. An individual's concrete existence (her "actuality") is not simply to be understood as something imposed upon her; rather, an essential dimension of human life is a horizon of possibility. A person is not to be understood as imprisoned by circumstance or capacity. His worth is not measured according to what he can do, for such boundaries cannot account for the extensive possibilities that his life offers. This dimension of Kierkegaard's theory of the subject offers a rich source for further reflection to disability studies, particularly with regard to his concern not to diminish the reality that every human person is indeed limited by certain "necessities" in their lives. He calls upon individuals to admit and accept their limitations, while at the same time to avoid evaluating their worth and their capacities based solely upon these limitations. This attention to both necessity and potentiality opens up a promising avenue into a sensitive area related to a theory of the disabled subject.

A theology of disability is offered still more of interest in this passage, since Kierkegaard argues that, in order to hold open the place for possibility in the realm of actuality, belief in God is necessary. Only for God are all things possible, and so, according to Kierkegaard, only God can prevent necessity from foreclosing on alternative prospects and opportunities. Possibility is the very oxygen the individual breathes, and the prayer of the healthy human subject. When coupled with Kierkegaard's discussion of sin as despair before God — as a lack of faith in possibility (**8.8**) — there are considerable resources offered here which might contribute a great deal to ongoing reflections on the spirituality of disability.

The two selections from *Purity of Heart* (**8.9**) and *Works of Love* (**8.10**) engage more immediately with prominent issues within disability studies. Once again, there is a danger that Kierkegaard's use of the term "sufferer" might be understood as indicating a paternalistic attitude that sometimes surfaces within the medical model of disability. But the tone of **8.10** neither idealizes suffering nor bewails it, and it does not focus on developing strategies to escape or cure it. Rather, the sole contribution that suffering serves here is to remind the busyness of the world that there is something more important than worldly achievement. This is a more elaborate articulation of the same message that Kierkegaard offers in his letters to Jette and Peter: true accomplishment, and the highest form of life, are to be found through relation to the Eternal, by being authentically oneself. Suffering does not enable this in any particular way, other than simply interrupting the busyness of the rest of life and offering the opportunity to attend to matters often left neglected.

The excerpt from *Works of Love* (**8.10**) opens up an ethical landscape within which issues of disability can be situated. Once again, Kierkegaard opposes establishing a scale upon which to value or measure human life, but here the case is deepened through an exploration of the dynamics of love. For him, insisting that a human being must possess certain traits in order to be "lovable enough" undermines the very concept of love itself. Kierkegaard is by no means ignorant of how difficult it is for humans to achieve this openness to the other, which is why once again the divine has a central role in his presentation of the work of love. In learning to love the unseen God, the individual is enabled to openly love those around him.

This text merits considerable scrutiny from the perspective of disability theory, for Kierkegaard's profound remarks on this topic are anything but mere sentimentality. One could read this short passage as confronting the views of a number of prominent critics. Against a perspective not unlike that of his contemporary Ludwig Feuerbach, who suggested that religion alienates humanity from its highest ideals by projecting them onto a divine being (Feuerbach 1957), Kierkegaard insists that loving the unseen God does not alienate human beings from others; "Such a thing can occur only to a hypocrite or to a deceiver in order to find an escape." Though he might agree that many people engage in such flight, he refuses to grant this behavior legitimacy. His perspective also challenges Sigmund Freud's insistence that "if I love someone, he must deserve it in some way. . . . He deserves it if he is so like me in important ways that I can love myself in him; and he deserves it if he is so much more perfect than myself that I can love my ideal of my own self in him" (Freud 1962, 56). Such a view is highly problematic, since the human beings that disability studies is concerned with often cannot aspire to represent our culture's narcissistic ideals. As such, Kierkegaard's theology of love merits a sustained and serious engagement by those committed to reflecting on the place and value of the disabled in contemporary society.

The homiletical excerpt from *Christian Discourses* (**8.12**) illustrates how Kierkegaard relativizes all worldly distinctions between human beings before his understanding of the Eternal. Elaborating on the famous text from the sixth chapter of the Gospel of Matthew, he again emphasizes how "the single individual" ought properly to focus on developing a healthy relationship with itself, rather than comparing itself to the standards of others, or seeking to achieve goals other than its own. The text reminds us again how Kierkegaard argues that it is possible to become oneself only through "holding fast to God." As we have read elsewhere in these excerpts, one's mediation by the abstract public can be interrupted only by a concrete other, and no such other escapes the confines of social conditioning besides the divine. In a text like this, a theology of disability will find an interesting approach to discussing a model (or "prototype") for a theological anthropology which avoids all the pitfalls of a limited notion of human essence or ideal.

The brief, parable-like concluding selection from *Stages on Life's Way* (**8.13**) is offered as an example of Kierkegaard's humor, and primarily of his ability to locate both the comic and the tragic in the same experiences. In an age of identity politics, in which rigid confrontations erupt between communities of difference, the spirit of this passage might contribute a healthy sense of the tragic-comic to disability studies, one that does not diminish its commitment to advocate for the concerns and needs of the disabled, while also avoiding the despair that can arise in the face of the inevitable frustrations, failures, and disappointments that the movement often experiences. Particularly noteworthy here is Kierkegaard's emphasis that the misunderstanding between these two different people (male and female) is "not due to some third factor," or to any ill will on the part of the other, but can often be — tragically, but also comically — inevitable. This makes it no less annoying or disappointing; but it may make it more tolerable. As such, perhaps there is a contribution offered to disability studies in this very basic outlook on relationships as well.

Such a perspective represents a promising resource for theologies of disability concerned with the agency and dignity of those with physical disabilities, although perhaps less so for those with mental disabilities. Kierkegaard's emphasis on inwardness and subjective awareness is not immediately translatable to the conditions of mental disability, although his celebration of the grace and beauty of the "birds of the air" offers some directions to explore (Kierkegaard 2009, 7-8). Some readers might also find that his emphasis on individual action and decision demonstrates insufficient emphasis on community and solidarity, which is frequently so important in discussions of disability. The final excerpt (**8.13**) — like his writings on love (see also **8.10**) — demonstrates how he does not intend to marginalize intersubjective relationships. Kierkegaard's work may not offer a great deal to constructing a social or political theology, but there is much here that can illuminate the challenges and struggles that individuals within such social movements must confront and overcome.

These limitations aside, Kierkegaard's writing represents a rich resource to disability theory and theology. His entirely non-instrumental approach to philosophy and theology seeks to develop a concept of subjectivity that takes individuality and difference seriously, while avoiding reliance upon theories of human essence or characteristics that are frequently part of humanistic or liberative models of discourse. Although Kierkegaard writes very little directly on or to people with disabilities, his thought offers many conceptual tools that might contribute to the ongoing development of a theology of disability.

REFERENCES

Primary Sources

Kierkegaard, Søren. 1997. *Christian Discourses: The Crisis and a Crisis in the Life of an Actress*, vol. XVII in Kierkegaard's Writings. Translated and edited by Howard V. Hong and Edna H. Hong. Princeton: Princeton University Press.

———. 1992. *Concluding Unscientific Postscript to Philosophical Fragments*, vol. XII in Kierkegaard's Writings. Translated and edited by Howard V. Hong and Edna H. Hong. Princeton: Princeton University Press.

———. 1969. *The Present Age*. Translated by Alexander Dru. London and Glasgow: Collins Clear-Type Press: The Fontana Library.

———. 1948. *Purity of Heart Is to Will One Thing*. Translated by Douglas V. Steere. New York: Harper & Row.

———. 1980. *The Sickness Unto Death*, vol. XIX in Kierkegaard's Writings. Translated and edited by Howard V. Hong and Edna H. Hong. Princeton: Princeton University Press.

———. 1978. *Søren Kierkegaard's Journals and Papers*, vols. 5 and 6. Translated by Howard V. Hong and Edna H. Hong. Bloomington and London: Indiana University Press.

———. 1988. *Stages on Life's Way*, vol. XI in Kierkegaard's Writings. Translated and edited by Howard V. Hong and Edna H. Hong. Princeton: Princeton University Press.

———. 2009. *Without Authority*, vol. XVIII in Kierkegaard's Writings. Translated and edited by Howard V. Hong and Edna H. Hong. Princeton: Princeton University Press.

———. 1962. *Works of Love*, vol. XVI in Kierkegaard's Writings. Translated by Howard V. Hong and Edna H. Hong. New York: Harper Torchbooks.

Secondary Sources

Adorno, Theodor W. 1989. *Kierkegaard: Construction of the Aesthetic*. Translated by Robert Hullot-Kentor. Minneapolis: University of Minnesota Press.

Barnes, Colin, Mike Oliver, and Len Barton, editors. 2002. *Disability Studies Today*. Cambridge: Polity Press.

Dupré, Louis. 1964. *Kierkegaard as Theologian.* London and New York: Sheed & Ward.

Feuerbach, Ludwig. 1957. *The Essence of Christianity.* Translated by George Eliot. New York: Harper & Row.

Freud, Sigmund. 1962. *Civilization and Its Discontents.* Translated by James Strachey. New York: W. W. Norton & Co.

Garff, Joakim. 2005. *Søren Kierkegaard: A Biography.* Translated by Bruce H. Kirmmse. Princeton and Oxford: Princeton University Press.

Haecker, Theodor. 1948. *Kierkegaard the Cripple.* Translated by C. Van O. Bruyn. London: Harvill Press.

For Further Reading

Evans, C. Stephen. 2006. *Kierkegaard on Faith and the Self.* Waco, Tex.: Baylor University Press.

Gowen, David J. 1996. *Kierkegaard as a Religious Thinker.* Cambridge: Cambridge University Press.

Hall, Amy Laura. 2002. *Kierkegaard and the Treachery of Love.* Cambridge: Cambridge University Press.

Hannay, Alastair. 2003. *Kierkegaard: A Biography.* Cambridge: Cambridge University Press.

Kierkegaard, Søren. 1998. *Encounters with Kierkegaard.* Edited by Virginia R. Laursen. Translated by Bruce H. Kirmmse. Princeton: Princeton University Press.

Rae, Murray. 2010. *Kierkegaard and Theology.* London and New York: T&T Clark.

Walsh, Sylvia. 2009. *Kierkegaard: Thinking Christianly in an Existential Mode.* Oxford: Oxford University Press.

Excerpts from the Writings of Søren Kierkegaard

Because of the way I have set up these excerpts, I have chosen to use parenthetical citation for the works I quote from — many of them volumes in the Kierkegaard's Writings series published by Princeton University Press. All citations refer to works listed in the Primary Sources.

PASTORAL LETTERS

8.1

Letter to his cousin, Hans Peter Kierkegaard, who is disabled (paralyzed completely on one side) [1848]. (Kierkegaard 1978, vol. 6, 83)

Dear Peter,

Happy New Year! I never go calling to offer my New Year greetings and send them in writing only rarely and as an exception — but you are among the exceptions. In recent years I have often thought of you, and I intend to do likewise in this one. Among the other thoughts or considerations I often have had and intend to go on having about you is this: that reconciled to your fate, with patience and quiet devotion, you carry out as important a task as the rest of us who perform on a larger or smaller stage, engage in important business, build houses, write copious books, and God knows what. Undeniably your stage is the smallest, that of solitude and inwardness — but *summa summarum,* as it says in *Ecclesiastes,* when all is said and done, what matters most is inwardness — and when everything has been forgotten, it is inwardness that still matters.

I wrote this some days ago, was interrupted, and did not manage to conclude it. Today your father visited me, and that circumstance once more reminded me to complete or at least put an end to what I had begun. For there was something more I wanted to add. If I were to give you any advice about life, or taking into consideration your special circumstances, were to commend to you a rule for your life, then I would say: Above all do not forget your duty to love yourself; do not permit the fact that you have been set apart from life in a way, been prevented from participating actively in it, and that you are superfluous in the obtuse eyes of a busy world, above all do not permit this to deprive you of your idea of yourself, as if your life, if lived in inwardness, did not have just as much meaning and worth as that of any other human being in the loving eyes of an all-wise Governance, and considerably more than the busy, busier, busiest haste of busyness — busy with wasting life and losing itself.

Take care of yourself in the new year. If you would enjoy visiting me once in a while, please do come. You are welcome.

Your Cousin
S.K.

8.2

Letter to his sister-in-law, Sophie Henriette ("Jette"), who suffered from severe illness and depression and was bed-ridden for thirty years [December 1847]. (Kierkegaard 1978, vol. 5, 425-27)

Dear Jette,

Thank you for your little letter which, in your own words, I must have before Christmas. I hasten to reply so that you may have my answer before New Year.

The period between Christmas and New Year is usually a particularly convenient time for me to receive letters, and a fortunate season for my correspondent, that is, if he thinks it fortunate to get a reply from me.

And now you are confined to bed again. Still, it was a sound and healthy — anything but sickly — decision to write to me right away as you did, even though you had not heard from me for so long. That, you see, is a favorable sign and makes me happy. "Last year at the same time you wrote a letter to me — but it was not sent." Then, you see, you were perhaps not bedridden, and yet your condition may have been more like that of a person who was.

Hence I am pleased on your behalf as well to have received this letter from you as a sign of health. Preserve it, and take care of it in the coming year, which God will surely make a happy one for you.

There is something closely connected with physical illness — that quiet, deeply painful, and slowly consuming worry which now turns over in agony on one side and imagines itself forgotten by others "who probably never give one a thought" and now turns over on the other side and is afraid that whatever one has to say or write will not be good enough. Oh, do banish that worry, which is especially dangerous for you because you are so frequently bedridden and constantly live in monotonous quiet. The person who is actively engaged in life soon forgets such thoughts, but the person who only sees little change around him may easily find that worrying almost becomes a necessity. When one lives in small rooms — as you know very well — they need frequent airing out; in the same way, when one entertains but few thoughts and has little diversion, then it is extremely important that what one inhales, spiritually understood, be good and beneficent and gentle and soothing thoughts.

You also need diversion, but diversion is not easily made available in monotony. And yet it is perhaps easier than one thinks if only one is willing. It is generally believed that what determines the direction of one's thoughts lies in the external and is the greater or lesser probability of this or that. But that is not so. That which determines the direction of one's thoughts lies basically in one's own self. He who has a tendency to melancholy, for example, most probably always finds unhappiness. Why? Because melancholy lies within him. In this hypothetical case there would be as great a probability of the opposite, perhaps even greater, but he arbitrarily breaks off and immediately has enough to be able to conclude that something unhappy will happen to him.

But what is it then to "have faith"? To have faith is constantly to expect the joyous, the happy, the good. But is not that an extraordinary and blessed diversion! Oh, what more does one need then? What I am about to say next might almost seem like a joke, but is in fact very serious and indeed sincerely meant for you. You are in some measure always suffering — hence the task lies right here: Divert your *mind; accustom yourself by faith to changing suffering into expectation of the joyous. It is really possible.* What is required is this flexibility in the quiet of the mind, which, whenever things go wrong for one, in that very instant begins all over again and says, "Yes! Yes! Next time it will work." Oh, if one were never to see another human being again — and that is far from your case — then one could *by faith conjure* up or forth a world of diversion into the loneliest room.

In general it is probably right to warn against self-love; still, I consider it *my duty to say to every sufferer* with whom I come into contact: *See to it that you love yourself.* When one is suffering and unable to do much for others, it is easy to fall prey to the melancholy thought that one is superfluous in this world, as others perhaps sometimes give one to understand. Then one must remember that *before God every person is equally important, without reservation equally important;* indeed, if there were any distinction, then one who suffers the most must be the closest object of God's care. And also in this lies infinite Godly diversion. But I will stop; I can truthfully say I have no more room. Take care of yourself, dear Jette. Happy New Year! Thank you for concluding the old one so beautifully by thinking of me. Greetings to Peter and to Poul.

Your devoted
S.K.

THE INDIVIDUAL AND THE ABSTRACT "PUBLIC"

8.3

The Individual and the Masses (Kierkegaard 1969, 57-62, 65)

The dialectic of the present age tends towards equality, and its most logical — though mistaken — fulfillment is leveling, as the negative unity of the negative reciprocity of all individuals.

It must be obvious to everyone that the profound significance of the leveling process lies in the fact that it means the predominance of the category of "generation" over the category of "individuality." In antiquity the total number of the individuals was there to express, as it were, the value of the outstanding individual. Nowadays the standard of value has been changed so that *equally,* approximately so and so many men go to one individual, and one need only be sure of having the right number in order to have importance. In antiquity the individual in the masses had no importance whatsoever; the outstanding individual signified them all. The present age tends towards a mathematical equality in which equally in all classes approximately so and so many people go to one individual. . . . Simply in order to put a passing whim into practice a few people add themselves together, and the thing is done — then they dare do it. For that reason not even a preeminently gifted man can free himself from reflection, because he very soon becomes conscious of himself as a fractional part in some quite trivial matter, and so fails to achieve the infinite freedom of religion. The fact that several people united together have the courage to meet death does not nowadays mean that each, individually, has the courage, for, even more than death, the individual fears the judgment and protest of reflection upon his wishing to risk something on his own. The individual no longer belongs to God, to himself, to his beloved, to his art or science; he is conscious of belonging in all things to an abstraction to which he is subjected by reflection, just as a serf belongs to an estate. . . .

The leveling process is not the action of an individual but the work of reflection in the hands of an abstract power. . . . The individual who levels down is himself engulfed in the process and so on, and while he seems to know selfishly what he is doing one can only say of people *en masse* that they know not what they do; for just as a collective enthusiasm produces a surplus which does not come from the individual, there is also a surplus in this case.

A demon is called up over whom no individual has any power and though the very abstraction of leveling gives the individual a momentary, selfish kind of enjoyment, he is at the same time signing the warrant of his own doom. Enthusiasm *may* end in disaster, but leveling is *eo ipso* the destruction of the individual. No age, and therefore not the present age, can bring the scepticism of that process to a halt, for as soon as it tries to stop it, the law of the leveling process is again called into action. It can therefore only be held up by the individual attaining the religious courage which springs from his individual religious isolation.

. . . The abstract leveling process, that self-combustion of the human race, produced by the friction which arises when the individual ceases to exist as singled out by religion, is bound to continue, like a trade wind, and consume everything. But through it each individual for himself may receive once more a religious education and, in the highest sense, will be helped by the *examen rigorosum* of the leveling process to an essentially religious attitude.

. . . For the leveling process is as powerful where temporary things are concerned as it is impotent where eternal things are concerned.

SUBJECTIVITY, TRUTH, INWARDNESS

8.4

The Subject and Objectivity (Kierkegaard 1992, 189-90, 193-94)

Whether truth is defined more empirically as the agreement of thinking with being or more idealistically as the agreement of being with thinking, the point in each case is to pay scrupulous attention to what is understood by being and also to pay attention to whether the knowing human spirit might not be lured out into the indefinite and fantastically become something such as no *existing* human being has ever been or can be, a phantom with which the individual busies himself on occasion, yet without ever making explicit to himself by means of dialectical middle terms how he gets out of this fantastical realm. . . .

If, in the two definitions given, being is understood as empirical being, then truth itself is transformed into a *desideratum* [something wanted] and everything is placed in the process of becoming, because the empirical object is not finished, and the existing knowing spirit is itself in the process of becoming. Thus truth is an approximating whose beginning cannot be established absolutely, because there is no conclusion that has retroactive power. On the other hand, every beginning, when it is *made* . . . , does not occur by virtue of immanental thinking but is *made* by virtue of a resolution, essentially by virtue of faith. That the knowing spirit is an existing spirit, and that every human being is such a spirit existing for himself, I cannot repeat often enough, because the fantastical disregard of this has been the cause of much confusion. May no one misunderstand me. I am indeed a poor existing spirit like all other human beings, but if in a legitimate and honest way I could be assisted in becoming something extraordinary, the pure I-I, I would always be willing to give thanks for the gift and the good deed. . . .

The way of objective reflection turns the subjective individual into something accidental and thereby turns existence into an indifferent, vanishing something. The way to the objective truth goes away from the subject, and while the subject and subjectivity become indifferent, the truth also becomes indifferent, and that is precisely its objective validity, because the interest, just like the decision, is subjectivity. The way of objective reflection now leads to abstract thinking, to mathematics, to historical knowledge of various kinds, and always leads away from the subjective individual, whose existence or non-existence becomes, from an objective point of view, altogether properly, infinitely indifferent. . . . At its maximum, this way will lead to a contradiction, and to the extent that the subject does not become totally indifferent to himself, this is merely an indication that his objective striving is not objective enough. At its maximum, it will lead to the contradiction that only objectivity has come about, whereas subjectivity has gone out, that is, the existing subjectivity that has made an attempt to become what in the abstract sense is called subjectivity, the abstract form of an abstract objectivity. And yet, viewed subjectively, the objectivity that has come about is at its maximum either a hypothesis or an approximation, because all eternal decision is rooted specifically in subjectivity.

But the objective way is of the opinion that it has a security that the subjective way does not have. . . . It is of the opinion that it avoids a danger that lies in wait for the subjective way, and at its maximum this danger is madness. In a solely subjective definition of truth, lunacy and truth are ultimately indistinguishable, because they may both have inwardness. But one does not become lunatic by becoming objective. At this point I might perhaps add a little comment that does not seem superfluous in an objective age. Is the absence of inwardness also lunacy? The objective truth as such does not at all decide that the one stating it is sensible; on the contrary, it can even betray that the man is lunatic, although what he says is entirely true and especially objectively true.

8.5

Human Existence (Kierkegaard 1980, 13-14)

A human being is spirit. But what is spirit? Spirit is the self. But what is the self? The self is a relation that relates to itself or is the relation's relating itself to itself in the relation; the self is not the relation but is the relation's relating to itself. A human being is a synthesis of the infinite and the finite, of the temporal and the eternal, of freedom and necessity, in short, a synthesis. A synthesis is a relation between two. Considered in this way, a human being is still not a self.

In the relation between the two, the relation is the third as a negative unity, and the two relate to the relation and in the relation to the relation; thus under the qualification of the psychical the relation between the psychical and the physical is a relation. If, however, the relation relates itself to itself, this relation is a positive third, and this is the self.

Such a relation that relates itself to itself, a self, must either have established itself or have been established by another.

If the relation that relates itself to itself has been established by another, then the relation is indeed the third, but this relation, the third, is yet again a relation and relates itself to that which established the entire relation.

The human self is such a derived, established relation, a relation that relates itself to itself and in relating itself to itself relates itself to another. This is why there can be two forms of despair in the strict sense. If a human self had itself established itself, then there could be only one form: not to will to be oneself, to will to do away with oneself, but there could not be the form: in despair to will to be oneself. The second formulation is specifically the expression for the complete dependence of the relation (of the self), the expression for the inability of the self to arrive at or be in equilibrium and rest by itself, but only, in relating itself to itself, by relating itself to that which has established the entire relation. Yes, this second form of despair (in despair to will to be oneself) is so far from designating merely a distinctive kind of despair that, on the contrary, all despair ultimately can be traced back to and be resolved in it. . . . The misrelation of despair is not a simple misrelation but a misrelation in relation so that the misrelation in that relation which is for itself also reflects itself infinitely in the relation to the power that established it.

The formula that describes the state of the self when despair is completely rooted out is this: in relating itself to itself and in willing to be itself, the self rests transparently in the power that established it.

THEOLOGY AND CHRISTIANITY

8.6

God and Inwardness (Kierkegaard 1992, 243-44, 249)

The direct relationship with God is simply paganism, and only when the break has taken place, only then can there be a true God-relationship. But this break is indeed the first act of inwardness oriented to the definition that truth is inwardness. Nature is certainly the work of God, but only the work is directly present, not God. With regard to the individual human being, is this not acting like an elusive author, who nowhere sets forth his result in block letters or provides it beforehand in a preface? And why is God elusive? Precisely because he is truth and in being elusive seeks to keep a person from untruth. The observer does not glide directly to the result but on his own must concern himself with finding it and thereby break the direct relation. But this break is the actual breaking through of inwardness, an act of self-activity, the first designation of truth as inwardness.

Or is it not the case that God is so unnoticeable, so hidden yet present in his work, that a person might very well live on, marry, be respected and esteemed as husband, father, and captain of the popinjay shooting club, without discovering God in his work . . . ?

If one were to portray such a person in an imaginary construction, he would be a satire of what it is to be a human being. It is really the God-relationship that makes a human being a human being, but this is what he would lack. Yet no one would hesitate to consider him an actual human being (for the absence of inwardness is not seen directly), although he would be more like a puppet character that very deceptively imitates all the human externalities. . . .

People in our day have forgotten what it means *to exist,* and what *inwardness* is, and that the misunderstanding between speculative thought and Christianity could be explained by that. I now resolved to go back as far as possible in order not to arrive too soon at what it means to exist religiously, not to mention existing Christianly-religiously, and in that way leave dubieties behind me. If people had forgotten what it means to exist religiously, they had probably also forgotten what it means to exist humanly.

8.7

Be Who You Are: On Necessity, Possibility, and God (Kierkegaard 1980, 35-41)

Possibility and necessity are equally essential to becoming (and the self has the task of becoming itself in freedom). Possibility and necessity belong to the self just as do infinitude and finitude. A self that has no possibility is in despair, and likewise a self that has no necessity.

. . . The philosophers are mistaken when they explain necessity as a unity of possibility and actuality — no, actuality is the unity of possibility and necessity. When a self becomes lost in possibility in this way, it is not merely because of a lack of energy. . . . What is missing is essentially the power to obey, to submit to the necessity in one's life, to what may be called one's limitations. Therefore, the tragedy is not that such a self did not amount to something in the world; no, the tragedy is that he did not become aware of himself, aware that the self he is is a very definite something and thus the necessary. Instead, he lost himself, because this self fantastically reflected itself in possibility. Even in seeing one*self* in a mirror it is necessary to recognize oneself, for if one does not, one does not see one*self* but only a human being. . . . Possibility is like a child's invitation to a party; the child is willing at once, but the question now is whether the parents will give permission — and as it is with the parents, so it is with necessity. . . .

If losing oneself in possibility may be compared with a child's utterance of vowel sounds, then lacking possibility would be the same as being dumb. The necessary is like pure consonants, but to express them there must be possibility. If this is lacking, if human existence is brought to the point where it lacks possibility, then it is in despair and is in despair every moment it lacks possibility. . . .

When someone faints, we call for water, *eau de Cologne,* smelling salts; but when someone wants to despair, then the word is: get possibility, get possibility, possibility is the only salvation. A possibility — then the person in despair breathes again, he revives again, for without possibility a person seems unable to breathe. At times the ingeniousness of the human imagination can extend to the point of creating possibility, but at last — that is, when it depends upon *faith* — then only this helps: that for God everything is possible. . . .

To lack possibility means either that everything has become necessary for a person or that everything has become trivial.

The determinist, the fatalist, is in despair and as one in despair has lost his self, because for him everything has become necessity. He is like that king who starved to death because all his food was changed to gold. Personhood is a synthesis of possibility and necessity. Its continued existence is like breathing, which is an inhaling and exhaling. The self of the determinist cannot breathe, for it is impossible to breathe necessity exclusively, because that would utterly suffocate a person's self. The fatalist is in despair, has lost God and thus his self, for he who does not have a God does not have a self, either. But the fatalist has no God, or, what amounts to the same thing, his God is necessity; since everything is possible for God, then God is this — that everything is possible. Therefore the fatalist's worship of God is at most an interjection, and essentially it is a muteness, a mute capitulation: he is unable to pray. To pray is also to breathe, and possibility is for the self what oxygen is for breathing. Nevertheless, possibility alone or necessity alone can no more be the condition for the breathing of prayer than oxygen alone or nitrogen alone can be that for breathing. For prayer there must be a God, a self — and possibility — or a self and possibility in a pregnant sense, because the being of God means that everything is possible, or that everything is possible means the being of God; only he whose being has been so shaken that he has become spirit by understanding that everything is possible, only he has anything to do with God. That God's will is the possible makes me able to pray; if there is nothing but necessity, man is essentially as inarticulate as the animals.

8.8

Sin as *the* Disability (Kierkegaard 1980, 22, 81-83, 85)

Just as a physician might say that there very likely is not one single living human being who is completely healthy, so anyone who really knows mankind might say that there is not one single living human being who does not despair a little, who does not secretly harbor an unrest, an inner strife, a disharmony, an anxiety about an unknown something or a something he does not dare to try to know, an anxiety about some possibility in existence or an anxiety about himself, so that, just as the physician speaks of going around with an illness in the body, he walks around with a sickness, carries around a sickness of the spirit that signals its presence at rare intervals in and through an anxiety he cannot explain. In any case, no human being ever lived and no one lives outside of Christendom who has not despaired. . . .

No doubt this observation will strike many people as a paradox, an overstatement, and also a somber and depressing point of view. But it is none of these things. It is not somber, for, on the contrary, it tries to shed light on what generally is left somewhat obscure; it is not depressing but instead is elevating, inasmuch as it views every human being under the destiny of the highest claim upon him, to be spirit; nor is it a paradox but, on the contrary, a consistently developed basic view, and therefore neither is it an overstatement. . . .

Sin is: before God in despair not to will to be oneself, or before God in despair to will to be oneself. . . .

The definition embraces every imaginable and every actual form of sin; indeed, it rightly stresses the crucial point that sin is despair (for sin is not the turbulence of the flesh and blood but is the spirit's consent to it) and is: before God. . . . The main point here is simply that the definition, like a net, embraces all forms. And this it does, as can be seen if it is tested by posing its opposite: faith. . . . Faith is: that the self in being itself and in willing to be itself rests transparently in God.

Very often, however, it is overlooked that the opposite of sin is by no means virtue. In part, this is a pagan view, which is satisfied with a merely human criterion and simply does not know what sin is, that all sin is before God. No, *the opposite of sin is faith,* as it says in Romans 14:23. . . .

The antithesis sin/faith is the Christian one that Christianly reshapes all ethical concepts and gives them one additional range. At the root of the antithesis lies the crucial Christian qualification: before God, a qualification that in turn has Christianity's crucial criterion: *the absurd, the paradox, the possibility of offense.* That this is demonstrated by every determination of what is Christian is extremely important, because offense is Christianity's weapon against all speculation. In what, then, lies the possibility of offense here? It lies in this, that a human being should have this reality: that as an *individual* human being a person is directly before God and consequently, as a corollary, that a person's sin should be of concern to God. The idea of the individual human being — before God — never enters speculation's mind. It only universalizes individual human beings fantastically into the race. That, in fact, was also the reason a disbelieving Christianity made out that sin is sin and that whether it is directly before God or not makes no difference at all. In other words, it wanted to get rid of the qualification *before God* and therefore worked out a higher wisdom that, curiously enough, however, was neither more nor less than what higher wisdom most often is: the old paganism.

There is so much talk about being offended by Christianity because it is so dark and gloomy, offended because it is so rigorous, etc., but it would be best of all to explain for once that the real reason that men are offended by Christianity is that it is too high, because its goal is not man's goal, because it wants to make man into something so extraordinary that he cannot grasp the thought. . . .

. . . Christianity teaches that this individual human being — and thus every single human being, no matter whether man, woman, servant girl, cabinet minister, merchant, barber, student, or whatever — this individual human being exists *before God,* . . . this human being who does not have the slightest illusion of being on intimate terms with this one or that one, this human being exists before God, may speak with God any time he wants to, assured of being heard by him — in short, this person is invited to live on the most intimate terms with God! Furthermore, for this person's sake, also for this very person's sake, God comes to the world, allows himself to be born, to suffer, to die, and this suffering God — he almost implores and beseeches this person to accept the help that is offered to him!

8.9

Those Whom Nature Has Wronged from Birth (Kierkegaard 1948, 160-69)

Let us speak of a whole life of sufferings or of some person whom nature, from the very outset, as we humans are tempted to say, wronged, someone who from birth was singled out by useless suffering: a burden to others; almost a burden to himself; and yes, what is worse, to be almost a born objection to the goodness of Providence. Alas, the career of many a busy man is described by and gives rise to fresh *busyness.* The contemplation of such an unfortunate one is an excellent antidote for busyness. *For just by observing such a sufferer, one comes to know unmistakably what the highest is.* But we will not speak carelessly or in passing, hastening away from the sight of this suffering, absorbed in rejoicing over our having been spared it. Neither shall we speak of it despondently.

To be sure it is wonderful to be a child, to fall asleep upon the mother's breast only to awaken to see the mother again; to be a child and to know only the mother and the toy! We laud the happiness of childhood. The very sight of it soothes us by its smile, so that even the one to whom fortune has been granted does not forget this down through the years. But, God be praised, it is not so ordered, that this should be the highest thing of all. It may be dispensed with without losing the highest thing of all. It may be absent without having lost the highest thing of all.

. . . But now the sufferer! Alas, there was no happy childhood for him. Of course a mother's love is faithful and tender, especially toward an ailing child. But a mother is also a human being. When he lay at his mother's breast, she did not gaze joyfully upon him. He saw that she was troubled. Sometimes when he wakened he noticed her weeping.

. . . When he was born there was no gladness or rejoicing, only fearful dismay; when he died there was no grief or affliction, only a melancholy joy. In this fashion his life was passed, or, to speak more accurately, is passed, for this is not an ancient fairy tale that I am telling . . . the same thing happens frequently. It lies close to us even though frivolity and sensuousness, worldly cleverness and godlessness wish to remain ignorant of it. It lies close enough to us even though they wish to keep away from any such unfortunate ones and to avoid all sober reminders not alone from the careless judgment of the storyteller's art, but also from the church and from the edifying insight that must certainly know that the Holy Scriptures have almost a predilection for the halt and the lame, the blind and the lepers. When the disciples began to seem "busy," Christ set a little child in their midst. The crowd that storms and blusters in the bewildered name of the century might well tempt a serious man to set just such an unfortunate sufferer in their midst. The sight of him certainly would not detain anyone that willed anything eternal; but busyness has nothing whatever to do with the Eternal.

He, the sufferer, took part in life — by living. But to his life one thing was unknown, a thing which in all relations of life, as in the passion of love, makes for happiness: to be able to give and to receive "like for like." This "like for like" he never received, and he himself could never give; for as a sufferer he was always the object of sympathy and compassion. . . . All through his life he could never do anything to repay others. . . .

Oh, you sufferer, wherever you may be, wherever you hide from the sight of men in order to spare them from being reminded of the pitiable, oh, do not forget that you, too, can accomplish something. Do not let your life consume itself in a futile counting up of the worthless sufferings of the days and years. You can still do — the highest thing of all. You can will to suffer all and thereby be committed to the Good. . . . Now you are indistinguishable from those whom you wish to be like — those that are committed to the Good. All are clothed alike, girded about the loins with truth, arrayed in the armor of righteousness and wearing the helmet of salvation! . . .

. . . But there is a force that is momentarily powerful. It is cleverness. . . . From its momentary standpoint, it has in view only a decision by which the suffering shall be brought to an end. But be assured, the Eternal does not heal in this fashion. The palsied man does not become whole, because he has been healed by the Eternal, nor the leper clean, nor the deformed made physically perfect. "But then it is a useless device, this help of the Eternal," cleverness suggests, "and what is still worse, is this decision, where the sufferer dedicates himself to his suffering, which indeed makes his condition hopeless" — because the decision renounces the juggling hope of temporal existence. . . .

When the sufferer actually takes his suffering to heart, then he receives help from the Eternal toward his decision. Because to take one's suffering to heart is to be weaned from the temporal order, and from cleverness and from excuses, and from clever men and women and from anecdotes about this and that, in order to find rest in the blessed trustworthiness of the Eternal. For the sufferer, it is as if one should liken him to a sick man who turns himself from side to side, and now at last discovers the position in which there is relief — even if the wish still pains. . . .

But the sufferer who does not wish to be healed by the eternal is double-minded. The double-mindedness in him is a disease that gnaws and eats away the noblest powers; the injury is internal and infinitely more dangerous than being deformed and palsied. This double-minded one wishes to be healed and yet does not wish to be healed: eternally, he does not wish to be healed. . . .

In relation to the sufferer, all double-mindedness has its ground in and is marked by the double-minded one's unwillingness to let go of the things of this world. In the same way the double-minded talk that is from time to time addressed to the sufferer may be recognized by the fact that it puts trust in the things of this world. It is only too often the case that the sufferer shrinks from receiving the highest comfort, and the speaker is ashamed to offer the highest consolation. Contrary to the truth, the consoling talk seeks to offer comfort by saying that the illness will soon be better — perhaps; and begs for a little patience. It coddles the sufferer a little, and says that by Sunday all will surely be well. Yet why give a pauper, if we may for a moment compare a sufferer with a pauper, silver or even counterfeit coin when one has a rich supply of gold to offer him? For the Eternal's comfort is pure gold.

8.10

Our Duty to Love Those We See (Kierkegaard 1962, 157-58, 161, 163-64)

It is a sad upside-downness . . . to talk on and on about how the object of love should be in order to be lovable enough, instead of talking about how love should be in order that it can love. . . .

. . . This discussion is about the duty of finding in the world of actuality those we can love in particular and in loving them to love the men we see. *When this is the duty, the task is not: to find — the lovable object; but the task is: to find the object already given or chosen — lovable, and to be able to continue finding him lovable, no matter how he becomes changed. . . .*

The matter is quite simple. Man shall begin by loving the unseen, God, for thereby he himself shall learn what it is to love. But the fact that he really loves the unseen shall be indicated precisely by this, that he loves the brother he sees. The more he loves the unseen, the more he will love the men he sees. It is not the opposite, that the more he rejects those he sees, the more he loves the unseen, for when this is the case, God is changed into an unreal something, a fancy. Such a thing can occur only to a hypocrite or to a deceiver in order to find an escape, or to one who misrepresents God, as if God were grasping for his own interest and his being loved, rather than that the holy God is gracious and therefore points away from himself, saying, as it were, "If you love me, love the men you see. Whatever you do for them you do for me." . . .

When it is a duty in loving to love the men one sees, *it holds true that in loving actual individual men one does not slip in a fanciful idea about how one thinks or could wish this man should be.* He who does this does not love the man he sees but again something invisible, or his own imagination, or something of that sort. . . .

If a man is going to fulfill the task to love by loving the men that he sees, he must not merely find those that he loves among actual human beings, but he must root out all double-mindedness and fastidiousness in loving them, so that in earnestness and truth he loves them as they are, so that he grasps the task in earnestness and truth: to find lovable the object which has now been given or chosen. We do not mean hereby to glorify a childish infatuation for the accidental characteristics of the beloved, still less a misplaced caressing indulgence. Far from it. The earnestness is precisely in this, that the relationship itself wills to strive with integrated powers against imperfection, to conquer deficiencies, to remove the heterogeneous. . . . One does not become alien to the other person because of his weakness or his error, but the union regards the weakness as alien. . . . When the fault or weakness makes the relationship more inward, not to entrench the fault but to conquer it, then you love the person you see. You see the error, but the fact that your relationship then becomes more inward indicates that you love the person in whom you see the fault or weakness or imperfection.

Just as there are hypocritical tears, hypocritical sighing and complaining over the world, so is there also hypocritical grief over the beloved's weaknesses and imperfections. It is so easy and sweet to wish the beloved to have all possible perfections, and if something is lacking it is again so easy and sweet to sigh and grieve and become self-important in one's supposedly pure and deep concern. On the whole, it is perhaps a more common form of lasciviousness selfishly to wish to make a show of the beloved or friend and to wish to despair over every trifle. But should this be regarded as loving the men that one sees? Ah, no, the men we see (and it is the same when others see us) are not perfect. And yet it is very often the case that one develops within himself this queasy weakness which is good only for loving the complete epitome of perfections. And yet, although we human beings are all imperfect, one very rarely sees the sound, strong, capable love which is good for loving imperfect beings, that is, the men we see.

When it is a duty in loving to love the men we see, *there is no limit to love. If the duty is to be fulfilled, love must be limitless. It is unchanged, no matter how the object becomes changed.*

8.11

Christianity: A Religion of the Marginalized (quotation from Garff 2005, 705-6)

If Christianity has any special affinity for anyone . . . then it is for those who suffer, the poor, the sick, the lepers, the mentally ill, and similar people, sinners, criminals. And look at what Christendom has done to them, see how they have been removed from life so as not to create a disturbance — earnest

Christendom. . . . Christ did not divide people in this manner; it was precisely for these people that he was pastor. . . . What has happened to Christianity in Christendom is like what happens when you give something to a sick child — and then a couple of stronger children come along and grab it.

8.12

Human Identity — God the Prototype (Kierkegaard 1997, 37-43)

> *Therefore I say to you, do not worry about your life, what you will eat and what you will drink, nor about your body, what you will wear. Is not life more than food, and the body more than clothing? Look at the birds of the air: they sow not and reap not and gather not into barns, and your heavenly Father feeds them. Are you not much more than they? But who among you can add one foot to his growth even if he worries about it? And why do you worry about clothing? Look at the lilies in the field, how they grow; they do not work, they do not spin. But I say to you not even Solomon in all his glory was clothed as one of them. (Matt. 6:25-29)*

The care of Lowliness: *This care the bird does not have.* Sparrows are divided into grey sparrows and yellow — or, if you please, gold sparrows, but this distinction, this classification "lowly/eminent" does not exist for them or for any one of them. The other birds do indeed follow the bird that flies at the head of the flock or to the right there is the distinction first and last, to the right and the left. But the distinction lowly/eminent does not exist. . . . And when the thousand voices sing in chorus, there certainly is one that strikes the note; there is distinction. But lowly/eminent, this distinction does not exist, and joy lives freely in the alternating of voices. It gratifies "the single individual" so indescribably to sing in chorus with the others; yet it does not sing to gratify the others; therefore it stops quite abruptly, pauses for a moment, until it is again inclined to join in — and to hear itself.

The bird, then, does not have this care. Why is this so? It is because the bird is what it is, is itself, is satisfied with being itself, is contented with itself. . . . In order to be, in order to have the joy of being, it does not have to walk the long road of first learning to know something about the others in order to find out what it is itself. . . .

It is the lily's and the bird's fortunate privilege that it is made so easy for them to begin to be, that once they have come into existence they have begun at once, they are immediately at full speed in being and there is no need at all for any preliminaries to the beginning, and they are not at all tested in that difficulty much discussed among people and portrayed as very perilous — the difficulty of beginning.

How, then, is the bird the teacher; where is the contact point of the instruction? . . .

This care the lowly Christian does not have. But he is different from the bird in having to be tested in this difficulty of the beginning, because he is aware of the distinction, lowly/eminent. He knows, and he knows that others know the same about him, that he is a lowly human being, and he knows what this means. He knows also what is understood by the advantages of earthly life, how very diverse they are, and alas, that they are all denied to him, that while they otherwise exist to manifest what the others are in these advantages, in his case they seem to be for the purpose of indicating how lowly he is. . . . What exists to indicate the greatness of the eminent seems from the other side to exist to indicate how very little the lowly one is. Oh, what a difficult beginning to existing or for coming to exist: to exist, then to come into existence in order first to exist. Oh, what a slyly concealed snare, one that is not set for any bird! It indeed seems as if in order to begin to be oneself, a human being first of all must be finished with what others are and by that find out then what he himself is — in order to be that. But if he falls into the snare of this optical illusion, he will never become himself. He walks on and on like the person who walks along a road that the passersby tell him definitely leads to the city but forget to tell him that if he wants to go to the city he must turn around. . . .

But the lowly Christian does not fall into the snare of this optical illusion. He sees with the eyes of faith; with the speed of faith that seeks God, he is at the beginning, is himself before God, is contented with being himself. He has found out from the world or from others that he is a lowly person, but he does not abandon himself to this knowledge; he does not lose himself in any worldly way, does not become totally engrossed in it; by holding fast to God with the reservedness of eternity, he has become himself. He is like someone with two names, one for all the others, another for his nearest and dearest ones; in the world, in his association with others, he is the lowly person. He does not pretend to be anything else, and neither is he taken to be anything else, but before God he is himself. . . . He is the lowly human being in the crowd of human beings, and what he is in this way depends on the relationship, but in being himself he is not dependent on the crowd; before God he is himself. From "the others" a person of course actually finds out only what the others are — it is in this way that the world wants to deceive a person out of becoming himself. "The others" in turn do not know what they themselves are either but continually know only what "the others" are. There is only one who completely knows himself, who in himself knows what he himself is — that is God. And he also knows what each human being is in himself, because he is that only by being before God. The person who is not before God is not himself either, which one can be only by being in the one who is in himself. If one is oneself by being in the one who is in himself, one can be in others, or before others, but one cannot be oneself merely by being before others. . . .

What, then, is the lowly Christian who before God is himself? He is a *human being.* Inasmuch as he is a human being, he in a certain sense is like the bird, which is what it is. . . .

But he is also a *Christian.* . . . To that extent he is not like the bird, because the bird *is* what it is. But one cannot become a Christian in this way; if one is a Christian, one must *have become* that. Consequently the lowly Christian has become something in the world; the bird, alas, cannot become something — it is what it is. The lowly Christian was a human being, just as the bird was a bird, but then he became a Christian; he became something in the world. And he can continually become more and more, because he can continually become more and more Christian. As a *human being* he was created in *God's image,* but as a *Christian* he has God as the *prototype.* . . . A prototype is certainly a summons, but what blessing! We even speak of good fortune when we say that there is something in the poet that summons him to write lyrics, but the prototype is an even more rigorous requirement, is an incentive for everyone who sees it, everyone for whom it exists. The prototype is a promise; no other promise is so reliable, because the prototype is indeed the fulfillment. There is no prototype before the bird, but the prototype exists before the lowly Christian, and he exists before his prototype — he can continually grow to resemble it more and more. . . .

If . . . at such a blessed moment when he is absorbed in his prototype, someone else looks at him, the other person sees only a lowly person before him; it was just the same for the prototype — people saw only the lowly person. He believes and hopes he will ever more and more approach a likeness of this prototype, who will only in the next life manifest himself in his glory. . . . He believes that this prototype, if he continually struggles to resemble him, will bring him again, and in an even more intimate way, into kinship with God, that he does not have God only as a creator, as all creatures do, but has God as his brother.

8.13

The Comic and the Tragic in Relations with the Other (Kierkegaard 1988, 420-21)

A deaf man is entering a meeting hall when the meeting is in progress; he does not want to disturb and therefore opens the big double door very gently. Unfortunately, a feature of the door is that it creaks. This he cannot hear; he believes he is doing it very well, and a long sustained creaking is produced by this slow opening of the door. People become impatient; someone turns around and shushes him: he thinks he may have been opening the door too fast, and the creaking continues. . . . There is a point of unity intimated here: he does not want to disturb, the assembly does not want to be disturbed, and he disturbs it. Add a dash of feeling and something else, and the result is the many situations over which one does not know whether to laugh or to cry. This is the tragic-comic. . . .

Now to my imaginary construction. I have placed together two heterogeneous individualities, one male and one female. . . . As soon as I posit a point of unity there can be plenty of misunderstanding. This point of unity is that they are united in loving each other. The misunderstanding, then, is not due to some third factor, as if they understood each other and were separated by some alien power — no, ironically enough, everything favors their misunderstanding. There is nothing to keep them from having each other and talking together, but right there the misunderstanding begins. . . . The conjunction in this misunderstanding is that they love each other, but in their heterogeneity this passion must express itself in essentially different ways, and thus misunderstanding must not come between them from outside but develops in the relationship itself that exists between them. The tragic is that the two lovers do not understand each other; the comic is that two who do not understand each other love each other.

9 *People Are Born from People: Willem van den Bergh on Mentally Disabled People*

Marjolein de Mooij

The fear of madness is leaving me to a great extent, as I see at close quarters those who are affected by it in the same way as I may very easily be in the future. . . . For though there are some who howl or rave continually, there is so much of real friendship here among them: they say we must put up with others so that the others will put up with us . . . and among ourselves we understand each other very well. For instance, I can sometimes chat with one of them who can only answer in incoherent sounds, because he is not afraid of me.

Van Gogh, *The Complete Letters of Vincent van Gogh*

So Vincent van Gogh wrote to his brother, Theo, from the hospital at St. Remy in 1889. His growing perception of the insane as individuals shows in both his letters and his paintings. During this period he began to paint portraits not only of his physicians, but also of the patients. He wrote, "At the moment I am working on a portrait of one of the patients here. It is curious that after one has been with them for some time and got used to them, one does not think of them as being mad any more" (Van Gogh 1959, 3:266).

Van Gogh's perception of his fellow patients displays genuine insight into insanity based on intense personal experience. In this he represents a radical break with the prevalent Romantic conception at that time — a conception that often focused on and valued extreme emotional states and the irrational over the rational — and so catalyzes a movement during the nineteenth century toward a more realistic view of the world.

It is at this turning point that we find the thought and works of Willem van den Bergh, the founder of the first institution for mentally disabled people in the Netherlands. Van den Bergh was a Romantic, but also a realistic Calvinist; a Protestant thinker who wanted to create a new world without losing the old one. While his views on mentally disabled people may sometimes be offensive, they are always "inclusive," for, according to Van den Bergh, disability is related to morality, or, more specifically, to sin. Since all people are sinners, disabled people are no different in this respect and should therefore not be classified as inferior. Thus the words of Calvin that point to one mankind and one common human nature turn out to be crucial in the formation of Willem van den Bergh's views on disability.

If we are to fully understand Van den Bergh's thinking, a bit of contextualization will be helpful. I will open by describing the cultural and theological context for thinking about the lives of mentally disabled people in the Netherlands in the nineteenth century. In the first section, I will briefly describe the Romantic world and its influence on contemporary perceptions of disabled people. In the second section, I will explore Romanticism and theology as they manifested themselves specifically in the Netherlands in the nineteenth century. The Romantic movement not only touched Protestant theology, but also played a major role in the preoccupation of Protestant thinkers with disabled, sick, and insane people. In the third and fourth sections, I will show how the thought of Van den Bergh exemplifies this changing cultural and theological context, melding Calvinism, Romanticism, and an understanding of the realities of Dutch society in order to provide answers to important questions and problems of the time. In the fifth section, I will show how Van den Bergh's works on mentally disabled people and their care are concrete and practical in their response to these problems. Finally, I will offer some suggestions about the ideas of Van den Bergh that remain relevant for our time.

I. The Romantic World

Romanticism refers not to a specific style but to an attitude of mind that may reveal itself in any number of ways.

H. W. Janson, *The History of Art*

Writings and paintings of the Romantic period reveal that insanity (mental disability being classified as a specific type of madness in that era) was a subject that deeply preoccupied the Romantic artist. Mental illness came to be seen in new, often sympathetic terms, and people greeted its manifestations with lively curiosity. How are we to understand this enhanced estimation of a side of the mind that had been pitied or abhorred in previous centuries?

Romanticism as a movement focused on psychological, internal realities, but ones with enormous power and influence on the external world. Its fascination with altered modes of perceiving and feeling is evident in the attention paid to unusual psychological conditions such as terror and violence. As Edmund Burke states in *A Philosophical Enquiry into the Origin of Our Ideas of the Sublime and the Beautiful* (1757),

> The ideas of pain, sickness, and death fill the mind with strong emotions of horror. . . . Whatever is fitted in any sort to excite the ideas of pain, and danger, that is to say, whatever is in any sort terrible, or is conversant about terrible objects, or operates in a manner analogous to terror, is productive of the strongest emotion which the mind is capable of feeling. (Burke 1958, 38-39)

The Romantic artist worshiped at the altar of emotions, and throughout the period one encounters a deep hunger for emotional experience and new intensities of feeling. It is as if reality could most intensely be experienced in situations of violence, ecstasy, or madness. Characteristic of Romantic "enthusiasts" was also a tendency to doubt the validity of facts: feeling and emotion were now seen as modes of perception and experience superior to intellect and reason (MacGregor 1989, 68).

It is perhaps paradoxical that while Romanticism was in some respects a public phenomenon, its essential nature tended to focus on experiences of a highly individual character, on inner states, and on the introspective perception of feeling, intuition, and emotion. Extreme individuality — the artist as outsider, rejecting and rejected by his society — is an essential component of the ideal of the Romantic writer and artist (MacGregor 1989, 71).

Another aspect of Romanticism is an adulation of nature and the natural. The insane were often seen as in some sense natural, as primitive beings uninhibited by the restraints imposed by reason and a society of conventional morality. Madness served as an excuse for the liberation of the instinct. The image of the madhouse — impressively painted by Francisco Goya and Henry Fuseli — can thus be understood as a vision of natural man unleashed and of the force of pure emotional intensity. "The instincts erupt

323

to the surface, the cruelest lusts clamor for satisfaction, the darkest passions proclaim their dominion — all this must be borne in mind when we think of the great madman whom the Romantic imagination produced" (Hoffmann 1961, 263).

But madness was also defined as a disease of the imagination./The world of the madhouse served as a warning for those who went too far in the search for intensity of experience and freedom from conventional morality and reason/After all, many Romantic writers held strongly negative views of madness. In the image of the lunatic they saw an allegory of the world gone mad, a microcosm expressive of the human condition. "In the nineteenth century, madness, crime, sensual orgies . . . were felt to be manifestations of a hell that was everywhere immanent" (Hoffmann 1961, 262).

In the Netherlands in the 1800s, the Romantic and the religious converged in a surprising way when a group of Protestants who were touched by Romanticism felt a deep need to awaken the world: this group is called "het Réveil" — "the awakening."

II. Het Réveil: Romanticism Meets Theology

In the 1820s and 1830s, following the revolutionary and Napoleonic periods, an anti-revolutionary and anti-liberal religious awakening movement formed in Holland under the name of het Réveil (Koenders 1996, 42).

Het Réveil is the Dutch-Calvinist variant of European revivalism which emerged as a group of intellectuals united to resist the spirit of rationalism. They were particularly concerned with religio-spiritual matters, setting the Gospel and the Bible against the revolution (Kluit 1970, 189-91). Isaac da Costa, a Jewish convert to Protestantism and a famous poet and essayist, became one of the principal figures of the movement. In 1823 he wrote the book *Bezwaren tegen den Geest dezer eeuw (Objections to the Spirit of Our Time)*, an anti-revolutionary and reactionary manifesto, the Calvinist counterpart of De Maistre's *Du Pape* of 1819.

This manifesto shows us many elements of the politically conservative movement in the nineteenth century which emerged in reaction to the French Revolution and to liberalism. On the one hand, the movement represented a huge protest not only against the revolution but also against Enlightenment rationalism, which was seen as a source of immorality, the belief in progress, and abstract moralistic thought that did not acknowledge the importance of tradition and history, but instead intended to reform the world on the basis of natural law. On the other hand, the movement embraced pre-revolutionary Europe, the *ancient régime* (which stood as the "conservative" standard, sanctified by God, tradition, and history [Von der Dunk 1978, 742]), and taught that man was a weak and sinful creature and therefore imperfect. The society of the nineteenth century, with its numerous social problems, was viewed by the movement as a permanent reality made so by God and thus not to be changed.

Réveil and Politics

It was the Protestant statesman and historian Guillaume Groen van Prinsterer — an important man in the Réveil group — who tried to transform the pure spiritual-cultural conservatism of the Réveil into political, Protestant conservatism (Kluit 1970; Koenders 1996, 51). In 1847, Groen outlined his ideas in *Ongeloof en Revolutie (Unbelief and Revolution),* explaining how he wished to transform the liberal state into a Protestant-Christian state where the Gospel should become the guiding principle of a national policy for the country and the whole social system (Von der Dunk 1978, 748).

Groen's efforts did not succeed in establishing a strong anti-revolutionary political faction. That became the main task for his successor, Abraham Kuyper, the clergyman, neo-Calvinist theologian, and (later) prime minister of the Netherlands, who organized a vigorous, active, anti-revolutionary party, established in 1879. For the Anti-Revolutionary Party, the doctrine of the sovereignty of spheres (the belief that every sphere or area of action — the familial, the religious, the economic, etc. — should attend to its own interests, and that these interests are equal to one another) was very important. Thus Abraham Kuyper rejected the French doctrine of popular sovereignty and the German doctrine of the sovereignty of the state. Instead, Kuyper wanted to honor the "intermediate institutions" in society (families, schools, the press, trade unions, etc.), which he saw as discrete spheres, discovered through Scripture and history, which are equally authoritative in God's ruling of the world.

Kuyper's thinking — strongly shaped by Groen and het Réveil, and exhibiting an evangelical and anti-revolutionary character, as well as an impressive social conscience — came together in his greatest theological act: the founding of the Reformed Churches in the Netherlands in 1892. The aims of this new church were to repristinate the old Dutch Reformed Church of the sixteenth century and to bring the church and her confessions back to the people. This would be a church for the "kleine luyden" (the common people), who would take responsibility for their own social problems.

Réveil and Social Concern

Réveil members tended to be socially distinguished and high-ranking, with a pietistic spirituality. They often came from an aristocratic social environment and had double and French names, like Guillaume Groen van Prinsterer. Their meetings — called *réunions* or *soirées religieuses,* which took place in the impressive houses of the members of the group — provided venues to listen to speeches, read the Bible, and talk about spirituality. Nevertheless, the people of the Réveil were also people of the nineteenth century — a century full of social problems that, while perhaps not having a direct effect on their lives, did not leave them untouched.

The social-conservative concern of the aristocracy for the lower classes, in combination with a deep wish to bring the Gospel to their society, gave an important impetus to many philanthropic works. The Réveil built hospitals, shelters for prostitutes, workhouses for women, homes for orphans, schools for children, and more. But note that all this was framed by an emphasis on individual piety and was limited to private philanthropy, which the doctrine of sphere sovereignty grounded in Scripture. The people of the Réveil reacted to what they saw in their own "neighborhood" and so restricted themselves to local actions. They did not work with the government or other authorities but stayed within their own circle of connections. They had no interest in these realms, and for theological reasons never sought to generate more structural solutions to their problems. The existing society was taken for granted and assumed to be a permanent reality established in its current configuration by God.

III. The Life of Willem van den Bergh

In 1850, the precise middle of the nineteenth century, Willem van den Bergh was born into a wealthy, Protestant family in The Hague. After attending gymnasium, he went to the University of Leiden to study law and theology. There, Van den Bergh became a close friend of Prince Willem Alexander, the son of King Willem III and Queen Sophia, and an admirer of Abraham Kuyper, who was then thirty-three years old. On finishing his studies, Van den Bergh went to Germany on several study tours (Van den Doel 1999, 18-19), and it was there that he observed several programs of charity and Christian education of the German evangelist Johann Wichern, the founder of the "Innere Mission." He also became acquainted with several important conservative leaders (Schram 1980, 46).

The visit to Germany made a strong impression on Van den Bergh, and he decided to write a dissertation on prostitution. Hendrik Pierson, manager of the shelters for prostitutes in Zetten, invited Van den Bergh to complete his research there, and Willem warmly accepted this invitation. In 1877 he finished his juridical dissertation, *The Battle Against Prostitution,* and two years later he wrote his theological dissertation, titled *Calvin and the Bond of Grace.* In 1879 Van den Bergh married Ida Pierson, the daughter of Hendrik Pierson.

After his marriage, Willem van den Bergh became a minister and moved to the vicarage in Schaarsbergen, where his two daughters, Diete Ida (1880) and Hermine Agnes (1881), were born. Shortly after the birth of their second child, Ida became sick with tuberculosis. In 1884, at the age of twenty-five, Ida died; in that same year, Willem himself also began to cough up blood (Van den Doel 1999, 21-22).

After the death of his wife, Van den Bergh moved to the village of Voorthuizen, where he started a long jurisdictional battle against the hierarchical structure of the Protestant Church of the Netherlands. He wanted a more democratic church that could change his society and would take care of the poor, and to this end, he worked closely with Abraham Kuyper, who later was to help found the Reformed Churches of the Netherlands.

The death of Ida inspired Van den Bergh to help people in a more practical way, and in 1884 he invited several churches to establish the Association for Christian Care of Insane People and Neuropaths, and to found an establishment for mentally disabled people in Veldwijk. It was also the deep wish of Van den Bergh to found an institution for mentally disabled children, and he worked hard to raise a school for them. His influence within the church and society increased, and in 1889 he accepted a chair at the Free University of Amsterdam. Unfortunately, he was never able to take up this post because tuberculosis had weakened his body, and his health was worsening. A long stay in a sanatorium in Switzerland was to no avail, and in 1890, at the age of forty, Willem van den Bergh died (Van den Doel 1999, 26-27).

IV. The Ideas of Willem van den Bergh

A broken and contrite heart, O God, you will not despise.

Psalm 51:19

These words — from Willem van den Bergh's favorite psalm — can be found on his tombstone and seem to suggest that he was a gloomy man with little confidence in his own work, a quite misleading impression. A wall of the church hall in Voorthuizen displays the complete text that Van den Bergh used when he delivered his first sermon there:

A broken and contrite heart, O God, you will not despise.
Do good to Zion in your good pleasure;
Build up the walls of Jerusalem.

Van den Bergh wished to build a new Jerusalem, to make a new society — a new society that was to be built from the "bottom up." He also believed that the initiative should come not from the state, but from a private venture of the churches called to take care of the needs of society.

Van den Bergh and the Réveil

Willem van den Bergh was deeply influenced by the people of the Réveil. Their conservative way of looking at their world, their pietistic spirituality, their genuine wish to help other people, and their desire to make Protestantism a constructive element of the Netherlands was foundational to his thought. However, he was also a man with his own pragmatic insights. In his opinion the care of the poor should be undertaken by the church, not the state, nor some wealthy individuals unable to provide the structural solutions that Van den Bergh sought. Like Kuyper, Van den Bergh honored the "intermediate institutions" headed by the local churches, and he believed it was the mission of the church to provide care when people could not help themselves. One might say that while Van den Bergh incorporated the ideas of the Réveil and its works in the Reformed Churches of the Netherlands, he looked beyond the Réveil and prepared it for the century to come.

Van den Bergh and John Calvin

Willem van den Bergh was a man of the Réveil, but he was also a Calvinist. Not only was his second dissertation on Calvin, but in his other works several aspects of Calvin's ideas also appear. As he developed his own concept of humanity, he searched the works of John Calvin for material to flesh out his own system. However, his approach was not accepted by everyone: as early as 1879, other professors were already criticizing Van den Bergh's theological dissertation, claiming that it was inappropriate to separate Calvin's various ethical-social conclusions from his dogmatic system (Van Dijk 1917, 275-339). This was, as we will see, an accurate assessment of Van den Bergh's theological approach.

In 1532, John Calvin wrote a commentary on *De Clementia* by the Roman philosopher Seneca. Commenting on the unity of humanity, Seneca states: "There is nobody — the Roman emperor says in the second chapter of the book — who by the name human only does not enjoy my favor, even if anything else would lack him" (Calvin 1969, 2). In his comment on these words, Calvin notes several groups that for certain reasons should be treated with mildness, such as the nobility, the clergy, the masses, and another group: "I think that they, who cannot defend themselves, are at least human beings and matter to me because they carry the same name" (Calvin, 11, 17).

Thus stoic ideas about the unity of humanity and common human nature that had become generally accepted in antiquity were appropriated by Calvin. However, Calvin adds a theological tenet: All people are one because they are all created after the image of God:

> The Lord enjoins us to do good to all without exception, though the greater part, if estimated by their own merit, are most unworthy of it. But Scripture subjoins a most excellent reason, when it tells us that we are not to look to what men in themselves deserve, but to attend to the image of God, which exists in all, and to which we owe all honor and love. (Calvin 1845-46, III, 7, 6)

Calvin asserted that the prime mark of the image of God is rationality. Willem van den Bergh, however, never mentions this distinctive mark in his works. It is likely that Calvin's emphasis on rationality did not fit into his Romantic way of thinking. To trust the intellect in any sense, including in the definitions of humanity, is a mistake, Van den Bergh insists. Science and compulsory school attendance do not bring the common happiness people are looking for, he added, because only God is capable of bringing peace and calmness to unhappy people (Van den Bergh 1885, 82-88). This agreement is typical of Van den Bergh's approach: the unity of humanity and the commonality of human nature are important themes in his work, but excerpts showing Calvin's emphasis on rationality are never quoted and are indirectly criticized.

Emphasizing that all people are one — being created in the image of God — has consequences for human action. One cannot be human without being open and obliging to other people, Calvin states:

> Therefore, whoever be the man that is presented to you as needing your assistance, you have no ground for declining to give it to him. Say he is a stranger. The Lord has given him a mark which ought to be familiar to you: for which reason he forbids you to despise your own flesh (Gal. 6:10) . . . Say he is unworthy of your least exertion on his account; but the image of God, by which he is recommended to you, is worthy of yourself and all your exertions. (Calvin 1845-46, III, 7, 6)

Every human being matters. Restating the Stoics, Calvin writes: "*Homines hominum cause esse genitos* — people are born from people. The fact that someone is my fellow is enough for me to feel connected with him or her." These thoughts color the notion of *humanitas* in Calvin: human life is inconceivable without fellowship. They also play an important role in Calvin's considerations of the state and church:

> All we wish to be understood at present is, that it is perfect barbarism to think of exterminating it [the civil government], its use among men being not less than that of bread and water, light and air, while its dignity is much more excellent. Its object is not merely, like those things, to enable men to breathe, eat, drink, and be warmed (though it certainly includes all these), while it enables them to live together; this, I say, is not its only object, but [also the prevention of idolatry] . . . that honesty and modesty be cultivated; in short, that a public form of religion may exist among Christians, and humanity among them. (Calvin 1845-46, IV, 20, 3)

Here we can see what Calvin means by a human life in a human society: it is a society where people are mutually connected and everyone is able to "breathe, eat, drink, and be warmed." Van den Bergh's interest was in what these ideas of Calvin's might mean for people with mental disabilities.

V. Van den Bergh on Mentally Disabled People

On the Origins of Insanity

On April 15, 1885, Willem van den Bergh gave the lecture *On the Origins of Insanity* at the first meeting of the Association for Christian Care of Insane People and Neuropaths. This lecture is a mix of theology and psychiatry, Calvinism and Romanticism, dreams and reality. *On the Origins of Insanity* consists of three major parts: the introduction, a discussion of the origins of insanity, and the conclusion.

The introduction to *On the Origins of Insanity* (**9.1**) displays several Romantic elements: insanity is interpreted as a manifestation of a perverting society (cf. Hoffmann 1961, 262). Van den Bergh also presents himself as an individualistic thinker, rejecting the world and the church of his time. Elements of the Réveil are also present: the deep wish to testify and bring the word of God to the people, the social-conservative sensitivity to care for people who cannot take care of themselves, and the strong awareness of humans as weak and sinful creatures. Finally, the introduction includes aspects of Calvin's thought on the unity of humanity and common human nature.

In the main part of the lecture (**9.2**), Van den Bergh connects theology and the origins of insanity. He reviews ten causes of insanity, explaining them in biblical terms. According to Van den Bergh, "scientific" reflections on insanity show us the actual truth of Scripture. He thus connects the heredity of insanity — while using scientific data and pointing to alcoholism — with the words in Exodus 20:5: "I, the LORD your God, am a jealous God, punishing the children for the sin of the fathers to the third and fourth generation of those who hate me." Here Romanticism and Realism are neatly meshed: the "facts" are told — the realities of the nineteenth century are presented — but they are placed in a Romantic and religious context. Reason is drawn into the project of supporting religion. The last part of the lecture (**9.3**) is a passionate cry to control the origins of insanity and a call for more compassion toward the insane. At the heart of the conclusion we again find Calvin's emphasis on the unity of humanity prominently cited.

"A Child without Parents or Name"

In 1884 Willem van den Bergh wrote the article "A Child without Parents and Name" in the magazine *Bouwstenen (Building Stones)*. The title of the article is an allusion to Christian social work in Van den Bergh's time, which had no link with the church and was therefore considered to be a child without parents (church) or name (identification). In his article, Van den Bergh examines care for people from a broad and Christian perspective. He raises and discusses several questions, giving answers that are often surprisingly modern and well-considered. We will examine four parts of this article: the articulation of the task, the importance of caring for people near us, the importance of taking care according to God's order, and the maxim that everyone should take care of others.

In the first part (**9.4**), Van den Bergh quotes the words of Abraham Kuyper on the "The Assignment of the Laborer." The assignment of the laborer is to be answered by the church in a structural way. There should be no help for individuals by individuals (here we find a form of criticism of the Réveil); the whole church is responsible for meeting the demands of social need. Van den Bergh then goes on to set these comments within a wider perspective. To Abraham Kuyper the social question concerns only the laborer, but Van den Bergh adds other people too: the orphan, the sick, the idiot, the drunk, the insane, and the soldier. These too also present needs to society, and the church's most important reason for existing is to respond to *everyone's* need.

In the second part (**9.5**), Van den Bergh draws our attention to those we encounter every day. He rejects the Christian social work of his time — the Internal Mission — because it did not pay attention to people near at hand. Why look for the needy far away and not nearby? Why only look for sinners and not for people less guilty? Why the preference for the exceptional and not the common man? Realism wins over Romanticism here. Van den Bergh accuses the Internal Mission of favoring the "gevallene en verlatene" ("fallen" people and those who are left behind) and forgetting the others who need help too. He also points to the hypocrisy of his time: some are conspicuous in their attempts to rescue the unmarried mother, but forget to close their saloons to those who made her fall; the fabric school may be lauded, but shouldn't the manufacturer be educated and taught to treat the laborers like people and not like machines?

In the next section (**9.6**), Van den Bergh presents a vision of what Christian care according to God's order should look like. People should be looked after in their own environment — their own home, family, village, town, church, and so on — and this environment should accord with the divine order. Van den Bergh argues that the estrangement of people from their context is damaging for them; therefore, institutions should understand and respect the factors that tie people together.

The acme of Christian care will be achieved when it evokes the compassion of religious communities to care for the people in their own sphere (**9.7**). Taking care is everyone's responsibility, and it starts within the family of each individual. For Willem van den Bergh, building a new world without losing the old one represents the best of Christian care. It is a melding of old and new concepts: the church will build hospitals and shelters, but it is even better when people solve the problems in their own houses.

Conclusion

Willem van den Bergh was a man of the nineteenth century who looked at his world with Romantic and realistic eyes. His world was different from ours, and his comments may sometimes seem naïve to us or even offensive, so that we can only reject, for example, the way he links growth in the population of the insane with the retardation of society. Although *On the Origins of Insanity* opens with the words of Deuteronomy 28:28 — "The Lord will afflict you with madness, blindness, and confusion of mind" — Van den Bergh never relates insanity directly to God, but always understands it to be the effect of some human behavior. Van den Bergh blames individual behavior for incrementally swelling the ranks of the insane: individuals have committed morally condemnable acts, they have let their faith turn into disbelief, and they have done so in a (modern) society that fosters the choices that lead to insanity.

In making these connections between insanity and morality, Van den Bergh is most obviously a man of his age. The correlation between the increase in insanity and the regression of society was common in the nineteenth century — indeed, insanity and morality had been connected since the Middle Ages (Le Goff 2006, 450). Unfortunately, Van den Bergh finds no reason to resist these accepted views, but a close reading of his lecture does reveal that while he uses harsh words to describe his society, he is very gentle in representing insane people themselves. How are we to understand this?

Although Van den Bergh espouses many of the traditional ideas of his time, he also interjects a Calvinist element. Insanity and morality are not the domain of insane people only; they include all mankind. All people are sinners and in a specific sense insane. Van den Bergh widens the definition of insanity and morality by turning the exclusive conceptions of both into inclusive ones. The common nature of mankind and the unity of humanity release mentally disabled people from a realm of social isolation: thus exclusivity turns into inclusivity. Showing care and compassion for mentally disabled people is a logical consequence of this inclusivity; as Calvin states, "I think that they, who cannot defend themselves, are at least human beings and matter to me because they carry the same name" (Calvin 1845-46, 17).

The works of Willem van den Bergh represent an engagement with the ideas of John Calvin and the views of nineteenth-century society. Van den Bergh was deeply touched by the social questions of his time and eventually formulated his own inclusive conception of humanity that called for a caring society with its own unique contours. This conception still has relevance for our time despite Van den Bergh's failure to develop his explicit critique of Calvin's rationalist definition of the image of God that he clearly believed was necessary. He dealt with this issue in his own way, ignoring the beliefs of Calvin he could not accept and tacitly correcting Calvin's concept of humanity as he built his own theological system.

"Homines hominum cause esse genitos," Calvin insisted. Willem van den Bergh acted on that statement as he worked for a better world, expressing his commitment to those who could not defend themselves.

REFERENCES

Primary Sources

Van den Bergh, Willem. 1885. *De oorzaken der krankzinnigheid.* Tract, publisher unknown. Unpaginated.

——. 1884. "Een ouderloos en naamloos kind." In *Bouwstenen, tijdschrift voor inwendige zending,* 3rd ed. Utrecht: C. H. E. Breijer, 35-82.

Secondary Sources

Arblaster, Paul. 2006. *A History of the Low Countries.* New York: Palgrave Macmillan.

Burke, Edmund. 1958. *A Philosophical Enquiry into the Origin of Our Ideas of the Sublime and the Beautiful.* London: Routledge & Kegan Paul.

Calvin, John. 1969. *Calvin's Commentary on Seneca's De Clementia.* Edited and translated by Ford L. Battles and André M. Hugo. Leiden: Brill.

——. 1845-46. *Institutes of the Christian Religion.* Edinburgh: Calvin Translation Society.

Foucault, Michel. 1965. *Madness and Civilization.* New York: Vintage Books.

Gilman, Sander L. 1982. *Seeing the Insane.* New York: John Wiley and Brunner-Mazel.

Hoffmann, Werner. 1961. *The Earthly Paradise: Art in the Nineteenth Century.* New York: G. Braziller.

Janson, H. W. 1962. *The History of Art.* New York: Abrams.

Kluit, Marie Elisabeth. 1970. *Het protestantse Reveil in Nederland en daarbuiten 1815-1865.* Paris, Amsterdam: n.p.

Koenders, Pieter. 1996. *Tussen Christelijk Reveil en seksuele revolutie: Bestrijding van zedeloosheid in Nederland met nadruk op de repressie van homoseksualiteit.* Amsterdam: IISG.

Le Goff, Jacques. 2006. *De cultuur van middeleeuws Europa.* Amsterdam: Wereldbibliotheek.

MacGregor, John M. 1989. *The Discovery of the Art of the Insane.* Princeton: Princeton University Press.

Schram, P. L. 1980. *Willem van den Bergh, 1850-1890* Amsterdam: Ton Bolland.

Van den Doel, Huibrecht G. 1999. *Het mallegat in de branding: Bewogen zorg op de Willem van den Bergh [1924-2024].* Noordwijk: Willem van den Bergh.

Van Dijk, Isaak. 1917. "De beoefening der Gereformeerde theologie in ons vaderland." In *Gezamenlijke Geschriften van Is. Van Dijk* I. Groningen: P. Noordhoff.

Van Gogh, Vincent. 1959. *The Complete Letters of Vincent van Gogh.* Greenwich, Conn.: New York Graphic Society.

Von der Dunk, Hermann. 1978. "Conservatism in the Netherlands." *Journal of Contemporary History* 13, no. 4 (October): 741-63.

Excerpts

All the excerpts following are translated from the Dutch by Reinder Bruinsma.

The Origins of Insanity

Willem van den Bergh. 1885. *De oorzaken der krankzinnigheid.* Unpaginated tract. Publisher unknown. Van den Bergh delivered this speech on April 15, 1885, in Utrecht, to introduce a discussion on this topic prior to the General Meeting of the Association of Christian Carers for the Insane and the Sufferers of Nervous Disorders (Algemeene Vereniging tot Christelijke Verzorging van Krankzinningen en Zenuwlijders).

9.1

"However, if you do not obey the Lord your God and do not carefully follow all his commands and decrees I am giving you today, all these curses will come upon you and overtake you. . . . The Lord will afflict you with madness, blindness and confusion of mind." Deuteronomy 28:15, 28.

"The causes of insanity." When we accept the Scriptures as norm, we discover that the term has a somewhat ambiguous meaning. What sort of insanity is intended? The Scriptures refer to a "darkening" of people's "understanding" (Ephesians 4:18), as a characteristic that is inherent in every human being. Thus, one might call Eve the first insane person, after her way of thinking and acting had become "estranged from the divine life." This would imply that all unregenerate human beings are insane and that Alexander von Oettingen (*Moral-Statistik,* second edition, 629) is justified in differentiating between the *"Geisteskrankheit,"* which is part of human nature, and the *"Seelenstörung,"* which nowadays is referred to as insanity.

Limiting ourselves to this latter aspect, and in particular to the Netherlands, we find that the increase of this kind of insanity is in all probability related to the spiritual decline that at present manifests itself all too clearly among God's children. They themselves are to blame for this increase, since (1) they do not sufficiently combat the causes of this illness, though God's

Spirit and His Word enable them to do so; (2) in the church, in the family circle, and in the inner chamber they so little plead the lot of these unfortunate sufferers before the merciful High Priest; (3) [and] they do not humble themselves enough under the divine judgments, which are also visible in the increase in the numbers of insane people and sufferers of nervous disorders.

Concerning this last point: very seldom the attention is focused on the fourfold Babel, under which those who confess Christ, regardless of the denomination they belong to, live at present in our country — without, alas, being weighed down by it. Because of some of the rules and laws that have been imposed, we find ourselves, corporately, not only in a spiritual, civil, and social, but also in a *medical* Babel. One only needs to be reminded of the rules with regard to prostitution, the coercion of vaccination, while recently also the new law to govern the supervision of the insane by the state has been introduced. According to this law the state supervision extends "to all insane people," with the exception of those who, "without being deprived of their freedom, are cared for in their own home, or in the house of their parents or spouses" (Art. 2 of the law of April 27, 1884; *Staatsblad* no. 96). If this supervisory role is indeed necessary, because of the abuses that have been found in connection with the care for these people by private persons, even by their own children, it is, on the one hand, a testimony to our lack of charity, and, on the other hand, a new step on the road that was opened in 1854 with the Law about Provisions for the Poor and was an indignity for the Christian churches, which, apparently, not only need the control of the state, but also its financial support to supplement their practice of charity. Thus, there cannot be an attitude of pride towards the state asylums or the supervisory role of the state. No, we must feel humbled by the fact that these are needed as a result of the folly of families, and the lack of faith and sluggishness on the part of the churches and Christendom in general.

From this we may, in fact, conclude that the asylum which has been planned for Christian care of the insane should be regarded as a *testimony,* rather than as having a *saving* character. For such an initiative is bound to carry a number of dangers with it: (1) it increases the number of organizations, local associations, meetings, and concern for funding, which, for a variety of reasons, in fact, might produce more insanity; (2) it will not affect the sources, but will only provide care for the unfortunate sufferers who drank from them; and (3) it will easily stimulate the kind of pride to which Daniel 4:30 refers, which might, according to verse 33, by way of punishment be followed by a greater degree of insanity. It is thus of immense importance that the institution presents a testimony. For, if it does, it deals with the real problem as it points to the actual causes of insanity. In so doing, it can become an instrument in the Lord's hands that will lead not only to a pursuit of humility, but also the labors of faith, as each person will have his assigned task. For that reason article 2b of the draft of the by-laws for the local chapters of the association, in particular — if it is actually accepted — may be so fruitful: "The purpose of the chapter is: *b* to promote, especially in the place where it has been established, the knowledge of, and interest for, the calling of Christians with regard to the insane, as well as, to contribute, according to its abilities and to the needs that exist and the opportunities that present themselves, to participate in this Christian care." One might, however, remark that this pertains to the calling of every church member, even if he does not hold membership in this association. The fact that this instruction must be specifically given, however, is one of the many signs of the deterioration of the church. Alas. The ignorance and lack of mercy that are addressed in this article are but two of the many diseases which afflict our churches. The situation is even aggravated by the illusion of so many that the neglect of duty and misery is not so serious. Yet, what has been said by a German author (Dr. C. W. van Roller), when he referred to physical insanity, may also be said of this spiritual insanity, as we might call it: "Healing will result if there is insight in the nature of the illness."[1] A similar statement comes from a Dutch physician (Dr. A. O. Tellegen): "Slowly the insane person is beginning to sense that something must be wrong with him. . . . This realization is the beginning of his improvement."[2]

It is likewise with the sins of our churches that we already mentioned with regard to the insane and insanity. Insight into the nature of the misery leads to a beginning of redemption. May God's people wake up from its imaginary righteousness — and the establishment of this institution may be a testimony to this — for then a deliverance from this medicinal Babylon may perhaps be on the horizon.

That is why this conference, where this testimonial character is so prominent, is so important. More than one testimony could provide the subject matter for a discussion. As this association is being established and will expand, the content which is seen in its work will be a testimony to (1) *the truth of the Word of God;* (2) *man's depravity as a result of Satan's influence;* (3) *the lack of compassion towards the unfortunate person in many a church community or family;* (4) *the unlimited power of our God manifested in works*

---

1. *De Heilanstalt Johannesberg bei Kaiserswerth*, 1993, p. 78.
2. *Pyschiatrische Bladen* (Dordrecht: H. R. van Elk), vol. II, section 1, p. 42.

338

of healing through our Lord Jesus Christ; (5) [and]*his willingness to use human beings in his service.*

9.2

Considering the topic that has been assigned to me — *the causes of insanity* — I would like, at this point, to link it to the testimony to *the truth of God's Word* with regard to these causes. Therefore, each of these causes will be discussed with reference to a word of Scripture.

But first, a few words about the study of the causes, or *the etiology of insanity.* I hesitate to tread upon this terrain; not only because I was given only a few weeks in which to prepare this lecture, while the study of this subject would require a lifetime, but also, because I suspected more than once that another light would be shed upon this illness and its description if it were approached through a discipline that is connected with the Word of God. Thus I will only report what I found in a few well-known handbooks of later date, apart from the two studies by van Roller and Tellegen, which were mentioned above: J. L. C. Schroeder van der Kolk: *Handboek van de Pathologie en Therapie der krankzinnigheid* (Utrecht: van der Post, 1863); Dr. W. Griesinger: *Die Pathologie und Therapie der psychischen krankheiten* (2nd edition; Stuttgart: Krabbe, 1867); Dr. R. von Krafft-Ebing: *Lehrbuch der Psychiatrie* (2nd edition; Stuttgart, 1883), especially vol. I, pp. 147-210; M. Morel: *Klinische studie over de zielsziekten,* translated from French by J. C. Rooseboom, vol. I (Utrecht: C. van der Post jr.); E. Gerdes, *Meerenberg en de krankzinningen* (Amsterdam: van Oosterzee, 1876) [. . .] and, finally, Dr. N. B. Donkersloot: *De krankzinnigheid, haar wezen, oorsprong, oorzaken, verschijnselen en voorbehoeding, in populairen vorm geschetst* (Amsterdam: Centen, 1881). This last work, which may be bought at a price of Dfl. 2.25, is useful for those who want to have some idea of what more recent authors think with regard to insanity, while the modern worldview which saturates it even more strikingly illustrates the truthfulness of the Holy Scriptures and will even more clearly put some remarkable statements about the causes of insanity above suspicion.

Today it is quite generally maintained: "Insanity is an illness; it is a disease of the brain; this proposition is the core of our contemporary view of insanity." This we find in Tellegen, p. 9. Donkersloot says (p. 105): "Insanity occurs only when the brain and its activities are disturbed. That the disease of the brain is not always discovered during an autopsy is often said to result from the fact that the visible traces of the disease may disappear soon after death, while also these may escape even the closest scrutiny." (See also Schroeder van der Kolk, pp. 97, 98.) The insanity is described as *idiopathic* when the disease originates in the brain itself, and as *sympathic* when it has been transferred from some other part of the body to the brain. It is felt that the question Who is insane? is more difficult to answer than the question What is insanity? Hence the various explanations.

With regard to the *causes,* we find a differentiation between *predisposing* or *exposing* and *accessory* causes (v. Krafft-Ebing, p. 149), or, as in the Dutch terms proposed by Donkersloot: *predisposing* (voorbeschikkende) and *facilitating* (gelegenheidgevende) of *existing* (opwekkende) causes: "A child of parents with tuberculosis may, for a considerable time, yes, even throughout its life, remain free from that particular illness, when the facilitating or exciting causes are absent; the child perhaps moved to a milder climate, chose a more healthy occupation, and it was thus only affected by a predisposition towards tuberculosis. The predisposition towards insanity operates in a similar way. Insanity will only emerge when this predisposition towards this disease is augmented by a facilitating cause" (Donkersloot, p. 70). It is remarkable how insanity also in other ways reminds us of tuberculosis: "The connection between these two diseases has already been established by science and is amply confirmed by experience." (See the essay "about diseases of the organs in the thorax in relationship to insanity" by W. F. Westereng, in the *Psychiatrische Bladen III,* p. 141.) Here we will limit ourselves in dealing with the causes of insanity to the opinion of a retired professor of psychiatry, who has a wealth of experience. He states that:

(1) Both the predisposing as well as the exciting causes are only of relative value;

(2) The causes must be ascertained in each particular case;

(3) No cause in isolation from other causes results in insanity; and

(4) The illness only manifests itself when these causes have resulted in a considerable change which may be detected in the psychological activities of the patient.

More than one author has remarked that what to many seemed to appear the *cause* of insanity is, in actual fact, only a result or one of the first signs of it (Tellegen, pp. 21, 26), or that the facilitating cause, to which usually such great value is attached, is often no more than a grain of sand which upsets the balance (Morel, p. 227). What completed the insanity is not always its cause; what led to its development is not by definition its *germ*. In addition, the causes are divided into physical or somatic and psychological (those that are linked to the body and those that are related to the soul).

If the Christian feels that these views do not sufficiently account for the Providence of God and the power of Satan, it becomes even more remarkable that, when we pursue the topic further, the truth of the Scriptures comes into even clearer focus.

This is apparent from:

The *first* cause: *the power of Satan*. We find an immediate link with John 8:44: the devil is a murderer from the beginning and a father of deceit. The statement by Donkersloot, in vol. III, p. 49, about the nature of insanity is very striking: "As soon as a man is struck by a loss of his senses, he undergoes something like an Ovidian metamorphosis. He no longer is who he was, but he is controlled by unknown forces that dictate what he says and does. Or to put it more succinctly: Insanity has the character of an evil spirit (demon). To state it in a practical manner: Such a human being ceases to *live*: he is *being lived*. Even the ancient popular expression for insanity, that is 'being possessed,' automatically includes the element of lack of freedom." It is remarkable how an expert uses this expression to describe the essence of insanity, but mistakenly refers to this term that we find in Scripture as merely a popular saying. Could one not also say that the increase in the incidence of insanity coincides with a constant decrease in faith in the existence and power of Satan?[3] Donkersloot describes on pages 156 and 157 in a realistic fashion how an insane person will, as his disease becomes more serious, lead the life of an animal, yes, the existence of a plant, and will experience total "darkness." This again reminds us not only of the work of Satan, which in the Scriptures is referred to as the darkness of this age, but also of the spiritual condition that we all inherit (Eph. 5:8).

The *second* cause of insanity is the hereditary nature of insanity, which to some extent reminds us of the threat that we find in the second commandment of the Law (Exod. 20:5): "I the LORD thy God am a jealous God, visiting the iniquity of the fathers upon the children unto the third and fourth generation of them that hate me." Von Krafft-Ebing is of the opinion (p. 172) that, "with the exception of tuberculosis, there is no sickness that

---

3. Rightly, this has recently been pointed out by the honorable Mr. P. J. Elout van Soeterwoude, on the occasion of his 80th birthday, when he said, among other things, in his reply to the Representatives of the Central Committee: "The Satan is active in appalling ways.... While Satan has not been spoken about from the pulpit for a long time, he works in more terrible ways than was ever imagined" (*Standaard,* August 13, 1865).

presents us with more examples than insanity." Among 111 cases of female patients that he treated, Tellegen found (p. 17) 45 cases in which heredity played no role, 21 in which one of the parents or grandparents was insane, 32 in which indirect heredity could be established, 10 in which the parents suffered from a nervous disorder, and 3 where the father was an alcoholic — thus there was no question of heredity in 40.5 percent, but there was such a connection in 59.5 percent. In general, the numbers that are reported vary from 4 up to 90 percent. This wide variety in numbers is due to the lack of agreement concerning the questions when we may speak of heredity. Tellegen already indicates heredity when one of the parents showed nervousness or was addicted to strong drink. In some cases, because of a kind of family pride among the surviving relatives, the physician will not mention that parents or grandparents were insane. In the meantime it should absolutely not be suggested that all children or grandchildren of insane parents or grandparents are doomed to insanity. "Mostly, only the tendency is inherited, the disposition towards insanity only developing into a disease when other unfavorable factors can exert their influence" (Tellegen, p. 20). Donkersloot believes that "one-fifth of all mental disorders can be traced to a hereditary disposition and in more than half of the cases is linked to the mothers rather than to the fathers" (p. 71).

The *third* cause one might mention is marriage between relatives, which is condemned by laws concerning marriage in Leviticus (18:6): "None of you shall approach to any that is near of kin to him, to uncover their nakedness: I am the LORD." Donkersloot cites some striking examples from which he draws this conclusion: "It will be sufficient to convince the reader that the unfortunate label that marriage between relatives often attaches to the children is more than a myth. But should someone, in defiance of what he knows, develop an interest in a niece or an aunt to which he is linked by a blood relationship, he would be wise to turn from her in time, lest he become an accomplice in creating offspring that, either physically or mentally, or both, will appear to the healthy youth around them as a lamentable creature." It may be, Donkersloot says (p. 71), that the unfavorable consequences will only emerge in the third or fourth generation, but then sometimes in a more serious form. Von Krafft-Ebing maintains that the relatively high percentage of insane persons among Jews and members of the aristocracy is due to marriages between relatives that occur for a variety of reasons.

The *fourth* cause is a bad upbringing, resulting from a neglect of the Lord's commandment: "And, ye fathers, bring your children up in the nurture and admonition of the Lord" (Eph. 6:4). Tellegen writes: "Among the causes that are related to heredity, a first place must be attributed to the education, that is, to the influence of the parental example" (p. 22). Morel emphasizes, in page 228, how "the activities of the brain of tender children will often bring about very serious disturbances in the central organ of our nervous system." Note that this is a warning addressed to those who promote nursery schools and to the parents who proudly delight in them! In just a few but striking words von Krafft-Ebing sketches the danger of inconsistency and carelessness in education (p. 180), which imply a neglect of the demands that the Scriptures present. Likewise, visiting places where the senses are excessively excited often has lamentable results (Morel, p. 236). Smoking, in particular, is to be considered harmful.

The *fifth* cause, neglect of the body, reminds us of the serious warning from Romans 12:1: You must *"present your bodies a living sacrifice, holy, acceptable unto God."* Although the body is intended as a shelter for the soul, the Christian should consider care for the entire body as commanded by Scripture. 1 Corinthians 12:23 points specifically to the fact that even our "less honorable members" possess "abundant comeliness." And Matthew 6 states it so clearly that the "body is more than raiment" — and yet how much more attention is given to procuring clothing than to care for the body. And even with respect to food and drink, to sleeping and labor and other natural activities, simple injunctions cannot with impunity be disregarded. Based on his own experience and that of others, Schroeder van der Kolk relates (pp. 91, 93) how "it has been convincingly shown how accumulated substances in the colon may have a sympathetic effect on the brain, which may lead to hallucinations." It has therefore been argued that three-eighths of the insane suffer from disorders in the abdomen. The sedentary life of scholars and excessive exertion due to intense labor, especially of the brain, and other factors must of necessity be harmful. Tellegen thus mentions (p. 29), among other things, inadequate nutrition and bodily weakness as so-called somatic causes that are directly linked to the body.

The *sixth* cause is connected with the previous one and may be referred to as *abuse of our bodies:* "If any man defile the temple of God, him shall God destroy" (1 Cor. 3:17). 1 Cor. 6:19 informs us that the body serves as such a temple. Sexual excesses and abuse of strong drink are mentioned by Donkersloot (pp. 87-94) among the primary causes of insanity. Foreign physicians also put tobacco in the same category. But Donkersloot is of the opinion that extensive contact with insane persons, both in and outside the asylum, has not provided him with enough evidence for the harmful effects of smoking. He puts, however, great emphasis on strong alcoholic drinks as producing the greatest contingent of insane people. In the report of the Dutch asylums for the insane (p. 180) it is stated that drunkenness has been the cause in 15.7 percent of the male patients and 2 percent of the female patients. Sexual excesses, masturbation, and abnormal practices with regard to the siring of children (referred to by Griesinger — p. 203, with the general term "diseases of the sexual organs") also have a prominent place among the causes of insanity. This reminds us of the wording used in the Heidelberg Catechism to describe the ninth commandment (question 108): "That we must live a chaste and disciplined life, whether in or outside the state of matrimony." Therefore the ministers of the Word, in particular, carry a heavy responsibility, both with regard to the marriage consecration and to confirmation classes, as well as the teachers in the schools and the parents at home.

The *seventh* cause may be found in an overburdening of the brain, as a consequence of disregard for the advice given in Rom. 12:3, *not to think more highly (of ourselves) than we ought to think.* Tellegen points out that in families that are highly gifted intellectually we find more idiotic people, while Donkersloot states (p. 77) "that the descendants of great geniuses, will, if they do not become insane, have a greater propensity towards mental imbalance." Similarly, many regard the civilization as one of the factors that are conducive towards insanity. Griesinger maintains (p. 142) that, according to the majority of today's psychiatric physicians, the increase in insanity has to do with the state of our modern society. And, after having given praise to true civilization (p. 80), he writes: "The civilization that is based on a relentless pursuit of sophisticated pleasures contributes to the development of mental disorders. Are not those who everywhere and always are seeking pleasure, who in their younger years lead a life full of sensuality — are they not the ones who spend the last part of their life in asylums for the insane? The craving for praise and honor, the longing for more material possessions, the constant ambition to be of importance make a strong demand on the activities of their brain. Miscalculations and wounded pride, which most of these people cannot avoid, will lead to disorders of their mental powers. This does not necessarily have to take the form of ruthless covetousness, but even entertaining thoughts about what it would mean to become rich, the excitement of continuous speculations and calculations, exhaust the nervous energy and lead the activities of the minds on a dangerous path." It has therefore been suggested that, relatively speaking, there are more cases of insanity in civilized countries than in the so-called uncivilized countries (Von Oettingen, p. 632). Von Krafft-Ebing states (p. 152) that "Insanity has become a much more frequent phenomenon in our modern society. This is already manifest in the increase in nervous disorders that result from a wrong life style" — which is confirmed in 2 Cor. 7:10: "The sorrow of the world worketh death."

The *eighth* cause is related to the previous one: *improper worries* that result from a neglect of the comforting promise *"Cast all your cares upon God, for he cares for you"* (1 Peter 5:7). With regard to the psychiatric problems that Tellegen had found in the women he had observed, he writes (p. 270): "After fear, among the girls of marriageable age, the termination in or opposition during their courtship, and among married women disasters in their marriage (such as the death of a child, immoral behavior of the husband, or grief about the undesirable behavior of children) are the most important factors." We find these causes also with men. Von Kraft maintains that most cases of insanity among women occur between the ages of 25 and 35, when their expectations prove to be unrealistic, while they occur among men between the ages of 35 and 50, when they are subject to the greatest exertion. It is also striking to find, on p. 168, a reference to the frequent occurrence of insanity among nannies. Are such facts not proof that unbelief is at the root of all kinds of misery, but also about the concerns about many things, while the one essential thing is forgotten?

The *ninth* cause is already characterized with a specific name which refers to one of the varieties of insanity, *megalomania,* as confirmation of the truth of these words of Scripture: "A man's pride will bring him low" (Prov. 29:23). Donkersloot writes (pp. 136, 132): "This form of insanity occurs most frequently in asylums; yes, it seems to be beyond doubt that there will invariably come a moment in the further development of the insanity when megalomania appears." But he rightly adds that those people who develop megalomania may outwardly be the most calm, but "one should not forget that those whose insanity is most serious and untreatable will often be the most tranquil, and that below the apparent self-confidence often the deepest disturbance of the mind remains hidden." Donkersloot also refers (p. 199) to the conclusions of the prominent physician Güntz: "Upon close observation we find among the causes of insanity: vanity, arrogance, thirst for honor, but also love for money, fondness of intrigue, addictions to games, religious fanaticism (I will return to this factor), and, furthermore, among those of the weaker sex, the yearning for adornment, flirtatiousness, extravagance, sexual drive, romantic or sentimental ideas and experiences, or whatever names these character weaknesses may be given — which, especially, threaten the favorite children of fortune. They undermine contentment, chase away peace of mind, occupy the thoughts, rob the will of its power to make decisions, or hinder its effectiveness." Even though in citing all these faults, we must, once again, be reminded of the fact that these are always merely *facilitating* causes, and that, rather than being the causes, they may be the results of mental disorders, we see here also the relationship between insanity and the deceit of Satan to destroy mankind in Paradise: "Ye shall be as gods" (Gen. 3:3).

We want to refer to the *tenth* cause with the label that is commonly used: religious fanaticism, but as explained and described in the Scriptures: "Satan himself is transformed into an angel of light" (2 Cor. 11:14). In the very fact that here the word religious is without a capital letter, it is indicated that serving the true God will never lead to fanaticism. However, religion that is centered upon man himself (see Col. 2:23), or idolatry, as it is referred to in the Catechism, question 95, does lead thereto. True religion can be a medicine against insanity, but never its cause. Tellegen emphasizes (p. 366) this as follows: "Religious mania is almost always merely a form in which insanity manifests itself. But I think that religion, if understood correctly, is rather to be seen as providing leverage against mental derangement, because it keeps the passions of the person in check instead of stimulating mental disorders." Von Kraft agrees (p. 156) "that this kind of religious mania is often only an indication of a sickly character disposition, and that, in particular, sensuality and sexual sins hide behind this external vale."

9.3

And thus we conclude that this final cause leads us back to the first: The power of Satan, which often misleads science by urging her to seek the cause of insanity where, in fact, its remedy may be found. Yet, this falsehood is already present in the slander which he made his servants utter against the Victor of Satan, Jesus Christ, when, according to John 10:20, many said of Him: "He hath a devil, and is mad, why hear ye Him?" We know what the others replied: "These are not the words of him that hath a devil. Can a devil open the eyes of the blind?"

This same Christ, who not just healed the blind, but also expelled the devils from the demon possessed, is the only Name given to man by which we may be saved, and the almighty Healer through whom, if it pleases Him, insane people may be restored. Even those who are not immediately involved in the care for the insane have been called to the task to fight against these causes through His Spirit and in accordance with His Word. This, however, presupposes that we know these causes, and that we realize that we have been guilty of downplaying their importance or even of strengthening them. Who can claim not to earn any blame? May everyone in view of his own experience add where he has been lacking, or correct where he has done wrong. May, most of all, parents, teachers, and educators, in their important role, but also each one of us personally, more closely scrutinize God's instructions in every domain and by His grace follow them. Much is said these days about reform in the church. May this everywhere become a reality, as in each place charity towards the insane, in your home, your environment, and your church, is restored, and as efforts are made to combat the causes of this disease, which are so diverse, but often regarded as of little importance, and for which God's Word offers both a description and a remedy. May God the Almighty grant this to us.

Voorthuizen, W. van den Bergh

A Child without Parents or Name

Willem van den Bergh 1884. "Een ouderloos en naamloos kind." In *Bouwstenen, tijdschrift voor inwendige zending,* 3rd ed. Utrecht: C. H. E. Breijer, 35-82.

9.4

Already a few years ago Dr. A. Kuyper said the following with regard to the "Labor Question," which at present is assuming a broader and more threatening form, and which was also touched upon last year in our Journal: "Every major issue in life, and in particular *'the question of the laborer'* arises from distress, from a misery, a complaint, and is, therefore, a cry for the healing balm for a painful wound in our human existence. How should we then imagine a church of Christ, without a heart for such suffering and without the urge to ensure that even in these circumstances her Lord, whom she worships, will shine forth in His saving and redeeming love? Is suffering humanity not precisely the field of labor that has been assigned to her, and are, in particular, not the 'insignificant ones on this earth' entrusted to her, in order that the church might especially manifest towards them the power of her comfort, the power of her life-giving principles, and the blessing of all that she is? For that reason God surely disapproves of the fact that the Church of

Christ, also in our lands, has distanced itself so languidly from this issue. We do not intend to denigrate in any way the accomplishments of Heldring and his followers. But one must come to the conclusion: Helping where an emergency has already risen, combating one particular social evil, and saving the individual, is not the same as dealing with the *social question as such* in a way that is inspired by our faith. And, the accomplishments of *some* do not acquit *the corporate Church*."[4]

Write, rather than "the question of the laborer," the question of the maid, the poor, the orphan, the sick, those who are neglected, fallen, imprisoned, those who serve in the army, or those who are blind, deaf, mute, the idiots, the insane, the drunkards, etc., and this very useful term will retain its meaning when applied to all associations, asylums, institutions, as something every local church should take to heart. Even abroad, and specifically in France, we heard a voice that addressed us in *"Le Signal"* on page 290 of last year's edition, where it was predicted that "the philanthropy in the church," preferably "the philanthropy of the church," will prove to be the key condition for its continued existence. . . .

I limit myself to describing the consequences of this character of the Home Missionary Movement, as referred to above, for *this movement itself* and for *the Church*. . . .

9.5

Let us first pay attention to the nature of the work that is the priority for the Home Missions Movement. This will also remind us of the accusation of sickliness, one-sidedness, and exaggeration that has often been directed against this work. This work originated among other things from the indignation regarding the kind of pharisaic attitude that haughtily passed by the publican and the sinner, the fallen and the neglected person, with the thought: "I thank Thee, Lord, that I am not like one of these" [Luke 18:11]. It was only right that the spirit of charity was awakened in His community of believers in the face of such trampling on the innocent, such lack of solidarity, this desperate need of God's mercy, that neglect of the task of honor that Christ gave to his disciples. But this reaction all too often led to an unhealthy predilection for what was fallen and left behind. "The healer prefers to en-

---

4. "De Arbeiderskwestie en de Kerk: An Essay about the Social Question," introduced by Dr. A. Kuyper (Amsterdam: B. van der Land, 1874), p. vii.

gage in a risky and experimental treatment, and the physician values in particular his serious patients. Likewise some Christians are far more interested in those who have wandered far, than in people who are less culpable, who tend to be forgotten in the midst of the urgent concerns for the sinful men and women. When there is a decent mother who needs help in raising her children, there is hardly anyone who shows any willingness to assist her. But, if there is an immoral woman who indicated that she may want to better her life, we find that, immediately, a human heart reaches out to provide help."[5]

Is there not some truth is this statement? Is it not a fact that in the midst of our busy work as a Martha, there is a stronger tendency to get involved with the extraordinary, rather than with the ordinary; to seek and focus on the more difficult rather than the easier task? Do we not see those who are eager to support attempts to save *the fallen, unwed mothers,* but forget to close their parlors or associations to those who cause these poor women to stumble, or to avoid in their own style of clothing or behavior what will have a direct influence on women of lower social rank? Are not some shelters for house maids initiated by women who in their own homes use their house maids only as "sources of labor" and who fail to ensure that these house maids find a true "shelter" in the home of the women who employ them, and is it not true that the desire to move elsewhere and to find a "higher" position is thwarted by their masters as capricious, arrogant, and insensitive? Is there no thought, when "serviceman's hostels" are founded — something we applaud — that god-fearing officers in the barracks and encampments ought, in fact, to be able to compensate for their men their longing for their parents; and is there no thought how greater attention for the homes from which the officers and soldiers are recruited could over time change the entire character of the army? Who among us does not praise the *nursery homes* of the deaconesses, the *Bethesda's* and the *Bethany's,* for what they have done both for soul and for body? But would, also in this case, prevention not have been much more practical than healing? And would it not be better to educate families to utilize cheap and simple means to improve their health, such as air, cold water, and bodily exercise and sensible food, in order that illnesses and ailments may be prevented and weak constitutions may be strengthened in accordance with the divine instructions? There is ample opportunity to get assistance and money for *neglected children,* but has enough thought been given to find ways to prevent this neglect, by paying attention to ill-advised education, and, yes, by more adequately showing in one's own

5. Dr. A. Kuyper, *Uit het Woord,* I, blz. 317.

family, how one must *lead* house maids and children in the fear of the Lord, and how one should personally *serve* Him and the neighbor in this respect? More and more nurseries for children are established, thus enabling women to take a job outside the house. But does this not undermine the family unit, and is this not a medicine that is worse than the disease that should have been combated in a less harmful manner? Large sums of money are collected for *orphans* and *half-orphans,* and institutions like Neerbosch, Bethel, De Goede Herder (the good shepherd), [and] the Martha-Stichting (Martha Foundation) are being established. But should we not, where appropriate, warn against the unwise marriages that people want to enter into, against harmful occupations, unhealthy houses, and pernicious life styles, that cause the premature death of parents. And should there not be a stronger pressure on family members, the neighborhood, and the environment to show charity and take these unfortunate ones who have been left behind in their care. We might take as an example how in the Transvaal region childless couples will often adopt these orphans and raise them as their own children.[6] Could this kind of charity perhaps explain the blessings that have been experienced by the Transvalers, but also solve the riddle why God has left so many couples without offspring? Schools established by factories are excellent, but should not rather the factories, and thus the factory owners, be the target of the Home Missions Movement, and should not, in the first place, these "sources of labor" be treated as human beings, and not as machines, which are each day started up and provided with the materials needed for the work, but that are otherwise left to fend for themselves?

And I could continue by pointing out how the youth societies and Sunday schools show evidence of fundamental deficiencies in the home, the work place, and the shop, which in no lesser degree demand our attention. And how the concern for drunkards and prisoners, on the one hand, and the blind, the deaf and the mute, the idiots, epileptics, and insane, on the other hand — however much we also welcome this — should remind us of those who are less culpable and miserable, but in no lesser need, in physical as well as in mental respect. One only needs to look at our extensive, in fact almost shepherdless, slums, our indigent dwellings in hovels, cellars, and attics, and at the lamentable situation of our factory workers, etc. And thus we may also point out how, out of concern for neglected and fallen people, we at times sacrifice those who by God's grace have not succumbed but are now swept along. Dickens mentions this problem with humor, though not always with

6. F. Lion Cachet, *De Worstelstrijd der Transvalers,* 1881, p. 426.

justice: how mothers neglect their family on behalf of Negroes or Indians on other continents. Yet, we find not only in England but also in the Netherlands various examples that show how this sickly predilection here referred to, or the disregard for the task that God has assigned us above anything else, has made many persons who work for the Missions into little usefulness for their environment, or even for society as a whole. . . .

9.6

In all manifestations of mercy it should be clear that these should be directed as much as possible to the circle that God has assigned to us: the home, the wider family, the village, the city, the church, etc., and that we should only assume new commitments that go beyond these divine instructions on a temporary and incidental basis. Most of today's associations, institutions, etc., do not sufficiently aim to keep these instructions, as much as possible, in mind. On the contrary, at times the focus is solely on strengthening and confirming the tie with the society or institution, even when one is no longer in its care. This means that often the only commitment demanded from those who send those who are in need is pecuniary rather than moral. If the needy person is affiliated with a church, at least this instruction from God remains applicable. But today we often notice that there is but little concern regarding the person's estrangement from home, family, domicile, and also church, and that this is extremely detrimental, in the first place, for those involved. . . .

9.7

In the meantime, the greatest danger for the church from the contemporary Home Missions Movement — even though it is done in good faith, with the conviction that one offers help — is not the undermining of the Diaconate. For suppose that all societies and associations were directly attached to the church or one of its offices — would that solve everything? Is it our ideal that the diaconate does everything and that it is forced to continuously expand and add departments and budgets? Who would want to argue for this? No, for in that case the result would only be — as in the parable to which I alluded — that the father would voluntarily transfer the education of the children to the house maid and the nanny, while he would waste away, inactively, without commitment to any work.

No, the danger is, in fact, that the local congregations or churches allow themselves to be indulged and thereby let themselves be robbed of its work and to forfeit its crown. All too often, in the discussion about the issue of Home Missions, only this question has been posed: How can we best help those who suffer, the needy and the destitute poor? It was forgotten that the churches themselves were seriously sick, not just in ecclesiastical matters, but also in the practice of mercy, precisely as a result of their own unresponsiveness and inactivity. If one does not work — and that applies also to spiritual work — one will find that one's hands lose their strength or reach for activities that are not allowed. Our homes, our families, and the other parties that were mentioned earlier now find themselves in that situation. And this is the great danger: things become too easy for us. The diaconate reaches its peak when it awakens in everyone, with the support of the preaching of the Word, the charity that springs from the church itself, to do those things in our own circle that would make action from the diaconate superfluous. The Home Missions Movement, however, opens all its doors, and is even less capable of guarding against the abuse of its services. And, as a result, we see the sad situation in the care for the sick that sometimes a deaconess is called, where a daughter, a house maid, or relative or someone else should have performed this task. Families send orphans readily and speedily to institutions, and can thus evade the sacrifice and self-renunciation which would otherwise be required of them. And this would apply to many other domains of life.

But does that, on the other hand, not mean, in accordance with God's Word, that the time when the *cripple* and the *blind* had to go around *begging* was also the time when charity declined, but that the Lord, in fact, sent the sick and the people who suffer all kinds of misery, not just with the intention that they should be cared for, but also with the aim that we should improve ourselves with regard to mercy, patience, and faith? *If that is so, the judgments over our church and our families are invoked rather than kept away by this systematic withdrawal from these activities instead of the promotion thereof.*

In addition we find that those who, because of the monetary contributions, can devote themselves to works of charity, will experience how they will be robbed of the crown for their labor. For when heart and eye have been detached from what one does, the financial aspect misses an underlying motive. This explains the blessing that comes upon local activities, in our own circle, for our own city or village.

"My Strength Is Made Perfect in Weakness":
Bonhoeffer and the War over Disabled Life

BERND WANNENWETSCH

Because Dietrich Bonhoeffer is already well-known for being the theologian who bravely resisted Hitler, it comes as little surprise to discover that he implacably resisted the Nazi machinery of death. We find him, for example, engaging directly with the issue of euthanasia with the distinctive theological clarity and passion for which he is justly known. In a detailed and penetrating discussion of this issue in his *Ethics,* Bonhoeffer arrives at this unambiguous judgment:

> Life created and preserved by God possesses an inherent right, completely independent of its social utility. . . . There is no worthless life before God, because God holds life itself to be valuable. Because God is the Creator, Preserver, and Redeemer of life, even the poorest life before God becomes a valuable life. (**10.6** [193])

While we might have expected him not to shy away from such controversial topics in his ethical writing, the exciting discovery as we investigate what he has to contribute to a theology of disability is that by penetrating into the deeper layers of the historical, biographical, and theological complex of his work, we find that the dignity of disabled life appears to be more than yet another "topic" for Bonhoeffer. Rather, it represents a focal point in which numerous key insights developed in his theological work coincide.

Bethel vs. Buchenwald: Embodiments of Rival Worldviews

Bonhoeffer's 1933 visit to Bethel near Bielefeld, a village that existed for the sole purpose of caring for the weak and fragile, assumes a symbolic role in that discovery. This visit was largely motivated by the theological work that he planned to undertake there with a group of fellow theologians of the Confessing Church — work on a draft that would lead to the so-called Bethel Confession, a forerunner of the Barmen Declaration. While the theologians' work on the confessional statement was meant to re-articulate the true marks of the church in a time of ecclesiological confusion, it was the firsthand experience of Bethel as a place of embodied neighborly love that made Bonhoeffer aware of the *reality* of "the church that still knows what the church can be about and what it cannot be about" (**10.1** [157]). Just after returning from a service in Bethel, in which a proto-celestial mélange of epileptics and other disabled people, elderly tramps, deaconesses and theology students, doctors, and pastors and their families worshiped together, Bonhoeffer wrote a letter to his grandmother Julie. In the letter he admitted that "for the first time" it really struck him how the lives of disabled persons revealed something of the truth of human existence — a truth that healthy people typically try to ignore. In particular, the situation of epileptic people, moving as they do between health and sickness, served as a strong reminder of the defenselessness that characterizes human life at its core. "Their situation of being truly defenseless perhaps gives these people a much clearer insight into certain realities of our human existence, the fact that we are indeed basically defenseless, than can be possible for healthy persons" (**10.1** [158]).

The way that Bonhoeffer reflected on his experience in and of Bethel gives us a good example of the concreteness that has become a hallmark of his theology (Dietrich Bonhoeffer Works [hereafter DBW] 6, 99). In his ecclesiological writings as well as in his ethics, Bonhoeffer constantly warns of the corrupting influence that idealist ideologies exert on theological thought. For him, the church is not an ideal community, but the real and material form of Christ's existence in the world (DBW 5, 27-47; cf. **10.4**). Every confessional statement that aims to articulate the nature of the church must not give in to "wishful thinking," but truthfully describe the reality of this institution that God has created and continues to sustain. There were certainly times in the course of the German church struggle when it was painfully difficult for Bonhoeffer to experience the reality of the church in which he believed, times when confessing that the church is one, holy, catholic, and apostolic had to be done *sub specie contrario,* in the face of the opposite impression. But here at Bethel, "sight" was given to him of the church as it actually existed "for others." For all the extraordinary features of life at Bethel that had made a lasting impression on him, Bonhoeffer still sensed that what he had come to experience here was far from the idyllic escape that we associate with a distant island. In a manner characteristic of his theological realism, he refused to understand Bethel, as many would have done, as a haven of humanitarianism so rare and other-worldly that its very existence as a place in the world only served to confirm that life outside this place could proceed undisturbed, according to the world's own very different rationality and social temperature. Instead of understanding Bethel as a ghetto of love, but a ghetto nevertheless, Bonhoeffer grasped its significance as a place of revelation, a place that revealed the reality of universal Christian brotherhood. It was an embodied recognition that all human life is essentially feeble, defenseless, and dependent, and so revealed neighborly love as the matrix of all human sociality. Bonhoeffer describes his Bethel experience as consonant with the gospel stories depicted in Rembrandt's "Hundred Guilder" etching: "There is nothing sentimental about any of this; it is tremendously real and natural. It knocks down some of the barriers with which we usually shut ourselves off from this world. Here it simply is a part of one's own life, as it is in reality" (**10.1** [158]).

On the basis of this ecclesiological realism, Bonhoeffer's resistance to the euthanasia programs of the Nazis was more than righteous outrage against inhumane politics and the grave infringements of human rights. The strong booster injection of ecclesiological realism he received at Bethel allowed Bonhoeffer to denounce the Nazi elimination of disabled life not simply as wrong or morally corrupt, but more precisely as "mad," as completely out of touch with reality. "What utter madness, that some people today think that the sick can or ought to be legally eliminated" (**10.1** [158]). Now the tables are being turned: For Bonhoeffer, it is not the mentally handicapped who are insane, but those who assume they can distinguish their own "healthy" existence from that of the handicapped in a way that actually severs the bond of all humanity, that eliminates those others who powerfully reveal the fundamental fragility of human life shared by everyone.

What the Bethel experience meant for Bonhoeffer might be best explained in terms of "the view from below," a concept that he developed as an afterthought to a letter for friends and fellow conspirators in 1942. In what has become the concluding paragraph in the letter that was later entitled "After Ten Years," Bonhoeffer explains a new epistemological principle that he discovered in the test and trials of living a faithful life under the Nazi regime:

It remains an experience of incomparable value that we have for once learned to see the great events of world history from below, from the perspective of the outcasts, the suspects, the maltreated, the powerless, the oppressed and reviled, in short from the perspective of the suffering. . . . That we come to see matters great and small, happiness and misfortune, strength and weakness with new eyes; that our sense for greatness, humanness, justice, and mercy has grown clearer, freer, more incorruptible; that we learn, indeed, that personal suffering is a more useful key, a more fruitful principle than personal happiness for exploring the meaning of the world in contemplation and action. (**10.2** [52])

The privileged epistemic perspective that Bonhoeffer discovered as he suffered together with the underprivileged allows access to spheres of reality and insights that cannot be gained otherwise. This is not to suggest that the view from below is a vantage point offering a more accurate view of affairs, but that it breaks up default modes of perception from within — it is no less than "seeing with new eyes." What Bethel revealed to Bonhoeffer was not only the true countenance of the church as the body of the Crucified One in the world, but also how "ambiguous" the default concepts of sickness and health actually are. "What we see as 'sick' is actually healthier, in essential aspects of life and of insight, than health is. And that the two conditions depend on one another is surely an essential part of the plan and the laws of life, which can't simply be changed to suit people's impertinence and lack of understanding" (**10.1** [158-59]).

When referring to "impertinence and lack of understanding" with regards to the "laws of life," as they have been ordered by the Creator, Bonhoeffer takes a thinly concealed swipe at the Nazi ideology of his day, in which the conflation of creature and creator resulted in the propagation of a new humanity in the form of the Aryan superhuman — a higher form of human life, which, Nazis believed, would come to fruition once it freed itself from the genetic ballast of lesser forms of human existence represented in the disabled.

It would be easy to underestimate the significance of the Bethel experience and indeed the symbolic role of the disabled for the ideological, theological, and political war in which Bonhoeffer was involved. But the question of the status of disabled life was to grow into a prime occasion for the *status confessionis* for the churches in Germany, a question about which the integrity of Christianity as a whole was explicitly understood to be at stake. But it was to take some time for this to become clear, first for political reasons, as the eugenics programs that were begun in 1933 were only later revealed as stage preparation for Hitler's further wars of extinction. The war on "bad genes" was first confined to the more physically and mentally obvious bearers of such genes but then moved on to Jews and other unwanted groups in society, ending finally in "total warfare" against other nations.

The status of disabled life also became a focus for the churches in exposing ideological conflicts. The Nazis' euthanasia policies revealed the spirit of their reign as deeply anti-Christian, as it exposed the rivalry of irreconcilable anthropologies and concepts of power and history. In the light of these clashing ideologies, we gain a sense of the symbolic significance that surrounded the quarrels over the appointment of the first bishop of the unified Reichs Church in 1933. It was no accident that those in the churches who opposed the growing influence of the German Christians presented as their candidate none other than the director of the Bethel Institute for the Physically and Mentally Handicapped, Friedrich Bodelschwingh the Younger. The reaction by a rival party marshaled by the German Christians is no less explicable in terms of a simple political blocking maneuver, as they wasted no time in mounting a campaign of lying and intimidation that eventually led to Bodelschwingh's resigning from this office (DBW 13, 5; Bethge 1999, 284).

The nasty campaign against Bodelschwingh made plain that those who bought into the Nazis' ideologies understood perfectly well the symbolic significance of Bethel as a social embodiment of Christian anthropology. This anthropology was seen as a major ideological obstacle to the kind of evolutionary progress that the Nazis meant to facilitate for the human race — a progress that included the necessity of places like Buchenwald. Meaning the "house of God" in Hebrew, Bethel's very name was an antithesis to the worship of the superhuman embodied in these places designed for sorting and purifying the human genome. Thus Buchenwald and the other concentration camps are best understood as the antithesis to Bethel: the "embodiment of the satanic worldview," as Eric Metaxas aptly puts it (Metaxas 2010, 504). While Bethel was a place where even the most feeble forms of human life were respected, loved, and cared for, Buchenwald was a place "where weakness was preyed upon and crushed" (Metaxas 2010, 504), where the best technological skills were exploited to perfect the machinery of death, where human skin was used to make wallets for members of the SS, where human heads were shrunken and given as gifts, and where soap was made from the fat of human beings.

The polar antithesis of "Bethel vs. Buchenwald" brings into relief many of the ideological, political, and theological battles fought through in the years of Hitler's regime. From the beginning of his reign in 1933, measures were introduced in piecemeal fashion that would eventually amount to an outright warfare against the weakest and most vulnerable members of society. This was undertaken first as an attack on "bad genes," as reflected in sterilization programs that had been legalized in the 1933 "Law for the Prevention of Genetically Ill Progeny." Under this law, some 400,000 people were sterilized by 1945, mimicking practices that had been established before in the United States and other Western countries (Pence 1990, ch. 9). The official commentary on this law stated that it "serves to establish the primacy and authority that the state has finally secured for itself in the area of life, marriage, and the family.... The National Socialist German government has shown thereby that it is prepared . . . to subordinate the interest of genetically diseased (erbkrank) individuals to the general welfare of the genetically healthy (erbgesund) German people and thereby to the flourishing of the German nation" (DBW 6, 179, n. 30).

The transition from eugenics to euthanasia, from war on "defective genes" to war on "unworthy life" itself, was accompanied by propaganda measures that increasingly employed martial rhetoric to characterize the existence of unworthy elements in German society as an "attack" against the health, welfare, and future of the German people. Once the wider population was "helped" to recognize the presence of one group of citizens as comprising an "attack" on the health of the whole society, as the designation of disabled persons as "useless eaters" suggested, other unwanted groups could be portrayed and seen as attackers, from Jews to gypsies to homosexuals. This trajectory of the Third Reich to extend the measures it justified as necessary to "defend" itself against such "attacks" from within later seamlessly merged into the outright military action it felt it had to undertake against "aggressions" from the outside.

It was therefore not by sheer coincidence that the beginning of the war in September 1939 coincided with an escalation to a new dimension of the war on bad genes and their bearers. The so-called Action T4, in the wake of which more than 200,000 physically or mentally handicapped persons were murdered, was initiated by a personal memo of Hitler's known as the "euthanasia decree." Hitler predated this memo explicitly to September 1, the exact date of the invasion of Poland, which began the Second World War. The entry in Hitler's personal notes read: "Reich Leader Bouhler and Dr. Brandt are charged with the responsibility for expanding the authority of physicians, to be designated by name, to the end that patients considered incurable according to the best available human judgment of their state of health, can be granted a mercy death" (Lifton 1986, 64). The linguistic cynicism in the expression "mercy death" was matched by the label of the euthanasia program as "T4," which reflected the location of its headquarters, which was based in the Berlin borough of Tiergarten and went under the euphemistic name Gemeinnützige Stiftung für Heil- und Anstaltspflege (Charitable Foundation for Cure and Institutional Care).

The country's war against other nations not only served as a cover for deflecting the public's awareness of these measures, but also offered a rationale for the intensification of these policies. Even those within the populace who might have harbored reservations about the notion of "life not worthy of living" were expected to acquiesce to the new order of priority that came with the necessities of warfare, when, for example, room needed to be made in hospitals for the care of wounded soldiers. For the contemporary reader who has become used to structurally similar arguments in recent debates on "assisted suicide," it may be uncomfortable to note that it was the Nazis who first perfected the type of pro-euthanasia argument which combined the subjective notion of "life not worth living" with objective concerns of rational distribution of means in health care. It was the Nazis who initiated a move to view care for the incurable and other forms of "defective life" primarily as a question of cost that needed to be weighed against other factors.

As Hitler's perfect sense of timing attested, Action T4 was a (more or less open) declaration of war against Bethel (as a type) that literally paved the road toward Buchenwald (as a type). This conjunction became apparent even at the most practical level, when the technologies of death that were first developed in the context of euthanasia programs would become refined and more extensively used as means of mass murder in concentration camps. The "transfers" of people from hospitals to more remote places "of care" was sometimes arranged in specially prepared vehicles, where the exhaust was pumped directly into the interior, so that when these vehicles had reached their destination, the passengers' corpses could be unloaded straight into the crematorium ovens. The pattern of the euthanasia "death vans" was later adopted on large scale for the gas chambers in the camps (Lifton 1986, ch. 2).

Since the euthanasia policies turned out to be among the most politically controversial measures of the regime, they had to be carried out under the cover of euphemistic terminology and a layer of deceptive public claims. Already from August 1939, every doctor and midwife had been required to register all newborns with genetic defects retrospectively to 1936. Action T4 took this to the next level by requesting hospitals and institutions of care such as Bethel to provide comprehensive collations of data about patients with hereditary diseases. Such requests were necessary, they were told, for the purposes of statistical accuracy and transfer to other institutions due to wartime demands. Soon after these transfers had been arranged, parents of these patients would receive a letter informing them of the death of their loved one by, say, pneumonia, with their ashes arriving shortly thereafter (Lifton 1986, 70).

The Bonhoeffer family was engaged in combating this particular strand of Nazi policies from very early on. Karl Bonhoeffer, who was a respected professor of psychiatry and neurology in Berlin, concentrated on writing psychiatric references and public declarations in order to keep cases of enforced sterilizations to a minimum (DBW 6, 293, n. 177). On March 24, 1940, in the heyday of Action T4, Dietrich arranged a meeting between his father, Karl, Paul Braune, director of the Bodelschwingh institutions at Lobethal, and Friedrich von Bodelschwingh. They discussed what could be done to stop the murdering of the most vulnerable members of society entrusted to these men's institutions (Schlingensiepen 2010, 258; DBW 16, 647). Shortly thereafter, Braune went to prison for writing a memorandum on the issue, but a broader front of protest originating primarily in the churches also solidified during that time. This movement of protestation eventually forced Hitler to officially end the euthanasia measures in August 1941, although they continued in secret until the end of the Third Reich (Bethge 1999, 688-89).

In his "Notes on the State of the Church in Europe," drafted after a conversation with Dietrich Bonhoeffer and sent to England in March 1941, Willem Visser't Hooft (who went on after the war to become the first secretary-general of the World Council of Churches) summarized the situation in Germany thus: "Euthanasia continues. Nobody knows how many people have been killed, but it is generally believed that the number is very large. There have been a number of courageous but ineffective protests, i.e., by Bishop Wurm, Cardinal Faulhaber, by some doctors. Bodelschwingh has refused to fill out the questionnaires which are used as a basis of selection, and so far no Bethel patients have been killed" (DBW 16, 178).

"My Strength Is Made Perfect in Weakness": The Christian Offense and Benevolence

Given the long-term engagement of Bonhoeffer's family in these matters, it is not surprising to find a high degree of alertness to the questions that we have described as the antagonism between Bethel and Buchenwald in

Bonhoeffer's theological writings. His sensitivity to the exemplary signifi-cance of Hitler's war on the disabled comes to the fore in a sermon that Bonhoeffer preached (in English) in St. Paul's Church, London, in 1934 (**10.3** [401-4]). Still moved by his first visit to Bethel, for which he had organized a collection from his London churches, and conscious of the growing war on "bad genes" in his home country as reflected in the eugenics laws of that year, Bonhoeffer chose to preach on only one verse from 2 Corinthians 12: "My strength is made perfect in weakness" (12:9).

In reading this sermon, it strikes us that all the major components that we might wish to nominate as comprising Bonhoeffer's "theology of disabled life" are present and densely woven together in this piece: the ideological battle over anthropology (superhuman vs. creature), the Christological grounding of a theological account of human existence, the self-critical question about the church's complicity, and the warning against the tempta-tion to a condescending approach to disabled life.

Bonhoeffer opens his sermon with a question, followed by a claim that highlights the foundational significance he attributes to the question of dis-ability for the "whole attitude toward life": "What is the meaning of weak-ness in this world, what is the meaning of physical or mental or moral weak-ness? . . . Have we ever realized that ultimately our whole attitude toward life, toward man and God depends on the answer to this problem?" (**10.3** [401]). Bonhoeffer finds the reason for this coincidence in the creaturely bond that unites all human beings, regardless of the respective degree of health or sick-ness, power or weakness that their lives assume at any given point in time, which is bound to change in unforeseeable ways. When people find the courage to resist distancing themselves from their disabled brothers and sis-ters and thus resist distancing themselves from the truth about all human life, they awaken to the fact that their own lives are as frail and mortal as these brothers and sisters, and that they are all what Alasdair MacIntyre has called "dependent rational animals." Translated into the framework of con-temporary discussions about the question of when human individuals may be considered "persons" with full and inalienable rights, the answer that we find in Bonhoeffer is simply the creaturely bond. "You are inseparably bound together with the unfortunate people, just because you are a man like them." Every human being is to be treated as a person, simply on the basis of his or her membership in the human race, which is marked by universal kin-ship. Or, as Bonhoeffer would put it about a decade later in his *Ethics*: "The question whether life, in the case of persons severely retarded from birth, is really *human* life at all is so naive that it hardly needs to be answered. It is disabled life, born of human parents, which can be nothing else than *human* life, however unfortunate" (**10.6** [195]).

Just as we recognize that this definition of "personhood" based on kinship and its power to encompass all forms of disability is controversial today, so Bonhoeffer recognized the rivalry which this theology of creation has had from the beginning with other worldviews:

> Against the new meaning which Christianity gave to the weak, against this glorification of weakness, there has always been the strong and indignant protest of an aristocratic philosophy of life which glorified strength and power and violence as the ultimate ideals of humanity. We have observed this very fight going on up to our present days. (**10.3** [402])

For Bonhoeffer, the Nazi cult of the "superhuman," which fueled the war on "defective" genes and forms of human life in "our present days," was part of a large-scale battle in human history between two rival anthropologies that were at odds with each other at the most foundational level.

It is striking to see how Bonhoeffer did not make the slightest effort in this sermon to combat or relativize the diagnosis of the major representative of "aristocratic philosophy," Friedrich Nietzsche, whose "Genealogy of Morals" accused Christianity of bringing about a deplorable re-valuation of all values by celebrating suffering and weakness over human strength and excellence. On the contrary, Bonhoeffer's own expressions echo Nietzsche's language on this point, whose philosophy he admired for its diagnostic sharpness: "So Christianity means a devaluation of all human values and the establishment of a new order of values in the sight of Christ" (**10.3** [403]). Instead of mounting an apologia for Christianity against Nietzsche's attack, by, for example, admitting where it had gone too far in promoting attitudes of self-sacrifice and the ready embrace of suffering, Bonhoeffer accepts both Nietzsche's framing of the battle and the necessity to actually fight this battle to the end. For Bonhoeffer, the theologically appropriate response to Nietzsche's philosophical attack and to those who crudely turned his inspiration into a political war on defective human life was not an apologia for Christianity, but an apologia for the weak: "Christianity stands or falls with its revolutionary protest against violence, arbitrariness, and pride of power and with its apologia for the weak. I feel that Christianity is rather doing too little in showing these points than doing too much. Christianity has adjusted itself much too easily to the worship of power. It should give much more offense, more shock to the world, than it is doing" (**10.3** [402]).

Inquiring into the reason for this "new conception of the meaning of weakness in the world," Bonhoeffer points to the Christological anchoring of any Christian anthropology:

> Our God is a suffering God. Suffering conforms man to God. The suffering man is in the likeness of God. "My strength is made perfect in weakness," says God. Wherever a man in physical or social or moral or religious weakness is aware of his existence and likeness with God, there he is sharing God's life, there he feels God being with him, there he is open for God's strength, that is God's grace, God's love, God's comfort, which passeth all understanding and all human values. (**10.3** [404])

In Christ as the new Adam, suffering and weakness have taken on a new, salvific meaning, and sharing in Christ's suffering, which for Bonhoeffer also meant sharing the plight of the weakest brothers and sisters as of Christ, is but an invitation to embrace grace.

In a move characteristic of someone with a strong pastoral sense and a sobriety in analyzing the state of affairs in church and society, Bonhoeffer does not confine his sermon to this portrayal of the great rivalry of anthropologies that come to clash over the question of disabled human life. It is clear where he thinks the church should stand in this battle, but he also points out that there are positions "between the Christian and the aristocratic view" that invite themselves as attempts at "mediation." It is one such position that he considers the most real and dangerous temptation for those who wish to distance themselves from the "aristocratic" view: "The most dangerous of these positions is the very common attitude of benevolence and beneficence" (**10.3** [403]). To hear Bonhoeffer mark out benevolence as a dangerous temptation for Christians must have been as disturbing to his hearers back then as it is to readers today. After all, does this classical virtue not look like the closest thing to the Christian calling to neighborly love? And had the preacher of these same words not asked his same hearers to give freely to the Bethel institutions and thus show benevolence by practicing beneficence? Bonhoeffer obviously felt the need to elaborate more on this warning: In any attempt to mediate neighborly love by translating (and hence narrowing) it into benevolence and beneficence, he explained,

> . . . the seriousness of the problem is not [at] all recognized. Weakness to them is nothing but imperfection. With all due respect for the real sacrifices that have been made in such a benevolent attitude, it must be said

frankly that this approach is wholly wrong and unchristian, for it means condescension instead of humility. (**10.3** [403])

The subtle though by no means marginal difference between neighborly love and benevolence, which Bonhoeffer pointed out, is still a decisive, if often unrecognized, underlying feature in discussions about disabled life today. Becoming alert to the differences between these two concepts will sensitize us, for example, to the problematic nature of the "inclusion" debate (cf. Wannenwetsch 2007). Should we "include" the disabled in the protective zone of the language of "personhood," a moral attitude which would still be based on a condescending "us-them" rationale, or should we instead summon those who consider themselves not disabled to find themselves included in the same frail and dependent human existence as God's creatures that the disabled exemplify?

Since this 1934 sermon offered us the unique opportunity to present the major threads of thought in Bonhoeffer's theology as they pertain to the question of disabled life in a highly condensed yet comprehensive manner, we can limit our discussion of the remaining excerpts by approaching them as elaborations of that sermon's themes. In a few final paragraphs we will point to other places in Bonhoeffer's work where these themes are developed or related to other theological insights or moral summons.

Fragments and Perfection: Christ the Revealer of True Humanity

As many of the ideological battles in which Bonhoeffer was involved centered on the question of what might count as a true, full, and wholesome human being, he repeatedly reflected on the fragmentary nature of human life and its fragmentary self-perception. At a time in his life when it had become increasingly clear to Bonhoeffer that his days were numbered after the failed plot against Hitler, he introduced an interesting new distinction in a letter from prison:

> What matters, it seems to me, is whether one still sees, in this fragment of life that we have, what the whole was intended and designed to be, and of what material it is made. After all, there are such things as fragments that are only fit for the garbage heap . . . and others which remain meaningful for hundreds of years, because only God could perfect them, so they must remain fragments. . . . If our life is only the most remote reflection of such

a fragment . . . then it is not for us, either to complain about this fragmentary life of ours, but rather even to be glad of it. (DBW 8, 306)

The difference between useless and necessary fragments is the latter's character as being "open to divine fulfillment" (DBW 8, 301). For Bonhoeffer, the refusal to assess human life in terms of its surface appearance as regards, for example, its varying degrees of organic or functional completeness is grounded in the expectation of a future completion that can come only from the one who brought each individual being into existence in the first place. No account of a "complete and wholesome" humanity can therefore be credible which takes no account of God's prerogative to perfect what he has begun. This insight is part of Bonhoeffer's discussion of the Christological determination of anthropological discourse. When Christ is confessed the Second Adam, then everything we think we know about humanity is judged by the revelation of true humanity in and through Christ, who became human in order to restore and perfect the fragments of human life that exist, both individually and socially.

For Bonhoeffer, human life cannot be understood in abstraction from "Christ as the origin, essence, and goal of life, of our life." As Bonhoeffer adds,

> Apart from the fact that we are creatures who are reconciled and redeemed, we can only arrive at biological or ideological abstractions. . . . There is no human being as such, just as there is no God as such; both are empty abstractions. Human beings are accepted in God's becoming human and are loved, judged, and reconciled in Christ, and God is the God who became human. (**10.7** [251, 253])

For Bonhoeffer, Christ, as the true image of God, is not the icon "of noble humanity but the Yes of God to real human beings" (DBW 6, 85). Thus, Christ was not seeking to be the perfect one "at the expense of human beings, nor, as the only guiltless one, to look down on a humanity perishing under its guilt" (DBW 6, 275). Instead, Christ is the vicarious representative for all human beings precisely by "entering" human frailty, dependency, and even guilt. With regards to the great rivalry over the true image of mankind in his time, Bonhoeffer chose to portray Christ as the revelation of true humanity precisely in terms of the anti-Superhuman.

If Christ is the revelation of true humanity, mediating, as it were, any truthful image that human beings might have of themselves, Bonhoeffer insists that Christ must also play a central role in mediating human relationships. This insight is particularly important, since human relationships are prone to be determined by an economy of desire that absorbs the otherness of the other into a fantasy image which we make of her. In his account of *Life Together*, in which Bonhoeffer reflected on the community experiment with his students in the Seminary at Finkenwalde, he distinguishes two rival types of love: emotional (or self-centered) love and spiritual love:

> Self-centered love constructs its own image of other persons, about what they are and what they should become. It takes the life of the other person into its own hands. Spiritual love recognizes the true image of the other person as seen from the perspective of Jesus Christ. It is the image Jesus Christ has formed and wants to form in all people. (**10.3** [44])

This distinction is of paramount importance for our understanding of Bonhoeffer's contribution to a theology of the disabled life. We ask: Is it not precisely that sort of love which he calls "emotional" — a love that actually rather loves the image we project onto others, often a condensed version of our own aspirations and anxieties — that makes the life of the disabled in our midst so difficult? Under the best of circumstances, "emotional love" leads to distinguishing "good" disabled persons, those who respond to care by "making progress," as opposed to others who don't reciprocate. Under less satisfying circumstances, however, this type of love will work toward a blatant call to exclusion for those that (appear to) have nothing to give back. Bonhoeffer observes,

> The exclusion of the weak and insignificant, the seemingly useless people, from everyday Christian life in community [Lebensgemeinschaft] may actually mean the exclusion of Christ; for in the poor sister or brother, Christ is knocking at the door. (DBW 5, 45-46)

Christ needs to mediate human relations in order to facilitate the involved parties' discovering Christ in the other by resisting their absorption into the chaotic, domesticating, and absorbing forces that dwell in economies of human desire if not given appropriate direction. "Spiritual love, however, comes from Jesus Christ; it serves him alone. It knows that it has no direct access to other persons. Christ stands between me and others" (DBW 5, 43).

Political Vocation: Taking a Public Stance on Behalf of the Weak

Bonhoeffer's public and political engagement for the disabled, the Jews, and other preyed-upon members of society under Hitler grew from his understanding that the Christian's prerogative is to share in Christ's own life and action. Hence, instead of "dull looking on" (DBW 8, 49), the Christian is called to act as "vicarious representative" and to open her mouth and hand for the powerless, attacked, and despised. Correspondingly, Bonhoeffer's concept of "responsible action" was based on a notion of vocation as political in nature, since God can at any time call the Christian to become a neighbor to the stranger. Therefore, the Christian cannot confine her responsibility to a narrow sphere of, say, professional duties:

> The boundary of vocation has been broken open not only vertically, that is, through Christ, but also horizontally, with regard to the extent of responsibility. Let us say I am a medical doctor, for example. In dealing with a concrete case I serve not only my patient, but also the body of scientific knowledge, and thus science and knowledge of truth in general. Although in practice I render this service in my concrete situation — for example, at a patient's bedside — I nevertheless remain aware of my responsibility toward the whole, and only thus fulfill my vocation. In so doing, it may come to the point that in a particular case I must recognize and fulfill my concrete responsibility as a physician no longer only at a patient's bedside, but, for example, in taking a public stance against a measure that poses a threat to medical science, or human life, or science in general. Vocation is responsibility, and responsibility is the whole response of the whole person to reality as a whole. (**10.8** [293])

Bonhoeffer understood the summons to speak up and act for the most vulnerable not only as the responsibility of the individual Christian, but as the communal vocation of the church which is called to be "Church for others." Acknowledging the manifold shortcomings of his own church to live up to this vocation and its failure to take a public stance against the dehumanizing policies of the Third Reich, Bonhoeffer composed a formula for a "confession of guilt" for the church, structured according to the Decalogue as a mirror of sin. Drawing on the precept against killing, the paragraph that pertains to our topic in particular reads as follows:

> The church confesses that it has witnessed the arbitrary use of brutal force, the suffering in body and soul of countless innocent people, that it

has witnessed oppression, hatred, and murder without raising its voice for the victims and without finding ways of rushing to help them. It has become guilty of the lives of the weakest and most defenseless brothers and sisters of Jesus Christ. (**10.5** [139])

One form which the public protest against Hitler's euthanasia programs took was a Petition to the Armed Forces, composed around December 1941. It was signed by Bonhoeffer, who had advised Friedrich J. Perels, who wrote down in twelve points examples of why "the hope of Protestant Christians that the antichurch measures would cease, at least for the length of the war, has been bitterly disappointed" (DBW 16, 240). Point 12 of this petition reads:

The killing of so-called unworthy lives, which has now become better known in the congregations and has claimed its victims from them, is viewed by Christians of all confessions with the deepest alarm and with revulsion, especially in connection with the general abrogation of the Ten Commandments and any security of law and thus as a sign of the anti-Christian stance of leading authorities in the Reich. (DBW 16, 245)

What Bonhoeffer understood, as did few others in his time, was that only those who respect God's commands have access to a freedom that saves from the various forms of idolatry — the worship of the self and the superhuman that eventually ends in the self-destruction of humanity. Because he did so, he was able to perceive and disdain the elimination of the weakest members of society as the firstfruits of such a self-destruction.

REFERENCES

Primary Sources

Bonhoeffer, Dietrich. 2009. *Berlin: 1932-1933. Dietrich Bonhoeffer Works* (hereafter DBW), Vol. 12. Edited by Larry L. Rasmussen. Translated by Isabel Best, David Higgins, and Douglas W. Stott. Minneapolis: Augsburg Fortress Press.

———. 2006. *Conspiracy and Imprisonment: 1940-1945.* DBW, Vol. 16. Edited by Mark Brocker. Translated by Lisa E. Dahill. Minneapolis: Augsburg Fortress Press.

———. 1997. *Creation and Fall: A Theological Exposition of Genesis 1–3* (first published as *Schöpfung und Fall*, 1937). DBW, Vol. 3. Edited by John W. de Gruchy. Translated by Douglas Stephen Bax. Minneapolis: Augsburg Fortress Press.

————. 2005. *Ethics* (first published as *Ethik* in 1949). DBW, Vol. 6. Edited by Clifford J. Green. Translated by Reinhard Krauss, Charles C. West, and Douglas W. Stott. Minneapolis: Augsburg Fortress Press.

————. 2010. *Letters and Papers from Prison.* DBW, Vol. 8. Edited by John W. de Gruchy. Translated by I. Best, L. E. Dahill, R. Krauss, and N. Lukens. Minneapolis: Augsburg Fortress Press.

————. 1995. *Life Together* and *The Prayerbook of the Bible* (first published as *Gemeinsames Leben,* 1939, and *Das Gebetbuch der Bibel,* 1940). DBW, Vol. 5. Edited by Geffrey B. Kelly. Translated by Daniel W. Bloesch and James H. Burtness. Minneapolis: Augsburg Fortress Press.

————. 2007. *London: 1933-1935.* DBW, Vol. 13. Edited by Keith W. Clements. Translated by Isabel Best. Minneapolis: Augsburg Fortress Press.

Secondary Sources

Bethge, Eberhard. 1999. *Dietrich Bonhoeffer: A Biography.* Revised and edited by Victoria J. Barnett. Minneapolis: Fortress Press.

Lifton, Robert Jay. 1986. *The Nazi Doctors: Medical Killing and the Psychology of Genocide.* New York: Basic Books.

Metaxas, Eric. 2010. *Bonhoeffer: Pastor, Martyr, Prophet, Spy.* Nashville: Thomas Nelson.

Pence, Gregory. 1990. *Classic Cases in Medical Ethics: Accounts of the Cases that Have Shaped Medical Ethics, with Philosophical, Legal, and Historical Backgrounds.* New York: McGraw-Hill.

Schlingensiepen, Ferdinand. 2010. *Dietrich Bonhoeffer, 1906-1945: Martyr, Thinker, Man of Resistance.* Translated by Isabel Best. London and New York: T&T Clark.

Wannenwetsch, Bernd. 2007. "Angels with Broken Wings: The Disabled as Key to the Recognition of Personhood." In *Theology, Disability, and the New Genetics.* Edited by John Swinton and Brian Brock. London: T&T Clark, 182-200.

Dietrich Bonhoeffer on Disability: Excerpts

The excerpts below are all taken from various volumes of Dietrich Bonhoeffer Works (DBW), specifically the series by Augsburg Fortress Press. The abbreviated citations refer to works listed in the Primary Sources.

10.1

DBW 12, 157-59

Letter to Julie Bonhoeffer, August 20, 1933

Dear Grandmama,

Here I am writing again to wish you a happy birthday, and I had been so sure that this time I would be able to come over at least for the day. But we have not yet finished our work, and it probably won't even be finished by Wednesday evening. However, I hope I will still be able to come up on Thursday for two days. I have to be back in Berlin by Sunday.

I hope you will have nice weather for your birthday party this Monday. With the great-grandchildren there as well, you will surely have a delightful time. I also hope you have had such a good rest these last few weeks that you have been able to put the recent disturbances behind you to some extent and can look forward to going back to Berlin. Then we will have at least part of September together in Berlin, in any case, before I go to London. I am trying to postpone my departure to October 15. I accepted the position without committing myself to a specific time.

The time here in Bethel has made a deep impression on me. Here we have a part of the church that still knows what the church can be about and what it cannot be about. I have just come back from the worship service. It is an extraordinary sight, the whole church filled with crowds of epileptics [158] and other ill persons, interspersed with the deaconesses and deacons who are there to help in case one of them falls; then there are elderly tramps who come in off the country roads, the theological students, the children from the lab school, doctors and pastors with their families. But the sick people dominate the picture, and they are keen listeners and participants.

Their experience of life must be most extraordinary, not having control over their bodies, having to be resigned to the possibility of an attack at any moment. Today in church was the first time this really struck me, as I became aware of these moments. Their situation of being truly defenseless perhaps gives these people a much clearer insight into certain realities of human existence, the fact that we are indeed basically defenseless, than can be possible for healthy persons. And it is just this abrupt alternation between standing there healthy and falling down sick which must be more conducive to this insight than being healthy all the time. Today in church I was constantly reminded of Rembrandt's "Hundred Guilder" etching and the gospel stories it illustrates. There is nothing sentimental about any of this; it is tremendously real and natural. It knocks down some of the barriers with which we usually shut ourselves off from this world. Here it simply is a part of one's own life, as it is in reality. It is said of Buddha that he was converted by an encounter with a seriously ill person. What utter madness when some people today think that the sick can or ought to be legally eliminated. It is almost like building a Tower of Babel and it must bring vengeance on us. Anyhow, our concept of sickness and health is pretty ambiguous. What we see as "sick" is actually healthier, in essential [159] aspects of life and of insight, than health is. And that the two conditions depend on each other is surely an essential part of the plan and the laws of life, which can't simply be changed to suit people's impertinence and lack of understanding.

Our work here is very enjoyable and also very demanding. We want to try to make the German Christians declare their intentions. I rather doubt we shall succeed. Even if, at this point, they make concessions in their official formulations, they are under such strong pressure that sooner or later any promises made are bound to break down. It is becoming increasingly clear to me that what we are going to get is a big, *völkisch* national church that in its essence can no longer be reconciled with Christianity, and that we must make up our minds to take entirely new paths and follow where they lead. The issue is really Germanism or Christianity, and the sooner the conflict comes out in the open, the better. The greatest danger of all would be trying to conceal this.

This has now turned into a long letter, and it's time for me to go to dinner. I wish you a good new year of life, dear Grandmama, and look forward to seeing you soon. My love to Karl Friedrich and Grete, and love and gratitude to you from

Dietrich

10.2

DBW 8, 52

"The view from below" in *Letters and Papers from Prison*

It remains an experience of incomparable value that we have for once learned to see the great events of world history from below, from the perspective of the outcasts, the suspects, the maltreated, the powerless, the oppressed and reviled, in short from the perspective of the suffering. If only during this time bitterness and envy have not corroded the heart; that we come to see matters great and small, happiness and misfortune, strength and weakness with new eyes; that our sense for greatness, humanness, justice, and mercy has grown clearer, freer, more incorruptible; that we learn, indeed, that personal suffering is a more useful key, a more fruitful principle than personal happiness for exploring the meaning of the world in contemplation and action. But this perspective from below must not lead us to become advocates for those who are perpetually dissatisfied. Rather, out of a higher satisfaction, which in its essence is grounded beyond what is below and above, we do justice to life in all its dimensions and in this way affirm it.

10.3

DBW 13, 401-4

> Sermon for the Evening Worship Service on 2 Corinthians 12:9 (London 1934): "My Strength Is Made Perfect in Weakness"

All philosophy of life has to give an answer to the question which presents itself everywhere in the world: What is the meaning of weakness in this world, what is the meaning of physical or mental or moral weakness? Have we ever thought about it at all? Have we ever realized that ultimately our whole attitude toward life, toward man and God depends on the answer to this problem? Even if we have never faced this question intellectually, do we know that actually we are bound to take an attitude towards it every day? What has remained unconscious with us shall become conscious now, conscious in the light of the word of God. There is a certain inclination in human nature to keep off from all problems that might make us feel uncomfortable in our own situation. We like to leave these questions in the darkness of subconscious action rather than to put it into the light of a clear and responsible intellectual attitude. We are all dealing with the problem of weakness every day, but we feel it somewhat dangerous to give account of our fundamental attitude. But God does not want us to put our head into the sand like ostriches, but he commands us to face reality as it is and to make a truthful and definite decision.

Someone might ask: Why is this problem of weakness so all-important? We answer: Have you ever seen a greater mystery in this world than poor people, ill people, insane people — people who cannot help themselves but who have just to rely on other people for help, for love, for care? Have you ever thought what outlook on life a cripple, a hopelessly ill man, a socially [402] exploited man, a colored man in a white country, an untouchable, may have? And if so, did you not feel that here life means something totally different from what it means to you and that on the other hand you are inseparably bound together with the unfortunate people, just because you are a man like them, just because you are not weak but strong, and just because in all your strength you will feel their weakness? Have we not felt that we shall never be happy in our life as long as this world of weakness from which we are perhaps spared — but who knows for how long — is foreign and strange and far removed from us, as long as we keep away from it consciously or subconsciously? (Bethel!)

Let us be truthful and not unreal, let us ask the question: What is the meaning of weakness in this world? We all know that Christianity has been blamed ever since its early days for its message to the weak. Christianity is a religion of slaves, of people with inferiority complexes; it owes its success only to the masses of miserable people whose weakness and misery Christianity has glorified. It was the attitude towards the problem of weakness in the world which made everybody into followers or enemies of Christianity. Against the new meaning which Christianity gave to the weak, against this glorification of weakness, there has always been the strong and indignant protest of an aristocratic philosophy of life which glorified strength and power and violence as the ultimate ideals of humanity. We have observed this very fight going on up to our present days. Christianity stands or falls with its revolutionary protest against violence, arbitrariness, and pride of power and with its apologia for the weak. I feel that Christianity is rather doing too little in showing these points than doing too much. Christianity has adjusted itself much too easily to the worship of power. It should give much more offense, more shock to the world, than it is doing. Christianity should take a [403] much more definite stand for the weak than to consider the potential moral right of the strong.

In the middle between the Christian and the aristocratic view there is a great variety of attempts to mediate between them. The most dangerous of these positions is the very common attitude of benevolence and beneficence. There the seriousness of the problem is not [at] all recognized. Weakness to them is nothing but imperfection. But this includes, of course, that the higher value in itself is strength and power. Strength and weakness are considered in the proportion of the perfect and in the imperfect. Here Christianity must protest. With all due respect for the real sacrifices that have been made in such a benevolent attitude, it must be said frankly that this approach is wholly wrong and unchristian, for it means condescension instead of humility. Christian love and help for the weak means humiliation of the strong before the weak, of the healthy before the suffering, of [the] mighty before the exploited. The Christian relation between the strong and the weak is that the strong has to look *up* to the weak and never to look down. Weakness is holy; therefore we devote ourselves to the weak. Weakness in the eyes of Christ is not the imperfect one against the perfect, rather is strength the imperfect and weakness the perfect. Not the weak has to serve the strong, but the strong has to serve the weak, and this not by benevolence but by care and reverence. Not the powerful is right, but ultimately the weak is always right. So Christianity means a devaluation of all human values and the establishment of a new order of values in the sight of Christ.

Here we have arrived at the last question: What is the reason for this new conception of the meaning of weakness in the world? Why is suffering holy? Because God has suffered in the world from man, and wherever he comes, he has to suffer from man again. God has suffered on the cross. It is therefore that all human suffering and weakness is sharing God's own suffering and weakness in the world. We are suffering: God is suffering much [404] more. Our God is a suffering God. Suffering conforms man to God. The suffering man is in the likeness of God. "My strength is made perfect in weakness," says God. Wherever a man in physical or social or moral or religious weakness is aware of his existence and likeness with God, there he is sharing God's life, there he feels God being with him, there he is open for God's strength, that is God's grace, God's love, God's comfort, which passeth all understanding and all human values. God glorifies himself in the weak as He glorified himself in the cross. God is mighty where man is nothing.

10.4

DBW 5, 42-46

From "Community" in *Life Together*

[42] There is, likewise, a "merely emotional" love of neighbor. Such love is capable of making the most unheard-of sacrifices. Often it far surpasses the genuine love of Christ in fervent devotion and visible results. It speaks the

Christian language with overwhelming and stirring eloquence. But it is what the apostle Paul is speaking of when he says: "If I give all I possess to the poor, and surrender my body to the flames" (1 Cor. 13:3) — in other words, if I combine the utmost deeds of love with the utmost of devotion — "but do not have love (that is, the love of Christ), I would be nothing" (1 Cor. 13:2). Self-centered love loves the other for the sake of itself; spiritual love loves the other for the sake of Christ. That is why self-centered love seeks direct contact with other persons. It loves them, not as free persons, but as those whom it binds to itself. It wants to do everything it can to win and conquer; it puts pressure on the other person. It desires to be irresistible, to dominate. Self-centered love does not think much of truth. It makes the truth relative, since nothing, not even the truth, must come between it and the person loved. Emotional, self-centered love desires other persons, their company. It wants them to return its love, but it does not serve them. On the contrary, it continues to desire even when it seems to be serving.

[43] Two factors, which are really one and the same thing, reveal the difference between spiritual and self-centered love. Emotional, self-centered love cannot tolerate the dissolution of a community that has become false, even for the sake of genuine community. And such self-centered love cannot love an enemy, that is to say, one who seriously and stubbornly resists it. Both spring from the same source: emotional love is by its very nature desire, desire for self-centered community. As long as it can possibly satisfy this desire, it will not give it up, even for the sake of truth, even for the sake of genuine love for others. But emotional, self-centered love is at an end when it can no longer expect its desire to be fulfilled, namely, in the face of an enemy. There it turns into hatred, contempt, and slander.

Spiritual love, however, begins right at this point. This is why emotional, self-centered love turns into personal hatred when it encounters genuine spiritual love that does not desire but serves. Self-centered love makes itself an end in itself. It turns itself into an achievement, an idol it worships, to which it must subject everything. It cares for, cultivates, and loves itself and nothing else in the world. Spiritual love, however, comes from Jesus Christ; it serves him alone. It knows that it has no direct access to other persons. Christ stands between me and others. I do not know in advance what love of others means on the basis of the general idea of love that grows out of my emotional desires. All this may instead be hatred and the worst kind of selfishness in the eyes of Christ. Only Christ in his Word tells me what love is. Contrary to all my own opinions and convictions, Jesus Christ will tell me what love for my brothers and sisters really looks like. Therefore, spiritual love is bound to the word of Jesus Christ alone. Where Christ tells me to maintain community for the sake of love, I desire to maintain it. Where the truth of Christ orders me to dissolve a community for the sake of love, I will dissolve it, despite all the protests of my self-centered love. Because spiritual love does not desire but rather serves, it loves an enemy as a brother or sister. It originates neither in the brother or sister nor in the enemy, but in Christ and his word. Self-centered, emotional love can never comprehend spiritual love, for spiritual love is from above. It is something completely strange, new, and incomprehensible to all earthly love.

Because Christ stands between me and an other, I must not long for un-mediated community with that person. As only Christ was able to speak to me in such a way that I was helped, so others too can only be [44] helped by Christ alone. However, this means that I must release others from all my at-tempts to control, coerce, and dominate them with my love. In their freedom from me, other persons want to be loved for who they are, as those for whom Christ became a human being, died, and rose again, as those for whom Christ won the forgiveness of sins and prepared eternal life. Because Christ has long since acted decisively for other Christians, before I could begin to act, I must allow them the freedom to be Christ's. They should encounter me only as the persons that they already are for Christ. This is the meaning of the claim that we can encounter others only through the mediation of Christ. Self-centered love constructs its own image of other persons, about what they are and what they should become. It takes the life of the other per-son into its own hands. Spiritual love recognizes the true image of the other person as seen from the perspective of Jesus Christ. It is the image Jesus Christ has formed and wants to form in all people.

Therefore, spiritual love will prove successful insofar as it commends Christ to the other in all that it says and does. It will not seek to agitate an-other by exerting all too personal, direct influence or by crudely interfering in one's life. It will not take pleasure in pious, emotional fervor and excite-ment. Rather, it will encounter the other with the clear word of God and be prepared to leave the other alone with this word for a long time. It will be willing to release others again so that Christ may deal with them. It will re-spect the other as the boundary that Christ establishes between us; and it will find full community with the other in the Christ who alone binds us to-gether. This spiritual love will thus speak to Christ about the other Christian more than to the other Christian about Christ. It knows that the most direct way to others is always through prayer to Christ and that love of the other is completely tied to the truth found in Christ. It is out of this love that John the disciple speaks: "I have no greater joy than this, to hear that my children are walking in the truth" (3 John 4).

Emotional love lives by uncontrolled and uncontrollable dark desires; spiritual love lives in the clear light of service ordered by the truth. Self-centered love results in human enslavement, bondage, rigidity; spiritual love creates the *freedom* of Christians under the Word. Emotional love breeds artificial hothouse flowers; spiritual love creates the *fruits* that grow healthily under God's open sky, according to God's good pleasure in the rain and storm and sunshine.

[45] The existence of any Christian communal life essentially depends on whether or not it succeeds at the right time in promoting the ability to distinguish between a human ideal and God's reality, between spiritual and emotional community. The life and death of a Christian community is decided by its ability to reach sober clarity on these points as soon as possible. In other words, a life together under the Word will stay healthy only when it does not form itself into a movement, an order, a society, a *collegium pietatis,* but instead understands itself as being part of the one, holy, universal, Christian church, sharing through its deeds and suffering in the hardships and struggles and promise of the whole church. Every principle of selection, and every division connected with it that is not necessitated quite objectively by common work, local conditions, or family connections is of the greatest danger to a Christian community. Self-centeredness always insinuates itself in any process of intellectual or spiritual selectivity, destroying the spiritual power of the community and robbing the community of its effectiveness for the church, thus driving it into sectarianism. The exclusion of the weak and insignificant, the seemingly useless people, from everyday Christian life in community [Lebensgemeinschaft] may actually mean the exclusion of [46] Christ; for in the poor sister or brother, Christ is knocking at the door.

10.5

DBW 6, 138-40

Ethics: Confession of Guilt

[138] The church confesses that it has not professed openly and clearly enough its message of the one God, revealed for all times in Jesus Christ and tolerating no other gods besides. The church confesses its timidity, its devia-

tions, its dangerous concessions. It has often disavowed its duties [Ämter] as sentinel and comforter. Through this it has often withheld the compassion that it owes to the despised and rejected. The church was mute when it should have cried out, because the blood of the innocent cried out to heaven. The church did not find the right word in the right way at the right time. It did not resist to the death the falling away [Abfall] from faith and is guilty of the godlessness of the masses.

The church confesses that it has misused the name of Christ by being ashamed of it before the world and by not resisting strongly enough the misuse of that name for evil ends. The church has looked on while injustice and violence have been done, under the cover of the name of Christ. It has even allowed the most holy name to be openly derided without contradiction and has thus encouraged that derision. The church [139] recognizes that God will not leave unpunished those who so misuse God's name as it does.

The church confesses it is guilty of the loss of holidays [Feiertag], for the barrenness of its public worship, for the contempt for Sunday rest.

It has made itself guilty for the restlessness and discontent of working people, as well as for their exploitation above and beyond the workweek, because its preaching of Jesus Christ has been so weak and its public worship so limp.

The church confesses that it is guilty of the breakdown of parental authority. The church has not opposed contempt for age and the divinization of youth because it feared losing the youth and therefore the future, as if its future depended on the young! It has not dared to proclaim the God-given dignity of parents against revolutionary youth and has made a very worldly-minded attempt "to go along with youth." Thus it is guilty of destroying countless families, for children's betraying their parents, of the self-divinizing of youth, and therefore of abandoning them to fall away from Christ.

The church confesses that it has witnessed the arbitrary use of brutal force, the suffering in body and soul of countless innocent people, that it has witnessed oppression, hatred, and murder without raising its voice for the victims and without finding ways of rushing to help them. It has become guilty of the lives of the weakest and most defenseless brothers and sisters of Jesus Christ.

[140] The church confesses that it has not found any guiding or helpful word to say in the midst of the dissolution of all order in the relationships of the sexes to each other. It has found no strong or authentic message to set against the disdain for chastity and the proclamation of sexual licentious-

ness. Beyond the occasional expression of moral indignation it has had nothing to say. The church has become guilty, therefore, of the loss of purity and wholesomeness among youth. It has not known how to proclaim strongly that our bodies are members of the body of Christ.

The church confesses that it has looked on silently as the poor were exploited and robbed, while the strong were enriched and corrupted.

The church confesses its guilt toward the countless people whose lives have been destroyed by slander, denunciation, and defamation. It has not condemned the slanderers for their wrongs and has thereby left the slandered to their fate.

The church confesses that it has coveted security, tranquility, peace, property, and honor to which it had no claim, and therefore has not bridled human covetousness, but promoted it.

The church confesses itself guilty of violating all of the Ten Commandments. It confesses thereby its apostasy from Christ. It has not so borne witness to the truth of God in a way that leads all inquiry and [141] science to recognize its origin in this truth. It has not so proclaimed the righteousness of God that all human justice must see there its own source and essence. It has not been able to make the loving care of God so credible that all human economic activity would be guided by it in its task. By falling silent the church became guilty for the loss of responsible action in society, courageous intervention, and the readiness to suffer for what is acknowledged as right. It is guilty of the government's falling away from Christ.

10.6

DBW 6, 175; 178-80; 185-86; 189-96; 206

Ethics: The Natural Life

[175] A decisive consequence follows from this. The natural can never be a construct of some part or some authority in the fallen world. Neither the individual nor any community or institution in the preserved world can set and decide what is natural. It has already been set and decided, and in such a way that the individual, the communities, and the institutions receive their respective share in it. What is natural cannot be determined by an arbitrary construct [Setzung]; instead, every arbitrary construct of this kind, whether by an individual, a community, or an institution, will inevitably be shattered

and will destroy itself against the natural that already exists. Injury and violation of the natural avenge themselves on the violator.

[178] Natural Life

Natural life is formed life. The natural is the form that inheres in and serves life. If life severs itself from this form, if it tries to assert itself in freedom from this form, if it will not allow itself to be served by the form of the natural, then it destroys itself down to its roots. Life that makes itself absolute, that makes itself its own goal, destroys itself. Vitalism ends inevitably in nihilism, in the destruction of all that is natural. In the strict sense, life as such is a nothing, an abyss, a ruin. It is movement without end, without goal, movement into nothingness. It does not rest until it has drawn everything into this annihilating movement. This vitalism is found in both individual and communal life. It arises from the false absolutizing of an insight that is essentially correct, that life, both individual and communal, is not only a means to an end but also an end in itself. God wills life and gives life a form in which it can live, because left to its own resources it can only destroy itself. At the same time, however, this form places life at the service of other lives and of the world; it makes life in a limited sense a means to an end.

[179] As there is a vitalistic absolutizing of life as an end in itself that destroys life, so there is an absolutizing of life as a means to an end that has the same result; this holds for both individual and community. We can call this error the mechanization of life. Here the individual is understood only in terms of usefulness [Nutzwert] to the whole, and the community only in terms of its use to an all-controlling institution, organization, or idea. The collective is the god to whom both individual and communal life is sacrificed in a process of total mechanization. Here life is extinguished, and the form that is meant to serve life assumes unlimited domination over life. Life's being an end in itself is defeated in every respect, and life sinks into nothingness. For as soon as mechanization has killed all life, from which alone it drew its energy, it must collapse itself.

Vitalism and mechanization, as described here, equally express a perhaps unconscious despair about natural life, an enmity to life, a weariness of life, an incapacity for life. Taste for the natural has yielded to the allures of the unnatural. Natural life stands between the extremes of vitalism and mechanization. It is at the same time life as an end in itself and as a means to an end. In Jesus Christ life as an end in itself expresses its createdness, and life as a means to an end expresses its participation in the kingdom of God [Gottesreich]. In the context of natural life, [180] accordingly, life as an end in itself is expressed in rights [Rechte], and life as the means to an end is expressed in duties. These rights and duties are both given with life. So for the sake of Christ and Christ's coming, natural life must be lived according to certain rights and certain duties. Where these rights and duties are denied, suspended, or destroyed, a serious obstacle is placed in the way of the coming of Christ. Here the gratitude that preserves the life we have received, and at the same time places this life in the service of the Creator, is attacked at its roots.

It may sound strange to *idealist* thought that a Christian ethic speaks first of rights and only then of duties. However, we take our stand here not with Kant, but with Holy Scripture. Therefore we must speak first of the rights of natural life; that means speaking first of what is given to life, and only then of what is demanded of it. God gives before God demands. It is not the creature but the Creator who is honored by respecting the rights of natural life. The wealth of God's gifts is acknowledged. There are no rights before God, but the natural, understood as a pure gift of God, becomes rights with respect to human beings. The rights of natural life are the reflection of the glory of God the Creator in the midst of the fallen world. They are not in the first place what human beings can lay claim to for their own interest, but what God guarantees. Duties spring from the rights themselves, as tasks [Aufgaben] from gifts [Gaben]. They are intrinsic to the rights. In treating natural life and speaking first of rights and then of duties we make space for the gospel in natural life.

[185] The Right to Bodily Life

Bodily life, which we receive through no action of our own, intrinsically bears the right to its preservation. This is not a right that we have stolen or earned for ourselves; it is in the truest sense a right that is "born with us," that we have received, that was there before our will, that rests in what actually exists [im Seienden]. Since by God's will human life on earth exists only as bodily life, the body has a right to be preserved for the sake of the whole person. Since all rights are extinguished at death, the preservation of bodily life is the very foundation of all natural rights and is therefore endowed with special importance. The most primordial right of natural life is the protection of the body [186] from intentional injury, violation, and killing. That may sound very sober and unheroic. However, the body does not exist in the first place to be sacrificed but to be preserved. That the right and duty to sacrifice the body can emerge from other and higher viewpoints presupposes the primordial right of the body to be preserved. Bodily life, like life as a whole, is both a means to an end and an end in itself. It is idealistic, but not Christian, to understand the body exclusively as a means to an end. The means can be disposed of as soon as the end is achieved. This corresponds to the view that the body is a prison of the immortal soul, which will leave the body forever at death. In Christian teaching the body has a higher dignity. The human being is a bodily being and remains so in eternity as well. Bodiliness and being human [Menschsein] belong indivisibly together. Thus, the bodiliness that God has willed as the form of human existence becomes an end in itself. This does not exclude the body from being subordinated to a higher end. But it is important that the rights of bodily life include its preservation not only as a means to an end but also as an end in itself. That the body is an end in itself is expressed within natural life in the joys of the body. If the body were only the means to an end, the human being would have no right to bodily joys. Bodily pleasure, then, could not be allowed to exceed a useful minimum. And that would have drastic results for Christian judgments about all the problems related to bodily life — problems of housing, food, clothing, recreation, play, and sexuality. But if the body is an end in itself, then there is a right to bodily joys, without subordinating them to a further, higher purpose. Part of the very essence of joy is that it is spoiled by thoughts about purpose.

[189] The first right of natural life is the protection of bodily life from arbitrary killing. We must speak of arbitrary killing wherever innocent life is deliberately killed. In this context every life that does not undertake a conscious attack on another life, and is not guilty of a crime worthy of death, is innocent. Accordingly, the killing of an enemy in war is not arbitrary; for even if the enemy is not personally guilty, the enemy still consciously takes part in the attack of another people on the life of my people and must therefore share the consequences of bearing the common guilt. The killing of a criminal who has encroached on another life is, of course, not arbitrary. Nor is the killing of civilians in war arbitrary when it is not directly intended, but is only the unfortunate result of a necessary military action. The killing of defenseless prisoners or the wounded, who are not capable of attacking my life, is arbitrary.

[190] The killing of an innocent person in passion or for some advantage is arbitrary. Every conscious killing of innocent life is arbitrary.

This last statement has not remained unchallenged. The problem that arises here is described by the concept of euthanasia. The basic question here is whether innocent life that is no longer worth living may be terminated in a painless manner. A double motivation underlies this question — concern for the sick, and concern for the healthy. Before we go into the substance of the question, however, we must establish as fundamental that any decision about the right to kill human life can never be made based on the sum of various grounds. Either *one* reason is so compelling that it leads to this decision, or the reason is not compelling. In that case, however, such a decision cannot be justified by adducing a number of additional reasons. The killing of another's life can only take place on the basis of unconditional necessity, and then it must be carried out even against any number of other reasons, even good ones. Never may the killing of another's life be one possibility among many, however well founded that possibility may be. Where there is even the smallest responsible possibility of allowing the other to stay alive, then the destruction of this life would be arbitrary killing — murder. Killing or sparing life are never equivalent alternatives in a decision. [191] The preservation of life has an incomparable priority over destruction. Life may claim all grounds to validate itself, while for killing there is only one single valid ground. Where this is not considered, one runs afoul of the Creator and Preserver of life. In supporting the right to euthanasia on several different grounds, one puts oneself in the wrong from the beginning, by admitting indirectly that there is no single absolutely compelling ground.

So, in dealing with this question, we must examine each of the grounds on its own terms and ask about its compelling character. We can never try to compensate for the weakness of one ground by bringing up another.

Does consideration for the incurably ill and the heavy burden of their suffering demand the deliberate ending of their lives by a humane form of death? Such a case takes for granted that the consent, that is, the wish, of the ill person must be presupposed. Where this wish has not been or cannot be clearly expressed, as, for example, by the severely retarded, or where even the desire for life is unmistakably expressed, one can no longer honestly speak of consideration for the ill. And who can gauge how strongly even the incurably mentally ill person, despite suffering, clings to life and how much happiness that person may achieve even in a miserable life? There are strong indications that in such people the affirmation of life is particularly strong and unrestrained. Here consideration for the ill person could not become grounds for the destruction of that life. Or, in the reverse case, when a severely depressive person asks for the ending of his or her life, may we then overlook the fact that this is the plea of an ill person who is not in control of himself or herself? To reply that this is also the case with the severely retarded person who hangs on to life disregards the fact that the right to life has priority over the right to kill.

But let us take the case of an incurably ill person who with a clear mind consents to, even yearns for, the ending of his or her life. Can such a wish constitute a compelling demand for the application of euthanasia? [192] Without doubt, one cannot speak of a compelling demand as long as the patient's life still makes demands of its own — in other words, as long as the physician is obligated not only to the will but also to the life of the patient. The question of the killing of another life is shifted here toward whether ending one's own life in the most severe illness is permitted and may be assisted. We will discuss this question in connection with the problem of self-murder.

The objection that physicians in some cases will no longer do everything possible to prolong life artificially raises a serious question. For example, perhaps they will not send a severely retarded tuberculosis patient to a sanatorium; this, it is argued, is no different from deliberately ending the patient's life. Still, it is important to hold firmly to the distinction between allowing to die and killing. In life in general, one cannot in every case use all conceivable means to postpone death, yet there remains a decisive difference between this and deliberate killing. One must therefore conclude that consideration for the ill person cannot be adequate grounds for killing human life.

Does concern for the healthy, then, make the killing of innocent life necessary? To answer this question in the affirmative presupposes that every life must have a certain utility [Nutzwert] for the community and that life is no longer justified when this usefulness ceases and may in a given case be destroyed. Even where one avoids this radical version of the idea, the right to life of those who are socially valuable is [193] evaluated differently from the socially worthless, even though in both cases nothing but innocent life is involved. But this different valuation evidently cannot be carried out in life, because it would have impossible consequences. It would forbid what one takes for granted, namely, the risking of socially valuable lives on behalf of lives that might be socially less valuable, for example, in war or in any situation in which life is at risk. This is enough to indicate that those of social value make no distinctions about rights of life. Precisely they will be ready to risk their own lives for those whom society values less — the strong for the weak, the healthy for the sick. Precisely those who are strong will not ask about the utility for themselves of the weak — although the weak might do so. Instead, the need of the weak will lead the strong to new tasks that develop their own social value. The strong will see in the weak not a lessening of their strength, but an incentive to higher deeds. The idea of destroying the life of one who has lost social utility [Nutzwert] comes from weakness, not from strength.

Above all, however, this idea comes from the false presupposition that life consists only in its social utility. This ignores the fact that life created and preserved by God possesses an inherent right, completely independent of its social utility. The right to life inheres in what exists [im Seienden] and not in some value or other. There is no worthless life before God, because God holds life itself to be valuable. Because God is the Creator, Preserver, and Redeemer of life, even the poorest life before God becomes a valuable life. Poor Lazarus, the leper who lay crippled before the door of the rich man while dogs licked his wounds — a man without any social utility, a victim of those who judge life only by its utility — is valued by God as worthy of eternal life. Where, other than in God, should the measure for the ultimate worth of a life lie? In the subjective affirmation of life? If so, then many a genius would be surpassed by an idiot. In the judgment of the community? If so, then it would soon be evident that judgment about socially valuable or worthless life would be abandoned to the need of the moment and therefore to [194] arbitrary action, and that now this group and now that group of people would fall victim to extermination. The distinction between valuable and worthless life sooner or later destroys life itself.

After this basic clarification something must still be said about the real social utility of seemingly useless, meaningless life. We cannot get around the fact that precisely this so-called worthless life of the incurably ill has elicited the greatest amount of social readiness for sacrifice and true heroism among the healthy, including physicians, caretakers, and relatives. Values of the highest real utility for the community have emerged precisely from such dedication of healthy life to sick life.

Of course, it cannot be denied that severe, incurable genetic diseases are a serious problem and even a certain danger for the community. The question, however, is whether this danger can be met only by exterminating these lives. The answer is definitely no. To quarantine such ill people is, from the perspective of health, an adequate means. Economically the care of such patients can never seriously impair the living standard of a people. A nation's expenditures for the care of such patients have never come close to expenditures on luxury goods. The healthy will [195] always be prepared to assume certain limited burdens for the sick, for the very natural reason that there is no certainty about their own future.

But must not incurable genetic disease also be seen as an attack on the existence of the community, like, for example, the attack of an enemy in war?

Here a double distinction must be noted. First, this attack can be countered by other means than the extermination of life. Second, in the case of those with genetic defects, we are dealing with innocent life. If one speaks here of guilt at all, it is certainly not the guilt of the sick, but of the community itself. It would be unbearable Pharisaism if the community should treat the sick as guilty and place itself in the right at the sick person's expense. Killing the innocent would be arbitrary in the extreme.

The question whether life, in the case of persons severely retarded from birth, is really *human* life at all is so naive that it hardly needs to be answered. It is disabled life, born of human parents, which can be nothing else than *human* life, however unfortunate. Indeed, the very fact that human life can appear so terribly distorted should make the healthy ponder. . . .

[196] The thesis that killing innocent sick life is permissible for the benefit of the healthy has its roots not in fundamental social, economic, or hygienic reasons, but in ideology [Weltanschauung]. A superhuman attempt is proposed in order to liberate the human community from seemingly meaningless sickness. A battle is fought against fate or, as we can also say, against the essence of the fallen world. One supposes that with rational means one can create a new, healthy humanity. At the same time, health is held to be the highest value to which all other values must be sacrificed. The rationalization and the biologization of human life unite in this vain undertaking, which destroys the right to life of all that is created and thereby, finally, destroys all human community.

If, then, we come to the conclusion that consideration for the healthy gives no right to kill innocent, sick life intentionally, the question of euthanasia receives a negative answer. Holy Scripture summarizes this judgment in the sentence, "Do not kill the innocent" (Exod. 23:7).

[206] Marriage involves acknowledging the right of life that will come into being, but this is not a right that is at the disposal of the married couple. Without the basic acknowledgment of this right, marriage ceases to be marriage and becomes a relationship. In acknowledging this right, however, space is given to the free creative power of God, who can will to let new life come forth from this marriage. To kill the fruit in the mother's womb is to injure the right to life that God has bestowed on the developing life. Discussion of the question whether a human being is already present confuses the simple fact that, in any case, God wills to create a human being and that the life of this developing human being has been deliberately taken. And this is nothing but murder.

10.7

DBW 6, 251-55

Ethics: Christ, true man

[251] We can no longer speak about our life other than in this relation to Jesus Christ. Apart from Christ as the origin, essence, and goal of life, of our life, and apart from the fact that we are creatures who are reconciled and redeemed, we can only arrive at biological or ideological abstractions. As a life that is created, reconciled, and redeemed, and that in Jesus Christ finds its origin, essence, and goal, our life is stretched out between the Yes and the No. Only in the Yes and the No can we recognize Christ as our life. It is the Yes of creation, reconciliation, and redemption, and the No of judgment and death over life that has fallen away from its origin, essence, and goal. However, no one who knows Christ can hear the Yes without the No and the No without the Yes. It is the Yes to what is created, to becoming, to growth, to flower and fruit, to health, to happiness, to ability, to achievement, to value, to success, to greatness, to honor, in short, the Yes to the flourishing of life's strength. It is the No to falling away from the origin, essence, and goal of life, which is always already inherent in all of these things. It is the No that means dying, suffering, poverty, [252] renunciation, surrender, humility, self-deprecation, and self-denial, and that, in these very forms, again already contains the Yes to new life. This new life does not disintegrate into a parallel Yes and No, as if, for example, a boundless expansion of vitality were to stand side by side with, yet unconnected to, an ascetic spiritual attitude to life, or as if what is "appropriate to creation" were simply to stand alongside what is "Christian." In such a scheme the Yes and No would lose its unity in Jesus Christ. Instead, this new life, which is *one* in Jesus Christ, is held between the Yes and the No so that in each Yes already the No is perceived, and in each No also the Yes. Both the flourishing of life's strength and self-denial, growth and death, health and suffering, happiness and renunciation, achievement and humility, honor and self-deprecation belong inextricably together in a living unity full of unresolved contradictions. Any attempt to isolate one from the other, to play one off against the other, or to appeal to one against the other is an unholy destruction of the unity of life. This then leads to the abstractions of a vitalistic ethic and a so-called ethic of Jesus, those well-known theories about autonomous areas of life that have nothing to do with the Sermon on the Mount. This approach tears apart the unity of life, and

though it seems to be accompanied by the pathos of an especially profound knowledge of reality because it casts a dark glow of tragic heroism on life, nevertheless it misses the reality of life as it is given in Jesus Christ. As a consequence of false abstractions, this kind of thinking remains stuck in eternally insoluble conflicts, which practical action is unable to leave behind and by which it is worn down. It is plainly evident that all this is completely foreign to the New Testament and to the sayings of Jesus. The activity of Christians does not spring from bitter resignation over the incurable rift between vitality and self-denial, between "worldly" and "Christian," between an "autonomous ethic" and the "ethic of Jesus" but from [253] the joy over the already accomplished reconciliation of the world with God, from the peace of the already accomplished work of salvation in Jesus Christ, from the all-encompassing life that is Jesus Christ. Because in Jesus Christ God and humanity became one, so through Christ what is "Christian" and what is "worldly" become one in the action of the Christian. They are not opposed to each other like two eternally hostile principles. Instead, the action of the Christian springs from the unity between God and the world, and the unity of life that have been created in Christ. In Christ life regains its unity. Although this takes place in the mutual contradiction of Yes and No, this is again and again overcome in the concrete activity of those who believe in Christ.

We now return to the question about the good. So far we can say that it is definitely not an abstraction from life, such as a realization of certain ideals and values that are independent of life, but life itself. Good is life as it is in reality, that is, in its origin, essence, and goal, life as understood by the statement: Christ is my life. Good is not a quality of life but "life" itself. Being good [Gutsein] means "to live."

This life is concrete in the contradictory unity of Yes and No that lies outside life itself, namely, in Jesus Christ. But Jesus Christ is the human being and God in one. The original and essential encounter with the human being and with God takes place in Jesus Christ. From now on it is no longer possible to conceive and understand humanity other than in Jesus Christ, nor God other than in the human form of Jesus Christ. In Christ we see humanity as a humanity that is accepted, borne, loved, and reconciled with God. In Christ we see God in the form of the poorest of our brothers and sisters. There is no human being as such, just as there is no God as such; both are empty abstractions. Human beings are accepted in God's becoming human and are loved, judged, and reconciled in Christ, and God is the God who became human.

So there is no relation to other human beings without a relation to God, [254] and vice versa. Again, only the relation to Jesus Christ is the basis for our relation to other human beings and to God. Just as Jesus Christ is our life, so we may now also say — from the vantage point of Jesus Christ! — that other human beings and that God are our life. This means, of course, that our encounters with others, like our encounters with God, are subject to the same Yes and No that is present in our encounter with Jesus Christ.

We "live" means that in our encounter with other human beings and with God, the Yes and the No are bound together in a unity of contradiction, in selfless self-assertion, in a self-assertion that is a surrender of myself to God and to other human beings.

We live by responding to the word of God addressed to us in Jesus Christ. It is a word that addresses our whole life. The answer, therefore, can also only be a complete one, one that is given with our whole life as it is realized in activities in particular cases. The life that encounters us in Jesus Christ as the Yes and the No to our life must be answered by a life that incorporates and unites this Yes and No.

This life, lived in answer to the life of Jesus Christ (as the Yes and No to our life), we call "responsibility" [*"Verantwortung"*]. This concept of responsibility denotes the complete wholeness and unity of the answer to the reality that is given to us in Jesus Christ, as opposed to the partial answers that we might be able to give, for example, from considerations of usefulness, or with reference to certain principles. In light of the [255] life that encounters us in Jesus Christ, such partial answers will not suffice, but only the complete and single answer of our life. Responsibility thus means to risk one's life in its wholeness, aware that one's activity is a matter of life and death.

10.8

DBW 6, 292-93

Ethics: Responsibility

[292] The question of the place and the limit of responsibility has led us to the concept of vocation. However, this answer is valid only where vocation is understood simultaneously in all its dimensions. The call of Jesus Christ is the call to belong to Christ completely; it is Christ's address and claim at the place at which this call encounters me; vocation comprises work with things

and issues [sachliche Arbeit] as well as personal relations; it requires "a definite field of activity" though never [293] as a value in itself but only in responsibility to Jesus Christ. By being related to Jesus Christ, the "definite
field of activity" is set free from any isolation. The boundary of vocation has
been broken open not only vertically, that is, through Christ, but also hori-
zontally, with regard to the extent of responsibility. Let us say I am a medical
doctor, for example. In dealing with a concrete case I serve not only my patient, but also the body of scientific knowledge, and thus science and knowledge of truth in general. Although in practice I render this service in my
concrete situation — for example, at a patient's bedside — I nevertheless remain aware of my responsibility toward the whole, and only thus fulfill my
vocation. In so doing, it may come to the point that in a particular case I
must recognize and fulfill my concrete responsibility as a physician no longer only at a patient's bedside, but, for example, in taking a public stance
against a measure that poses a threat to medical science, or human life, or
science in general. Vocation is responsibility, and responsibility is the whole
response of the whole person to reality as a whole. This is precisely why a
myopic self-limitation to one's vocational obligations in the narrowest sense
is out of the question; such a limitation would be irresponsibility. The nature
of free responsibility rules out any legal regulation of when and to what extent human vocation and responsibility entail breaking out [Durchbrechen]
of the "definite field of activity." This can happen only after seriously considering one's immediate vocational obligations, the dangers of encroaching on
the responsibilities of others, and finally the total picture of the issue at
hand. It will then be my free responsibility in response to the call of Jesus
Christ that leads me in one direction or the other. Responsibility in a vocation follows the call of Christ alone.

11 This *Ability: Barth on the Concrete Freedom of Human Life*

DONALD WOOD

I.

Already during his lifetime, Karl Barth enjoyed (and resisted) a reputation as one of the few truly great theologians of the modern Christian church — a figure for whom comparisons with Augustine, Aquinas, Calvin, and Schleiermacher were not transparently absurd. Forty years after his death, his work remains a touchstone in several fields of theological inquiry; but not, significantly, in disability theology.

Any number of reasons might be given for the general lack of extended engagement with Barth in more recent writing on the theology of disability: a prevailing tendency toward correlationist theology in some leading texts in the field, for example, and the sheer scale and complexity of Barth's writing, which places unusual demands on its readers and often proves an obstacle to its reception. Most importantly, disability simply is not a major theme in Barth's own work. While he fully recognized that the physical, mental, and emotional capabilities of human beings vary widely, and that these variances matter, he rarely devoted direct and sustained attention to them in writing.

Some readers have seen this as a symptom of a more general material problem in Barth's theology, arguing that his Christologically focused, scripturally ordered account of human being remains too far removed from ordinary human experience, not least the social vulnerability and personal suffering of the sick or disabled. Such claims invite quite careful consideration. Barth certainly worried about what he considered undisciplined appeals to experience in certain strands of Christian theology, convinced that they often obscured the sheer comprehensiveness of the claim of the gospel on creaturely life. For Barth, the inclusion of all human beings — and therefore of every individual human being — in the covenant of grace attested by membership in the Christian church was theologically basic. Other modes of human self-identification (in terms of race, nationality, socio-economic status, membership in a voluntary society or interest group, and so on) had their proper place, but they were in no sense foundational (11.12). Thus Barth would have felt profound unease at the suggestion that the experience of the disabled was theologically normative, or that the gospel must serve a given politics of disability. That said, Barth was keenly aware of the impact of physical limitation and psychological impairment in human life. And he thought deeply about the ways in which a theological account of human nature could impact upon the medical and pastoral care of the marginalized and suffering. In this connection we might note the appropriation of Barth's work in the pastoral theology of Eduard Thurneysen (see Thurneysen 1959) and, within the medical community, in the widely influential vision of holistic patient care developed by Richard Siebeck and the Heidelberg School (see Baier 1988). In light of these and other features of Barth's biography, we have every reason to think quite carefully before accepting the claim that Barth's theology never really touches the ground.

We can secure this point most directly by referring to the story of an encounter between Barth and his friend Heinrich Vogel, the German Lutheran systematic theologian. (The story comes in multiple, conflicting versions; this follows the account in Busch 1986, 92-93.) Vogel and Barth were discussing the Christian hope for creaturely fulfillment and perfection in the kingdom of God. The question between them was how to account for the transformation that each believed would take place when the kingdom was finally and fully revealed. Vogel wanted to speak straightforwardly of a wholly new creative act of God, one in which the painful limitations of this life would be left behind. And he had deep personal reasons for doing so. His daughter was severely disabled, and his theological commitments resonated with his wish as a father that there — in God's new creation — his daughter would be freed from present restriction: "She will walk!" To which Barth replied, No, that makes it sound as if God has made a mistake in your daughter's case, one which he is obliged to put right. "Is it not a much more beautiful and powerful hope," Barth asked, "that something becomes apparent there that at present we cannot understand at all — namely that *this* life was not futile, because it is not in vain that God has said to it: 'I have loved: *you!*'?" And, he added, the final revelation of the truth and meaning of this life will involve a radical re-ordering of prevailing cultural values: "*She* will sit at the head of the table, while we — if we are granted a seat at all — will have to sit right down at the other end."

This story, like many of the occasional comments on physical limitation and mental disturbance in Barth's correspondence and sermons, is at once evocative and elusive. And we can hardly draw from it detailed conclusions about Barth's posture either toward disabled persons or toward any given theology of disability. But as it stands, it at least suggests that Barth had something interesting to say about the complex of questions with which disability theology has to do, and it invites further consideration of the ways in which this and other express statements about the identity and destiny of the disabled relate to the theological commitments regarding human creatures developed at length in Barth's mature doctrinal and ethical writing, above all in the *Church Dogmatics.*

One word of caution: Readers coming to Barth with a precise, fixed account of "disability" in mind and looking for resources in his theology to help further develop a particular vision of disablement will almost certainly come away disappointed. Put more positively: Barth's theology may prove most interesting and fruitful precisely where his formulations and conceptual moves fail to map neatly onto more familiar discussions in the field. Our first and perhaps most demanding interpretative task, then, simply is to let him speak in his own terms. The brief summary that follows takes up one aspect of this work by way of high-level commentary on Barth's doctrine and ethics of creation. As it stands, it offers no more than the barest introduction to an account of human being and agency that occupies many hundreds of pages of conceptually demanding, descriptively rich prose. A fuller treatment would involve much wider reading in the *Church Dogmatics,* not least in the magisterial doctrine of reconciliation. And while not everyone will welcome the advice to read even more of Barth, there really is no substitute for engaging him directly and at length. For those who do wish to persevere, the bibliography offers some initial guidance.

II.

Whatever else it does, the term "disability" serves as one way of indicating the intersection of the individual and society. It highlights and problematizes the fact that we live together as people whose physical, mental, and emotional capacities vary widely; and that we do so as *people* — as those who belong together by virtue of some commonality which renders our differences meaningful. When we speak of a person having a disability, or of a person being disabled, we may refer primarily to the individual who in one way or another does not exhibit the full capabilities of a "normal" human being; or we may refer to the society within which "disability" appears in various forms — as a term of legal protection, architectural accommodation, educational or medical provision, and so on. In either case, we are speaking of human beings in relation, presuming both the unity and the diversity of life together. This unity in light of which the variances of individual capability and social recognition take meaningful form traditionally is indicated by the term "human being" or "human nature." But even where these specific terms are problematized, it is always and precisely of *humanity* that we have to do when we speak of the disabled. Thus a theology of disability always presumes and from time to time is called upon to give an explicit account of the human.

This is not merely a general observation about the grammar of disability talk. It is a way of drawing attention to the fact that if we are to understand and rightly appropriate what Barth has to say — more or less directly — about disability, we need to recognize and appreciate the highly distinctive way in which he renders the specific reality and shape of the life of human creatures.

We can begin by noting the distinction Barth draws between the reality of human being and the appearance or phenomena of the human (11.1; cf. *Church Dogmatics* [CD] III/2, 71-302). On Barth's account, what we directly experience, recognize, and attempt to control in human life is not the true essence of the human; it is the appearance of humanity under conventional forms and conditions. Psychology, sociology, and the life sciences all have to do with this appearance, with the phenomena of the human, and in doing so they offer legitimate and serviceable if always provisional indications of the various ways in which human life appears to exist and can continue to do so. Theology, on the other hand, makes claims about the reality and truth of the human — about human beings as they truly and really exist from and for God the creator. Insofar as theology thinks and speaks of humanity, "it does not apprehend or explain an appearance of human essence, but the reality; not its outward features, but its most inward; not a part but the whole" (*CD* III/2, 20). Barth's point is not that real human life is separate from visible life, located in some idealized transcendent sphere, disconnected from and unaffected by the give-and-take of daily human commerce. Still less is humanity an ideal to which each person approximates, so that one may be deemed more or less fully human. The one, real life given each human creature by God is fully human life, and it is always visible, historical, embodied life, lived as a succession of individual moments and as the sum of those moments. But this life is life — *from God*. And because it speaks of human life *sub specie divinitatis*, Christian theology can and must claim knowledge not simply of what human beings appear to be but of what they truly are.

It does so because it has been given knowledge of true human being by God, the giver of life. Theology speaks truly of humanity, then, when it attends to divine revelation, and concretely when it attends to revelation as authoritatively attested by holy scripture. The articulation of true human identity is thus for Barth primarily an *exegetical* task. The question is not "Given the evident diversity of human life, how can we speak of 'normal' human being?"; but, quite simply, "How does Scripture render the human?" It does so, Barth claims, not by offering a comprehensive view of the world within which the lineaments of "biblical man" can be traced, but by directing all of its energies to identifying one man among all others: Jesus Christ. "The nature of the man Jesus alone is the key to the problem of human nature. This man is man" (*CD* III/2, 43; **11.2**).

This is not to say that Jesus is the only human being, as if confession of his true and original humanity simply displaces talk of other human beings. On the contrary, a scripturally governed account of the identity of the one man Jesus Christ demands and enables a theologically confident recognition of the reality and true character of all other human beings. "We cannot really look at Jesus without — in a certain sense through him — seeing ourselves also" (*CD* III/2, 48). We are because he is; we are who we are because of who he is; and we know ourselves as the ones we really are insofar as we know him as the one he is. This affirmation of the ontological and so also the epistemological priority of the man Jesus Christ entails a negation: precisely because we are and know ourselves in him, we do not exist and cannot know ourselves otherwise. Barth simply resists the widespread assumption that we can and should know ourselves directly — an assumption underlying appeals to personal experience and analyses of cultural dynamics in much recent work in disability theology (see, e.g., Eiesland 1994) and medical ethics (see Baumann-Hölzle 1999). For Barth, human sinfulness, precisely because it involves our resistance to the gracious will of the creator, entails the most serious self-contradiction and self-alienation; in despising covenant fellowship with God, we obscure and forfeit our being as his human creatures. Nevertheless, our sin does not finally determine our identity, "as though human nature had been changed into its opposite, and by sinning the human being had in some sense suffered a mutation into a different kind of creature" (*CD* III/2, 37; **11.2**). Humanity is upheld in being by God and hidden in Christ, the true man. Thus the only secure basis for genuine human self-knowledge is God's word — God's address to us in Jesus Christ. "It is either through him that we know what we truly are as human beings or we do not know it at all. Our self-knowledge can only be an act of discipleship" (*CD* III/2, 53).

In short, the guiding question in a theological account of human being is not "Who are we?" but "Who is he?" — that is, who is this one man Jesus Christ from whom and for whom all other human beings live? In his doctrine of creation, Barth organizes his description of Jesus' identity under four main headings: Jesus is the man for God; he is the man for others; he is the whole man; and he is the Lord of time. In all this, Jesus is the subject of his history, the one who freely enacts his identity. And as with Jesus, so also *(mutatis mutandis)* with us: As Jesus is the man for God, to be human is to be from and with God in Jesus Christ — to be graciously chosen and called by God for a unique service, and gratefully to respond to God's election and summons in worship, confession, and prayer. As Jesus is the man for others, to be human is to live with other human beings in relations of mutual affirmation, enjoyment, and honor. As Jesus is whole man, to be human is to live as the soul of one's body — to encounter God and others as a single, internally ordered, and just so truly rational subject. And as Jesus is the Lord of time, to be human is to live in time — to live within the limitations set by God, and to live within them in hope and good cheer.

To live an authentically human life, then, means to live before God and with others, within the conditions of creaturely existence established and maintained by the creator. It is to live the distinctively human life that God gives — or, more precisely, lends — entirely on God's terms. The gift of life is embracing and purposive, bearing with it the command to *live*. This command is what has been called an "imperative of reality" (Webster 2004, 156), a directive that confirms and illuminates the true being of its recipients. So the order "You must go and live this life which God has granted you" is as such an invitation: "Come live this life of yours." And repeatedly throughout his ethics of creation Barth presses home the point that because the command of God is his permission, it evokes genuinely free obedience, a joyful and humble acceptance of human life as a distinct creaturely reality graciously willed and effected by God.

III.

"Real man lives with God as his covenant partner" (CD III/2, 202). In determining human life as life-for-covenant-fellowship, God chooses not to confront his human creatures as a force of nature or a brute fact. Rather, he *addresses* human beings, calling forth their free, spontaneous response. Human life is, on Barth's account, precisely because it is life given by God, irreducibly active life, the life of a properly independent agent. "The Word of God, demanding hearing and obedience, presupposes a productive subject, a being capable of making for himself a new beginning with his being, conduct, and action . . . of planning something new and his very own, corresponding to what he has heard from God and therefore achieved through obedience. The Word of God as it is spoken to man thus constitutes his knowledge of himself as such a free subject of his life" (*CD* III/4, 330; **11.5**).

What are we to make of this? Barth's point in this and similar passages clearly is not to specify human identity so as to deny the full, authentic humanity of, for instance, the profoundly mentally disabled — those whom we ordinarily would not describe as agents capable of intentionally enacting their own life histories. But his language may well prove unsettling on this score, precisely in its apparent lack of awareness of the limits of such talk in the presence of the profoundly disabled (see, e.g., Reinders 2008). We can sharpen the point. Elsewhere, Barth assumes — again without heavy investments but also without evident concerns — the cogency of the classical identification of man as rational animal: "It may indeed be seen and said that man is an animal being, and that as such he consists in the union of an organic body with a living soul, but that in contradistinction to the soul of other animal beings this soul is gifted with reason, which can also be described as *vis intellectus,* as the capacity to think and know" (*CD* III/2, 76). On first glance, such passages in Barth, with their stress on rationality, freedom, independence, and spontaneity as basic markers of human identity, may appear simply corrosive of a theological account of severe physical or mental disability. And we may think the problems compounded insofar as Barth characterizes the limits of humanity in terms of the reciprocal recognition of individuality and spontaneity: "these are the two points by which one man recognizes another most surely, or at any rate impressively, as someone like himself, namely by the fact that he is so definitely this man, and lives as man in this distinctive freedom. As he himself acts and reacts specifically and spontaneously as a rational creature, so does also the other. And as the other does, so does he" (*CD* III/4, 331).

Any straightforward reading of Barth will recognize these moments in his account of human being and acknowledge that he simply does not share the sensitivities which underlie much recent disability talk. But we must also acknowledge that Barth's own position is rather more complex and nuanced than may at first appear. While Barth believes, for example, that human solidarity may well be expressed in the form of mutual relations between free individual subjects, he also affirms that these human relations follow upon a prior divine determination that secures their reality and character (11.5). In other words, Barth does not finally claim that the limits of "humanity" coincide with the experience of shared communicative acts, or in the manifest presence of the rationality that such acts presuppose. The affirmation of human nature, or the recognition of human solidarity (against which individual or collective differences — including various forms of disability — become meaningful), is not finally a conclusion from experience. Human solidarity is a function of God's creative and redemptive works — his enacted will that we be toward him with others precisely in the true man Jesus Christ. "Humanity" thus is not an infinitely malleable term, to be deployed at will as a matter of political or cultural expediency. Distinctively human life in all instances and in every instance is a gift of the God to whom each person is fully known as the one he or she is and will be.

Of course this does not resolve all the questions which may arise when we attempt to appropriately discern and live toward the limits of human life. But it does open up space for Barth to speak of these limits in a rather more relaxed way than might otherwise be the case. To say that human life is a function of the divine address, which both unites and individualizes all human beings, is to say that God *alone* fully knows *how* he relates to each individual person. Human life before God is, in short, a *mystery* (*Geheimnis*). Negatively, this means that we are not able to specify the mode of God's relations to every creature. But to speak of the "mystery" of human life is not simply or even primarily to indicate the limits of our knowledge of ourselves and others; it is above all a positive theological affirmation: God wills, accompanies, and upholds creaturely life at every moment, in all its forms, and he knows his creation originally, fully, and truthfully. Just so, our knowledge is derivative and partial, and it is truthful only as it approximates God's own knowledge, which God shares and withholds from us according to his own counsel, which always intends our good.

This recognition of the mystery of life from God forestalls any political determination or utilitarian calculation of the worth of an individual life. Thus Barth's rejection of the National Socialist eugenics program, with its classification of the socially unproductive as *Lebensunwert,* "unworthy of life" (on which see Klee 1983; Barnett 1992, 104-21). In a passage excerpted here (11.10), Barth addresses a specific political moment, and in doing so uses language that perhaps no longer falls easily from our lips. (See the more general critique of postwar German-language disability talk, including its equation of disability and suffering, in Poole 2002.) But for our present purposes, the key point is simply to note how Barth's basic doctrinal affirmation — life always is given (on loan) by God — generates a basic ethical rule: All human life must be recognized as divine gift and so *respected.* In Barth's usage, to "respect" life means, first, to receive life with an appropriate humility, wonder, and modesty. Second, it means actively to confirm one's own life and the life of others, to will to live and to live together with all those to whom God has given life. And this is one place where Barth's ethics of creation can generate direct discussion of the politics of disability: the function of the state that respects human life as God's gift is to support and protect the life of all its members, especially those who are not able to earn and spend, produce and consume. This is not to say, however, that the state must value every individual life infinitely, or that its main task with regard to the disabled is to nurture medical technologies and practices that serve no other purpose than to indefinitely prolong the lives of each of its citizens (cf. Hauerwas 1994, 156-76). Rather, a proper respect for human life involves a recognition of its limits: human life "is not divine life, but creaturely. It is not the eternal life promised to man, but temporal" (*CD* III/4, 397). Precisely as this finite, creaturely life, human life in all its forms must be respected and protected.

If the respect for life has this political moment, demanding social policies and cultural institutions that tend toward the flourishing of all members of a community, it also has a more directly personal dimension. To respect life means to will actively to receive and continue the life one has been lent; in short, to will to be *healthy.* Health, on Barth's account, means the capacity to live as the rational subject of one's own history, "the power to be as man exercised in the powers of the vital functions of soul and body" (*CD* III/4, 371; 11.6). "Health," in other words, is a term that names the psycho-physical condition of effective human moral agency, the freedom of the voluntary subject who acts toward deliberately adopted ends in a given social location (11.7). And it functions in contrast to "sickness," a more or less significant and evident weakness or impairment of the power of a freely directed life. Sickness, and the death to which it inevitably leads, is to be seen in two ways. On the one hand, sickness always meets us and must be understood in terms of human sinfulness "as an element and sign of the power of chaos and nothingness, and therefore as an element and sign of the judgment of God falling on humanity" (*CD* III/4, 368). In this respect, sickness is simply to be resisted, through prayer and the active deployment of other suitable preventative and restorative means. On the other hand, once again, simply by virtue of the fact that it is creaturely life, life on loan from God, human life always is bounded, and the characteristic faculties and capacities of human life are given by God to be exercised and developed for specific ends within appointed limits. The creator intends human life in a determinate context — a specific living space *(Lebensraum)*. And while this means above all that each person faces a temporal limitation, and confronts the signs of aging which accompany the movement toward death, the point has more general application: a person must always live *this* life, in *these* circumstances, and this specificity belongs to the goodness of creation. So creaturely life in all its "hard actuality" — including that aspect of life which Barth called its "shadow side" (**11.4**) — really may be grasped as the one life given each of us, the unique arena in which we may recognize and praise the faithfulness of the creator (**11.8**).

IV.

Thus far, we have sketched Barth's depiction of the true human creature which comes to light in the gospel; of human life in correspondence to its divine determination for fellowship with God and with others; and of the demand that human life in all its forms be embraced precisely in its limitations. Along the way, we have seen some of the ways in which Barth's theology of human being may, more or less directly, be brought into constructive engagement with contemporary disability theology. It remains in this final section to speak briefly of some ways in which such a conversation may attend to Barth's eschatology and ecclesiology — to his talk of the church which exists in the time between Christ's ascension and his return by and for the sake of the gospel in love, joy, and hope.

We can begin by noting that for Barth the church of Jesus Christ — that human society which serves the gospel through its unified witness to the works of the Triune God — is a community of love. Concretely, the church cares for the sick among it, offering what assistance it can so that each member of the community may, in the measure that he or she is able, join in the church's common service. In the church, the distinction between the "able" and the "disabled," the "healthy" and the "sick" is at once affirmed and sanctified by continually renewed acts of mutual comfort and support. The members of this community belong to each other in the service of the gospel. They recognize each other, then, not primarily as "able" and "disabled" — still less as "privileged" and "deprived" or as "oppressor" and "victim" — but as brothers and sisters in Christ, as those called together for a common purpose, who therefore really may fulfill their commission together (**11.11**; cf. *CD* III/4, 500). Barth's remarkable sermon on Acts 3 (**11.13**) may be read as making a similar point: it is the prerogative and task of the physically disabled to embody that condition — radical dependence upon the saving presence of God announced in the apostolic gospel — that faith recognizes as constitutive of the life of the entire community. Just so, the whole church learns to know itself anew as it shares in the praise and joins in the confession of its disabled members: we are "the church of the lame under the Word."

The life of this community is marked everywhere by joy. This joy ("really the simplest form of gratitude"; *CD* III/4, 376) cannot be manufactured; it is not a communal achievement, a "Pelagian optimism" that overreaches the difficult facts toward a false conceptual peace with a fallen world (see Mangina 2001, 148). But even in full recognition of the often painful constrictions of life, Barth argues, one may be truly joyful, and may hold oneself open for joy in communities of common gratitude and anticipation. In doing so, one is liberated to live as himself, as the one he is, patiently and hopefully exercising what capacities he has, neither despairing of his own (dis)abilities, nor grasping after the powers more clearly enjoyed by another. A theology of disability, we might say, also stands under the sign of the Tenth Commandment (**11.9**).

And, finally, those who rejoice together are united in hope, looking forward to the final revelation of the mystery of their life which now is hidden in Jesus Christ. That is, the church looks forward to the coming of the kingdom and so to the resurrection of the dead to eternal life. And here we come back to the story of Barth's conversation with Heinrich Vogel regarding the proper object of Christian hope for the disabled.

Barth belongs to a significant stream of modern theology which speaks of the Resurrection not as the inauguration of a new episode within human history so much as the revelation of the truth and eternal reality of this present life. "Eternal life is not another, second life, beyond the present one. It is *this* life, but the *reverse side* which God sees although here and now it is hidden from us — this life in its relation to what he has done for the whole world, and therefore for us too, in Jesus Christ. We thus wait and hope, even in view of our death, to be *revealed* with him" (Barth 1975, 9; cf. *CD* III/4, 338; 11.3). It is easy to misread Barth here, and it is important to note that he does not conceive our eschatological redemption as the emergence of an altered perspective on a world left fundamentally unchanged. For Barth, revelation never is an abstractly epistemological notion, simply the communication of further knowledge about a given state of being. The revelation of our lives with Christ in glory involves a genuine transformation of all things and so also of each individual life (see Oblau 1988, 155-61).

That said, Barth did not live long enough to fully develop his account of our eschatological transformation, and in many ways the material available to us remains unsatisfying. Here theological reflection on the resurrection hope of the profoundly mentally disabled may prove a particularly fruitful point of engagement with his work. One might wonder, for example, how the exchange between Barth and Vogel might read if the disability in question had less to do with a predominantly physical limitation and more to do with the ability to know oneself and self-consciously to communicate with others. In the case of the profoundly mentally disabled, we may ask, what sort of healing must be entailed to enable one to recognize the truth and meaning of this present life? This is a question about the eschatological perfection of the church's fellowship which Barth does not directly address. But if we wish to affirm that each individual is raised to active, self-aware participation in the church's praise of God's glory, we may be led to reconsider the distinction between Barth's vision of human destiny and what Vogel called "the ontological understanding of the eschatological promise" (Vogel 1973, 61). However this may be, contemporary theologies of disability may also profit from further reflection on the eschatological commitment that lies nearest the center of Barth's own concerns: the rigorous insistence that Christian hope must be hope in *God,* not in some projection of our future lives — whether we envision this as the radical transcendence of present limitations or assume the undisturbed continuance of our current self-understandings.

More generally, renewed engagement with Barth's theology provides occasion for fresh consideration of important questions about the sources and norms of Christian theology. Much recent disability theology, for example, rightly has attended closely to firsthand accounts of those living as and with disabled persons. But questions remain regarding the ways in which these accounts authorize and discipline Christian speech and theological reflection about the identity of God, human nature, and fitting forms of communal life. In this regard, Barth's Trinitarian theology of revelation and his articulation of the Reformational scripture principle may serve as a counterpoint to strongly correlationist statements of theological intent and as a provocation to a sharpened disciplinary self-understanding among all those working in this field.

REFERENCES

Primary Sources

Barth, Karl. 1975. *Briefe, 1961-1968*. Edited by Jürgen Fangmeier and Hinrich Stoevesandt. Zurich: Theologischer Verlag.

————. 1956-75. *Church Dogmatics*. Originally published as *Die kirchliche Dogmatik*, 1932-70. Edited by T. F. Torrance and G. W. Bromiley. Edinburgh: T&T Clark.

————. 1971-present. *Gesamtausgabe*. Zürich: TVZ.

————. 1996. *Predigten, 1935-52*. Edited by Hartmut Spieker and Hinrich Stoevesandt. Zurich: TVZ.

Secondary Sources

Baier, Hartmut. 1988. *Richard Siebeck und Karl Barth — Medizin und Theologie im Gespräch. Die Bedeutung der theologischen Anthropologie in der Medizin Richard Siebecks*. Göttingen and Zurich: Vandenhoeck & Ruprecht.

Barnett, Victoria. 1992. *For the Soul of the People: Protestant Protest against Hitler*. New York: Oxford University Press.

Baumann-Hölzle, Ruth. 1999. *Autonomie und Freiheit in der Medizin-Ethik. Immanuel Kant und Karl Barth*. Freiburg and Munich: Verlag Karl Alber.

Busch, Eberhard. 1986. *Glaubensheiterkeit. Karl Barth: Erfahrungen und Begegnungen*. Neukirchen-Vluyn: Neukirchener.

Eiesland, Nancy. 1994. *The Disabled God: Toward a Liberatory Theology of Disability*. Nashville: Abingdon Press.

Hauerwas, Stanley. 1994. "Communitarians and Medical Ethicists: Or, Why I Am None of the Above," and "Killing Compassion," in *Dispatches from the Front: Theological Engagements with the Secular*. Durham and London: Duke University Press.

Klee, Ernst. 1983. *"Euthenasie" im NS-Staat: Die "Vernichtung lebensunwerten Lebens."* Frankfurt: S. Fischer.

Mangina, Joseph. 2001. *Barth on the Christian Life: The Practical Knowledge of God*. New York: Peter Lang.

Oblau, Gotthard. 1988. *Gotteszeit und Menschenzeit: Eschatologie in der Kirchlichen Dogmatik von Karl Barth*. Neukirchen-Vluyn: Neukirchener Verlag.

Poole, Carol. 2002. "'The (Im)Perfect Human Being' and the Beginning of Disability Studies in Germany: A Report." *New German Critique* 86: 179-90.

Reinders, Hans. 2008. *Receiving the Gift of Friendship: Profound Disability, Theological Anthropology, and Ethics.* Grand Rapids: Wm. B. Eerdmans.

Thurneysen, Eduard. 1959. "Arzt und Seelsorger in der Begegnung mit dem leidenden Menschen." In *Medicus Viator. Fragen und Gedanken am Wege Richard Siebecks.* Edited by Paul Christian and Dietrich Rössler. Tübingen: J. C. B. Mohr.

Vogel, Heinrich. 1973. *Freundschaft mit Karl Barth. Ein Porträt in Anekdoten.* Zurich: TVZ.

Webster, John. 2004. *Barth,* 2nd ed. London and New York: Continuum.

Excerpts

The excerpts from Barth's multi-volume *Church Dogmatics* collected here refer to the Torrance and Bromiley edition (Edinburgh: T&T Clark, 1956-75), whose translations I have adapted on the basis of the original German (*Die kirchliche Dogmatik* [Zürich: EVZ, 1932-70]). I have retained its so-called generic use of the English term "man" — a decision which implies no judgments about Barth's own complex understanding of male-female relations. An expanding array of academic lectures, sermons, letters, and other occasional material is available in the *Gesamtausgabe* (Zürich: TVZ, 1971-), some of which is available in translation.

11.1

Church Dogmatics III/2, 13, 19, 25-26

The Word of God essentially encloses a specific view of humanity, an anthropology, an ontology of this *particular* creature. This being the case, we must accept this view in faith, reflect it in the confession of faith, and develop it as a perception of faith. . . .

As God speaks his Word, he not only establishes the fact but reveals the truth of his relationship to this, the human creature. The description of this relationship, the account of its history, forms the content of holy scripture. This does not give us any description or recount any history of the relationship between God and the rest of the cosmos. God alone and humanity alone are its theme. This is the distinction of man which makes him the object of theological anthropology.

But anthropology has a special task. It is the task of dogmatics generally to present the revelation of the truth of the relationship between God and man in the light of the biblical witness to its history as a whole. Anthropology confines its enquiry to the human *creatureliness* presupposed in this relationship and made known by it, i.e., by its revelation and biblical attestation. It asks what kind of a being it is which stands in this relationship with God. Its attention is wholly concentrated on the relationship. Thus it does not try to look beyond it or behind it. It knows that its insights would at once be lost, and the ground cut from beneath it, if it were to turn its attention elsewhere, abstracting from this relationship. Solely in the latter as illuminated by the Word of God is light shed on the creatureliness of man. Thus theological anthropology cleaves to the Word of God and its biblical attestation. But in the revealed relationship between God and man genuine light is thrown, not only on God, but also on man, on the essence of the creature to whom God has turned in this relationship. . . .

Theological anthropology expounds the knowledge of man which is made possible and necessary by the fact that man stands in the light of the Word of God. The Word of God is thus its *foundation*. We hasten to add that for this very reason it expounds the *truth* about human nature. As man becomes the object of its knowledge in this way, it does not apprehend or explain an appearance of human being, but the reality; not its outward features, but its most inward; not a part but the whole. . . .

The differentiation [between a theological anthropology and a working model of human being in the natural sciences] consists simply in the fact that theological anthropology has not to do merely with man as a phenomenon but with *man himself;* not merely with his possibilities, but with his *reality*. It is in this way, in the light of God's Word and therefore in the light of truth, that he is known by it. Hence it may not frame its principles merely as temporarily and relatively valid hypotheses; as contributions to the wider investigation of the nature of man and the development of a technique for dealing with these questions. It has a responsibility to make the *truth-claim*. . . . This does not mean that it cannot err, that it does not need continually to correct and improve itself. But in virtue of its basis and origin it concerns itself with the real man. It not only comments on him, it *denotes* him. It gives him his *name*. Interpreting him, it is concerned with the relation of this creature to God, and therefore with his *inner reality* and *wholeness*. This is something which the anthropology of exact science cannot do. How can it understand man as the creature of God? The fact that he is this does not belong to what is seen of man by exact science, to the external features which it can investigate and present, or to the sum of the parts in which he is present to it. Even the fact that man is God's *creature,* standing as such in a special relation to God, is a fact that is not accessible to human thought and perception otherwise than through the Word of God. And this is even more true of the inner reality, the manner, and the how of this relation. It is from within this context that theological anthropology must interpret man. But in so doing it interprets man himself, his reality. For what he is as the creature of God, what he is in his relation to God — that is he himself, that is his reality. As theological anthropology concerns itself with this reality, it is fully aware of its own shortcomings, but it raises the claim to truth. Scientific anthropology cannot do this, even when its exponents have occasionally (or not just occasionally) to be taken seriously as obedient hearers of the Word of God; more seriously perhaps than theologians occupied on the other side. For if they are to fulfill the function of theological anthropology, they must look beyond the phenomenal man who is the object of exact science to the real man perceptible in the light of God's Word. In other words, they must become seekers asking and answering theological questions. And if there is no reason why the scientist who is obedient to God's Word should not look beyond the phenomenon of man to the real man — if indeed it is self-evident that this should be the case — and that to this extent he should become more or less basically a theologian, it is still true that what he does as a scientist, a physiologist, a psychologist, etc., can be no substitute for what theology has to do at this point. Where it is simply a question of man as a *phenomenon* — and exact science as such can go no further — there can be no perception of man as the creature and covenant-partner of God, and therefore of his true reality and essence, and the task of theological anthropology is thus untouched. Hence we cannot admit that scientific anthropology has already occupied the ground we propose to cover. On this side, too, the way is clear for the enquiry which we must undertake from our own particular standpoint. . . .

Church Dogmatics III/2, 41-44

"As the man Jesus is himself the revealing Word of God, he is the source of our knowledge of the nature of man as created by God." The attitude of God in which the faithfulness of the creator and therefore the unchanging relationships of the human being created by him are revealed and knowable is quite simply his attitude and relation to the *man Jesus:* his election of this man; his becoming and remaining one with him; his self-revelation, action, and glorification in him and through him; his love addressed to him and through him to those who believe in him and to the whole of creation; his freedom and sovereignty which in this man find their creaturely dwelling and form, their bearer and representative. He is God as even in his eternal Godhead he became this man in his human creatureliness. This is God's attitude towards sinful man. He answers or reacts to the sin of man by this relation to the man Jesus. Everything else that the biblical testimony to this divine answer and reaction discloses has at this point its beginning, center, and goal, and receives from it its light and explanation. And our hearing and reception of this testimony are true and right and clear and effective when we allow ourselves to be enlightened and instructed at this point. The Word of God is the gospel of Jesus Christ. That is, it is the revelation of God's attitude to this man. As it reveals this, it reveals sin in its terrible gravity and judges it with supreme force, showing man that he cannot atone for it, and delivering him by assuring him in his heart that God himself atones for it, and showing how he does this. In God's attitude to this man the decision is made that the divine grace is primary and the sin of man secondary, and that the primary factor is more powerful than the secondary. Recognizing that it is made at this point, we cannot contradict the order which it establishes. We are forbidden to take sin more seriously than grace, or even as seriously as grace. At this point there is disclosed the merciful will of God, who chides and judges but cannot forget man because of his sin, who even in his wrathful judgment on his sin has not ceased to be his creator, or to be free to justify his creature, knowing him as the being whom he created out of nothing according to his wisdom. At this point it may be seen how God sees man in spite of and through his sin, and therefore how we ourselves are incapable of seeing him. What is impossible with man but possible with God emerges at this point, namely, the vision of our being which can be distorted by sin but not destroyed or transmuted into something different, because even in its sinful distortion it is held in the hand of God, and in spite of its corruption is not allowed to fall. . . .

The nature of the man Jesus alone is the key to the problem of human nature. This man is man. As certainly as God's relation to sinful man is properly and primarily his relation to this man alone, and a relation to the rest of mankind only in him and through him, he alone is primarily and properly man. If we were referred to a picture of human nature attained or attainable in any other way, we should always have to face the question whether what we think we see and know concerning it is not a delusion, because with our sinful eyes we cannot detect even the corruption of our nature, let alone its intrinsic character, and are therefore condemned to an unceasing confusion of the natural with the unnatural, and vice versa. We do not have to rely on these vague ideas, and we are not therefore condemned to this confusion, because true man, the true nature behind our corrupted nature, is not concealed but revealed in the person of Jesus, and in his nature we recognize our own, and that of every man.

But we must really keep to the human nature of Jesus. Thus we may not deviate from it, nor may we on any account rely upon, nor take for granted, what we think we know about man from other sources. We must form and maintain the conviction that the presupposition given us in and with the human nature of Jesus is exhaustive and superior to all other presuppositions, and that all other presuppositions can become possible and useful only in connection with it.

We have thus to formulate the theological enquiry into the nature of man in the following terms. *What is the creaturely nature of man* to the extent that, looking to the revealed grace of God and *concretely to the man Jesus, we can see in it a continuum unbroken by sin, an essence which even sin does not and cannot change?* It is the special and characteristic task of theological anthropology to consider this question. In so doing, it does not prevent other anthropological discussion. But it cannot be blocked or diverted by any other. Here lies its freedom and objectivity. Even in its investigation of human nature, its enquiries are not based on any creaturely insight into the creature. It places the contemplative and reflective reason of the creature in the service of the creator's knowledge of the creature revealed by God's own Word. . . . If we rightly consider the special difficulty of a theological anthropology, there can be no question of any other point of departure. But the choice of this point of departure means nothing more nor less than *the founding of anthropology on Christology.*

In so doing, we leave the traditional way, which was to try first to establish generally what human nature is, and on this basis to interpret the human nature of Jesus Christ in particular. Our whole approach to the relation between human sin and human nature has led us irresistibly in the opposite direction. Human sin excludes us from understanding human nature except by a new disclosure through the perception of divine grace addressed to man and revealing and affirming true humanity in the midst of human sin, i.e., a disclosure which is genuinely new, involving faith in the divine revelation. But if we ask where we may find an authentic revelation in this respect, we are not led to man in general but to man in particular, and in supreme particularity to the one man Jesus. Thus, contrary to the usual procedure, we must first enquire concerning this one man, and then on this basis concerning man in general. In His own person He is *God's* Word to *men,* of divine *and* human essence, man in immediate confrontation and union with God, and therefore immediately the *real* man, and the revelation of the *truth* about men.

11.3

Church Dogmatics III/2, 633

Man as such . . . has no beyond. Nor does he need one, for God is his beyond. Man's beyond is that God as his creator, covenant-partner, judge, and savior, was and is and will be his true counterpart in life, and finally and exclusively and totally in death. Man as such, however, belongs to this world. He is thus finite and mortal. One day he will only have been, as once he was not. His divinely given promise and hope and confidence in this confrontation with God is that even as this one who has been he will share the eternal life of God himself. Its content is not, therefore, his liberation from his this-sidedness, from his end and dying, but positively the glorification by the eternal God of his natural and lawful this-sided, finite and mortal being. He does not look and move towards the fact that this being of his in his time will one day be forgotten and extinguished and left behind, and in some degree replaced by a new, other-sided, infinite and immortal being after his time. More positively, he looks and moves towards the fact that this being of his in his time, and therewith its beginning and end before the eyes of the gracious God, and therefore before his own eyes and those of others, will be revealed in all its merited shame but also its unmerited glory, and may thus be eternal life from and in God. He does not hope for redemption from the this-sidedness, finitude, and mortality of His existence. He hopes positively for the revelation of its redemption as completed in Jesus Christ, namely, the redemption of his this-sided, finite and mortal existence. This psycho-physical being in its time is *he himself*. He himself as this being makes himself guilty of judgment and the curse. He himself as this being is freed by the crucifixion of Jesus from his guilt and thus released from the judgment and curse of death. He himself is here and now concealed and imperceptible and inconceivable in this freedom, and waits for its revelation. But again he himself as this being clings here and now to God as the one who as the creator has set him these limits and given him this allotted span, and who now in the concrete form of the appearance and work of Jesus Christ is his only full and perfect hope. And he himself as this being knows that already in the totality of his own this-sided existence, above and beyond which there is no other, he is claimed by and belongs and is committed and thankful here and now to the God who as his gracious judge and therefore his savior from death is his true beyond. This view of human nature, with its frank recognition of the fact that it ends as well as begins, will be most important for our understanding of the divine command and the bearing of Christian ethics, giving to human life an importance as something which will one day be completed and not be continued indefinitely, and therefore to that which is required of it an urgency which would obviously be lacking if we set our hopes on deliverance from the limitation of our time, and therefore on a beyond, instead of on the eternal God Himself.

11.4

Church Dogmatics III/3, 296-97

It is true that in creation there is not only a Yes but also a No; not only a height but also an abyss; not only clarity but also obscurity; not only progress and continuation but also impediment and limitation; not only growth but also decay; not only opulence but also indigence; not only beauty but also ashes; not only beginning but also end; not only value but also worthlessness. It is true that in creaturely existence, and especially in the existence of man, there are hours, days, and years both bright and dark, success and failure, laughter and tears, youth and age, gain and loss, birth and sooner or later its inevitable corollary, death. It is true that individual creatures and men experience these things in most unequal measure, their lots being assigned by a justice which is curious or very much concealed. Yet it is irrefutable that creation and creature are good even in the fact that all that is exists in this contrast and antithesis. In all this, far from being null, it praises its creator and Lord even on its shadowy side, even in the negative aspect in which it is so near to nothingness. If he himself has comprehended creation in its totality and made it his own in his Son, it is for us to acquiesce without thinking that we know better, without complaints, reproach, or dismay. For all we can tell, may not his creatures praise him more mightily in humility than in exaltation, in need than in plenty, in fear than in joy, on the frontier of nothingness than when wholly oriented toward God? For all we can tell, may not we ourselves praise him more purely on bad days than on good, more surely in sorrow than in rejoicing, more truly in adversity than in progress? It can, of course, be otherwise. But need it always be? If not, if there may also be a praise of God from the abyss, the night and misfortune, and perhaps even from the deepest abyss, the darkest night and the greatest misfortune, why should we doubt the hidden justice which apportions the distinctions and contrasts to ourselves and others? How surprised we shall be, and how ashamed of so much improper and unnecessary disquiet and discontent, once we are brought to realize that all creation both as light and shadow, including our own share in it, our puny and fleeting life, was laid on Jesus Christ as the creation of God, and that even though we did not see it, without and in spite of us, and while we were shaking our heads that things were not very different, it sang the praise of God just as it was, and was therefore right and perfect. We aspire to be Christians, and no doubt in some small measure we are, but is it not strange that only in our few better moments can we make anything either theoretically or practically of the truth that the creation of God in both its aspects, even the negative, is his good creation?

11.5

Church Dogmatics III/4, 329-32

As God addresses man, it is decided, and man is reassured, that his life possesses a definite origin. He lives his life. He is the soul of his body. He is the living individual. He is the one who moves in time, constant yet changing. The Word of God is not spoken merely to a psycho-physical individual in time which is simply the functioning organ of another author or element in his movement, but to a subject who is himself at all points the author, accomplishing this movement freely, independently, and spontaneously. The Word of God, demanding hearing and obedience, presupposes a productive subject, a being capable of making for himself a new beginning with his being, conduct, and action (irrespective of his co-existence and connection with other beings), of planning something new and his very own, corresponding to what he has heard from God and therefore achieved through obedience. The Word of God as it is spoken to man thus constitutes his knowledge of himself as such a free subject of his life. Otherwise what would be the sense of God speaking to him and not simply disposing of him? Speaking to him, God appeals to his independence. It is a creaturely and therefore not an absolute independence. It cannot in any sense compete with that of God. Hence we cannot say that his life is his own. Together with its independence, it belongs to the One who alone is truly independent. The fact that he himself may and should live his life is one of the things which have been entrusted to him and over which he has no ultimate control, and he must not try to usurp it. It is from the man who in all his freedom belongs to God that hearing and obedience are demanded. But the fact remains that, as it demands this from him, it discloses and reveals the fact that in his freedom he belongs to God. . . .

Yet obviously we cannot fully describe what human existence and life are as such — for they cannot really be considered schematically — without recalling the twofold determination on which they are truly based and by which they are properly characterized as human. We first remember his determination for freedom before God. Life is lent to man under the determination for this freedom. . . . Life as such . . . means to live for the one to whom it belongs and from whom it has been received as a loan. Life, human life, thus hastens as such towards freedom before God, and only *per nefas*, and never according to its own nature, can it depart from this direction or take the opposite one. We must accept the fact that, in respect of this natural direction of his life towards God, man is not its owner and lord. Together with everything else which determines and characterizes his life, the fact that it is orientated to God is also and particularly God's creation and loan. But we can understand even human life as such only if we gather, not from speculation but from the event of its confrontation by the Word of God, that it too, without any cooperation of its own but by nature and from the very first, has this vertical direction. . . .

The other equally original determination of human existence is that of freedom in fellowship. In every significant and characteristic point, life is a possession lent to every man as such, to each in a different way, in a specific time and place, but the same gift to all. To be sure, it is not a collective act. The singularity as well as the spontaneity in which it may be lived militates against such a view. But even its singularity and spontaneity belong to the manner in which it is the same for all. And it is worth noting that these are the two points by which one man recognizes another most surely, or at any rate impressively, as someone like himself, namely, by the fact that he is so definitely this man, and lives as man in this distinctive freedom. As he himself acts and reacts specifically and spontaneously as a rational creature, so does also the other. And as the other does, so does he. Human life obviously cannot be lived otherwise than as a life which by its very nature consists in solidarity with those who have also to live it in their own way as it is lent to them. The natural and historical relations in which he stands to them are only the concrete conditions in which this solidarity achieves form, and is visible, and becomes a problem, to him and them. They ensure that this solidarity will not be overlooked and forgotten. But the equality and interrelatedness of all human life consists in its essence and not primarily in these relations. We therefore do not base our knowledge of it on any supposition derived from analogies. They might be unreliable. They can also be evaded. But as God addresses man, he also speaks to him through the solidarity which exists between him and other men. What God says to him applies to him, but to him only as a creature that has others of his kind. For he says it to him as he who is the creator of each and all men, who as such *mutatis mutandis,* at other times and places, has also addressed, addresses, and will address others with a different emphasis, content, and commission. However differently and specifically he may thus address each individual, when addressed by him each recognizes himself in the other, and therefore necessarily, compulsorily, and definitively, and again as a revelation of his creative will, as a disclosure of a determination which by its very nature is peculiar to human life. Thus the fact that man is determined for fellowship is very far from being an accident. From this standpoint, human life as such takes place with a view to freedom in fellowship and therefore in the interrelatedness of one man with the other who also in accordance with his place and time can and must live it in all its singularity. Only *per nefas,* and not according to its nature, could it break free from this interrelationship and be lived in opposition to it. Man's life is also to be understood in this respect as God's creation and loan. No power, no possibility of rebellion against God or other men, is given to the individual by the fact that there are so many like him. To the understanding of human life belongs also the insight guaranteed by the Word of God that, again without his own cooperation, it has by nature this horizontal direction.

11.6

Church Dogmatics III/4, 357-59

Included in the will to live there is a will to be healthy which . . . like the will to live is demanded by God and is to be seriously achieved in obedience to this demand. By health we are not to think merely of a particular physical or psychical something of great value that can be considered and possessed by itself and therefore can and must be the object of special attention, search, and effort. Health is the strength to be as man. It serves human existence in the form of the capacity, vitality, and freedom to exercise the psychical and physical functions, just as these themselves are only functions of human existence. We can and should will it as this strength when we will not merely to be healthy in body and soul but to be man at all: man and not animal or plant, man and not wood or stone, man and not a thing or the exponent of an idea, man in the satisfaction of his instinctive needs, man in the use of his reason, in loyalty to his individuality, in the knowledge of its limitations, man in his determination for work and knowledge, and above all in his relation to God and his fellow-men in the proffered act of freedom. We can and should will this, and therefore we can and should will to be healthy. For how can we will, understand, or desire the strength for all this unless in willing it we put it into operation in the smaller or greater measure in which we have it? And in willing to be man, how can we put it into operation unless we also will and seek and desire it? We gain it as we practice it. We should therefore will to practice it. This is what is demanded of man in this respect.

Though we cannot deny the antithesis between health and sickness when we view the problem in this way, we must understand it in its relativity. Sickness is obviously negative in relation to health. It is partial impotence to exercise those functions. It hinders man in his exercise of them by burdening, hindering, troubling, and threatening him, and causing him pain. But sickness as such is not necessarily impotence to be as man. The strength to be this, so long as one is still alive, can also be the strength and therefore the health of the sick person. And if health is the strength for human existence, even those who are seriously ill can will to be healthy without any optimism or illusions regarding their condition. They, too, are commanded, and it is not too much to ask, that so long as they are alive they should will this, i.e., exercise the power which remains to them, in spite of every obstacle. Hence it seems to be a fundamental demand of the ethics of the sick bed that the sick person should not cease to let himself be addressed, and to address himself, in terms of health and the will which it requires rather than sickness, and above all to see to it that he is in an environment of health. From the same standpoint we cannot count on conditions of absolute and total health, and therefore on the existence of men who are already healthy and do not need the command to will to be so. Even healthy people have great need of the will for health, though perhaps not of the doctor. Conditions of relative and subjectively total ease in relation to the psycho-physical functions of life may well exist. But whether the man who can enjoy such ease is healthy, i.e., a man who lives in the power to be as man, is quite another question which we need only ask, and we must immediately answer that in reality he may be severely handicapped in the exercise of this power, and therefore sick, long before this makes itself felt in the deterioration of his organs or their functional disturbance, so that he perhaps stands in greater need of the summons that he should be healthy than someone who already suffers from such deterioration and disturbance and is therefore regarded as sick in soul or body or perhaps both. And who of us has not constantly to win and possess this strength? A fundamental demand of ethics, even for the man who seems to be and to a large extent really is "healthy in body and soul," is thus that he should not try to evade the summons to be healthy in the true sense of the term.

On the same presupposition it will also be understood that in the question of health we must differentiate between soul and body but not on any account separate the two. The healthy man, and also the sick, is both. He is the soul of his body, the rational soul of his vegetative and animal body, the ruling soul of his serving body. But he is one and the same man in both, and not two. Health and sickness in the two do not constitute two divided realms, but are always a single whole. It is always a matter of the man himself, of his greater or lesser strength, and the more or less serious threat and even increasing impotence. It is he who has been predominantly ill and he who may be predominantly well. Or it is he who must perhaps go the opposite way from predominant health to predominant sickness. It is he who is on the way from the one or the other. Hence he does not have a specific healthy or sick life of the soul with particular dominating or subjugated, unresolved, or resolved inclinations, complexes, ties, prohibitions, and impulses, and then quite apart from this, in health or sickness, in the antithesis, conflict, and balance of the two, an organic vegetative and animal life of the body. On the contrary, he lives the healthy or sick life of his soul in his body and with the life of his body, so that in both, and in their mutual relationship, it is a matter of his life's history, his own history. Again, he does not have a specific physical life in the sound or disordered functions of his somatic organs, his nervous system, his blood circulation, digestion, urination, and so on, and then in an upper story a separate life of the soul. But he lives the healthy or sick life of his body together with that of his soul, and again in both cases, and in their mutual relationship, it is a matter of his life's history, his own history, and therefore himself. And the will for health as the strength to be as man is obviously quite simply, and without duplication in a psychical and physical sphere, the will to continue this history in its unity and totality. A man can, of course, orientate himself seriously, but only secondarily, on this or that psychical or physical element of health in contrast to sickness. But primarily he will always orientate himself in this contrast toward his own being as man, toward his assertion, preservation, and renewal (and all this in the form of activity) as a subject. In all his particular decisions and measures, if they are to be meaningful, he must have a primary concern to confirm his power to be as man and to deny the lack of power to be this. In all stages of that history the question to be answered is: "Will you be made whole?" (John 5:6), and not: "Will you have healthy limbs or be free of their sickness?" The command which we must always obey is the command to stand upright and not to fall.

11.7

Church Dogmatics III/4, 363

The principle *mens sana in corpore sano* [a sound mind in a sound body] can be a highly short-sighted and brutal one if it is only understood individually and not in the wider sense of *in societate sana* [in a sound society]. And this extension cannot only mean that we must see to it that the benefits of hygiene, sport, and medicine are made available for all, or at least as many as possible. It must mean that the general living conditions of all, or at least of as many as possible, are to be shaped in such a way that they make not just a negative but a positive preventative contribution to their health, as is the case already in varying degrees with the privileged. The will for health of the individual must therefore take also the form of the will to improve, raise, and perhaps radically transform the general living conditions of all men. If there is no other way, it must assume the form of the will for a new and quite different order of society, guaranteeing better living conditions for all. Where some are necessarily ill the others cannot with good conscience will to be well. Nor can they really do it at all if they are not concerned about neighbors who are inevitably sick because of their social position. For sooner or later the fact of this illness will in some way threaten them in spite of the measures which they take to isolate themselves and which may be temporarily and partially successful. When one person is ill, the whole of society is really ill in all its members. In the battle against sickness the final human word cannot be isolation but only fellowship.

11.8

Church Dogmatics III/4, 372-73

Man does not possess the power to be as man in the same way as God has his power to be as God, nor does he have power over his vital functions as God has his power as creator, ruler, and merciful deliverer of his creature. It does not belong to him to be and to live as God. Rather, he may see the goodness of God the creator in the fact that to his life and strength and powers a specific space to live is allotted — that is, a limited *time.* He may and should exercise them in it and not in the field of the unlimited. They are adapted for it, for development and application within it. Within its confines he may and should be as man in their possession and exercise. Within its confines he stands before God, and at the limit of this span God is mightily for him and is his hope. Just because it is limited, it is a kind of natural and normal confirmation of the fact that by God's free grace man may live through him and for him, with the commission to be as man in accordance with the measure of his strength and powers, but not under the intolerable destiny of having to give sense, duration, and completeness to his existence by his own exertions and achievements, and therefore in obvious exclusion to the view that he must and may and can by his own strength and powers eternally maintain, assert, and confirm himself, attaining for himself his own dignity and honor. The eternal God himself guarantees all this, and tells him he does so by giving him a life that is temporal and therefore limited. In this way it always remains in God's hand both in its splendor and in its triviality. In itself and as such this fact cannot be an object of complaint, protest, or rebellion, nor can the fact that man must make the concrete discovery that his life and therefore his health and strength and powers are not an unlimited reality, but that he is restricted in their possession and exercise, that weakness is real as well as strength, that there is destruction as well as construction, impairment as

417

well as development. This is all the more terrible because it is just from this direction that we find ourselves threatened by death and judgment. But is it really surprising and shocking in itself? The life of man, his commission, and his strength to fulfill it are not limited accidentally but by God, and therefore not to his destruction but to his salvation. Inevitably, then, he always in some way comes up concretely against this boundary of his life. Inevitably he must grow old and decline. Inevitably he must concretely encounter his creator and Lord and therefore God's omnipotence and mercy. But is it merely a question of necessity? In the correct sense, is it not true to say that, no less than in his unimpeded movement within these confines, this is also a possibility? May it not be that genuine freedom to live can and must be concretely realized in the fact that in the *restriction* he is shown that neither his life nor he himself is in his own hand, but that he is in God's hand, that he is surrounded by him on all sides, that he is referred wholly to him, but also that he is reliably upheld by him? Does not this freedom begin at the very point where we are confronted by the hard actuality of the insight that "Christ will be our consolation"? But what if sickness as the concrete form of weakness, of destruction, of the impairment of his strength and powers, of growing old and declining, is the hard actuality which ushers in this genuinely liberating insight? What if it is not only the forerunner and messenger of death and judgment, but also, concealed under this form, the forerunner and messenger of the eternal life which God has allotted and promised to the man who is graciously preserved and guided by him within the confines of his time?

11.9

Church Dogmatics III/4, 394

The capacity of each individual is in reality as incalculable and uncontrollable as he is in himself. It can be known and decided only by God. If a man says: "I cannot," he must remember that he might well be able to do today what he quite honestly thought he could not do yesterday. But if he says: "I can," he must consider that he might not be able to do today or ever again what he was confident he could do yesterday. In neither case has he perhaps realized what is given to him. In both he must perhaps make new discoveries, whether positive or negative, in relation to his capacity. In both the decision must be made in relation to the God who has created, sustains, guides, and knows him. The genuine art of living is learned along the way of such human decisions in relation to God, of such discovery of the limits within which a man may be powerful and beyond which he can only condemn himself to powerlessness, seeing that God has prescribed and set them for him.

11.10

Church Dogmatics, III/4, 423-24

Has society as constituted and ordered in the state a right to declare that certain sick people are "not worthy of living" *(Lebensunwert)* and therefore to resolve and execute their death? We have in view the incurably infirm, the insane, imbeciles, the deformed, persons who by nature or accident or war are completely immobilized and crippled and therefore "useless." The question whether human society has the right to extinguish the life of such people is to be answered by an unequivocal *No.* . . . This is a type of killing which can *only* be regarded as murder, i.e., as a wicked usurpation of God's sovereign right over life and death. A human life not (or no longer) marked by a capacity to work, to earn, to consume, or perhaps even to communicate is *not* for this reason a life "not worth living," least of all because it cannot make a recognizable active contribution to the life of the state, but can only directly or indirectly be a burden to it. The worth of such life is God's *secret.* Those in the surrounding area and in the human community as a whole may not find anything in it, but in no case does this mean they are authorized to terminate it through a forceful negation. For who sees into the inner and essential thing of such a human life? Who can know whether it may not be far more precious in the eyes of God and whether it may not in eternity be revealed as far more glorious than that of hundreds of healthy workers and peasants, technicians, scientists, artists, and soldiers so dear to the state? Nor is it any argument that the state may and should permit a similar verdict in certain cases, e.g., the imposition of a capital sentence on criminals or as a defensive measure in times of war. The incurably infirm or the cripple is not a criminal or an enemy of the state against whom the state may claim this right in self-preservation. He might well be to some extent a victim of the gaps and deficiencies in the existing order of society and state. It may well be that society and the state really owe him much *compensation.* In any case he is not an aggressor, but a *suffering* member of society and the state. As such he has been entrusted to the very particular protection and support of the community. No community — no family, no village, and so also no state —

is really strong if it will not carry its weak and even its very weakest members. They belong to it no less than the strong, and the quiet work of their maintenance and care, which might seem useless on a superficial view, is perhaps far more effective than common labor, culture, or historical conflict in knitting it closely and securely together. On the other hand, a community which regards and treats its weak members as a hindrance, and even proceeds to their extermination, is on the verge of collapse. The killing of the weak for the sake of the others hampered by their weakness can only rest on a *misconception* of life — *life* which in its specific form, and therefore even in its weakness, is always given by God, and which should therefore be to others an object of *respect* [*Ehrfurcht*]! And the result of this misconception can only be murder, and not in any sense obedience to the command of God. Indeed, the misconception itself, the whole idea of the "life not worth living," is already transgression.

11.11

Church Dogmatics III/4, 499-502

Those summoned to participate first in the external service of the community, then in the internal, are human persons, men and women, old and young, healthy and sick, relatively independent and relatively dependent from the social standpoint, more educated and less, of different outlooks, stronger and weaker even in faith, loyalty, zeal, and patience. They can be truly and solidly bound together only by the Lord and his Spirit, or, seen from below, only by their mutual perception of the kingdom of God. There may and will be other relations between them, whether erotic, domestic, friendly, intellectual, economic, social, or political. For different reasons they may and will in varying degrees interest, need, suit, or like one another. But for all their strength these relations are not absolutely necessary, nor can they be maintained unconditionally. It is not these relations which cement the Christian community together. What decisively and consistently binds the people united in it is their common vocation, i.e., the horizontal relation created among them by the fact that in their own place and manner they are all in the same vertical relation. The recognition, expression, and realization of this relation between man and man is the act by which the community continually constitutes and renews itself as a human society. Does a Christian see in another Christian a relative in blood or spirit, a fellow-man in the same situation or on the same level of taste, morality, or piety, a sympathetic, stimulating, and helpful contemporary and companion? He may well see in him either these things or others of the same kind. But these things are not what really counts. What really counts is quite simply that a Christian sees in another Christian a man who like himself is called to faith, obedience, and service, and who is therefore his brother, and that he thus recognizes that he is united with and under an obligation to him as a brother. Under obligation to do what? The only answer worth considering is: to grant to and secure for this other as much of the freedom physically and spiritually necessary for his life in service as a creature, as one man can grant to and secure for another, and he specifically to and for this other. No man, not even the Christian, can give another the freedom of the children of God, the freedom of the Spirit. But for the life of service there is also needed a measure of creaturely freedom, of psycho-physical freedom, of space to breathe and move, of joy, of opportunity for expression and development.

This is the freedom which one Christian grants to and secures for the other within the limits of his ability, but to the extent of these limits. In his place and manner he sees the other set in the same service as himself. He affirms his existence as that of his brother. He is grateful for it. He rejoices at it. But he also perceives the limitation, frailty, and burden of his creatureliness. He realizes how restricted he is in his freedom and therefore how threatened in his service. He certainly cannot help him in every need, but he can do so in some things, and perhaps in many. He gives this help as he can, perhaps in words or perhaps without, perhaps by simply letting him do as he pleases, perhaps by strong and definite action, perhaps by standing responsibly at his side, and always with the intention that he should become and be and remain free for his service, and on the basis of the fact that he is a brother, that they have the same Father and Lord, and that from him they have received the same commission. This is Christian love. It is active brotherly love. It builds and sustains the community as a human society. It is as such that it should accept its service in the world. Only as such can it do so. Yet this active love is also the action in which every member of the community is summoned to direct co-operation at some point. In the person of one, or several, or perhaps many fellow-Christians standing in some need either of freedom or of more freedom, the inner history of the community enters the common sphere of vision. Everyone has an ability or talent, a personal freedom, whereby he may assist others to the same. No one can redeem another. But each has the task of loosing others, even if these others be only Christians who happen to be in his vicinity. Each has the task of releasing them in some small measure from their creaturely existence, of lightening, cheering, and strengthening them as he is able and to the very best of his ability. To help them in this way to be free for service is itself service. In this form service is both proposed to each and demanded of each.

There can be no doubt that active as distinct from contemplative or meditative brotherly love is the most difficult form of Christian service, not necessarily because it may sometimes demand great sacrifices of time and strength and even external possessions, but because Christian service in this form is so indirect and unpretentious, because as service of the Lord in the person of the brother it seems to lack almost entirely the direct splendor of an endeavor on his behalf and for his cause. For often, and in the strict sense always, it is so difficult to recognize in the other a man who has the same calling and who is therefore a brother. Often, and in the strict sense always, it is difficult to see here genuine service, and the common Lord and his Spirit. His limitation, frailty, and burden are easily seen. But are they really the limitation, frailty, and burden of one whom it is worthwhile to help by granting and securing his freedom and loving him as a brother? Does he look like someone of whom something important is to be expected, so that it is essential to help him? Is there really a brother in respect of whom we do not have sound reasons for letting love grow cold or preventing it from growing warm? What can make him so interesting to me, when he is obviously only a man and hardly known by me (if at all) even as a Christian, that I must love him, and indeed love him actively? This is, of course, a resigned and despairing question which shows that I myself am obviously only a man, and probably hardly known to the other as a Christian. This is the very difficulty of this form of service. Active brotherly love demands a kind of double leap. The fact that the brother is also a man cannot be overlooked. It has to be acknowledged. But it is precisely as a man that he needs the freedom to be able to be a Christian, and it is to this end that I am summoned to help him in his humanity. Again, it is quite true that as his brother I am only a man. But it is as a man that I am summoned to do what is Christian. At this point the origin of every call and admission into the community, and of every existence in it in faith, is very concretely revealed and tested and must prove itself. We remember the sharp statement of 1 John. Without loving God, no one can love the brethren. But what is this love for God if one does not also love the brethren, and love them actively? There can be no contesting the fact that this most difficult form of service is not just one among others. If it is not the basis, it is at least the *conditio sine qua non* of all Christian service. The Christian community is powerless to do what it should do in this world if the people assembled in it try to deny this service, the service of brotherly love. Of what help to them is even the most serious participation in its life in freedom and order, in strength and sobriety, in its service under and by the Word, to what purpose is all their participation in its external service, and how can it be cooperation in the fulfillment of the task of the community, if the Christian, or pretended Christian as he really is, evades that which constitutes cooperation? There can be no cooperation except in active brotherly love. Only as this is practiced does the community edify itself. Only in the measure in which he practices it does the individual participate in its edification as demanded of him. If he does not seem to practice it, the question is pertinent whether his admission into the community and therefore his faith, his recognition of the kingdom of God, are true and genuine.

11.12

Church Dogmatics IV/3.1, 362-64

In the first instance we are not contemporaries of the great and little personages of the history of the world or culture or even the church, of their lives and acts and opinions, of their enterprises and achievements as more or less authentically reported in the press and by radio. In the first instance we are contemporaries of Jesus Christ and direct witnesses of his action, whether with closed or open or blinking eyes, whether actively or passively. More closely and properly than any other — indeed, he alone closely and properly in the full sense — he is the neighbor of every other person, the Good Samaritan for all of us who have so obviously fallen among thieves. And incomparably more important and incisive and significant than anything that may happen to the world in East or West, or to any one of us by way of good or ill and with or without our co-operation, is that which comes upon the world and each of us with the fact that Jesus Christ as the light of life, as the Word of the covenant of grace, but also as the future judge of the living and the dead, passes actively through the midst at every hour, the hope of us all in the promise of the Spirit addressed to all. And the part of all humanity and each individual in this positive sign of the middle period and situation of his *parousia,* presence, and revelation is that wittingly or unwittingly we are alongside and with him. His today is really ours, and ours his. Nor does this mean only that what he does today and what we do proceed along two specific and separated lines. He goes on our way and we on his. Hence he does not do what he does without us, nor we without him. Our action is wholly ours, yet it is determined by his. There is thus no altering the fact that the events, forms, and relationships of the public and private action which apparently (but only apparently) fill this intervening time, that our great and little successes and defeats and advances and retreats and enlightenments and obfuscations and joys and sorrows, stand in a relationship which may perhaps be suspected, not to say perceived, only infrequently by a few, which may be more near or distant, which may be one of opposition or concord, which may seem to be colorless and indefinite, but which is still a very real relationship to the movement in which he passes through our midst, striding through our time from his commencement to his goal. No man eats or drinks, wakens or sleeps, laughs or cries, blesses or curses, builds or destroys, lives or dies, outside this relationship. Whether we affirm, deny, or ignore his prophetic work, whether we resist or further it, whether we serve or hinder it, we all take part in it as the occurrence which truly and properly fills this time of ours. He and he alone knows infallibly how we do this. The manner in which we have done, do, and will do so is written in the book of life which will not be opened until the last day, and which will then perhaps contain many surprising data. The positive thing, however, about the lives of all of us here and now in our time is that we do actually take part in the *parousia,* presence, and revelation of Jesus Christ as the hope of us all, in the promise of the Spirit addressed to us all. Nor do we do so merely incidentally and externally, but centrally and internally, though externally, too, as those who, existing in time, are encircled by the glory of the mediator. It may be added that in this relationship to him, whatever form it may take, we are indissolubly linked with one another. It may also be added that in it we are linked with all to whom he was present before our time as his way was also theirs and theirs his, but also with all those whose way he will share after our time. In the relationship to him the history of present, past, and future is thus a single whole in which nothing did or will escape him, in which none could or can flee from him or slip from his grasp, i.e., break free from the relationship. As he lives in relationship to us in our time, we live in relationship to him together with all the men of our own and all times, there being no separation between them and us nor us and them. The day of his revelation in its final form will concretely reveal this. But since our day is a day of his revelation as the hope of us all, a day of the promise of the Spirit, it is already true and actual in this day of ours, and thus to be reckoned with in all seriousness and with all joy.

11.13

Sermon on Acts 3.1-10, delivered to the German-speaking Reformed congregation in the Madeleine Church, Geneva, on 14 June 1936. In Karl Barth, *Predigten 1935-52* (Zurich: TVZ, 1996), 34-46. Translated by Donald Wood.

We have heard a story of the temple. It was the temple of the one, true, living God of Israel. It was — how should it be otherwise, since besides this one God there is no other? — the temple to which we all belong, as certainly as we are baptized into the name of Jesus Christ and are called to the hearing of his Word. The temple is the one, holy, catholic, apostolic church. In this temple sacrifices, prayers, and teaching took place. Indeed, prayers, teaching, sermons, instruction in Christianity are offered up to this day. Here we have to do with God, with the soul and its eternal salvation, with the kingdom of God; here we think of days past and of the mighty deeds which God has done for the fathers. . . . But what, in the end, does it all mean? . . . Is it a matter of necessities or merely of customs with which we could, in a pinch, do without? Is it a matter of the truth or perhaps only of beautiful illusions? . . . What do we know of what the church really is? What we perceive of ourselves in this regard is in each one of us a very curious mixture of yes and no, of considerations sincere and insincere, obedient and arbitrary. No decision is reached here by and from us. What the church is *was* and *is* decided. The story that we have heard concerns just this decision. . . .

"And there was a man, lame from birth, who was borne and carried; and daily they set him before the temple gate that is called 'the beautiful gate,' so that he might beg alms of those who went into the temple." So here is a man who cannot stand and cannot walk. One who — without the ability to move, wholly unfree, stuck like a stump to the ground — must spend his days utterly dependent upon that bit of assistance provided by another. Is it life at all, human life, that is lived here? Is it not rather an image and prelude of death as it one day, when we lie under the earth, will rule over us all? . . .

"At once his legs and ankles were strengthened . . . he walked and leapt and praised God." Of whom is all this recounted? Of the lame man, of the man who had lived for forty years as a dead man, of the person whom we all know so well — whom we know only too well. Of him it is said, and we must hear it said of him: As the one he is, in his lameness, he suddenly is caught, enclosed, raised, supported by healing power. He is able to do what he never could do. He does what he never has done before. He no longer lives in the shadow of death. No, he walks in the light of eternal life. The same and no longer the same! The same and yet a wholly other! . . . He himself has become a living sign of the glory of God. . . .

"And he went . . . into the temple, and everyone saw him walking and praising God." . . . Now it is decided what the church is: The church is the lame man to whom the Word of God has come. Or better: the Word of God which has come to the lame man to raise and support him, to establish him, to set him in motion, to make him his own and to deal with him as with his own. The Word with the lame man: that is the church — with the lame man who is no hero, no wise or great man; but one who can and must now walk, live, and praise God, not on his own power but because he now has become the lame man with, in, and under the Word. This Word . . . the Word with, in, and under which this lame man must walk, leap, live, and praise God — it comes also to us, we who are gathered here today as the church. Consequently we do not need first to ask where and who the lame man is. We must henceforth become companions of this lame man if we would respond to this story as it requires: "I believe in the Holy Spirit; one, holy, catholic Christian church; the forgiveness of sins; the resurrection of the flesh; and one eternal life. And I believe that I am and eternally will remain a living member of this church, the church of the lame under the Word."

12 *Women, Disabled*

JANA BENNETT

The dissonance raised by the nonacceptance of persons with disabilities and the acceptance of grace through Christ's broken body necessitates that the church find new ways of interpreting disability.

Nancy Eiesland, *The Disabled God*

Women are disabled. This is not simply the notion that some women have disabilities (in the way that I myself am a woman with a hearing loss), but that the very fact of being a woman is a disability. I have no doubt that there are people who might find this statement offensive. People with disabilities (as commonly understood) might find it so because it would seem to lessen difficulties, pains, and real encumbrances that disability entails. Some feminists might do so because it would seem to emphasize some of the very stereotypes of women that they wish to overcome: that women are weak and irrational.

Yet I do not make this statement to be provocative so much as to highlight that women's problems have been curiously similar to those experienced by people with disabilities. By many feminist accounts, Nancy Eiesland's quote above could easily apply to women, substituting "women" for "persons with disabilities." The woman-disability connection exists in part because feminists often write about the ways in which women wrestle with bodies that are limiting and frustrating, and the ways in which Christians have contributed to poor theology and oppressive practices about those bodies. As Doreen Freeman writes, "Looking through the Hebrew and Christian scriptures and writings of the tradition, it is hard to tell women apart from disabled people" (Freeman 2002, 74). Writers over the centuries have noted that women bleed, are missing (apparently) some key anatomy, and are not rational — just as those with disabilities have wounds that don't heal, may be missing some parts of their anatomy, and may not present themselves as rational. Feminist and disability theologians alike critique thought that suggests "normal" is a young, physically muscular, perfectly formed adult male body, which by default is rational. Bodies are especially difficult and frustrating for those who are patronized or persecuted because of them, so in this sense, perhaps women and people with disabilities have similar concerns and points to share with each other. Although thoughts about disability and women may well be intertwined, disability theologians and feminist theologians rarely reference each other except in passing.

Of course, I have a caveat to all this. Saying that women are disabled does not thereby mean that women intuitively have a greater understanding of what it means to live in a wheelchair or any host of other ways in which bodies can be disabling. That women (and men) have reflected on bodily frustrations about gender in ways that intersect with work done by disability theologians does not yield a universal account of disability. And yet, I think that feminists and disability theologians can learn something from each other. My aim in this chapter, therefore, is to tell a story about feminist theology in terms of thinking about disability. My telling of the story highlights the similarity of questions and observations made for both and *also* indicates some of the ways in which feminism and disability theology have not been good for each other. Ultimately, I make the case that naming women as disabled, even with all the caveats, opens a space for a better theological anthropology — a better understanding of who we are as God's creatures.

The three excerpts I have chosen help me tell this story (though not exhaustively). The first excerpt is written by Rosemary Radford Ruether, a Catholic theologian currently working at Graduate Theological Union, who offers a survey of several kinds of feminism and proposes her own liberatory model of feminism. The second excerpt is by Nancy Eiesland, a disability theologian most known for her book *The Disabled God*. Eiesland taught at Candler School of Theology and was interested in how feminist theology intersected with liberation models of disability. The third excerpt is from Sarah Coakley, who teaches at Harvard Divinity School. Unlike Ruether and Eiesland, Coakley has taken questions about bodies in postmodern directions, following the work of feminist theorists like Judith Butler.

I offer an additional note about "feminism" here. The word usually refers to twentieth-century and twenty-first-century academics, activists, and others concerned for women's political and economic rights (such as the right to get a divorce on the same terms as men can), as well as the ways in which history and culture have often made women out to be lesser beings. The word therefore involves several diverse collections of ideas and people, so that contemporary scholars speak of *"feminisms"* in the plural.

If there is a common issue that unites these diverse feminisms together, I think it may well be concern for bodies. Different feminist perspectives will variously approach what "the body" means, but all have confronted the inescapable fact that humans exasperatingly inhabit bodies that mark and limit them. Feminist theologies therefore provide an excellent opportunity for thinking through various approaches toward disabled bodies.

The Body to Be Surpassed

This history begins with many people's realization that Jewish and Christian traditions have long considered both women and those with disabilities to be troublesome. At least as far back as the Grimké sisters (nineteenth century), women have wondered what it is about their bodies that prohibits them from working outside the home, from seeking ordination, and from having equal legal rights (and even authority) over men. Creation, in Genesis, looms large: Eve is taken from Adam's side and is therefore inferior to Adam, because he was made directly by God. Even from her very birth, then (at least according to the second creation account), Eve has a body that is inferior to Adam's, just as those with disabilities are seen as having inferior bodies. Moreover, being a woman is linked to sin, just as disability has often been linked to sin. Eve is the first one to eat the fruit from the forbidden tree, and thus she and all women bear the blame for sin being brought into the world, just as in ancient Hebrew tradition, disability was seen as evidence of sin.

In 12.1, Rosemary Radford Ruether traces the development of these scriptural ideas through the broader Christian tradition. She notes, for example, Augustine's sense of woman's "bodily representation of inferior, sinprone self [so] that he regards her as possessing the image of God only secondarily" (Ruether 1993, 95). Thomas Aquinas strengthens Augustine's view in her account, because he accepts a view of women as inferior because they are reversed versions of men (*Summa Theologica* I.92). Women's genitalia are inward, receptive cavities — the reverse of men's. Men's genitalia are outward, more clearly present, and add to the sense that men are less passive. The Reformers did nothing to change bodily representations of women; in

429

fact, they even more strongly counted the Fall as the reason for the loss of women's equality with men. Women's subjugation is punishment for crimes committed at creation.

And so, according to tradition, these troublesome bodies cannot be ordained. Leviticus 21:16-23 says:

> The LORD spoke to Moses, saying: "Speak to Aaron and say: No one of your offspring throughout their generations who has a blemish may approach to offer the food of his God. For no one who has a blemish shall draw near, one who is blind or lame, or one who has a mutilated face or a limb too long, or one who has a broken foot or a broken hand, or a hunchback, or a dwarf, or a man with a blemish in his eyes or an itching disease or scabs or crushed testicles."

According to this passage and others in Leviticus and Numbers, women may not be priests, but neither may those who are disabled. (For further discussion, see Christopher Newell 2007, 328.) Feminist theologians and disability theologians alike have taken on the task of reading scripture with their own respective eyes. Consider Phyllis Trible's *Texts of Terror,* which examines stories in Hebrew scriptures for what they have to say about women, though their focus is often on men.

Added to all this is a question about salvation. The importance of Jesus is that he is the God-man, taking on human flesh, becoming one with us, and therefore offering both the possibility of salvation from sin and unification and restored friendship with God. But this point of theology has led some to ask how it is that a male savior can save women. The second part of the excerpt from Ruether addresses this question. Jesus took on only male flesh, so is there not a way in which he is saving only men? In terms of disability, people do not generally speak of Jesus as disabled, so likewise, how is it that Jesus identifies enough with deafness to offer salvation to those with hearing loss? If Jesus is envisioned as somewhat disabled, it is on the cross, and his suffering is seen as virtuous — a problem for some feminists and disability theologians. Why glorify suffering, particularly when women and the disabled suffer at the hands of a patriarchal, able-bodied society?

The self-doubt raised by these questions and assumptions leads in part to a desire to get beyond these troublesome bodies. The predominant medical model of disability supposes that we might be able to surpass disability, in a sense, by healing it. Gene therapy, cochlear implants, and other medical interventions are designed to give the appearance, if not the reality, of a whole, non-disabled body. At heart, the medical model presupposes that the problem is the person with the disability, that the disabled person wants to overcome that disability, and that medicine and/or scientific advancements provide a way to surpass otherwise disabled bodies.

Likewise, the medical model of disability applies to women. Several authors have noted the ways in which childbirth and periods have become part of the realm of doctors, to be properly attended to by scientifically trained people who see pregnancy, labor, and periods as illnesses. Jennifer Block discusses the episiotomy, for example. There was a common belief in the mid-twentieth century that episiotomies were necessary because babies were too big to pass through the vagina. People failed to note, however, that the birth canal only seemed too small when women were lying on their backs in bed, which was and is the normal birth position in most hospitals. But for centuries, women had been giving birth in a variety of other positions, including squatting and standing. Those positions allow the pelvis to widen to the greatest degree possible, enabling women to give birth much more easily than when lying down. Yet under new hospital protocol, women were given episiotomies surgically, which actually increased the time they needed for recovery and which could lead to infections and problems with bladder and bowel control. By the early 1980s, the Center for Disease Control in the United States did a study that determined conclusively that there was no scientific basis for episiotomies, and yet that had been the medical standard for decades because doctors saw women's bodies as inadequate (Block 2007, 28-30). Another example might be the Seasonale birth control pill, touted as a way for a woman to have a period only four times a year, to "fix" the problem that is menstruation. Via pharmaceuticals, women can limit their own limits and presumably surpass much that is wrong with being in female bodies.

Why not embrace these visions to surpass bodies? A medical model that allows a person to surpass a body in such a way that one could "pass" as not-disabled or not-woman is a ticket to greater freedoms, greater enjoyment of life, and salvation in *this* life. Why would feminists object to anything that would permit women to have better lives, free of regular periods and painful childbirth? Why should theologians of disability object to a medical model of disability that might, in fact, allow for ordination of those who do not have hands or perfect limbs?

Indeed, some forms of feminism undergird this desire to get beyond bodies. In excerpts **12.2** and **12.3**, Ruether discusses some of these "egalitarian Christologies" that wish to transcend bodiliness. For example, she discusses what she names "eschatological feminism" (excerpt **12.2**), exemplified

431

by some early Gnostic groups which developed the idea that being Christian required surpassing bodies in favor of spiritual lives focused on the world to come, which, as these Gnostics saw it, would be egalitarian. Ruether critiques this stance, however. While she is sympathetic to an egalitarian view, she is concerned by the exclusive focus on the future and not the here and now. Thus, Ruether does not share the optimism of Elaine Pagels, another prominent feminist scholar who sees Gnostic texts as liberating for women.

Liberal feminism (excerpt 12.3) represents another egalitarian Christology stemming from the secular version of liberalism. Mary McClintock Fulkerson describes the main ideas of liberalism: "the primacy of individuals, the value of individual autonomy and choice, a state limited to the function of protecting the rights and freedoms of individuals, and a neutral posture toward any account of the good in order to protect a plurality of views" (Fulkerson 1994, 5). (Under liberalism's influence, some concluded that men and women could be equal because both were autonomous individuals and had rationality and moral reasoning in common.)

The benefit of liberalism is that it envisions equality as a historical possibility, so, unlike Gnostic views, it allows for and even foments revolution with the aim of equality. But who provides the basis for that equality? Equality has often meant urging women to take on male roles, which then further suppresses women. Ruether makes her critique of liberalism along this line, and that critique stands against the medical model of disability as well. It presumes a liberal view of bodies in its attempt to help all be "equal," which means that we are all autonomous, rational creatures. Yet Ruether claims that this focus is exclusive even as it seeks to universalize all humans, because the focus on rationality and autonomy means that other valid (perhaps better) accounts of humans are left out.

Thus far, I have suggested that for feminist theologians, women and people who are disabled stand together against prevalent presumptions about bodies. The initial issues that the Christian tradition raised and the arguments made against those issues are such that it is almost impossible to distinguish between the issues of women's bodies and disabled bodies.

The One Human Body

One solution to attempting to surpass bodies is to embrace them. Lisa Isherwood, a postmodern theologian particularly concerned with body theology, writes, "I think we have to take incarnation much more seriously, to take the flesh as the place where the utopian vision of heaven is felt and lived — we have to enflesh the Christ that we are baptized into and profess to believe in" (Isherwood 2007). Far from being an object to surpass, the body is something to celebrate, according to many feminists and disability theologians. A focus on Paul's vision that Christians are one body in Christ and that there are many members in the one body allows for different bodies to be appreciated as gifts. Paul's words here provide a popular early feminist scripture that supports many ways of being, both male and female.

Alongside this celebratory view of bodies comes the "social model" (as opposed to the medical model), which sees that disability exists only where social structures prevent a person from fully interacting. Thus, for example, as a person with a hearing loss, I do not have a disability when I am among a community of people who also speech read (and speak in "speech read"), because then I can understand and be understood perfectly. Likewise, the person in a wheelchair does not have a disability if he is able to wheel himself into a building that is built with wheelchair access (with a ramp and wide doorways). In these instances, it is society itself that accommodates to disability without trying to "fix" it but instead seeing it as a gift, whether that is society at large, or a simple, small society of speech-readers.

This social model of disability has some parallel strands in theological discourse and feminist thought. In the 1970s, some feminists began to think in terms of "cultural feminism" or "gynocentric feminism." Ruether names and describes this kind of feminism as "romantic" in excerpt 12.4. Romantic feminism will often name women as the peacekeepers, as gentle and nurturing caregivers, and therefore as having no disability. On this account, women bring unique gifts to humanity by their very woman-ness. Mary Aquin O'Neill writes of this form of feminism:

> There is a male way of being and a female way, and these can be known from an examination of the bodies of the two and given a fair degree of specificity. Thus men are supposed to be, by nature, active, rational, willful, autonomous beings whose direction goes outward into the world; women are to be passive, intuitive, emotional, connected beings whose natural inclination is inward. (O'Neill 1993, 149)

Many romantic feminists (Ruether discusses two types — conservative and reformist romantics) see these differences in men and women as simply part of their complementary nature. That is, humans share one nature, and men and women together demonstrate what that nature is. Men need women to fill in gaps, and vice versa: men have roles and habits that are complementary to women's. We cannot be fully human without knowing ourselves in relation to members of the other gender, and so what it means to be fully human is to be in relationship with each other as men and women. Thus, men and women together comprise the many members of the one body of which Paul speaks.

One problem that gynocentric feminism presents for thinking about disability is the "ethic of care" that it has developed. The "ethic of care" views women's unique gift to humanity as forming relationships with each other that emphasize care of others. This is opposed to other ethical theories like those of Immanuel Kant and John Rawls, which focus on rationality and justice, often from male perspectives that overlook women's ideas and work as valid. From the viewpoint of a theology of disability, however, there is a concern with seeing women as the caregivers, particularly of people with disabilities. For one thing, an ethic of care reinforces the idea that people with disabilities are different and therefore in need of more care than people without disabilities. Another argument against the ethic of care is that it may produce worry about whether a person can truly care for another or not. Jackie Leach Scully writes, "Parents might believe, rightly or wrongly, that they can better care for a child who is more rather than less like themselves: better able to anticipate their needs, to create strong emotional bonds, and to provide some appropriate guidance as they grow . . ." (Scully 2003, 277).

Likewise, Ruether does not see romantic feminism as the solution for understanding bodies. In excerpt 12.5, she makes the case that the best from liberal and romantic feminisms ought to be combined to create what she names "liberatory feminism." Liberating women means making use of symbols and tradition in new, freeing ways. Thus, Ruether examines the traditional Christian doctrine of Christ (excerpt 12.6) and answers definitively that a male savior can save women. (Some of Ruether's counterparts, like Mary Daly, will disagree.) As Ruether sees it, the traditional masculine symbol of Christ becomes a powerful force for liberation because Jesus, far from upholding societal standards that approved of male superiority, always supported those with marginalized bodies, especially women.

Multiplying Bodies

Other feminists questioned this view of the "one body," though, recognizing that for all that feminists might have achieved, there were some women who had not benefited from liberation. Liberal and gynocentric feminisms arose from mainly white, educated women and tended to universalize "woman" to suggest that all women everywhere experienced what Ruether, as a white Christian woman, experienced. By the late 1970s and into the 1980s, women who did not share that background began to question the underlying assumptions that white women made about other women, and the ways in which oppression took many forms. While white women might be oppressed, that did not mean they were not also guilty of oppressing others or overlooking significant concerns.

The move toward understanding the feminist movement as a collection of many feminisms came in part out of the desire of women of other races, ethnicities, and classes to consider how gender politics worked. What it means to be a "body" began to have multiple answers for feminist scholars as well as theologians. Dualisms were no longer the problem. There was not woman versus man, but African-American woman in relation to African-American man, African-American woman in relation to white man, Asian woman in relation to Asian man, and so on.

Likewise, feminists concerned with disability took similar trajectories, realizing that theology cannot simply take white feminist strands and pull them in a thoroughgoing, uncritical way into thought about disability. For one thing, many of those associated with women's and gendered studies have a concerted focus on abortion that many disability activists find annihilating. As Nancy Eiesland recounts,

> Not long ago I gave a guest lecture in a feminist ethics course at a mainline seminary in the United States. The participants in the class were enthusiastic about understanding the social and ethical issues raised by women with disabilities until I noted that many people with disabilities were critical of the antidisability bias present in some feminist pro-choice arguments. A student asked, "Wouldn't you agree that it is a woman's right to decide whether she wants to have a disabled child?" (quoted in Elshout 1994, 114)

Eiesland attempted to point out that that pattern of thought was one of the problems that those with disabilities have in modern culture. Eiesland's conversation not only highlights the points of departure between disability theology and feminist theologies, but also raises up the inseparability of disability theology and feminist thought. The idea that a woman has an inalienable right to choose for her own body comes crashing into the concern that such a focus stems from "able-ism." Prevailing feminist thought presupposes that the woman is able-bodied and wouldn't/couldn't/shouldn't care for a baby that would be disabled.

For those with disabilities, the theological problem with feminists and abortion is not just that disabled fetuses are often the ones deemed necessary to be aborted, which is offensive to those with disabilities. It is also that the background of much feminist thought presumes a certain amount of choice with respect to bodies, and autonomy over those bodies. These are liberal assumptions that stem from Enlightenment thought. African-American women, too, have struggled with this issue. (See Dorothy Roberts' book titled *Killing the Black Body*.)

Indeed, a conversation I once had with my ear doctor highlights the tension. When I was pregnant, the doctor recommended genetic testing, and presumed that even though I have a hearing loss, I obviously wouldn't want to bring a baby into the world who has a hearing loss. From the doctor's point of view, this was *my* decision to make, since I am the one responsible for my child-bearing capacity. Yet this view is uniquely offensive, for it suggests that what is worthwhile about my body is that it is rational, and that therefore as a rational creature I should recognize that disability is wrongheaded. It also presumes that as a woman, I bear the sole responsibility for the marks of my own child-bearing body, without recognizing that what I do with my body does, in fact, affect others. If I "choose" to abort a baby with a hearing loss, what is that saying to other women, other people with disabilities, about their own bodies? While seeming to support my autonomy, the doctor's statement also belies that our strongly anti-disabled culture controls people's views about who should and should not be born, and judges what "rational" people would and would not do.

Excerpt **12.7**, from Nancy Eiesland's groundbreaking work *The Disabled God,* makes a further point about disability and feminism. Eiesland begins by discussing what she calls "contextual Christology," by which she means and presumes that God cares about people where they are, as they are. God does not love and care for a vague notion of universal humanity, but actually cares for each person as he/she is, and the way God does that is incarnationally. God incarnate — God's becoming flesh and blood in Jesus Christ — would be maimed, bruised, and yes, disabled, on the cross, and so experienced and thus knows firsthand what it is like to be disabled. Indeed, salvation comes *because* of the disability, and for Eiesland this is liberatory.

Eiesland recognizes feminist concerns here: that the same body that dies on the cross happens to be male, and so does not experience the bodiliness of being a woman. Eiesland agrees that women cannot support an image of

Christ that only undergirds white male privilege (that is, to see Christ as a white male is to privilege whiteness as the mode of Christ's salvation for humanity). Nonetheless, she thinks that feminists run too far in directions which suggest that Christ was not human or that Christ was not divine. For Eiesland, the point instead is that Jesus Christ is a "survivor" and lived physically in this world. Rather than attempting to surpass or "erase" our bodiliness, Christ in his physicality "removes the barriers which constrain our bodies, keep us excluded, and intend to humiliate us" (12.7, 103). Indeed, in her excerpt Eiesland speaks strongly against those who advocate divine healing of people with disabilities, for that insinuates that Christ matters only in a spiritual way. Spiritual healing presumes that if one has enough faith, the body will be healed and surpassed. But Eiesland says no — God's love for us is deeper than wanting us to surpass our broken bodies. God loves us *because of* those broken bodies, and even becomes disabled in the Incarnation. Eiesland's excerpt closes with a commentary on all these proliferating theologies — feminist, African-American, Latin American — that celebrates the diverse, many-membered Body of Christ in a Pentecostal (Acts 2) way. These new bodies of Christ simply represent "the corporate enactment of the resurrection of God" (12.7, 105).

The Playful Body

After the assertion of Eiesland and others that the many-membered Body of Christ is not a chaos after all, some scholars wondered whether bodies can have any meaning whatsoever. If the disabled God means something to me but not to you because you do not share my bodily experiences, then do we really have any shared understanding of what it is to say that we profess belief in "one Lord Jesus Christ," of whose body we are a part?

Accordingly, some postmodern scholars have probed the "we" assumptions — that is, the idea that "we" have a shared view of the world. They say there is no longer any "grand narrative" (another way to understand "grand narrative" might be to see it as "cultural assumptions" about the way the world is) in which all people can participate, like the story that Christianity tells about what the world is. The world, on the Christian view, is fallen, in need of redemption, and that redemption comes in the person of Jesus Christ. Once, people held that narrative as true, but now, in our secular culture, we cannot assume that acquiescence to the story. In the absence of a grand narrative, how is a person to think about and understand the world?

The answers of some postmodern thinkers have related to the idea that the meaning of the world is constructed by societies or by power structures. What it means to be a woman in the United States is constructed by our sense of what a woman should look like, and we develop that sense through television, movies, what we read, what girls tell each other in the bathroom in junior high, what boys tell girls on dates, what magazines suggest about how to dress, wear makeup, and act, and on and on. However, if we were to be in another culture — say, the culture in Saudi Arabia — our understanding of what it means to be a woman would be constructed in a very different way. Postmodern theorists take this idea still further, proclaiming that gender is a fluid concept within a culture itself, that what it means to be a man or a woman is not definitively set by biological bodies. (See Judith Butler's book titled *Bodies That Matter*.)

Sarah Coakley's essay comprises the final excerpts in this chapter and demonstrates one feminist theologian's use of this postmodern view of bodies that is fluid and performative. In much of her work, Coakley uses sources such as Gregory of Nyssa to show how they offer a surprising account of gender and bodies, surprising because feminists like Ruether have tended to see these authors as patriarchal more often than not. For example, Gregory discusses virginity as a way to be "fecund," but not in the sense that married men and women bear children. Ascetics give birth to spiritual children, even to the point of "giving birth to ourselves by our own free choice in accordance with whatever we wish to be, whether male or female, molding ourselves to the teaching of virtue or vice" (Coakley 2002, 164).

In excerpt **12.8**, Coakley takes on arguments against women's ordination (she herself is an ordained Anglican priest), namely those of Mary Douglas and Hans Urs von Balthasar. Douglas and Balthasar both maintain that ordination of women is problematic because of the gender binaries that God has put forth. Christ is the bridegroom of the church, the bride; the feminine qualities that women have are already superior to the masculine qualities that men have because women can be Marian in the sense of totally assenting to God's will. Balthasar argues, "The Catholic Church is perhaps humanity's last bulwark of genuine appreciation of the difference of the sexes" (quoted in Sarah Coakley 2004, 85).

Coakley thinks that Douglas and Balthasar have both hit on important points about what it means to be a woman or a man, but she also thinks that their arguments against ordination belie another, more interesting meaning. Balthasar sees, for example, that the male priesthood takes on both masculine and feminine characteristics, though he is physiologically male. Coakley finds this fascinating, for she agrees: a priest's role displays the fluidity of gender, but it causes her to ask why women, too, couldn't be part of this gender-bending, this playfulness with bodies.

In the final excerpt (**12.9**), then, Coakley describes the motions of her body as she celebrates the Eucharist and finds that she herself experiences fluid gender play. She remains a woman, and yet she takes on both femininity and masculinity. On Coakley's view, this gender fluidity shows God's breaking into our world and transforming it, even while also keeping the world as it is. Such a claim is good news for us, with our limited human bodies, because it gives us a way of understanding how our bodies might be limited and frustrating, but also capable of transcendence and transformation.

Perhaps Coakley's view of bodies is the most empowering and realistic of the feminist theologies presented. Rather than seeing a body, with all its limits, weaknesses, and troubles, as something to be surpassed, or conversely as something to be wholeheartedly embraced, Coakley offers both. Could this be a way of recognizing that while humans cannot get outside of their bodies, there are still many ways in which bodies can be "played" beyond seeing a person with a disability as someone with a broken body that needs something done to it?

Conclusion

Women are disabled. I hope that by this point, my readers will see that making this statement opens up a broad range of views about women, disability, and especially bodies, views that are both positive and negative. Yet the danger in this statement — and indeed in an essay of this kind — is to make it seem that all these differing points about feminist theologians have mostly to do with women and, as a sideline, with disabled people.

Isn't this all academic nonsense if it doesn't say something helpful? Aren't these mere mind games for academics (ironically) if discussions about bodies don't lead to something concrete? The point of studying feminist theology and bodies is to consider whether, from these particular points of view that *don't* arise from studying Karl Barth and the church fathers, Ruether, Eiesland, Coakley, and others are saying something truthful about human bodies. If we are reading them well, these theologians should cause us all to wonder and ask questions about our bodies — "Am I, too, a disabled body somehow?" — regardless of whether we fit into neat categories called "woman" or "disabled."

A world that sees "normal" bodies as young, athletic, healthy, and male (or women's bodies as smooth, sleek, thin sex objects) — is not a world that understands itself as God does. "Normal" bodies require no help. Yet the prophets say that God views the world as fallen and in need of redemption. In that view, how can there truly be a "normal" body? Indeed, it could be said that Christianity makes all of our bodies abnormal. Jesus Christ's salvation of us involves making us part of a new body that is strangely his (even his broken, bruised body on the cross), and yet comprised of all Christians — past, present, and future.)

The truthful speech that feminist theologians offer about bodies should push us all to consider ourselves as disabled in some way, needing to be redeemed by a Christ whose own body is broken. Bodily redemption is not perfection in the way that patriarchal culture has often defined it.

The other lesson of feminist theologies and their wide-ranging discussion of bodies should be to add humility into the equation. To say "I am disabled" should not thereby lead to the mistaken notion that somehow I might now understand what it means to be blind or autistic. Rather, the very diversity of feminist theologies on the issue of bodies ought to spur us to understand that we do not fully understand, nor are we done with the need for seeking understanding of others around us.

References

Primary Sources

Coakley, Sarah. 2004. "The Woman at the Altar: Cosmological Disturbance or Gender Subversion?" *Anglican Theological Review* 86, no. 1 (Winter): 75-94.

Eiesland, Nancy. 1994. *The Disabled God: Toward a Liberatory Theology of Disability.* Nashville: Abingdon Press.

Ruether, Rosemary Radford. 1983; revised, 1993. *Sexism and God-Talk: Toward a Feminist Theology.* Boston: Beacon Hill Press.

Secondary Sources

Block, Jennifer. 2007. *Pushed: The Painful Truth about Childbirth and Modern Maternity Care.* Cambridge, Mass.: Da Capo Lifelong Books.

Coakley, Sarah. 2002. "The Eschatological Body: Gender, Transformation, and God." In *Powers and Submissions: Spirituality, Philosophy, and Gender.* Oxford: Blackwell Publishers.

Elshout, Elly, et al. 1994. "Roundtable Discussion: Women with Disabilities: A

Challenge to Feminist Theology." *Journal of Feminist Studies in Religion* 10, no. 2 (Fall): 99-134.

Freeman, Doreen. 2002. "A Feminist Theology of Disability." *Feminist Theology* 10, no. 29 (January): 71-85.

Fulkerson, Mary McClintock. 1994. *Changing the Subject: Women's Discourses and Feminist Theology.* Minneapolis: Fortress Press.

Isherwood, Lisa. 2007. "What's God Got to Do with It?" *Feminist Theology* 15, no. 3 (May): 265-74.

Newell, Christopher. 2007. "Disabled Theologians and the Journeys of Liberation Where Our Names Appear." *Feminist Theology* 15, no. 3 (May): 322-45.

O'Neill, Mary Aquin. 1993. "The Mystery of Being Human Together." In *Freeing Theology: The Essentials of Theology in Feminist Perspective.* Edited by Catherine Mowry LaCugna. San Francisco: HarperSanFrancisco.

Scully, Jackie Leach. 2003. "Drawing Lines, Crossing Lines: Ethics and the Challenge of Disabled Embodiment." *Feminist Theology* 11, no. 3 (May): 265-80.

Thomas Aquinas. 1981. *The Summa Theologica of St. Thomas Aquinas.* London and New York: Christian Classics.

For Further Reading

Butler, Judith. 1993. *Bodies That Matter: On the Discursive Limits of Sex.* First edition. New York: Routledge.

Creamer, Deborah Beth. 2009. *Disability and Christian Theology: Embodied Limits and Constructive Possibilities.* New York: Oxford University Press.

hooks, bell, and Cornel West. 1991. *Breaking Bread: Insurgent Black Intellectual Life.* Cambridge, Mass.: South End Press.

Isherwood, Lisa, and Elizabeth Stuart. 2000. *Introducing Body Theology.* Cleveland: Pilgrim Press.

Lacquer, Thomas. 1990. *Making Sex: Body and Gender from the Greeks to Freud.* Cambridge, Mass., and London: Harvard University Press.

Roberts, Dorothy. 1998. *Killing the Black Body: Race, Reproduction, and the Meaning of Liberty.* New York and Toronto: Vintage.

Trible, Phyllis. 1984. *Texts of Terror: Literary-Feminist Readings of Biblical Narratives.* Minneapolis: Fortress Press.

Excerpts

12.1

Rosemary Radford Ruether. *Sexism and God-Talk: Toward a Feminist Theology.* Boston: Beacon Hill Press: 1983; revised, 1993. Chapter 4: "Anthropology: Humanity as Male and Female," 93-98.

When we examine the theological tradition we see an ambiguity in the way *imago dei*/sin has been correlated with maleness and femaleness. On the one hand, deeply rooted in Christian thought is an affirmation of the equivalence of maleness and femaleness in the image of God. This has never been denied, but it has tended to become obscured by a second tendency to correlate femaleness with the lower part of human nature in a hierarchical scheme of mind over body, reason over passions. Since this lower part of the self is seen as the source of sin — the falling away of the body from its original unity with the mind and hence into sin and death — femaleness also becomes linked with the sin-prone part of the self. . . .

  This ambiguous structure of Christian anthropology expresses what today might be called a "case of projection." Males, as the monopolizers of theological self-definition, project onto women their own rejection of their "lower selves." Women, although equivalent in the image of God, nevertheless symbolize the lower self, representing this in their physical, sexual nature. This notion that woman, in her physical, sexual nature, not only symbolizes but incarnates lower human nature and tendency to sin seldom fails to revert to the theological definition of woman's equivalence in the image of God. Woman in her essential nature is seen as having less of the higher spiritual nature and more of the lower physical nature. She is an "inferior mix" and, as such, is by nature non-normative and under subjugation.

Patriarchal Anthropology

The patriarchal Christianity that came to dominate the Christian Church in classical orthodoxy never went so far as to completely deny women's participation in the image of God. To link woman only with the sin-prone part of the self would have been to deny her any redeemability. Christianity would have become a males-only religion to be entered by rejection of women as bearers of sin. At times, in theological definitions, and, even more, in popular diatribe, Christian churchmen came perilously close to this view of woman as sin. While allowing woman baptism, patriarchal theology stressed her "greater aptness" for sin and her lesser spirituality. As an "inferior mix," woman can never as fully represent the image of God as a man who is seen as representing the rational and spiritual part of the self.

Even in the original, unfallen creation, woman would have been subordinate and under the domination of man. Normatively and ideally, the woman should have deferred to the man, who represents, in greater fullness than herself, the principle of "headship," mind or reason. He, in turn, should regard her as representing the part of himself that must be repressed and kept under control by reason to prevent a fall into sin and disorder. According to most traditional Christian theology, this would have been the case even in "paradise." Within sinful, fallen, historical conditions, however, woman's suppression must be redoubled. Proneness to sin and disorder is no longer potential but actual, and woman is particularly responsible for it. Within history, woman's subjugation is both the reflection of her inferior nature and the punishment for her responsibility for sin.

This pattern of patriarchal anthropology can be illustrated in the entire line of classical Christian theology from ancient to modern times. I mention here particularly Augustine, Aquinas, Luther, and Barth.

Augustine is the classical source of this type of patriarchal anthropology. Although elements of it are present in the New Testament and in earlier patristic theologians, Augustine expresses all aspects of it explicitly. He is, in turn, the source for this type of anthropology for the later Western Christian tradition, both Catholic and Protestant, which looks to Augustine as the font of orthodoxy. Although Augustine concedes woman's redeemability and hence her participation in the image of God, it is so overbalanced by her bodily representation of inferior, sin-prone self that he regards her as possessing the image of God only secondarily. The male alone possesses the image of God normatively. Thus in his discussion of the image of God, reflected in the Trinity, Augustine says:

> How then did the apostle tell us that man is the image of God and therefore he is forbidden to cover his head, but that the woman is not so and therefore she is commanded to cover hers? Unless forsooth according to that which I have said already, when I was treating of the nature of the human mind, that the woman, together with her own husband, is the image of God, so that the whole substance may be one image, but when she is re-

443

ferred to separately in her quality as a helpmeet, which regards the woman alone, then she is not the image of God, but as regards the male alone, he is the image of God as fully and completely as when the woman too is joined with him in one. (*De Trinitate* 7.7.10)

Aquinas continues the Augustinian tradition. But he makes woman's "symbolism" of the inferior side of the self literal by accepting a biological theory of woman's inferiority. Aquinas adopted the Aristotelian definition of woman as a "misbegotten male." According to Aristotelian biology, the male seed provides the "form" of the human body. Woman's reproductive role contributes only the matter that "fleshes out" this formative power of the male seed. Normatively, every male insemination would produce another male in the "image" of its father. But by some accident, this male form is sometimes subverted by the female matter and produces an inferior or defective human species, or female. This inferiority touches the entire nature of woman. She is inferior in body (weaker), inferior in mind (less capable of reason), and inferior morally (less capable of will and moral self-control).

This inferiority has been deepened by sin, according to Aquinas. But even in the original created state, woman's defective nature meant that she was by nature servile and under subjection. This creates a problem for Aquinas: why would woman have been created at all, given that God should not have created anything defective in the original plan of things? Aquinas concludes that woman, although defective and misbegotten in her individual nature, nevertheless belongs to the overall "perfection" of nature because of her role in procreation. It is for this and this alone that a separate female member of the human species has been created by God; for any form of spiritual help, man is better served by a companion of the same sex than by woman.

In Aquinas's words, domination and subjugation in human relations are "twofold": In the social order that arose after sin, the ruler uses subjects for the benefit of the ruler, but even before sin there was also inequality. Males naturally excel at the higher faculty of reason; females have less rational capacity and are less capable of moral self-control. Good order requires that the naturally superior rule the naturally inferior.[1] Aquinas also believes in

---

1. Thomas Aquinas, *Summa Theologica*, pt. 1, q. 92, art. 1. See also Kari Børresen, *Subordination and Equivalence: The Nature and Role of Women in Augustine and Thomas Aquinas* (Washington, D.C.: University Press of America, 1981; originally published in French in 1968).

class hierarchy and slavery as necessary for social order. For him these servile relations have become necessary because of sin; but male-female hierarchy was not just a product of sin; it was a part of the natural order created by
God.

The Reformation brought slight modifications, but no essential change
in this line of patriarchal anthropology. Luther draws on the monastic and
mystical tradition in asserting that, in the original creation, Eve would have
been equal with Adam. Luther suggests that the original Eve cannot even be
known by reference to the present nature of woman:

> For the punishment that she is now subjected to the man was imposed on
> her after sin and because of sin, just as the other hardships and dangers
> were: travail, pain, and countless other vexations. Therefore Eve was not
> like the woman of today; her state was far better and more excellent, and
> she was in no respect inferior to Adam, whether you count the qualities of
> the body or those of the mind.[2]

Woman, through the Fall and in punishment for the Fall, lost her original equality and became inferior in mind and body. She is now, within fallen
history, subjected to the male as her superior. This subjugation is not a sin
against her but her punishment for her sin. It is the expression of divine justice. Any revolt, or even complaint, against it by woman is a caviling refusal
to accept the judgment of God. . . .

Thus Luther's use of the doctrine of original equality of Eve with Adam
does not become a source for theological re-evaluation of woman's historical
subjugation. On the contrary, it simply deepens the reproach of her as one
whose sinfulness lost this original equality and merited the punishment of
subjugation.

The Calvinist tradition connects equivalence and subordination differently from both Luther and the earlier Catholic tradition. In Calvinism,
women not only were but are equivalent with men in the image of God. In
their essential nature, women have as much capacity for conscience and
spiritual things as do men. The subordination of women to men is not an expression of an inferiority either in nature or in fallen history. Rather it reflects the divinely created social order by which God has ordained the rule of
some and the subjugation of others: rulers over subjects, masters over ser-

2. Martin Luther, *Lectures on Genesis,* Gen. 2:18, in *Luther's Works,* vol. 1, ed. Jaroslav
Pelikan (St. Louis: Concordia Publishing House, 1958), 115.

vants, husbands over wives, parents over children. This hierarchical order is not a reflection of differences of human nature but rather of differences of appointed *social office*. The man rules not because he is superior but because God has commanded him to do so. The woman obeys not because she is inferior but because that is the role God has assigned her. Social offices are necessary for good order in society. . . .

12.2

Rosemary Radford Ruether. *Sexism and God-Talk*. Chapter 4: "Anthropology: Humanity as Male and Female," 99-101.

Eschatological Feminism

Eschatological feminism is a perspective that developed parallel and even earlier than patriarchal Christianity, during the late first and second centuries. It is a way of interpreting what Elisabeth Schüssler Fiorenza has called the "egalitarian counter-cultural trend" of early Christianity. It has generally been connected with mystical ascetic sects and movements, condemned as heretical, although it has never been entirely absent from orthodox asceticism and mysticism. Remnants of it continue throughout monastic theology. It bursts forth again in Protestantism among left-wing mystical, Utopian, and millenarian sects, such as the mysticism of Jacob Boehme, the German Rappites, or the Anglo-American Shakers.

Eschatological feminism affirmed the restored equality of men and women in Christ by referring to an original transcendent anthropology that existed before the fall into the finite condition characterized by sexual dimorphism. Male and female were equal in this transcendent state. This idea takes several forms in early Christian Gnosticism. In one version original humanity was united in a spiritual androgene. Adam was both male and female, united and whole. The fall of Adam represents the splitting apart of this androgynous humanity into sexual maleness and femaleness. This also signifies the fall into mortality, finitude, and death; hence the necessity for sexual reproduction to compensate in history for the loss of immortality. Christ represents the restored androgynous Adam. He makes available to the redeemed the original lost humanity. Salvation consists of transcending our sexual, bodily nature through ascetic practices and recovering our spiritual, androgynous nature. This also signifies the escape from mortal into immortal existence. Celibacy typically is seen as the key expression of redeemed humanity that has left the world and is preparing for Heaven.

Gnosticism can easily fall into an androcentric androgyny that correlates with the male part of the original androgynous humanity with spirituality and the female with carnality. In orthodox male monasticism this androcentric androgyny would then reinforce the sort of patriarchal anthropology we have discussed. But Gnosticism also suggests that there is a spiritual femaleness as well as a carnal femaleness. God is both male and female. Holy Wisdom, the female persona of God, mediates the fall into bodiliness and also the escape from creation into redeemed spiritual life. In the words of Shaker theology, "We have a Mother as well as a Father in Heaven." Redeemed humanity as male and female represents the reuniting of the self, in both its spiritual masculinity and its spiritual femininity, against the splitting into sexual maleness and sexual femaleness. . . .

Eschatological feminism implicitly agrees that the subordination of women in society is unchangeable within history. Sexuality, the division into gender, splits spiritual humanity and brings about the subordination of woman to man. Whether divinely mandated or the result of sin, patriarchy is of the nature of historical existence. Original equality restored in Christ, therefore, cannot change this historical condition; it can only free one to escape from it into a transcendent sphere.

12.3

Rosemary Radford Ruether. *Sexism and God-Talk*. Chapter 4: "Anthropology: Humanity as Male and Female," 102-3.

Liberal Feminism

Liberal feminism has roots in both Biblical and scholastic anthropology, but it represents a radical remodeling of the patriarchal component of these traditions under the impact of the eighteenth-century Enlightenment. Liberalism rejects the classical tradition that identified nature or the order of creation with patriarchy. Instead it identifies nature or order of creation with the original unfallen *imago dei* and affirms the equivalence of all human beings in this original creation. All human beings, male and female, share a common human nature, characterized by reason and moral conscience. Liberalism takes a minimalist rather than an exalted view of the human nature that all human beings share equally. It is not a question of whether all people are geniuses or saints. Rather, the common possession of reason and moral conscience means simply that, as the eighteenth-century French philosopher Condorcet puts it, "that men are beings with sensibility, capable of acquiring moral ideas and of reasoning on these ideas." From this possession of a common human nature flows equal rights in society, according to Condorcet: "So women, having these same qualities, have necessarily equal rights. Either no individual of the human race has genuine rights or else all have the same; and he who votes against the right of another, whatever the religion, color or sex of that other, has henceforth abjured his own."[3]

Liberalism secularizes the doctrine of the *imago dei*. The equivalence of male and female refers to the actual capacities of men and women as finite, historical persons. Whence then come patriarchy and the distortion of equality into domination and subjugation? Liberalism interprets this not as a fall into bodily, finite existence but as a fall into injustice. Historical injustice has distorted the original equivalence of all human beings and has created instead hierarchical societies of privilege and deprivation, domination and exploitation. The common rights of all persons to property and to participation in the government have been distorted into inherited privileges of the few based on false concepts of innate superiority. The rest of humanity — lower classes, nonwhite races, and women — have been deprived of their human rights and reduced to subjugation.

12.4

Rosemary Radford Ruether. *Sexism and God-Talk*. Chapter 4: "Anthropology: Humanity as Male and Female," 104-8.

Romantic Feminism

In contrast to liberal feminism, romantic feminism stresses the differences between male and female as representative of complementary opposites:

3. "Condorcet's Pleas for the Citizenship of Women," *The Fortnightly Review* 13, no. 42 (June 1870): 719-20. Translated from *Journal de la Société de 1789*, 3 July 1790.

femininity and masculinity. In contrast to patriarchal anthropology, romantic feminism takes its definition of femaleness not from carnality and sin but from spiritual femininity, that is, intuitive spirituality, altruism, emotional sensitivity, and moral (sexual) purity. These ideas of spiritual femininity are particularly developed in Mariology. But Mariology, in classical Catholicism, is set against historical women as representatives of carnal femaleness. Mary was the spiritual lady in whose service one rejected real (carnal) females. In Protestantism and bourgeois Catholicism, Mariological femininity is partly secularized to characterize the ideal nature of women, especially middle-class wives or "good Christian women."

Romanticism comes close to reversing the traditional patriarchal correlation of *imago dei* and fallen humanity with spiritual maleness and carnal femaleness. Instead it is the female who represents, in a purer and less ambiguous way, the original goodness of humanity as *imago dei*. This does not mean that men do not also possess this good human nature originally. But because they have to enter the sphere of power, competition, and sin, the good human nature becomes obscured in men. Men, as makers of history, take on the nature of historical humanity characterized by force and domination. Women, as those forbidden to enter the sphere of force and domination, retain more of the original purity and goodness of human nature. Women, shielded from history, are *less fallen* than men. They are more capable of altruistic, loving, self-giving life, less prone to the sins of egoism that are a sinful but necessary part of historical existence. . . .

Conservative Romanticism

Conservative romanticism correlates the sphere of altruism, purity, and love with the home and the realm of pride, egoism, and sin with the public sphere of politics, war and work. Woman, although ideally the exponent of a higher, more loving humanity, possesses this good nature only in a fragile and vulnerable way. She can preserve her goodness only by the strictest segregation in the home, by eschewing all participation in the realm of public power. If woman leaves the home to take up a traditional male occupation, she will straightway lose this good femininity and become a she-male, a monstrous virago, or will become debased to carnal femaleness, fallen woman. . . .

JANA BENNETT

Reformist Romanticism

Reformist romanticism agrees with conservative romanticism in the belief in woman's purer and less ambiguous nature and its correlation with her role as nurturer of husband and children in the home. Unlike conservative romanticism, it takes more literally the view of the good nature of woman as innate rather than as something woman might lose if she enters the sphere of power. Reformist romanticism shares with liberalism the belief that the higher nature of humanity can be a basis for reform of social institutions rather than just a call to escape from them into a separate and more spiritual sphere. For reformist feminism, the bourgeois ideal of the family is seen as a launching pad for a mission into the world to uplift and transform it to the higher standards of goodness, peace, and loving service of womanhood and the home.

Woman's mission to uplift not just men but male institutions to the higher standards of the home was expressed in the most wide-ranging programs of social reform during the era of the Social Gospel in late-nineteenth-century America. Leaders like Frances Willard of the Women's Christian Temperance Union were particularly effective in converting the language of conservative romanticism into the program of reformist romantic feminism. Women as educators of children must become founders of schools, particularly for infants and small children. As mothers, women have a natural interest in orphanages to provide homes for the homeless. As the keepers of cleanliness, they should extend themselves in all sorts of campaigns against dirt and disorder in society, ranging from physical dirt to political corruption. . . .

Unlike conservative romanticism, however, reformists don't think women can accomplish this vision by staying at home and uplifting men on a private level. Women must enter the world and use their higher instincts to change its social structures and relationships. To do this, they must have power. They need the vote and the right to education and political office. . . .

12.5

Rosemary Radford Ruether. *Sexism and God-Talk.* Chapter 4: "Anthropology: Humanity as Male and Female," 109-10.

Toward a Feminist Anthropology Beyond Liberalism and Romanticism

Contemporary feminism inherits the traditions of both liberal and romantic feminism. It becomes divided and confused over the opposite values and directions espoused by each viewpoint. Both liberalism and romanticism are inadequate and yet both testify to important truths that I wish to affirm. A more adequate feminist anthropology would be one that finds a creative synthesis between the two. Liberal feminism too readily identifies normative human nature with those capacities for reason and rule identified with men and the public sphere. It claims that women, while appearing to have lesser capacities for these attributes, actually possess them equally; they have simply been denied the opportunity to exercise them. Opening up equal education and equal political rights to women will correct this and allow women's suppressed capacities for reason and rule to appear in their actual equivalence to men's.

There is important truth to this. Women, through the opening of equal education and political rights, have indeed demonstrated their ability to exercise the "same" capacities as men. But liberalism does not entirely recognize the more complex forms of women's psychological and economic marginalization that result in only token integration of women into "equal" roles in the public sphere. Liberalism assumes the traditional male sphere as normative and believes it is wrong to deny people access to it on the basis of gender. But once women are allowed to enter the public sphere, liberalism offers no critique of the modes of functioning within it.

Romanticism, in contrast, recognizes the moral ambiguity of the roles traditionally associated with masculinity. It idealizes the home, the private sphere of interpersonal relations, and places of "unspoiled nature" outside of urbanization and industrialization as havens of a more integrated humanity. It idealizes women precisely in their segregation from this ambiguous world. It tends to overlook the ambiguity and violence present in the sphere of private relationships, both the violation of women to keep them there and the way in which unexpressed angers and frustrations from the work world can be unleashed in the home. Altruism and service, while compensating women for acquiescence to relations of domination, also become a means of passive aggression masquerading as "helping others."

Romanticism is not entirely wrong in believing there are clues to a better humanity in the virtues relegated to women and the home in bourgeois society. But these virtues exist in deformed and deforming ways within the institutionalization of "woman's sphere." Moreover, the capacities traditionally associated with men and with public life also contain some important human virtues that women should not be forbidden to cultivate.

Thus neither masculinity traditionally defined nor femininity traditionally defined discloses an innately good human nature, and neither is simply an expression of evil. Both represent different types of alienation of humanity from its original potential. Socially, both home and work represent realms of corruption. If women will not be automatically redeemed by being incorporated into male political power and business in its present form, men will not automatically be redeemed by learning to nurture infants and keep house. . . .

12.6

Rosemary Radford Ruether. *Sexism and God-Talk.* Chapter 5: "Christology: Can a Male Savior Save Women?" 135-38.

A Feminist Christology?

. . . Fundamentally, Jesus renews the prophetic vision whereby the Word of God does not validate the existing social and religious hierarchy but speaks on behalf of the marginalized and despised groups of society. Jesus proclaims an iconoclastic reversal of the system of religious status: The last shall be first and the first last. The leaders of the religious establishment are blind guides and hypocrites. The outcasts of society — prostitutes, publicans, Samaritans — are able to hear the message of the prophet. This reversal of social order doesn't just turn the hierarchy upside down; it aims at a new reality in which hierarchy and dominance are overcome as principles of social relations.

Jesus revises God-language by using the familiar *Abba* for God. He speaks of the Messiah as servant rather than king to visualize new relations between the divine and the human. Relation to God no longer becomes a model for dominant-subordinate relations between social groups, leaders, and the led. Rather, relation to God means we are to call no man "Father, Teacher, or Master" (Matt. 23:1-12). Relation to God liberates us from hierarchical relations and makes us all brothers-sisters of each other. Those who would be leaders must become servants of all.

Women play an important role in this Gospel vision of the vindication of the lowly in God's new order. It is the women of the oppressed and marginalized groups who are often pictured as the representatives of the lowly. The dialogue at the well takes place with a Samaritan woman. A Syro-Phoenician woman is the prophetic seeker who forces Jesus to concede redemption to the Gentiles. Among the poor it is the widows who are the most destitute. Among the ritually unclean, it is the woman with the flow of blood who exhorts healing for herself contrary to the law. Among the morally outcast, it is the prostitutes who are the furthest from righteousness. The role played by women of marginalized groups is an intrinsic part of the iconoclastic, messianic vision. It means that the women are the oppressed of the oppressed. They are the bottom of the present social hierarchy and hence are seen, in a special way, as the last who will be first in the Kingdom of God.

This role is quite different from doctrines of romantic complementarity. The Gospels do not operate with a dualism of the masculine and feminine. The widow, the prostitute, and the Samaritan woman are not representatives of the "feminine," but rather they represent those who have no honor in the present system of religious righteousness. As women they are the doubly despised within these groups. They carry the double burden of low class and low gender status. The protest of the Gospels is directed at the concrete sociological realities in which maleness and femaleness are elements, along with class, ethnicity, religious office, and law, that define the network of social status.

Jesus as liberator calls for a renunciation, a dissolution, of the web of status relationships by which societies have defined privilege and deprivation. He protests against the identification of this system with the favor or disfavor of God. His ability to speak as liberator does not reside in his maleness but in the fact that he has renounced this system of domination and seeks to embody in his person the new humanity of service and mutual empowerment. He speaks to and is responded to by low-caste women because they represent the bottom of this status network and have the least stake in its perpetuation.

Theologically speaking, then, we might say that the maleness of Jesus has no ultimate significance. It has social symbolic significance in the framework of societies of patriarchal privilege. In this sense Jesus as the Christ, the representative of liberated humanity and the liberating Word of God, manifests through *kenosis of patriarchy* the announcement of the new humanity through a lifestyle that discards hierarchical caste privilege and speaks on behalf of the lowly. In a similar way, the femaleness of the social and religiously outcast who respond to him has social symbolic significance as a witness against the same idolatrous system of patriarchal privilege. This system is unmasked and shown to have no connection with favor with God. Jesus, the homeless Jewish prophet, and the marginalized women and men who respond to him represent the overthrow of the present world system and the sign of a dawning new age in which God's will is done on earth.

But this relation of redeeming Christ and redeemed women should not be made into ultimate theological gender symbols. Christ is not necessarily male, nor is the redeemed community only women, but a new humanity, female and male. We need to think in terms of a dynamic, rather than a static, relationship between redeemer and redeemed. The redeemer is one who has been redeemed, just as Jesus himself accepted the baptism of John. Those who have been liberated can, in turn, become paradigmatic, liberating persons for others.

Christ, as the redemptive person and Word of God, is not to be encapsulated "once-for-all" in the historical Jesus. The Christian community continues Christ's identity. As vine and branches Christic personhood continues in our sisters and brothers. In the language of early Christian prophetism, we can encounter Christ *in the form of our sister.* Christ, the liberated humanity, is not confined to a static perfection of one person two thousand years ago. Rather, redemptive humanity goes ahead of us, calling us to yet incompleted dimensions of human liberation.

12.7

Nancy Eiesland. *The Disabled God: Toward a Liberatory Theology of Disability.* Nashville: Abingdon Press, 1994, 100-105.

Theological Implications of the Disabled God

The symbol of Jesus Christ, the disabled God, has transformative power. It is the experience of Christ from below as a corporeal experience. The power of the disabled God is the seemingly inherent contradiction this God embodies. This revelation of God disorders the social-symbolic order, and God appears in the most unexpected bodies. The disabled God does not engage in a battle for dominance or create a new normative power. God is in the present social-symbolic order at the margins with people with disabilities and instigates transformation from this de-centered position.

The disabled God repudiates the conception of disability as a consequence of individual sin. Injustice against persons with disabilities is surely sin; our bodies, however, are not artifacts of sin, original or otherwise. Our bodies participate in the imago Dei, not in spite of our impairments and contingencies, but through them. The conflation of sin and disability causes problems for the interpretation of the resurrected Jesus Christ. What is the significance of the resurrected Christ's display of impaired hands and feet and side? Are they the disfiguring vestiges of sin? Are they to be subsumed under the image of Christ, death conqueror? Or should the disability of Christ be understood as the truth of incarnation and the promise of resurrection? The latter interpretation fosters a reconception of wholeness. It suggests a human-God who not only knows injustice and experiences the contingency of human life, but also reconceives perfection as unself-pitying, painstaking survival.

The resurrected Jesus Christ in presenting impaired hands and feet and side to be touched by frightened friends alters the taboo of physical avoidance of disability and calls for the followers to recognize their connection and equality at the point of Christ's physical impairment. Christ's disfigured side bears witness to the existence of "hidden" disabilities as well. Historically, interpretations of the "pierced" side of Jesus have emphasized the tragedy of innocent suffering. But understanding the internal damage wrought by hacking swords as part of God's eternal existence necessitates a deromanticization of interpretations of Christ's impaired body and a recognition of the population of people who identify with Christ's experience of disabilities, hidden and displayed, as part of our hidden history. For many people whose hidden disabilities keep them from participating fully in the church or from feeling full-bodied acceptance by Christ, accepting the disabled God may enable reconciliation with their own bodies and Christ's body the church. Hence, disability not only does not contradict the human-divine integrity, it becomes a new model of wholeness and a symbol of solidarity.

Feminist criticisms of the symbolism of Jesus as the male Galilean and lordly Christ — a problematic image for women — notwithstanding, the image of Jesus Christ, the disabled God, is not inherently oppressive for

455

women, particularly women with disabilities. The disabled God provides a new way of identifying with the physical reality of Jesus. Clearly feminists and marginalized people cannot continue to support an

> image of Christ [which] is manipulated in the praxis of privilege (by those on the top, representatives of white male gentry) not only to symbolize the suffering servant, with whom those on the bottom can identify in terms of passive acceptance of suffering; but also, because Christ is God, to symbolize the rulership of all that is established, the guardian and custodian of all human and "natural" resources.[1]

Nonetheless, one need not move from a rejection of this image of Christ to a negation of either the physical presence or the divinity of Jesus Christ. Jesus Christ, the disabled God, is not a suffering servant or a conquering lord. Rather, this contextualization of Jesus enables that "the Christ understood as the stranger, the outcast, the hungry, the weak, the poor, [and I would add the person with disabilities] makes the traditional male Christ (Black and White) less significant."[2] The significance of the disabled God is not primarily maleness, but rather physicality. Jesus Christ the disabled God is consonant with the image of Jesus Christ the stigmatized Jew, person of color, and representative of the poor and hungry — those who have struggled to maintain the integrity and dignity of their bodies in the face of the physical mutilation of injustice and rituals of bodily degradation.

Jesus Christ the disabled God is not a romanticized notion of "overcomer" God. Instead, here is God as survivor. Here language fails because the term "survivor" in our society is contaminated with notions of victimization, radical individualism, and alienation, as well as with an ethos of virtuous suffering. In contradistinction to that cultural icon, the image of survivor here evoked is that of a simple, unself-pitying, honest body, for whom the limits of power are palpable but not tragic. The disabled God embodies the ability to see clearly the complexity and the "mixed blessing" of life and bodies, without living in despair. This revelation is of a God for us who celebrates joy and experiences pain not separately in time or space but simultaneously.

The disabled God is God for whom interdependence is not a possibility

---

1. Carter Heyward, *Our Passion for Justice* (New York: Pilgrim Press, 1984), 145.

2. Jacquelyn Grant, *White Women's Christ and Black Women's Jesus: Feminist Christology and Womanist Response* (Atlanta: Scholars Press, 1989), 219.

to be willed from a position of power, but a necessary condition for life. This interdependence is the fact of both justice and survival. The disabled God embodies practical interdependence, not simply willing to be interrelated from a position of power, but depending on it from a position of need. For many people with disabilities, too, mutual care is a matter of survival. To posit a Jesus Christ who needs care and mutuality as essential to human-divine survival does not symbolize either humanity or divinity as powerless. Instead, it debunks the myth of individualism and hierarchical orders, in which transcendence means breaking free of encumbrances and needing nobody and constitutes the divine as somebody in relation to other bodies.

This disabled God makes possible a renewal of hope for people with disabilities and others who care. This symbol points not to a utopian vision of hope as the erasure of all human contingency, historically or eternally, for that would be to erase our bodies, our lives. Rather, it is a liberatory realism that maintains a clear recognition of the limits of our bodies and an acceptance of limits as the truth of being human. This liberatory realism also calls for a realization of the necessity of a social and interpersonal transformation that does not surrender to cynicism and defeatism any more than the limits of our bodies suggest that we should do nothing. It locates our hope in justice as access and mutuality, a justice that removes the barriers which constrain our bodies, keep us excluded, and intend to humiliate us. It also situates our hope in the reality of our existence as ones with dignity and integrity. Hope is the recollection and projection that even our nonconventional bodies, which oftentimes dissatisfy us and fail us, are worth the living. It is knowing that the so-called curses sometimes feel like blessings.

The image of the disabled God proceeds from Jesus Christ's embodied commitment to justice as rightly ordered interpersonal and structural relations. This is the God who indicts not only deliberate injustice, but unintended rituals of degradation that deny the full personhood of marginalized people. Moreover, Jesus Christ, the disabled God, disorders the social-symbolic orders of what it means to be incarnate — in flesh — and confirms that "normal" bodies, like impaired bodies, are subject to contingency. And it is a contingency born not of tragedy or sin but of ordinary women and embodied unexceptionably. This representation of God does not gloss over the suffering enacted against bodies as the consequence of injustice; rather, it posits that our bodies cannot be subsumed into injustice or sin.

The disabled God defines the church as a communion of justice. Jesus Christ, the disabled God, is, as Jürgen Moltmann writes,

The one who is to come is then already present in an anticipatory sense in history in the Spirit and the word, and in the miserable and the helpless. His future ends the world's history of suffering and completes the fragments and anticipations of his kingdom which are called the church.[3]

Thus the church, which depends for its existence on the disabled God, must live out liberating action in the world. The church finds its identity as the body of Christ only by being a community of faith and witness, a coalition of struggle and justice, and a fellowship of hope. This mission necessitates that people with disabilities be incorporated into all levels of participation and decision-making.

Jesus Christ as the disabled God provides a symbolic prototype and opens the door to the theological task of re-thinking Christian symbols, metaphors, rituals, and doctrines so as to make them accessible to people with disabilities and remove their able-bodied bias. . . . Liberating our theology from biases against people with disabilities is a process that will require tremendous and continual commitment to identifying with the disabled God in our midst. Even in the process of developing the symbol of Jesus Christ, disabled deity, I have heard numerous objections. Individuals who are heavily invested in a belief in the transcendence of God constituted as a radical otherness will undoubtedly find this representation disconcerting. The theological implications of the disabled God resist the notion of power as absolute control over human-divine affairs. For people with disabilities who have grasped divine healing as the only liberatory image the traditional church has offered, relinquishing belief in an all-powerful God who could heal, if He would, is painful. Yet who is this god whose attention we cannot get, whose inability to respond to our pain causes still more pain? This god is surely not Emmanuel — God for us. The second objection some have expressed is that the articulation of a model of God that incorporates disability signals runaway confusion in the church, and they insist that a halt should be called on all representational language for God. With the emergence of African American, feminist, gay-lesbian, and Latin American liberation theologies in recent history, models of God have proliferated. Yet this representational proliferation does not portend chaos; rather, it is the corporate enactment of the resurrection of God. The body of God is becoming alive, vivified by an insurrection of subjugated knowledges. This resurrection happens, however, only when these

---

3. Jürgen Moltmann, *The Church in the Power of the Spirit: A Contribution to Messianic Ecclesiology* (San Francisco: Harper & Row, 1977), 132.

emerging models of God are more than simply new names for the same symbolic order. The challenge for the Christian is to engage one or more "names" of God and to follow these images into the worlds they open.

Bearing Our Bodies

For me, and I hope, other people with disabilities, as well as for some able-bodied people, the presence of the disabled God makes it possible to bear a nonconventional body. This God enables both a struggle for justice among people with disabilities and an end to estrangement from our own bodies.

12.8

Sarah Coakley. "The Woman at the Altar: Cosmological Disturbance or Gender Subversion?" *Anglican Theological Review* 86, no. 1 (Winter 2004): 75-79.

Introduction and Forecast

In this paper, I wish to develop a speculative line of argument about the nature of the priesthood and its putative connection to eroticism and gender identification. And I want to do this in a way that embraces, rather than eschews, the traditional symbolism of the eucharist as the enactment of nuptial love between Christ and the church. This strategy might seem to be a high-risk one for a feminist theologian and woman priest, and indeed it is: it consciously walks right into the fanned flames of passion surrounding the question of female ordination in conservative Roman Catholic and Orthodox circles, where the very idea of women priests is still denounced as intrinsically gender disordered, indeed as cosmically disturbing to the supposedly "natural" arrangement of sex binaries.[1]

1. The official Roman Catholic pronouncements against the ordination of women can conveniently be found in The Congregation for the Doctrine of the Faith, From *"Inter Insigniores"* to *"Ordinatio Sacerdotalis"* (Washington, D.C.: United States Catholic Conference, 1998). Recent Eastern Orthodox positions are represented in Thomas Hopko, ed., *Women and the Priesthood* (Crestwood, N.Y.: St. Vladimir's Seminary Press, rev. ed., 1999). Both volumes rehearse and discuss the theme of the presumed "unnaturalness" of female priesthood.

A much safer strategy for a feminist theologian, it would seem, would be the *sanitization* of this heady nexus of themes (communion, desire, priestly enactment) by repressing or de-essentializing the symbolism of Christ and his bride, the church. Such a sanitization can be attempted, and of course has been, many times over. The arguments for such sanitization are certainly not without worth, and perhaps should be mentioned here at the start. Three such lines of approach come to mind. One may either, first, on *scriptural* or *theological* grounds, declare erotic symbolism to be disconnected from the New Testament evidence about the institution of the eucharist, only later imposed as a questionable hermeneutical veneer, and now in any case inappropriate to post–Vatican II Catholic ecclesiological sensibilities about the "pilgrim church." Or second, one may urge on *moral grounds* — which today of course are peculiarly pressing — that this nexus fatally confuses the arenas of sexual desire and desire for God in ways inclined subliminally to promote abuse. Or, third, one may insist on an even quicker disposal technique for the nuptial metaphor by taking a stand against it on secular *gender theoretical* grounds, and seeing it as intrinsically misleading precisely because it is sustaining of repressive and stereotypical "gender binaries."

In what follows, however, I shall be exploring none of these well-worn arguments, however important one may judge them to be. Rather, I want to conduct a different sort of thought experiment. I want to see what happens if we relentlessly *pursue* the very logic of the opponents of women priests, that is, if we look more deeply into this problematic nexus of eroticism, gender roles, and priestly mediation of Christ's presence. And (to anticipate my conclusions) I shall be arguing that it is vital so to look — rather than to look *away*: for when we probe the implications of the Christ/church nuptial model more attentively, and reflect on how the priest acts as mediator of that relationship, we shall find it impossible to "fix" the priest as "masculine" alone: the conservative argument fails precisely in the complexities of its enactment. On the contrary, I shall argue, the priest is in an inherently fluid gender role as beater of the liminal bounds between the divine and the human. But in representing *both* "Christ" *and* "church" (that is the first rejoinder to the conservatives), the priest is not simply divine/"masculine" in the first over human/"feminine" in the other, but *both* in *both*. Yet this is not, as is sometimes argued, a form of "androgyny" that either flattens "difference" or downplays erotic meaning. For in the course of the liturgy, the priest moves implicitly through these different roles, strategically summoning the stereotypical gender associations of each, but always destabilizing the attempt to be "held" in one or the other.[2] In short, the gender binaries that *appear* to be being re-valorized liturgically (God/active/"masculine," versus human/receptive/"feminine") are actually being summoned in order subtly to be undermined.[3]

Finally, if I am right, a significant part of the undeniably "erotic" tug of the priest's position at the altar lies in this very destabilization, a gesturing towards a divine "order" of union and communion beyond the tidy human attempts at gender characterization and binary division. Yet the delicacy of such a gesturing cannot simply be predicated on an ideological gender egalitarianism, on the forced *repression* of "difference"; in this the conservative opponents of women's ordination are right. Where they fail is in the attempt to "freeze" the gender binaries back into an order that their very own insights betray.

In short, I shall in this paper seem to be hoisting the remaining opponents of women's ordination on their own petard. Yet that would actually be a somewhat misleading reading. For I offer these reflections less in the spirit of antagonism than of rapprochement; to admit the irreducible significance of the nuptial metaphor is already to have found a deep point of contact and agreement. It is also to have located the source of the profound erotic passion that fuels the disagreement in the first place. Ecumenical advance can therefore only be achieved by attention to this nexus, not avoidance.

Finally, in this introduction, let me admit an element of autobiography in the way this argument has developed, for it has implications for what might be called the epistemological underpinnings of the line of thought to be traced. I must own that I could scarcely have dreamed up this particular collection of ideas in advance of my own ordination to the priesthood (which happened fairly recently, in July 2001). I had already, to be sure, done a lot of research on the connection between prayer (especially contemplative prayer), eroticism, and the development of Trinitarian doctrine in the pa-

2. The emphasis on the *"strategic"* summoning of stereotypical binaries here is important, lest I be misheard as simply recommending their continuation. As will emerge as my argument unfolds, I am presuming that such human binaries do, and will, continue to exercise us in some form, both culturally and theologically; thus "strategic" attention to them, rather than a forced attempt at their obliteration or repression, is in my view required *en route* to their liturgical transformation.

3. A subthesis of this paper will thus be a concomitant questioning of the modern liturgical tendency to "fix" the priest behind the altar in almost unvarying facial availability to the people; here, for contemporary Roman Catholicism in particular, the danger of a "play-acting" of the Christ role, *qua* male, becomes extreme.

tristic era.[4] So my work was already attuned to the problematic nexus of sexual desire and desire for God, a nexus that shows us, I believe, why communion with the divine always tends to summon the erotic metaphor. But my investigation of *liturgical,* and specifically eucharistic, prayer in this context had been regrettably slight.[5] It was only in learning to celebrate the eucharist myself, in immersing myself in something of the history of eucharistic enactment, and in so doing finding that I had to make a host of apparently minor choices nonetheless encoded with immense theological significance, that I began fully to appreciate the gender and erotic latency of the eucharistic act. Any new priest will be aware of the intensity of these choices. How to modulate one's gestures, whether to use manual acts (and if so, of what sort), how to dispose one's body in prayer, whether to elevate the elements, where in one's voice to pitch one's chanting: all these questions assumed for me levels of significance, both theological and in relation to my own sense of self as a woman, that could hardly be gainsaid, and went beyond mere consideration of the liturgical text and rubric into the more nebulous but intuitive category of ritual performance. Further decisions which were to affect not only my liturgical activity but my general life as a priest also impinged: what sort of clerical dress to choose, what shoes, whether to mix clerical collar and lay clothes, whether to wear any makeup or jewelry, how to wear my hair — none of these decisions are without considerable impact on the nexus of themes described at the outset of this paper, as any reflective priest will surely admit.

Such emerging insights in my case were intensified by my own rather odd arrangement of belonging, as an Anglican priest of the diocese of Oxford, to two very different parishes — one in England, one in North America — as well as to an ecumenical divinity school. In the summer, I am a curate at Littlemore, outside Oxford. John Henry Newman built the church there before his subsequent conversion to Rome, and fixed a stone altar inexorably into the east end so that perforce one celebrates with one's back to the people.[6]

---

4. Some aspects of these themes are explored in a preliminary way in *Powers and Submissions: Philosophy, Spirituality, and Gender* (Oxford: Blackwell, 2002), but are treated in more detail in the first volume of my systematics: *God, Sexuality, and the Self: An Essay "On the Trinity"* (Cambridge: Cambridge University Press, forthcoming).

5. I discuss the Trinitarian shape of the eucharistic prayer briefly in "Why Three? Some Further Reflections on the Origins of the Doctrine of the Trinity," in Sarah Coakley and David A. Pailin, eds., *The Making and Remaking of Christian Doctrine* (Oxford: Oxford University Press, 1993), 29-56, at 45.

6. The original stone altar and reredos of 1836, installed by Newman, were later moved

I had expected to find this offensive as a feminist, but oddly, for reasons that will become clearer as we proceed, I found it impinged on the gender implications of the rite with surprisingly positive effect. In my parish in Waban, Massachusetts, in contrast, and at Harvard Divinity School, different forms of celebration are in use, which for the most part keep the priest facing the people (except on high days and holy days at Waban, when one circumambulates the altar to cense it). To these apparently insignificant details I shall return in the last section of this paper.

12.9

Sarah Coakley. "The Woman at the Altar," 87-93.

The Woman at the Altar: Beating the Bounds of Gender Liminality

I said at the start of this essay that I was set on demonstrating that the priest is in "an inherently fluid gender role as beater of the liminal bounds between the divine and the human." . . . If an acknowledgment of the significance of the nuptial metaphor calls forth an awareness of the erotic aura of the priest's mediating of the boundary between the divine and the human, then wherein lies the distribution of the "natural" signs (in Douglas's anthropological terms) of "masculinity" and "femininity" in the priest's negotiation of this boundary?[1] And what difference is made to the liturgical perception of this negotiation if the priest can be female as well as male?

---

back to accommodate a choir and larger chancel; see George F. Tull, *Littlemore: An Oxfordshire Village, Then and Now* (Rotherham: The King's England Press, 2002), 17-27. Apparently Newman himself, having opted for his contentiously "Roman" stone altar, nonetheless celebrated "north end," in traditional Anglican mode.

1. By now it may be clear that the "binary" of divine/human needs rather careful distinction from the *gender* "binary" of "masculine"/"feminine" (since *different* understandings of "difference" are at stake). The conservative position, as we have shown at some length, sees the latter as irreducibly, and immovably, connected to the former as a "natural" sign, and the eucharist as liturgically performing this supposedly immovable given of gender difference. My view, in contrast, is that while the first "binary" of "difference" (of transcendent divine gift and human response) must always be summoned and "re-presented" in the eucharist, its effect — rightly understood — is actually one of destabilizing and transforming static societal gender roles; there is *alteration,* not "re-fixing," of gender as a result. The "world" is disturbed and transformed. Thus, there is a paradox here: the "erotic" metaphor

My answer to this will involve . . . pointing to three dimensions of priestly eucharistic enactment which may not always *obviously* convey messages about gender, but in my view subliminally are doing so. My conclusion, to anticipate, will be that the woman's presence as priest in these negotiations makes it impossible any more to count these gender destabilizations as reversals that merely prove the patriarchal "rule." Rather, these destabilizations can now be seen as endemic to the life of transformation into God to which the eucharist invites us. Let me explain a little further with my three chosen liturgical examples.

First, recall my remark that I was startled to discover, in celebrating east-facing at Littlemore, that far from finding myself offended by this position as a feminist,[2] I actually found the east position curiously releasing. I think I can now give a theological account of this, as follows. When the priest has her back to the people, it is symbolically clear that she is adopting the position of "offering" on behalf *of* the laity: she is facing Godwards, representing the *laos*. In the terms of the old "natural signs" (which, as Mary Douglas argues, cannot be repressively obliterated, but must rather — in my view — be resummoned and strategically destabilized), the priest is "feminine" in this posture — supremely Marian, as Balthasar would see it. But when she turns around, whether to greet (at the *sursum corda*), or to offer the consecrated elements, or to bless, she has moved to the other side of the divide, representing Christ, offering God to the people — again, in the terms of the nuptial metaphor, both summoning and destabilizing the "masculine" posture of the bridegroom's self-gift. Without these bodily reversals and movements in the liturgy, I suggest, something deeply significant to the enactment of this destabilization is lost. When I am stuck, fixed behind the altar west-facing throughout, I also contribute unwittingly to a gender fixing

---

for the eucharist is still irreducible and ontologically basic (because founded in the divine *eros* for the human); but its irreducibility does not reside in its leaving gender *as it is*. One might say that its normativity consists in the way it *subverts* such "normativity" at the human level.

From this it follows that my use in this essay of the metaphor of "beating the bounds" of gender is also playful and paradoxical. Normally "bounds" are "beaten" in order to re-establish a clear *demarcation* between territories. But in my view, the priest at the *limen* between the divine and the human is "re-presenting" a *transgression* of the boundary between the human and the divine that occurs, transformatively, in the Incarnation, and is found to have implications, too, for the transformation of static gender binaries.

2. The classic feminist case *against* "hierarchy" and east-facing celebration may be found in Nancy Jay, *Throughout Your Generations Forever* (Chicago: University of Chicago Press, 1992).

that blocks the play of liminality those older movements conveyed. As I suggested at the outset, it is not — and never was — that the priest *only* represented Christ, and the people *only* the church. Rather, by moving from one role and its evocations to the other, even the male priest "played" with a destabilization of associated gender binaries. What the female priest now makes impossible, in my view, in her same play of movements, is the use of this play as a reversal that merely reestablishes its opposite; *her* destabilization is more confounding even than a "ritual of reversal," and so gestures to the endlessness of the movement of gender subversion at the gateway between the divine and the human.

Such a claim is bold, I am aware; but I have a second, related, reflection about the dangers of a fixed west-facing pose, and it is one I share with Orthodox commentators such as (most recently) Kallistos Ware, in an essay charting his change of mind on the question of women's ordination to an open-minded and potentially positive one.[3] It is that the west-facing "stuck" position, along with the manual acts that often attend it, unnecessarily intensifies the visually "iconic" dimension of the priest's role as being in persona Christi; the problem then may arise for the congregation that this person's appearance (old, young, male, female, blonde, bespectacled, spotty) seems incongruous as "representative" of Christ. What again is lost here is the capacity for labile "play" over which way is being "faced" — towards God or towards the church — and thus which gender association concomitantly summoned and queried.

My third and last liturgical focus I take from a fascinating — albeit speculative — analysis in a recent doctoral dissertation by Ludger Viefhues[4] of the implicit gender significance of the censing of the altar at the offertory at high mass. . . . His fundamental argument, however, is that the movement of the priest and his/her assistants around the altar, and the concomitant censing, is both establishing a close association between the priest and the altar, as locus of vertical divine presence, but also simultaneously destabilizing such an association by the subordination of the priest to the center of action on the altar, also indicated by the movement of the censing. That priestly gender associations are also here subliminally being both enacted and destabilized is part of Viefhues's argument: the "traditional" hier-

---

3. Kallistos Ware, "Man, Woman, and the Priesthood of Christ," in Thomas Hopko, ed., *Women and the Priesthood* (Crestwood, N.Y.: St. Vladimir's Seminary Press, rev. ed., 1999), 5-53, at 47-49.

4. Ludger Viefhues, "Cavell, the Skeptic and the Diva: The Human Self between Gender and Transcendence," Ph.D. thesis, Harvard University, December 2001, at 289-91.

archy of gender, he suggests, is implicitly summoned but also dissolved, just as the ritual power of the priest is both enacted and subordinated through the complex movements of the censing.

Conclusions

Let me now sum up what I have, and have not, been arguing in this essay. I set out to explore the classic gender associations of the nuptial metaphor for the eucharist, and argued that rather than repressing and rejecting this "erotic" theological zone, we would do well to explore its fullest implications. In the course of an interrogation of Mary Douglas's and Hans Urs von Balthasar's reasons for the rejection of women priests, I argued that their very own insights pointed to an internal critique: the logic of the nuptial metaphor's outworking leads to a priestly destabilization of normative gender binaries rather than the opposite. However, the "fixing" or "freezing" back of such binaries, which has classically attended the liturgical play in destabilizing them, becomes, I argued, impossible once a real-life woman is at the altar; in that sense, we must conclude that her presence represents a cosmological disturbance, in the original terms of the debate. It is not just that she is a woman dressing up as a man dressing up as a woman (though sartorial details are certainly significant in this "play"), but rather that the gender fluidity that the male priest has always enjoyed *qua* liturgically liminal can no longer be a means of "leaving *everything else* as it is." Offensive as this logic must inevitably be to conservatives, whether Roman Catholic, Anglo-Catholic, or Orthodox, it has the merit of meeting such opponents in their own chosen zone of nuptial reflection of working relentlessly through to the end that the theology suggests. If I am right, then the sort of perpetual destabilization of gender binaries that Nyssa glimpsed in his last writings is what the spiritual "end" may be. . . .

What I have laid before you in this essay, then, should not be seen as a proposal about sexual ethics, but rather a theory about that mysterious liminality of priestly enactment, a liminality that can through God's grace be a point of both mediation and transformation, a disturbing remaking, indeed, of the order of the world — both cosmological and personal. Insofar as the world is thus re-ordered, we know that the Spirit has broken in, and the Word made flesh; for what, after all, is the Incarnation itself, if not the greatest "cosmological disturbance" that the "world" has known?

13 Being with the Disabled:
Jean Vanier's Theological Realism

HANS S. REINDERS

Communion is rooted in reality, not in dreams or illusions.

Jean Vanier, *Our Journey Home*

Introduction

In his book *Befriending the Stranger,* Jean Vanier introduces his readers to L'Arche with the following words: "In the communities of L'Arche we live and journey together, men and women with disabilities and those who feel called to share their lives with them. We are all learning the pain and joy of community life, where the weakest members open hearts to compassion and lead us into deep union with Jesus. We are learning to befriend them, and through and with them, to befriend Jesus" (Vanier 2010a, vii). With this introduction, Vanier sums up in his own words what L'Arche is about. It is about a journey in which people with disabilities have taken the lead in showing how to find God. Striking in Vanier's voice, here as elsewhere in his writings, is his tone. It is surely one of his greatest gifts to speak profoundly about the message of the Gospel in plain and simple language. This is not to accommodate the people he speaks to by using "easy, accessible language." Rather, it is the other way around. Being with people who are intellectually disabled has taught him that the truth about human life before God is in fact plain and simple. There is absolutely no reason to make it complicated. On the contrary.

So he tells us about Luisito, a man with severe disabilities who was left alone when his mother died. Luisito used to live in the streets of Santo Domingo before he came to L'Arche. His home was a small hut near a Catholic church. "From time to time the neighbors would give him something to eat, but no one was really committed to him," Vanier explains. "He was dirty and smelly; his body was twisted; he could not walk, nor talk. People found it difficult to look at him; he disturbed them. Yet today he is one of the founding members of L'Arche in Santo Domingo" (Vanier 2010a, vii). Vanier continues,

> That is the mystery; the secret of the Gospel of Jesus: Luisito renders Jesus present! It seems foolish to say that. Much that I say may well seem quite foolish because the gospel is truly a message of folly. It is so simple, so amazing, that it is difficult to believe it is true. (Vanier 2010a, 2-3)

There are many such little stories in Vanier's writings. He tells them again and again to open our eyes to what is in his view the essence of Christian witness: the people on whom our world has turned its back reveal the mystery of Jesus — like the Samaritan woman, for example. (See **13.10**.)

The profound impression that Vanier's words leave on his audience stems from the fact that he simply tells us what he believes and why. He does not present us with a theory, nor has he any interest in philosophical or theological systems. The profundity of Vanier's speech is of a different nature. Whatever he speaks of is spoken from a heart that has learned to look at itself in truth (**13.20-21**). His words are witness to Augustine's insight that knowing God and knowing oneself in truth are two sides of the same coin. He regards his ability to speak to people's hearts and minds as an aspect of the mystery of the Word, saying, "It is funny how often people tell me: 'You never say anything that I haven't heard before.' It is as if the Word enters the depth of their hearts and puts into words what people in fact already know it reveals. In fact you do not teach anything; you only make people realize that they know" (quoted in Spink 2006, 106). What is extraordinary in his witness, however, is the mediating role that Vanier has recognized in people with intellectual disabilities in learning to know God, and to know himself.

Notwithstanding the fact that he is a great storyteller, Vanier is primarily concerned with the reality of human life, particularly with regard to our relationship with God. Some things are true about me, whether I like it or not, and there is no way of coming closer to God unless I am prepared to face them. Vanier reflects upon the fact that there is no way of bearing fruit in our lives unless we face the reality of our own pain and anxiety. Quoting from the prophet Hosea, he writes,

> We are often frightened of reality because reality can be painful and a source of disappointment. We tend to escape into a world of illusions and to seek refuge in dreams. We bury ourselves in ideas and theories. . . . We run away from our Valley of Achor[1] which is the place of our greatest and most intimate pain. Yet that is the very place that God calls us to enter so that it may be transformed into a door of hope. (Vanier 2010a, 5-6)

This metaphorical valley is the place where we do not want to go or look because it hurts. It is a place of bitterness, of fear, and shame. However, the Valley of Achor is not necessarily an interior space. It is often represented by people that disturb us because they embody pain. Insofar as they remind us of our own pain, we fear their presence. To allow such people into our lives is to become witness to their misery, which is what most people refuse to do. But the good news of the Gospel, as Vanier explains, is that if we do become witness to their misery and pain, these people will turn into a "door of hope." It is crucial to Vanier's reading that these interior and exterior worlds are connected. Sharing his life with disabled people has taught him that healing their pain was impossible as long as he was not prepared to go into the darkness of his own heart and accept the things about himself that he would rather avoid facing.

Realism

When Vanier started the first community of L'Arche, he had no idea what he was doing. He had no plan ("That's not my way"; Vanier 1995a, 16) for what he was about to start under the guidance of his spiritual mentor, Father Thomas Philippe. The only thing he had was a calling that committed him to the people he had seen in Saint Jean les Deux Jumeaux, a mental hospital south of Paris. He heard the outcry of its inmates. As Vanier recalls, he saw the question in their gestures: "Will you come back? Do you love me?" More than anything else these people longed to be accepted by someone. He found

---

1. Hosea 2:15. The "Valley of Achor" is a place of misfortune that JHWH brought upon the Israelites (Josh. 7:24-26).

himself called to respond (Vanier 1995a, 15; Vanier 2010b, 19-20), a calling he later came to refer to as his being called into the church's *mission,* as he explains in the chapter on that topic he added to the revised version of *Community and Growth* (**13.1**).

As a result, he found himself some time later living in a house with two men who came from Saint Jean and who became the "core members" of the first community of L'Arche. This was in 1964. Now that L'Arche is in its fifth decade, this calling has been heard and answered by many people, inspired by Vanier's example, so that now there are over 130 L'Arche communities in the world today.

There is a growing literature celebrating Vanier as a spiritual leader (see Spink 2006). In that capacity his work has been acknowledged throughout the world and has been honored, for example, by John Paul II. Within this literature one finds ample proof of the extraordinary gifts of this man. In this chapter I do not want to contribute to this literature, however. Instead I want to highlight Vanier as a theological thinker, notwithstanding the fact that he is a trained philosopher. The present project tracing Christian voices on disability offers a suitable occasion to do so because it will show in what sense Vanier's voice is unique in the Christian literature in this area.

More specifically, I will attempt to describe Vanier's thought in terms of what I propose to name his theological realism. Whatever it is that must be said positively about L'Arche, it is not to be understood as an ideal of Christian morality. Nor is L'Arche properly understood as the realization of a preconceived form of Christian life. When Vanier and Father Philippe started, there was no preconceived idea (Vanier 1995a, 22). L'Arche is lived rather than thought of, so that when in Vanier's work we encounter a profound Christian vision, it is important to realize that it is only in hindsight that this vision emerged. Put differently, Vanier's life in L'Arche has guided and developed his reading and writing, not the other way around. In the beginning was the deed.

Following a suggestion recently made by Stanley Hauerwas (Hauerwas 2010), I will pursue this Wittgensteinian reading of L'Arche to explain why Vanier's account of being with people with disabilities *could not* have been preconceived. The reason is that the experience of sharing his life with disabled people proved to be crucial to Vanier's vision, which he only gradually learned to understand. Looking back to the formative period of L'Arche, Vanier labels it "open to providence and daily life" (Vanier 1995a, 22). He had a deep awareness that L'Arche was God's project, so that to attend to daily affairs and to look out for what came his way was a call of faith:

The hand of God was clearly present at the foundation of each of our communities — and that is still true today. God continued to watch over us throughout these years. When I think of those foundations, I see how everything was given: a sign or a gift led us to another sign, another gift. It was as if we were walking on a road without knowing quite where it was leading. (Vanier 1995a, 53)

God was working through the reality of their daily lives in their communities. Vanier's way was to respond to a calling rather than to project a grand vision. In other words, L'Arche had to be lived before it could be envisioned. In his own unpretentious manner, Vanier recognizes this when he says, "I am one of those people who first make a decision and then afterwards discover their reasons for doing so. This concerns a symbolic rather than a rational domain. It goes very, very deep" (quoted in Spink 2006, 73). This complicates introducing his work, of course, since most of the readers of the present volume will encounter Vanier only through his writings. This introduction is an attempt to make the selected texts by Vanier more intelligible as reports from and on this singular life.

Crucial to my reading of Vanier's work — and of the writings from L'Arche in general — is the observation that the "core members" of their communities are frequently mentioned in their capacity as "our teachers" (cf. Vanier 1991, 96-97; 2010a, 46; also Nouwen). To understand L'Arche, it is crucial to understand what is meant by that expression. It is only when this expression is properly understood that it will be clear why L'Arche is misconceived as the realization of a preconceived Christian ideal that is lived by morally gifted people. Vanier and his friends in L'Arche would certainly maintain that they have been blessed with very special people, but they would not mean this in a moral sense. The key notion in their view is that more than anything else, people with disabilities can open the door to our hearts. Before this opening can be celebrated, however, there is a truth about our selves that needs to be faced (**13.3**). Sharing our lives with such people may teach us a few things about ourselves and our moral character that otherwise may remain hidden beneath the surface. (For Nouwen's account of this notion, see Reinders 2008, 340-45.)

Obviously, since the people they speak of are referred to as *intellectually* disabled, their role as teachers cannot be taken in an intentional sense. Teaching is not what they think they are doing, nor do they have any awareness that they are doing it. So the question is how to explain the notion of teaching as it appears in the writings from L'Arche. Elsewhere I have discussed the same notion as it appears in one of Søren Kierkegaard's sermons on the Gospel of Matthew where he uses it in a similar context (Reinders 2010). Kierkegaard speaks about the lilies in the fields and the birds in the sky as our "teachers" — our "divinely appointed teachers," to be precise. We can learn from the lilies and the birds what it means to receive our lives as a good and perfect gift. This we learn from their *being,* which Kierkegaard explains in terms of being content with what they are. As we will see, Vanier speaks analogously about people with disabilities as our teachers. Most of them cannot take responsibility for their own lives, while many of them would barely survive being out in the world on their own. Their role as our teachers is a quality of who they are rather than an intentional pedagogical strategy.

To give an account of Vanier's views on what it is that the communities of L'Arche learn from people with disabilities as their teachers, I will present Vanier's answer to this question, as indicated, in terms of his theological realism. "Realism" in this connection does not refer to a strand of theological metaphysics in a technical sense, although there certainly is an element to its meaning corresponding with it. Christian understanding is an afterthought with which we respond to how God works his works in our lives.[2] I call Vanier's realism "theological" in the sense that his views are guided by the question of how the reality of Christ works in our lives.[3] As we will see, the discovery of L'Arche is that its members are guided by "the poor" in learning to become friends with God.

---

2. I take it that "theological realism" as a technical term refers to the philosophical view according to which the word "God" refers to a reality independent of human thought, language, and belief. (See Cobb 2003.) In view of Vanier's claim that the reality of L'Arche precedes understanding, and that its practice is a response to the reality of Christ as presented by people with disabilities, Vanier would undoubtedly call himself a realist in this metaphysical sense. The very point of naming these people as their teachers is that, according to Vanier's thinking, the reality of God cuts right through our thoughts, language, and beliefs.

3. This means that the subject matter of Vanier's theological realism has nothing to do with the doctrine of Christian realism as represented by Reinhold Niebuhr. Christian realism is the view that the nature of (political) power forbids Christians to act on the primacy of love as a moral principle. "The Christian ethic cannot be simply love, for men live in history, and 'perfect love' in history has not fared well" (Niebuhr 1932, 22). Therefore Christian love is tragic, according to Niebuhr, because when practiced in a society governed by power relations, its fate will inevitably be death on the cross. Presumably Vanier would say that Christian love, as exemplified by the cross, gives true life, even though it will not be the kind of life that is known to the world of power.

The Poor

Understanding why and how the poor are "guiding" explains also why the acceptance of poverty is key to Vanier's theological realism. The reason is simple. People with disability are usually poor. If you want to share your life with them — be with them instead of serving them from your privileged position of power — you will share in their poverty. Many people might think that someone from a well-to-do Canadian family of diplomats and officers might best help others by sharing his wealth. But Vanier wanted to share in a more thoroughgoing way than this, and he saw that in order to share his life with disabled people, he had to accept their poverty (**13.21**). So when the writings of L'Arche address people with disabilities as "the poor," this term is intended to reflect the language of the Beatitudes, but inflected in a very concrete and material sense.

Reading through the various accounts of the early days of L'Arche, one gets the impression that at this point Father Thomas Philippe's influence on Vanier is particularly significant. Even though he was a Roman Catholic priest with orthodox theological views, Father Philippe commanded respect and authority among his flock because he shared the poor conditions of their existence in rural France (Spink 2006, 58). He occupied two small rooms in Trosly-Breuil without a kitchen and a stove; and he decided that one of the rooms should be a chapel. His livelihood depended largely on the support of the villagers.

Poverty in Vanier's writings is not only an economic condition, however, because it has also a spiritual meaning in the sense that the poor are deprived of the goods that nourish the soul such as friendship and fellowship. They share a deep wound because of being rejected and abandoned.[4] And of course, poverty never comes alone; it brings sickness, weakness, and all kinds of social evils with it, like abandonment, abuse, and homelessness. It is therefore not surprising that when Vanier sets out to describe the spirituality of L'Arche communities in his book *The Heart of L'Arche,* his first move is toward Jesus as the one who brought good news to the poor. Jesus' message is new, according to Vanier, because he does not just preach to serve the poor but becomes one of them. Referring to how Jesus confronts the established order in his society and then is convicted and killed by it, Vanier writes,

---

4. Vanier was deeply convinced that Father Thomas Philippe shared this condition of spiritual woundedness too. Later in his life Philippe was barred from celebrating mass because of a conflict with his bishop. See Spink 2006, 55-58.

Jesus is condemned to death and dies in total abjection. He is mocked by all. The man of compassion becomes a man in need of compassion, a poor man. Jesus overturns the established order: he urges people not simply to do good to the poor but to discover God hidden in the poor, to discover that the poor have the power to heal and free people. (Vanier 1995b, 21)

Following Father Thomas Philippe, who introduced Vanier to the world of the poor in the mental hospital that he served as a priest, Vanier and his friends accepted the condition of poverty as part of what responding to the call of these people demanded. But that was only the beginning of their journey together. What he had not yet grasped was the reversal of roles that gradually became the essence of L'Arche: the poor as the ones who reveal the work of God and in doing so become "teachers." As we remember from the story about Luisito, one of the founders of L'Arche in Santo Domingo, the mystery of Jesus is identified as the mystery of the poor. They have the power to heal our wounds.

Illusions

People often come to L'Arche to assist in the community because they want to help people with intellectual disabilities. Vanier does not want to question their motive to help, but he does encourage the assistants in L'Arche to question such motives themselves. While in itself commmendable, the desire to be good to other people can easily become self-serving, particularly when it is fueled by the presumption that one's role in the community is to give. People entering L'Arche with this presumption have to learn something that, according to Vanier, is essential for its community, namely, that the marginalized and the despised — "the poor" — have something to give. This has to be learned, because without it, true community is impossible. The virtuous motives that make people want to be good to others often betray a hidden sense of superiority; they assume for themselves the role of "giver" and assign the other person to the role of "receiver." After all, giving can easily be a gesture of power (see Reinders 2008, 335-40). Consequently, realizing that there is something to be received from the "core members" is a major task for newly arrived assistants. Vanier explains,

Those who come because they feel they have something to offer to people who are weak and poor often get a shock when they start to become conscious of the weaknesses and limitations in themselves and the other assistants. It is always easier to accept the weakness of people with a handicap — we are there precisely because we expect it — than our own weakness, which often takes us by surprise! (Vanier 1991, 131)

One of the weaknesses and limitations that must be confronted quite early is the presumption of superiority. Vanier tells us how he had to discover this presumptuousness in himself very early in the beginning of L'Arche when his two new friends made him feel that he was pushing them around. Coming from a family within which discipline and authority were highly valued, he discovered that his desire to answer the call of Jesus did not stop him from thinking that he was in charge (Spink 2006, 69-70).

The weaknesses and limitations that have to be confronted become even more serious when the motive of doing good to others gets frustrated because the other refuses to receive the gift (**13.5**). Vanier tells us about his experience when he lived in La Forestière, a home for profoundly disabled people, among whom was Lucien. Lucien had lost his mother, who was the only person in Lucien's life who knew how to read his body language. When his mother died, he was put in a hospital, where he was left alone. When he came to L'Arche, he faced his assistants with constant screaming while he allowed no one to touch him in order to calm him down. Vanier describes his own feelings about this experience:

> The pitch of Lucien's screaming was piercing and seemed to penetrate the very core of my being, awakening my own inner anguish. I could sense anger, violence, and even hatred rising up within me. I would have been capable of hurting him to keep him quiet. It was as if a part of my being that I had learned to control was exploding. It was not only Lucien's anguish that was difficult for me to accept but the revelation of what was inside my own heart — my capacity to hurt others — I, who had been called to share my life with the weak, had a power of hatred for a weak person! (**13.16**)

This story becomes even more powerful when we realize that when Vanier had this awakening, he had been a community leader of Trosly-Breuil for fourteen years! He must have been among the most experienced of assistants in La Forestière, but he still was susceptible to fits of rage against someone as vulnerable as Lucien. This tells us what Vanier has in mind when he insists that truth in self-knowledge is crucial. It also tells us that the insistence on self-knowledge in order to face one's own weaknesses and limitations proves that the community of L'Arche is not a community designed for moral heroes. On the contrary, moral heroes are likely to be the least disposed to suspect their own motives. As Vanier warns them, "We want to see only good qualities in ourselves and other assistants." An important task, therefore, is to face the truth about ourselves — but as Vanier points out, it is "painful . . . for us to look reality in the face, to discover our own fragility and our capacity for anger and hatred. The temptation is so great to avoid or run away from those who reveal our inner limits and brokenness" (**13.17**). In our responses to Vanier's work we sometimes have a tendency to speak in endearing terms about the recognition of our own weakness and vulnerability, which apparently puts us on a par with marginalized people such as the disabled. There is nothing endearing about vulnerability, however. Marginalized people have no reason to exalt their own weakness. Therefore the possibility must be faced that, again, there are gestures of power involved in this exaltation. Vanier at any rate has a different aim. The point in recognizing our own limitations and weaknesses is related to that true self-knowledge, without which no growth is possible.[5]

> One of the most important things for growth in people and in communities is precisely this dedication to truth, even (and maybe especially) if it hurts. There is no growth when we live in falsehood and illusion; when we are frightened to let the truth be uncovered and seen by ourselves and others. So we often hide our fears, our injustices, our incompetence, our hypocrisy. (Vanier 1991, 135)

Teachers

Speaking of *illusions,* in this connection, Vanier suggests that people are not deliberately hiding their darker side. His view seems to be that most people are misguided, rather than deceitful, about their own motives. They fear the pain of confrontation. "We tend to live in a world of illusions with regard to ourselves," he says. "We so easily judge others but have trouble seeing ourselves as we really are" (**13.6**). If this conjecture is right, it explains why

5. In this respect Vanier seems to argue within an Aristotelian framework that is quite similar to Alasdair MacIntyre's argument about human fragility and vulnerability. See MacIntyre 1999, 1-10.

Vanier's work is constantly turning toward learning, developing, and growing as a human being. It also explains why we need teachers of an exceptional kind. Indeed, when people are afraid to confront their hidden fears, the question arises who will lead them in opening up.

The writings of L'Arche point to the "core members" of their communities, "the poor," as their "teachers." Vanier explains the logic of this move in two steps, which he names the first and second "call." The first call occurs when people decide to enter into a covenant and choose community life. As Vanier explains, we start from the motive of wanting to do something for other people, "or to prepare ourselves to do wonderful and noble things for the Kingdom. We are appreciated and admired by family, by friends, or by the community" (Vanier 1991, 139). Particularly the experience of being appreciated and admired indicates the temptation to let self-serving motives determine our actions. The motive of being good to others gets mixed up with the desire to be praised and admired. As was discussed before, however, the presence of mixed motives can easily lead us astray when it comes to the attitude with which we approach the ones we seek to help. When we perceive them as marginalized and excluded from society — as is the case in L'Arche communities — then we will have a strong tendency to regard them as needing our help. The harder we push to help others, the more likely they will resist. Things start to get difficult. The desire to be praised is frustrated by the very people we want to help. We begin to doubt our ability to participate in community life. Fear of failure arises.[6] That is when the second call comes, according to Vanier:

> The second call comes later, when we accept that we cannot do big or heroic things for Jesus; it is a time of renunciation, humiliation, and humility. We feel useless; we are no longer appreciated. If the first passage is made at high noon, under a shining sun, the second call is often made at night. We feel alone and are afraid because we are in a world of confusion. (Vanier 1991, 139)

The sabbatical stay in La Forestière was a time of growth for Vanier himself: there he experienced something like a second call. Particularly his experience with Eric, a young man who was completely deaf and blind, and who

---

6. At this point Henri Nouwen's account about his own experience in serving Adam as a personal assistant is very illuminating, particularly because of the meticulous observations the author makes about his own motivations (Nouwen 1997, 42-46).

could not speak or walk, became very important. Eric's physical state of being was normally one of high muscular tension, and he could relax only when he felt the healing energy of love. Vanier had to learn that Eric's fear of being rejected could not be overcome as long as he would not open his own heart. He had to overcome his own fear of being rejected (Spink 2006, 184-85). In La Forestière Vanier learned to see himself in such a way that the distinctions between "helper" and "helped" vanished. He found a tenderness in Eric that could only be ascribed to trust. That was an important lesson that he had been taught by one of the most vulnerable people in their community. Vanier comments,

> I can only continue when I accept that God has made a covenant between Eric and myself. Because of this covenant we are responsible to one another. If God has done this, then He will also help us to deepen our relationship. He will offer me His grace and give me patience to accept my own darkness, and He will help me to trust that someday it will disappear. (quoted in Spink 2006, 186)

This is the moment when the "core members" of L'Arche are introduced in their capacity as teachers. "They evangelize us," Vanier says (Vanier 1995b, 50). They reveal qualities of the heart in the friendship and love they spontaneously give. Paradoxically, Vanier traces these qualities to aspects of their being that are usually regarded as defining their disabilities.[7] Lacking in skills of social adaptation, they are not governed by social conventions. "They are not interested in anyone's position or rank, but they are perceptive about people's hearts. . . . They live in the present moment" (Vanier 1995b, 33).[8] They are not longing for a past or dreaming about a future but are relying on what there is here and now. Because of their qualities of the heart, according to Vanier, people with intellectual disabilities are capable of awakening the hearts of others. In one of his accounts of the first years of L'Arche in Trosly-Breuil, Vanier recalls that in the midst of the many difficulties the

---

7. See Vanier's *Our Journey Home* (1997), where he explains the "paradox of L'Arche: People with mental handicaps, so limited physically and intellectually, are often more gifted than others when it comes to the things of the heart and to relationships. In a mysterious way they can lead us to the home of our hearts" (x).

8. Incidentally, Vanier describes God's relationship with us in similar terms: "God knows me today just as I am. God does not live in the past or in the future but in the 'now' of the present moment. God sees me in my present reality as I am in each present moment" (2010b, 32).

community faced, he began to see the contribution of people with disabilities. Amid crises and even violent outbursts of rage, the community discovered that these people were not only the cause of problems but also — and primarily — a source of friendship and joy. "Their thirst for friendship, love, and communion leaves no one indifferent: either you harden your heart to their cry and reject them, or you open your heart and enter into a relationship built on trust, simple, tender gestures, and few words. Hidden in those who are powerless is a mysterious power: they attract and awaken the heart" (Vanier 1995, 26). So the second call that Vanier distinguishes in the process of growth is the call to leave behind false pretenses about the superiority of helping and giving, and to open up to the experience of receiving, primarily from those who we never expected had something to give (**13.19**).

As Vanier explains time and again, answering this second call is not a matter of strength, but of accepting that people with disabilities as "the poor" present the mystery of Jesus to us (see, **13.18**; also Vanier 1995b, 43). Jesus tells us that whoever welcomes the poor welcomes him, and whoever welcomes him welcomes the Father. The mystery of Jesus is the Word made flesh, God with us, and this most decisively in the presence of someone like Eric! "By identifying himself with the poor and the weak, Jesus reminds us that he identifies with all that is poor and weak in each of us" (Vanier 1995b, 45). Thus we have no reason to hide our weaknesses but need instead to turn to Jesus, which, according to Vanier, is how we find the presence of God. Speaking about Jesus' encounter with the Samaritan woman, he says that we often experience the presence of God most strongly when we are with people who are marginalized — in his own case, people with profound disabilities. "The mystery Jesus revealed to the Samaritan woman is the mystery contained in the life of each of us: if we drink from the source of life, which is Jesus, we too will become a source of life; we will bring life, the very life of God, into our world" (**13.14**).

Conclusion

Compared with other accounts of the connections between theology and disability, Vanier's work, strikingly enough, shows only a limited interest in issues of freedom and self-determination. Whereas, for example, accounts originating from liberation theology put all their emphasis on empowering people with disabilities to shape their own lives, Vanier prefers the language of strength in weakness as a way to build community. While there is nothing in his view that prevents him from supporting empowerment as a way to enable people to find their own strength, Vanier's primary aim is not to create equal opportunities for people with disabilities to help them shape their own future. In focusing on community as the primary goal, he courts a particular kind of problem, a problem that each of these communities frequently faces. It is the problem of attracting people who want to spend time in L'Arche to sort out their own unresolved issues. As is testified by his book *Community and Growth,* Vanier is very well aware of the danger inherent in this. Assistants coming to L'Arche often are themselves complex characters that have a lot to sort out in their lives. Given the inevitable asymmetry in levels of vulnerability, the danger is that "core members" become entangled in problems they don't need. Issues of unstable assistants can take too much of their limited energy. In this respect it is important to consider how Vanier's thinking is relatively defenseless against this risk to the extent that it invites assistants to face their own weakness and pain. The transition from the "first call" to the "second call" amounts to something like a rite of passage, without which assistants will not be able to participate in community life.

The danger, in other words, lies in an inheritance of Christian thought and practice in which the poor are "instrumentalized" (cf. Reynolds 2008, 16). It has often been noticed in the Christian tradition that people with intellectual disability have a particular standing in the eyes of God. In fact, there is a long history of Christian speech about "holy innocents" (cf. Scheerenberger 1983), a notion that has often been taken as a calling to charity: the "poor" enable us to become better people in responding to God, which to some extent explains why charity has received a bad reputation in recent times (Reinders 2008, 317-22). In a sense, Vanier continues this tradition, which creates the problem signaled here. But it must be added that he changes it at the same time. As long as we hear the first call to assist people with disability (in the sense of doing good *to* them), but fail to hear the second call (learning to be *with* them), we most likely will continue the hypocrisy that marks the history of charitable institutions. To the extent that learning to be with them focuses on self-knowledge, the danger exists that this is turned into an end in itself. As my reading has tried to show, however, finding oneself in truth is never an end in itself for Vanier, but is the way of opening one's heart to find Christ.

The account of Vanier's work presented here shows his particular contribution to reflecting theologically on intellectual disability. Self-knowledge is essential to what being with persons with intellectual disabilities can teach us, not in the sense of showing us how to become better people, but in the sense of knowing the truth about ourselves without illusions. We will not succeed in being with them — and enjoy life with them, and find time for celebration — unless we learn to face the hidden fears in our own hearts, which will break the bonds of our hypocrisy. The hard lesson for Christians who grow up in a culture that abrogates the reality of the Cross to which Christian faith attests is how to avoid the sentimentalism of being moved by one's own feelings for the poor. Vanier's message is as simple as it is confrontational: go live with them, and you will soon find out whether you are truly a neighbor of the poor. He frequently speaks about the story of Jesus' encounter with the Samaritan woman as told in the Gospel of John (4:7-38), but the insight he contributes might as well be taken from Jesus' story of the Good Samaritan as told in the Gospel of Luke (10:30-37). The point of the story is not to recommend the moral feelings of someone who helped a victimized man; it is to raise the question of who is the true neighbor to that man. Vanier's theological realism teaches that God's truth about our lives is tangible in the victimized Christ, who is present in the lives of victimized people. There is no way to find this truth that does not lead us to them.

References

Primary Sources

Vanier, Jean. 1995a. *An Ark for the Poor: The Story of L'Arche.* Toronto: Novalis.

———. 1999. *Becoming Human.* London: Darton, Longman & Todd.

———. 2010a. *Befriending the Stranger* (first published as *La source des larmes,* 2001). Mahwah, N.J.: Paulist Press.

———. 1989. *Community and Growth,* rev ed. (originally titled *La communauté: Lieu du Pardon et de la Fête,* 1989). London: Darton, Longman & Todd.

———. 1995b. *The Heart of L'Arche: A Spirituality for Every Day.* Toronto: Novalis.

———. 1997. *Our Journey Home.* Maryknoll, N.Y.: Orbis Books.

———. 2010b. "What Have People with Learning Disabilities Taught Me?" In *The Paradox of Disability: Responses to Jean Vanier and L'Arche Communities from Theology and the Sciences.* Edited by Hans S. Reinders. Grand Rapids: Wm. B. Eerdmans.

Secondary Sources

Cobb, John B. Jr. 2003. "Theological Realism." This essay was presented at a meeting of the American Academy of Religion, Atlanta, in 2003. It can be accessed at http://www.religion-online.org (accessed 08-18-2008).

Hauerwas, Stanley. 2010. "Seeing Peace: L'Arche as a Peace Movement." In *The Par-*

adox of Disability: Responses to Jean Vanier and L'Arche Communities from Theology and the Sciences. Edited by Hans S. Reinders. Grand Rapids: Wm. B. Eerdmans, 113-26.

MacIntyre, Alasdair. 1999. *Dependent Rational Animals: Why Human Beings Need the Virtues*. Peru, Ill.: Carus Publishing.

Niebuhr, Reinhold. 1932. *Moral Man and Immoral Society*. New York: Harper & Collins.

Nouwen, Henri. 1997. *Adam: God's Beloved*. Maryknoll, N.Y.: Orbis Books.

Reinders, Hans S. 2008. *Receiving the Gift of Friendship: Profound Disability, Theological Anthropology, and Ethics*. Grand Rapids: Wm. B. Eerdmans.

————. 2010. "Watch the Lilies of the Field: Theological Reflections on Profound Disability and Time." In *The Paradox of Disability: Responses to Jean Vanier and L'Arche Communities from Theology and the Sciences*. Edited by Hans S. Reinders. Grand Rapids: Wm. B. Eerdmans, 154-68.

Reynolds, Thomas E. 2008. *Vulnerable Communion: A Theology of Disability and Hospitality*. Grand Rapids: Brazos Press.

Scheerenberger, R. C. 1983. *A History of Mental Retardation: A Quarter Century of Promise*. Baltimore: Paul H. Brookes.

Spink, Kathryn. 2006. *The Miracle, the Message, the Story: Jean Vanier and L'Arche*. Mahwah, N.J.: Paulist Press.

Excerpts

13.1

Jean Vanier, *Community and Growth*, rev. ed. London: Darton, Longman & Todd, 1989, 84-85, 86-87.

Coming Together for a Purpose

Jesus first of all called men and women to him and told them: "Leave all, come and follow me." He chose them, loved them, and invited them to become his friends. That is how it all began, in a personal relationship with Jesus, a communion with him.

Then he brought together the twelve he had called to become his friends; they started to live together in community. Obviously it was not always easy. They quickly began to quarrel, fighting over who should be first. Community life revealed all sorts of jealousies and fears in them. Then Jesus sent them off to accomplish a mission: *to announce* good news to the poor, *to heal* the sick, and *to liberate* by casting out demons. He did not keep them with him for long, but sent them out so that they would have an experience of life flowing out from them: an experience of giving life to people and an experience of their own beauty and capacities if they followed him and let his power act in and through them.

The pains of community are situated between the joy of this communion and friendship with Jesus and the joy of giving life to others: the mission.

If people come together to care for each other, it is because they feel more or less clearly that as a group they have a mission. They have been called together by God and have a message of love to transmit to others.

When two or three come together in his name, Jesus is present. Community is a sign of this presence: it is a sign of the Church. Many people who believe in Jesus are in some degree of distress: battered wives, people in mental hospitals, those who live alone because they are too fragile to live with others. All these people can put their trust in Jesus. Their suffering is a sign of his cross, a sign of a suffering Church. But a community which prays and loves is a sign of the resurrection. That is its mission. . . .

Communities can produce things, make cheese, beer, or wine; they can show new and better methods of agriculture; they can build hospitals and schools; they can further culture through their books, libraries, or art. However, these things do not necessarily give life; and the mission of a community is to give life to others, that is to say, to transmit new hope and new meaning to them. Mission is revealing to others their fundamental beauty, value, and importance in the universe, their capacity to love, to grow, and to do beautiful things and to meet God. Mission is transmitting to people a new inner freedom and hope; it is unlocking the doors of their being so that new energies can flow; it is taking away from their shoulders the terrible yoke of fear and guilt. To give life to people is to reveal to them that they are loved just as they are by God, with the mixture of good and evil, light and darkness that is in them: that the stone in front of the tomb, in which all the dirt of their lives has been hidden, can be rolled away. They are forgiven; they can live in freedom.

Jesus wants each one of us individually to bear fruit, but he also wants us to bear much fruit in community, and then we become his disciples (John 15).

All living beings give life. Thus from generation to generation we have birds, fish, animals, trees, flowers, and fruit; [from] the incredible fecundity of creation a life flows from one being to another. Man and woman together give life, conceiving and giving birth to a child.[1] And [these are] just the physical and biological aspects of procreation. Once the baby is born, and even before birth, the parents give life to the child, and reveal to him/her its beauty by the way they welcome and love it. Or else they may bring inner death to the child, making it feel ugly and worthless through the way they reject or over-protect it. Through love and tenderness, through welcome and listening, we can give life to people.

Jesus' whole message is one of life-giving. He came to give life and give it abundantly. He came to take away all the blockages that prevent the flow of life. The glory of God, wrote Irenaeus in the second century, is people fully alive, fully living. Jesus came to announce good news to the poor, freedom to the oppressed and imprisoned, and sight to the blind. He came to liberate, to open up new doors and avenues; he came to take away guilt, to heal, make whole and to save. And he asks his disciples to continue this mission of life-giving, of fecundity and of liberation. That is the mission of every Christian community. . . . Mission is to bring the life of God to others, and this can only be done if communities and people are poor and humble, letting the life of God flow through them.

13.2

Community and Growth, 93-95

The Yearning for God and the Cry of the Poor

In all ages and in many religions, people have come to live together, yearning and searching for communion with God. Some of these communities were founded on the mountain tops or in desert lands, far away from the hustle

1. Jean Vanier, *Man and Woman He Made Them* (London: Darton, Longman & Todd; New York: Paulist Press; and Strathfield, NSW: St. Paul's Publications, 1985).

and bustle of cities. Life in these communities is frequently austere, directed essentially toward a personal relationship with God and to acts of common worship and work. Other communities — particularly those in the Christian heritage — were founded to serve the poor, the lost, the hungry, and those in need in the ghettos and the hustle and bustle of cities.

The quest for the eternal, all-beautiful, all-true, and all-pure, and the quest to be close to the poor and most broken people appear to be so contradictory. And yet, in the broken heart of Christ, these two quests are united. Jesus reveals to us that he loves his Father, and is intimately linked to him; at the same time he is himself in love with each person and in a particular way with the most broken, the most suffering, and the most rejected. To manifest this love, Jesus himself became broken and rejected, a man of sorrows and of anguish and of tears; he became the Crucified One.

And so, communities formed in his name will seek communion with the Father through him and in him; they will also seek to bring good news to the poor, and liberation to the oppressed and the imprisoned.

Within the Church, over the ages, one or the other aspect of this double mission has been emphasized, according to the call of God in different times and places, but both are also present. There are those who are called to the desert or the mountain top to seek greater union with God through the Crucified One; and their prayer will flow upon the broken and the crucified ones of this world. And there are those called to give their lives for and with the crucified and broken ones in the world; and they will always seek a personal and mystical union with Jesus so that they may love as he loves.

Every community and every family are called to live both forms of mission, but in different ways: to pray and to be present in a special way to the smallest and the weakest within their own community or outside it, according to their individual call. God is the fountain from whom we are all called to drink, and this source of life is meant to flow, through each of us, upon all those who thirst: "As the Father has loved me, so I love you . . . my commandment is that you love one another as I love you" [John 15:9-10].

Some people drink first of the waters flowing from God and then discover that they are called to give water to the thirsty. Others begin by giving water to the thirsty but soon find that their well is empty; they then discover the sources of water flowing from the heart of God which become in them "a source of water welling up into eternal life" [John 4:14].

Seen in this way, community life is not something extraordinary or heroic, reserved only for an elite of spiritual heroes. It is for us all; it is for every family and every group of friends committed to each other. It is the most human way of living; and the way that brings the greatest fulfillment and joy to people. As people live in communion with the Father, they enter more and more into communion with one another; they open their hearts to the smallest and weakest. Being in communion with the smallest and the weakest, their hearts are touched and the waters of compassion flow forth; in this way they enter more deeply into communion with the Father.

Sometimes it is easier to hear the cries of poor people who are far away than it is to hear the cries of our brothers and sisters in our own community. There is nothing very splendid in responding to the cry of the person who is with us day after day and who gets on our nerves. Perhaps too we can only respond to the cries of others when we have recognized and accepted the cry of our own pain.

When we know our people, we also realize that we need them, that they and we are interdependent; they open our hearts and call us to love. We are not better than they are — we are there together, for each other. We are united in the covenant which flows from the covenant between God and his people, God and the poorest.

13.3

Community and Growth, 95-97

Jesus Is the Poor

Jesus reveals an even greater unity between the personal contemplation of the Eternal and the personal relationship and bonding with people who are broken and rejected. This is perhaps the great secret of the Gospels and the heart of Christ. Jesus calls his disciples not only to serve the poor but to discover in them his real presence, a meeting with the Father. Jesus tells us that he is hidden in the face of the poor, that he is in fact the poor. And so with the power of the Spirit, the smallest gesture of love towards the least significant person is a gesture of love towards him. Jesus is the starving, the thirsty, the prisoner, the stranger, the naked, the homeless, the sick, the dying, the oppressed, the humiliated. To live with the poor is to live with Jesus, to live with Jesus is to live with the poor (cf. Matt. 25). "Whosoever welcomes one of these little ones in my name, welcomes me; and whosoever welcomes me, welcomes the Father" (Luke 9:48).

People who gather to live the presence of Jesus among people in distress are therefore called not just to do things for them, or to see them as objects of charity, but rather to receive them as a source of life and of communion. These people come together not just to liberate those in need, but also to be liberated by them; not just to heal their wounds, but to be healed by them; not just to evangelize them, but to be evangelized by them.

Christian communities continue the work of Jesus. They are sent to be a presence to people who are living in darkness and despair. The people who come into these communities also respond to the call and the cry of the weak and oppressed. They enter into the covenant with Jesus and the poor. They meet Jesus in them.

Those who come close to people in need do so first of all in a generous desire to help them and bring them relief; they often feel like saviors and put themselves on a pedestal. But once in contact with them, once touching them, establishing a loving and trusting relationship with them, the mystery unveils itself. At the heart of the insecurity of people in distress there is a presence of Jesus. And so they discover the sacrament of the poor and enter the mystery of compassion. People who are poor seem to break down the barriers of powerfulness, of wealth, of ability, and of pride; they pierce the armor the human heart builds to protect itself; they reveal Jesus Christ. They reveal to those who have come to "help" them their own poverty and vulnerability. These people also show their "helpers" their capacity for love, the forces of love in their hearts. A poor person has a mysterious power: in his weakness he is able to open hardened hearts and reveal the sources of living water within them. It is the tiny hand of the fearless child which can slip through the bars of the prison of egoism. He is the one who can open the lock and set free. And God hides himself in the child.

The poor teach us how to live the Gospel. That is why they are the treasures of the church.

In l'Arche, assistants discover that they are called to announce good news to people in need and to reveal to them the immense love God has for them. Sometimes these assistants truly lead people with a handicap over the threshold and into faith. But once over the threshold, people with a handicap truly lead the assistants deeper into faith; they become our teachers.

13.4

Community and Growth, 97-98

The Cry for Love

When I came to Trosly-Breuil, that small village north of Paris, I welcomed Raphael and Philippe, I invited them to come and live with me because of Jesus and his Gospel. That is how l'Arche was founded. When I welcomed those two men from an asylum, I knew it was for life; it would have been impossible to create bonds with them and then send them back to a hospital, or anywhere else. My purpose in starting l'Arche was to found a family, a community with and for those who are weak and poor because of a mental handicap and who feel alone and abandoned. The cry of Raphael and of Philippe was for love, for respect, and for friendship; it was for true communion. They of course wanted me to do things for them, but more deeply they wanted a true love; a love that seeks their beauty, the light shining within them; a love that reveals to them their value and importance in the universe. Their cry for love awoke within my own heart and called forth from in me living waters; they make me discover within my own being a well, a fountain of life.

In our l'Arche community on the Ivory Coast, we welcomed Innocente. She has a severe mental handicap. She remains in many ways like a child only a few months old. But her eyes and whole body quiver with love whenever she is held in love; a beautiful smile unfolds on her face, and her whole being radiates peace and joy. Innocente is not helped by ideas, no matter how deep or beautiful they may be; she does not need money or power or a job; she does not want to prove herself; all she wants is loving touch and communion. When she receives the gift of love, she quivers in ecstasy; if she feels abandoned, she closes herself up in inner pain — the poorer a person is, old or sick or with a severe mental handicap or close to death, the more the cry is solely for communion and friendship. The more then the heart of the person who hears the cry, and responds to it, is awoken.

Other people we have welcomed in l'Arche are more capable and are able to grow in different ways. However, their fundamental need remains the same as Innocente's: communion and friendship, not a possessive friendship but one that gives life and calls them to growth. Love is not opposed to competence. Love is always competent. And, of course, that love is such that it encourages some people to walk on their own, to leave the community, to risk the pain of separation for greater growth.

13.5

Community and Growth, 98-101

Inner Pain

The cry for love and communion and for recognition that rises from the hearts of people in need reveals the fountain of love in us and our capacity to give life. At the same time, it can reveal our hardness of heart and our fears. Their cry is so demanding, and we are frequently seduced by wealth, power, and the values of our societies. We want to climb the ladder of human promotion; we want to be recognized for our efficiency, power, and virtue. The cry of the poor is threatening to the rich person within us. We are sometimes prepared to give money and a little time, but we are frightened to give our hearts, to enter into a personal relationship of love and communion with them. For if we do so, we shall have to die to all our selfishness and to all the hardness of our heart.

The cry for love that flows from the heart of people in need is mixed with pain, anguish, and sometimes agony. They are so fearful of not being lovable; they have suffered so much from oppression and rejection. If this call for love awakens compassion in the hearts of those around them, their fears and anguish and inner pain can also awaken fears and inner pain in those who hear the cry. That is why it is so hard and so frightening to meet people who are inwardly broken. Their anguish seems to awaken anguish and pain in those around them.

In l'Arche, many assistants have felt this inner pain, which can provoke anger and even hatred for the weak person; it is terrible when one feels surging up inside oneself the powers of darkness and of hate. No wonder some want to run away and others try to forget; some try to cover up; others ask for help from a wise guide. The latter discover then that, in their own brokenness, they are truly brothers and sisters with the people they came to serve. They discover too that Jesus is not hidden in the poor around them, but in the poor person within their own being.

People come to l'Arche to serve the needy. They only stay if they have discovered that they themselves are needy, and that the good news is announced by Jesus to the poor, not to those who serve the poor.

Mission, then, does not imply an attitude of superiority or domination, an attitude of "We know, you don't, so you must listen to us if you want to be well off. Otherwise you will be miserable." Mission springs necessarily from poverty and an inner wound, but also from trust in the love of God. Mission is not elitism. It is life given and flowing from the tomb of our beings which has become transformed into a source of life. It flows from the knowledge that we have been liberated through forgiveness; it flows from weakness and vulnerability. It is announcing the good news that we can live in humility, littleness, and poverty, because God is dwelling in our hearts, giving us new life and freedom. We have received freely; we can give freely.

As long as there are fears and prejudices in the human heart, there will be war and bitter injustice. It is only when hearts are healed, and become loving and open, that the great political problems will be solved. Community is a place where people can live truly as human beings, where they can be healed and strengthened in their deepest emotions, and where they can walk towards unity and inner freedom. As fears and prejudices diminish, and trust in God and others grows, the community can radiate and witness to a style and quality of life which will bring a solution to the troubles of our world. The response to war is to live like brothers and sisters. The response to injustice is to share. The response to despair is a limitless trust and hope. The response to prejudice and hatred is forgiveness. To work for peace in community, through acceptance of others as they are, and through constant forgiveness, is to work for peace in the world and for true political solutions; it is to work for the Kingdom of God. It is to work to enable everyone to live and taste the secret joys of the human person united to the eternal.

Mission will always imply struggle: the struggle between the forces of evil that seek to divide — pushing people and groups into isolation and loneliness and then into a closed world of fear, insecurity, and aggression — and the force of love and trust, which open up people and groups to forgiveness, humility, and understanding, to compassion and mutual acceptance, to unity and peace. This struggle is within each person and each community, and between the community and the world surrounding it. Communities which live this call and mission will always be counterculture. The world with its false values will try to isolate them, make them look silly or utopian, or else it will try to infiltrate them with its false values so that they lose their spirit and enthusiasm, becoming rich and secure.

Living communities will always be persecuted in one way or another. Their members must be aware of the gravity of the struggle. They must be prepared to live the struggle with courage and in prayer. Satan and the evil spirits do not want loving communities to exist. So they will do everything they can to discourage, wound, and ultimately destroy them.

In order to be able to meet Jesus in moments of communion with those who are broken and in need, one must also meet him in prayer and in the Eucharist. "He who eats my body and drinks my blood, lives in me and I in him" [John 6:56].

Through the years, I am discovering that there is no contradiction between my life with those in need and my life in prayer and union with God. Of course Jesus reveals himself to me in the Eucharist, and I need to spend time with him in silent prayer. But he reveals himself too in this life with my brothers and sisters. My fidelity to Jesus is also realized in my fidelity to my brothers and my sisters of l'Arche and especially the poorest. If I give retreats, it is because of this covenant, which is the basis of my life. The rest is only service.

Some people in the church consecrate themselves to God in a life of prayer and adoration. Others have a mission to announce the good news or act mercifully in the name of the Church. I sense that my own place in the Church and in human society is to walk with the poor and the weak, so that each of us develops and we sustain each other in fidelity to our own deepest growth, on our own journey towards a greater internal freedom and sometimes external autonomy.

13.6

Jean Vanier. *Befriending the Stranger* (first published as *La source des larmes*, 2001). Mahwah, N.J.: Paulist Press, 2010, 51.

Touching Our Wounds
As we take time alone with Jesus,
as we listen to his call,
we discover his love
but we also touch our pain and our sense of loss.
We tend to live in a world of illusion with regard to ourselves.
We so easily judge others
    but have trouble seeing ourselves as we really are.
Either we feel that we are extraordinary or else we feel that we are
    no good.
There is much inside of us that we do not want to look at.
People with alcohol problems, for example, rarely recognize or
    admit that they are addicted.
Jesus wants to teach us to know ourselves
    with our gifts, with our beauty,
with our deepest desire to love,
with our pain, our fragility, our vulnerability.

13.7

Befriending the Stranger, 51

Let's look once again at the Samaritan woman
    and her encounter with Jesus. [John 4:7-38]
She is one of the most wounded people in the whole gospel.
She belongs to a rejected race
and her own people seem to have cast her aside.
I often wondered why she came to fetch water "at noon."
In countries like hers, women usually go to collect water early in
    the morning
when the sun is not yet too hot.
They usually go at about the same time
so that they can all meet and talk around the well,

share about their lives,
>their difficulties, their children, their husbands.
If a woman of ill repute arrives, tension can arise.
Others make remarks or make fun of her or move away from her.
She does not feel comfortable;
she does not feel she belongs to this little community of village
>women;
she does not share their way of life nor the same concerns.
She scandalizes them.
I think that is why the Samaritan woman comes at noon,
>even though the sun is at its zenith.
But maybe I am mistaken.
When I meet her in heaven I will ask her if what I said about her
>was true.
I won't be a bit surprised if she tells me that I completely missed
>the point,
and that she had come at that late hour simply because she had
>overslept!!
It is clear, however, that her situation made it difficult for her
to meet others in public places as well as in places of worship.
She was a broken woman,
rejected by the sanctimonious people around her;
she must have thought that God too had rejected her.
Maybe she was from a broken background
>that had only known misery:
no family, no home, no stable love, no security,
a situation that filled her with sadness and anger and locked her in
>guilt and revolt.
Maybe she felt sad and angry with herself, with her children,
>and with the people around her.

13.8

Befriending the Stranger, 52

John's Gospel tells us that Jesus is tired
and so sits down near the well of Jacob in Samaria.
It is moving to sense Jesus' exhaustion, his humanity.

He is so "like us in all things except sin."
We need to pay close attention to Jesus in his humanity,
be close to him in his tiredness.
He can show us how to live our tiredness and our humanity.
The woman arrives with a jug on her head or shoulder to fetch
     water.
Jesus turns to her and asks: "Give me to drink."
He does not begin by telling this woman to get her act together
but rather by expressing his need and asking if she can help him.

The fact that this encounter takes place at a well is significant.
Scripture tells us about three other important encounters
     that took place near a well
and that were sealed in a deep covenant.
The first involved Abraham's servant who was sent to find a wife
     for Abraham's son.
When the servant reaches the well he meets Rebecca and says:

     "Give me something to drink" (cf. Gen. 24).

The second concerned the meeting between Jacob and Rachel (cf. Gen. 29).
The third was Moses and Zipporah (cf. Exod. 2).
At the well in Samaria,
     Jesus himself meets this broken, rejected woman
and reveals to her her value, her importance;
reveals that she can become a source of life and be fruitful.

13.9

Befriending the Stranger, 53

This Samaritan woman truly existed
     and Jesus really spoke to her.
One day, in heaven, we too will be able to meet and speak to her!
We must be careful of interpretations of the gospel
     which are only symbolic.
They can be interesting but it is important to look at the facts,
     at the concrete reality,

and see what they tell us.
The Samaritan woman is both a reality and a symbol
(like others in Scripture),
because she teaches us something about humanity
    and about our own selves.
She tells us something important about those who are weak,
    broken, excluded, marginalized;
all those we usually do not want to see
    or that we pretend do not exist,
those we put away in institutions and prisons
    out of sight of the rest of society;
those who are hidden in slum areas.

13.10

Befriending the Stranger, 54

This woman also lives within each one of us;
she is the wounded, broken part of our being
    that we hide from others,
and even from our own selves.
She symbolizes the place of guilt in us
from which are born many of our attitudes and actions —
consciously or unconsciously.
This sense of guilt can even urge us to be heroic and generous
in order to redeem ourselves.
It can also push us into anger
    and dependence on drugs and alcohol.
If we do not let God penetrate
    into the shadow areas of our being,
they risk governing our lives.

I remember talking about the Samaritan to a group
in which there was a woman with a serious alcohol problem.
She used to go through times of abstinence
but then would fall back into drinking.
She would stop again and again and then start drinking.
After my talk she came up to me and said:

"Now I understand. There are two women living inside me.
The one who drinks
and the one who, when she is not drinking,
refuses to look at the wounded part of me,
as if it was too dirty for God to love.
I deny that that part exists
    and I only speak to God about the bright side of me.
I understand now that I have to let God meet
    the wounded, broken woman inside of me
and let him enter into all the dirt inside me."
Without realizing it and in her own rough language
    she was uttering the words of John in the prologue to his Gospel:
    "the light came into the darkness."

If we deny the existence of darkness within ourselves
because we think we are pure,
then the light cannot come into us.
So too, if we think we are only darkness, unworthy of God,
we close up in our darkness;
we cut ourselves off from the light
and prevent it from entering into our lives.

13.11

Befriending the Stranger, 55

This is precisely the mystery of the Incarnation:
God wants to enter into our very being.
God knows how wounded we are.
God knew how broken the woman from Samaria was,
the hurt she had lived with, perhaps from birth;
just as God knows the wounds of our early childhood.
God is aware of the world of darkness, fear, and guilt
    that develops in our lives
even before we become aware of it.
God yearns to enter precisely into that part of our being
that is obscure, broken, and in pain
in order to liberate us.

This Samaritan woman lives in me and in you,
in all those parts of our being where we feel guilty
    of not loving others as we should.
Men often do not know how to love and care for their wives,
or women for their husbands, and they feel guilty.
Parents often feel they do not love their children enough,
or children their parents.
We are all caught up in the same inability to love.
When Jesus speaks to this woman, he is speaking to you and to me.

Jesus sits down by the well, in a position below the woman,
    more humble than the woman.
He has to look up at her — he has to look up at her in me;
then he shows me his need: **"Give me something to drink."**
Our reaction is generally like hers:
"How can you, Jesus, ask me for something!
How can you come to one who feels so weak and broken!
I'm too insignificant, too unworthy,
    for you to ask something of me."

This is our spontaneous reaction
just like Peter's reaction at the washing of the feet:
"It is not possible that you put yourself lower than me!"
Then Jesus says to the Samaritan woman:
    "If you but knew the gift of God . . ."
If we only knew the gift of God. . . .

In order for us to listen to God saying "Give me to drink";
in order for us not to run away from him;
in order for us to accept and be open
    to our wounds as well as to our gifts —
we need time and we need silence.

13.12

Befriending the Stranger, 56

To Discover the Source of Living Water
This encounter between Jesus and the Samaritan woman
    announces a covenant.
It is a moment of communion, of tenderness and of truth.
Jesus is going to reveal to her
    that she will find the waters to quell her thirst,
not only in Jacob's well
but within her inner "well," her own heart, her deepest self.

> "If you but knew the gift of God
> and who it is that is saying to you, 'Give me to drink,'
> rather you would have asked him
> and he could have given you living water" (John 4:10).

She is surprised by his words and does not understand:

> "Lord," she says, "you have no bucket to draw from the well
> and the well is deep.
> Where will you find the living water?
> Are you greater than our Father Jacob, who gave us this well,
> drank from it himself, and gave water to his family and all the
> animals?" (vv. 11-12).

Jesus replies:

> "Whoever drinks of the waters that I will give,
> will never be thirsty."

Then he adds some of the most extraordinary words in the whole gospel:

> "The waters that I will give will become [in that person] a
> spring of water
> welling up in eternal life" (v. 14).

This extraordinary promise was made to this wounded, broken
    woman of Samaria;

this woman full of guilt.
Jesus tells her that she will become a spring of water for others.
She will give them new life, the very life of God,
for water is a symbol of life.
He is telling her: "You will bear much fruit."

13.13

Befriending the Stranger, 57

Jesus yearns for us to become fully alive
and so to communicate life to others.
The giving of life is one of the most amazing mysteries of creation.
Spiders give birth to spiders
    who in turn give birth to other spiders and so on.
Giraffes give birth to giraffes, apples to apples:
there is an infinite, uninterrupted flow of life.

There are of course different ways of giving life.
There is first of all the biological transmission of life:
a man and woman unite and give birth to a child.
That physical birth is only the beginning.
In order for a child to grow and develop
    and to communicate life in turn to others,
he/she needs security, love, and tenderness.
A child needs to live in a stable relationship of love,
a bonding with his mother, his father, and others around him/her.
We human beings are made for love,
called to live covenant relationships
within which we give life to one another.

It does not really matter if a mother spider does not love her baby
    spiders!
But if a child has not known a special, unique love,
the life of the child is in danger.
This love is not an ideal but a real struggle day after day.
We are all struggling to grow in love.
No parent, no person, is perfect.

But each one of us, with our personal stories,
is called to growth in love.

13.14

Befriending the Stranger, 58-60

When I was thirteen I lived a very strong experience
    which was like a new birth for me —
my third "birth" . . . the first one being my birth day, the second
    my baptism. . . .
I wanted to enter the Royal Naval School in England.
War was already raging and we were living in Canada.
I would have to cross the Atlantic
at a time when one out of every five boats
    was being sunk by German submarines.
I went to see my father and told him what I wanted to do.
He asked me why.
I am not sure what I answered
    but I will never forget what he said to me:
"I trust you.
If that is what you want, you have to do it."

That day, with those words, my father gave me new life.
I experienced a sort of rebirth.
If my father had confidence in me
that meant I could have confidence in myself.

If he had told me to wait until I was older
    and had more experience,
I probably would have waited
but I would have lost confidence in my own intuitions.
His reply "I trust you" not only gave me confidence in myself,
but it has helped me throughout my life to trust others.

When we love someone, we give life to that person.
When we love, we trust
and reveal to people their value, their beauty,

and their capacity to give life to others.
When Jesus told this woman that she would become a
"spring of water welling up in eternal life,"
he was revealing to her the deep hidden source of life in her.
We do not always recognize this spring of life within us.
We know that we have a certain intelligence
and are aware of our emotions, desires, and compulsions,
but we are often unaware of the deep well, the sanctuary of love,
　　within us,
and our capacity to love with the very love of God.
We may in fact be frightened of this loving tenderness
　　that we sense rising within us
because we see it as a weakness
or as something linked only to our sexuality.
This can fill us with confusion.

Yet within this very gentleness and tenderness of our hearts,
there is a presence of God.
We often experience this most strongly
when we are with people with profound disabilities.
The mystery Jesus revealed to the Samaritan woman
is the mystery contained in the life of each one of us:
if we drink from the source of life, which is Jesus,
we too will become a source of life;
we will bring life, the very life of God, into our world.
Thus we fulfill the deepest desire of Jesus for us:
his desire that we become men and women who are fully alive.

13.15

Befriending the Stranger, 60-61

To Welcome the Person within Us
Who Is Weak and Poor
The Samaritan woman was confused; she did not understand.
She says to Jesus:
"Lord, give me these waters that I may not thirst" (John 4:15).

Jesus changes the conversation:
"**Go and call your husband and come back**" (v. 16).

Jesus is so gentle and understanding.
He does not judge or condemn this woman.
He simply wants to draw her attention to her wounds, her fragility,
and to show her the place of pain and sadness
that she has been hiding from others and even from herself.

"**I have no husband,**" she replies.
"**You are right in saying, 'I have no husband,'**" says Jesus,
"**for you have had five husbands
and the man you have now is not your husband.
What you have said is true**" (vv. 17-18).
That little phrase "**What you have said is true**" is important.

Jesus wants to help her to discover the truth of her being,
to realize who she is, with all her brokenness;
to show in this way that he does not judge her or condemn her.
The only thing that matters is that we be truthful;
that we do not let ourselves be governed by lies and by illusion.
Once she has accepted the truth of her being, she can become a
    spring of life.
It is only when we have accepted the truth of our being
that we, like the Samaritan woman, can begin to walk
    the path of inner wholeness.

We need to touch the truth of who we are.
It is then, as we grow gradually into the acceptance of our wounds
    and fragility,
that we grow into wholeness,
and from that wholeness, life begins to flow forth
    to others around us.

It is important to take time to be silent, to be alone with Jesus,
to look at the reality of who we are,
be in contact with our hidden places of pain,
and little by little we can become a friend of our weakness.

13.16

Befriending the Stranger, 61-62

In 1980, when I left the role of community leader in Trosly,
I lived a year at "La Forestiere," one of our homes
for ten men and women with profound disabilities.
I have told you about Eric, but there was also Lucien.
Lucien was born with severe mental and physical disabilities.
He cannot talk or walk or move his arms.
His body is a bit twisted,
     and he has to remain in his wheelchair or in his bed.
He never looks anyone directly in the eyes.
Lucien's father died when he was twelve.
He lived the first thirty years of his life with his mother,
who cared for him and understood him and his needs;
she could interpret all his body language.
He was at peace and felt secure with her.
One day she fell sick and had to go to the hospital.
Lucien was put into another hospital
and was plunged into a totally strange and unknown world;
he had lost all his familiar points of reference;
no one seemed to understand him.
Screams of anguish rose up in him
     which were unbearable to hear.
Finally he came to "La Forestiere."
When faced with his constant screaming, we felt quite powerless.
If we tried to touch him to calm him down,
this very touch seemed to increase his anguish.
There was nothing to do but to wait.

The pitch of Lucien's scream was piercing
and seemed to penetrate the very core of my being,
awakening my own inner anguish.
I could sense anger, violence, and even hatred rising up within me.
I would have been capable of hurting him to keep him quiet.
It was as if a part of my being that I had learned to control
     was exploding.
It was not only Lucien's anguish

that was difficult for me to accept
but the revelation of what was inside my own heart —
my capacity to hurt others —
I who had been called to share my life with the weak,
had a power of hatred for a weak person!

13.17

Befriending the Stranger, 62-63

That experience, and other similar experiences, helped me towards
    a better understanding of the mothers of "battered children";
women who have been abandoned by their husbands or partners;
an abandonment which gives rise to loneliness,
    anguish, and depression within them.
They usually have to work for a living
    and are bringing up their children alone.

When they come home from a full day's work, they are tired;
they have just enough energy to make dinner
    and to put the children in front of the television!
But children of course need more than that.
They are yearning for love and attention and presence.
So they start crying, even screaming.
The mother is exhausted; her inner "well" is empty.
Their cry for attention and love reveals her own need for love.
There is so much anguish and inner pain in her
that she ends up by hitting one of the children
in order to make him be quiet —
and especially to liberate her own anguish!

How painful it is for us to look reality in the face,
to discover our own fragility
    and our capacity for anger and hatred.
The temptation is so great to avoid or run away from
those who reveal our inner limits and brokenness.
The roots of much racism, rejection, and exclusion are here.
It is important not to run away,

but to find someone with whom we can speak about these shadow
     areas of our being,
these inner "demons," the "wolf" within us,
someone who can help us not to be controlled by them
so that they no longer haunt our lives.

13.18

Befriending the Stranger, 63-65

When I was living in the Forestiere, I was given a text by Carl
     Jung, the analytical psychologist and disciple of Freud.
It was a letter he had written to a young Christian woman which
     I quote from memory.
He said something like this, referring to the words of Jesus in
     Matthew 25:

I admire Christians,
because when you see someone who is hungry or thirsty,
you see Jesus.
When you welcome a stranger, someone who is "strange,"
you welcome Jesus.
When you clothe someone who is naked, you clothe Jesus.
What I do not understand, however,
is that Christians never seem to recognize Jesus
in their own poverty.
You always want to do good to the poor outside you
and at the same time you deny the poor person
living inside you.
Why can't you see Jesus in your own poverty,
in your own hunger and thirst?
In all that is "strange" inside you:
in the violence and the anguish that are beyond your control!
You are called to welcome all this, not *to deny* its existence,
but to accept that it is there and to meet Jesus there.

Jung's letter helped me to realize
     that I cannot welcome and receive Jesus

unless I welcome my own weakness, my poverty
    and my deepest needs.
I cannot accept the wounds of Innocente, Eric, and Lucien
unless I am open and accept my own wounded self and seek help.
Can I truly be compassionate towards them
    if I am not compassionate towards myself?

The mystery of the weak and the broken is that they call forth
not only the deep well of love and tenderness in us
but also the hardness and darkness.
Jesus calls us not only to welcome the weak and the rejected,
    like Claudia and Lucien,
but also the weak and the broken person within us
and to discover the presence of Jesus within us.

That is the meaning of the words of Jesus
    to the woman from Samaria:
"What you have said is true."
In order for us to be men and women who give life to others,
we have to live in the truth of who we are;
we have to find an inner wholeness,
no longer to deny or ignore our wounds
    but to welcome them
and to discover the presence of God
    in these very places of our own weakness.

13.19

Jean Vanier. *Becoming Human.* London: Darton, Longman & Todd, 1999, 83-84.

From Exclusion to Inclusion

How do we move from exclusion to inclusion?

When I talk about "inclusion" of people, whether they are those with disabilities, beggars like Lazarus, or people suffering from AIDS, I am not talking only about starting up special schools or residences or creating good soup kitchens or new hospitals. These are, of course, necessary. I am not just saying that we should be kind to such people because they are human beings. Nor is it a question of "normalizing" them in order that they can be "like us," participate in church services, and go to the movies and the local swimming pool. When I speak of the inclusion of those who are marginalized, I am affirming that they have a gift to give to all, to each of us as individuals, to the larger forms of human organization, and to society in general.

The excluded, I believe, live certain values that we all need to discover and to live ourselves before we can become truly human. It is not just a question of performing good deeds for those who are excluded but of being open and vulnerable to them in order to receive the life that they can offer; it is to become their friends. If we start to include the disadvantaged in our lives and enter into heartfelt relationships with them, they will change things in us. They will call us to be people of mutual trust, to take time to listen and be with each other. They will call us out from our individualism and need for power into belonging to each other and being open to others. They will break down the prejudices and protective walls that gave rise to exclusion in the first place. They will then start to affect our human organizations, revealing new ways of being and walking together. . . .

13.20

Becoming Human, 85-88

The Heart

The heart, the metaphorical heart, the basis of all relationships, is what is deepest in each one of us. It is my heart that bonds itself to another heart; it leads us out of the restricted belonging, which creates exclusion, to meet and love others just as they are. A little child is only heart; he thrives off relationships; his joy is in relationships; he grows through relationships. When he is in communion with someone he trusts, he is safe, he is someone, someone unique and important. He is thus empowered, for the rest of his life, to be open to others, and to bring this sense of empowerment into his work.

To work means to be energetic, strong, and active, cooperating with others; communion means to be vulnerable and tender; it means opening one's heart and sharing one's hopes and pain, even all that is failure or brokenness.

If my heart is broken, I can quickly feel crushed and fall into depression, unable to work. Or, I may refuse all relationships and throw myself savagely into work. If my heart is fulfilled, it will shine through my work.

We've all seen the transforming power of love. The most hardened, embittered person sees themselves and sees life in a new way when they fall in love and when they know that they are loved. It is easy to recognize a man or a woman in love. Aggressive or depressive tendencies seem to disappear. They move towards a gentle openness. Instead of protecting themselves behind barriers, they make themselves open and welcoming. A new freedom, kindness, and tenderness become evident.

My point is that a human being is more than the power or capacity to think and to perform. There is a gentle person of love hidden in the child within each adult. The heart is the place where we meet others, suffer, and rejoice with them. It is the place where we can identify and be in solidarity with them. Whenever we love, we are not alone. The heart is the place of our "oneness" with others.

The way of the heart implies a choice. We can choose to take this path and to treat people as people and not just as machines. We can see the cook in a hotel simply as somebody who is paid to cook well or as a person with a heart, who has children, and who might be living painful relationships and is in need of understanding and kindness. To treat each person as a person means that we are concerned for them, that we listen to them, and love them and want them to become more whole, free, truthful, and responsible.

To speak of the heart is not to speak of vaguely defined emotions but to speak of the very core of our being. At the core, we all know we can be strengthened and rendered more truthful and more alive. Our hearts can become hard like stone or tender like flesh. We have to create situations where our hearts can be fortified and nourished. In this way, we can be more sensitive to others, to their needs, their cries, their inner pain, their tenderness, and their gifts of love.

Our hearts, however, are never totally pure. People can cry out to be loved, especially if as children they were not loved. There are "loving" relationships that are unhealthy because they are a flight from truth and from responsibility. There are friendships that are unhealthy because one is too frightened to challenge one's friend. These are the signs of the immature heart. An immature heart can lead us to destructive relationships and then to depression and death.

It is only once a heart has become mature in love that it can take the road of insecurity, putting its trust in God. It is a heart that can make wise decisions; it has learned to discern and to take risks that bring life. It can meet other people inside and outside the place of belonging. It can meet people who have been excluded. It is the heart that helps us to discover the common humanity that links us all, that is even stronger than all that bonds us together as part of a specific group. The heart, then, forgoes the need to control others. The free heart frees others.

Heart-to-heart relationships where God is present are more important than the approbation of society or of a group. Belonging to a group is important; it is the "earth" in which we grow. Sometimes we have to forego group approval and even accept rejection, if it should happen, in order to follow what the ancients called "scientia cordis," the science of the heart, which gives the inner strength to put truth, flowing from experience, over the need for approval. The science of the heart permits us to be vulnerable with others, not to fear them but to listen to them, to see their beauty and value, to understand them in all their fears, needs, and hopes, even to challenge them if need be. It permits us to accept others just as they are and to believe that they can grow to greater beauty. The mature heart does not seek to force belief on others; it does not seek to impose a faith. The mature heart listens for what another's heart is called to be. It no longer judges or condemns. It is a heart of forgiveness. Such a heart is a compassionate heart that sees the presence of God in others. It lets itself be led by them into uncharted land. It is the heart that calls us to grow, to change, to evolve, and to become more fully human.

13.21

Becoming Human, 88-91

The Way of the Heart

I discovered the "way of the heart" in l'Arche, as a way of putting people first, of entering into personal relationships. This way of approaching each individual, of relating to each one with gentleness and kindness, was not easy for me. I joined the navy when I was very young, just thirteen, a highly impressionable age. All my training was geared to help me to be quick, competent, and efficient, and so I became. As a naval officer, and even later, after I had left the navy, I was a rather stiff person, geared to the goals of efficiency, duty, prayer, and doing good to others and to philosophical and theological studies. My energies were goal-oriented.

From the beginning, in 1964, l'Arche has been truly a learning experience for me. It has brought me into the world of simple relationships, of fun and laughter. It has brought be back into my body, because people with disabilities do not delight in intellectual or abstract conversation. There are times when, of course, conversation with them is serious; we need to talk about fundamental realities of life such as birth, death, sexuality, prayer, and justice. They need times of work where they can see what they can accomplish. Leisure times are centered [on] fun, games, and celebrations. There is not a life centered on the mind. So it is that the people with intellectual disabilities led me from a serious world into a world of celebration, presence, and laughter: the world of the heart.

When we are in communion with another, we become open and vulnerable to them. We reveal our needs and our weaknesses to each other. Power and cleverness call forth admiration but also a certain separation, a sense of distance; we are reminded of who we are not, of what we cannot do. On the other hand, sharing weaknesses and needs calls us together into "oneness." We welcome those who love us into our heart. In this communion, we discover the deepest part of our being, the need to be loved and to have someone who trusts and appreciates us and who cares least of all about our capacity to work or to be clever and interesting. When we discover we are loved in this way, the masks or barriers behind which we hide are dropped; new life flows. We no longer have to prove our worth; we are free to be ourselves. We find a new wholeness, a new inner unity.

I love to watch little children playing and chatting among themselves. They do not care what people think. They do not have to try to appear to be clever and important. They know they are loved and are free to be themselves. As they grow into adolescence and adulthood, they become more self-conscious. They lose a certain freedom, which they may find again later, when they rediscover that they are loved and accepted just as they are and are no longer obsessed by what others may think of them.

Spiritual masters in sacred scripture often tell stories to reveal trusts and to awaken hearts. Jesus spoken in parables; Hasidic Jews and Sufi Teachers tell tales; Hindu scripture is full of stories. Stories seem to awaken new energies of love; they tell us great truths in simple, personal terms and make us long for light. Stories have a strange power of attraction. When we tell stories, we touch hearts. If we talk about theories or speak about ideas, the mind may assimilate them, but the heart remains untouched.

To witness is to tell our story. In l'Arche, we love to tell our stories and how people with disabilities have transformed us, stories that reveal their love and simplicity and that speak of their courage, pain, and closeness to God. It is hard to be interesting if we speak in general terms about those with disabilities; people are not always terribly interested. It is the story of a specific person that touches the listener.

When we hear stories of others who have lived as we have lived and how they have risen up from the drab and found hope, we, too, find hope. Stories of transformation from death to life sow seeds of hope.

14 The Importance of Being a Creature: Stanley Hauerwas on Disability

JOHN SWINTON

For over thirty years, Stanley Hauerwas has been reflecting theologically on issues of disability. He is convinced that understanding the lives of people with profound intellectual disabilities is crucial for enabling the faithful interpretation and practice of Christian theology and for developing a proper understanding of what it means to be church. It is important to note that Hauerwas's thinking on disability precedes much of the contemporary political and theological literature that has come to make up the field known as "disability theology." Hauerwas is not a disability theologian in the sense of many who currently identify themselves as such, particularly those who have been influenced by the goals of disability studies, with its strong emphasis on politics and political intervention as the most appropriate way of enabling the acceptance and participation of people with disabilities within church and society (see Eiesland 1994; and Jana Bennett, chapter 12, this volume). Hauerwas begins with the assumption that political philosophies based on the premises of modernity and worked out within liberal democracies, that is, systems of democracy based on individual rights and freedoms, can offer little in terms of protection or meaningful inclusion for people with severe intellectual disabilities. The goals of autonomy, rights, independence, equality, power, and freedom are precisely the types of social goods that are not available to people with such disabilities. Not only can they not access the political system in order to participate in change; they are also deeply vulnerable to that system. As reading **14.1** indicates, the same equality, freedom, and choice that enable people to choose *for* people with disabilities allows people the freedom *not to choose* to be for them. The politics of modernity cannot bring about the kinds of change that the disability studies perspective desires. This places Hauerwas in quite a different position from other theologians writing about disability.

Profound and Complex Intellectual Disability

In order to understand how and why Hauerwas focuses on disability, we need to be clear about precisely what form of disability he concentrates on. Hauerwas's interest is not in disability per se; his interest is in a form of disability within which people encounter a quite specific set of experiences. He usually refers to this form of disability as "mental retardation" and/or "mental handicap." The precise content of these terms is never explicitly defined, though implicit assumptions can easily be drawn out. Hauerwas's focus is on the experiences of people who have severe intellectual disabilities. This group of human beings is deemed to have limited communication skills, restricted or no self-care skills, and significant intellectual and/or cognitive difficulties; it is also assumed that they will require some kind of full-time care throughout their lives. Importantly, the experiences of this group are the *exact opposite* of the goals and ideals of modernity and liberal democracy. People with these life experiences are not free, autonomous individuals who are able to narrate their own stories or live independently of others. They will never be autonomous; they will never participate in the political process; they cannot actively seek after rights and power; and they will never attain freedom in the political sense of this term. As such, they cannot and do not share in the capacities that modernity indicates are fundamental for fulfilled human living. Within modernity the lives of such people become unintelligible. It is therefore not disability in general that forms Hauerwas's focus, but this particular type of disability that has become highly problematic within modernity.

Shifting the Questions

Hauerwas identifies himself as a theologian and an ethicist. However, his interest is not in solving ethical dilemmas at the edges of life. Rather, his focus is on challenging the presuppositions which underpin situations and contexts and which cause particular questions to arise. For example, rather than framing abortion as an ethical dilemma, Hauerwas asks why it is that Christians might consider the option of killing babies in the first place. For something to be a dilemma, it needs first to be an option; if it is not an option, it cannot become a dilemma. Why would Christians perceive killing unborn children as an option which then causes a dilemma? Such questioning and challenging of presuppositions leads readers to re-think why it is that they think what they do in the ways that they do.

This approach is important for understanding Hauerwas's perspective on disability. Hauerwas does not see people with profound intellectual disabilities in terms of ethical dilemmas. The question is not "What can we do about the problem of the disabled?" Rather, the important issue is why we see disability as a problem or an ethical dilemma in the first place. This challenges us to do two things. First, we must ask whether there actually *is* a problem to be solved or an ethical dilemma to be resolved. Second, if there is, then the question becomes "Whose problem is it?" Is disability the problem which raises the dilemma, or is the modern mind-set that has taught us to perceive disability in particular ways the real problem? Hauerwas focuses on the latter. Hauerwas's interest is therefore on the presuppositions that lie within and beneath particular commonly held assumptions about profound intellectual disability.

Redescribing situations in order to disclose hidden presuppositions forms a central aspect of Hauerwas's theological task. He describes his basic approach as a "theology of indirection":

> I have tried to resist the temptation to make theology another set of ideas that can be considered in and of themselves. For example, anyone concerned to discover what "my" doctrine of God might be or what my "theological anthropology" entails will look in vain for an essay or book on those theological topics. But this does not mean I do not think about questions classically associated with the doctrine of God or theological anthropology; I try to write about such issues in relation to material practices that exemplify what is at stake. My reflections on the challenge the mentally handicapped present to some of our most cherished conceits about ourselves is best understood as my attempt to develop a theological anthropology. In brief, I "use" the mentally handicapped to try to help us understand what it means for us to be creatures of a gracious God. For I think it a profound mistake to assume that a strong distinction can be drawn between those who are mentally handicapped and those who are not mentally handicapped once it is acknowledged that we are equally creatures of God, who, as Augustine observed, created us without us, but who refuses to save us without us. (quoted in Swinton 2005, 192)

Hauerwas wants his readers to be clear that his theology contains classic doctrinal assertions presented *indirectly,* but no less illuminatively. In the case of disability, he does this by using the experience of people with profound intellectual disabilities to re-describe both God and human beings in opposition to false representations presented within modernity. One way in which we can understand Hauerwas's reflections on disability is that they represent *his indirect but nonetheless intentional attempts to present a theological anthropology based on a radical assertion of human creatureliness, and to identify the material practices that exemplify what is at stake in making such a claim truthful.*

Whose Suffering? The "Problem" of Disability

A useful place to begin to explore Hauerwas's thinking on disability is through his reflections on suffering. Hauerwas asks the apparently obvious question: "Why is it that the term 'suffering' frequently comes to be associated with profound intellectual disabilities?" As readings **14.2** and **14.3** highlight, this association is so close and acute that individuals and societies rarely question its authenticity. At first glance our moral obligation to prevent suffering seems obvious:

> No one should will that an animal should suffer gratuitously. No one should will that a child should endure an illness. No one should will that another person should suffer from hunger. No one should will that a child should be born retarded. That suffering should be avoided is a belief as deep as any we have. That someone born retarded suffers is obvious. Therefore, if we believe we ought to prevent suffering, it seems we ought to prevent retardation. (Hauerwas 1986, 164)

It seems "obvious" that people with intellectual disabilities suffer; therefore, it is "obvious" that preventing the existence of such lives is the most appropriate, compassionate, and right thing to do. However, the simple fact that "compassionate" acts of prevention often mean the elimination of the subject should alert us to the possibility that there might be more at issue here than immediately meets the eye. When we begin to explore precisely what is meant by the "suffering of the retarded" (i.e., when we look at the presuppositions behind such a statement), things begin to look different.

How Do "the Retarded" Suffer?

There are many different ways in which people suffer. We get cancer, we experience pain, and we are struck by natural tragedies such as storms and earthquakes. We naturally try to avoid such tragic circumstances and treat their victims with compassion and care; we take care not to live in areas that are prone to earthquakes; we try to encourage people not to smoke and to eat well and so forth. All of these are appropriate preventative and interventionist strategies that we engage in our attempts to avoid suffering. However, Hauerwas suggests that the suffering which we presume to be experienced by people with profound intellectual disabilities is taken to be of a different order.

And yet, there is nothing inherent within the experience of profound intellectual disability which necessitates the term "suffering." People with such disabilities can have very good and fulfilled lives: they can experience relationships and love; they can engage in joyful activities; and they can make and receive genuine contributions to families and to society. They may suffer, as all people may do, but being intellectually disabled is not in itself a necessary source of suffering. So why are people so prone to using the term "suffering" in relation to such lives?

The Social Nature of Suffering

Suffering is not something that is simply located within the bodies of particular individuals. Suffering is a social concept (**14.2, 14.3**). As such, it has a particular meaning that is tied to the context within which a person's experience is named and lived out. We suffer because of the types of people we encounter, the societies within which we live, and the expectations that we have for our lives — what Hauerwas describes as our "life projects." Within modernity, one mode of suffering comes from our inability to achieve that which we presume to be central to our self-identified life projects. "Not only is what we suffer relative to our projects," says Hauerwas, "but how we suffer is relative to what we have or wish to be" (Hauerwas 1986, 166). If this is so, it is not too difficult to see why people trained in the practices and worldview of modernity can easily attribute suffering to intellectual disability. Such a disability is inevitably perceived as a significant constraint on a person's life project, to the extent that it nullifies cultural perceptions of what a worthwhile life project might actually look like.

It may well be that those forms of suffering we believe we should try to prevent or to eliminate are those that we think impossible to integrate into our life projects, socially or individually. It is exactly those forms of suffering which seem to intrude uncontrollably into our lives which appear to be the most urgent candidates for prevention. Thus, our sense that we should prevent those kinds of suffering that we do not feel can serve any human good. (Hauerwas 1986, 167)

Our attribution of the term "suffering" to people with profound intellectual disabilities relates to the fact that "we" (i.e., those who do not carry the weight of the label "profoundly intellectually disabled") could not imagine ourselves in "their" situation. In fact, Hauerwas says,

> . . . we have no way to know what the retarded suffer as retarded. All we know is how we imagine we would feel if we were retarded. We thus often think that we would rather not exist at all than to exist as one retarded. As a result we miss the point at issue. For the retarded do not feel or understand their retardation as we do, or imagine we would, but rather as they do. (Hauerwas 1986, 174)

The problem is that the modern imagination presumes that the criteria that underpin liberal democratic societies have provided for us an accurate description of that which is essential for authentic human living. To lose such valuable social goods (autonomy, freedom, independence, choice, etc.) would be worse than death. Put slightly differently, modern people have a tendency to project their own fears and concerns for themselves and what they expect from their lives onto the life experiences of people with severe intellectual disabilities. And Hauerwas is very clear about how wrong this is:

> We have no right or basis to attribute our assumed unhappiness or suffering to them. Ironically, therefore, the policy of preventing suffering is one based on a failure of imagination. Unable to see like the retarded, to hear like the retarded, we attribute to them our suffering. (Hauerwas 1986, 101)

Projected interpretations of the experiences of people with severe intellectual disabilities are quite different from lived interpretations of that experience. A narrative of loss is not the same as a narrative of being. The primary loss within the lives of people with profound intellectual disabilities is not the loss of intellect; rather, it is the loss of value placed on them by a society whose systems of valuing render them worthless and frightening. If people with profound intellectual disabilities suffer, it is because modern minds have constructed the meaning of the term "suffering" in ways which make their normal ways of being in the world highly problematic. Hauerwas draws our attention to the "narrative of being" and urges us to explore what that narrative might tell us about what human beings are, who God is, and what it might mean to be a faithful church within modernity.

Intellectually disabled people live lives that cannot be made sense of within the values, beliefs, and assumptions of modernity. Either we reject their experience as aberrant and/or meaningless, or we listen to that experience and allow what we hear to challenge our presuppositions and assumptions. Within modernity our lives are deemed meaningful only to the extent that they are meaningful to ourselves. We are assumed to be the authors of our own lives. As Hauerwas puts it, "The project of modernity was to produce people who believe they should have no story except the story they choose when they have no story" (Hauerwas 1995, 4). But Christians belong within a story which is not of their own making. We are creatures, created beings, who are wholly dependent on God for all things:

> As Christians we know we have not been created to be "our own authors," to be autonomous. We are creatures. Dependency, not autonomy, is one of the ontological characteristics of our lives. That we are creatures, moreover, is but a reminder that we are created with and for one another. We are not just accidentally communal, but we are such by necessity. We are not created to be alone. . . . For Christians the mentally handicapped do not present a peculiar challenge. That the mentally handicapped are constituted by narratives they have not chosen simply reveals the character of our lives. (Hauerwas 1999, 16)

Reading 14.4 develops this key point. Within modernity, dependence is perceived to be the antithesis of the good life. Individualism with all of its accretions is presumed to be the norm for authentic human living. That being so, the lives of people with intellectual disability stand in sharp, negative tension with cultural expectations. However, the essence of the Christian tradition is that human beings are wholly dependent. Far from being an indication of a lack of human fulfillment, the lives of people with intellectual disabilities are in fact a reminder of the true state of *all* human beings. Their existence is nothing more (and nothing less) than a concentrated vision of normality.

Reflection on the lives of people with profound intellectual disabilities is therefore a context for learning what it means to be a creature. Learning to be a creature means to recognize that our existence and the existence of the universe itself are gifts. If all is gift, then dependency is our natural state. Hauerwas reminds us that the lives of people with profound intellectual disabilities, far from being problematic, marked by suffering, or raising ethical dilemmas, in fact inform us of what human living is *really* like (14.5).

At the core of Hauerwas's theology is a mode of theological realism wherein there is an inherent assumption that the narrative of creation, redemption, cross, and resurrection is *actually the way that the world is*. The gospel is *the* revelation of the nature of the world that God gives to Christians, a revelation which equips them to see the world as it is and not as it appears. Within such a worldview, autonomy is inevitably an illusion, a culturally shaped projection of our desires and fantasies. Our encounters with people who have profound intellectual disabilities remind us of a fundamental theological truth that modernity has hidden from us: *It is dependency and not autonomy that is one of the ontological characteristics of our lives.* This theological truth as it is embodied in the lives of people with profound intellectual disabilities reveals the true character of all of our lives. In this way Hauerwas marks out the lives of people with profound intellectual disabilities as *paradigmatic* rather than *exceptional*; their needs are *ordinary* rather than *special*.

Thus the presence of people with profound intellectual disabilities does not pose a challenge or a problem, as if such lives required special justification. Rather, people with profound intellectual disabilities are gifts bearing gifts, to be welcomed rather than questioned. The Christian story produces practices of welcoming which make the reception of such gifts possible.

Bearing Witness

It is important to restate that Hauerwas's writings on disability are not intended simply as a theological defense of disabled lives. Rather, his reflections are aimed at drawing our attention to theological truths that are applicable to *all* people. He is making strong theological truth-claims based on the experience of disability: "I have used the mentally handicapped as *material markers* to show that Christian speech can and in fact does make claims about the way things are" (Hauerwas 1999, 17 [emphasis added]). Christian theology informs us clearly that we are creatures in the ways outlined previously. Such a claim requires witness before it can become intelligible. The fact that people with profound intellectual disabilities exist and live out lives of total dependency is a "material marker," a physical marking point within human history, which indicates that it is actually possible to live as dependent creatures. In a real sense, people with profound intellectual disabilities bear witness to the truth of the gospel.

Critical Reflections

Hauerwas's thinking on issues of disability is undoubtedly an important contribution to theology in general and to the field of disability theology in particular. It is not, however, without its problems. Hauerwas has come under some criticism from within the disability community because of his continuing use of terms that are considered outdated, such as "mentally retarded" and "mentally handicapped." It would be unfair to level this criticism with regard to the work he produced in the sixties and seventies. However, the use of such terms in his later work is an unhelpful distraction; at this point he was writing within a social context in which the oppressive and destructive nature of these particular labels has been brought sharply to our attention by those who have been forced to bear their consequences.

There are, however, deeper concerns than political correctness. If disability is a gift that leads us to understand our true state as human beings, then why does Hauerwas seem to support the suggestion that we should do all we can to prevent disability? (Hauerwas 1986, 176). If people with intellectual disability are gifts, as reading 14.6 indicates, why should we not rejoice that they are born "retarded" rather than "normal"? Why should the presence of such people "destroy our plans and fantasies about what we wish our children to be"? In the footnotes to his essay "Suffering the Retarded: Should We Prevent Retardation?" Hauerwas seems to imply that the problem relates to the "inevitable" frustration that parents experience at having a "retarded" child; the fact that such a child cannot "get better" is inevitably a problem and, by implication, a mode of suffering. However, as Hazel Morgan points out, the reality is that parents respond to disabled children in a variety of different ways. Some love them immediately; other struggle.[1] The assertion that disabled children inevitably bring such frustration cannot be sustained.

It could be argued that Hauerwas's apparently contradictory position is

---

1. Hazel Morgan, "Thoughts on Suffering: A Parent's View," in *Critical Reflections on Stanley Hauerwas' Essays on Disability*, ed. John Swinton (New York: Haworth Press, 2005).

due to his disinterest in the question of whether or not having disabled children is morally good or bad; rather, his focus is on what the experience of profound disability reveals about the ways in which we describe humans and God and the practices that emerge from such understanding. To criticize him for this apparently contradictory position is to risk detracting from his more important theological points. This would not be unfair comment. Hauerwas does not claim to be a practical theology, and the intentions of his writings are theological rather than pastoral. Nevertheless, it may be that Hauerwas's focus suggests that people with profound disabilities are merely useful vehicles for his broader theological probject (Hauerwas 1999, 1), which raises significant issues regarding the pastoral utility of his position.

One of the problems is that Hauerwas's personal memory of people with disability is distant (Hauerwas 1999, 13). This admission is important. His interest falls not on *particular* disabled individuals or even on specific families; rather, his attention is focused on the *category* of profound intellectual disability and how the experiences associated with it have become problematic within modernity. By the term "category" I simply mean a collection of things sharing some common attributes. This observation has two important consequences. First, the language he uses to address this category becomes unimportant. If the terms "mental handicap" and "mental retardation" are offensive to people, that is not the point. The category is the point, not the individuals who bear the weight of the category. The problem with this approach is that there is no such thing as "mental handicap," "mental retardation," or even "profound intellectual disability" apart from the individuals who carry these labels. Such terms are simply ways of naming specific forms of human difference that have become problematic within cultures at particular moments in time. This is at least part of Hauerwas's point. Yet throughout his writings he seems to assume that such categories exist and can be identified and written about in an academic context. This tendency to reify "handicap" and "retardation" is problematic. As we have seen, it allows Hauerwas to slip between various positions regarding the moral status of disabled persons. In focusing on the category of disability, he tends to lose sight of the implications of certain statements for unique individuals.

Second, this tendency to work with a category rather than with persons leads to a clear "us" and "them" dynamic that has significant theological and practical consequences. John O'Brien astutely picks up on this point. Why does Hauerwas seem to perceive "the retarded" as a distinct group of people, like Hungarians or Texans? (in Swinton 2005, 49). Precisely who are "they," and in what way are "they" not like "us"? If the "mentally handicapped" are in fact gifts that reveal the true nature of human beings, then this implicit process of reification and separation into "us" and "them" has significant consequences. Take, for example, this passage from Hauerwas:

> That such fellow-feeling is possible does not mean that they are "really just like us." They are not. They do not have the same joys we have nor do they suffer just as we suffer. But in our joys and in our sufferings they recognize something of their joy and their suffering, and they offer to share their neediness with us. Such an offer enables us in quite surprising ways to discover that we have needs to share with them. We are thus freed from the false and vicious circle of having to appear strong before others' weakness, and we are then able to join with the retarded in the common project of sharing our needs and satisfactions. As a result we discover we no longer fear them. (Hauerwas 1986, 103)

This is a somewhat startling exercise in distancing and "other-ing." One might be forgiven for thinking that this piece referred to an encounter with a person from another planet rather than a revelation from God of the true nature of human beings! What sense is there in Hauerwas's suggestion that "the retarded" "do not experience suffering or joy in the way 'we' do" in the light of their status as gifts and their revelation of the true nature of human being? How does he know that they don't have life projects in precisely the way in which modernity insists people should have? And why would he presuppose they do not? One might well ask if people who live with or work closely with people with profound intellectual disabilities would come to the same conclusions. "They are not like us" may work at the level of academic argument *about* disability, but it makes little sense in terms of the relational realities of life *with* disabled people.

This clear separation of people with disabilities from "us" not only has obvious implications for how "we" relate to "them" on a temporal level; it also has significant theological implications. It could of course be argued that Hauerwas's point is that people with profound intellectual disabilities are somehow closer to God and that the "us" and "them" dynamic is designed to challenge those who consider themselves to be normal but who are clearly abnormal when perceived through the lens of the values of the kingdom of God. This is one way in which the following passage could be read:

> Quite simply, the challenge of learning to know, to be with, and care for the retarded is nothing less than learning to know, be with, and love God.

God's face is the face of the retarded; God's body is the body of the retarded; God's being is that of the retarded. For the God we Christians
must learn to worship is not a god of self-sufficient power, a god who in
self-possession needs no one; rather, ours is a God who needs a people,
who needs a son. Absoluteness of being or power is not a work of the God
we have come to know through the cross of Christ. (Hauerwas 1986, 104)

Here Hauerwas seems to directly equate profound intellectual disability with
Godliness. It would appear that "they" are closer to the likeness of God than
"we" are, not only in terms of their social experiences (helplessness, dependency, vulnerability, etc.), but also somehow ontologically.

At one level this suggestion has positive force. No longer can we assume
that the image of God is somehow owned by those who claim the status of
"normal." In this sense Hauerwas's idea is protective and constructive. However, the problem is this: If God's face is the face of the "retarded," then where
is the face of the "non-retarded"? Are disabled people to be equated with the
"holy innocents" specially blessed by God? If so, then the "us" and "them"
not only relates to the fact that "they" come from Texas and "we" come from
Kansas, but suggests that "they" are like God and "we" are not! The separation is not simply relational but has now been given divine sanctification.
Quite apart from the obvious empirical observation that people with profound intellectual disabilities can be far from godly in the way that they behave and live out their lives, such a statement serves further to distance intellectually disabled people from people who consider themselves to be
normal. If "we" are not like "them" and "they" are like God, then what might
that say about "us" in relation to "them" and to God?

Having said all of that, there is a tension between Hauerwas's statement
about the otherness of people with profound intellectual disabilities and his
more recent statements (such as 14.7). It is difficult to assess why this shift
has occurred. However, I would hypothesize that there has been a shift in his
thinking since he began to engage with the work of Jean Vanier and reflect
on the lived experience of the L'Arche communities (see Chapter 13 in this
volume). This may have grounded Hauerwas's thinking in important ways
and enabled him to recognize the significance of the people behind the category (Hauerwas, Vanier, and Swinton 2008). His focus on the L'Arche communities as living paradigms of how the church should be has given his work
on disability a sense of embodiment, awareness, and liveliness that is beginning to counter some of the difficulties highlighted above (Hauerwas in
Reinders 2010).

Nevertheless, it is less clear why it seems to be assumed that it is the task of Vanier and the L'Arche communities to live out and reveal the truth of the gospel on behalf of others. As Hans Reinders has observed, why would an Aristotelian such as Hauerwas assume that Jean Vanier, L'Arche, or any other person or group should live out the life of the kingdom on his or her behalf? It is simply not enough to write about disability or the L'Arche communities. These things must be lived. If Christianity is unintelligible without witness, then the natural conclusion of Hauerwas's position on disability is that he, along with all others who claim the status of disciples, should live their lives in deep connection with people who have profound intellectual disabilities. Can a powerful academic working in one of the most prestigious universities in the world truly model that which he has learned from people with profound intellectual disabilities and from the life and work of someone like Jean Vanier? This is not intended as a polemical question. Nor is it one that can be aimed only at Hauerwas. What is so for him is so for me and for many of us. Noticing the real state of human beings is helpful; living this new reality is crucial. Looking at disability is interesting; living with the disabled requires a faithful response to a vocational call that God offers to all who claim the identity of disciple.

REFERENCES

Primary Sources

Hauerwas, Stanley. 1994a. "The Church and the Mentally Handicapped: A Continuing Challenge to the Imagination." In *Dispatches from the Front: Theological Engagements with the Secular*. Durham and London: Duke University Press, 1994, 177-87.

————. 1977. "Having and Learning to Care for Retarded Children." In *Truthfulness and Tragedy: Further Investigations into Christian Ethics*. Notre Dame: University of Notre Dame Press, 156-63.

————. 1994b. *Naming the Silences: God, Medicine, and Suffering*. Grand Rapids: Wm. B. Eerdmans.

————. 1995. "Preaching as Though We Had Enemies." *First Things* 53 (May): 45-49.

————. 2010. "Seeing Peace: L'Arche as a Peace Movement." Unpublished paper presented at the Templeton Foundation conference in Trosly, Paris, France, 2007. Published in revised form in *The Paradox of Disability: Responses to Jean Vanier and L'Arche Communities from Theology and the Sciences*. Edited by Hans Reinders. Grand Rapids: Wm. B. Eerdmans, 113-27. (The passage quoted in this chapter was presented in the original paper, but modified in the published version. However, the original version makes the point more effectively for current purposes.)

————. 1988. *Suffering Presence: Theological Reflections on Medicine, the Mentally Handicapped, and the Church.* Edinburgh: T&T Clark, 159-82.

————. 1999. "Timeful Friends: Living with the Handicapped." In *Sanctify Them in the Truth: Holiness Exemplified.* Edinburgh: T&T Clark; Nashville: Abingdon Press, 143-56.

————. 2001. *With the Grain of the Universe: The Church's Witness and Natural Theology.* Grand Rapids: Brazos Press.

Hauerwas, Stanley, Jean Vanier, and John Swinton. 2008. *Living Gently in a Violent World: The Prophetic Witness of Weakness.* Downers Grove, Ill.: InterVarsity Press.

Secondary Sources

Amato, J. A. 1990. *Victims and Values: A History and a Theory of Suffering.* New York: Praeger.

Eiesland, Nancy. 1994. *The Disabled God: Toward a Liberatory Theology of Disability.* Nashville: Abingdon Press.

Nagel, Thomas. 1979. *Mortal Questions.* Cambridge: Cambridge University Press. See especially pp. 24-38.

Spink, Kathryn. 2006. *The Miracle, the Message, the Story: Jean Vanier and L'Arche.* Mahwah, N.J.: Hidden Spring.

Swinton, John, editor. 2005. *Critical Reflections on Stanley Hauerwas' Essays on Disability: Disabling Society, Enabling Theology.* New York: Haworth Press.

Vanier, Jean. 2001. *Befriending the Stranger* (first published as *La source des larmes,* 2001). Mahwah, N.J.: Paulist Press.

Williams, Bernard. 1981. *Moral Luck.* Cambridge: Cambridge University Press.

Excerpts

14.1

Stanley Hauerwas. "Community and Diversity: The Tyranny of Normality." In *Suffering Presence: Theological Reflections on Medicine, the Mentally Handicapped, and the Church*. Edinburgh: T&T Clark, 1986, 212-14.

At a social level we also can run into some misleading claims about what we are doing. For example, many of us fighting for better treatment for the retarded use the language of securing the rights of the retarded. To be sure, the language of rights has a moral and social significance, but we must use it carefully, for too often in our political system it is the battle cry of one group against another. When used in this manner it transforms what should be this society's moral commitment into an issue comparable to a conflict between businesses and labor. If we are to use the language of rights, we must do so only as a means to protect the retarded from those who would treat them, for either cruel or sentimental reasons, with less than respect.

I think it is important, therefore, that we remember that the language of rights is dependent on a more profound sense of community that forms our commitment to the retarded. Speaking as the "outsider," I want to suggest that the retarded help us understand some crucial things about what it means to be a community that enhances us all. Put differently, many talks about the retarded are about what we should be doing for them, but I am suggesting that they do something for us that we have hardly noticed. Namely, they force us to recognize that we are involved in a community life that is richer than our official explanations and theories give us the skill to say.

For example, we usually associate movements towards justice in our society with the language of equality. We assume to be treated equally is to be treated justly, but on reflection we may discover that is not the case. Often the language of equality only works by reducing us to a common denominator that can be repressive or disrespectful. This can perhaps be seen most clearly in terms of the black struggle for civil rights. That struggle began with a justified call to be treated equally — to have the opportunity to enjoy the same rights of all Americans that blacks were denied on the basis of their color. But, black Americans soon discovered that it was not enough to be treated equally if that treatment meant they must forget what it means to be black. Being black is just who they are. To be "black" is to be part of a history that should be cherished and enhanced. No one wants to pay the price of being treated equally if that means they must reject who they are — that is, if they must reject their roots. We find the same kind of movement today among those born Hungarian, Spanish, or (the ultimate good) Texan. In other words, none of us want to be treated equally if that means we lose our distinctiveness.

Now it seems to me that our commitment to having the retarded in our society embodies a richer sense of community than the language of equality provides. For the retarded, in a profounder way than being black, Hungarian, Pole, or even Texan, call us toward a community of diversity and difference. Such a community is a community of equality, but not in the way that equality makes us forget our differences. Rather, in a community of equality our differences help each of us to flourish exactly as different people.

There should be no mistake about it: a community of diversity that enhances differences is indeed a hard enterprise to sustain. We are creatures that fear difference. The fact that the other is not as we are means that there may be something wrong with us. The only solution is to make them as much like us as possible or to make them live apart.

Most of us learn to deal with this demand to be like everyone else — we have the power. It should be said, however, that we are not nearly as successful as we think, as too often we voluntarily accept the other's definition of us. The most stringent power we have over another is not physical coercion but the ability to have the other accept our definition of them. But the retarded are often in the unfortunate position of not having the power to resist those who would make them like us.

This consideration, I think, must make us a little cautious about being too enthusiastic about the "principle of normalization" that is currently so popular among those who work with the retarded. It is of course true that the retarded deserve to do what they are able — to dress themselves, to spend their own money, to decide to spend their money foolishly or wisely, to date, to fall in love, and so on. But the demand to be normal can be tyrannical unless we understand that the normal condition of our being together is that we are all different. If we are to be a good community we must be one that has convictions substantive enough not to fear our differences and, indeed, to see that we would not be whole without the other being different than us.

14.2

Stanley Hauerwas. "Suffering the Retarded: Should We Prevent Retardation?" In *Suffering Presence*, 163-68.

We must ask what the "prevent retardation" campaign would mean for this group? If a society were even partially successful in "eliminating" retardation, how would it regard those who have become retarded? Since retardation was eliminated on grounds of being an unacceptable way of being human, would the retarded who live in a society be able to recognize the validity of their existence and willing to provide the care they require? Of course it might be suggested that with fewer retarded there would be more resources for the care of those remaining. That is no doubt true, but the question is whether there would be the moral will to direct those resources in their direction. Our present resources are more than enough to provide good care for the retarded. That we do not provide such care can be attributed to a lack of moral will and imagination. What will and imagination there is comes from those who have found themselves unexpectedly committed to care for a retarded person through birth or relation. Remove that and I seriously doubt whether our society will find the moral convictions necessary to sustain our alleged commitment to the retarded.

To reckon whether this is mere speculation, consider this thought experiment. We live at a time when it is possible through genetic screening to predict who has the greatest likelihood of having a retarded child, particularly if that person marries someone of similar genetic characteristics. It has become a general policy for most of the population to have such screening and to choose their marriage partner accordingly. Moreover, amniocentesis has become so routine that the early abortion of handicapped children has become the medical "therapy" of choice. How would such a society regard and treat a couple who refused to be genetically screened, who refused amniocentesis, and who might perhaps have a less than normal child? Would such a society be happy with the increased burden on its social and financial resources? Why should citizens support the birth and care of such a child when its existence could easily have been avoided? To care for such a child, to support such "irresponsible" parents, means only that the "truly" needy will be unjustly deprived of care in the interest of sustaining a child who will never "contribute to societal good." That such an attitude seems not unreasonable to many people also suggests that in our current situation a campaign to "prevent retardation" might have negative implications for those who are retarded, as well as those who may have the misfortune to be born retarded or become retarded in the future.

Suffering and the Retarded

But surely there is something wrong with these observations, as they seem to imply that since we can never ensure that no one will be born or become retarded, then we should not even try to prevent retardation. On such grounds it seems we cannot change our lives to ensure that few will be born retarded so that those who are retarded now and in the future will not be cruelly treated and may even receive better care. That is clearly a vicious and unworthy position. We rightly seek to prevent those forms of retardation that are preventable. To challenge that assumption would be equivalent to questioning our belief that the world is round or that love is a good thing. Like so many things that seem obvious, however, if we ask *why* they seem so, we are often unable to supply an answer. Perhaps they seem obvious precisely because they do not require a reason for holding them.

I suspect that at least part of the reason it seems so obvious that we ought to prevent retardation is the conviction that we ought to prevent suffering. No one should will that an animal should suffer gratuitously. No one should will that a child should endure an illness. No one should will that another person should suffer from hunger. No one should will that a child should be born retarded. That suffering should be avoided is a belief as deep as any we have. That someone born retarded suffers is obvious. Therefore if we believe we ought to prevent suffering, it seems we ought to prevent retardation. Yet like many other "obvious" beliefs, the assumption that suffering should *always* be prevented, if analyzed, becomes increasingly less certain or at least involves unanticipated complexity. Just because it implies eliminating subjects who happen to be retarded should at least suggest to us that something is wrong with our straightforward assumption that suffering should always be avoided or, if possible, eliminated. This is similar to some justifications of suicide: namely, in the interest of avoiding or ending suffering a subject wills no longer to exist. Just because in suicide there is allegedly a decision by the victim does not alter the comparison with some programs to prevent retardation: both assume that certain forms of suffering are so dehumanizing that it is better not to exist.

As I have indicated above, this assumption draws upon some of our most profound moral convictions. Yet I hope to show that our assumption that suffering should *always* be prevented is a serious and misleading over-simplification. To show why this is the case a general analysis of suffering is required. We assume we know what suffering is because it is so common, but on analysis, suffering turns out to be an extremely elusive subject. Only once that analysis has been done will we be in a position to ask if the retarded suffer from being retarded or whether the problem is the suffering we feel the retarded cause us.

The Kinds and Ways of Suffering

"To suffer" means to undergo, to be subject. But we undergo much we do not call suffering. Suffering names those aspects of our lives that we undergo and which have a particularly negative sense. We suffer when what we undergo blocks our positive desires and wants. Suffering also carries a sense of "surdness": it denotes those frustrations for which we can give no satisfying explanation and which we cannot make serve some wider end. Suffering thus names a sense of brute power that does violence to our best-laid plans. It is not easily domesticated. Therefore, there can be no purely descriptive account of suffering, since every description necessarily entails some judgment about the value or purpose of certain states.

No doubt the intensity of our own suffering or of our sympathy for others' suffering has reinforced our assumptions that we have a firm grip on its meaning. Yet it is certainly not clear that the kind of suffering occasioned by starvation is the same as that of cancer, though each is equally terrifying in its relentless but slow resolution in death. It is interesting that we also use *suffer* in an active sense of "bearing with," permitting, or enduring. While such expressions do not eclipse the passive sense associated with suffering, they at least connote that we do not associate suffering only with that for which we can do nothing.

Perhaps this is the clue we have been needing to understand better the nature of suffering. We must distinguish between those forms of suffering that happen to us and those that we bring on ourselves or that are requisite to our purposes and goals. Some suffering which befalls us is integral to our goals, only we did not previously realize it. We tend to associate pain, however, with that which happens to us, since it seems to involve that which stands as a threat to our goals and projects, rather than as some means to a further end. In like manner, we suffer from illness and accidents — thus our association of pain with sickness and physical trauma. Of course pain and illness are interrelated, because most of the time when we are ill we hurt, but it is also true that conceptually pain and illness seem to stand on that side of suffering that is more a matter of fate than choice.

This distinction helps us to see the wider meaning of suffering. We not only suffer from diseases, accidents, tornadoes, earthquakes, droughts, floods — all those things over which we have little control — but we also suffer from other people, from living here rather than there, from doing this kind of job — all matters we might avoid — because in these instances we see what we suffer as part of a large scheme. This latter sense of "suffer," moreover, seems more subjective, since what may appear as a problem for one may seem an opportunity for another. Not only is what we suffer relative to our projects, but how we suffer is relative to what we have or wish to be (Nagel 1979; Williams 1981).

Without denying the importance of the distinction between forms of suffering that happen to us and those that we instigate as requisite to our goals, we would be mistaken to press it too hard. Once considered, it may not seem as evident or as helpful as it first appeared. For example, we often discuss how what at the time looked like something that happened to us — something we suffered — was in fact something we did, or at least chose not to avoid. Our increasing knowledge of the relation of illness to life-style is enough to make us think twice before drawing a hard-and-fast distinction between what happens to us and what we do.

But the situation is even more complex. We often find that essential in our response to suffering is the ability to make what happens to me mine. Cancer patients frequently testify to some sense of relief when they find out they have cancer. The very ability to name what they have seems to give them a sense of control or possession that replaces the undifferentiated fear they had been feeling. Pain and suffering alienate us from ourselves. They make us what we do not know. The task is to find the means to make that which is happening to me mine — to interpret its presence (even if such an interpretation is negative) as something I can claim as integral to my identity. No doubt our power to transform events into decisions can be the source of great self-deception, but it is also the source of our moral identity.

Please note: I am not suggesting that every form of pain or suffering can or should be seen as some good or challenge. Extreme suffering can as easily destroy as enhance. Nor do I suggest that we should be the kind of people who can transform any suffering into benefit. We rightly feel that some forms of suffering can only be acknowledged, not transformed. Indeed, at this point I am not making any normative recommendations about how we should respond to suffering; rather, I am suggesting the distinction between the suffering which happens to us and the suffering which we accept as part of our projects is not as clear as it may at first seem. More important is the question of what kind of people we ought to be so that certain forms of suffering are not denied but accepted as part and parcel of our existence as moral agents.

In spite of our inability to provide a single meaning to the notion of suffering or to distinguish clearly between different kinds of suffering, I think this analysis has not been without important implications. It may well be that those forms of suffering we believe we should try to prevent or to eliminate are those that we think impossible to integrate into our projects, socially or individually. It is exactly those forms of suffering which seem to intrude uncontrollably into our lives which appear to be the most urgent candidates for prevention. Thus our sense that we should try to prevent suffering turns out to mean that we should try to prevent those kinds of suffering that we do not feel can serve any human good. Even this way of putting the matter may be misleading. Some may object that while it is certainly descriptively true that we find it hard to integrate certain kinds of suffering into our individual and social lives, that ought not to be the case. The issue is not what we do, but rather who we ought to be in order to be capable of accepting all suffering as a necessary aspect of human existence. In viewing our life narrowly as a matter of purposes and accomplishments, we may miss our actual need for suffering, even apparently purposeless or counter-purposeful suffering. The issue is not whether retarded children can serve a human good, but whether we should be the kind of people, the kind of parents and communities that can receive, even welcome, them into our midst in a manner that allows them to flourish.

But it may be objected that although this latter way of putting the issue seems to embody the highest moral ideals, in fact, it is deeply immoral because the suggestion that all forms of suffering are capable of being given human meaning is destructive to the human project. Certain kinds of suffering — Hiroshima, Auschwitz, wars — are so horrible that we are able to preserve our humanity only by denying them human significance. No "meaning" can be derived from the Holocaust except that we must do everything we can to see that it does not happen again. Perhaps individuals can respond to natural disasters such as hurricanes and floods in a positive manner, but humanly we are right to view these other destructions as a scourge which we will neither accept nor try to explain in some positive sense.

Our refusal to accept certain kinds of suffering, or to try to interpret them as serving some human purpose, is essential for our moral health. Otherwise we would far too easily accept the causes of suffering rather than trying to eliminate or avoid them. Our primary business is not to accept suffering, but to escape it, both for our own sake and our neighbor's. Still, in the very attempt to escape suffering, do we not lose something of our own humanity? We rightly try to avoid unnecessary suffering, but it also seems that we are never quite what we should be until we recognize the necessity and inevitability of suffering in our lives.

To be human is to suffer. That sounds wise. That sounds right, that is, true to the facts. But we should not be too quick to affirm it as a norm. Questions remain as to what kind of suffering should be accepted and how it should be integrated into our lives. Moreover, prior to these questions is the even more challenging question of why suffering seems to be our fate. Even if I knew how to answer such questions, I could not try to address them in this paper. (Indeed, I suspect that there can be no general answer that does not mislead as much as it informs.) But perhaps by directing our attention toward the retarded we can better understand why and how suffering is never to be merely "accepted" and yet why it is unavoidable in our lives.

14.3

"Suffering the Retarded: Should We Prevent Retardation?" In *Suffering Presence*, 161-63.

It has become increasingly recognized that disease descriptions and remedies are relative to a society's values and needs. Thus "retardation" might not "exist" in a society which values cooperation more than competition and ambition. Yet the increasing realization that retardation is a social designation should not blind us to the fact that the retarded do have some quite specifiable problems peculiar to them and that their difference requires special forms of care. It is extremely important how we put this if we are to avoid two different perils. The first, assuming that societal prejudice is embodied in all designations of retardation, seeks to aid the retarded by preventing discriminatory practices in a manner similar to the civil rights campaigns for blacks and women. Because the retarded are said to have the same rights as anyone, in this view all they require is to be treated "normally." Without denying that the retarded have "rights" or that much good has been done under the banner of "normalization," I believe this way of putting the matter is misleading and risks making the retarded subject to even greater societal cruelty. Would it not be unjust to treat the retarded "equally"? Instead, retardation ought to be so precisely understood that those who are thus handicapped can be accommodated as they need. But that may be a reason for avoiding the word *retardation* altogether. As I have already noted there are so many different ways of being retarded, so many different kinds of disabilities and corresponding forms of care required that to isolate a group as "retarded" may be the source of much of the injustice we perpetrate on those whom we identify as "not normal."

The second peril is that of oppressive care, a kind of care based on the assumption that the retarded are so disabled they must be protected from the dangers and risks of life. Such a strategy subjects the retarded to a cruelty fueled by our sentimental concern to deal with their differences by treating them as something less than human agents. Too often this strategy isolates the retarded from the rest of society in the interest of "protecting" them from societal indifference. As a result they are trained to be retarded. The challenge is to know how to characterize retardation and to know what difference it should make, without our very characterizations being used as an excuse to treat the retarded unjustly. However, we see this is not just a problem for the retarded, but a basic problem of any society, since societies are only possible because we are all different in skills and different in needs. Societies must find ways to characterize and institutionalize those differences so that we see them as enhancing rather than diminishing each of our lives. From this perspective the retarded are a poignant test of a society's particular understanding of how our differences are relevant to and for achievement of a common good.

The various issues I have raised can be illustrated by pointing to one final fallacy that the film[1] underwrites. It gives the impression that retardation is primarily a genetic problem recognized at, or soon after, birth. But that is simply not the case. Half the people who bear the label "retarded" do so as the result of some circumstance after their conception and/or birth. Many are retarded due to environmental, nutritional, and/or accidental causes. To suggest, therefore, that we can eliminate retardation by better prenatal care or more thorough genetic screening and counseling is a mistake. Even if we were all required to have genetic checks before being allowed to marry, we would still have some among us that we currently label as "retarded."

---

1. Hauerwas is considering an informational film (produced by the Amercian Association of Retarded Citizens) on the topic of the prevention of disability, a film that presumes the equation of disability and suffering. *Editors' note.*

14.4

Stanley Hauerwas. "Timeful Friends: Living with the Handicapped." In *Sanctify Them in the Truth: Holiness Exemplified*. Edinburgh: T&T Clark, 1998, 147-48.

As Christians we know we have not been created to be "our own authors," to be autonomous. We are creatures. Dependency, not autonomy, is one of the ontological characteristics of our lives. That we are creatures, moreover, is but a reminder that we are created for and with one another. We are not just accidentally communal, but we are such by necessity. We were not created to be alone. We cannot help but desire and delight in the reality of the other, even the other born with a difference we call mentally handicapped. Our dependency, our need for one another, means that we will suffer as well as know joy. Our incompleteness at once makes possible the gifts that make life possible as well as the unavoidability of suffering. Such suffering, moreover, may seem pointless. [See Hauerwas 1990 for a further development of this point.] Yet, at least for Christians, such suffering should not tempt us to think our task is to eliminate those whose suffering seems pointless. Christians are, or at least should be, imbedded in a narrative that makes possible a sharing of lives with one another that enables us to go on in the face of the inexplicable. For Christians the mentally handicapped do not present a peculiar challenge. That the mentally handicapped are constituted by narratives they have not chosen simply reveals the character of our lives. That some people are born with a condition that we have come to label as being mentally handicapped does not indicate a fundamental difference between them and the fact that we must all be born. The question is not whether we can justify the mentally handicapped, but whether we live any longer in a world that can make sense of having children. At the very least, Christians believe that our lives are constituted by the hope we have learned through Christ's cross and resurrection that makes morally intelligible the bringing of children into a world as dark as our own.

I have not made these arguments to try to convince people constituted by the narratives of modernity that they should believe in God. Such an argument could not help but make God a *deus ex machina* which not only demeans God, but God's creation as well. Rather, my concern is to help Christians locate those practices that help us understand better why our willingness to welcome the mentally handicapped should not be surprising given the triune nature of the God we worship. In other words, I have used the mentally handicapped as material markers necessary to show that Christian speech can and in fact does make claims about the way things are. Theologically, thinking about the mentally handicapped helps us see, moreover, that claims about the way things are cannot be separated from the way we should live. By subjecting the mentally handicapped to this agenda, one might object, am I not also exemplifying the desperate attempt I have criticized in others to find some "meaning" in the existence and care of the handicapped? I would obviously like to answer with a quick denial, but as I indicated above, the question rightly continues to haunt me. That it does so, I think, is partly because I am not sure how one rightly responds to such a challenge.

14.5

Stanley Hauerwas. "The Church and the Mentally Handicapped: A Continuing Challenge to the Imagination." In *Dispatches from the Front: Theological Engagements with the Secular.* Durham and London: Duke University Press, 1994, 181-85.

On Children, the Church, and the Mentally Handicapped

Of course, learning to live joyfully with the Annas and the Boyces draws on the resources of other practices that make their presence intelligible in relation to other practices that constitute who we are and desire to be. For example, consider an issue that at first may seem foreign to the question of how we should care for the mentally handicapped — namely, why we have children in the first place. I often used to begin a course in the theology and ethics of marriage with the question "What reason would you give for yourself or someone else for having a child?" Few students had thought about the question, and their responses were less than convincing: that is, children should manifest their love for one another as a hedge against loneliness, for fun, and/or to please grandparents. Often, one student finally would say that he or she wanted to have children to make the world better. The implicit assumption behind this reason was that the person who spoke up would have superior children who, having received the right kind of training, would be enabled to help solve the world's problems. Such reasoning often appears morally idealistic. However, its limitations can be revealed quickly by showing its implications for the mentally handicapped. For people who want to have superior children in order to make the world better are deeply threatened by the mentally handicapped. If children are part of a progressive story about the necessity to make the world better, these children do not seem to fit. At best, they only can be understood as deserving existence insofar as our care of them makes us better people. Such attitudes about having children reveal a society with a deficient moral imagination. It is an imagination correlative to a set of practices about the having and care of children that results in the destruction of the mentally handicapped. The fundamental mistake regarding parenting in our society is the assumption that biology makes parents. In the absences of any good reason for having children, people assume that they have responsibilities to their children because they are biologically "theirs." Lost is any sense of how parenting is an office of a community rather than a biologically described role.

In contrast, Christians assume, given the practice of baptism, that parenting is the vocation of everyone in the church whether they are married or single. Raising children for Christians is part of the church's commitment to hospitality of the stranger, since we believe that the church is sustained by God across generations by witness rather than by ascribed biological destinies. Everyone in the church, therefore, has a parental role whether or not they have biological children.

For Christians, children are neither the entire responsibility nor the property of parents. Parents are given responsibility for particular children insofar as they pledge faithfully to bring up those children, but the community ultimately stands over against the parents reminding them that children have a standing in the community separate from their parents. Therefore, the ways in which mentally handicapped children are received in such a community should be strikingly different from how they are received in the wider society. For the whole burden of the care for such children does not fall on the parents; rather, the children now are seen as gifts to the whole community. At the very least, the church should be the place where parents and mentally handicapped children can be without apologizing, without being stared at, without being silently condemned. If others act as if we ought to be ashamed for having such children among us, then those others will have to take on the whole church. For this is not the child of these biological parents, but this child is the child of the whole church, one whom the church would not choose to be without. Moreover, as this child grows to be an adult, she, just as we all do, is expected to care as well as to be cared for as a member of the church. Such a child may add special burdens to the community but on the average not more than any child. For every child, mentally handicapped or not, always comes to this community challenging our presuppositions. Some children just challenge us more than others as they reveal the limits of our practices. Christians are people who rejoice when we receive such challenges, for we know them to be the source of our imaginations through which God provides us with the skills to have children in a dangerous world. The church is constituted by a people who have been surprised by God and accordingly know that we live through such surprises.

The church, therefore, is that group of people who are willing to have their imagination constantly challenged through the necessities created by children, some of whom may be mentally handicapped. The church is constituted by those people who can take the time in a world crying with injustice to have children, some of whom may turn out to be mentally handicapped. We can do that because we believe this is the way God would rule this world. For we do not believe that the world can be made better if such children are left behind.

I am aware that this view of the church's treatment of the mentally handicapped is overly idealized. But I believe I am indicating the potential contained in common Christian practice. Moreover, the presence of the mentally handicapped helps Christians rediscover the significance of the common, because the handicapped call into question some of our most cherished assumptions about what constitutes Christianity. For example, often in Christian communities a great emphasis is placed on the importance of "belief." In attempts to respond to critiques of Christian theology in modernity, the importance of intellectual commitments often is taken to be the hallmark of participation in the church. What it means to be Christian is equivalent to being "ultimately concerned" about the existential challenges of human existence and so on. Yet the more emphasis that is placed on belief, particularly for individuals, the more the mentally handicapped are marginalized. For what the mentally handicapped challenge the church to remember is that what saves is not our personal existential commitments, but being a member of a body constituted by practices more determinative than my "personal" commitment. I suspect this is the reason why mentally handicapped people often are better received in more "liturgical" traditions — that is, traditions which know that what God is doing through the community's ritual is more determinative than what any worshiper brings to or receives from the ritual. After all, the God worshiped is the Spirit that cannot be subject to human control. The liturgy of the church is ordered to be open to such wildness by its hospitality to that Spirit. What the mentally handicapped might do to intrude onto that order is nothing compared to what the Spirit has done and will continue to do. Indeed, the presence of the mentally handicapped may well be the embodiment of the Spirit.

Nowhere is the individualistic and rationalistic character of modern Christianity better revealed than in the practice of Christian education. For example, religious education is often the attempt to "teach" people the content of the Christian faith separate from any determinative practices. What it means to be Christian is to understand this or that doctrine. Yet if the church is the community that is constituted by the presence of the mentally handicapped, we know that salvation cannot be by knowing this or that but rather by participating in a community through which our lives are constituted by a unity more profound than our individual needs. From such a perspective the mentally handicapped are not accidental to what the church is about, but without their presence the church has no way to know it is church — that the church is body. If the word is preached and the sacraments served without the presence of the mentally handicapped, then it may be that we are less than the body of Christ.

Mentally handicapped people are reminders that belief and faith are not individual matters, but faith names the stance of the church as a political body in relation to the world. We are not members of a church because we know what we believe, but we are members of a church because we need the whole church to believe for us. Often, if not most of the time, I find that I come to be part of the community that worships God not as a believer or as a faithful follower of Christ, but as someone who is just "not there." I may not be a disbeliever, but I am by no means a believer either. By being present to others in church I find that I am made more than I would otherwise be — I am made one in the faith of the church; my body is constituted by the body called church.

The mentally handicapped remind us that their condition is the condition of us all insofar as we are faithful followers of Christ. The church is not a collection of individuals, but a people on a journey who are known by the time they take to help one another along the way. The mentally handicapped constitute such time, as we know that God would not have us try to make the world better if such efforts mean leaving them behind. They are the way we must learn to walk in the journey that God has given us called Kingdom. They are God's imagination, and to the extent we become one with them, we become God's imagination for the world.

14.6

Stanley Hauerwas. "Having and Learning to Care for Retarded Children." In *Truthfulness and Tragedy: Further investigations into Christian Ethics.* Quoted in John Swinton, ed., *Critical Reflections on Stanley Hauerwas' Essays on Disability: Disabling Society, Enabling Theology.* New York: Haworth Press, 2005, 156-57.

The Retarded as Gifts

Thus we must learn to accept the retarded into our lives as a peculiar and intense form of how we should regard all children. They are not, to be sure, the kind of children we would choose to have, for we would wish on no one any unnecessary suffering or pain. But they are not different from other children insofar as any child is not of our choosing.

Children, Suffering, and the Skill to Care

It is of course true that retarded children destroy our plans and fantasies about what we wish our children to be. They thus call us to reality quicker than most children, as they remind us that the plans we have for our children may not be commensurate with the purpose for which we have children at all. Thus these retarded children are particularly special gifts to remind us that we have children not that they be a success, not for what they may be able to do for the good and betterment of mankind, but because we are members of a people who are gathered around the table of Christ.

I want to be very clear about this. I am not suggesting that Christians should rejoice that their children are born retarded rather than normal. Rather, I am suggesting that as Christians the story that informs and directs why we have children at all provides us with the skill to know how to welcome these particular children into our existence without telling ourselves self-deceiving stories about our heroism for doing so. For such heroic stories can also serve to subject the retarded child to forms of care that they should not be forced to undergo. For example, such heroic stories can lead us to forms of sentimental care and protection that rob these children of the demands to grow as they are able. For the love of the retarded, like any love, must be hard if we are to not stifle the other in overprotective care. Or to care for these children as if they are somehow specially innocent — that is, "children of God" — is to rob them of the right to be the kind of selfish, grasping, and manipulative children other children have the right to be. Retarded children are not to be cared for because they are especially loving, though some of them may be, but because they are children. We forget that there is no more disparaging way to treat another than to assume that they can do nothing wrong.

14.7

Stanley Hauerwas. "Seeing Peace: L'Arche as a Peace Movement." In *The Paradox of Disability: Responses to Jean Vanier and L'Arche Communities from Theology and the Sciences.* Edited by Hans S. Reinders. Grand Rapids: Wm. B. Eerdmans, 2010, 113-19.

How L'Arche Makes Peace Visible

One of the gifts L'Arche offers Christians and non-Christians alike is its enabling us to visualize peace. Some may find this remark odd since L'Arche did not begin as a peace movement and, furthermore, the primary work of L'Arche does not seem to be about peace. Moreover, apart from questions about L'Arche there is the matter of *seeing* peace. Why do we need to *see* peace? We need to see peace because we have been taught that violence is the norm and peace the exception. In calling attention to L'Arche as a peace movement, therefore, I hope to show that peace is not an ideal waiting to be realized. Rather, peace is as real — as concrete — as the work of L'Arche. By seeing the realization of peace in the communities of L'Arche, we are more able to see and enact peace in our own lives.

Christianity, like peace, is not an idea. Rather, it is a bodily faith that must be seen to be believed. As we pray following the Eucharist, we "eat this body" and "drink this blood" so that we might become "living members of your Son our savior Jesus Christ." We partake of the bread and wine as the body and blood of Christ because in doing so we are taken up into Christ's vision of his creation. Given this vision we look for Christ's presence in the world to help us live into our calling as members of His body. L'Arche, a community built on faith, turns out to be a lens that helps us see God's peace in the world.

By suggesting L'Arche is a peace movement I do not think I am forcing a category on L'Arche, or Jean Vanier. Vanier has increasingly identified working for peace to be one of the primary purposes of L'Arche. The same is true for the various zones of L'Arche around the world. For example, the recent newsletter of L'Arche USA Zone identified its Zone Mandate by focusing on four major themes:

- Fostering vocation in L'Arche by continuing to build structures and processes that support long-term membership in our communities;
- Announcing L'Arche and the gifts of people with disabilities in order to help build a more peaceful and just world;
- Deepening our relationships of solidarity within the Federation of L'Arche, especially with our communities in Latin America and the Caribbean; and
- Exploring new models for living the Mission that respond to current realities facing our communities (L'Arche USA, 2006, 2).

It is by no means clear, however, how "announcing" the gifts of people with disabilities can help "build a more peaceful and just world." The phrase "in order" in the second theme seems to suggest a causal connection between the work of L'Arche and the work of peace, but it remains vague as to how we should understand the relation between those two tasks. Nor is it apparent how the four themes are interrelated. How does building structures and processes that support long-term vocations serve to sustain a more peaceful world? Why is deepening relationships within the Federation of L'Arche so important, particularly as the work of peace?

I believe there are good answers to these questions to be found in the work of Jean Vanier. Accordingly, by drawing on his work I will try to spell out how Vanier understands L'Arche to be a movement for peace. I should warn the reader in doing so [that] Jean Vanier will often sound very much like John Howard Yoder's understanding of Christian non-violence. I do not think that is accidental because Jean Vanier and John Howard Yoder do strike many of the same chords, though in quite different keys.

Vanier, particularly after September 11, 2001, has increasingly and explicitly emphasized that one of the essential tasks of L'Arche is to exemplify peace. With his usual insight into the complex character of our lives he often calls attention to fear as the source of our violence. The fear that dominates our lives is not in the first instance the fear of an enemy, unless it is acknowledged that each of us is the enemy, but rather the fear that is the source of violence is the fear that makes us unwilling to acknowledge the wounded character of our lives. L'Arche, a place where the wounds of each person cannot avoid being exposed and thus hopefully healed, becomes a context where we can learn the patient habits necessary for being at peace. Vanier knows such an understanding of peace may not have results for creating a more peaceful world at the international level, but he suggests "we are all called to become men and women of peace wherever we may be — in our family, at work, in our parish, in our neighborhood" (quoted in Spink 2006, 225).

Though Vanier's modesty about the work of L'Arche not being a strategy designed to end the scourge of war is admirable, I want to suggest that L'Arche is exactly the kind of peace work we so desperately need if our imaginations are to be capable of conceiving what peace might look like at the international level. One of the problems with being an advocate of peace, and I am a pacifist, is the widespread presumption that violence is the rule and peace the exception. The pacifist, therefore, is assumed to bear the burden of proof because violence is thought to be necessary for the maintenance of a relatively just and secure order. The question addressed to the pacifist, "What would you do if . . . ?" allegedly shows the unworkability of a commitment to peace. L'Arche is the way I believe that question must be answered.

Vanier and the work of L'Arche help us see that peace is a deeper reality than violence. However, this vision — a vision that enables us to see that peace is a deeper reality than violence because we were created to be at peace — requires training. It turns out our teachers are the core members of L'Arche whose gift is their unprotected vulnerability. In learning to live with those whom we call "the disabled" we learn to recognize questions such as "Would it not have been better if a person so disabled would not have been born?" are not questions we are tempted to ask if we have learned to view our world through the lens L'Arche provides. For the answers, even the most humane answers to such questions, too often disguise a violence cloaked in the language of compassion.

The Mystery of Suffering

I need to explain this last remark, because it is important for understanding the kind of peace found in L'Arche. Crucial for our learning to be at peace with ourselves and one another is the ability to accept the mystery of suffering. But it turns out that is exactly what we have lost the ability to do.

In an extraordinary but unfortunately not well-known book, *Victims and Values: A History and a Theory of Suffering,* [Joseph] Amato argues that modernity is marked fundamentally by a transformation of how suffering is understood and responded to (Amato 1990). Amato observes that all human cultures must give meaning to suffering, but a fundamental shift in attitudes toward suffering occurred in the Enlightenment. The shift was characterized by a social sympathy for those who suffer which led to reform movements that resulted in much social good. But that same sympathy confronted by more victims than can be cared for also led to a battle over the value of suffering.

Just at the time when people developed a universal sympathy for all those who suffer, thus the significance given to the status of being a victim, they also increasingly came to believe that suffering is not an inevitable part of human experience. Thus the presumption shared by increasing numbers of people that it is wrong not to be happy. Jeremy Bentham exemplifies this attitude by his attempt to develop a social calculus that aims to do nothing less than remove all unnecessary suffering from human experience (Amato 1990, 79). Hidden, however, in this humanism is a violence against all who suffer in ways that their suffering cannot be eliminated. In the name of sympathy for the sufferer we must eliminate those who cannot be "cured." It is against this violence that Vanier set his face by insisting on the mystery of suffering. Vanier observes,

> Jesus did not come into the world to explain suffering nor to justify its existence. He came to reveal that we can all alleviate pain, through our competence and our compassion. He came to show us that every pain, every hurt we experience can become an offering, and thus a source of life for others in and through Jesus' offering of love to the Father. (Vanier 2001, 89)

Vanier's great gift, the gift of L'Arche, is to teach us to see pain, to enter into the pain of others, without wanting to destroy those who suffer. In *Befriending the Stranger,* Vanier tells the story of Lucien, who was born with severe mental and physical disabilities. He could not talk and his twisted body meant he had to spend his life in a wheelchair or the bed. He lived the first thirty years of his life with his mother, who could interpret his body language. He was at peace with his mother, but she fell ill, requiring hospitalization. Losing all points of reference, screams of anguish possessed him. He came to "La Forestiere," but his constant screaming continued and nothing seemed to work to calm him. Vanier confesses that Lucien's screams pierced the very core of his being, forcing him to recognize that he would be willing to hurt Lucien to keep him quiet. Vanier had to recognize that he, someone who thought he had been called to share his life with the weak, had in his heart the capacity to hate a weak person (Vanier 2001, 62).

The work of L'Arche is dangerous as it tempts us to rage against those we are committed to "help." So when Vanier tells us that "it is important to enter into the mystery of pain, the pain of our brothers and sisters in countries that are at war, the pain of our brothers and sisters who are sick, who are hungry, and who are in prison," he puts us at great risk (Vanier 2001, 87). To face the mystery of pain means we must confront the violence we harbor in our hearts created by a world we cannot force to conform to our desires. Vanier observes, "The only thing that matters is that we be truthful; that we do not let ourselves be governed by lies and by illusion" (Vanier 2001, 61). But to face the truth about ourselves — the truth that we desire to eliminate those in pain — is no easy task. Yet without such truth there can be no peace.

Acknowledgments

The authors, editors, and publisher gratefully acknowledge permission to quote material from the following publications:

CHAPTER 1

Excerpts from Basil the Great's *Ascetical Works*. Translated by Sr. M. M. Wagner. Fathers of the Church, vol. 9. Copyright © 1999 by Catholic University of America Press. Reprinted with permission.

Excerpts from Gregory of Nyssa's *On the Love of the Poor, 2*. Translated by Susan R. Holman. In Susan R. Holman, *The Hungry Are Dying*. Copyright © 2001 by Susan R. Holman. Reprinted with permission of Oxford University Press.

Excerpts from Gregory of Nazianzus's *Oration 14*. Translated by Brian E. Daley, S.J. In Brian E. Daley, *Gregory of Nazianzus*. Copyright © 2006 by Brian E. Daley, S.J. Reprinted with permission of Taylor & Francis Books, UK.

CHAPTER 2

Excerpts from Augustine's *A Treatise on the Merits and Forgiveness of Sins, and on the Baptism of Infants*. In *The Nicene and Post-Nicene Fathers*. First Series, vol. 5. Edited by Philip Schaff. Grand Rapids: Wm. B. Eerdmans, 1978. Reprinted with permission.

Excerpts from Augustine's *Tractates on the Gospel of John, 1–10*. Translated by John Rettig. Copyright © 1988 by Catholic University of America Press. Reprinted with permission.

Excerpts from Augustine's *The Trinity*. Translated by Edmund Hill. Copyright © 1991 by Augustine Heritage Institute. Excerpts reprinted with permission of New City Press/Augustinian Heritage Institute.

Excerpts from Augustine's *The City of God against the Pagans*. Edited and translated by R. W. Dyson. Copyright © 1998 by Cambridge University Press. Reprinted with permission.

CHAPTER 3

Excerpts from Thomas Aquinas's *Summa Theologica*. English translation by the Fathers of the English Dominican Province. Copyright © 1981 by Ave Maria Press. Reprinted with permission.

Excerpts from Thomas Aquinas's *On Evil (De Malo)*. English translation by Richard Regan. Edited and with an introduction and notes by Brian Davies. Copyright © 2003 by Brian Davies and Richard Regan. Reprinted with permission of Oxford University Press.

CHAPTER 4

Excerpts from Denise Levertov's "On Belief in the Physical Resurrection of Jesus." In *Sands of the Well*. Copyright © 1994, 1995, 1996 by Denise Levertov. Reprinted with permission of New Directions Publishing Corporation.

Excerpts from Julian of Norwich's *Revelations of Divine Love (The Short Text)*. Abridged edition. Translated by Elizabeth Spearing. Translation copyright © 1998 by Elizabeth Spearing. Reprinted with permission of the Penguin Group.

CHAPTER 5

Excerpts from Martin Luther's "Sermon on the Man Born Blind." In *Luther's Works: American Edition*, vol. 51. Translated by John W. Doberstein. Copyright © 1959 by Augsburg Fortress Press. Reprinted with permission.

Excerpts from Martin Luther's "Lectures on Galatians." In *Luther's Works: American Edition*, vol. 27. Translated by R. Jungkuntz. Copyright © 1964, 1992 by Concordia Publishing House. Reprinted with permission.

Excerpts from Martin Luther's "Whether One May Flee from a Deadly Plague." In *Luther's Works: American Edition*, vol. 43. Translated by C. J. Schindler. Copyright © 1968 by Augsburg Fortress Press. Reprinted with permission.

CHAPTER 6

Excerpts from John Calvin's "Draft Ecclesiastical Ordinances." In *Calvin: Theological Treatises*. Translated and with an introduction and notes by J. K. S. Reid. Philadelphia: Westminster Press, 1954. U.S. rights to quote excerpts from this work were granted by Hymns Ancient & Modern Ltd. All other rights were granted by SCM Press.

Excerpts from John Calvin's *Institutes of the Christian Religion*. Edited by John T. McNeill. Translated and indexed by Ford Lewis Battles. Copyright © 1960 by W. L. Jenkins. Reprinted with permission of Westminster John Knox Press.

Acknowledgments

Excerpts from *Calvin: Commentaries*. Translated and edited by Joseph Haroutunian in collaboration with Louise Pettibone Smith. Reprinted with permission of Baker Publishing Group, 1974.

Excerpts from *John Calvin's Sermons on the Ten Commandments*. Edited and translated by Benjamin W. Farley. Copyright © 1980 by Benjamin W. Farley. Reprinted with permission of Baker Publishing Group.

John Calvin's "Letter to Monsieur de Richebourg." In *John Calvin: Writings on Pastoral Piety*. Edited and with translations by Elsie Anne McKee. Copyright © 2001 by Elsie Anne McKee. Reprinted with permission of Paulist Press/Copyright Clearance Center.

CHAPTER 7

Excerpts from Hegel's *Philosophy of Mind: Being Part Three of "The Encyclopaedia of the Philosophical Sciences"* (1830). Translated by William Wallace. Copyright © 2007 by Oxford University Press. Reprinted with permission.

Excerpts from Hegel's *Elements of the Philosophy of Right*. Edited by Allen W. Wood. Translated by H. B. Nisbet. Copyright © 1991 by Cambridge University Press. Reprinted with permission.

Excerpts from Hegel's *Lectures on the Philosophy of Religion*, vol. 1: *Introduction and the Concept of Religion*. Edited by Peter C. Hodgson. Translated by R. F. Brown, P. C. Hodgson, and J. M. Stewart, with the assistance of J. P. Fitzer and H. S. Harris. Copyright © 1988 by Oxford University Press. Reprinted with permission.

Excerpts from Hegel's *Lectures on the Philosophy of Religion*, vol. III: *The Consummate Religion*. Edited by Peter C. Hodgson. Translated by R. F. Brown, P. C. Hodgson, and J. M. Stewart with the assistance of H. S. Harris. Copyright © 2008 by Oxford University Press. Reprinted with permission.

CHAPTER 8

Excerpts from *Søren Kierkegaard's Journals and Papers*. Volumes 5 and 6. Edited and translated by Howard V. Hong and Edna H. Hong. Copyright © 1968 and 1978, respectively. Reprinted with permission of Indiana University Press.

Excerpts from Kierkegaard's *Purity of Heart Is to Will One Thing*. English translation copyright © 1938 by Harper & Brothers; copyright renewed 1966 by Douglas V. Steere. Reprinted with permission of HarperCollins Publishers.

Excerpts from Kierkegaard's *The Sickness Unto Death*. Translated and edited by Howard V. Hong and Edna H. Hong. Copyright © 1941 by Princeton University Press; copyright renewed in 1969. Reprinted with permission of Princeton University Press.

Excerpts from Kierkegaard's *Concluding Unscientific Postscript to Philosophical Fragments*. Translated and edited by Howard V. Hong and Edna H. Hong. Copyright © 1992 by Princeton University Press. Reprinted with permission.

Excerpts from Kierkegaard's *Works of Love*. Translated by Howard V. Hong and Edna H. Hong. Copyright © 1946 by Princeton University Press. Reprinted with permission.

Excerpt from *Søren Kierkegaard: A Biography* by Joakim Garff. Copyright © 2007 by Princeton University Press. Reprinted with permission.

Excerpts from Kierkegaard's *Stages on Life's Way*. Translated and edited by Howard V. Hong and Edna H. Hong. Copyright © 1940 by Princeton University Press; copyright renewed in 1968 and 1988. Reprinted with permission of Princeton University Press.

CHAPTER 10

Excerpts from Dietrich Bonhoeffer Works, vol. 12: *Berlin: 1932-1933*. Edited by Larry Rasmussen. Translated by Isabel Best and David Higgins. Copyright © 2009 by Augsburg Fortress Press. Reprinted with permission.

Excerpts from Dietrich Bonhoeffer Works, vol. 13: *London: 1933-1935*. Edited by Keith Clements. Translated by Isabel Best. Copyright © 2007 by Augsburg Fortress Press. Reprinted with permission.

Excerpts from Dietrich Bonhoeffer Works, vol. 5: *Life Together* and *The Prayerbook of the Bible*. Edited by Geffrey B. Kelly. Translated by Daniel W. Bloesch and James H. Burtness. Copyright © 1995 by Augsburg Fortress Press. Reprinted with permission.

Excerpts from Dietrich Bonhoeffer Works, vol. 6: *Ethics*. Reproduced by permission of Hymns Ancient and Modern Ltd. Reprinted with the permission of Scribner, a Division of Simon & Schuster, Inc., from *Ethics* by Dietrich Bonhoeffer, translated from the German by Neville Horton. Copyright © 1955 by SCM Press Ltd. Copyright 1955 by Macmillan Publishing Company. All rights reserved.

CHAPTER 11

Excerpts from Barth's *Church Dogmatics* III/2. Edited by G. W. Bromiley and T. F. Torrance. Copyright © 2004 by Continuum International Publishing Group. Reprinted by kind permission of Continuum International Publishing Group.

Excerpts from Barth's *Church Dogmatics* III/3. Edited by G. W. Bromiley and T. F. Torrance. Copyright © 2010 by Continuum International Publishing Group. Reprinted by kind permission of Continuum International Publishing Group.

Excerpts from Barth's *Church Dogmatics* III/4. Edited by G. W. Bromiley and T. F. Torrance. Copyright © 2004 by Continuum International Publishing Group. Reprinted by kind permission of Continuum International Publishing Group.

Excerpts from Barth's *Church Dogmatics* IV/3.1. Edited by G. W. Bromiley and T. F. Torrance. Copyright © 2010 by Continuum International Publishing Group. Reprinted by kind permission of Continuum International Publishing Group.

CHAPTER 12

Excerpts from Rosemary Radford Ruether's *Sexism and God-Talk: Toward a Feminist Theology.* Copyright © 1983, 1993 by Rosemary Radford Ruether. Reprinted with permission of Beacon Press.

Excerpts from Nancy Eisland's *The Disabled God: Toward a Liberatory Theology of Disability.* Copyright © 1994 by Abingdon Press. Reprinted with permission.

Excerpts from Sarah Coakley's "The Woman at the Altar: Cosmological Disturbance or Gender Subversion?" *Anglican Theological Review* 86, no. 1 (Winter 2004): 75-94. Reprinted with permission.

CHAPTER 13

Excerpts from Jean Vanier's *Community and Growth.* Copyright © 1989 by Jean Vanier. Reprinted with permission from Darton, Longman & Todd, London.

Excerpts from Jean Vanier's *Befriending the Stranger.* Copyright © 2005 by Jean Vanier. Reprinted with permission from Darton, Longman & Todd, London.

Excerpts from Jean Vanier's *Becoming Human.* Copyright © 1998, 2008 by Jean Vanier. Reprinted with permission from Darton, Longman & Todd, London.

CHAPTER 14

Excerpts from Stanley Hauerwas's *Suffering Presence: Theological Reflections on Medicine, the Mentally Handicapped, and the Church.* Copyright © 1986 by University of Notre Dame Press. Reprinted with permission.

Excerpts from Stanley Hauerwas's "The Church and the Mentally Handicapped: A Continuing Challenge to the Imagination." In *Dispatches from the Front: Theological Engagements with the Secular.* Copyright © 1994 by Duke University Press. All rights reserved. Reprinted with permission.

Excerpts from Stanley Hauerwas's "Having and Learning to Care for Retarded Children." In *Truthfulness and Tragedy: Further Investigations into Christian Ethics.* Copyright © 1977 by University of Notre Dame Press. Reprinted with permission.

Index of Authors

Index of Subjects

Index of Scripture